Th
Yo

Humphreys' Family Proceedings

Humphreys'
Family Proceedings

Twentieth Edition

**General Editor
David Salter**

THOMSON

SWEET & MAXWELL

First Edition 1946
Twentieth Edition 2002

Published in 2002
Sweet & Maxwell Limited of
100 Avenue Road, Swiss Cottage, London NW3 3PF
http://www.sweetandmaxwell.co.uk
Computerset by Servis Filmsetting Ltd, Manchester
Printed by T. J. International, Padstow, Cornwall

A CIP Catalogue Record
for this book is available
form the British Library

ISBN 0421 748206

Contents

Preface

Humphreys' Matrimonial Causes was first published in 1946, when divorce procedure was radically reformed to cope with the thousands of broken marriages which were part of the aftermath of the Second World War. From the seventh edition, which appeared in 1964, *Humphreys'* was edited by Hugh Collins, former Chief Clerk of Birmingham District Registry and County Court, to whom our thanks are due for the firm foundations laid during the seventeen years of his editorship. The 16th–18th editions were prepared by members of the family law department of Booth & Co (now Addleshaw Booth & Co). This partnership was then extended to members of the National Family Law Group (formerly the Norton Rose M5 Family Law Group) for the 19th and current editions.

In November 1993, after 47 years, the title of *Humphreys'* was changed for the first time to reflect the implementation of the Family Proceedings Rules 1991. This emphasised the procedural nature of the book, which remains unchanged. It is nonetheless hoped that the treatment of non-procedural matters will be of assistance to the busy practitioner. This book can only act as a first port of call in more complex situations. The reader is thus referred to standard words such as *Rayden & Jackson on Divorce*, Butterworths' *Family Law Service* or, in specialised topics, to works such as *Matrimonial Property and Finance* (Duckworth), to which cross-references are contained in this text.

The field of family law continues to change at a rapid pace. Since the publication of the 19th edition in October 1996, the Protection from Harassment Act 1997, the Human Rights Act 1998, the Welfare Reform & Pensions Act 1999 and the Child Support, Pensions and Social Security Act 2000 have, by way of example, gone on to the statute book. Further, the face of family finance was changed dramatically in October 2000 by the House of Lords decision in *White v White* [2000] 2 FLR 981. In addition, there has been a notable increase in judicial guidance on a wide range of procedural matters.

As always, we must express our thanks to Nicola Thurlow and her colleagues at Sweet & Maxwell for all their assistance in enabling us to deliver the manuscript almost on time!

The law is stated so far as possible as at November 1, 2002.

November 2002   **David Salter**
                                                                                                      Leeds

Contributors

General Editor: David Salter MA, LLM
Partner, Addleshaw Booth & Co, Leeds

Michael Bacon MA, FALCD, MAE, QDR
Michael Bacon Associates, Peterborough

Roger Bamber MA
Partner, Mills & Reeve, Cambridge

Lisa Bartlett MA
Solicitor, Mills & Reeve, Cambridge

Jane Bridge LLB
Barrister (non-practising) and Mediator FMA, UKFM; Consultant to
Mills & Reeve, Cambridge

Alison Bull LLB
Senior Solicitor, Addleshaw Booth & Co, Manchester

Eleanor Harding MA, LLB
Senior Solicitor, Addleshaw Booth & Co, Leeds

Angela Moores
Senior Solicitor, Addleshaw Booth & Co, Leeds

Nicola Turner LLB
Solicitor, Addleshaw Booth & Co, Leeds

Philip Way BA (Hons)
Partner, Addleshaw Booth & Co, Leeds

David Whittaker LLB (Hons)
Associate, Williscroft & Co, Bradford

Table of Cases

Table of Statutes

Table of Statutory Instruments

Table of Practice Directions

Table of Conventions

Chapter 1

Jurisdiction

1 Preliminary considerations

Statutes, rules and practice directions: the sources 1.01

This book deals with family proceedings in divorce county courts and the Family Division of the High Court with special reference to district registries. It does not attempt to discuss the jurisdiction of family proceedings courts (formerly magistrates' courts).

The principal *statutes* concerned with these proceedings are:

Married Women's Property Act 1882, s.17 (MWPA 1882, s.17);

Family Law Reform Act 1969 (FLRA 1969);

Matrimonial Causes Act 1973 (MCA 1973);

Domicile and Matrimonial Proceedings Act 1973 (DMPA 1973);

Inheritance (Provision for Family and Dependants) Act 1975 (I(PFD)A 1975);

Child Abduction Act 1984 (CAA 1984);

Matrimonial and Family Proceedings Act 1984 (MFPA 1984);

Child Abduction and Custody Act 1985 (CACA 1985);

Family Law Act 1986 (FLA 1986);

Family Law Reform Act 1987 (FLRA 1987);

Children Act 1989 (CA 1989);

Maintenance Enforcement Act 1991 (MEA 1991);

Child Support Acts 1991 and 1995 and the Child Support, Pensions and Social Security Act 2000 (CSA 1991, CSA 1995 and CSA 2000);

Family Law Act 1996 (FLA 1996);

Trusts of Land and Appointment of Trustees Act 1996 (ToLATA 1996);

Protection from Harassment Act 1997 (PHA 1997);

Human Rights Act 1998 (HRA 1998);

Council Regulation (EC) No. 1347/2000 of May 29, 2000 on jurisdiction and the recognition and enforcement of judgments in matrimonial matters and in matters of parental responsibility for children of both spouses ("Brussels II").

1.02   The principal *rules* of procedure for these proceedings are:

> Rules of the Supreme Court 1965 (RSC);
>
> County Court Rules 1981 (CCR);
>
> Family Proceedings Rules 1991 (as amended) (FPR);
>
> Civil Procedure Rules 1998 (CPR 1998) (see below as to which parts of these rules are applicable to family proceedings);
>
> Family Proceedings (Miscellaneous Amendments) Rules 1999;
>
> Family Proceedings Fees Order 1999 (as amended).

The CPR 1998 do not apply to "family proceedings" as defined by Matrimonial and Family Proceedings Act 1984, s.32 with the exception of the following:

> (*a*) costs, as provided for in the Family Proceedings (Miscellaneous Amendments) Rules 1999.
>
> (*b*) Expert evidence in ancillary relief proceedings, as provided for in FPR 1991, r.2.61C.

1.03   The CPR do, however, apply to other forms of family process and a detailed table of the procedural rules applicable under each relevant statute is set out in the notes to FPR, r.1.3 in *The Family Court Practice 2002.*

Practice directions and *notes* are issued usually by the President or Senior District Judge of the Family Division regulating procedure in family proceedings. If issued with the concurrence of the Lord Chancellor, they are binding on district registries and divorce county courts (FPR, r.10.22).

1.04   *Jurisdiction under MCA 1973 and FPR*: Definitions are contained in FPR, r.1.2.

Family proceedings are defined by MFPA 1984, s.32 as family business, which means business of any description, which, in the High Court, is for the time being assigned only to the Family Division under the Supreme Court Act 1981, s.61 and Sch.1 (MFPA 1984, s.32). Business so assigned to the Family Division includes all matrimonial causes and, in short, causes and matters relating to legitimacy, maintenance of minors, adoption and proceedings under CACA 1985, FLA 1986, CA 1989 and CSA 1991 (as amended). The Lord Chancellor may direct that other business be assigned to the Division under the Supreme Court Act 1981, s.61.

Cause means a *matrimonial cause* as defined by MFPA 1984, s.32 as amended by FLA 1986 or proceedings under MCA 1973, s.19 (FPR, r.1.2). A matrimonial cause is therefore an action for divorce, nullity, judicial separation or presumption of death and dissolution of marriage.

Matrimonial proceedings are those proceedings in which divorce county courts have jurisdiction pursuant to MFPA 1984, ss.33–35 (FPR, r.1.2(7)).

The terms *family proceedings* and *matrimonial proceedings* both include a wide range of proceedings and have different meanings in different statutes.

1.05   Certain county courts are designated *divorce county courts.* Every matrimonial cause must be commenced in a divorce county court and must be heard and determined in that or another such court unless transferred to the High Court under MFPA 1984, s.39 or the County Courts Act 1984, s.41 (transfer by order of the High Court). All divorce county courts are designated courts of trial thereby having jurisdiction to try a matrimonial cause.

Certain divorce county courts are to be designated by the Lord Chancellor under MFPA 1984, s.33(4) as having jurisdiction in matters arising under Pt III of the MFPA 1984 (financial relief after overseas divorce, etc). No such order has as yet been made.

The jurisdiction of a divorce county court is exercisable throughout England and Wales: the residential address of either party does not have to be within the district of the court.

A list of divorce county courts is to be found at Appendix 1.

Outside London, matrimonial proceedings pending in the High Court are **1.06** dealt with in *district registries* and are tried before a judge at *divorce towns*. A list of divorce towns is also set out at Appendix 1.

District registries are in the same office as the local county courts. Not all county court offices have district registries. For the purpose of the FPR, a district registry means any district registry having a divorce county court within its district (FPR, r.1.2). Such district registries are indicated in the list of divorce county courts at Appendix 1.

The *principal registry* means the principal registry of the Family Division of the High Court in London (MFPA 1984, s.42; FPR, r.1.2). It is treated as a divorce county court in respect of proceedings there, which would otherwise be commenced in a county court (FPR, r.1.4).

As to the jurisdiction of courts to try proceedings under CA 1989, see below at para.11.02.

2 Jurisdiction to entertain proceedings

The jurisdiction of the courts of England and Wales in divorce, judicial sep- **1.07** aration, nullity and presumption of death and dissolution derives from DMPA 1973, s.5(2). Section 5(2) of the DMPA 1973 was amended by Council Regulation (EC) No. 1347/2000 of May 29, 2000 on jurisdiction and the recognition and enforcement of judgments in matrimonial matters and in matters of parental responsibility for children of both spouses ("Brussels II"), which came into force on March 1, 2001. The provisions of Brussels II were brought into effect by the European Communities (Matrimonial Jurisdiction and Judgments) Regulations 2001 with consequential amendments to the FPR being brought into effect pursuant to the Family Proceedings (Amendment) Rules 2001.

DMPA 1973, s.5(2) covers the jurisdiction of the courts in divorce and judicial separation in all cases and not just those with a European element, *i.e.* those to which Brussels II is directly relevant.

The courts of England and Wales have jurisdiction to entertain proceed- **1.08** ings:

(*a*) *for divorce or judicial separation* if and only if:

  (i) the court has jurisdiction under Brussels II (see below) or;
  (ii) no court of a contracting state to Brussels II has jurisdiction under Brussels II and either of the parties to the marriage is domiciled in England and Wales on the date when the proceedings are begun.

  The sole jurisdictional basis for the issue of divorce or judicial separation proceedings in cases where Brussels II does not apply is now domicile, as the previous alternative criterion of habitual residence in England and Wales for one year has been abolished.

1.09   (b) for *nullity of marriage* if and only if:

(i) the court has jurisdiction under Brussels II (see below); or

(ii) no court of a contracting state to Brussels II has jurisdiction under Brussels II and either of the parties to the marriage is domiciled in England and Wales on the date when proceedings are begun, or died before that date and either was at death domiciled in England and Wales or had been habitually resident in England and Wales throughout the period of one year ending with the date of death (DMPA 1973, s.5(3)).

(c) for *presumption of death and dissolution of marriage* if and only if the petitioner:

(i) is domiciled in England and Wales on the date when proceedings are begun; or

(ii) was habitually resident in England and Wales throughout the period of one year ending with that date (DMPA 1973, s.5(4)).

Brussels II is confined to proceedings relating to divorce, legal separation or nullity and has no impact on the pre-existing law relating to petitions for presumption of death and dissolution of marriage.

3   Jurisdiction under Brussels II

1.10   Since March 1, 2001 Brussels II has regulated the jurisdiction of the courts of the contracting states in matters relating to divorce, legal separation and nullity. The contracting states are all members of the EU other than Denmark, which declined to participate in the new regime. The contracting states are therefore, Belgium, Germany, Greece, Spain, France, Ireland, Italy, Luxembourg, the Netherlands, Austria, Portugal, Finland, Sweden and the United Kingdom. The United Kingdom includes Scotland, Northern Ireland and Gibraltar, but not the Channel Islands or the Isle of Man.

1.11   Pursuant to Article 2 of Brussels II, in matters relating to divorce, legal separation or marriage annulment, jurisdiction lies with the courts of the member state:

(a) in whose territory:

(i) the spouses are habitually resident; or

(ii) the spouses were last habitually resident, in so far as one of them still resides there; or

(iii) the respondent is habitually resident; or

(iv) in the event of a joint application, either of the spouses is habitually resident; or

(v) the applicant is habitually resident if he or she resided there for at least a year immediately before the application was made; or

(vi) the applicant is habitually resident if he or she resided there for at least six months immediately before the application was made and is either a national of a Member State in question or, in the case of the United Kingdom and Ireland, has his "domicile" there.

(*b*) Jurisdiction shall lie with the courts of the Member State of the nationality of both spouses, or in the case of the United Kingdom and Ireland, of the "domicile" of both spouses. (For the purpose of Brussels II "domicile" has the same meaning as it has under the legal systems of the United Kingdom and Ireland; see below).

Article 8(1) provides a fallback position which is that if none of the grounds **1.12** in Article 2 apply, jurisdiction will be determined by each Member State in accordance with its own laws. Therefore if none of (i) to (vi) above apply and no other Member State has jurisdiction, the additional ground of the domicile of one spouse in England and Wales is still available without either spouse being resident in England and Wales. The alternative ground of habitual residence in England and Wales for a period of 12 months, which was available prior to Brussels II coming into force, has been abolished.

The reference to "joint application" at (iv) above would have applied to divorce proceedings issued in England and Wales had Part II of the Family Law Act 1996 been brought into force, but is of no application as the law currently stands.

There is no order of preference as to the six bases of jurisdiction available under Brussels II which are listed above.

Even where a divorce involves no foreign element whatsoever, a petition **1.13** issued in the courts of England and Wales must set out the basis for jurisdiction by reference to Brussels II with effect from September 3, 2001 pursuant to the Family Proceedings (Amendment) Rules 2001, r.43. See Chapter 22. The provisions of Brussels II, as incorporated by DMPA 1973, apply to any individual who seeks to invoke the jurisdiction of the courts of England and Wales and does not apply solely to EU citizens.

Brussels II is not retrospective and will not affect the jurisdiction of the courts in any proceedings already issued prior to March 1, 2001. Nor does it affect the grounds for divorce, which are still determined by the law of the individual state.

Article 5 provides that where a court has jurisdiction pursuant to Articles 2 to 4 of Brussels II, that court also has jurisdiction to accept a "counterclaim", *i.e.* in English proceedings, an answer and/or cross-petition.

Brussels II makes provision for the jurisdiction of the courts of contracttracting states in matters relating to "parental responsibility" for the children of both spouses, where the court is already seised of matrimonial proceedings under Article 2 as described above. These matters are not discussed in this chapter. Reference should be made to Article 3 of Brussels 11.

4 Definition of domicile and habitual residence

Domicile

Domicile is the legal relationship between a person and a country subject to **1.14** one system of law arising either from his residence there with the intention of making it his permanent home or from its being, or having been, the domicile of some person upon whom he is for this purpose legally dependent. A person can only have one domicile at any time.

A person acquires at birth a *domicile of origin* being, in the case of a legitimate child, that of his father when the parents are both alive and living together at that date.

A legitimate child born after the death of his father, or an illegitimate child, takes his mother's domicile of origin as his own (*Udny v Udny* (1869) L.R. 1 Sc. & Div. 441). As to the domicile of origin of a child whose parents are alive but living apart, see DMPA 1973, s.4 and below. A domicile of origin is never destroyed. It may be displaced by a different domicile of choice but will revive when that new domicile is abandoned until a further domicile of choice is acquired.

1.15   A person who is not under a disability may acquire a *domicile of choice* by voluntarily residing in another country with the intention of continuing to reside there indefinitely, unless and until something happens to make him change his mind, coupled with the absence of a genuine intention of returning to reside permanently in the country in which he was hitherto domiciled (*Russell v Russell* [1957] 1 All E.R. 929; *Re Fuld's Estate* (No. 3) [1968] P.675; *Buswell v IRC* [1974] 2 All E.R. 520; *IRC v Bullock* [1976] 3 All E.R. 353).

The fact that a person has not resided in a country for many years does not necessarily mean that he has abandoned his domicile of choice if there is evidence that his state of mind indicated an intention to return to live there (*Irvin v Irvin* [2001] 1 F.L.R. 178).

A child becomes capable of acquiring a domicile of choice either when he attains the age of 16 or marries under that age (DMPA 1973, s.3). Until such capacity is acquired, a child has a *domicile of dependence* related to that of his parents. Initially, the domicile of dependence will be the same as the child's domicile of origin; however, the domicile of dependence will change when that of one or other of his parents changes.

1.16   A legitimate child's domicile will normally change with that of his father or, after his father's death, with that of his mother. An illegitimate child or one whose parents are separated (where he is living with his mother) has a domicile of dependence changing with that of his mother (DMPA 1973, s.4).

A married woman does not after January 1, 1974 have a domicile dependent upon her husband (DMPA 1973, s.1(1)). However, a woman who was married before January 1, 1974 and then had her husband's domicile by dependence is to be treated as retaining that domicile (as a domicile of choice, if it is not also her domicile of origin) unless and until it is changed by acquisition or revival of another domicile (DMPA 1973, s.1(2)).

Habitual residence

1.17   Habitual residence refers to what is a settled practice or usual. *Rayden and Jackson* 17th ed (paragraph 2.27) says:

> "the expression 'habitual residence' indicates the quality of the residence rather than its duration and requires an element of intention to reside in the country in question. The word 'habitual' denotes a regular physical presence which must endure for some time. Quality is indicated rather than length; intention is not the determining factor although an element of this is required. The expression is not to be treated as a term of art with some special meaning, but, rather, is to be understood according to the ordinary and natural meaning of the two words it contains".

In *Nessa v Chief Adjudication Officer* [1999] 2 F.L.R. 1116 the House of Lords held that as a matter of ordinary language, a person is not habitually resident unless he has taken up residence and lived there for a period. It was a question of fact whether and when habitual residence had been established. There is no fixed period which will determine habitual residence but some period of residence is required in addition to voluntary presence in a country with the settled purpose of establishing residence. In deciding whether a period of residence was sufficient to qualify as habitual residence, bringing possessions, doing everything necessary to establish residence before coming, having a right of abode, seeking to bring family, durable ties with the country of residence or intended residence and many other factors had to be taken into account. Habitual residence does not require continual physical presence subject to *de minimis* absences (*Oundjian v Oundjian* [1979] 1 F.L.R. 198).

A person can have *two habitual or ordinary residences at the same time* but **1.18** must spend an "appreciable" part of the relevant year in a country in order to qualify for habitual residence (*Ikimi v Ikimi* [2001] Fam. Law. 660).

Habitual residence terminates when a person leaves a country with the settled intention not to return see (*C v S* [1990] 2 F.L.R. 442, *D v D* [1996] 1 F.L.R. 574 and *Re M* [1996] 1 F.L.R. 887).

A *child's habitual residence* will usually be dependent upon the person in **1.19** whose care he is but cannot be altered by an unlawful act such as abduction (*Re H* [1991] 1 All E.R. 836). For a useful analysis of a child's habitual residence see *Re M* [1993] 1 F.L.R. 495; *D v D* [1996] 1 F.L.R. 574; and *Re M* [1996] 1 F.L.R. 887. A child's habitual residence cannot be changed unilaterally by one parent where another parent also has parental responsibility. Where only one parent has parental responsibility, and that parent has a settled intention at the time the child leaves the jurisdiction that the child should reside in another country on a long term basis, then the child will lose his or her habitual residence in the first country, even if that parent remains habitually resident there. However, there must be clear evidence of a settled intention (see *In Re V (Jurisdiction, habitual residence)* [2001] 1 F.L.R. 253). There is no real distinction between habitual and ordinary residence (*Kapur v Kapur* [1984] F.L.R. 920; *V v B* [1991] 1 F.L.R. 266, *Ikimi v Ikimi* [2001] Fam. Law. 660).

See further *Rayden and Jackson* (17th ed), pp.37–72.

5   Concurrent proceedings outside England and Wales

Where there are concurrent proceedings issued in a country outside England **1.20** and Wales, the applicable rules which regulate whether the English proceedings should be stayed will depend on where those other proceedings are taking place. The law is set out below under three headings:

(*a*) proceedings in the "related jurisdiction" of Scotland, Northern Ireland, the Channel Islands or the Isle of Man;

(*b*) proceedings in a Contracting State to Brussels II;

(*c*) proceedings elsewhere in the world.

(*a*)   Obligatory stay: concurrent proceedings in Scotland, Northern Ireland, the Channel Islands or the Isle of Man ("the related jurisdiction")

Pursuant to DMPA 1973, Sch.1, s.8(1), where there are continuing proceed- **1.21** ings begun after January 1, 1974 in Scotland, Northern Ireland, the Channel Islands or the Isle of Man and it appears, on the application of a party to the marriage, before the beginning of the trial or first trial of the main suit in proceedings that:

(*a*) proceedings for *divorce* or *nullity* are continuing in a related jurisdiction; and

(*b*) the parties to the marriage have resided together after its celebration; and

(*c*) the place where they resided together when the proceedings in England and Wales were begun, or where they last resided together before the proceedings were begun, is in the related jurisdiction; and

(*d*) either of the parties was habitually resident in the related jurisdiction throughout the year ending with the date on which they last resided together before proceedings were begun in England and Wales,

then the court must order the proceedings in England and Wales to be stayed (see for example *T v T* [1992] 1 F.L.R. 43).

1.22 The court is not obliged to stay the proceedings other than to the extent that they are divorce proceedings (DMPA 1973, Sch.1, para.8(2)). The court may grant a discretionary stay in respect of other proceedings.

An application by a party in proceedings for divorce for an obligatory stay must be made to a district judge, who may determine the application or refer it to a judge as in the case of ancillary relief (FPR, r.2.27(1)). In the divorce county court, the application is made either ex parte or on notice under CCR 1981, Ord. 13, r.1 where at least two clear days' notice will be required. Where proceedings are in the High Court, application is by summons (FPR, r.10.9). No affidavit is required in the first instance although the court may direct evidence to be adduced.

(*b*) Obligatory stay: concurrent proceedings in a contracting state to Brussels II

1.23 Pursuant to Article 11(1) of Brussels II, where proceedings involving the same cause of action and between the same parties are brought before the courts of different Member States, the court second seised shall of its own motion stay its proceedings until such time as the jurisdiction of the court first seised is established.

An identical duty to stay proceedings applies to proceedings for divorce, legal separation or marriage annulment *not* involving the same cause of action but involving the same parties and brought before the courts of a different Member State (Art.11(2)), for example, divorce proceedings brought in one state and nullity proceedings brought in another.

1.24 The crucial date is the date on which the court of the first Member State is deemed to be "seised", defined in Article 11(4) as:

(*a*) at the time when the document instituting the proceedings, or an equivalent document, is lodged with the court, provided that the applicant has not subsequently failed to take the steps he was required to take to have service effected on the respondent, or

(*b*) if the document has to be served before being lodged with the court, at the time when it is received by the authority responsible for service, provided the applicant has not subsequently failed to take the steps he was required to take to have the document lodged with the court.

1.25 *Obligation to stay*: Where the jurisdiction of the court first seised is established, the court second seised must decline jurisdiction in favour of the court first seised (Art.11(3)). Article 7 provides that a spouse who (a) is habitually resident in the territory of a Member State or (b) is a national of a Member State, or in the case of the UK and Ireland has his domicile within a Member State, may be sued in another Member State only in accordance with articles 2 to 6 of Brussels II. This refers to the position of the prospective Respondent.

The court first seised has *exclusive jurisdiction* irrespective of any other con- **1.26**
sideration or argument as to forum conveniens. The party who is the first to issue proceedings will, therefore, secure the jurisdiction of their choice.

Article 9 requires the court to declare of its own motion that is has no jurisdiction if it is seised of a case over which another Member State has jurisdiction and it has no jurisdiction.

The court first seised will remain seised until the proceedings, including any appeal that may be pending have ended (*A v. L (Jurisdiction Brussels II)* (2002) (1 IFLR 1042).

Brussels II does not provide for spouses to be able to regulate, by way of a premarital contract, which state will have jurisdiction in the event of divorce proceedings.

(c) Discretionary stay: concurrent proceedings abroad where Brussels II does not apply

Where there are continuing proceedings begun after January 1, 1974 in any **1.27**
country outside England and Wales *other than a contracting state to Brussels II* and it appears to the court before the beginning of the trial or first trial of the main suit in any matrimonial proceedings, that is, proceedings for divorce, judicial separation, nullity, a declaration as to the validity of a marriage or a declaration as to the subsistence of a marriage, that:

(*a*) any proceedings in respect of the marriage in question, or capable of affecting its validity or subsistence, are continuing in another jurisdiction; and

(*b*) the balance of fairness (including convenience) as between the parties to the marriage is such that it is appropriate for the proceedings in the other jurisdiction to be disposed of before further steps are taken,

then the court may, if it thinks fit, order that the proceedings in England and Wales be stayed, or be stayed so far as they consist of the kind of proceedings in the other jurisdiction (DMPA 1973, Sch.1, para.9(1)).

In considering the balance of fairness and convenience, the court must **1.28**
have regard to all relevant factors, including the convenience of witnesses and any delay or expense resulting from a stay (DMPA 1973, Sch.1, para.9(2)). The court will also take into account any loss of financial advantage if proceedings were continued abroad although such factors will not mitigate against a stay of the English proceedings provided that "substantial justice" can be done to the parties in the courts of the foreign jurisdiction (*Gadd v Gadd* [1985] 1 All E.R. 58; *Thyssen-Bornemisza v Thyssen-Bornemisza* [1985] 1 All E.R. 328; *De Dampierre v De Dampierre* [1987] 2 All E.R. 1; *R. v R.* [1994] 2 F.L.R. 1036) *Breuning v Breuning* [2002] IFLR 888). The fact that an impecunious party is eligible for public funding in England, but ineligible in the foreign jurisdiction with which the proceedings have the most real and substantial connection, is not a ground on which the court should refuse to stay proceedings (*Connelly v RTZ Corp plc* [1996] 1 All E.R. 500).

A prenuptial contract giving one country jurisdiction in the event of matrimonial proceedings, or made under the law of one country, can be an influential factor (*S v S* [1997] 2 F.L.R. 100, *C v C* [2001]1 F.L.R. 624).

1.29   The burden is not on the applicant for a stay to establish that there is another available forum which is clearly or distinctly more appropriate than the English court; the test is simply the statutory test of whether the balance of fairness supports the grant of a stay (*Butler v Butler* [1997] 2 F.L.R. 311).

An application for a discretionary stay *must* be made to a judge (F.P.R., r.2.27(2)) and should be made *at the outset* (*Mansour v Mansour* [1989] Fam. Law. 190 and *K v K* [1999] 1 F.L.R. 969). However, the fact that there is a delay in making an application for stay is not necessarily fatal to that application and each case will turn on its particular facts (*W v W* [1997] 1 F.L.R. 257).

Application is made either *ex parte* or on notice in the divorce county court and by summons in the High Court (FPR, r.10.9).

6   Stays: general considerations

1.30   The court's inherent power to stay proceedings in the circumstances described above is not prejudiced by DMPA 1973 (s.5(6)(b)), thereby enabling the court to order a stay even where there are no proceedings abroad. The court may in exceptional circumstances restrain foreign proceedings being pursued by way of an injunction. The power will be exercised with great discretion and only where it is oppressive or vexatious to continue the proceedings abroad (see *M v M* [1997] 2 F.L.R. 263). As an alternative, an undertaking may be sought from the respondent to the application not to pursue the proceedings abroad pending the outcome of the application for a stay of the proceedings in England and Wales. (See Butterworth's *Family Law Service* C[22]; *Hemain v Hemain* [1988] 2 F.L.R. 388).

1.31   *Stay on directions for trial*: Where it appears to the district judge on reading the papers when giving directions for trial that there are continuing proceedings outside England and Wales, he may direct an appointment before the judge for consideration of a stay (FPR, r.2.27(3)).

1.32   *Duty to give notice of continuing proceedings*: There is a duty to furnish particulars to the court of any proceedings which a party knows to be continuing in another jurisdiction and are in respect of the marriage or capable of affecting its validity or subsistence (DMPA Sch.1, para.7). See Chapter 2 in relation to information to be supplied in the divorce petition. Where a party omits to give notice of proceedings continuing in another jurisdiction, the court may declare that the person has failed in his duty to furnish particulars of those proceedings and the court may consider the question of a stay *at any time* (DMPA 1973, Sch.1, para.9(4)).

1.33   *Conditions imposed upon a stay*: The court may impose conditions upon a stay, for example in *K v K* [1999] 1 F.L.R. 969 where a stay of English proceedings was made conditional upon the husband providing a sum to cover the wife's reasonable legal and travel costs for proceedings in Germany, to avoid injustice to the wife where she was entitled to public funding in England but would not have this benefit in Germany.

1.34   *Discharge of stay*: Where a stay, whether obligatory or discretionary, is in force, the court may, if it thinks fit, on the application of a party, discharge the order staying the proceedings if it appears that the other proceedings outside

England and Wales are stayed, or concluded, or that a party to those other proceedings has delayed unreasonably in prosecuting them (DMPA 1973, Sch.1, para.10(2)). The application may be made to a district judge, who may determine the application or refer it to a judge as in the case of ancillary relief (FPR, r.2.27(5)).

7 Effect of stays and the court's power to provide interim financial and protective relief

1.35

Article 12 of Brussels II provides that in urgent cases, the courts of a Member State shall not be prevented from taking such provisional, including protective measures in respect of persons or assets in that State as may be available under the law of that State even if, under Brussels II, the court of another Member State has jurisdiction as to the substance of the matter. The court's pre-existing powers to grant protective relief in support of proceedings issued in any other jurisdiction are therefore not affected by Brussels II.

Where a stay of proceedings issued in England and Wales has been granted, only where circumstances need to be dealt with urgently may the court make or extend an order for maintenance pending suit, an order for periodical payments for children, a lump sum order for children, an order as to custody and education of children under MCA 1973, an order under CA 1989, s.8 and Sch.1 or an order restraining a person from removing a child out of England and Wales or out of the care of another person. The court does not have the power to make such orders where provision for those matters has been made in an order made in another jurisdiction, except an order restraining a person from removing a child out of England and Wales or out of the care of another person (DMPA 1973, Sch.1, para.11).

Unless the stay is removed or discharged, such existing orders (other than a lump sum) cease to have effect on the expiration of three months from the beginning of the stay, although such orders can be extended (DMPA 1973, Sch.1, para.11).

1.36

Where proceedings are stayed when there is an order in force in another jurisdiction (or when such an order subsequently comes into force) providing for periodical payments for a spouse or child or any provision which could be made under CA 1989, s.8, then an order in the stayed proceedings making such provision for a spouse or child ceases to have effect from the imposition of the stay or the date the order in the other proceedings comes into force in so far as provision is made in the other order for the spouse or child (DMPA 1973, Sch.1, para.11).

An order under MCA 1973, s.24A(1) requiring the proceeds of sale of property to be used for securing periodical payments in favour of a child also ceases to have effect. These provisions apply *only* to proceedings for divorce, judicial separation or nullity, and then only where they are stayed by reference to proceedings for divorce, judicial separation or nullity in the related jurisdiction (DMPA 1973, Sch.1, para.11).

8 Split forum and the jurisdiction of the courts in matters of ancillary relief where there are concurrent proceedings

The fact that the jurisdiction of the court in relation to, for example, a divorce is determined by the court in which proceedings are issued first pursuant to **1.37**

Brussels II does not necessarily mean that financial matters between spouses will also be concluded in that jurisdiction. With the advent of Brussels II, there may now be a trend towards splitting the forum for hearing the divorce and ancillary relief proceedings. The courts of England and Wales may make a stay order in relation to ancillary relief proceedings, enabling financial proceedings to take place abroad, notwithstanding the fact that the divorce will be pronounced here because of Brussels II.

The leading case is *D v P (Forum conveniens)* [1998] 2 F.L.R. 25, in which ancillary relief proceedings following the grant of an English decree of divorce were stayed in circumstances in which neither party lived in England and there was a form of separation agreement which was still operative in Italy. The Italian court had jurisdiction on the issue of the children's maintenance and the English court held that it would be unsatisfactory to have proceedings for the wife's maintenance dealt with separately from the Italian proceedings. An application for a stay of the English ancillary relief proceedings was therefore granted under the court's inherent jurisdiction. See also *W v W (Financial relief: Appropriate forum)* [1997] 1 F.L.R. 257, *K v K* [1999] 1 F.L.R. 969. Note that in *D v P and K v K*, Brussels II would now apply).

1.38   Brussels II does not affect the recognition and enforcement of maintenance obligations within the EU. Brussels I (The Brussels Convention on Jurisdiction and Enforcement in Civil and Commercial matters 1968, incorporated into English domestic law by the CJJA 1982, as amended from March 1, 2001 by Council Regulation No. 44/2001 of December 22, 2000 on jurisdiction and the recognition and enforcement of judgments in civil and commercial matters) provides for reciprocal enforcement of maintenance, including lump sum maintenance. These provisions are not dealt with in this chapter. See para 15.85 below.

9 Polygamous marriages

1.39   A polygamous marriage entered into outside England and Wales after July 31, 1971 is void, where either party was at the time of the marriage domiciled in England and Wales (MCA 1973, s.11(d)).

Section 47 of the MCA 1973 enables matrimonial relief to be granted (*e.g.* divorce or nullity) and declarations concerning the validity of a marriage (*i.e.* Pt III of FLA 1986) to be made, although the marriage in question was polygamous.

R.3.11 of the FPR provides for the additional matters which must be stated in a petition, originating application or originating summons in respect of a polygamous marriage. The court may order an additional spouse to be added as a party to the proceedings or be given notice of the proceedings (FPR, r.3.11(3)). An order may be made at any stage of the proceedings, either on the application of any party or by the court of its own motion. Where an additional spouse is mentioned in a petition or an acknowledgment of service of a petition, the petitioner must, on making an application in the proceedings or, if no application has been made, on making a request for directions for trial, ask for directions as to whether the additional spouse be added as a party or be given notice of the proceedings (FPR, r.3.11(4)). Such an additional spouse is entitled to be heard without filing an answer or affidavit (FPR, r.3.11(5)).

10 Recognition of overseas decrees: divorce, annulment and separation

The law relating to recognition of overseas decrees of divorce, annulment and **1.40** legal and judicial separation is contained in Pt II of FLA 1986 for cases to which Brussels II does not apply (*i.e.* where recognition is sought of a decree granted in a country outside the EU other than Denmark). Where Brussels II applies, it takes precedence over the code of recognition in Pt II of the FLA 1986. The law is set out below under three headings:

(*a*) recognition of decrees granted in the British Islands.

(*b*) recognition of decrees granted in contracting states to Brussels II.

(*c*) recognition of decrees granted abroad in a state other than a contracting state to Brussels II.

(*a*) Divorces, annulments and judicial separations granted in the British Islands

No divorce or annulment obtained in any part of the British Islands will be **1.41** regarded as effective in any part of the UK unless granted by a court of civil jurisdiction, unless saved by the provisions of FLA 1986, s.52(4) and (5)(a) (FLA 1986, s.44(1)). Subject to the court's discretionary power to refuse recognition contained in FLA 1986, s.51, the validity of any divorce, annulment or judicial separation granted by a court of civil jurisdiction in any part of the British Islands must be recognised throughout the UK (FLA 1986, s.44(2)). British Islands means the UK, the Channel Islands and the Isle of Man (Interpretation Act 1978, s.5, Sch.1).

Refusal of recognition: Grounds for non-recognition of divorces, annulments **1.42** and judicial separations are set out in section 51 of FLA 1986 and these are detailed below paras 1.56 *et seq*. However, there are certain grounds which are not applicable in the context of recognition or non-recognition of a decree granted in the British Islands. The court cannot refuse to recognise a decree granted in the British Islands on the grounds that the rules of natural justice have been breached, or that there is no official certificate, or as a matter of public policy, (FLA 1986, s.51(3) being applicable to overseas divorces or legal separations only).

(*b*) Recognition of divorces, annulments and legal separations granted in contracting states to Brussels II

Chapter III of Brussels II provides for the recognition and enforcement of **1.43** judgments of Member States. A "judgment" is defined by Article 13 as a divorce, legal separation or marriage annulment, whatever that may be called, including a divorce, order or decision.

"Judgment" includes the determination of the amount of costs and expenses of relevant proceedings but not property or maintenance orders or other ancillary measures. It includes settlements approved by the court in the course of proceedings and which are enforceable in the Member States.

Procedure: No special procedure is required for a judgment given in a Member **1.44** State to be recognised. However, any interested party may apply for a decision that the judgment be or not be recognised (Article 14). Pursuant to Article 22 and Annex 1 of Brussels II, an application in England and Wales for a declaration of enforceability shall be submitted to the High Court.

Article 23(1) provides that the procedure for making the application shall be governed by the law of the Member State in which enforcement is sought. The following documents shall be attached to the application:

(*a*) a copy of the judgment which satisfies the conditions necessary to establish its authenticity

(*b*) a certificate issued by the court at the request of the applicant using the form for judgments in matrimonial matters (Annex IV to Brussels II)

(*c*) in the case of a judgment given in default, proof of service on the defaulting party of the document instituting proceedings and any document indicating that the defendant has accepted the judgment unequivocally.

(Articles 32 and 33 Brussels II).

Appeals: Article 26 of Brussels II provides for an appeal procedure.

Grounds for refusal of recognition under Brussels II

1.45   Article 18 of Brussels II provides that the recognition of a judgment relating to a divorce, legal separation or a marriage annulment may not be refused because the law of the Member State in which such recognition is sought would not allow divorce, legal separation or marriage annulment on the same facts.

Article 15 provides limited grounds for non-recognition. A judgment shall not be recognised:

(*a*) if such recognition is manifestly contrary to public policy

(*b*) where it was given in default of appearance and the respondent was not served, or not served in sufficient time, with the appropriate documents

(*c*) if it is irreconcilable with a judgment given in proceedings between the same parties in the Member State in which recognition is sought

(*d*) if it is irreconcilable with an earlier judgment given in another Member State or in a non-Member State between the same parties, provided that it would have been recognised under the law of the Member State.

Article 15(2) provides separate grounds for non-recognition of a judgment relating to parental responsibility but this is not dealt with in this chapter. See chapter [ ].

(*c*)   Recognition of overseas divorces, annulments and legal separations granted outside contracting states to Brussels II

1.46   Part II of the FLA 1986 provides a code of recognition for decrees granted in non-Brussels II countries (*i.e.* Denmark and all countries outside the EU).

Part II of the FLA 1986 is retrospective and applies to an overseas divorce, annulment or legal separation obtained at any time (FLA 1986, s.52(1)).

The law and procedure relating to declarations of status (Pt III of the FLA 1986) is discussed in chapter 13.

Subject to FLA 1986, ss.45(2), 51 and 52, the validity of an overseas divorce, annulment or legal separation must be recognised in the UK if, and only if, it is entitled to recognition by virtue of FLA 1986, ss.46–49 or any other enactment (FLA 1986, s.45). Pt II of the FLA 1986 distinguishes between overseas divorces, annulments or legal separations *obtained by means of proceedings* and those *obtained otherwise than by proceedings* ("extra-judicial" divorces, etc).

For the purpose of FLA 1986, s.46, a party to a marriage is domiciled in a country if he was domiciled in that country either according to the law of that country in family matters or according to the law of the part of the UK in which the question of recognition arises (FLA 1986, s.46(5)).   **1.47**

Obtained by proceedings: The validity of an overseas divorce, annulment or legal separation obtained by means of proceedings must be recognised if the divorce, annulment or legal separation is effective under the law of the country in which it was obtained and at the relevant date either party to the marriage: **1.48**

    (*a*) was habitually resident in the country in which the divorce, annulment or legal separation was obtained; or

    (*b*) was domiciled in that country; or

    (*c*) was a national of that country

(FLA 1986, s.46(1)(10)). The "relevant date" means in this context the date of commencement of proceedings (FLA 1986, s.46(3)(a)).

The foreign divorce must have been obtained by one set of proceedings initiated in the same country as that in which the divorce was ultimately obtained (*Berkovits v Grinberg (Att-Gen intervening)* [1995] 2 All E.R. 681).

Ordinarily a talaq divorce, which is a unilateral pronouncement by one spouse, is not the product of judicial or other proceedings for the purpose of the FLA 1986. However in *El Fadl v El Fadl* [2000] 1 F.L.R. 175, where Lebanese law required a talaq to be registered with the Sharia court, that registration process was held to be properly described as "proceedings" for the purpose of section 46(1) of the FLA 1986, even though no judicial decision of that court was required. This will not apply where the talaq has been pronounced outside the state in which it is registered, for example in *Sulaiman v Juffali* [2002] IFLR 479, where the husband pronounced a bare talaq in England which was then registered with the Sharia court in Saudi Arabia. This was held not to be an "overseas divorce" within the meaning of section 45(1) of the FLA 1986, and therefore not entitled to recognition.   **1.49**

Where recognition depends upon habitual residence or domicile in a country comprising territories in which different systems of law are in force in matters of divorce, annulment or legal separation, each territory is to be treated as a separate country (FLA 1986, s.49(1),(2)). However, where recognition depends upon nationality, the divorce, annulment or legal separation must also be effective throughout the country in which it was obtained (FLA 1986, s.49(3)(a)).

A pronouncement of a divorce, annulment or legal separation can be "effective" within the meaning of s.46 of the FLA 1986, even though it may have lacked jurisdictional basis in the country in which it was granted if it would be recognised by that country under some other legal principle such as estoppel (*Kellman v Kellman* [2000] 1 F.L.R. 785).   **1.50**

Where in the case of an overseas annulment, proceedings are commenced after the death of either party to the marriage, the jurisdictional requirements of FLA 1986, s.46(1)(b) are satisfied if the deceased satisfied any of them at the date of his death (FLA 1986, s.46(4)).

1.51 *Obtained otherwise than by proceedings*: The validity of an overseas divorce, annulment or legal separation obtained otherwise than by means of proceedings must be recognised if:

> (*a*) it is effective under the law of the country in which it was obtained;
>
> (*b*) at the relevant date:
>
> > (i) each party to the marriage was domiciled in that country; or
> >
> > (ii) either party to the marriage was domiciled in that country and the other party was domiciled in a country under whose law it is recognised as valid; and
>
> (*c*) neither party to the marriage was habitually resident in the UK throughout the period of one year immediately preceding that date (FLA 1986, s.46(2)).

See, for example, *Wicken v Wicken* [1999] 1 F.L.R. 293 where it was determined by way of expert evidence that a "divorce letter" given by a husband to a wife in the Gambia was effective under Gambian law and would be recognised by the English court.

1.52 For the purpose of section 46(2) of the FLA 1986 "the relevant date" means the date on which the overseas divorce, annulment or legal separation was obtained (FLA 1986, s.46(3)(b)).

Where a country comprises territories in which different systems of law are in force in matters of divorce, annulment or legal separation, the recognition requirements as to domicile have effect as if each territory were a separate country (FLA 1986, s.49(1) and (4)).

In the case of an overseas annulment obtained after the death of either party to the marriage, domicile is determined as at the date of that party's death (FLA 1986, s.46(4)).

1.53 *Cross-proceedings*: Where there have been cross-proceedings, the validity of an overseas divorce, annulment or legal separation obtained either in the original proceedings or in the cross-proceedings must be recognised if the jurisdictional requirements of FLA 1986, s.46(1) (habitual residence, domicile or nationality) are satisfied in relation to the date of the commencement either of the original proceedings or of the cross-proceedings, and the validity of the divorce, annulment or legal separation is otherwise entitled to recognition under Pt II of the FLA 1986 (FLA 1986, s.47(1)).

1.54 *Divorces following legal separations*: Where an overseas legal separation is entitled to recognition under FLA 1986, s.46 or 47(1) and is converted, in the country in which it was obtained, into a divorce which is effective under the law of that country, the validity of the divorce will be recognised whether or not it would itself be entitled to recognition by virtue of those provisions (FLA 1986, s.47(2)). The provisions of FLA 1986, s.49(2)–(4), referred to above, dealing with jurisdictional requirements where a country comprises territories in which different systems of law are in force in matters of divorce etc, also apply.

1.55 *Proof of facts relevant to recognition*: For the purpose of deciding whether an overseas divorce, annulment or legal separation obtained by proceedings is entitled to recognition under FLA 1986, ss.46 and 47, any finding of fact made (whether expressly or by implication) in the proceedings and on the basis of which jurisdiction was assumed in the proceedings is, if both parties to the marriage took part in the proceedings, conclusive evidence of the fact found, and, in any other case, sufficient proof of that fact unless the contrary is shown (FLA 1986, s.48(1)). A "finding of fact" includes a finding as to habitual residence, domicile (under the law of the country in which the divorce, etc. was obtained) or nationality (FLA 1986, s.48(2)). Habitual residence and domicile are to be determined as if each territory were a separate country (FLA 1986, s.49(5)). Nothing in Pt II of the FLA 1986 is to be construed as requiring the recognition of any finding of fault made in any proceedings for divorce, annulment or separation or of any maintenance, custody or other ancillary order made in such proceedings (FLA 1986, s.51(5)). A party to the marriage who has appeared in judicial proceedings is treated as having taken part in them (FLA 1986, s.48(3)).

Grounds for refusal of recognition where Brussels II does not apply

These provisions apply to decrees granted in the British Islands and to decrees granted abroad in a state other than a contracting state to Brussels II (*i.e.* Denmark or any country outside the EU). **1.56**

By FLA 1986, s.51, the court is given a discretionary power to refuse recognition in certain circumstances. A distinction is drawn between divorces, annulments and judicial separations granted by a court of civil jurisdiction in any part of the British Islands and overseas divorces, annulments or legal separations. The effect of the distinction is that the court cannot refuse to recognise a divorce, annulment or judicial separation granted elsewhere in the British Islands on the grounds that the rules of natural justice have been breached or that there is no official certificate or as a matter of public policy (FLA 1986, s.51(3)).

Section 51 of the FLA 1986 provides a discretionary power for the court to refuse recognition of a pronouncement of divorce, annulment or legal separation on any of five grounds:

(1) *Res judicata principle*: A divorce, annulment or judicial separation granted by a court of civil jurisdiction in any part of the British Islands or an overseas divorce, annulment or legal separation may be refused recognition (subject to FLA 1986, s.52) if it was granted or obtained at a time when it was irreconcilable with a decision determining the question of the subsistence or validity of the marriage of the parties previously given (whether before or after the commencement of Pt II of FLA 1986). The decision must have been made by a court of civil jurisdiction in that part of the UK where recognition is sought or by a court elsewhere whose decision is recognised or entitled to be recognised in that part of the UK (FLA 1986, s.51(1)). **1.57**

Recognition cannot, however, be refused on the *res judicata* principle where the validity of a divorce, annulment or separation has been decided upon by any competent court in the British Islands before Pt II of FLA 1986 came into force (FLA 1986, s.52(2)(b)).

(2) *No subsisting marriage*: The validity of a divorce or judicial separation granted by a court of civil jurisdiction in any part of the British Islands or an overseas divorce or legal separation may be refused rec- **1.58**

ognition (subject to FLA 1986, s.52) in any part of the UK if the divorce or separation was granted or obtained at a time when, according to the law of that part of the UK (including its rules of private international law and Pt II of FLA 1986), there was no subsisting marriage between the parties (FLA 1986, s.51(2)); *D v D* [1994] 1 F.L.R. 38).

1.59   (3) *Breach of principles of natural justice*: The validity of an overseas divorce, annulment or legal separation which has been obtained by proceedings may (subject to FLA 1986, s.52) be refused recognition if it was obtained:

> (*a*) without such steps having been taken for giving notice of the proceedings to a party to the marriage as, having regard to the nature of the proceedings and all the circumstances, should reasonably have been taken; or
> (*b*) without a party to the marriage having been given (for any reason other than lack of notice) such opportunity to take part in the proceedings as, having regard to those matters, he should reasonably have been given (FLA 1986, s.51(3)(a)); *D v D* [1994] 1 F.L.R. 38).

1.60   (4) *No official certificate*: The validity of an overseas divorce, annulment or legal separation obtained otherwise than by proceedings may (subject to FLA 1986, s.52) be refused recognition:

> (*a*) if there is no official document certifying that the divorce, annulment or legal separation is effective under the law of the country in which it is obtained; or
> (*b*) where either party to the marriage was domiciled in another country on the date when the divorce, etc. was obtained, there is no official document certifying that it is recognised as valid under the law of that other country (FLA 1986, s.51 (3)(b)). "Official" means that the document must be issued by a person or body appointed or recognised for the purpose of giving such a certificate under the law of the country concerned (FLA 1986, s.51(4)).

1.61   (5) *Public policy*: The validity of an overseas divorce, annulment or legal separation, whether or not obtained by means of proceedings, may be refused recognition if to do so would be manifestly contrary to public policy (FLA 1986, s.51 (3)(c)).

Fraud in itself is not a ground for the refusal of recognition and the motive for the divorce is generally irrelevant in the exercise of the court's discretion, although the fact that one party had deceived the other and the foreign court may be such a ground (*Eroglu v Eroglu* [1994] 2 F.L.R. 287).

11   Effect of recognition or non-recognition

1.62   *Financial relief*: If a marriage has been dissolved or annulled or the parties legally separated by judicial or other proceedings overseas which are entitled to be recognised as valid in England and Wales, either party will be able to apply to the court for leave to apply for financial relief under Pt III of the MFPA 1984. Such applications are discussed at paras 13.19 to 13.31.

Capacity to marry: Where, in any part of the UK a divorce or annulment has **1.63** been granted by a court of civil jurisdiction, or the validity of a divorce or annulment is recognised by Pt II of FLA 1986, the fact that the divorce or annulment would not be recognised elsewhere will not preclude either party to the marriage from remarrying in that part of the UK or cause the remarriage of either party (wherever the remarriage takes place) to be treated as invalid in that part (FLA 1986, s.50).

Findings in previous proceedings: Recognition under Pt II of FLA 1986 does **1.64/5** not require the court to recognise any finding of fault made in proceedings for divorce, annulment or separation or of any maintenance, custody or other ancillary order made in any such proceedings (FLA 1986, s.51(5)).

Wills: The Wills Act 1837, s.18A (added by the Administration of Justice Act **1.66** 1982, s.18(2)) provided for the lapse of any devise or bequest or appointment as executor upon divorce or annulment in the case of the will of a testator dying after December 31, 1982. Section 18A(1)(a) and (*b*) was amended by section 3 of the Law Reform (Succession) Act 1995 in relation to a will made by a person dying on or after January 1, 1996, regardless of the date of the will or the date of the dissolution or annulment. It now provides that the provisions of the will appointing the former spouse as executor or trustee, conferring a power of appointment and devising or bequeathing an interest in property to a former spouse shall take effect or pass as if the former spouse had died on the date on which the marriage was dissolved or annulled. The amended s.18A applies to any divorce or annulment entitled to recognition in England and Wales under Part II of the FLA 1986, by virtue of section 53 of that Act.

See further *Rayden and Jackson,* 17th ed., pp.442–443.

12   Time restrictions on presentation of petitions for divorce or nullity

Divorce: No petition for divorce may be presented before the expiration of one **1.67** year from the date of the marriage (excluding that actual date: *Bamford v Bamford* [1956] C.L.Y. 2831). This is an absolute bar. A petition when presented may nevertheless be based upon matters which occurred during the first year of marriage (MCA 1973, s.3 as substituted by MFPA 1984, s.1).

Nullity: Nullity suits under s.12(c) (lack of consent), (*d*) (mental disorder), (*e*) **1.68** (venereal disease) and (*f*) (pregnancy per alium) of the MCA 1973 (voidable marriages) must be commenced within three years from the date of marriage, unless leave for the institution of proceedings after the expiration of that period is granted. A judge may grant such leave where he is satisfied that the petitioner has at some time during the first three years of marriage suffered from a mental disorder within the meaning of the Mental Health Act 1983 and it is considered just in all the circumstances to grant leave. An application for leave may be made after the expiration of the period of three years from the date of marriage (MCA 1973, s.13, as amended by MFPA 1984, s.2 and Sch.2, para.2).

Judicial separation: A petition for judicial separation can be filed at any time **1.69** after the date of marriage. The one year time bar in MCA 1973, s.3 applies only to petitions for divorce and not to petitions for judicial separation. As to the effect of the time restriction on the amendment of a petition for judicial separation to one for divorce, see para. 4.01 *et seq.*

13   Commencement of proceedings

1.70   Every matrimonial cause must be commenced in a divorce county court (MFPA 1984, s.33(3)) or in the principal registry in London (MFPA 1984, s.42(1)).

Every cause must be begun by petition (FPR, r.2.2(1)) and may be presented in any divorce county court (FPR, r.2.6(1)). A list of these county courts appears at Appendix 1. There is no requirement for the Petitioner to reside in the county court district of the chosen divorce county court.

Where there is before a divorce county court or the High Court a petition which has not been dismissed or otherwise disposed of by a final order, another petition by the same party in respect of the same marriage may not be presented without leave being granted on an application made in the pending proceedings. No such leave, however, is required where it is proposed, after the expiration of the period of one year from the date of the marriage, to present a petition for divorce alleging such of the facts mentioned in MCA 1973, s.1(2) as were alleged in a petition for judicial separation presented before the expiration of that period (FPR, r.2.6(4)).

1.71   Omission to obtain leave to file a petition when there is a first petition undisposed of is an irregularity which the court may set aside and leave can be given retrospectively (*Cooper v Cooper* [1964] 3 All E.R. 167).

The second petition must be filed in a divorce county court. If the first petition is proceeding in the High Court, an application should be made for an order to transfer the new petition to the same court. If the first petition is in the course of being heard, an order may be made by the district judge of the county court (FPR, r.10.10) or by the judge hearing the petition in the High Court (Supreme Court Act 1981, s.26).

See further *Rayden and Jackson* 17th ed. para.10.11.

A person is not prevented from presenting a petition for divorce by reason only that the petitioner or respondent has at any time, on the same facts or substantially the same facts, been granted a decree of judicial separation. The court may treat the previous decree as sufficient proof of any adultery, desertion or other fact by reference to which it was granted, but evidence must be received from the petitioner (MCA 1973, s.4).

As to the commencement of proceedings under CA 1989, see Chapter 11.

Chapter 2

Petitions

1 Contents of petition

Although the form of petition is no longer prescribed, every petition must **2.01** contain the information required by Appendix 2 to the FPR unless otherwise directed. It has been the common practice to use the forms of petition supplied by law stationers, although it was not necessary to do so (*Practice Direction*, August 9, 1971 [1971] 3 All E.R. 288). Computer generated forms are generally acceptable and may indeed be preferred as they should only contain relevant information. The paragraphs in the petition should be numbered. A general form of petition is to be found in Appendix [ ] Form [ ] and a standard form of petition (Court Form D8), together with notes for guidance, may be obtained free of charge from the principal registry or any divorce county court.

The information required in a petition (for divorce, judicial separation, nullity or presumption of death and dissolution) is set out in the following paragraphs, which are prefixed by the same letter, (*a*), (*b*), (*bb*), (*c*), etc. as in FPR App. 2, para.1.

   (*a*) *The names of the parties to the marriage and the date and place of the* **2.02** *marriage*: The place of marriage should be stated so as to be strictly in accordance with the marriage certificate which is filed. If two marriage ceremonies have taken place, details of the first must be given and it is advisable to include details of the second. The court will decide which ceremony created the marriage, that ceremony being recited in the decree (*Thynne v Thynne* [1955] 3 All E.R. 129). The name and status of the wife immediately before the marriage do *not* have to be stated, but this is commonly done (*e.g.* Sarah Brown, then Sarah Jones, a spinster). Any differences between the petition and the marriage certificate should be explained. The correct names of the parties must be stated in full. If the name appearing on the marriage certificate is incorrect, this must be shown and the error corrected, *e.g.* "John James Smith, in the marriage certificate wrongly described as John Smith". Where a party has changed his or her name by deed poll or otherwise, the names as altered should be given first, *e.g.* "Sarah Smith, formerly Brown, who has since the marriage changed her name to Smith" (the husband's name being Brown). The title of the suit would read *"Sarah Smith (formerly Brown) v John Brown"*.

   (*b*) *The last address at which the parties to the marriage have lived together as husband and wife.*

2.03   (*bb*) *Jurisdiction – Brussels II*

Where it is alleged that the court has jurisdiction under the Council regulation (Brussels II), the grounds of jurisdiction under Article 2(1) of the Council regulation should be stated. Following the Family Proceedings (Amendment) Rules 2001, r.43 a new para.3 must with effect from September 3, 2001 be included in a petition:

The court has jurisdiction under article 2(1) of the Council Regulation on the following ground(s) [*tick/mark applicable box*]

❏ (a) The Petitioner and the Respondent are both habitually resident in England and Wales.

❏ (b) The Petitioner and the Respondent were last habitually resident in England and Wales and the [Petitioner/Respondent] still resides there.

❏ (c) The Respondent is habitually resident in England and Wales.

❏ (d) The Petitioner is habitually resident in England and Wales and has resided there for at least one year immediately prior to the presentation of the petition. [*Give the address(es) where the Petitioner lived during that time and the length of time lived at each address*]

❏ (e) The Petitioner is domiciled and habitually resident in England and Wales and has resided there for at least six months immediately prior to the presentation of the petition. [*Give the address(es) where the Petitioner lived during that time and the length of time lived at each address*]

❏ (f) The Petitioner and the Respondent are both domiciled in England and Wales.

[*Or if none of the above apply*]

❏ (g) The court has jurisdiction other than under Council Regulation on the basis that no contracting state has jurisdiction under the Council Regulation and the [Petitioner/Respondent] is domiciled in England and Wales on the date when the petition is issued.

See paras 1.10–1.13 for further discussion of Brussels II.

2.04   (*c*) *Domicile*: Where it is alleged that the court has jurisdiction, other than under the Council regulation, based on domicile, the petition must state the country in which the petitioner is domiciled and, if that country is not England and Wales, the country in which the respondent is domiciled.

See paras 1.14–1.16 for further discussion of domicile.

2.05   (*d*) *Habitual residence*: Where it is alleged that the court has jurisdiction, other than under the Council regulation, based on habitual residence, the petition must state:

(i) the country in which the petitioner has been habitually resident throughout the period of one year ending with the date of the presentation of the petition; or

(ii) if the petitioner has not been habitually resident in England and Wales, the country in which the respondent has been habitually resident during that period, with details in either case, including the addresses of the places of residence and the length of residence at each place.

See paras 1.17–1.19 for further discussion of habitual residence.

(*e*) *The occupation and residence of the petitioner and the respondent*: The respondent's occupation or address may simply be given as "unknown", if such is the case: see p.[00] *et seq* as to service. See p.[00] where it is considered necessary to omit any information from the petition which is required by FPR, App.2. **2.06**

(*f*) *Whether there are any living children of the family*: See (*h*) below as to the definition of a child of the family. If there are living children, the petition should state:

(i) the number of such children and the full names (including surname) of each and his date of birth or (if it is the case) that he is over eighteen; and

(ii) in the case of each child over the age of sixteen, whether he is receiving instruction at an educational establishment or undergoing training for a trade, profession or vocation.

If the name of the child does not indicate the sex, this should be stated.

(*g*) *Other children*: Whether (to the knowledge of the petitioner in the case of a husband's petition) any other child now living has been born to the wife during the marriage and, if so, the full names (including surname) of the child and his date of birth or, if it is the case, that he is over eighteen. **2.07**

(*h*) *Whether there is any dispute as to a child of the family*: If it is the case that there is a dispute concerning whether a living child is a child of the family.

"Child of the family" in relation to the parties to a marriage, means (MCA 1973, s.52(1)):

(i) a child of both those parties; and

(ii) any other child, not being a child who is placed with those parties as foster parents by a local authority or voluntary organisation, who has been treated by both of those parties as a child of their family.

If a petition refers to "issue", "children of the marriage", etc. without saying whether there are other children of the *family,* directions will not be given for trial until a suitable amendment has been made (*Practice Note* April 16, 1959 [1959] 2 All E.R. 163). **2.08**

"Child", in relation to one or both of the parties to a marriage, includes an illegitimate child of that party or, as the case may be, of both parties (MCA 1973, s.52(1)).

If a child of the parties has been legitimised, particulars should be given of the circumstances. If the parties have adopted a child, or if a child of the parties has been adopted, this should be stated in the paragraph dealing with other proceedings affecting the marriage or children of the family (see (*i*) below).

If a child of the family is a ward of court, this should be disclosed in the petition. If wardship proceedings or any other proceedings in the High Court, a county or a family proceedings court relating to a child of the family are begun after the petition has been presented, a statement to that effect must be filed (FPR, r.2.40(2)). A transfer may then be appropriate (MFPA 1984, ss.38 and 39 and *Practice Direction* June 5, 1992 [1992] 3 All E.R. 151.

Where there is a dispute regarding any statement made in accordance with paras (*f*), (*g*) and (*h*) above, the respondent is required to give particulars of the facts relied on in an answer where one is filed, unless otherwise directed (FPR, r.2 15(2)).

2.09   For the court's special duty to consider the children of the family and arrangements made for them, and its power to order that a decree may not be made absolute or a decree of judicial separation be made until the court so orders, see paras 5.15–5.16.

(*i*) *Other proceeding*: Whether or not there are or have been any other proceedings in *any court* in England and Wales or elsewhere with reference to the marriage, or to any child of the family, or between the petitioner and the respondent with reference to any property of either or both of them and, if so:

   (i)   the nature of the proceedings;
   (ii) the date and effect of any decree or order; and
   (iii) in the case of proceedings with reference to the marriage, whether there has been any resumption of cohabitation since the making of the decree or order.

2.10   Where there has been a previous suit, the file in that case is required to be placed with the current cause for use at any hearing. The attention of the court officials should be drawn to the previous proceedings. If the suit was filed in London or in a different county court or registry, they will arrange for the previous file to be sent to the county court or registry where the fresh suit is proceeding.

The issue of a summons, even though withdrawn before the hearing, must be set out. Full particulars are necessary, including any variation of the original order. If any child of the family has been adopted, the adoption proceedings should be mentioned and details should be given unless the details appear in another paragraph. Particulars of wardship proceedings should be included.

(*ia*) *Child Support Act 1991*: If any applications have been made under the CSA 1991 for a maintenance calculation in respect of any child of the family, the date of any such application and details of the calculation made must be included.

2.11   (*j*) *Proceedings continuing outside England and Wales:* If there are any proceedings continuing in any country outside England and Wales which relate to the marriage or are capable of affecting its validity or subsistence the following information should be included:

(i) particulars of the proceedings, including the court in or tribunal or authority before which they were begun;
(ii) the date when they were begun;
(iii) the names of the parties;
(iv) the date or expected date of any trial in the proceedings; and
(v) such other facts as may be relevant to the question whether the proceedings on the petition should be stayed under Sch.1 to DMPA 1973.

Any proceedings which are not instituted in a court of law in that country, but are instituted before a tribunal or other authority having power under the law having effect there to determine questions of status must be included. Proceedings are to be treated as continuing if they have been begun and have not been finally disposed of.

(k) *Agreements for the support of the respondent, petitioner or children*: **2.12** Where the fact on which the petition is based is five years' separation, whether any, and if so what, agreement or arrangement has been made or is proposed to be made between the parties for the support of the respondent or, as the case may be, the petitioner or any child of the family. Although not required by FPR this could also be pleaded in any petition where it is thought desirable to record an agreement at an early stage, especially if under MCA 1973, s.1(2)(d) consent has been given on agreed terms as to ancillary relief.

(l) *In the case of a petition for divorce, that the marriage has broken down irretrievably*: See para. 2.17 *et seq.*

(m) *The fact alleged by the petitioner for the purposes of MCA 1973, s.1(2)* **2.13** *or the ground on which relief is sought*: The fact alleged by the petitioner for the purposes of MCA 1973, s.1(2) or, where the petition is not for divorce or judicial separation, the ground on which relief is sought, together in any case with brief particulars of the individual facts relied on must be included but not the evidence by which they are to be proved.

In the case of a petition alleging unreasonable behaviour (MCA 1973, s.1(2)(b)), where the cause is defended, the district judge may, of his own motion besides on the application of any party, order particulars to be given when he gives directions for trial (FPR, r.2.26).

(n) *The information required by FPR, r.3.11(2) relating to polygamous* **2.14** *marriages*: See pp.[00] for where this is applicable.

A petitioner who intends to rely on Civil Evidence Act 1968, ss.11–12 must state his intention in the petition with particulars (FPR, r.2.4).

2 Application to omit information from form of petition

Where it is desired to omit any information required by FPR, App.2, the peti- **2.15** tion should be filed without such information, but before service is effected an ex parte application must be made to a district judge for leave for the petition to stand. If leave is refused, the district judge should make an order requiring the petition to be amended.

The application should normally be supported by affidavit, although this is in the discretion of the district judge. In the case of an application for the omission of the petitioner's address, the affidavit should state the address, but if it is omitted, or if an affidavit is dispensed with, the petitioner's solicitor should lodge with the court a written note of the address. If leave is granted, an order is drawn up and should provide that the affidavit or statement of the address, as the case may be, be sealed up and not inspected without leave of a district judge. A copy of the order is served with the petition. The outside of the court file is marked to indicate that leave has been granted for non-disclosure of the petitioner's address. Neither the envelope containing the address nor any public funding certificate granted to the petitioner may be made available to any party who seeks to inspect the file, except by leave of a district judge in person.

2.16 Care must be taken that the effect of the order is not nullified by information given in other documents, *e.g.* by giving the name of the school attended by a child in the statement as to the arrangements for children. Subsequent affidavits should commence: "I, , the petitioner in this cause (having been granted leave for my address not to be disclosed in the petition) make oath, etc." (*Practice Directions* April 11, 1968 [1968] 2 All E.R. 88 and May 8, 1975 [1975] 2 All E.R. 384).

FPR, r.10.21, which dispenses with the need for any party to reveal the address of their private residence save by order of the court, does not apply to petitions.

3   Divorce and proof of irretrievable breakdown

2.17 In a petition for divorce it must be alleged: "The said marriage has broken down irretrievably" (FPR, App.2, para.1(1)). This paragraph would not be applicable in the case of a petition for presumption of death and dissolution, unless there is an alternative prayer to dissolve the marriage on the grounds of irretrievable breakdown on the proof of desertion or of separation.

The next paragraph of the petition should contain the facts as related to MCA 1973, s.1(2) which sets out the bases of proof of irretrievable breakdown. Separate sub-paragraphs follow giving brief particulars of the individual facts relied on but not the evidence by which they are to be proved. It is not necessary to show that the basis of proof relied upon *caused* the irretrievable breakdown (*Buffery v Buffery* [1988] 2 F.L.R. 365). A strong presumption of irretrievable breakdown arises once one of the bases of proof has been proved. It is open to a respondent in a defended suit to rebut this presumption (*Santos v Santos* [1972] 2 All E.R. 240; *Mustafa v Mustafa* [1975] 3 All E.R. 355).

It is sufficient for the petitioner to prove irretrievable breakdown at the date of the hearing of the suit (*Pheasant v Pheasant* [1972] 1 All E.R. 587).

2.18 A petitioner may rely under MCA 1973, s.4(1) and (2) on a previous decree of judicial separation or an order under the Domestic Proceedings and Magistrates' Courts Act 1978 or any corresponding enactments in Northern Ireland, the Isle of Man or the Channel Islands as sufficient proof of any adultery, desertion or other fact by reference to which it was granted in order to establish irretrievable breakdown. However, a decree of divorce cannot be granted without evidence being received from the petitioner. A certified copy of the decree or order must be produced upon seeking directions or at the hearing.

Adultery (MCA 1973, s.1(2)(a)): The petition alleges that the respondent **2.19** has committed adultery and that the petitioner finds it intolerable to live with the respondent. Brief particulars of the individual facts relied on must be stated, indicating the date(s) and place(s) involved. (See Appendix 2, form 2)

Adultery is a voluntary act of sexual intercourse involving some penetration, however slight, between a man and a woman one of whom at least is married but not to the other (*Clarkson v Clarkson* (1930) 46 T.L.R. 623; *Dennis v Dennis* [1955] 2 All E.R. 51). The adultery will be involuntary as against a party who is incapable of giving a valid consent, eg by reason of insanity (*Redpath v Redpath* [1950] 1 All E.R. 600; *S v S* [1961] 3 All E.R. 133).

The acknowledgment of service (Form M6) which is annexed to the copy **2.20** petition for service contains the question (no.5) "Do you admit the adultery alleged in the petition?" If the answer is "Yes", it will be treated by the court as an admission upon which the petitioner is entitled to rely. In this case the acknowledgment of service must be signed by the respondent even if it is also signed by his or her solicitor. In such circumstances, it is no longer necessary to prove adultery by a confession statement signed by the respondent or co-respondent or by the evidence of an enquiry agent given by affidavit. Proof of adultery in undefended causes is discussed further on pp. [00].

Where the person with whom the adultery is alleged to have been committed *has been named,* he or she must be joined in the proceedings as co-respondent, whether the respondent is a husband or wife (MCA 1973, s.49), unless the court otherwise directs (FRR, r.2.7(1)).

It is no longer necessary for a petitioner to name the person with whom the respondent is alleged to have committed adultery, even if that person's identity is known to the petitioner (FPR, r.2.7(1)). However, some county courts remain unprepared to accept a petition based upon adultery where a co-respondent has not been named.

If the petition alleges that the respondent has been guilty of rape upon a **2.21** person named, that person is not made a co-respondent unless the court so directs (FPR, r.2.7(2)). Where a petition contains a charge of adultery with a girl under sixteen years of age, an application should be made under FPR, r.2.9(11) for directions whether she should be served (*Practice Direction* December 15, 1960 [1961] 1 All E.R. 129). The fact that it is no longer necessary to name an alleged adulterer or adulteress should severely restrict the number of occasions when it is necessary to name a minor. If it is considered necessary to name a minor, directions of the court should be applied for.

Where a person named as an adulterer or adulteress, or upon whom rape has been committed, has died before the filing of the petition, this must be stated. He or she is not made a party to the proceedings (FPR, r.2.7(5)) and the name does not appear in the title to the suit.

By the Civil Evidence Act 1968, s.12(1) (as amended by FLRA 1987, s.29)) a **2.22** subsisting finding in any family proceedings that a person has committed adultery, or was found or adjudged to be the father of a child in relevant proceedings (as defined by the Civil Evidence Act 1968, s.12(5), as amended by the Courts and Legal Services Act 1990, s.115, Sch.16, para.2(1)) before any court in England and Wales is admissible in evidence in civil proceedings for the purpose of proving that he committed the adultery to which the finding relates, or is or was the father of that child. Birth of a child of which the husband is not the father will be sufficient evidence of the wife's adultery. Proof of paternity is discussed on para. 6.47 *et seq*. If such a finding is relied upon to prove adultery in later family proceedings in the High Court or a divorce county court, a transcript (if any) of the judgment (or an appropriate extract) recording the finding will be required by the court at the hearing. Any party to the original proceedings may order the transcript from the official shorthand writer (FPR, r.10.15(5)). Any other person requiring such a transcript may make application to a district judge under (FPR, r.10.15(6)) for permission for the official shorthand writer to supply the copy (*Practice Direction* [1969] 2 All E.R. 873). If a petitioner intends to adduce such evidence, he must include a statement of his intention in the petition together with particulars (FPR, r.2.4).

2.23   A party is not entitled to rely on adultery committed by the other, if after that adultery became known to him, the parties lived with each other for a period or periods totalling together in excess of six months (MCA 1973, s.2(1)). A petitioner is treated as still relying upon the adultery after decree nisi until decree absolute so that cohabitation after the decree nisi will justify rescission of the decree nisi (*Biggs v Biggs* and *Wheatley* [1977] 1 All E.R. 20). Suspicion does not amount to knowledge for the purposes of this subsection (*Kemp v Kemp* [1961] 2 All E.R. 764). Adultery in this context means an act of adultery so that, where adultery is continuing, eg because of cohabitation, the six-month period will only run from the last act of adultery (*Carr v Carr* [1974] 1 All E.R. 1193). Where it became known to one party that the other has committed adultery, but section 2(*l*) does not apply, and the petitioner relies on that adultery, the fact that the parties have lived with each other after that time must be disregarded in determining whether the petitioner finds it intolerable to live with the respondent (MCA 1973, s.2(2)). A husband and wife are treated as living apart unless they are living with each other in the same household, and references to living with each other are construed as references to their living with each other in the same household (MCA 1973, s.2(6)).

2.24   Since the petitioner has to satisfy the court that, in addition to the respondent having committed adultery, the petitioner finds it intolerable to live with the respondent, the facts may be such that the petitioner is in a position also to satisfy the court, under MCA 1973, s.l(2)(*b*), that the respondent has behaved in such a way that the petitioner cannot reasonably be expected to live with the respondent. This might be pleaded in addition or in the alternative or the petitioner may choose to rely solely upon unreasonable behaviour because of the effect of MCA 1973, s.2(1) (see above).

It is not necessary to show that the petitioner finds it intolerable to live with the respondent because of the adultery (*Cleary v Cleary* [1974] 1 All E.R. 498; *Carr v Carr* [1974] 1 All E.R. 1193).

2.25   *Unreasonable behaviour (MCA 1973, s.1(2)(b))*: The petition alleges that the respondent has behaved in such a way that the petitioner cannot reasonably be expected to live with the respondent.

"Unreasonable behaviour" is a broad concept. The test is whether a right-thinking person would conclude that this particular petitioner could not reasonably be expected to live with this particular respondent. The respondent's behaviour must be examined for its effect upon the petitioner in the light of the temperaments and characters of the parties. Regard must therefore be had to the effect of the behaviour of *this* respondent on *this* petitioner (*Livingstone-Stallard v Livingstone-Stallard* [1974] 2 All E.R. 766; *O'Neill v O'Neill* [1975] 3 All E.R. 289; *Buffery v Buffery* [1988] 2 F.L.R. 365; *Birch v Birch* [1992] 1 F.L.R. 564). The respondent to a divorce petition based upon unreasonable behaviour has the right to oppose it and have the allegations made properly proved to the satisfaction of the court to the civil standard on the balance of probabilities (*Butterworth v Butterworth* [1997] 2 F.L.R. 336).

Examples of unreasonable behaviour may be *positive or negative, e.g.* physical violence towards the petitioner or children, violent temper, causing financial deprivation to the petitioner, verbal abuse, drunkenness, drug taking, persistent nagging, refusal to have sexual intercourse, excessive or unreasonable sexual demands or an improper relationship with another person. Desertion alone cannot amount to unreasonable behaviour (*Stringfellow v Stringfellow* [1976] 2 All E.R. 539). Involuntary actions caused by the mental illness of the respondent may constitute negative unreasonable behaviour even though they are outside the respondents' control (*Katz v Katz* [1972] 3 All E.R. 219; *Thurlow v Thurlow* [1975] 2 All E.R. 979).

2.26 Particulars (with date, time, place, occasion and brief details of conduct) of say, half a dozen of the most serious incidents, including the most recent, should be sufficient to satisfy the court. Nevertheless, it should be indicated that there were other incidents, if such was the case. Particulars of the respondent's disposition are usually pleaded first in general terms, *e.g.* violent temper, meanness. Particulars are then given of specific incidents in chronological order concluding with the separation, if appropriate (see Appendix 2 form 3). The effect of the respondent's behaviour on the petitioner should be pleaded.

Where the petitioner alleges that the respondent has behaved in such a way that the petitioner cannot reasonably be expected to live with him, but the parties to the marriage have lived with each other for a period or periods after the date of the occurrence of the final incident relied on by the petitioner, and held by the court to support the allegations, that fact is disregarded in determining whether the petitioner cannot reasonably be expected to live with the respondent, if the length of that period or of those periods together was six months or less (MCA 1973, s.2(3)). References to the parties to a marriage *living with each other* are construed as references to their living with each other in the same household (MCA 1973, s.2(6)). The court has a discretion to disregard longer periods of cohabitation, and that discretion will be exercised according to the length of and reason for continued cohabitation (*Bradley v Bradley* [1973] 3 All E.R. 750).

2.27 *Desertion (MCA 1973, s.1(2)(c)):* The petition alleges that the respondent has deserted the petitioner for a continuous period of at least two years immediately preceding the presentation of the petition.

Desertion can be defined as separation with the intention of bringing cohabitation permanently to an end when the intention is without both just cause and the consent of the other party. Desertion may be constructive: constructive desertion occurs when one spouse by his conduct compels the other to leave (*Sickert v Sickert* [1899] P.278). Desertion will come to an end if:

(*a*) the parties agree to live apart;

(*b*) the obligation to cohabit has itself been brought to an end by a decree of judicial separation or an order under the Matrimonial Proceedings (Magistrates' Courts) Act 1960 containing a non-cohabitation clause subject to MCA 1973, s.4(5);

(*c*) the parties resume cohabitation or mutually intend so to do;

(*d*) there is condonation;

(*e*) the party who is in desertion makes a bona fide offer to resume cohabitation which is unreasonably refused;

(*f*) a just cause for leaving supervenes.

2.28   The date and circumstances of the desertion should be pleaded. If constructive desertion is alleged, particulars of the conduct relied on should be pleaded
in separate sub-paragraphs as in an unreasonable behaviour position (see
Appendix 2, form 4).

It should be noted that "presentation" means the date of filing, not the date
of the petition. If spouses separated on February 6, 2000 and the petition was
filed on February 6, 2002, the petition was presented a day too early. If a
decree is granted, it is not a nullity in the absence of an appeal (*Warr v Warr*
[1975] 1 All E.R. 85).

The court may treat a period of desertion as having continued even at a time
when the deserting party was incapable of continuing the necessary intention
if the evidence before the court is such that, had the party not been so incapable, the court would have inferred that his desertion continued at that time,
e.g. if a respondent had been sentenced to a term of imprisonment (MCA
1973, s.2(4)).

2.29   In considering whether the period during which the respondent has been in
desertion has been continuous, any one period (not exceeding six months) or
any two or more periods (not exceeding six months in all), during which the
parties lived with each other, does not count as part of the period of desertion
(MCA 1973, s.2(5)).

When a petition for divorce follows a decree of judicial separation, or an
order containing a provision exempting one party to a marriage from the obligation to cohabit with the other, then, for the purposes of the petition, a
period of desertion immediately preceding the institution of the proceedings
for that decree or order will, if the parties have not resumed cohabitation, and
the decree or order has been continuously in force since it was granted, be
deemed immediately to precede the presentation of the petition (MCA 1973,
s.4(3)).

The court may treat as a period during which the respondent deserted the
petitioner any period during which the respondent was excluded from the matrimonial home by an injunction granted by the High Court or a county court
or an order made under MHA 1983, ss.1 or 9 or the Domestic Proceedings and
Magistrates' Courts Act 1978, s.16(3) (MCA 1973, s.4(4)).

*Two years' separation and respondent consents to decree being granted (MCA
1973, s.1(2)(d))*: The petition alleges that the parties to the marriage have
lived apart for a continuous period of at least two years immediately preceding the presentation of the petition and the respondent consents to a decree
being granted. The date and circumstances of the separation should be
pleaded. (See Appendix 2, form 5).

2.30   Section 2(5) of the MCA 1973 and the decision in *Warr v Warr* [1975] 1
All E.R. 85 also apply to MCA 1973, s.1(2)(*d*). The parties are treated as
living apart unless they are living with each other, which means living with
each other in the same household (MCA 1973, s.2(6)). If living apart while
under the same roof, it is necessary to show that two households have been
created so that not only is there a cessation of sexual intercourse, but an
absence of any sharing of domestic duties, such as cleaning or cooking
(*Mouncer v Mouncer* [1972] 1 All E.R. 289; *Fuller v Fuller* [1973] 2 All E.R.
650).

The acknowledgment of service (Form M6) which is annexed to the copy
petition for service contains the question (no.5): "Do you consent to a decree
being granted?" The notice of proceedings (Form M5) is also annexed to the

copy petition for service. This form contains information (para.4) pursuant to MCA 1973, s.2(7) enabling the respondent to understand the consequences of a decree being granted, such as that the respondent's right to inherit from the petitioner if he or she dies without having made a will ceases on a decree being made absolute. Para.4 indicates that a respondent's right to take any gift under the petitioner's will or to act as an executor will cease upon decree absolute, unless a contrary intention appears in the will (Wills Act 1837, s.18A (added by Administration of Justice Act 1982, s.18(2)). Para.4 also informs the respondent, in the case of divorce, that the making absolute of the decree will end the marriage, thereby affecting any right to a pension which depends upon the marriage continuing and that the state widow's pension will not be payable when the petitioner dies, and that any rights of occupation the respondent may have in the matrimonial home under FLA 1996 will cease, unless the court directs otherwise during the subsistence of the marriage. The paragraph also states that other consequences may follow, depending upon the respondent's particular circumstances, and that the respondent should obtain legal advice from a solicitor about these.

Where a respondent wishes to indicate to the court before the hearing that he consents to the grant of a decree under MCA 1973, s.1(2)(d), he must file a notice to that effect signed by himself *personally.* An acknowledgment of service containing a statement that the respondent consents to the grant of a decree will be treated as such a notice if the acknowledgment is signed by the respondent (if the respondent is acting in person), or by the respondent *as well* as the solicitor if the respondent is represented by a solicitor (FPR, r.2.10(1)). Where this is not the case, some other clear and positive act of consent is required (*McG v R* [1972] 1 All E.R. 362; *Matcham v Matcham* (1972) 6 Fam. Law. 212). **2.31**

The respondent may give notice to the court that he does not consent to a decree being granted or that he withdraws any consent which he has already given (FPR, r.2.10(2)). Where such notice is given, the petition is automatically stayed.

The two-year period will only commence when one party has decided the marriage is at an end: hence question 6 in Form M7(d) (affidavit of petitioner in support of petition) (*Santos v Santos* [1972] 2 All E.R. 246). **2.32**

S.10 of the MCA 1973 contains provisions enabling a decree nisi granted under MCA 1973, s.1(2)(d) to be rescinded at any time prior to decree absolute when the respondent has been misled about any matter taken into account when giving consent as well as provisions protecting the financial position of the respondent.

There will usually be an agreement as to costs (*e.g.*, claim for half or no costs) because consent may be validly given on condition that the respondent is not liable for costs (*Beales* v *Beales* [1972] 2 All E.R. 667). The proper order for costs is that the costs are shared by the respondent being ordered to pay half of the costs of the petitioner (*Hymns v Hymns* [1971] 3 All E.R. 596).

Five years' separation (MCA 1973, s.1(2)(e)): The petition alleges that the parties to the marriage have lived apart for a continuous period of at least five years immediately preceding the presentation of the petition. The date and circumstances of the separation should be pleaded. (See Appendix 2, form 6) Section 2(5) and (6) of the MCA 1973 and the decision in *Warr v Warr* [1975] 1 All E.R. 85 (see p.[00]) also apply to MCA 1973, s.1(2)(e). **2.33**

Para.1(k) of App.2 to the FPR requires the petition to state whether any, and if so what, agreement or arrangement has been made or is proposed to be made for the support of the respondent or any child of the family. This requirement enables the court to consider the terms of an agreement when an application for ancillary relief is made.

The respondent may oppose the grant of a decree nisi on the grounds that the dissolution will result in grave financial or other hardship to him and that it would in all the circumstances be wrong to dissolve the marriage (MCA 1973, s.5(1)). This defence only operates when the court makes no finding on any of the other bases of proof contained in MCA 1973, s.1(2) (MCA 1973, s.5(2)(*a*)).

2.34   Grave financial hardship has usually involved loss of pension rights. Other grave hardship has involved allegations that a wife will suffer social ostracism or loss of status consequent upon divorce (*Banik v Banik* [1973] 3 All E.R. 45; *Rukat v Rukat* [1975] 1 All E.R. 343; *Balraj v Balraj* (1980) 11 Fam. Law. 110).

Costs are not usually awarded (*Chapman v Chapman* [1972] 3 All E.R. 1089) except where one party has plainly been unreasonable and so has increased the costs (*Wright v Wright* [1973] 3 All E.R. 932). The court would still have a discretion in the ordinary way to make an order for costs in ancillary relief proceedings (*Grenfell v Grenfell* [1978] 1 All E.R. 561).

4   Judicial separation (MCA 1973, s.17)

2.35   A petition for judicial separation may be presented to the court by either party to a marriage on the ground that any such fact as is mentioned in MCA 1973, s.1 (2) exists, *i.e.*, any such fact as must be proved in order to support a decree for divorce. Judicial separation may be of use where a petitioner has religious objections to divorce or as a means to preserve pension entitlement. Ss.2, 6 and 7 of the MCA 1973 (supplemental provisions as to facts alleged, provisions designed to encourage reconciliation and consideration by the court of agreements and arrangements) apply as they do to a petition for divorce with the necessary modifications (MCA 1973, s.17). However, MCA 1973, s.5 (defence of grave financial or other hardship when petition based upon five years' separation (MCA 1973, s.1(2)(*e*)) and MCA 1973, s.10 (rescission of decree nisi where respondent misled and consideration for respondent's financial position) do *not* apply to petitions for judicial separation. In contrast, MCA 1973, s.4(4) (desertion to continue when certain exclusion orders in force) does apply.

The provisions of Pt II of the MCA 1973 as to ancillary relief apply to decrees of judicial separation in the same way as to decrees of divorce but with certain amendments:

2.36   (1) The court is not obliged to have regard to benefits (for example, a pension) which would be lost only on dissolution or annulment (MCA 1973, s.25(2)(*h*)).

        (2) There are limited powers to vary property adjustment orders made under MCA 1973, s.24(1) (*b*), (*c*) and (*d*) (MCA 1973, s.31(2)(*e*) and s.31(4)).

        (3) The court has no power to make a pension sharing order (MCA 1973, s.24B(1)).

        (4) A party should not be penalised by a reduction in ancillary relief

because such relief is ancillary to judicial separation rather than divorce.

It should be noted that the legislation does not prevent a party seeking **2.37** further orders for ancillary relief upon a subsequent divorce. For example, subject to any agreement reached between the parties, the court may make a lump sum order ancillary to a decree of judicial separation and a further lump sum order ancillary to a subsequent divorce.

The prayer reads "that he (or she) may be judicially separated from the respondent".

The procedure and requirements are the same as those required for a petition for divorce. A precedent for a petition is at Appendix 2, form 1. The special procedure applies as it does to divorce (see para. 5.03 *et seq.*).

On a petition for judicial separation, the court is not concerned to consider **2.38** whether the marriage has broken down irretrievably, and if it is satisfied on the evidence of any such fact as is mentioned in MCA 1973, s.1(2), it must (subject to MCA 1973, s.41 which relates to restrictions on decrees affecting children) grant a decree of judicial separation (MCA 1973, s.17(2)), which is a single decree (i.e., unlike divorce, it is not granted in two stages: nisi and absolute).

An application may be made by consent for the rescission of a decree of judicial separation where a reconciliation has been effected (FPR, r.2.48(1)).

There is no time bar on the presentation of a petition for judicial separation.

The effect of a decree of judicial separation is that the petitioner is no longer obliged to cohabit with the respondent and that if either party dies intestate after the decree his or her property devolves as if the other party had been dead (MCA 1973, s.18(1) and (2)).

5 Nullity

Distinction between void and voidable marriages: A void marriage is one that **2.39** will be regarded as never having taken place and can be so treated by both parties without the necessity of any decree annulling it. A voidable marriage is one that will be regarded as a valid subsisting marriage until a decree annulling it has been pronounced by a court of competent jurisdiction (*De Reneville v De Reneville* [1948] 1 All E.R. 56).

Marriages before August 1, 1971: See MCA 1973, Sch.1, Pt II.

Void marriages: A marriage celebrated after July 1971 31, may be *void* only on **2.40** the following grounds (MCA 1973, s.11):

(1) *Not valid under Marriage Acts*—That it is not a valid marriage under the provisions of the Marriages Acts 1949 to 1986 where:

(a) the parties are within the prohibited degrees of relationship; or
(b) either party is under the age of sixteen; or
(c) the parties have intermarried in disregard of certain requirements as to the formation of marriage.

(2) *Bigamy*—That at the time of the marriage either party was already lawfully married.

(3) *Not male and female*—That the parties are not respectively male and female (*Corbett v Corbett* [1970] 2 All E.R. 33; *W v W (Nullity)* [2000] 3 FCR 748; *Bellinger v Bellinger* [2001] 3 F.C.R. 1).

(4) *Polygamous marriages*—In the case of a polygamous marriage entered into outside England and Wales, that either party was at the time of the marriage domiciled in England and Wales. In such a case a marriage may be polygamous although at its inception neither party has any spouse additional to the other (*Hussain v Hussain* [1982] 3 All E.R. 369).

2.41 *Voidable marriages*: A marriage celebrated after July 31, 1971 may be *voidable* only on the following grounds (MCA 1973, s.12) subject to the bars contained in MCA 1973, s.13 (see below):

2.42

(1) *Incapacity*—That the marriage has not been consummated owing to the incapacity of either party to consummate it (*Baxter v Baxter* [1947] 1 All E.R. 387; *Harthan v Harthan* [1948] 2 All E.R. 639; *Corbett v Corbett (otherwise Ashley)* [1970] 2 All E.R. 33).

(2) *Wilful refusal*—That the marriage has not been consummated owing to the wilful refusal of the respondent to consummate it (*Horton v Horton* [1947] 2 All E.R. 871).

(3) *Lack of consent*—That either party to the marriage did not validly consent to it, whether in consequence of duress, mistake, unsoundness of mind or otherwise (*Szechter v Szechter* [1970] 3 All E.R. 905; *Hirani v Hirani* (1982) 4 F.L.R. 232; *Militante v Ogunwomoju* [1993] 2 F.C.R. 355).

(4) *Mental disorder*—That at the time of the marriage either party, though capable of giving a valid consent, was suffering (whether continuously or intermittently) from mental disorder within the meaning of the Mental Health Act 1983 of such a kind or to such an extent as to be unfitted for marriage (*Bennett v Bennett* [1969] 1 All E.R. 539).

(5) *Venereal disease*—That at the time of the marriage the respondent was suffering from venereal disease in a communicable form (*C v C* (1962) 106 Sol. Jo. 959). Venereal disease has been defined in the Venereal Disease Act 1917, s.4 as "syphilis, gonorrhoea or soft chancre" for the purposes of that Act and does not cover other diseases, *e.g.* AIDS. However, venereal disease or AIDS could be used to evidence a petition for divorce based upon adultery or unreasonable behaviour.

(6) *Pregnancy per alium*—That at the time of the marriage the respondent was pregnant by some person other than the petitioner (*Smith v Smith* [1947] 2 All E.R. 741).

2.43 *Bars to relief where marriage is voidable*: In proceedings instituted after July 31, 1971 the court may not grant a decree of nullity on the ground that the marriage is *voidable*, if the respondent satisfies the court:

(*a*) that the petitioner, with knowledge that it was open to him to have the marriage avoided, so conducted himself in relation to the respondent as to lead the respondent reasonably to believe that he would not seek to do so (*D v D* [1979] 3 All E.R. 337); *and*

(*b*) that it would be unjust to the respondent to grant the decree (*Harthan v Harthan* [1948] 2 All E.R. 639); (MCA 1973, s.13(1)).

The court may not grant a decree of nullity by virtue of MCA 1973, s.12 on **2.44** the grounds of lack of consent, mental disorder, venereal disease, or pregnancy per alium, unless the proceedings were instituted within *three* years from the date of the marriage (MCA 1973, s.13(2)) or leave is granted under MCA 1973, s.13(4) and (5).

The court may not grant a decree of nullity by virtue of MCA 1973, s.12 on the grounds mentioned of venereal disease or pregnancy per alium, unless it is satisfied that the petitioner was at the time of the marriage ignorant of the facts alleged (MCA 1973, s.13(3)).

Foreign marriages: MCA 1973, s.14 provides that the English law of nullity **2.45** applies to marriages which take place after July 31, 1971, but preserves the power of the courts to apply foreign law, if the rules of private international law so require. It also preserves the power to apply the law and rules as to void marriages outside England and Wales under common law or under the Foreign Marriages Acts 1892 to 1947 as amended by the Foreign Marriage (Amendment) Act 1988.

Effect of decree of nullity: A decree of nullity granted after July 31, 1971 on the ground that a marriage is voidable operates to annul the marriage only as respects any time after the decree has been made absolute, and the marriage is treated as if it had existed up to that time (MCA 1973, s.16). In the case of a void marriage, it is unnecessary to obtain a decree of nullity, as the marriage is regarded as never having taken place. However, it is advisable to obtain a decree if only to enable the court to exercise its powers to make orders for ancillary relief. Such powers may be required whether the marriage is found to be void or voidable.

Whether a nullity decree was granted before or after July 31, 1971, a child **2.46** of a voidable marriage is legitimate (MCA 1973, s.16 and MCA 1973, Sch.1, Pt II, para.12). A child of a void marriage, whenever born (but see *F and F v AG and F* [1980] Fam. Law. 60; *Re Spence* [1990] 2 F.L.R. 278), is legitimate if:

(*a*) at the time of the insemination resulting in the birth; or

(*b*) where there was no such insemination, at the time of the child's conception; or

(*c*) at the time of the celebration of the marriage, if later than the insemination or the conception;

both or either of the parties reasonably believed that the marriage was valid and the child's father was domiciled in England and Wales at the time of the birth or, if he died before the birth, immediately before his death (Legitimacy Act 1976, s.1(1), (2) as amended by FLRA 1987, s.28). A reasonable belief in this context can extend to a mistake as to law (Legitimacy Act 1976, s.1(3) added by FLRA 1987, s.28). In relation to a child born after April 4, 1988, when FLRA 1987, s.28 came into force, one of the parties to the marriage is presumed to have held a reasonable belief, unless the contrary is shown (Legitimacy Act 1976, s.1(4) as added by FLRA 1987, s.28).

Form of petition and procedure: For a form of petition, see Appendix 2, form 7. **2.47**

In proceedings for nullity the names of the parties should be stated in the same manner as in proceedings for divorce. The practice of including as an alias name the surname of the wife prior to the marriage is unnecessary (*Practice Direction* June 12, 1973 [1973] 2 All E.R. 880).

Wilful refusal and incapacity may be pleaded in the alternative. If grounds exist, the petition may contain an alternative prayer for divorce, *e.g.* in a petition based on wilful refusal there may be ah alternative prayer for dissolution based upon desertion.

Where proceedings are brought under MCA 1973, s.12(*e*) (venereal disease) or section 12(*f*) (pregnancy per alium), the petition must state whether the petitioner was at the time of the marriage ignorant of the facts alleged (FPR, App.2, para.2).

2.48   The special procedure relating to divorce suits does *not* apply to nullity suits. Sections 1(5), 8 and 9 of the MCA 1973 (which relate to the granting of a decree in two stages (nisi and absolute), the intervention of the Queen's Proctor and the general powers of the court after decree nisi) apply to nullity proceedings (MCA 1973, s.15).

The bar on presenting a petition within a year of the marriage under MCA 1973, s.3 does not apply to nullity.

6   Presumption of death; dissolution of marriage (MCA 1973, s.19)

2.49   There is a common law presumption of death where a spouse has been missing for seven years. Whilst it may be safe to rely on this presumption, *e.g.* to obtain a grant of probate, reliance for the purposes of remarriage would be unsafe where there would remain a risk that a subsequent marriage would be void. This consequence may be avoided by seeking a decree of presumption of death and dissolution of marriage. The decree is not only declaratory as to the presumption of death; it also dissolves the marriage and therefore affects rights of inheritance under a will or on intestacy.

The petition alleges that reasonable grounds exist for supposing that the other party to the marriage is dead. If satisfied that reasonable grounds exist, the court may grant a decree of presumption of death and dissolution of marriage. The paragraph setting out the relief may be as follows:

> "reasonable grounds exist for supposing that the respondent has died on or since the day of 199 ."

The petition must then particularise:

     (*a*) the last place at which the parties cohabited;

     (*b*) the circumstances in which the parties ceased to cohabit;

     (*c*) the date when, and the place where, the respondent was last seen or heard of; and

     (*d*) the steps which have been taken to trace the respondent (FPR, App.2, para.3). The prayer may be worded:

> "that the court will presume that the respondent is dead and that the said marriage may be dissolved".

2.50   An alternative prayer for divorce based upon desertion (MCA 1973, s.1(2)(*c*)) or upon living apart for at least five years (MCA 1973, s.1(2)(e)) may be considered desirable but dispensing with service upon the respondent.

The petitioner must prove that reasonable grounds exist for supposing the respondent to be dead. He will fail if he only proves that it is a mere matter of speculation unless there has been an absence of seven years or more and nothing has happened to give the petitioner reason to believe that the respondent was living (MCA 1973, s.19(3)). Relief is discretionary (*Thompson v Thompson* [1956] 1 All E.R. 603). The decree may be granted before seven years have elapsed if the court is satisfied that reasonable grounds do exist for presuming death (*Chard v Chard* [1956] 3 All E.R. 721).

Enquiries can be made through The Contributions Agency, the Department **2.51** of Work and Pensions, Room 101B, Special Section A, Longbenton, Newcastle upon Tyne, NE98 1YX. (Tel: 0191 213 5000). The Department will forward a letter addressed to the missing spouse at the last known address, if sufficient details are given. (See further, para. 3.43 *et seq.*)

Collusion or other conduct which may previously have been a bar to relief in matrimonial proceedings does not constitute a bar to the grant of a decree under MCA 1973, s.19.

Sections 1(5), 8 and 9 of the MCA 1973 (which relate to the granting of a decree in two stages (nisi and absolute), the intervention of the Queen's Proctor and general powers of the court after decree nisi) apply (MCA 1973, s.19(4)).

The court has power to grant ancillary relief if the party presumed dead is subsequently found to be alive (*Deacock v Deacock* [1958] 2 All E.R. 633). In other cases, the surviving spouse will have to rely upon the Inheritance (Provision for Family and Dependents) Act 1975 because of the effect of the decree on rights of inheritance.

7   Ancillary relief

Applications for ancillary relief in a petition are included in the prayer (FPR, **2.52** App.2, para.4(*a*)). Application for the following relief must be made in the petition:

(*a*) an order for maintenance pending suit;

(*b*) a financial provision order;

(*c*) a property adjustment order;

(*d*) pension sharing order.

If it is not made then, an application may be made later by leave of the court or upon agreed terms (FPR, r.2.53(2)).

An application for an avoidance of disposition order or a variation order need not be included in the petition.

8   Conclusion of petition

Every petition must conclude with: **2.53**

(1) A prayer setting out particulars of the relief claimed including any claim for costs and any application for ancillary relief which it is intended to claim.

The prayer *may* include any application for an order under any provision of Pt I or Pt II of the CA 1989 with respect to a child of the family, although it is no longer necessary to do so (Family Proceedings (Amendment No 2) Rules 1992, r.23).

(2) The names and address of the persons who are to be served with the petition, indicating if any of them is a person under disability.

2.54 Where a solicitor has agreed to his name and address being used as the address for service when a petitioner sues in person, but subsequently the solicitor wishes to withdraw his agreement, he should notify the court to this effect, give the petitioner's last known address and certify that he has notified the petitioner of the withdrawal of his agreement (*Practice Direction* April 12, 1979 [1979] 2 All E.R. 45).

The prayer for *divorce* is that the said marriage may be dissolved; in *nullity,* in the case of a *void* marriage, that the marriage may be declared void; and in the case of a *voidable* marriage, that the marriage may be annulled; *in judicial separation,* that the petitioner may **2.55** be judicially separated from the respondent.

Costs cannot be allowed, unless claimed in the prayer. It is therefore important to ensure that a prayer for costs is included if the petitioner wishes to recover the costs of the proceedings from the respondent. If the petitioner subsequently decides not to pursue the prayer for costs or to seek only half costs or costs in an agreed amount, the affidavit in support of petition should so state.

(3) The petitioner's address for service which, where the petitioner sues by a solicitor, must be the solicitor's name or firm and address.

Where the petitioner, although suing in person, is receiving legal advice from a solicitor, the solicitor's name or firm and address may be given as the address for service if he agrees. In any other case, the petitioner's address for service shall be the address of any place in England or Wales to which documents for him may be delivered or sent (FPR, App.2, para.4(*c*)).

9   Parties

2.56 R.2.7(1) of the FPR provides that where a petition alleges that the respondent (whether husband or wife) has committed adultery, the person with whom the adultery is alleged to have been committed shall be made a co-respondent unless:

(*a*) that person is not named in the petition; or

(*b*) the court otherwise directs.

2.57 However, where a petition alleges that the respondent has committed rape upon a person named, that person is not made a co-respondent unless the court so directs (FPR, r.2.7(2)). Service relating to adultery with a child is discussed on para. 2.21 *et seq.*

In every case in which adultery is alleged against any person not made a party to the suit, or in which the court considers that that person should be made a party to the suit in his interest, the court may allow that person to intervene (MCA 1973, s.49(5)).

Any application for directions under the above paragraphs may be made ex parte if no notice of intention to defend has been given (FPR, r.2.7(4)). Applications are by affidavit. A fee of £30 is payable. Attendance is sometimes required. If notice of intention to defend has been filed, then application is by notice of application in the county court or by summons in the High Court, in either case supported by affidavit. A fee of £30 is payable.

R.2.7(3) also provides that where a petition alleges that the other party to the marriage has been guilty of an improper association (other than adultery) with a person named, the court may direct that the person named be made a co-respondent in the case, and for that purpose the district judge may give notice to the petitioner and to any other party who has given notice of intention to defend, of a date and time when the court will consider giving such a direction.

R.2.7(1) and (3) do not apply where the person named has died before the filing of the petition (FPR, r.2.7(5)). **2.58**

Where adultery (including condoned adultery) or a reasonable belief of adultery is alleged as part of unreasonable behaviour in a petition under MCA 1973, s.1(2)(*b*), it is not necessary to name the third party, even if his or her identity is known. If, however, he or she *is* named in these circumstances, the alleged adulterer must be made a party as correspondent.

It is unnecessary to join a man admitted by a wife to be the father of her child if no allegation is made against him by the husband (*Practice Direction* December 3, 1935).

10 Signing of petition

Every petition must be signed by counsel if settled by him/her and, if not, by the petitioner's solicitor in his/her own name or the name of his/her firm, or by the petitioner if he sues in person (FPR, r.2.5). Counsel's signature to the draft is sufficient and his name may be printed at the end of the petition, this being the practice in the High Court. **2.59**

Chapter 3

Commencement and Service of Proceedings

1 Filing the petition

3.01 Every cause is begun by petition (FPR, r.2.2(1)). A petition is presented by filing it in the court office together with the documents referred to below and may be presented to any divorce county court irrespective of the addresses of the parties (FPR, r.2.6(1) and (5)).

The requirements for filing a petition are as follows (FPR, r.2.6):

(1) Petition and copy for each person to be served.

(2) Certificate of marriage, unless otherwise directed on an application made ex parte (FPR, r.2.6(2)).

(3) Certificate with regard to reconciliation in Form M3, unless otherwise directed on an application made ex parte, if the petition is for divorce or judicial separation and a solicitor is acting (FPR, r.2.6(3)). No certificate is required if the petitioner is "fee exempt" as defined in section 4 of the Family Proceedings Fees Order 1999 (*e.g.* being in receipt of public funding or quantifying benefits).

3.02 (4) Statement as to arrangements for children of the family in Form M4 and any medical report referred to therein, when applicable, with copy for service on respondent spouse (FPR, rr.2.2(2) and 2.6(5)). No copy is required for service on a co-respondent.

(5) Legal funding certificate, if any, and a notice of issue of legal funding certificate, with a copy for each person to be served.

(6) If petitioner is under disability, necessary authority of next friend (FPR, rr.9.2, see paras 3.11 *et seq.*).

(7) A copy of any magistrates' or other court order or maintenance assessment under the Child Support Act 1991 referred to in the petition. (Whilst this is not a strict requirement of FPR, r.2.6, it may be considered desirable to annex any relevant orders to the petition on filing as well as exhibiting them to the petitioner's affidavit.)

(8) Fee of £150. If FPR, r.2.6(4) applies (*i.e.* on presenting with leave a second petition where there is an earlier petition which has not been dismissed or disposed of) a fee of £50 is payable.

The petition is numbered by the court official, who returns Form D9H to the party issuing, stating the number of the petition.

A court office is not entitled to refuse to accept a petition because it is considered not to be drafted in accordance with the rules. The proper course is for the matter to be brought to the attention of the district judge (*Allford v Allford* [1964] 3 All E.R. 220).

2 Marriage certificate

Unless otherwise directed on an application made ex parte, a certificate of the **3.03** marriage to which the cause relates must be filed with the petition (FPR, r.2.6(2)).

There are four ways of obtaining a certified copy of a marriage certificate:

(*a*) From the Register Office for the area in which the marriage was celebrated (fee: £6.50).

(*b*) Where a marriage has been celebrated in a church and the register is kept by the church and has not yet been lodged at the Register Office, a certificate can be obtained direct from the church. The fee is variable.

(*c*) From the Family Records Centre, No. 1 Myddleton Street, Islington, London EC1R 1UW. It is necessary to attend in person and the fee is £6.50, or £22.50 for the priority service in which the certificate can be collected the next day.

(*d*) From the Registrar General, General Register Office, P.O. Box 2, Southport, Merseyside PR8 2JD by making a written request or by telephoning 0870 2437788 (fee: between £8 and £27 depending on the information supplied by the applicant and the level of service chosen).

An application to file a petition without a marriage certificate is normally **3.04** made ex parte by affidavit, *e.g.* if no certificate can be obtained. Such an application may be granted if the petitioner or his solicitor gives an undertaking to file the certificate subsequently.

The certificate of marriage may not be taken off the court file without leave except when:

(*a*) a petition is dismissed and a further petition between the same parties is presented in the same court;

(*b*) a decree of judicial separation has been granted and a petition for divorce between the same parties is presented in the same court.

When a petition is dismissed following a reconciliation, an ex parte consent application may be made for the release of the marriage certificate.

The celebration of a marriage outside England and Wales and its validity **3.05** under the law of the country where it is celebrated may, if the existence and validity of the marriage is not disputed, be proved by the evidence of one of the parties to the marriage and the production of a document purporting to be:

(*a*) a marriage certificate or similar document issued under the law in force in that country; or

(*b*) a certified copy of an entry in a register of marriages kept under the law in force in that country (FPR, r.10.14(1)).

When a document is not in English, it must be accompanied by a translation certified by a notary public or authenticated by affidavit, unless otherwise directed (FPR, r.10.14(2)). Subject to the direction of the district judge, a foreign marriage certificate may be accepted without a translation being available in the first instance. An undertaking may be required by the district judge
3.06 that a translation be filed before directions for trial are given.

R.10.14 of the FPR does not preclude the proof of a marriage in accordance with the Evidence (Foreign, Dominion and Colonial Documents) Act 1933 as amended, which relates to the admissibility of entries contained on foreign registers, or in any other authorised manner, *e.g.* proof of foreign law by expert evidence (FPR, r.10.14(3)). This does not affect the power of the judge at the trial to refuse to admit any evidence if in the interests of justice he thinks fit to do so (FPR, r.2.28(2)). For the requirements for authentication of copies of entries in marriage registers abroad, see *Rayden and Jackson* (17th ed.), p. 122 *et seq.*

3   Certificate with regard to reconciliation (Form M3)

3.07 Where a solicitor is acting for a petitioner for divorce or judicial separation, a certificate in Form M3 must be filed with the petition, unless otherwise directed on an application made ex parte (FPR, r.2.6(3)). Such an application is made by affidavit to the district judge. A fee of £30 is payable. The form is a certificate completed by the solicitor for the petitioner to say whether he has or has not discussed with the petitioner the possibility of a reconciliation and whether he has or has not given him or her the names and addresses of persons qualified to help effect a reconciliation. There is no requirement that either or both of these questions be answered affirmatively for the reasons discussed below. The form should be signed by a solicitor who has the conduct of the case, but it is accepted if it is signed in the firm's name. Form M3 is prescribed in FPR, Appendix 1 and is reproduced in Appendix 2, form 8. This rule gives effect to MCA 1973, s.6(1). It does not apply to a nullity petition.

If at any stage of proceedings for divorce it appears to the court that there is a reasonable possibility of a reconciliation, the court may adjourn the proceedings for such period as it thinks fit to enable attempts to be made to effect such a reconciliation (MCA 1973, s.6(2)). This section also applies to proceedings for judicial separation (MCA 1973, s.17(3)).

3.08 *Practice Direction*: October 4, 1972, as amended on October 19, 1972 [1972] 3 All E.R. 768 states that it is not necessary for the names of individuals qualified to help effect a reconciliation to be given to the petitioner by his solicitor; and that the following organisations and persons will be regarded as persons qualified to help effect a reconciliation for the purposes of the section:

> any marriage guidance council affiliated to Relate (formerly the National Marriage Guidance Council);
>
> any centre of the Catholic Marriage Advisory Council;
>
> the Jewish Marriage Council, 23 Ravenhurst Avenue, London NW4 4EE (tel:0208 203 6311) and Levi House, Bury Old Road, Manchester M8 6FX;
>
> any probation officer;

any Church of England clergyman nominated by the diocesan bishop (the names of such clergyman are available from the diocesan office whose address is in the *Church of England Yearbook*); and

Ministers of Free Church denominations nominated by the General Superintendent of the Baptist Union, by chairmen of the Methodist Districts or by moderators of the provinces of the United Reformed Church (Congregational and Presbyterian) whose names are available from the General Secretary, Free Church Federal Council, 27 Tavistock Square, London WC1H 9HH (tel: 0207–387–8413).

Local organisations may be found in the Yellow Pages. The *Practice* **3.09** *Direction* emphasises that the above list is not exclusive, and in the particular circumstances of any case there may be others who should be regarded as qualified within the section. It also emphasises that the object of MCA 1973, s.6 and FPR, r.2.6(3) is to ensure that the parties seek guidance when there is a sincere desire for a reconciliation. Reference to a marriage guidance counsellor is not a formal step which must be taken in all cases irrespective of the prospects of a reconciliation. Hence, both limbs of the certificate in Form M3 may, in appropriate cases, be completed in the negative.

The court may refer a case to a CAFCASS officer where there is a reasonable possibility of a reconciliation or where there are ancillary proceedings in which mediation might serve a useful purpose (*Practice Direction* 27 January 1971 [1971] 1 All E.R. 894).

4   Statement as to arrangements for children

Where a petition for divorce, nullity or judicial separation discloses that there **3.10** is a minor child of the family who is under 16 or who is over that age and receiving instruction at an educational establishment or undergoing training for a trade or profession, the petition must be accompanied by a written statement containing the information required by Form M4 in FPR, App.1, to which must be attached a copy of any medical report mentioned in the statement (FPR, r.2.2(2)). The statement sets out the arrangements made or proposed to be made for the children. The statement must be signed by the petitioner personally, even where a solicitor is acting.

The statement must, if practicable, be agreed with the respondent. Circumstances in which it would not be practicable to agree the statement with the respondent might include where the respondent is untraceable or where there is a genuine fear of physical violence. It is bad practice for a proposed respondent, to whom a statement has been sent for possible agreement, to mount a "pre-emptive strike" by issuing a petition without any attempt at agreeing the statement (see the Law Society Family Law Protocol 2002).

The courts do not require a certificate or other evidence that an attempt has been made to secure the respondent's agreement to the statement.

Full information should be provided in the statement ensuring that all **3.11** matters referred to in the italicised notes in Form M4 have been adequately covered, as appropriate.

A respondent may file in the court office a written statement of his own views on the present or proposed arrangements for the children whether or not he agreed the statement filed by the petitioner. There is no prescribed form for

such a statement and Form M4 need not be used. On receipt of such a statement from the respondent, the proper officer sends a copy of it to the petitioner (FPR, r.2.38(1)). The statement from the respondent should, if
practicable, be filed within the time limit for giving notice of intention to
defend and in any event before the district judge considers the arrangements
or proposed arrangements for the upbringing and welfare of the children of
the family under MCA 1973, s.41(1) (FPR, r.2.38(2)).

5 Public funding

3.12   Legal Help or Legal Representation may be granted in respect of divorce proceedings pursuent to the funding code under the Access of Justice Act 1999,
although the score of such public funding is often limited see Chapter 17 generally

6 Persons under disability

3.13   *Definitions* "*Person under disability*" means a person who is a minor or a
patient (FPR, r.9.1(1)).
       "*Patient*" means a person who, by reason of mental disorder within the
meaning of the Mental Health Act 1983, is incapable of managing and administering his property and affairs (FPR, r.9.1(1)).
       "*Mental disorder*" means mental illness, arrested or incomplete develop-
ment of mind, psychopathic disorder and any other disorder or disability of
mind (Mental Health Act 1983, s.1(2)).
       Disability is governed by FPR, r.9.1–9.5, RSC Ord. 80, CCR Ord. 10 and
the Court of Protection Rules 2001 (SI 2001/824).
       The Enduring Powers of Attorney Act 1985 enables a power of attorney to
be created in a form prescribed under the Act (Enduring Powers of Attorney
(Prescribed Forms) Regulations 1990), which survives any supervening mental
incapacity and thus avoids the need to apply to the Court of Protection for the
appointment of a receiver (Court of Protection (Enduring Powers of
Attorney) Rules 2001 as amended and *Practice Direction* March 14, 1986
[1986] 2 All E.R. 41 apply).
3.14   *Conduct of proceedings*: Except as otherwise provided, a person under disability may begin and prosecute any family proceedings only by his next friend and
may defend such proceedings only by his guardian ad litem (FPR, r.9.2(1)).
       R.9.2A of the FPR enables a minor to begin, prosecute or defend proceed-
ings without a next friend or guardian ad litem in certain circumstances.
Other examples of where a next friend may not be required include FPR,
r.3.20(3) (application for consent to marry) and FPR, r.7.4(8)(*a*) (judgment
summons on behalf of a minor). Except as otherwise provided by FPR, r.9.2,
it is not necessary for a guardian ad litem to be appointed by the court (FPR,
r.9.2(1)).
       Where a person is authorised under Pt VII of the Mental Health Act 1983
to conduct legal proceedings in the name of the patient or on his behalf (*i.e.*
authorised by the Court of Protection), that person is entitled to be next friend
or guardian ad litem of the patient in any family proceedings to which his
authority extends (FPR, r.9.2(3)).

When a petitioner is a person under disability, the heading of the petition is **3.15** "A B a minor (*or* patient) by C D his next friend" but the title of the cause is simply "A B (by his next friend)". Where a person under disability defends or intervenes, he is described as "E F a minor (*or* patient) by Y Z his guardian ad litem" and appears in the title as "E F (by his guardian)".

When a minor attains the age of eighteen years before the hearing, an application should be made by notice of application (county court) or by summons (High Court) supported by affidavit for the next friend or guardian ad litem to be discharged. A fee of £30 is payable.

The Official Solicitor will, in the absence of any other willing and suitable **3.16** person, act as next friend or guardian ad litem of an adult party under a disability, *i.e.* a patient as defined above (see *Practice Note: Official Solicitor: Appointment in Family Proceedings* [2001] 2 F.L.R. 155). It should be noted that in relation to minors, CAFCASS Legal has taken over many of the responsibilities for representing children which the Official Solicitor previously had. Reference should be made to the Practice Note referred to above and to the CAFCASS *Practice Note: officers of CAFCASS Legal Services and Special Casework: Appointment in Family Proceedings* [2001] 2 F.L.R. 151 for details of when it is appropriate for CAFCASS Legal or the Official Solicitor to act.

No person's name may be used in any proceedings as next friend of a person **3.17** under disability unless he is the Official Solicitor, or the following documents are filed:

(*a*) a written consent to act by the proposed next friend or guardian ad litem; or

(*b*) where the person under disability is a patient and the proposed next friend or guardian ad litem is authorised under Pt VII of the Mental Health Act 1983 to conduct the proceedings in his name or on his behalf, an office copy, sealed with the seal of the Court of Protection, of the order or other authorisation made or given under Pt VII; and

(*c*) except where the proposed next friend is authorised as mentioned in para (*b*) above, a certificate signed personally by the solicitor acting for the person under disability:

  (i) that he knows or believes that the person to whom the certificate relates is a minor or patient stating (in the case of a patient) the grounds of his knowledge or belief and, where the person under disability is a patient, that there is no person authorised as above; and

  (ii) that the person named in the certificate as next friend or guardian ad litem has no interest in the cause or matter in question adverse to that of the person under disability and that he is a proper person to be next friend or guardian (FPR, r.9.2(2) and (7)).

Both consent and certificate may be contained in the same document. No fee is payable.

For form of consent of next friend or guardian ad litem and certificate, see *Rayden and Jackson* (17th ed.), forms 56.144 and 56.145 and *Butterworth's Family Law Service* precedents 2E[21501] and [21502].

3.18   *Defending proceedings*: Except where proceedings are taking place in the absence of a next friend or guardian ad litem in accordance with FPR, r.9.2A, no notice of intention to defend may be given, or answer or affidavit in answer filed, by or on behalf of a person under disability unless the person (acting as guardian ad litem) giving notice or filing the answer or affidavit is the Official Solicitor, or has been appointed by the court to be guardian ad litem, or has filed documents similar to those required in the case of a next friend (see above) (FPR, r.9.2(6)).

The consent of any proposed guardian ad litem and a certificate of fitness should be obtained before the hearing. The order will make such provision as is necessary for giving notice of intention to defend and the filing of an answer.

The Official Solicitor or other guardian ad litem cannot consent on behalf of a patient to a decree being granted under MCA 1973, s.1(2)(*d*). The test for capacity to give a valid consent for a divorce is the same as the test for contracting marriage (*Mason v Mason* [1972] 3 All E.R. 315).

3.19   *Guardian ad litem—Official Solicitor*: Where a person entitled to defend any family proceedings is a patient and there is no person authorised under Pt VII of the Mental Health Act 1983 to defend the proceedings in his name or on his behalf then:

> (*a*) the Official Solicitor must, if he consents, be the patient's guardian ad litem, but at any stage of the proceedings an application may be made, on not less than four days' notice to the Official Solicitor, for the appointment of some other person as guardian;
>
> (*b*) in any other case, an application may be made on behalf of the patient for the appointment of a guardian ad litem.

There must be filed with the application the documents required in r.9.2(7) (FPR, r.9.2(4)).

3.20   Where there is difficulty in obtaining the consent of a person suitable and willing to act, the Official Solicitor may consent to be appointed. He must be approached as a preliminary step. If he acts, he may require an undertaking as to costs. The address of the Official Solicitor is 81 Chancery Lane, London WC2A 1DD (tel: 0207–911–7127).

It is suggested that immediately on filing the petition, a letter should be sent to the Official Solicitor requesting his consent to act as guardian ad litem of the respondent or person entitled to intervene. When the consent is received, the petition endorsed with notice in Form M24 (reproduced in Appendix 2, form 9), should be sent by post to the Official Solicitor.

The petitioner may be called upon to give the Official Solicitor an undertaking to pay his costs. Unless the petitioner is publicly funded, this will take the form of a personal undertaking by the solicitor and the court's attention should be drawn to this to ensure that it is not ignored if a limit is placed upon the costs which the petitioner is ordered to pay.

3.21   *Service (FPR, r.9.3)*: Where a document, to which FPR, r.2.9 (petition and documents to be served like a petition) applies, is required to be served on a person under disability, it must be served as follows:

> (*a*) in the case of a minor who is not also a patient, on his father or guardian or, if he has no father or guardian, on the person with whom he resides or in whose care he is;

(*b*) in the case of a patient:

    (i) on the person (if any) who is authorised under Pt VII of the Mental Health Act 1983 to conduct in the name of the patient or on his behalf the proceedings in connection with which the document is to be served; or

    (ii) if there is no person so authorised, on the Official Solicitor if he has consented under FPR, r.9.2(4) to be guardian ad litem of the patient; or

    (iii) in any other case, on the person with whom the patient resides or in whose care he is.

However, the court may order that a document, which has been, or is to be, served on the person under disability or on a person other than one mentioned in (*a*) or (*b*) above, shall be deemed to be duly served on the person under disability (FPR, r.9.3(1)).

3.22 A document to which FPR, r.2.9 applies (*i.e.* a petition and documents to be served like a petition) must be endorsed with a notice in FPR, Appendix 1, Form M24 (see Appendix 2, form 9). After service has been effected, unless the Official Solicitor is the guardian ad litem of the person under disability, or the court otherwise directs, the party at whose instance the document was served must file an affidavit by the person on whom the document was served, stating whether the contents of the document were, or its purport was, communicated to the person under disability and, if not, the reasons for not doing so (FPR, r.9.3(2)). For the form of affidavit see Appendix 2, form 9.

Where a petition, answer, originating application or originating summons has been served on a person whom there is reasonable ground for believing to be a person under disability, and no notice of intention to defend has been given or answer or affidavit in answer filed on his behalf, the party at whose instance the document was served must, before taking any further steps in the proceedings, apply to a district judge for directions as to whether a guardian ad litem should be appointed to act for that person. On any such application the district judge may, if he considers it necessary to protect the interests of the person served, order some proper person to be appointed his guardian ad litem (FPR, r.9.2(5)). The district judge has a discretion as to whether or not a guardian should be appointed (*M (SE) v M* (SV) [1965] 3 All E.R. 656). He will require evidence that the person is *prima facie* a patient (*Wickens v Wickens* [1952] 2 All E.R. 98).

3.23 The application is to the district judge by notice of application in form D11 (county court) or by summons (High Court). A fee of £30 is payable. For the form of application, see Appendix 2, forms 21 and 22. The application should be supported by an affidavit stating that the petition (or as the case may be) has been served on the respondent, that the respondent has neither given notice of intention to defend nor filed an answer (or as the case may be), and that there is reasonable ground for believing the respondent to be under disability.

As to service upon a girl under 16 years of age against whom there is an allegation of adultery in a petition, see paras 2.19–2.22.

Where a decree nisi is granted on a petition served on a minor without complying with the FPR, the decree will be voidable until made absolute (*John v John and Goff* [1965] 2 All E.R. 222). Where a patient is similarly served, the situation may be remedied after service, *e.g.* by the appointment of a guardian ad litem (*Cutbush v Cutbush* (1893) 37 S.J. 685).

7 Representation of children

3.24 While it is the norm for children to be represented by a children's guardian in public law proceedings, which are not dealt with in this book, in most private law family proceedings the child will not be independently represented. However there are circumstances where it is appropriate for a child to be represented separately and provision is made for this in FPR, r.9.2, 9.2A and 9.5. It should be noted that the terms "next friend" and "guardian ad litem" have been retained within these provisions of the FPR and have not been replaced with the term "children's guardian" which applies in most other family proceedings following the advent of CAFCASS.

Without next friend or guardian ad litem (FPR, r.9.2A): Subject to FPR, r.9.2A(4) (next friend or guardian ad litem already appointed), where a child is entitled to begin, prosecute or defend any proceedings under CA 1989 or the inherent jurisdiction of the High Court, he may do so without a next friend or guardian ad litem where:

> (1) He has obtained the leave of the court for that purpose (FPR, r.9.2A(1)(*a*)); or
>
> (2) A solicitor:
>
>> (*a*) considers that the child is able, having regard to his understanding, to give instructions in relation to the proceedings; and
>> (*b*) has accepted instructions from the child to act for him in the proceedings and, where the proceedings have begun, is so acting (FPR, r.9.2A(1)(*b*)).

3.25 Where a child already has a next friend or guardian ad litem and wishes to prosecute or defend the remaining stages of the proceedings without a next friend or guardian ad litem, he may apply to the court for leave to do so (FPR, r.9.2A(4)).

A child is entitled to apply for leave of the court under FPR, r.9.2A(1) or r.9.2A(4) without a next friend or guardian ad litem either:

> (*a*) by filing a written request for leave setting out the reasons for the application; or
>
> (*b*) by making an oral request for leave at any hearing in the proceedings (FPR, r.9.2A(2)).

On considering a written request for leave under FPR, r.9.2A(1)(*a*) the court must either:

> (1) Grant the request, whereupon the court clerk must inform the child and, where the leave relates to the prosecution or defence of existing proceedings, the other parties to those proceedings; or
>
> (2) Direct that the request be heard ex parte, whereupon the court clerk must fix a hearing date and give notice to the child (FPR, r.9.2A(3)). If leave is granted, notice must be given to the other parties to proceedings already begun (FPR, r.9.2A(7)).

On considering a written request for leave under FPR, r.9.2A(4) and for the **3.26** removal of a next friend or guardian ad litem, the court must either:

(1) grant the request if satisfied that the next friend or guardian does not oppose it, whereupon the court clerk must inform the child and next friend or guardian ad litem concerned and all other parties to the proceedings; or

(2) direct that the request be heard, whereupon the court clerk must fix a hearing date and give notice to the child and next friend or guardian ad litem (FPR, r.9.2A(5)). If leave is granted, notice must be given to the other parties to the proceedings (FPR, r.9.2A(7)).

Where the court is considering whether to grant leave either under FPR, r.9.2A (1)(*a*) or 9.2A(4) (and in the latter case the removal of a next friend or guardian ad litem), it must grant the leave sought and, as the case may be, remove the next friend or guardian ad litem if it considers that the child concerned has sufficient understanding to participate as a party in the proceedings without a next friend or guardian ad litem (FPR, r.9.2A(6)). For a useful discussion as to when a child may have sufficient understanding to do so, see *Re S (A Minor) (Independent Representation)* [1993] 2 F.L.R. 437. See also *Guide to Good Practice for Solicitors Acting for Children*; (5th ed., 2000) Solicitors Family Law Association. The complexity of the proceedings and whether the child intends to instruct a solicitor are clearly of relevance.

Any leave granted under FPR, r.9.2A(1)(*a*) may be revoked where the court **3.27** considers that the child does not have sufficient understanding to participate as a party in the proceedings concerned without a next friend or guardian ad litem (FPR, r.9.2A(8)). This may arise where the nature of the proceedings changes or where the court is of the opinion that leave should not have been granted after all.

Where a solicitor is acting for a child in proceedings in which he is prosecuting or defending without a next friend or guardian ad litem by virtue of FPR, r.9.2A(1)(*b*) and either of the conditions specified in that rule cease to be fulfilled, he must inform the court immediately (FPR, r.9.2A(9)).

Where the court revokes any leave under FPR, r.9.2A(8) or the conditions **3.28** specified in FPR, r.9.2A(1)(*b*) are no longer fulfilled, it may, if it considers it necessary in order to protect the interests of the child, order that some proper person be appointed his next friend or guardian ad litem (FPR, r.9.2A(10)).

A child may be of sufficient understanding to begin, prosecute or defend proceedings without a next friend or guardian ad litem in any event. He may, nevertheless, wish to do so (FPR, r.9.2A(11)(*a*)). If the child disagrees with his next friend or guardian ad litem as to what is in his best interests, it is open to the child to seek to remove him.

Separate representation (FPR, r.9.5): Without prejudice to FPR, r.2.57 (which **3.29** provides for separate representation of children on certain applications for a variation of settlement order and ancillary relief) and FPR, r.9.2A (which allows a child in certain circumstances to participate in proceedings without a next friend or guardian ad litem), if in any family proceedings it appears to the court that any child ought to be separately represented, the court may appoint an officer of CAFCASS, the Official Solicitor or some other proper person (provided, in either of the latter two cases, that he consents) to be the guardian ad litem of the child with authority to take part in the proceedings on the child's behalf (FPR, r.9.5(1)).

Reference should be made to the *CAFCASS Practice Note* [2001] 2 F.L.R. 151 and the *Official Solicitor Practice Note* at [2001] 2 F.L.R. 155 for an explanation as to the circumstances in which the Official Solicitor or CAFCASS Legal will act for a child. As from April 1, 2001, the Official Solicitor no longer represents children who are the subject of family proceedings other than in exceptional circumstances and after liaison with CAFCASS. However the Official Solicitor will act as next friend or guardian ad litem for a child whose own welfare is not the subject of family proceedings, *e.g.* a child intervener in divorce or ancillary relief proceedings. Other examples are given in the Practice Note

3.30   A guardian ad litem should be appointed where a conflict of interests exists between the parent and child (*Re A (A Child)(Contact: Separate Representation)* [2001] 1 F.L.R. 715). Examples of other circumstances in which a child may need party status are given in the CAFCASS Practice Note referred to above.

See *Re H* [1993] 1 F.L.R. 440 and *Re P* [1996] 1 F.L.R. 486 for guidance as to when it is appropriate for a child to be separately represented from his siblings and the guardian ad litem. An order may be made by the court of its own motion or on the application of a party or of the proposed guardian ad litem (FPR, r.9.5(2)). The court may at any time direct that an application be made by a party and may stay the proceedings until the application has been made (FPR, r.9.5(3)).

3.31   Unless otherwise directed, a person appointed to be the guardian ad litem of a child is treated as a party for the purpose of any rule of the FPR requiring a document to be served on or notice to be given to a party to the proceedings (FPR, r.9.5(5)).

Where separate representation for children is required in family proceedings, the children should be joined as parties to those proceedings (*L v L (Minors)(separate representation)* [1994] 1 F.L.R. 156).

3.32   Solicitors who have been consulted by a child (or an adult under a disability) wishing to request the Official Solicitor to act should write to the Official Solicitor setting out the background to the proposed case and explaining why there is no other willing and suitable person to act as next friend or guardian ad litem. Where the Official Solicitor is invited by the court to act in pending proceedings, an order appointing the Official Solicitor should be expressed as being made subject to his consent. The documents to be forwarded to the Official Solicitor in those circumstances are detailed in the *Practice Note* at 2 F.L.R. [2001] 155.

As to the appointment of a guardian ad litem where there is an issue of paternity, see paras 6.49–6.51.

8   Service of petition and accompanying documents

3.33   *Postal and personal service*: A copy of every petition must be served by post or personally on every respondent or co-respondent (FPR, r.2.9(1)). Service may be effected:

(*a*) where the party to be served is a person under disability, through the petitioner (see paras 3.21–3.25);

(*b*) in any other case, through the court, or if the petitioner so requests, through the petitioner (FPR, r.2.9(2)).

Personal service may in no case be effected by the petitioner himself (FPR, r.2.9(3)).

A copy of the petition which is to be served through the court is served by post. Bailiff service as referred to in FPR, r.2.9(4) and (7) is no longer available following the introduction of the CPR 1998.

The court annexes to each copy of the petition for service a notice in form **3.34** M5 with form M6 attached (see below). Any notice of issue of legal funding certificate is also attached. A copy of Form M4 (statement as to arrangements for children) and of any medical report are also served with the petition on the respondent spouse alone (FPR, r.2.6(6), r.2.2(2)).

The notice in Form M5 is a notice of proceedings and Form M6 is an acknowledgment of service in the form of a questionnaire. Form M5 informs the party served what steps he must take to acknowledge service and to defend the cause should he so wish, indicating that he must complete and send the acknowledgment of service to reach the court within seven days after his receipt of the notice. The respondent spouse may wish to file a written statement of his views on the present and proposed arrangements for any children of the family.

Where a petition is sent by an officer of the court, he must note the date of posting in the records of the court (FPR, r.10.5(1)).

Except in special circumstances, service by post must be attempted and charges for personal service will not be allowed on assessment of costs, unless postal service has failed.

If there is a doubt whether the respondent will acknowledge service **3.35** promptly, it might be considered advisable to serve through the petitioner's solicitor rather than to have postal service through the court. In this case, a letter could be sent to the respondent explaining the circumstances and enclosing a stamped addressed envelope for the return of the acknowledgment of service to the court.

Personal service is useful where the respondent has no fixed address but is traceable, *e.g.* by an enquiry agent, or where speed is of the essence. The court may require a letter on filing the petition requesting its return together with the accompanying documents for personal service. See paras 3.36–3.43 below as to affidavits of service.

Where an acknowledgment of service is returned to the court office, the court clerk must send a copy of it to the petitioner (or solicitor) (FPR, r.2.9(8)).

Deemed service: A copy of a petition is deemed to be duly served if: **3.36**

(a) an acknowledgment of service in Form M6 is signed by the party to be served or by a solicitor on his behalf and is returned to the court office; and

(b) where the form purports to be signed by a respondent spouse, his signature is proved at the hearing or, where the cause is undefended, in the petitioner's special procedure affidavit (FPR, r.2.9(5)).

Where a copy of a petition has been sent to a party and no acknowledg- **3.37** ment of service has been returned to the court office, the district judge, if satisfied by affidavit or otherwise that the party has nevertheless received the document, may direct that the document shall be deemed to have been served on him (FPR, r.2.9(6)). This does not apply to a petition alleging two years' separation coupled with the Respondent's consent, unless a written statement from the Respondent confirming that consent is produced (FPR, r.2.9(6A)). Such an affidavit seeking a deemed service order might indicate that the petitioner has served the respondent with the divorce petition or exhibit a letter from the respondent's solicitors indicating that their client has passed the petition to them. For a suggested form of affidavit, see Appendix 2, form 11.

3.38   See paras 3.21–3.22 as to deemed service on a person under a disability.

Personal service: Where a copy of the petition has been served personally on a party and no acknowledgment of service has been returned to the court office, service must be proved by filing an affidavit showing, in the case of a respondent spouse, the server's means of knowledge of the identity of the party served (FPR, r.2.9(7)).

Identification may be by means of:

(1) a recent clear photograph exhibited to the affidavit (and, if possible, signed by the respondent at the time of service) and proved at the hearing to be that of the respondent;

(2) the signature of the person served obtained at the time of service, being proved subsequently by petitioner to be that of the respondent;

(3) the personal knowledge of the process server, the petitioner or some other person present that the person served is the spouse of the petitioner;

(4) the admission of the person served that he is the spouse of the petitioner.

3.39   In (3) and (4) the full circumstances and means of knowledge and such corroborative evidence as is available (*e.g.*, the production by the person served of some document establishing his identity or the volunteering by him of details only likely to be known to the respondent) must be set out in the affidavit or certificate of service.

The photograph should be endorsed with the title and number of the cause. After service the process server should endorse the photograph with words such as "I used this photograph to identify AB" and sign it.

The affidavit of service has to show the server's means of knowledge only in the case of a respondent and not in the case of a co-respondent (FPR, r.2.9(7)).

3.40   A form of affidavit of service is not prescribed by the FPR. A suggested form of affidavit of service is reproduced in Appendix 2, form 12.

When an acknowledgment of service has been returned to the court office, an affidavit of service is not required.

3.41   *Service on solicitors*: Where a document is required by the FPR to be sent to any person who is acting by a solicitor, service must, subject to any other direction or order, be effected:

(*a*) by sending the document by first class post to the solicitor's address for service; or

(*b*) where that address includes a numbered box at a document exchange, at that exchange or at a document exchange which transmits documents every business day to that document exchange. Any document which is left at a document exchange is, unless the contrary is proved, deemed to have been served on the second day after the day on which it is left (FPR, r.10.2(2)); or (*c*) by fax in accordance with FPR r.10.2(1)(*c*). The transmission confirmation slip should be retained.

Where no other mode of service is prescribed, directed or ordered, service may additionally be effected by leaving the document at the solicitor's address (FPR, r.10.2(3)). A suggested form of affidavit of service is reproduced in Appendix 2, form 12. N.B. Confirmation should be obtained from the solicitor that he is instructed to accept service of a petition on behalf of a respondent before service is effected.

Service on persons acting in person: Subject to FPR, r.10.3(3) and to any other **3.42** direction or order, service of a document on anyone acting in person must be effected by sending the document by first class post to the address for service given by him or, if he has not given an address for service, to his last known address (FPR, r.10.3(1)). Subject to FPR, r.10.3(3) where no other mode of service is prescribed, directed or ordered, service may additionally be effected by delivering the document to him or by leaving it at the address specified above (FPR, r.10.3(2)).

Where it appears to the district judge that it is impracticable to deliver the document to the person to be served and that, if the document were left at, or sent by post to, the address specified above, it would be unlikely to reach him, the district judge may dispense with service (FPR, r.10.3(3)). Dispensing with service is discussed further at paras 3.53–3.61.

9 Disclosure of addresses

Government departments: Arrangements have been made whereby the court **3.43** may request an address from the records of the Department for Work and Pensions, the Office for National Statistics, the Passport Office or The Ministry of Defence to trace:

(*a*) the address of a person in proceedings against whom another person is seeking to obtain or enforce an order for financial provision either for himself or herself or for the children of the former marriage; and

(*b*) the whereabouts of a child, or the person with whom the child is said to be, in proceedings under CACA 1985 or in which a custody or residence order is being sought or enforced.

Practice Direction February 13, 1989 [1989] 1 All E.R. 765 refers to a "custody order" as defined in Pt I of the FLA 1986. The CA 1989, however, substituted "Part I order" for "custody order" which covers a significantly greater range of orders, including all orders available under the provisions of CA 1989, s.8.

Requests for such information will be made officially by the district judge. Full details are set out in *Practice Direction* February 13, 1989 [1989] 1 F.L.R. 307.

The request, in addition to giving the information mentioned below, must certify:

(*a*) in financial provision applications either:

(i) that a financial provision order is in existence, but cannot be enforced because the person against whom the order has been made cannot be traced; or

    (ii) that the applicant has filed or issued a notice, petition or originating summons containing an application for financial provision which cannot be served because the respondent cannot be traced. The expression "financial provision order" is widely defined in the *Practice Direction*.

    (*b*) in wardship proceedings that the child is the subject of wardship proceedings and cannot be traced and is believed to be with the person whose address is sought.

3.44 *Department for Work and Pensions (formerly Department of Social Security)*: The department most likely to be able to assist is the Department for Work and Pensions. The applicant's solicitor will be asked to supply as much as possible of the following information about the person sought:

    (*a*) national insurance number;

    (*b*) surname;

    (*c*) forenames in full;

    (*d*) date of birth (or, if not known, approximate age);

    (*e*) last known address, with date when living there;

    (*f*) any other known address(es) with dates;

    (*g*) if the person sought is a war pensioner, his war pension and service particulars (if known);
and in application for financial provision:

    (*h*) exact date of marriage;

    (*i*) wife's forenames.

3.45   Enquiries should be sent by the district judge to the Inland Revenue, National Insurance Contributions Office, Special Section A, Room BP1101, Longbenton, Newcastle upon Tyne NE98 1ZZ (0191 213 5000).

The department will be prepared to search if given full particulars of the person's name and date of birth. The chances of accurate identification are increased by the provision of further identifying information. Second requests for records to be searched, provided that a reasonable interval has elapsed, will also be met by the Department for Work and Pensions.

Where, in the case of applications for financial provision, the wife is in receipt or has been in receipt of income support, it would be advisable in the first instance to make enquiries of the manager of the local social security office for the area in which she resides in order to avoid possible duplication of enquiries.

3.46 *Office for National Statistics: National Health Service Central Register*: The Office for National Statistics administers the National Health Service Central Register for the Department of Health. The records held in the central register include individuals' names, with dates of birth and NHS number, against a record of the Family Practitioner Committee area where the patient is currently registered with an NHS doctor. The central register does not hold individual patients' addresses, but can advise courts of the last Family Practitioner Committee area registration. Courts can then apply for information about addresses to the appropriate Family Practitioner Committee for independent action.

When application is made for the disclosure of Family Practitioner Committee area registrations from these records, the applicant's solicitor should supply as much as possible of the following information about the person sought:

(*a*) NHS number;

(*b*) surname;

(*c*) forenames in full;

(*d*) date of birth (or, if not known, approximate age);

(*e*) last known address; (*i*) mother's maiden name.

The district judge sends enquiries to the Office for National Statistics, National Health Service Central Register, Smedley Hydro, Trafalgar Road, Southport, Merseyside PR8 2HH.

Passport Office: If all reasonable enquiries including the above methods have **3.47** failed to reveal an address, or if there are strong grounds for believing that the person sought may have made a recent application for a passport, enquiries may be made to the Passport Office. The applicant's solicitor should provide as much of the following information about the person as possible:

(*a*) surname;

(*b*) forenames in full;

(*c*) date of birth (or, if not known, approximate age);

(*d*) place of birth;

(*e*) occupation;

(*f*) whether known to have travelled abroad, and, if so, the destination and dates;

(*g*) last known address, with date living there;

(*h*) any other known address(es), with dates.

The applicant or his solicitor must also undertake in writing that informa- **3.48** tion given in response to the enquiry will be used solely for the purpose for which it was requested, that is, to trace the party in connection with the making or enforcement of a financial provision order or in tracing a child in connection with residence or wardship proceedings, as the case may be.

Enquiries should be sent with the undertaking to the Chief Passport Officer, UK Passport Services, Globe House, 89 Eccleston Square, London SW1V 1PN.

Ministry of Defence: Where a person sought is known to be serving or to have **3.49** recently served in any branch of HM Forces, a solicitor may obtain the address for service of financial provision or residence and wardship proceedings direct from the appropriate service department. The list of addresses and details required are contained in *Practice Direction* February 13, 1989 [1989] 1 All E.R. 765, which also contains details of the undertaking required for the release of the address. (*N.B.* The procedure for discovering the service address and for obtaining assistance to arrange personal service is prescribed in CPR 1998 PD6 Annex).

Alternatively, service of process may be effected on the commanding officer of a serviceman but will be ineffective if the commanding officer certifies that the serviceman is under orders for active service abroad and it would be impossible for him to attend the hearing and return in time to embark for service or he has deserted or is absent without leave (Armed Forces Acts 1971, s.62 and 1981, s.18 amending Army Act 1955, s.153, Air Force Act 1955, s.153 and Naval Discipline Act 1957, s.101).

3.50 *Other departments*: Records held by other departments are less likely to be of use. If an address may be known to another department, application may be made to it by the district judge, all relevant particulars available being given. If an address can be supplied, the district judge will release this to the applicant's solicitor (or the applicant if acting in person) against an undertaking to use it only for the purpose of the proceedings.

These arrangements do not apply to the service of petitions which do *not* contain any application for financial provision, etc. The earlier arrangements, whereby the Department for Work and Pensions will at the request of the solicitor forward a letter (and, therefore, a petition enclosed with it) by ordinary post to a party's last known address, remain in force in such cases (*Registrar's Circular* July 6, 1965).

10   Substituted service and dispensing with service (FPR, r.2.9(9), (10) and (11))

3.51 FPR, r.2.9(9) provides that an application for leave to *substitute* some mode of service other than personal service or service by post, or to substitute notice of the proceedings by advertisement or otherwise, must be made ex parte by lodging an affidavit setting out the grounds on which the application is made. However, no order giving leave to substitute notice of the proceedings by advertisement may be made unless it appears to the district judge that there is a reasonable probability that the advertisement will come to the knowledge of the person concerned. The form of the advertisement is settled by the district judge.

Subject to the proviso with regard to substituted service by advertisement, substituted service may be ordered even where there is no likelihood that the document served would reach or come to the knowledge of the person concerned: *Abbey National plc v Frost* [1999] 1 W.L.R. 1080, CA.

3.52 Where it is impracticable to serve a party in accordance with FPR, r.2.9 or it is otherwise necessary or expedient to dispense with service on the respondent or any other person, the district judge may make an order *dispensing* with such service. An application for such an order must be made in the first instance ex parte by affidavit, but the district judge may, if he thinks fit, require the attendance of the petitioner on the application (FPR, r.2.9(11)).

Thus, if service by post is not effective because an acknowledgment of service has not been returned, personal service may be effected or attempted. If personal service cannot be effected because the person to be served is evading service, an application by affidavit may be made for substituted service, if appropriate. If proof of service is still not available, an application might be made under FPR, r.2.9(11) to dispense with further service. The procedure relating to both types of application is discussed below.

Applications in the case of a person whose whereabouts are unknown to the petitioner differ essentially from those where a person is evading service. Where the petitioner, or other applicant, cannot show that there is a reasonable probability that the other party will be likely to see an advertisement in a particular paper, and no other form of substituted service seems likely to be effective, application may be made for an order dispensing with service. **3.53**

Substituted service: An affidavit (or affidavits) is (are) required. A fee of £30 is payable. For the form of affidavit, see *Butterworths Family Law Service*, precedent [21607]. **3.54**

If substituted service by advertisement is proposed, the affidavit must show that there is a reasonable probability that the advertisement will come to the knowledge of the person concerned (FPR, r.2.9(9)). It seems that normally only one insertion should be directed, but this is a matter for the district judge. The order is drawn up by the court.

The applicant or his solicitor should lodge a draft of the advertisement for settling by the district judge. For the form of advertisement and form of order for substituted service, see *Butterworth's Family Law Service*, precedent [21609] and [21608].

Arrangements for the insertion of the advertisement and payment for it are made by the applicant or his solicitor, either direct, or through any advertising agent. **3.55**

If no reply is received after the specified time, the applicant or his solicitor lodges at court the settled draft and a copy of the newspaper containing the advertisement, after which the cause proceeds in the usual way.

Where a communication is received from the respondent indicating his address, the court will send him a copy of the petition and accompanying documents, or as the case may be. If an acknowledgment of service is subsequently received, regard must be had to the time allowed for giving notice of intention to defend. Otherwise, the cause may proceed after expiry of the time specified in the advertisement.

Substituted service by advertisement is now comparatively rare because of the cost involved. Other modes of substituted service will depend on the circumstances and may include, for example, service at the address of a relative whom the respondent is known to visit. **3.56**

An order for substituted service, validly obtained and properly complied with, cannot be challenged even if the respondent never received the relevant document. However, such an order will not have been properly obtained if the applicant has failed to disclose to the court all information relevant to the application. In such circumstances, the order for substituted service and any subsequent decree nisi will be set aside (*Clifford v Clifford* [1985] F.L.R. 732).

Dispensing with service: An application should be made ex parte in the first instance supported by an affidavit setting out the grounds of the application. The court office supplies the form of affidavit as form D13B with notes of guidance, reproduced at 56.158 in *Rayden and Jackson* (17th ed.) A fee of £30 is payable. **3.57**

For form of application, see Appendix 2, form 13.

The affidavit should set out in detail the facts relied on to support the claim that every reasonable line of enquiry has already been tried but without success. Details of the enquiries must be given, such as enquiries from relations, friends, neighbours, place of employment, trade unions, magistrates' courts (if there have been proceedings there), government departments (see above). It is not sufficient to say that "all enquiries have been made" or that "the petitioner knows of no means of getting in touch with the respondent". **3.58**

In *Purse v Purse* [1981] 2 All E.R. 465, because the enquiries had been insufficient the order dispensing with service was treated as defective, rendering consequent decrees voidable.

3.59 On requiring the attendance of the petitioner on the application, the district judge may indicate what particular enquiries should be pursued or direct a specific mode of substituted service before dispensing with service.

The order is drawn up by the court.

In the case of a person acting in person, the district judge may dispense with service of any document where it appears impracticable to deliver the document to the person to be served and that, if the document were left at, or sent by post to, the address given for service or, if no such address has been given, to his last known address, it would be unlikely to reach him (FPR, r.10.3(3)).

11 Service out of England and Wales (FPR, r.10.6)

3.60 Leave is not required to serve any document in family proceedings out of England and Wales.

The document may be served in accordance with FPR (*i.e.* by post, personally or by substituted service) in the same manner as if the address had been in England and Wales, or it may be served in accordance with RSC Ord. 11 rr.5, 6 and 8 (if the proceedings are pending in the High Court) or in accordance with CCR Ord. 8, rr.8–10 and RSC Ord. 11, r.10 (which enables county court documents to be sent to the Senior Master for service abroad in accordance with CCR if the proceedings are pending in a divorce county court). R.10.6 of the FPR sets out in detail how RSC Ord. 11, and CCR Ord. 8 are modified in respect of family proceedings.

3.61 Council Regulation (EC) NO. 1348/2000 of May 29, 2000 on the service in the Member States of judicial and extrajudicial documents in civil and commercial matters applies to the service of documents within the European Union This has been incorporated into the CPR by SI2001/1388. This Regulation does not affect the service of petitions within the EU by post in accordance with FPR, but provides additionally for service of judicial documents on persons residing in another Member State through "transmitting agencies" and "receiving agencies" to be appointed by each Member State. A standard form of request for such service is provided in the Annex to the Regulation. All documents to be served out of England and Wales under the regulations are to be transmitted via the foreign process office of the High Court. The Regulation is only applicable where the address of the person to be served with the document is known.

3.62 Where difficulty is experienced in serving a respondent or other person abroad, consideration might be given to applying for an order dispensing with service under FPR, rr.2.9(11) or 10.3(3).

Where a petition is to be served on a person abroad by posting it from this country, and there is reasonable ground for believing that the person to be served does not understand English, the petition must be accompanied by a translation, approved by the district judge, of the notice in Form M5 in the official language of the country in which service is to be effected or, if there is more than one official language, in any one of those languages which is appropriate to the place where service is to be effected. However, a translation is not required if the official language, or one of the official languages, is English (FPR, r.10.6(4)(*b*)). A notarial translation of the notice or a translation certified by the person making it to be a correct translation and stating his name, address and qualifications for so certifying may be accepted.

Where a petition is to be served out of England and Wales, the time within which the person served must give notice of intention to defend, which will vary from country to country, is determined having regard to the practice under RSC, Ord. 11, r.4(4). Notice in Form M5 is amended accordingly (FPR, r.10.6(4)). The number of days which has to be substituted for the seven days in para.1 of Form M5 is calculated in accordance with RSC Ord. 11 r.4 and can be seen in the table at 11.23 in *Rayden and Jackson* (17th ed.) pp.366–367.

Where a document specifying the date of hearing of any proceedings has to be served out of England and Wales, the date must be fixed having regard to the time limit for giving notice of intention to defend if the document were a petition (FPR, r.10.6(5)).

12 Service of other originating proceedings and pleadings

R.2.9 of the FPR applies to the service of a petition. The rules as to service of **3.63** a petition contained in the FPR also apply to certain other originating proceedings, *e.g.* applications under the MWPA 1882, s.17 (FPR, r.3.6(11)) (FPR, r.3.8(2)) or an originating summons or application under MCA 1973, ss.35 or 36 (FPR, r.3.5(2)). In the absence of specific provisions as to service in the FPR, the RSC or CCR will apply as appropriate. For further information see *Butterworth's Family Law Service* 2A(381).

R.2.9 of the FPR also applies to service of a husband's or wife's answer to a petition or other subsequent pleading on a party cited (FPR, r.2.16)).

See also Chapter 4 (supplemental petition, amended petition, answer, amended answer, supplemental answer, reply and subsequent pleadings).

13 Service of decrees and orders

See paras 7.07 *et seq.*   **3.64**

Chapter 4

Pleadings and Procedure

1 Amended and supplemental petitions (FPR, r.2.11)

4.01 In general, a *supplemental petition* is used to add particulars, allegations or acts which occurred after the date of the original petition. A supplemental petition forms part of the original petition and effects an amendment to it. For form of petition, see Appendix 2, form 14.

In general, *amendment* of a petition is used to add or amend particulars, allegations or acts which arose before the date of the petition, or to make alterations and additions not connected with allegations (including, *e.g.* substitution of prayer for divorce instead of judicial separation, or birth of a child after date of petition).

An amendment of a petition substituting a prayer for divorce instead of a prayer for judicial separation can only be made if the judicial separation petition was filed in excess of one year after the date of the marriage. The amendment becomes part of the original petition and would otherwise be in breach of MPFA 1984, s.3 (divorce within one year of marriage; *Butler v Butler, The Queen's Proctor Intervening* [1990] 1 F.L.R. 114).

4.02 Where a period of two years' separation expires *after* the filing of the original petition, it is not possible to obtain a decree on the sole basis of separation by way of amending the petition or filing a supplemental petition. The two years' separation must immediately precede the petition and therefore it will be necessary to file a second petition (which will require leave unless the original petition is discontinued). The same principle would apply to a period of five years' separation or two years' desertion.

The general principle is that all the amendments should be allowed so as to ensure that all real matters in controversy between the parties are before the court, provided that this can be done without injustice to the other parties. Amendments alleging fraud are no different in this respect from any other amendments (*Atkinson v Fitzwalter* [1987] 1 All E.R. 483).

4.03 *Requirements*: A supplemental *or* amended *petition* may be filed without leave at any time before an answer is filed but thereafter only with leave (FPR, r.2.11(1)(*a*) and (*b*)).

No pleading may, however, be filed or amended, whether or not an answer has been filed, without leave once directions for trial have been given (FPR, r.2.14).

Application for leave to amend a petition by adding a claim for ancillary relief may be made at any time up to the hearing; reservice of the petition will normally be ordered (*Practice Note* [1957] 1 All E.R. 860).

4.04 An application for leave to file a supplemental petition or to amend a petition:

(*a*) may, if every other party consents in writing to the supplemental petition being filed or to the petition being amended, be made by lodging in the court office the supplemental petition or a copy of the petition as proposed to be amended; and

(*b*) must, in any other case, be made on notice (or in the High Court, by summons), to be served, unless otherwise directed, on every other party (FPR, r.2.11(2)).

The district judge may, if he thinks fit, require an application for leave to be supported by affidavit (FPR, r.2.11(3)).

Procedure

Where no leave required: The court will require: 4.05

(*a*) amended petition showing proposed amendments in red or supplemental petition, with one copy for each party to be served;

(*b*) notice of issue of legal funding certificate, if any, for any additional party;

(*c*) fee of £50.

The court completes Form M5 with Form M6 attached for each party to be   4.06
served, inserting the word "amended" or "supplemental" before the word "petition" where appropriate.

If service is not to be effected through the court, the necessary documents for service are returned to the petitioner (or solicitor).

Where leave is required: If the application is *by consent*:   4.07

(*a*) amended petition, showing proposed amendments in red, or supplemental petition, with one copy for each party to be served;

(*b*) consents of other parties in writing;

(*c*) notice of issue of legal funding certificate, if any, for any additional party;

(*d*) affidavit, if required by district judge.

(*e*) fee of £50.

Consents may be endorsed on the amended or supplemental petition filed.
If the application is *not by consent*:   4.08

(*a*) notice of application, if in county court, or summons, if in High Court, and copy for each party to be served;

(*b*) proposed amended or supplemental petition;

(*c*) affidavit, if required by district judge;

(*d*) Fee of £80.

After the hearing, if leave is granted,

(*a*) copy amended or supplemental petition for each party to be served and a copy to be filed if the copy filed with the application is not suitable;

(*b*) notice of issue of legal funding certificate, if any, for any additional party.

4.09   Amendments are to be shown in red in such a way that it should be apparent from the document what amendments have been effected. The original matter to be deleted should be typed in black and ruled through in red, and new matter should be typed in red. On copy documents, amendments should be shown by underlining the amendments in red.

For forms of application, see Appendix 2, forms 15 and 16.

4.10   After inserting the place, date and time of hearing, one copy of the notice of application (or summons) is returned. All other parties must be served at least two clear days before the date of hearing (RSC Ord. 32, r.3 and CCR Ord. 13, r.1(2). If leave is granted, the order is drawn up by the court and a copy sent to the petitioner or his solicitor. The order granting leave must:

(*a*) where any party has given notice of intention to defend, fix the time within which his answer must be filed or amended; and

(*b*) where the order is made after directions for trial have been given, provide for a stay of the hearing until after the directions have been renewed (FPR, r.2.11(4)).

4.11   An order to amend need not specify the amendment but should be in the terms, "be at liberty to amend the petition in accordance with the copy lodged". The court endorses in the top right-hand corner of the first page of the amended petition and copies, "This is the petition as amended pursuant to order dated".

An order to file a supplemental petition will be in the terms: "be at liberty to file the supplemental petition dated the day of 20". The court endorses in the top right-hand corner of the supplemental petition and copies, "Leave to file granted by order dated".

If, when an order is made (*e.g.* at the hearing) there is no copy of the petition available suitable to be filed, the judge may accept an undertaking from the solicitor to lodge a satisfactory copy and the drawing of the order will usually be delayed until such a copy is available. In the case of a minor amendment at a hearing, the judge may grant leave to amend dispensing with reservice. Where an order to amend is made at a hearing, the drawing of the decree nisi should not be delayed because of the absence of a copy suitable for filing. Under the special procedure, minor amendments may be sought by the petitioner in the affidavit in support in the answer to question 2.

4.12   After leave has been granted, copies of the amended or supplemental petition for every person to be served are lodged for sealing, if they have not already been lodged. Form M5 with Form M6 attached is prepared by the court for each person to be served. These forms should have the word "amended" or "supplemental", as appropriate, inserted before the word "petition". A copy of the order is also served. Notice of issue of any legal funding certificate is required for any additional party.

Unless otherwise directed, a copy of the supplemental or amended petition, together with a copy of the order (if any) must be served on every respondent and co-respondent named in the original petition or in the supplemental or amended petition (FPR, r.2.11(7)).

4.13   Service, unless otherwise directed, is effected in accordance with the rules which apply to the original petition (FPR, r.2.11(8)). A direction may be sought for service to be effected solely by delivery of the amended or supplemental petition.

An application to re-amend is dealt with in the same manner, save that re-amended matters are typed or underlined in green.

2 Notice of intention to defend (FPR, r.10.8)

Form M6 is the acknowledgment of service. The form also contains questions **4.14** for the person served to answer, which indicate whether he intends to defend the proceedings.

Any reference in FPR to a notice of intention to defend is a reference to an acknowledgment of service in Form M6 containing a statement to the effect that the person by whom or on whose behalf it is signed intends to defend the proceedings to which the acknowledgment of service relates. Any reference to giving notice of intention to defend is a reference to returning such a notice to the court office (FPR, r.10.8(1)). Form M6 is attached to Form M5 (notice of proceedings), which is served with the petition.

References in the FPR, in the case of a petition, to the time limit for giving notice of intention to defend are references to seven days after service of the petition (FPR, r.10.8(2)(*a*)). Accordingly, the notice in Form M5 instructs the person served to detach the acknowledgment of service in Form M6 and send it so as to reach the court office within seven days after he (or she) receives it.

R.2.12(1) of the FPR provides that an answer to a petition must be filed **4.15** within 21 days from the expiration of the time limited for giving notice of intention to defend (*i.e.* 28 days). Accordingly, if the person served wishes to defend the proceedings and has consequently answered Yes to question 4 in Form M6, Form M5 informs him that he must file an answer, together with a copy for every other party, within 28 days after receipt. Other questions are contained in Form M6 which the person served may answer in order to give notice of his intention as to costs, ancillary relief and matters relating to children.

When completing a form M6 in response to a petition issued after Council Regulation (EC) No.1347/2000 (Brussels II) came into force in England and Wales on March 1, 2001 the person served must answer questions as to jurisdiction (see para. 1.10 *et seq.*).

Form M6 requires the person served to give an address within England and **4.16** Wales for service even if that person does not reside within England and Wales. However, the address need not be within the district of the divorce county court or district registry. The court should be informed should a party subsequently wish to change his address for service.

If the person served has instructed a solicitor, the solicitor should sign Form M6. The respondent must, however, also sign the form where:

(*a*) in the case of a petition based on adultery, he admits the adultery alleged and answers Yes to question 5; or

(*b*) in the case of a petition based on two years' separation coupled with consent, he consents to a decree and answers Yes to question 6; or

(*c*) he agrees with the proposals for the children of the family set out in Form M4 and answers Yes to question 10(*c*).

4.17   If the time limit for notice of intention to defend has expired, such notice should only be given with leave, and before directions for trial are given. In practice, notices are often given late without any issue being raised by the petitioner.

A person may give notice of intention to defend notwithstanding that he has already returned to the court office an acknowledgment of service not constituting such a notice (FPR, r.10.8(3)), providing that the notice is given within the time limits prescribed by FPR, r.10.8(2) or that leave has been granted to extend the time for giving such notice.

When an acknowledgment of service is returned to the court office a copy of it is sent to the petitioner (FPR, r.2.9(8)).

3   Consent to the grant of a decree (FPR, r.2.10)

4.18   Where, before the hearing of a petition alleging two years' separation coupled with the respondent's consent to a decree being granted, the respondent wishes to indicate that he consents to the grant of a decree, he must do so by filing a notice to that effect signed by him *personally*. An acknowledgment of service containing a statement of consent is treated as such a notice if the acknowledgment is signed:

>   (*a*) by the respondent if he is acting in person; or

>   (*b*) if he is acting by a solicitor, by the respondent as well as by the solicitor (FPR, r.2.10(1)).

4.19   Where there is no acknowledgment of service signed by the respondent and it is alleged that he consents to a decree being granted, there must be clear evidence that *express* consent has been given (*McG v R* [1972] 1 All E.R. 362). Some form of written consent will usually suffice.

A respondent may give notice to the court either that he does not consent to a decree being granted, or that he withdraws any consent which has already been given (FPR, r.2.10(2)). The respondent must also give notice to the petitioner. For form of notice, see Appendix 2, form 17. Where such notice is given and none of the other facts under MCA 1973, s.1(2) is alleged in the petition, the proceedings on the petition must be stayed and the court must then give notice of the stay to all parties (FPR, r.2.10(2)). No date is specified by the rules by which notice of withdrawal of consent must be given. It is, however, unlikely that withdrawal will prove to be effective once the decree nisi has been pronounced. In certain circumstances, the court may hold the respondent to his previously-given consent (*N v N* [1992] 1 F.L.R. 266).

4   Answer

4.20   A party may be debarred from defending a petition if they have previously entered into a proper agreement with the petitioner agreeing not to do so at a future stage (*N v N* [1992] 1 F.L.R. 266).

Requirements: A respondent or co-respondent who:

(*a*) wishes to defend the petition or to dispute any of the facts alleged in it;

(*b*) being the respondent, wishes to make in the proceedings any charge against the petitioner in respect of which the respondent prays for relief; or

(*c*) being the respondent to a petition to which MCA 1973, s.5(1) applies, wishes to oppose the grant of the decree nisi on the ground mentioned in that subsection,

must, within twenty-one days after the expiration of the time limited for giving notice of intention to defend (*i.e.* seven days), file an answer to the petition (FPR, r.2.12(1)). An answer may only be filed after this period has expired if leave has been given (although see also FPR, r.2.14 below). Leave should be given unless the court regards the contents of an answer to be an abuse of process, for instance, where it is seen as being frivolous or irrelevant. The length of the delay will clearly be significant (*Lawlor v Lawlor* [1995] 1 F.L.R. 269).

MCA 1973, s.5(1) applies where the petitioner alleges five years' separation; **4.21** the section allows the respondent to oppose the grant of a decree on the ground that the dissolution of the marriage will result in grave financial or other hardship and that it would in all the circumstances be wrong to dissolve the marriage. This statutory defence is discussed in further detail at para. 9.38 *et seq.*

An answer may be filed, notwithstanding that the person filing the answer has not given notice of intention to defend (FPR, r.2.12(2)). Any reference to a person who has given notice of intention to defend is construed as including a reference to a person who has filed an answer without giving notice of intention to defend (FPR, r.2.12(3)).

An answer may not be filed without leave after directions for trial have been given (FPR, r.2.14, although see also FPR, r.2.12 above). Application for leave is to a district judge and should be supported by affidavit (*Spill v Spill* [1972] 3 All E.R. 9). For form of application or summons, see Appendix 2, form 18. The situation which arises where a respondent wishes to defend and directions have been given to enter a cause in the special procedure list is discussed on para. 5.11–5.12.

When the answer is filed the cause will remain in the county court unless it **4.22** is transferred to the High Court under the provisions of MFPA 1984, s.39 and *Practice Direction* June 5, 1992 [1992] 3 All E.R. 151. For this purpose the principal registry is treated as a divorce county court (see para. 4.43 *et seq.*).

If, on the filing of an answer, the cause becomes defended, the petitioner becomes eligible to apply to the Legal Services Commission for a certificate for legal representation (full representation).

R.2.12 of the FPR applies with the necessary modifications to a party cited as it applies to a co-respondent (FPR, r.2.16(2)).

A respondent will often disagree with certain allegations made in a petition, but nevertheless accept that the marriage has irretrievably broken down. A respondent who, in such circumstances, allows the petition to proceed undefended may wish to record his reasons for doing so in a formal letter to the petitioner and/or the court. An answer need not be lodged where a respondent simply wishes to oppose a prayer for costs, ancillary relief or in relation to any children of the family.

Contents of answer (FPR, r.2.15): There need be no particular form of answer **4.23** and a letter in the nature of an answer must be accepted as such. The letter or answer may contain all manner of irrelevant matters. Where there is doubt whether any document should be treated as an answer, the matter is referred to a district judge. It is open to the petitioner to apply to the court for directions or such order as will meet the case.

If an allegation is admitted which would entitle the other party to a decree, the court will grant a decree on the undisputed allegation (*Grenfell v Grenfell* [1978] 1 All E.R. 561).

An admission *may* adversely affect a party in ancillary proceedings in that an estoppel may be raised against him. It is doubtful, however, whether this would apply to proceedings relating to children where the child's interests are paramount and should not be prejudiced by any estoppel existing between the father and mother. In maintenance proceedings, a party's claims will not be prejudiced by not pursuing a prayer in the divorce proceedings or by refraining from an attempt to set up matters which might theoretically have constituted a bar to the decree (*Porter v Porter* [1971] 2 All E.R. 1037). For further discussion of estoppel in family proceedings, see Butterworth's *Family Law Service* 4A [818].

4.24   Where an answer (or reply or subsequent pleading) contains more than a simple denial of the facts stated in the petition (or other pleading), the answer (or reply) must set out with sufficient particularity the facts relied on, but not the evidence by which they are to be proved (FPR, r.2.15(1)). An answer containing only a simple denial may be appropriate (*Haque v Haque* [1977] 3 All E.R. 667). It will not, however, constitute a cross petition (see below).

If an answer is filed by the husband or wife which is more than a simple denial of the facts, it must contain, in relation to the facts in the answer, the information required in the case of a petition by FPR, App.2, para.1(*k*)—*i.e.* where one of the facts is based on five years' separation, it must state whether any, and if so what, agreement or arrangement has been made or is proposed to be made between the parties for the support of the respondent or petitioner or any children of the family (FPR, r.2.15(1)).

4.25   Unless otherwise directed, an answer by a husband or wife, who disputes any statement required by FPR, App.2, para.1(*f*), (*g*) and (*h*) to be included in the petition, must contain *full* particulars of the facts relied on (FPR, r.2.15(2)). These paragraphs require certain information as to any living children of the family, as to any other living child born to the wife during the marriage and of any dispute whether a living child is a child of the family; see p.[00].

Where a respondent intends to adduce evidence under the Civil Evidence Act 1968, ss.11 or 12 that a person was convicted of an offence or was proved to have committed adultery in matrimonial proceedings or was found or adjudged to be the father of a child in relevant proceedings before any court in England and Wales or in former affiliation proceedings before any court in the UK, he must include in his answer a statement of his intention with particulars, as is required by FPR, r.2.4 in the case of a petition (FPR, r.2.15(6)). This applies to all pleadings with the necessary modifications.

Where a petition or other pleading includes a statement that the petitioner intends to adduce evidence under the Civil Evidence Act 1968, ss.11 or 12, then if a respondent or other opposite party:

(*a*) denies the conviction, finding or adjudication to which the statement relates; or

(*b*) alleges that the conviction, finding or adjudication was erroneous; or

(c) denies that the conviction, finding or adjudication is relevant to any issue in the proceedings,

he must make the denial or allegation in his answer or other pleading (FPR, r.2.15(5)).

Any cross-prayer in an answer follows the form of petition. An answer **4.26** must conclude, where appropriate, with a cross-prayer setting out particulars of the relief claimed. These particulars must include any application for ancillary relief and *may* include any application for an order under Parts I or II of the CA 1989 with respect to a child of the family. It is not necessary to include in the answer any claim for costs against the petitioner (FPR, r.2.15(3)). A claim for costs against *any other* party, however, must be included in the prayer.

An answer may contain a cross-prayer for relief different to that sought in the petition, *e.g.* judicial separation where the petition is for divorce (MCA 1973, s.20). If the decree claimed by way of a cross-prayer is not an answer to the allegations in the petition (*e.g.* a cross-prayer for divorce in answer to a nullity petition) it must be pursued by way of cross-petition, rather than solely by answer, the pleading being designated an answer and cross-petition and the prayer being prefaced "and by way of cross-petition".

Where an answer contains a prayer for relief, it must contain the information **4.27** required by FPR, App.2, para.1(*j*) in the case of the petition, in so far as it has not been given by the petitioner (FPR, r.2.15(4)). The sub-paragraph deals with proceedings in any country outside England and Wales; see para. 2.11.

An answer (or other pleading) must be signed as in the case of a petition, by counsel if settled by him, and if not, by the respondent's solicitor in his own name or in the name of his firm, or by the respondent if he acts in person (FPR, r.2.15(6)). Counsel's name is usually typed in capital letters on the answer which is filed, the draft having been signed by him.

As regards allegations against a third person in an answer (or other pleading), the rules as to parties to the proceedings or persons named and the rules as to service (FPR, rr.2.7 and 2.9) which apply to a petition also apply to an answer (or other pleading), except that for references to a correspondent there are substituted references to a party cited (FPR, r.2.16(1)).

Unless otherwise directed, the name of the party cited must be added to the heading of the cause.

Filing of answer: A party who files an answer (or reply or subsequent pleading) must also file a copy for service on every opposite party (FPR, r.2.17). The fee payable is £100.

If the party is publicly funded, notice of issue of the legal funding certificate should be lodged for service with the copy answer on the other parties. The legal funding certificate and copy of notice of issue for the court and any amended certificate should be filed immediately.

Service of answer: The court sends by post the documents as follows: **4.30**

(a) to the petitioner, copy answer and notice of issue of legal funding certificate, if any;

(b) to a party cited in the answer, if any, copy answer, Forms M5 and M6 (notice of proceedings and acknowledgment of service) and notice of issue of legal funding certificate, if any;

(c) to other parties, copy answer and notice of issue of legal funding certificate, if any (FPR, r.2.17).

4.31   The rules of service on a co-respondent to a petition apply to a party cited in an answer (FPR, r.2.16(1)) and a district judge may direct or order service otherwise than by post. Where the answer alleges an improper association with a person named, the district judge will consider whether that person should be made a party under FPR, r.2.7(3) as in the case of a petition.

Amended answer and supplemental answer: FPR, r.2.11, which applies to amended and supplemental petitions, applies with the necessary modifications to the filing of a supplemental answer and the amendment of an answer, other pleading or other document (FPR, r.2.18).

5   Reply and subsequent pleadings (FPR, r.2.13)

4.32   A petitioner may file a reply to an answer within 14 days of receiving a copy of the answer. If the petitioner does not file a reply to an answer, he is, unless the answer prays for a decree, deemed on requesting directions for trial to have denied every material allegation of fact made in the answer (FPR, r.2.13(1) and (2)).

No pleading subsequent to a reply may be filed without leave (FPR, r.2.13(3)). A fee of £60 is payable on an application for leave.

The rules as to the contents of a reply and for service are the same as those for an answer (FPR, r.2.15).

No reply or other pleading may be filed without leave after directions for trial have been given (FPR, r.2.14). Leave in this case is obtained as in the case of an answer.

6   Proceeding on answer alone

4.33   Where relief is claimed in an answer and the petitioner does not proceed with the suit, the respondent, if he wishes to proceed on the allegations in his answer, may apply to the district judge for the proceedings arising on the prayer in the petition to be stayed, and for the cause to proceed on the prayer in the answer (for form see Appendix 2, form 19). The requirements for proceeding on the answer alone are as follows:

(*a*) notice of application;

(*b*) copy of notice of application (if not by consent);

(*c*) a fee of £30 is payable if the application is by consent and £60 if it is not.

Upon a successful order being made, the respondent proceeds with the answer as if it were a petition. If there is no reply or answer to the respondent's answer or cross-petition or such reply or answer has been struck out, the cause becomes undefended. If the cause was proceeding in the High Court, it should normally be transferred to the county court on becoming undefended (*Practice Direction* June 5, 1992 [1992] 3 All E.R. 151; see para. 4.43 *et seq.*).

The respondent applies for directions for trial.

Prayers for ancillary relief and in relation to children, etc in the petition remain unstayed, unless a stay is specifically sought and conceded (*Registrar's Direction* June 3, 1958).

7 Cross-decrees

If the parties consent, the district judge may deal with cross-petitions under **4.34** the "special procedure" on the basis that a decree is granted on the prayer of both the petition and the answer and neither prayer is then defended. A notice of application, if in the county court, or summons, if in the High Court, should be lodged endorsed with the other party's consent, asking for the cause to proceed undefended on both the prayer of the petition and the prayer of the answer. The matter is dealt with by the district judge on a without notice basis.

The relevant fee is £30.

8 Consolidation

Where there are separate petitions by husband and wife or two petitions by **4.35** the same petitioner which should be consolidated (in some cases one should be stayed or dismissed), either party may apply for consolidation when the pleadings are complete and ready for application to be made for directions for trial. In default, the court may give notice to attend to show cause why the suits should not be consolidated. The suits must be proceeding in the same court or registry and therefore it may be necessary to transfer one suit pursuant to FPR, r.10.10. The effect of consolidation will be that one suit becomes "the leading suit", the titles of both suits are amended, and the petitioner in the leading suit may apply for directions for trial.

The practice on consolidation of petitions is discussed in Butterworth's *Family Law Service* 2A[583] to [589].

9 Particulars (FPR, r.2.19)

A party on whom a pleading has been served may, in writing, request the party **4.36** whose pleading it is to give particulars of any allegation or other matter pleaded and, if that party fails to give particulars within a reasonable time, the party requiring them may apply for an order that the particulars be given (FPR, r.2.19(1)). The initial request may be made either by letter or by formal pleading, as long as it is in writing. Should the request not be complied with within a reasonable period of time, application should then be made to a district judge with a copy of the original request attached. Application is made on notice in the county court and by summons in the High Court. The fee is £60.

The request or order in pursuance of which the particulars are given must be incorporated with the particulars given in reply, each item of the particulars following immediately after the corresponding item of the request or order (FPR, r.2.19(2)).

A party giving particulars, whether in pursuance of an order or otherwise, **4.37** must at the same time file a copy of them (FPR, r.2.19(3)).

Particulars must be signed as in the case of a petition (FPR, r.2.15(6)).

If an order directing that particulars be given is not complied with, application may be made to a district judge to strike out the pleading or the relevant allegations.

A party who consents to an order for particulars pursuant to a request cannot later refuse to provide some of the particulars requested (*Fearis v Davies* (1986) *The Times*, June 5).

In a defended cause in which the petitioner alleges that the respondent has behaved in such a way that the petitioner cannot reasonably be expected to live with the respondent, the district judge may, of his own motion on giving directions for trial or on the application of any party made at any time before trial, order or authorise the party who has made the request for or obtained such directions to file a schedule of the allegations and counter-allegations made in the pleadings or particulars. The allegations must then, unless otherwise directed, be listed concisely in chronological order, each counter-allegation being set out against the allegation to which it relates, and the party filing the schedule must serve a copy of it on any party who has filed a pleading (FPR, r.2.26). The fee payable if application is made is £60. The same procedure should be adopted where the cause is proceeding on the respondent's answer.

10 Disclosure

4.38 FPR 1991, r.2.20 applies the former RSC Order 24 (relating to the discovery and inspection of documents) with certain amendments to a *defended* cause begun by petition and pending in the High Court or county court. Since RSC Ord. 24 has not been carried into Sch.1 to the CPR 1998 (which provides for disclosure and inspection at Part 31), references to RSC Ord. 24 must be taken to be references to that rule as in force at April 26, 1999, the date immediately prior to the CPR 1998 coming into force.

The parties may agree to dispense with or limit disclosure or, in default of agreement, either party may make an application for the same purpose (RSC, Ord. 24, r.2(5)). Each party must, within fourteen days after the pleadings are deemed to be closed, make and serve on the other party a list of the documents which are or have been in his possession custody or power relating to any matter in question in the action (RSC, Ord. 24, r.2(2)). There is no requirement to file the list at court. Pleadings are deemed to be closed after the expiration of fourteen days after service of the answer (FPR, r.2.20(2)). This may mean that a petitioner is obliged to make and serve his list of documents before he has filed his reply to the respondent's answer (for which he is allowed 28 days).

4.39 Where a party fails to make disclosure by service of a list of documents without order, a party may apply for an order for disclosure and, if required, an affidavit verifying the list. An order may be for general disclosure or limited to specific documents or issues (RSC, Ord. 24, r.3).

The court may dismiss or adjourn an application for disclosure where satisfied that disclosure is not necessary or not yet necessary and will in any case refuse an order if it is not necessary either for fairly disposing of the cause or for saving costs (RSC Ord. 24, r.8).

The list of documents must contain a notice stating a time within seven days after service when and where the documents may be inspected (RSC Ord. 24, r.9). The party requiring a list of documents may at any time before directions for trial request verification by affidavit (RSC Ord. 24, r.2(7)).

4.40 Where a pleading or affidavit refers to a document, a party may serve a notice requiring the document to be produced for inspection on the party whose pleading or affidavit it is. The party on whom such a notice is served must within four days of service serve on the other party a notice stating a time within seven days and the place at which such documents as he does not object to produce may be inspected, stating, if appropriate, the grounds of objection (RSC Ord. 24, r.10). If a party fails to comply with the rules as to inspection, the court may make an order for production for inspection (RSC Ord. 24, r.11).

Any party who is entitled to inspect any documents may at or before the time when inspection takes place serve on the party who is required to produce such documents a notice (which must contain an undertaking to pay the reasonable charges) requiring him to supply a copy of any documents to be produced (RSC Ord. 24, r.11A(1)). The party on whom such a notice is served must supply the copy requested within seven days of receipt of the request together with an account of the reasonable charges (RSC Ord. 24, r.11A(2)). Where a party fails to supply any copy documents requested in accordance with RSC Ord. 24, r.11A(1), the court may, on the application of either party, make such order as it thinks fit (RSC Ord. 24, r.11A(3)).

Discovery and inspection in relation to ancillary relief are discussed at para. 9.79 *et seq.*

11   Interrogatories

FPR 1991, r.2.21 applies the former RSC Ord. 26 (relating to discovery by **4.41** interrogatories) with certain amendments to a *defended* cause begun by petition and pending in the High Court.

No order is required to serve interrogatories which are necessary either for disposing fairly of the cause or for saving costs (see *Hall v Sevalco Ltd* [1996] P.I.Q.R. P344 as to the test of necessity which has to be satisfied). A party may otherwise seek leave to serve interrogatories on another party, although the circumstances when this should prove to be necessary will be limited. Interrogatories can be served twice without any order. A copy of the proposed interrogatories must be filed when they are served under RSC Ord. 26, r.3(1) (service without order) or when a summons for an order under RSC Ord. 26, r.1(2) is issued (FPR, r.2.21(2)).

Where a *defended* cause is pending in the county court, CCR Ord. 14, r.11 **4.42** applies the provisions of the former RSC Ord. 26. If an application for leave to serve interrogatories is necessary, it is made on notice and if leave is granted, the order is drawn up and served by the court (FPR, r.2.21(3); former CCR Ord. 14, r.11(2) and (3)).

There is no special protection for any party against whom adultery is alleged (*Nast v Nast* [1972] 1 All E.R. 1171; *C v C* [1973] 3 All E.R. 770).

12   Transfer and distribution of proceedings between the High Court and county court

Introduction: Every matrimonial cause must be commenced in a divorce **4.43** county court and heard and determined in that or another such court unless or except to the extent that it is transferred to the High Court under MFPA 1984, s.39 or CCA 1984, s.41 (MFPA 1984, s.33(3)). A cause is no longer automatically transferred to the High Court when an answer is filed and will only be transferred if it comes within the provisions of *Practice Direction* June 5, 1992 [1992] 3 All E.R. 151 given under MFPA 1984, s.37 (see below).

For the transfer of proceedings under CA 1989, see FPR r.4.6 and Children (Allocation of Proceedings) Order 1991 (as amended) discussed at para. 11.23 *et seq.*

4.44   *Transfer from High Court to county court (MFPA 1984, s.38)*: The following family proceedings are transferable at any stage wholly or partly from the High Court to a county court either of the court's own motion or on the application of any party to the proceedings:

> (*a*) all family proceedings commenced in the High Court which are within the jurisdiction of a county court or divorce county court (for definition of family proceedings, see para. 1.04); and

> (*b*) wardship proceedings, except applications for an order that a minor be made, or cease to be, a ward of court or any other proceedings which relate to the inherent jurisdiction of the High Court with respect to minors; and

> (*c*) all family proceedings transferred from a county court to the High Court under MFPA 1984, s.39 or County Courts Act 1984, s.41 (transfer by order of High Court); and

> (*d*) all matrimonial causes and matters transferred from a county court otherwise than as mentioned in (*c*) above

4.45   Proceedings will be transferred to the county court or divorce county court as the High Court directs. The transfer does not affect any right of appeal from the order directing the transfer nor does it affect the right to enforce in the High Court any order made before the transfer. Where proceedings are transferred, the county court has jurisdiction to award any relief which could have been awarded by the High Court.

4.46   *Transfer to High Court from county court (MFPA 1984, s.39)*: The following family proceedings are transferable at any stage wholly or partly from a county court to the High Court either of the court's own motion or on the application of any party to the proceedings:

> (*a*) all family proceedings commenced in a county court or divorce county court; and

> (*b*) all family proceedings transferred from the High Court to a county court or divorce county court under MFPA 1984, s.38.

4.47   *Transfer of a cause or an application in a cause (FPR, r.10.10)*: Where a cause or an application in a cause is pending in the High Court, it may be transferred to another registry by a district judge of that registry or by a judge (FPR, r.10.10(1)). Where a cause or application is pending in the county court, it may be transferred to another county court (FPR, r.10.10(2)).

Before making an order for the transfer of an application in a cause, the court must consider whether it would be more convenient to transfer the cause itself (FPR, r.10.10(3)).

The transfer may be made either of the court's own motion or on the application of any party to the proceedings.

Procedure: A transfer under MPFA 1984, ss.38 and 39 or under FPR, **4.48** r.10.10(1) and (2) must not be made unless the parties have consented to such an order or have had the opportunity of being heard on the question (FPR, r.10.10(4) and (6)).

Where the parties, or any of them, wish to be heard, the court must give the parties notice of a date, time and place at which the question will be considered (FPR, r.10.10(5) and (6)).

Application is made to the district judge on notice in the county court and by summons in the High Court. The fee is £60. For detailed procedure, see FPR, r.10.11 discussed at para. 4.54.

Practice Direction June 5, 1992 [1992] 3 All E.R. 151: These directions are **4.49** given under MFPA 1984, s.37 and apply to all family proceedings which are transferable between the High Court and county court under MFPA 1984, ss.38 and 39. They supersede the directions given on April 6, 1988 [1988] 2 All E.R. 103 save in respect of family proceedings concerning children pending immediately before October 14, 1991.

The following proceedings are not subject to the *Practice Direction* and may be *heard and determined in the High Court alone*:

(*a*) CA 1989 and the Adoption Act 1976, which are governed by the Children (Allocation of Proceedings) Order 1991 (as amended);

(*b*) an application that a minor be made, or cease to be, a ward of court;

(*c*) MFPA 1984, Pt III (application for financial relief after overseas divorce, etc) (para.1(*a*) and (*b*));

(*d*) a claim for a declaration of incompatibility under s.4 of the Human Rights Act 1998; or

(*e*) an issue which may lead to the court considering making such a declaration.

Family proceedings to which these directions apply (including interlocutory **4.50** proceedings) must be dealt with in the High Court where it appears to the court seized of the case that by reason of the *complexity, difficulty* or *gravity* of the issues they ought to be tried in the High Court (para.2(1)).

The following proceedings must be dealt with in the High Court unless the *nature of the issues of fact or law* raised in the case makes them more suitable for trial in a county court than in the High Court:

(*a*) petitions under MCA 1973, s.1(2)(*e*) which are opposed pursuant to section 5 of that Act;

(*b*) petitions for presumption of death and dissolution of marriage under MCA 1973, s.19;

(*c*) proceedings involving a contested issue on domicile;

(*d*) applications under DMPA 1973, s.5(6) (staying of matrimonial proceedings in England and Wales if concurrent proceedings in another country (see para. 1.20 *et seq.*));

(*e*) applications to restrain a respondent from taking or continuing with foreign proceedings;

(*f*) suits in which the Queen's Proctor intervenes or shows cause and elects trial in the High Court;

    (*g*) proceedings in relation to a ward of court in which:

        (i) the Official Solicitor is or becomes the guardian ad litem of the ward (now the "children's guardian") or of a party to the proceedings;

        (ii) a local authority is or becomes a party;

        (iii) an application for blood tests is made;

        (iv) an application is opposed on the grounds of want of jurisdiction;

        (*v*) there is a substantial foreign element;

        (vi) there is an opposed application for leave to take the child permanently out of the jurisdiction or where there is an application for temporary removal of a child from the jurisdiction and it is opposed on the ground that the child may not be duly returned;

    (*h*) interlocutory applications involving:

        (i) Freezing injunctions;

        (ii) directions as to dealing with assets outside the jurisdiction;

    (*i*) petitions in respect of declarations under FLA 1986, Pt III (declarations of status: see para. 13.01 to 13.11) (para.2(2)(*a*)–(*i*)).

4.51   Proceedings in the county court for an order within (*a*) to (*i*) above must be heard and determined in the High Court where either the county court or any party to the proceedings considers that any such orders mentioned below, if made, should be recognised and enforced in Scotland or Northern Ireland under FLA 1986, Pt I. These orders are those made by the county court in the exercise of its jurisdiction relating to wardship so far as it determines the living arrangements of a child or provides for the education of, or contact with, a child (para.3).

    In proceedings where *periodical payments*, a *lump-sum* or *property* are in issue, the court must have regard in particular to the following factors when considering whether the complexity, difficulty or gravity of the issues are such that they ought to be tried in the High Court:

    (*a*) the capital values of the assets involved and the extent to which they are available for, or susceptible to, distribution or adjustment;

    (*b*) any substantial allegations of fraud or deception or non-disclosure;

    (*c*) any substantial contested allegations of conduct.

4.52   An appeal in such proceedings from a district judge in a county court must be transferred to the High Court where it appears to the district judge, whether on application by a party or otherwise, that the appeal raises a difficult or important question whether of law or otherwise (para.4).

    Subject to the provisions of the *Practice Direction*, family proceedings may be dealt with in a county court (para.5).

    Proceedings which fall to be dealt with in a court different to that in which they are pending in accordance with the provisions of the *Practice Direction* must be transferred to that court unless to do so would cause *undue delay* or *hardship* to any party or other person involved (para.6).

    The jurisdiction to determine the venue of proceedings which may be transferred to the High Court under the *Practice Direction* lies with the county court in the first place. A decision of the county court on venue is subject to challenge by appeal in the normal way (*Re N and L (Minors) (Adoption Proceedings: Venue*) [1987] 2 All E.R. 732). The appeal should be brought before the county court proceeds to hear the case on its merits (*Re P (Minors*) [1990] 2 F.L.R. 335).

Removal of proceedings to the High Court under County Courts Act 1984, s.41: **4.53** The power of the High Court or a judge thereof under the County Courts Act 1984, s.41 to order the removal to the High Court of family proceedings pending in a divorce county court may be exercised by a district judge of the principal registry or by the district judge of any district registry having that county court within its district. The power is without prejudice to Supreme Court Act 1981, s.29 (power to issue prerogative orders) and is to be exercised in relation to family proceedings in accordance with any directions given under MFPA 1984, s.37.

Procedure on transfer of cause or application (FPR, r.10.11): Where any cause **4.54** or application is ordered to be transferred from one court or registry to another, the proper officer of the first mentioned court or registry must, unless otherwise directed, give notice of the transfer to the parties (FPR, r.10.11(1)).

In relation to proceedings which, after the transfer, are to continue in the principal registry, the transfer is construed as a provision for High Court proceedings to be treated as pending in a divorce county court; or as a provision for county court proceedings no longer to be treated as pending in a divorce county court, as the case may be (FPR, r.10.11(2)).

Proceedings transferred from a divorce county court to the High Court proceed, unless the order of transfer otherwise directs, in the registry nearest to the divorce county court from which they are transferred, but there is also power to order the transfer of the proceedings to a different registry (FPR, r.10.11(3)).

If the divorce county court and the district registry to which the proceedings are transferred, or vice versa, are in the same office, the proceedings remain where they are and are dealt with by the same district judge and court officials. Therefore, the court reference number remains unaltered but the name of the court in the title is changed.

Transfer to High Court to enforce an order (FPR, r.7.3): An order made by a **4.55** divorce county court in family proceedings, except an order for periodical payments or recovery of arrears of periodical payments, may, on an application made without notice by affidavit by the person entitled to enforce the order, be transferred to the High Court. The transfer takes effect on the filing of the application. Where an order is transferred, it carries the same force and effect as if it were an order of the High Court.

13 Applications (FPR, r.10.9)

Except where rules otherwise provide, every application in family proceedings **4.56** must be made to a district judge and must be made by summons if the proceedings are pending in the High Court or, if the proceedings are pending in a divorce county court, must be made by application in accordance with CCR Ord. 13, r.1 which is applied by FPR 1991, r.10.9.

The application must be served at least two clear days before the hearing, unless otherwise provided (RSC Ord. 32, r.3 and CCR, Ord. 13, r.1(2)). For form of notice, see Appendix 2, form 21 and for form of summons, form 22.

Most applications are supported by affidavit. Without notice applications are usually made on affidavit.

4.57   On the issue of a summons or application before a judge at the Royal Courts of Justice in which the applicant is represented and which is expected to last in excess of one day, a Notice of Estimate (available from the Clerk of the Rules at the Royal Courts of Justice and from the principal registry) indicating the length of hearing must be lodged with the Clerk of the Rules. The procedure is set out in full in the *Practice Direction* March 1, 1984 [1984] 1 All E.R. 783.

4.58   Business which will be taken at the Royal Courts of Justice during the Long Vacation is governed by an annual practice direction, the most recent being *Practice Direction* April 25, 2002 (the only citation for which at the date of publication being the Solicitors Journal vol.146, no.18, p.106LB). During the Long Vacation, Family Division business is usually restricted to the following categories:

> (*a*) injunctions;
>
> (*b*) committals to, and release from, prison;
>
> (*c*) any application relating to children when the estimated length of hearing does not exceed one day (the estimate must be signed by the solicitor making the application or by counsel instructed);
>
> (*d*) any other matter which has been certified by a district judge as being fit for vacation business subject to the estimated length of hearing not exceeding one day (a certificate signed by the solicitor making the application, or by counsel if instructed, must be supplied to the district judge that in his opinion (giving reasons and a time estimate) the matter is such that it must be dealt with during the vacation);
>
> (*e*) if so directed by a High Court judge, any matters where the estimated length of hearing is in excess of one day.

4.59   Whether the Clerk of the Rules lists an application within category (*c*) above or a district judge accepts an application within category (*d*) as vacation business will be entirely a matter for their discretion. Where the application falls within category (*e*), application for the appropriate direction should be made to the applications judge.

For the procedure when lodging sworn statements at the principal registry, see para. 6.11.

An application is issued in the district registry or divorce county court where the cause is pending. If the hearing is to take place before a judge in another town, the court official may obtain an appointment by telephone, but practice varies. The court file in all cases is sent immediately by the court officials to the local court office for the place where the hearing is to take place or to the Principal Clerk, Principal Registry of the Family Division (First Avenue House, 42–49 High Holborn, London WC1V 6NP), as the case may be.

4.60   Where the cause is proceeding in the High Court, the district judge of the registry for the divorce town at which a cause has been set down for trial may, if it appears to him to be desirable having regard to the proximity of the date of trial or otherwise, exercise any jurisdiction of the district judge of the registry where the cause is proceeding (FPR, r.2.34(1)).

Where the words "liberty to apply" are used, a fresh notice of application or summons must be issued for a subsequent application. The fee is £60. In special cases such as liberty to apply for further directions under a summons for directions or as to terms of compromise or minor terms where property is settled, a fresh notice of application or summons is not required and no further fee is payable (*Practice Direction* March 4, 1980 [1980] 1 All E.R. 1008).

14 Time

R.1.5 of the FPR governs the calculation of any period of time fixed by the FPR, any rules applied by them or by any decree, judgment, order or direction for doing any act. Where the FPR do not apply, RSC Ord. 3 and CCR Ord. 13 apply. **4.61**

Where an act is required to be done not less than a specified period and before a specified date, the period excludes the day on which the act is done and the day by which it had to be done (FPR, r.1.5(2)).

Where an act is required to be done within a specified period from or after a specified date, the period excludes the specified date (FPR, r.1.5(3)).

Saturday, Sunday, Christmas Day, Good Friday and bank holidays are excluded for calculating periods of seven days or less (FPR, r.1.5(4) and (6)).

Where the time fixed for doing an act in the court office expires on a day on which the office is closed, and for that reason the act cannot be done, the act will still be in time if done on the next day on which the office is open (FPR, r.1.5(5)). **4.62**

Time may be extended by the court or by consent (RSC Ord. 3, r.5; CCR Ord. 13, r.4). Special rules apply to proceedings under CA 1989 (see para. 11.34).

Ord. 3, r.6 of the RSC, which requires a party to give notice of intention to proceed after a year's delay, does not apply to any proceedings pending in the High Court (FPR, r.10.18).

15 Medical inspection (nullity) (FPR, rr.2.22 and 2.23)

Incapacity: In proceedings for nullity on the ground of *incapacity* to consummate the marriage, the petitioner *must* apply to the district judge to determine whether medical inspectors should be appointed to examine the parties, except that an application is not to be made in an *undefended* cause: **4.63**

(*a*) if the husband is the petitioner; or

(*b*) if the wife is the petitioner and:

(i) it appears from the petition that she was either a widow or divorced at the time of the marriage in question, or

(ii) it appears from the petition or otherwise that she has borne a child, or

(iii) a statement by the wife that she is not a virgin is filed,

but an application must still be made where the petitioner is alleging his or her own incapacity (FPR, r.2.22(1)(2)).

The above applies equally where the cause is proceeding on the respondent's answer or where the allegation is made only in the answer with the modification that references to the petitioner are construed as references to the respondent (FPR, r.2.22(3)). **4.64**

An application by the petitioner is made:

(*a*) where the respondent has not given notice of intention to defend, after the time limit for giving notice has expired (*i.e.* seven days after service of the petition);

(*b*) where the respondent has given notice of intention to defend, after the expiration of the time allowed for filing his answer (*i.e.* 28 days after service of the petition) or, if he has filed an answer, after it has been filed (FPR, r.2.22(4)).

4.65 The application must be served where the respondent has given notice of intention to defend but otherwise it may be heard ex parte (FPR, r.2.22(7)). The requirements are:

(*a*) if pending in county court, notice of application (and copy);

(*b*) if pending in High Court, summons (and copy). For form, see Appendix 2, form 23;

(*c*) a fee of £60.

No affidavit is required.

An application by the respondent is made after he has filed an answer (FPR, r.2.22(4)).

If the party required to make an application fails to do so within a reasonable time, the other party may, if he is prosecuting or defending the cause, make the application (FPR, r.2.22(5)).

The court may, if it thinks fit at the hearing, appoint one or two medical inspectors to examine any party not previously examined or to examine further any party (FPR, r.2.22(9)).

4.66 *Wilful refusal*: In proceedings for nullity on the ground that the marriage has not been consummated owing to the *wilful refusal* of the respondent, either party *may* apply to the district judge for the appointment of medical inspectors to examine the parties (FPR, r.2.22(6)).

The application must be served where the respondent has given notice of intention to defend but otherwise it may be heard ex parte (FPR, r.2.22 (7)).

The requirements are as follows:

(*a*) if pending in county court, notice of application and copy;

(*b*) if pending in High Court, summons and copy. For form, see Appendix 2, form 23.

(*c*) a fee of £60.

No affidavit is required.

4.67 *Medical inspectors*: The names of doctors who act as medical inspectors are supplied from a rota kept in the court office. Inspectors should not act in cases in which they have previously advised either of the parties professionally. An up-to-date list of medical inspectors who may be appointed appears in the Family Division Compendium at the principal registry.

As to medical inspection abroad and parties in H M Forces abroad, see *Registrar's Circular*, April 12, 1949.

Usually only one inspector is appointed unless good reason exists for appointing two inspectors, for instance, in a defended case where the wife does not wish to be examined by a male inspector.

Women doctors: Where a wife objects to being examined by a man, she may **4.68** request that a female doctor should be appointed to examine her. The solicitor for the wife should inform his client of her right to request such an appointment and should satisfy the district judge at the hearing of the summons or application that she has been so informed. A woman doctor is not to be appointed to examine the husband if either he or the inspector objects (*Practice Direction* July 5, 1971 [1971] 2 All E.R. 1310).

Procedure after order made: The court draws the order and sends copies to **4.69** both parties. The court also sends to the applicant's solicitor forms of statement of identification of party and certificate by inspector for completion at the medical examination.

The time and date of the examination are fixed by the inspector in consultation with the solicitors concerned. The medical examination must be held at the consulting room of the medical inspector, or of one of them if more than one, but the district judge may, on the application of a party, direct that the examination of the party be held at the court office or at such other place as the district judge thinks convenient (FPR, r.2.23(1)).

The party who has obtained the order, or who has conduct of the proceed- **4.70** ings where an order is made at the court's discretion, must serve on the other party notice of the date, time and place of the examination (FPR, r.2.22(10)). The practice under the former rules was to endorse the order as follows

> "Take notice that it has been arranged to carry out the examination referred to in this order on the day of , 20 at o'clock at [*place at which examination is to be held*]."

A copy of the order with endorsement of the appointment for the examination is served on the respondent. Service is in accordance with FPR, rr.10.2 and 10.3, that is, on the party's solicitor, or, if no solicitor is acting for the party, then by leaving the notice at the party's address or by sending it there by post.

A party to be examined has to be identified to the inspector. A party presenting himself for examination must sign, in the presence of the inspector, a statement that he or she is the person referred to as the petitioner or respondent, as the case may be, in the order for examination. At the conclusion of the examination the inspector or inspectors must certify on the statement that it was signed in his or their presence by the person who has been examined (FPR, r.2.23(2)).

The medical inspector sends his report to the court with the copy order and **4.71** completed form of statement of identification. A photocopy of the report may be supplied to the parties on payment of the usual fees (FPR, r.2.23(3)),

A supplementary report may be requested by either party upon notice to the other party and is dealt with in the same way as the original report.

In an undefended cause, it is not necessary for the inspector (or inspectors) to attend at the trial to give evidence unless so directed (FPR, r.2.23(4)).

In a defended cause, if the inspector's report is accepted by both parties, **4.72** notice to that effect must be given by the parties to the district judge and to the inspector (or inspectors) not less than seven clear days before the day fixed for trial. It will not then be necessary for the inspector (or inspectors) to attend (FPR, r.2.23(5)).

In a defended cause either party giving notice to the inspector that his attendance to give evidence is not required must also notify the other side. Unless a medical inspector has been told by both parties that he is not required to give evidence he will be entitled to assume that he must be present in court (*Practice Direction* November 18, 1968 [1968] 3 All E.R. 828).

Where the evidence of inspectors is not given at the trial, an inspector's report is treated as information furnished to the court by a court expert and is given such weight as the court thinks fit (FPR, r.2.23(6)). If an inspector has to attend the hearing, the solicitor should arrange for his attendance.

4.73   At the hearing of proceedings for nullity on the ground of incapacity the court may, if it thinks fit, appoint a medical inspector or two medical inspectors to examine any party who has not been examined or to examine further any party who has been examined (FPR, r.2.22(9)).

Fees due to a medical inspector are payable by the party at whose instigation he was appointed. The solicitors should liase with the inspectors as to their fees. In a defended cause, unless both parties give notice that the medical inspector is not required, the liability for fees remains where it originated. Exceptionally, in a cause listed as undefended on a respondent's answer, the liability for the inspector's fees for attending the hearing will fall on the respondent, who can avoid the liability only by having given the appropriate notice to the medical inspector (*Practice Direction* November 18, 1968 [1968] 3 All E.R. 828).

16   Change of solicitor

4.74   In proceedings pending in the High Court, RSC Ord. 67 applies; in proceedings pending in a divorce county court, CCR Ord. 50, r.5 applies. Notice of change in county courts is in CCR, form N434.

Practice Direction March 8, 1977 [1977] 1 All E.R. 844, states that a solicitor is required to file a notice of *acting* (CCR, Form N434 adapted), where he is acting for a limited purpose (*e.g.* because public funding has only been granted in respect of financial provision or opposed applications in proceedings relating to children), or a notice of *change*, where he is instructed generally in the proceedings. Notice must be filed at court and served on the other parties. In the event of there being a notice of acting for a limited purpose, there may be occasions where there are two addresses for service of a party.

Where public funding has been granted, the legal funding certificate must be filed and notice of its issue sent to the other parties.

4.75   Where a solicitor ceases to act and no notice of change of solicitor or notice of intention to act in person has been given, the solicitor may apply by summons in the High Court or on notice in the county court for his name to be removed from the record. The application must be served on the party for whom he has ceased to act but must not be served on any other party (*Re Creehouse Ltd* [1982] 3 All E.R. 659). The notice or summons must state the grounds of the application (RSC Ord. 67, r.6; CCR Ord. 50, r.5(4)).

Chapter 5

Directions and Setting Down

1   Introduction

The procedure for the giving of directions and setting down of a cause will   **5.01**
depend upon whether that cause is defended or undefended and, if undefended, whether it comes within the provisions of the special procedure.

A cause is *defended* if it is a cause which is not an undefended cause (FPR,
r.1.2(1)).

A cause is *undefended* if:

(*a*) no answer has been filed, or any answer filed has been struck out; or

(*b*) the cause is proceeding only on the respondent's answer, and no reply
or answer to the respondent's answer has been filed, or any such reply
or answer has been struck out; or

(*c*) it is a cause to which FPR, r.2.12(4) applies (relief sought under MCA
1973, s.12(*d*) (nullity on ground of mental disorder)) and in which no
notice has been given under that rule or any notice so given has been
withdrawn; or

(*d*) it is a cause in which an answer has been filed claiming relief, but in
which no pleading has been filed opposing the grant of a decree on
the petition or answer or any pleading or part of a pleading opposing the grant of such relief has been struck out; or

(*e*) it is a cause not within (*a*) to (*d*) above in which a decree has been pronounced (FPR, r.1.2(1)).

2   Time to apply for directions for trial

The relevant times to apply are given in the following table. The relevant times   **5.02**
for filing notice of intention to defend and answer (if such notice has been
given) in the case of every party cited and other respondent must also have
expired.

(See para. 4.61 as to computation of time).

Circumstances	Relevant Times
No notice of intention to defend filed	At the expiration of the time for filing such a notice
Notice of intention to defend filed	At the expiration of the time for filing an answer with no answer having been filed
Answer filed ● application by petitioner	After filing his reply or deciding not to do so
● application by respondent	At the expiration of the time for filing the reply

3 Special procedure in undefended suits of divorce and judicial separation

5.03 An undefended cause for divorce or judicial separation, whether pending in the county court or High Court, will be dealt with after close of pleadings by way of the special procedure, unless otherwise directed. A direction may, for example, be given that an undefended petition be heard in open court because the district judge is not satisfied that the petitioner has sufficiently proved the contents of the petition. "Special" is a misnomer as only a small number of undefended causes are not dealt with under this procedure. Special procedure is now said to be the ordinary procedure. The causes to which the special procedure does *not* apply are:

(*a*) defended causes;

(*b*) nullity proceedings.

Entry in the Special Procedure List

5.04 *Request for directions*: Rr.2.24(3) and 2.36 of FPR and *Practice Direction* March 1, 1977 [1977] 1 All E.R. 845 apply.

Unless otherwise directed, the petitioner or, if proceeding on the respondent's answer, the respondent must file with the request for directions for trial an affidavit:

(*a*) containing the information required by Form M7(*a*), M7(*b*), M7(*c*), 7M(*d*) or M7(*e*) (whichever is appropriate). The affidavit must be set out as far as possible in the order in the form and must be accompanied by any corroborative evidence on which the petitioner intends to rely; and

(*b*) verifying, with such amendments as the circumstances may require, the contents of any statement of arrangements filed by the petitioner under FPR, r.2.2(2).

5.05 Requirements are as follows:

(*a*) request for directions for trial (special procedure) (supplied by the court as Form D84);

(*b*) affidavit in Form M7(*a*) to (*e*);

(*c*) further affidavits (if any) or other evidence in corroboration;

(*d*) if there is any change in proceedings continuing in any country outside England and Wales, a statement giving particulars of the change (FPR, r.2.27(4)). Where it is not clear whether the proceedings issued abroad are "continuing", the party applying for directions should at least draw the attention of the court to the existence of the proceedings (*Krenge v Krenge* [1999] 1 F.L.R. 969).

As to ancillary relief, see below.

The solicitor for a petitioner does not have any duty to warn the respondent that he is applying for directions, unless he has previously agreed to do so (*Statement of the Law Society* (1986) *L.S. Gaz.* November 19, p.3474 following *Walker v Walker* [1987] 1 F.L.R. 31).

Where more than one fact is relied on, it is preferable to lodge separate affidavits rather than combine two or more forms into one affidavit.

The forms of affidavit are as follows:

Form M7(*a*), s.1(2)(*a*) (adultery);

Form M7(*b*), s.1(2)(*b*) (unreasonable behaviour);

Form M7(*c*), s.1(2)(*c*) (desertion);

Form M7(*d*), s.1(2)(*d*) (two years' separation coupled with consent);

Form M7(*e*), s.1(2)(*e*) (five years' separation).

The affidavit should be prepared carefully with precision, be as full and **5.06** informative as possible and not treated as a formality (*Newman v Newman* [1984] F.L.R. 835). Any alterations or additions to the facts pleaded in the petition should be fully dealt with in the affidavit. This will most commonly be the deletion of a prayer for costs, or a change of address of either party. However, the objectives of the special procedure are simplicity, speed and economy. District judges should therefore prefer substance to mere form so that, provided the petition and affidavit in support fulfil the essential requirements of the FPR, surplus matters should be ignored (*R v Nottingham County Court, ex p. Byers* [1985] 1 All E.R. 735).

Any corroborative evidence on which the petitioner intends to rely must be lodged with the affidavit. Enquiries should be made of the court as to corroborative evidence required, as the practice varies from court to court.

In adultery cases, any confession by the respondent or co-respondent **5.07** (including, if such be the case, an admission contained in the acknowledgment of service) should be exhibited to the petitioner's affidavit. The acknowledgment of service should be exhibited in a cause to which MCA 1973, s.1(2)(*d*) relates to prove the respondent's consent to a decree being granted. If it is not possible to produce an acknowledgment of service signed by the respondent, for example, due to his incapacity, such evidence as is available of the respondent's consent should be produced either by way of exhibit or separate affidavit. Court orders relating to previous proceedings concerning the parties or the children should be exhibited. Any unsworn documents (*e.g.* a medical report) should also be exhibited.

5.08 If the district judge is satisfied on the following matters, he must give directions for trial by entering the cause in the special procedure list (FPR, r.2.24(1)):

(*a*) that a copy of the petition (including any supplemental or amended petition) and any subsequent pleading has been duly served on every party required to be served and where that party is a person under disability, that any affidavit required by FPR, r.9.3(2) has been filed;

(*b*) if no notice of intention to defend has been given by any party entitled to give it, that the time limited for giving such notice has expired;

(*c*) if notice of intention to defend has been given by any party, that the time allowed him for filing an answer has expired;

(*d*) if an answer has been filed, that the time allowed for filing any subsequent pleadings has expired;

(*e*) in a case to which the MCA 1973 s.1(2)(d) applies the respondent under FPR, r.2.10(1) has given notice to the court that he consent to a decree being granted (FPR, r.2.24 (3)).

(*f*) that where proceedings which are in respect of the marriage or which are capable of affecting its validity or subsistence are continuing outside England and Wales it is not necessary to determine the question of whether a stay of the petition ought to be imposed under DMPA 1973, Sch.1, para.9 (FPR, r.2.27(3))(*i.e.* a discretionary stay in cases to which Brussels II does not apply, see Chap.1). If the issue needs to be determined he must fix a date, time and place for the consideration of the question by the judge and give notice thereof to all parties. If there has been a change in the information given in the petition or other pleadings as to proceedings outside England and Wales, a statement must be filed by the party making a request for directions for trial (FPR, r.2.27 (4)).

5.09 In the case of an undefended cause proceeding on the respondent's answer, the rule has effect as if for references to petitioner and respondent, there were references to respondent and petitioner (FPR, r.2.24(7)).

Disposal of causes in the Special Procedure List

5.10 As soon as practicable after the cause has been entered in the special procedure list, the district judge considers the evidence which has been filed. If the district judge is satisfied that the petitioner has sufficiently proved the contents of the petition and is entitled to a decree, he makes and files a certificate to that effect. If he is not satisfied, he may either give the petitioner an opportunity of filing further evidence, or remove the cause from the special procedure list. Further evidence will normally be in the form of an affidavit. It is rare for the District Judge to hear oral evidence but it may sometimes be possible to arrange a directions appointment at which matter can be clarified. The district judge may direct that the cause be heard in open court, failing which the petitioner (or the respondent) may apply for directions for trial in the usual way (FPR, r.2.36(1)). A request for directions for trial (Form D21 (divorce county court) or D267 (principal registry)) must then be lodged in accordance with the general procedure. The court notifies the petitioner accordingly. Refusal of a certificate is an interlocutory order from which an appeal will lie to a judge. The advantage of an appeal is, that by means of a relatively simple process in chambers the question of whether or not the certificate should have been signed can be heard by the judge and it is hoped that, if there are any irregularities on the pleading, they can be resolved. The alternative, if the judge has not already so directed, is to apply for directions for trial in open court (*R v Nottingham County Court*, ex p. *Byers* [1985] 1 All E.R. 735).

Where a district judge is satisfied that the petitioner is entitled to a decree and grants a certificate, a day is fixed for the pronouncement of a decree by a district judge, or judge, in open court at a court of trial. The court office sends to each party notice of the day and place so fixed, together with a copy of the certificate. It is not necessary for any party to appear on the day except to object to a claim for costs (FPR, r.2.36(2)). In this case the petitioner should attend to support his claim for costs.

Once the certificate has been made and filed, the district judge or judge who **5.11** is sitting in open court for the pronouncement of decrees is bound to grant the decree. If a respondent wishes to defend the cause and apply for time to file an answer, he must apply to the district judge to set aside the certificate and for leave to file an answer out of time. The application should be supported by an application giving reasons for the delay in filing or change of mind and should exhibit a draft answer. The district judge has a discretion in the matter. The general rule is that the application should be refused unless there are substantial grounds for believing that the decree, if granted, would have been obtained *contrary to the justice of the case* (*Owen v Owen* [1964] 2 All E.R. 53). However, the court must be alert to the problems encountered by the respondent under the special procedure in that a respondent is not given notice of when the district judge will be considering his certificate (*Day v Day* [1979]2 All E.R. 187). Where a respondent fails (through ignorance or lack of proper legal advice) to file an answer within the prescribed time, the court should, on an application to file an answer out of time, exercise its discretion in favour of the applicant where it is satisfied that if it does so, the result might well be different (*Mitchell v Mitchell* [1983] 3 All E.R. 621). This principle applies even if the district judge's certificate has already been granted (*Moosa v Moosa* (1983) 4 F.L.R. 131). In any event, where there is some fundamental vice (*e.g.* non-service of the petition), the certificate will be set aside automatically because any decree pronounced on the strength of it would be void (*Ebrahim v Ali* [1983] 3 All E.R. 615). A district judge should not set aside a certificate of his own motion, but should give the parties an opportunity to be heard (*Barry v Barry* [1984] Fam. Law. 178). The courses open to a judge or district judge on the hearing fixed for the pronouncement of the decree are:

(*a*) to adjourn the cause for a fixed period to enable the necessary application to be made, if the merits require an adjournment;

(*b*) to set aside the certificate and give leave to file an answer out of time, if there is before the court a properly constituted application of which notice has been given to the other party; or

(*c*) to refuse the application to set aside the certificate and pronounce the decree nisi (*Day v Day* [1979] 2 All E.R. 187; *Sims v Sims* (1979) 10 Fam. Law. 16; *Sandholm v Sandholm* (1979) 10 Fam. Law. 150; *Back v Back* (1979) 10 Fam. Law. 183; *Khawaja v Khawaja* (1980) 125 SJ 115; *Kissel v Kissel* (1980) 3 F.L.R. 65).

5.12   As to setting aside the decree nisi, see paras 7.19–7.22 and for applications for rehearing, see para. 7.16–7.18. As to persons under a disability and the special procedure, see *Bonnesen v Bonnesen* [1989] Fam. Law. 230.

Within 14 days after the pronouncement of a decree, any person may inspect the certificate and the evidence filed and may bespeak copies on payment of the prescribed fee (FPR, r.2.36(4)).

5.13   *Costs*: Where the petition contains a prayer for costs, the district judge may, if satisfied that the petitioner is entitled to costs, include in his certificate a statement to that effect. If he is not satisfied, he may refer the prayer for costs to the judge or district judge who is to pronounce the decree. He must give to any party who objects to paying costs notice that, if he wishes to proceed with his objection, he must attend before the court on the day fixed for the pronouncement of the decree (FPR, r.2.36(3)(*b*); *Hird v Hird* (1981) 11 Fam. Law. 244). The notice is in Form D84A, although many courts inform the parties by way of a standard letter.

It should be remembered that Form M5 gives notice to the respondent or co-respondent that an objection to a claim for costs cannot be entertained, unless grounds are given which would form a valid reason for not paying costs. Form M6 (acknowledgment of service) requires that the grounds for objecting to paying costs are to be stated in the acknowledgment. Nonetheless, a respondent or co-respondent may be heard on the question of costs whether or not he has returned an acknowledgment of service indicating his wish to be heard (FPR, r.2.37(2)). In some cases, the prayer for costs is withdrawn in the affidavit in Form M7 in consequence of an objection contained in the acknowledgment of service.

The court may at any time order any party objecting to a claim for costs to file and serve on the party making the claim a written statement setting out the reasons for his objection (FPR, r.2.37(1)). Some courts make such an order of their own motion. A copy of the statement will then be sent by the court to the other party as a result of which the prayer for costs may be withdrawn by letter.

5.14   *Consent order as to financial provision*: Where agreement has been reached as to an order regarding financial provision, the petitioner may, if desired, when applying for directions for trial, lodge two copies of the draft order one of which is signed by both parties, of, if represented by solicitors, by their solicitors together with a statement of information as required by FPR, r.2.61. The draft order will be perused by the district judge when he considers the evidence, and if he is of the opinion that an order should be made in the terms of the draft, or that terms of agreement be filed and made a rule of court, he will include a statement to this effect in his certificate. If there are matters which need to be clarified, he will request the petitioner or his solicitor to deal with them before he issues his certificate. The agreement will be made into an order supplemental to decree nisi by the judge or district judge when he pronounces the decree. If the district judge intended his order to come into effect after decree nisi, but it was wrongly dated by the court staff prior to the decree nisi, the date can be amended under the slip rule (*Pounds v Pounds* [1994] 1 F.L.R. 775). It should be borne in mind that periodical payments orders, lump sum orders and property adjustment orders for a petitioner or respondent can be made only on or after decree nisi but cannot take affect until decree absolute (MCA 1973, ss.23(5), 24(3)). Alternatively, application for ancillary relief, by consent or otherwise, may be made to a district judge in the normal way after the decree has been pronounced (*Practice Directions* September 26, 1972 [1972] 3 All E.R. 704 and March 7, 1977 [1977] 1 All E.R. 845).

Arrangements for the children of the family: Where there are children to whom **5.15**
MCA 1973, s.41 applies, the district judge will, unless an application under Pts
I or II of the CA 1989 is pending, consider whether there are any children of
the family and, if so, whether the court should exercise any of its powers under
the CA 1989 with respect to any of them (FPR, r.2.39(1)). If the district judge
is satisfied that there are no such children, or that there are such children but
no exercise of such power is required, he will certify accordingly and the court
will send a copy of the certificate to the petitioner and the respondent (FPR,
r.2.39(2)).

Where the district judge is not so satisfied he may direct: **5.16**

(a) that the parties file further evidence relating to the arrangements for
the children; or

(b) that a welfare report be prepared with regard to the children, or any
of them; or

(c) that the parties, or any of them, must attend before him at the date,
time and place specified in the direction (FPR, r.2.39(3)).

4 Disposal of causes to which the special procedure does not apply

Request for directions for trial: In any cause begun by petition, before it may **5.17**
be set down for trial or hearing the petitioner or a party who is defending the
cause must request the district judge to give directions for the trial of the cause
(FPR, r.2.24(1)). Forms of request may be supplied by the court office.

If the petition relates to a lawfully polygamous marriage, directions must be
asked for, if there has been no previous application as to adding an additional
spouse as a party (FPR, r.3.11 (4); see para. 1.39).

As under the special procedure the district judge considers the matter listed
at para. 5.08 under FPR, r.2.24(1).

In proceedings for nullity the district judge must also consider: **5.18**

(i) whether any application required by FPR, r.2.22(1) has been made
for the appointment of medical inspectors in petitions for nullity on
the grounds of incapability;

(ii) where an order for the medical examination of the parties has been
made under FPR, r.2.22, the notice of the appointment for the examination has been served and the report of the inspector or inspectors
has been filed (FPR, r.2.24(1)).

Where a petition for nullity has been presented on the ground that at the time **5.19**
of the marriage the respondent was suffering from mental disorder within the
meaning of the Mental Health Act 1983 of such a kind or to such an extent as to
be unfit for marriage, then the petitioner may not proceed with the cause without
leave of the district judge (FPR, r.9.4(1)). This applies whether or not the respondent gives notice of intention to defend. Leave for this purpose is obtained by
notice of application in Form D11 (general notice of application) in the county
court, or by summons in the High Court. The district judge may make it a condition of granting leave that some proper person be appointed to act as children's
guardian. Persons under disability are discussed further on paras 3.13–3.23.

5.20 *Directions for trial*: If a cause is not entered in the special procedure list, the district judge must give directions by requiring it to be set down for trial and notice given to every party that he has done so (FPR, r.2.24(5)). However, in the case of a defended cause, the district judge may treat the request for directions as a summons or application for directions. This will enable him to give such directions with regard to:

(*a*) the future course of the cause;

(*b*) any application made therein for ancillary relief or for an order relating to a child;

(*c*) the provision of evidence relating to the arrangements or proposed arrangements for the children of the family,

as appear to be necessary or desirable to secure the just, expeditious and economical disposal thereof. In this case the court must give notice of the date, time and place when the request will be considered (FPR, r.2.24(4)).

5.21 Unless the court otherwise orders, the directions given must include a direction to the petitioner to file an affidavit verifying, with such amendments as the circumstances require, the contents of any statement of arrangements filed by the petitioner under r.2.2(2) (FPR, r.2.24(6)).

If it is necessary for the district judge to exercise his powers under MCA 1973, s.41, he will do so after receipt of a request for directions for trial, or if he has treated the request for directions for trial as a summons or application for directions, and has subsequently given a direction for the provision of evidence relating to the arrangements or proposed arrangements for the children of the family, after the provision of such evidence (FPR, r.2.24(4) and r.2.39(1)). (See further para. 7.09 *et seq.*)

5.22 Upon receipt of the request for directions for trial, a pre-trial review is usually fixed before a district judge to ascertain the true state of the case and to give such directions as are necessary for its just, expeditious and economic disposal. The personal attendance of the parties is normally desirable. The purpose of the appointment is to enable parties to compose their differences and concentrate on the main issues in dispute (*Practice Direction* December 19, 1978 [1979] 1 All E.R. 112).

Directions for trial are requested on Forms D21 (undefended) and D121 (defended)(in practice, an amended Form D21 is often used instead) by either the petitioner or any party who is defending a cause begun by petition (FPR, r.2.24(1)).

Directions for trial determine the place of trial (FPR, r.2.25(1)) and once directions have been given, no further pleading may be filed without leave (FPR, r.2.14). As to directions as to allegations in a defended cause under MCA 1973, s.1(2)(*b*), see para. 4.37.

5.23 In an *undefended* cause, other than a case to which the special procedure applies, the request for directions must state:

(*a*) the place of trial desired;

(*b*) the place where the witnesses whom it is proposed to call reside;

(*c*) an estimate of the probable length of trial; and

(*d*) any other fact which may be relevant for determining the place of trial (FPR, r.2.25(2)).

In a *defended* cause, the party intending to make a request for directions for **5.24** trial must, not less than eight days before making his request, give notice of the place of trial desired to every other party who has given notice of intention to defend and, if the party intending to make the request is the respondent, to the petitioner. The notice must state the number of witnesses to be called on behalf of the party giving notice and the places (not necessarily addresses) where he and his witnesses reside. If any party to whom notice is given does not consent to the place of trial specified in the notice, he may, within eight days after receiving it, apply to the district judge to direct trial at some other place. If he does consent to the place so specified, he must, within that period, send to the party by whom the notice was given a statement signed by his solicitor (or by him, if he is acting in person) indicating that the notice has been received and specifying the number of witnesses to be called on his behalf and the places (but again not necessarily the addresses) where he and his witnesses reside (FPR, r.2.25(3)& (4)).

Where in the case of a *defended* cause no application is made for trial at **5.25** some other place as indicated above, the request for directions by a party must state:

(a) the place of trial desired;

(b) the number of witnesses to be called on his behalf and the places where he and his witnesses reside;

(c) if it be the case, that no statement has been received from any party (naming him) to whom notice was given under FPR, r.2.25(3) (indicating that he has received the notice and giving particulars of his witnesses); and

(d) an estimate of the probable length of the trial.

The party making the request must file any statement sent to him by any **5.26** other party under FPR, r.2.25(4) as to witnesses (FPR, r.2.25(5)).

If circumstances arise tending to show that any estimate of the probable length of trial given in the request for directions is inaccurate, a further estimate must be filed (FPR, r.2.25(6)).

In an *undefended* cause the requirements are as follows:

(a) request in Form D21 (divorce county court) or Form D267 (principal registry) (supplied by court);

(b) proof of service, if any required, including that of any order for medical inspection.

(c) if there is any change as to proceedings continuing in any country outside England and Wales, a statement giving particulars of the change (FPR, r.2.27(4)).

In a *defended* cause the requirements are: **5.27**

(a) request in Form D121 (or amended D21)(divorce county court or district registry) or Form D266 (principal registry);

(b) proof of service, if any required, including that of any order for medical inspection;

   (*c*) statement, if any, from any party under FPR, r.2.25(4) as to witnesses, any order for medical inspection;

   (*d*) if there is any change in proceedings continuing in any country outside England and Wales, a statement giving particulars of the change (FPR, r.2.27(4));

   (*e*) The fee of £30.

5   Place of trial (FPR, r.2.25(7), (8) and r.2.32)

5.28   A petition may be heard, according to circumstances at:

   (*a*) a court of trial;

   (*b*) a divorce town;

   (*c*) the Royal Courts of Justice (in London).

A petition pending in a divorce county court is tried at a *court of trial*, which includes the Royal Courts of Justice. A divorce county court is designated as a court of trial by the Lord Chancellor pursuant to MFPA 1984, s.33(1) (FPR, r.1.2(1)). All divorce county courts are also courts of trial (see Appendix 1 which lists divorce county courts).

5.29   *Divorce town*, in relation to family proceedings, means a place at which sittings of the High Court are authorised to be held outside the Royal Courts of Justice for the hearing of those proceedings or proceedings of the class to which they belong (FPR, r.1.2(1)). A list of divorce towns appears at Appendix 1.

A petition pending in the High Court (in a district registry or the principal registry in London) is tried at a divorce town or at the Royal Courts of Justice. Not all district registries are registries for divorce towns.

5.30   Most defended causes will remain and proceed to trial in a divorce county court, unless transferred to the High Court for trial where it appears that by reason of the complexity, difficulty or gravity of the issues involved they ought to be tried in the High Court (see further para. 4.43 *et seq.*).

Where, on a request for directions for trial in a cause pending in a divorce county court, it appears that a child is a ward of court, the party making the request is asked whether the wardship is still subsisting. If the wardship is subsisting, the district judge considers whether the whole or part of the proceedings should be transferred to the High Court under MFPA 1984, s.39 (see also *Practice Direction* June 5, 1992 [1992] 3 All E.R. 151 and para. 4.43 *et seq.*). Before making an order of his own motion, the district judge must give the parties an opportunity of being heard (FPR, r.10.10(4), (5), (6)).

5.31   In determining the place of trial, the district judge must have regard to all circumstances of the case so far as it is possible for him to do so on the basis of the information available to him, including the convenience of the parties and their witnesses, the costs likely to be incurred, the date on which the trial can take place, and the estimated length of the trial (FPR, r.2.25(7)).

Directions determining the place of trial of any cause may be varied by the district judge of the court or registry in which the cause is proceeding on the application of any party to the cause (FPR, r.2.25(8)). However, in the case of a petition pending in the High Court, a judge or the district judge of the registry for the divorce town at which any cause has been set down for trial may, where it appears to him that the cause cannot conveniently be tried at that town, order that it be tried at some other divorce town. This power may be exercised by the judge or district judge of his own motion or on the application of a party. However, an order must not be made unless the parties have either had an opportunity of being heard or consented to such an order. Where the parties, or any one of them, desire to be heard, the district judge must give the parties notice of a date, time and place at which the question will be considered (FPR, r.2.32(4)).

5.32 The district judge of the registry for the divorce town at which a cause has been set down for trial or, in the case of a cause set down for trial at the Royal Courts of Justice, a district judge of the principal registry may, if it appears to him to be desirable having regard to the proximity of the date of trial or otherwise, exercise in the cause any jurisdiction of the judge of the registry in which the cause is proceeding (FPR, r.2.34(1)).

Petitions for a declaration of marital status, parentage, legitimacy or legitimation or overseas adoption under FLA 1986, Pt III may be begun in the High Court or any county court. The county court jurisdiction is not restricted to divorce county courts. There is no longer any requirement that trial should take place at the Royal Courts of Justice.

6 Notice of setting down and hearing

5.33 Except with the consent of the parties, or by leave of a judge, no cause (whether defended or undefended) may be tried until after the expiration of ten days from the date on which directions for trial were given. This does not apply to a cause in the special procedure list (FPR, r.2.35).

5.34 *Divorce county court*: Where the cause is pending in a divorce county court other than the principal registry (not being a cause to which the special procedure applies) and is to be tried at that court, the district judge shall if he considers it practicable to do so, give directions for trial fixing the date, the place and, as nearly as may be, the time of the trial, giving notice thereof to every party to the cause, if it is practicable to do so (FPR, r.2.24(2)). Notice of the hearing is sent to every party in Form D23. If the hearing is not fixed at once, notice of setting down in Form D22 is sent and the notice of hearing is sent later.

In any other case, excluding causes to which the special procedure applies or defended causes dealt with under FPR, r.2.24(4) (see p.[ ]), the district judge must give directions for trial by setting the cause down for trial and giving notice that he has done so to every party to the cause (FPR, r.2.24(5)). Notice of setting down in Form D22 (county court) or Form D122 (High Court)(in practice, an amended D22 is often used instead)is sent.

5.35 Where a cause pending in a divorce county court is set down for trial at another divorce county court, the court file is sent to the district judge of the county court where the hearing is to take place. As soon as practicable, the district judge of the court of trial must send notice of the hearing to every party (FPR, r.2.32(5)). Notice of hearing is in Form D23.

A date for the hearing of a case set down in the county court list for hearing at the Royal Courts of Justice will be fixed by the Clerk of the Rules at the Royal Courts of Justice (*Practice Direction* April 10, 1968 [1968] 2 All E.R. 123). Causes set down for hearing at the Royal Courts of Justice are listed weekly and such lists are posted outside the office of the Clerk of the Rules. Causes are arranged in order of setting down and causes set down at either the district registries or divorce county courts are listed according to the date the court file was received in the Principal Registry. The lists show the number assigned to each case. There are separate lists for the High Court. The numbers assigned to causes in the county court list are prefixed by letter. On the cause being set down, notice is given to the parties informing them of the list number assigned to the case. The party who applied for directions for trial in county court cases are notified of the arrangements existing for listing or fixing the case for hearing (*Rayden and Jackson*, 17th ed., pp.392–393.)

5.36   *High Court*: Where a cause is pending in the High Court is set down for trial, and is not to be tried in the divorce town for the registry in which it is proceeding, the court file is sent to the registry for the place where the cause is to be tried or to the principal as the case may be.

In defended causes the court sends a form of list of witnesses (Form D24) to be completed by the parties attending and to be returned to the court before the date of hearing.

5.37   The arrangements for notifying the parties of the date of hearing at the divorce town vary and enquiries should be made locally if the arrangements are not known. Some courts give a fixed date of hearing when the cause is entered in the list. Others prepare a warned list containing the names of all cases to be dealt with in a specified period, usually a week. Copies of the list are sent to the solicitors acting on each side. Notification is then given, usually by telephone, a day or two in advance of the actual hearing date.

In the Royal Courts of Justice, in the High Court a date is listed by the Clerk of the Rules as in the County Court. Causes in the High Court are numbered without prefixes and all parties, rather than just the part applying for directions for trial, are notified of the arrangements existing for listing or fixing the case for hearing. (*Rayden and Jackson*, 17th ed, pp.392–393)

7   Trial of issue

5.38   It may be necessary to decide a preliminary issue (e.g., as to jurisdiction or paternity) before deciding the main suit or ancillary matters. Where directions are given for the separate trial of an issue and those directions have been complied with:

    (*a*) if the issue arises on an application for ancillary relief or with respect to any child or alleged child of the family, the district judge proceeds as if the issue were a question referred to a judge on an application for ancillary relief and FPR, r.2.65 applies;

    (*b*) in any other case, the district judge sets the issue down for trial and FPR, r.2.32(5) and (6) apply as if the issue were a cause (FPR, r.2.33).

5.39   Under FPR, r.2.66 (in the case of ancillary relief or with respect to children), the district judge fixes a date and time for the hearing and gives notice to the parties. The hearing takes place in chambers, unless otherwise directed. If the cause is pending in the High Court and proceeding in a district registry which is not in a divorce town, the hearing takes place at such divorce town as in the opinion of the district judge is the nearest or most convenient.

Under FPR, r.2.32 (in other cases), where the issue is set down for trial at another divorce county court, the court file is sent to the clerk of the court of trial, and he gives notice of the date and time for trial. If the cause is pending in the High Court, the court file is sent to the Royal Courts of Justice, or to the registry for the divorce town, as the case may be, where the trial is to take place, and the hearing is fixed as for a petition. Other issues covered by FPR, r.2.33(*b*) are tried in open court (*B(LA) v B(CH)* (1975) Fam. Law. 158).

In a cause pending in a county court, the court may order the cause to be **5.40** transferred to the High Court where it thinks it desirable having regard to all the circumstances, including the difficulty or importance of the issue (MFPA 1984, s.39, FPR, r.10.10(6) and *Practice Direction* June 5, 1992 [1992] 3 All E.R. 151 (see pp.79–84).

An order for the trial of an issue should state whether the issue is to be tried in open court or in chambers and who shall be the plaintiff in the trial. Directions might also be given:

(*a*) as to the place of trial if the cause is not proceeding in a district registry which is in a divorce town;

(*b*) as to the appointment of the Official Solicitor as children's guardian;

(*c*) for blood tests;

(*d*) for affidavits or oral evidence.

A draft issue should be drawn up by the solicitor for the plaintiff and sent **5.41** to each defendant, who should endorse it with his approval. The agreed draft issue should be lodged in or sent to the court in which the cause is proceeding for settling. The settled draft issue will be returned to the solicitor for the plaintiff. An engrossment of the settled draft should be sent in duplicate by the plaintiff to each defendant, who should endorse one copy to the effect that he has accepted service and return it to the plaintiff.

In order to set the issue down, the settled draft and engrossed copy should be sent to the court office (Room G34, if the cause is proceeding in the principal registry). If the issue is to be heard in open court the same procedure will apply as for a cause. If the hearing is to be in chambers, a notice of the hearing will be sent to each party by the court (*Practice Direction* November 11, 1975 [1975] 3 All E.R. 959).

(The precedents given in the Practice Direction appear as Forms 24, 25 and 26 in Appendix 2.)

Chapter 6

Evidence

1 Introduction

6.01 Evidence is the means by which a fact in issue in proceedings is proved to the satisfaction of the court. Certain rules dictate how such evidence is brought before the court.

FPR rr.2.28 to 2.31 and 10.12 to 10.14 apply. FPR, r.1.3(1) provides that, subject to the provisions of those rules, the County Court Rules 1981 and the Rules of the Supreme Court 1965 apply, as appropriate, to family proceedings in the county court and in the High Court. Family proceedings are defined by Matrimonial and Family Proceedings Act 1984, s.32. Family proceedings include divorce proceedings.

6.02 Evidence can take many formats including by affidavit, witness statement, or written expert evidence. The general rule however (subject to what is said below) is that evidence of witnesses at a trial of a cause begun by petition must be proved by the examination of witnesses orally and in open court (FPR, r.2.28(1)).

Practitioners should note that, whilst the Civil Procedure Rules 1998 (CPR) are not intended to apply formally in family proceedings, a district judge may well be influenced by such aspects as the overriding objective, case management and the provisions relating to expert evidence when considering how a case within the family proceedings should proceed.

CPR does apply, in part, to costs and expert evidence in relation to ancillary relief proceedings *Family Proceedings (Miscellaneous Amendments) Rules 1999 SI 1999/1012.*

2 Evidence within the divorce proceedings

6.03 Divorce proceedings remain one of the rare types of proceedings still commenced by petition (FPR, r.2.2(1)). The FPR provide exactly what must be contained with the petition FPR, r.2.3 (see para. 2.02). It is necessary to prove within divorce proceedings that there is a marriage in existence, that the marriage has irretrievably broken down and to provide full details of the fact(s) relied upon to prove this.

(i) Evidence of marriage

6.04 The existence of a marriage is proved by filing the marriage certificate at court with the petition. In the case of a marriage which took place outside England and Wales a marriage certificate or similar document issued under the law in force in that country must be filed. A certified copy of an entry in a register of marriages kept under the law in force in that country may also be acceptable evidence (FPR, r.10.14). Additional evidence may be required by the court.

(ii) Convictions and findings of adultery as evidence

A petitioner who, in reliance on the Civil Evidence Act 1968, ss.11 or 12, **6.05** intends to adduce evidence that a person:

    (*a*) was convicted of an offence by or before a court in the UK or by a court martial there or elsewhere (s.11); or

    (*b*) was found guilty of adultery in any matrimonial proceedings or was found to be the father of a child in relevant proceedings before any court in England and Wales or was adjudged to be the father of a child in affiliation proceedings before a court in the UK (s. 12 as amended by Family Law Reform Act 1987, s.29),

for the purpose of proving an offence was committed or adultery took place must include in his petition a statement of his intention (FPR, r.2.4(1)). This must contain particulars of:

    (*a*) the conviction, finding or adjudication and the date thereof;

    (*b*) the court or court martial which made the conviction, finding or adjudication and, in the case of a finding or adjudication, the proceedings in which it was made; and

    (*c*) the issue in the proceedings to which the conviction, finding or adjudication is relevant.

These provisions also apply to a respondent's answer and to any subsequent pleadings with the necessary modifications (FPR, r.2.15(5)).

"Matrimonial proceedings", "relevant proceedings" and "affiliation proceedings" have the same meaning as in the Civil Evidence Act 1968, s.12(5) (as amended) (FPR, r.2.4(2)).

There is no need to rely on the Civil Evidence Act 1968, s.12, where the pre- **6.06** vious proceedings were between the same parties. The finding in the earlier proceedings is conclusive evidence. Where the Civil Evidence Act 1968, s.12 does apply, the previous finding will be sufficient evidence unless the contrary is proved (Civil Evidence Act 1968, s.12(2)).

Where a party intends to rely on a previous decree or order of a magistrates' court in this country or in Northern Ireland, the Isle of Man or the Channel Islands, MCA 1973, s.4(1) and (2) still requires evidence from the petitioner, even though the previous decree or order is to be treated as sufficient proof of the allegations upon which it is based.

3 Proof of adultery in undefended causes

(i) Confession statement   6.07

In undefended proceedings for divorce in which it is alleged that the respondent has committed adultery, a statement in writing signed by the respondent admitting the adultery can be put in evidence, the respondent's signature being identified by the petitioner. This should form sufficient evidence of the adultery without the need for further evidence (*Practice Direction* July 27, 1973 [1973] 3 All E.R. 180).

At common law, a confession of adultery is only evidence against the person who makes it and is not evidence against the other party to the alleged adultery. This may change if it is made in the presence of that other party in such circumstances that the reaction of the other party makes it evidence against him or her or unless it is made on oath in court (*Spring v Spring*) [1947] 1 All E.R. 886.

As to hearsay evidence and the Civil Evidence Act 1995, see further para. 6.36 below.

(ii) Acknowledgment of service

6.08   The acknowledgment of service (Form M6) contains a question giving the respondent and co-respondent an opportunity to admit the adultery alleged in the petition when acknowledging service of the divorce petition. If the answer is "Yes", the party, as well as any solicitor who may be acting for him or her, must sign the acknowledgment of service. If the respondent admits the adultery within the acknowledgment of service form, it will be unnecessary for the petitioner to file affidavit evidence from an enquiry agent or other person or for the petitioner's affidavit to exhibit the confession statement(s).

In most special procedure cases, if there is no acknowledgment of service admitting adultery from the co-respondent or other form of confession, he will be dismissed from the suit and no order for costs made against him. The form of order will read: "The respondent has committed adultery with a person against whom the adultery is not proved".

6.09   There is no requirement in the FPR to name a co-respondent in divorce proceedings, which rely on the fact of adultery, even if the petitioner is aware of the identity of the potential co-respondent. If a co-respondent is named, he/she will be made a party to proceedings (FPR, r.2.7(1)). However, some district judges may require further evidence to be filed where no co-respondent has been named. In this event, the petitioner should file supplemental evidence indicating either the reason for not wishing to name the co-respondent and giving further particulars of the adultery or provide details of the enquiries made to trace and identify the co-respondent.

It is usual for direct evidence of adultery to be made available by a respondent. However, where it is necessary to rely upon circumstantial evidence, the court will require proof of an opportunity to commit adultery coupled with an inclination to do so (*Ross v Ellison (or Ross)* [1930] A.C. 1), for example due to cohabitation.

(iii) Further evidence

6.10   Where for some reason the evidence of an enquiry agent is necessary in a defended cause, it should normally be filed by way of affidavit. Leave to bring such evidence may be sought from the judge at the hearing, where directions for trial in open court have been given, without any prior application to the district judge (*Practice Direction* July 27, 1973 [1973] 3 All E.R. 180). If this practice is not adhered to, the enquiry agent's costs may not be recoverable.

Where a co-respondent is under the age of 16 years, it is present practice to request a direction under FPR 1991, r.2.7(1)(b) as to whether the minor should be made a co-respondent and/or served with the petition (*Practice Direction* December 15, 1960 [1961] 1 All E.R. 129).

4 Evidence by affidavit

Evidence must be given by affidavit, instead of or in addition to a witness statement if this is required by the court, a provision contained in any other Rule, a practice direction or other enactment. **6.11**

Despite the introduction of the Civil Procedure Rules (CPR) for civil proceedings, these do not generally apply to family proceedings. Rules of the Supreme Court (RSC) and County Court Rules (CCR) in their original form (*i.e.* those rules in force immediately before April 26, 1999) apply in so far as they are not inconsistent with the FPR.

RSC Ord. 38, r.1 provides the general rule that any fact requiring to be proved at trial by the evidence of a witness must be proved by examination of that witness orally and in open court. This rule is followed by FPR, r.2.28(1) and is subject to the provisions of the Civil Evidence Act 1995. Furthermore, FPR, r.2.28 provides that nothing in that rule affects the power of the judge at trial to refuse to admit any evidence if in the interests of justice he thinks fit to do so. **6.12**

An affidavit is a written sworn statement signed by a person (the deponent) which is used as evidence of the matters deposed of. In family proceedings it is often the case that the affidavit or statement stands as evidence in chief. The deponent or witness is then cross- examined on the content of the affidavit at trial. For details of the practice direction on affidavits see next page.

(i) Evidence by way of affidavit without an order

On any application made in a county court by way of an originating application, or an application in the course of the proceedings (CCR Ord. 13, r.1) in a divorce county court, or on any application made in the High Court by way of an originating summons, notice or motion, evidence may be filed by affidavit (RSC Ord. 41) unless the rules otherwise provide, or the court otherwise directs (FPR, r.10.12). **6.13**

However, the court may, on the application of any party, order the attendance for cross-examination of the person making any such affidavit. Where such an order has been made and the witness does not attend, his affidavit may not be used as evidence without the leave of the court (FPR, r.10.12). The judge has power at the trial to refuse to admit the evidence by affidavit if in the interests of justice he thinks fit to do so (FPR, r.2.28(2)).

(ii) Content of an affidavit

The content of an affidavit is of utmost importance bearing in mind that it may stand as evidence in chief. Whilst affidavits are not of themselves pleadings, they generally contain detailed information relating to the issues between the parties. An affidavit may contain only such facts as the deponent is able, of his own knowledge, to prove (RSC Ord. 41 r.5(1); CCR Ord. 20, r.10, and *Practice Direction* of January 31, 1995 (*Case Management*) [1995]1 F.L.R. 456). **6.14**

Furthermore, if the affidavit contains hearsay evidence the source of the information must be declared or good reason given for not doing so.

If the court finds any part of an affidavit to be superfluous, or oppressive, it can order that part of the affidavit be struck out. If part of the affidavit is considered to be privileged again it can be struck out (RSC Ord. 41 r.6).

Any person who provides affidavit evidence should be available for cross examination at the hearing of the cause.

(iii)   Practice

6.15   When drafting affidavits, particular regard should be had to RSC Ord. 41 and (*Practice Note* July 21, 1983 [1983] 3 All E.R. 33) which apply to proceedings in the Court of Appeal and the High Court, and CCR Ord. 20, r.10 which applies to proceedings in the county court.

Affidavits should be produced in a format to comply with the requirement to mark the top right-hand corner of the first page and backsheet of every affidavit and exhibit with specified details: see Appendix 2, form 27. Non-compliance with these requirements may result in the affidavit being rejected or a costs penalty.

Affidavits may be produced on one side of the paper providing they are bound in book form and the printed, written or typed sides of the paper are numbered consecutively (RSC Ord. 41, r.1(5)).

6.16   Where evidence is given by one party on affidavit and the other party is a litigant in person, the court has a duty to advise the litigant in person of his right to challenge the affidavit evidence by cross-examination and to give him an opportunity to do so (*Harris v Harris* [1986] 1 F.L.R. 12).

As to the admission of evidence outside that contained in the original affidavit and the position of witnesses other than parties in proceedings for financial provision, see *Ladd v Marshall* [1954] 3 All E.R. 745; *Krywald v Krywald* [1988] 2 F.L.R. 401.

Where a party wishes to file an affidavit or other document in connection with an application in any cause or matter proceeding in the Principal Registry for which a hearing date has been fixed, the affidavit or other document must be lodged in the Principal Registry not less than fourteen clear days before the appointed hearing date (*Practice direction* February 20, 1987 [1987] 1 All E.R. 546).

6.17   If it is not possible to file the affidavit at least fourteen clear days in advance, the affidavit or other document should be lodged as soon as possible before the hearing in the case of an application before the judge or, in the case of an application before a district judge, it should be handed to the clerk to that district judge immediately before the hearing.

If the practice direction is not observed, costs may be disallowed or be ordered to be paid personally by the defaulting solicitor and the affidavit may not be considered at all by the judge (*Practice Direction* February 1, 1984 [1984] 1 All E.R. 684).

(iv)   Affidavit evidence with no attendance by witness by order

6.18   A court may order that the affidavit of any witness may be read at the trial on such conditions as the court thinks reasonable (FPR, r.2.28(3)(*a*)). Where a party to the suit or a witness is abroad, or cannot attend the hearing due to illness or other sufficient reason, an application can be made for evidence to be given by affidavit. The application should be made to a district judge, ex parte, by filing an affidavit in those circumstances if no notice of intention to defend has been given, or if the petitioner and every party who has given notice of intention to defend consents to the order sought, or if the cause is undefended and directions for trial have been given. An ex parte application in a cause or matter proceeding in the Principal Registry should be made to the district Judge at least fourteen days before the hearing. In any other case, the application should be made to the Judge at the trial (*Practice Directions* October 31 1972 [1972] 3 All E.R. 910 and January 12, 1981 [1981] 1 All E.R. 323). The application should be made on notice in Form D11 in a divorce county court or by summons in the High Court supported by affidavit: see Appendix 2, form 21. The consent of any party should be lodged. The fee will be £30 if the application is made with consent of other parties, or £60 if no such consent if filed.

Where an application is made before trial for an order that the affidavit of a witness may be read at the trial, or that evidence of any particular fact may be given at the trial by affidavit, a copy of the proposed affidavit to be read, must be submitted with the application. This should be exhibited to the affidavit in support of the application, although the actual affidavit itself should not be marked as an exhibit. Where the affidavit is sworn before the hearing of the application and sufficiently states the grounds on which the application is made, no other affidavit is required FPR, r.2.28(5).

The affidavit, in support of the application where non-attendance is antici-   **6.19** pated, is usually made by the party's solicitor (unless, of course, the only affidavit relied on is that of the witness under FPR, r.2.28(5)). The affidavit must state the grounds on which the application is made (FPR, r.2.28(4)). The affidavit should also state the deponent's means of knowledge of the whereabouts of the petitioner or witness concerned and, if illness is a reason, a medical certificate is material and necessary.

The district judge has a discretion in considering the application and will consider, inter alia, the right of the other party to cross-examine and whether evidence should be taken before an examiner.

If the affidavit to be read at the hearing is not filed before the application is dealt with, the order should provide that it is to be filed not less than fourteen days (or such other time as the district judge may think fit) before the hearing and should impose a stay until it is filed (*Practice Directions* July 24, 1956, unreported and [1981] 1 All E.R. 323, para.3).

5   Orders for evidence otherwise than by affidavit

The court may order that the evidence of any particular fact shall be given at   **6.20** the trial in such manner as may be specified in the order and in particular:

(*a*) by statement on oath of information or belief; or

(*b*) by the production of documents or entries in books; or

(*c*) by copies of documents or entries in books; or

(*d*) in the case of a fact which is or was a matter of common knowledge either generally or in a particular district, by the production of a specified newspaper containing a statement of the fact (FPR, r.2.28(3)(*b*)).

The rule would also enable evidence to be given by other means, such as audio or video tape.

An application to the district judge for such an order must be made ex parte by filing an affidavit if no notice of intention to defend has been given, or if the petitioner and every party who has given notice of intention to defend consents to the order sought, or if the cause is undefended and directions for trial have been given (FPR, r.2.28(4)). Otherwise, application is made by notice of application in Form D11 (county court) or by summons (High Court).

The Bankers' Book Evidence Act 1879 provides for obtaining evidence of bank records. The Banking Act 1987 extends the old definition of what can be obtained to include modern forms of records, including computer records. The Act does not extend to correspondence, cheques and paying-in slips (*Williams v Williams* [1988] 1 F.L.R. 455).

6   Evidence by deposition (FPR, r.2.29)

(i)   Authority to provide evidence by way of deposition

6.21   If it is likely that a witness may be unable to attend trial, the court has a discretionary power to order that evidence may be taken earlier than trial where it appears necessary for the purposes of justice. The usual grounds upon which an order might be made are thought generally to be where the witness is too old or decrepit to attend a trial or might die before trial, or is so ill as to be no prospect of his being able to attend trial, or where a female witness is pregnant and likely to be delivered about the time of the trial, or if the witness is likely to leave the country before trial. In such cases orders are often made by consent.

Any party to a cause begun by petition may make an application to the court for the examination on oath of any person under CCR Ord. 20, r.13 or (if the cause is pending in the High Court) under RSC Ord. 39, r.1.

6.22   Rule 13 of the CCR Ord. 20 and RSC Ord. 39, rr.1–14 apply respectively with the appropriate modifications (FPR, r.2.29). Those rules set out the procedure to be adopted for evidence by way of depositions. It will not be possible to use any deposition taken as evidence at trial unless the deposition was taken in accordance with an order under RSC Ord. 39, r.1.

The order of the court allowing the deposition may contain terms, such as the provision of discovery prior to the examination, which appear necessary to the court for the purposes of the examination (RSC Ord. 39 r.1 (2)).

An examiner may not include in the deposition any opinion as to a witness's credibility, but may make a special report to the court (*In the Estate of Wipperman* [1953] 1 All E.R. 764; RSC Ord. 39/13/1; CCR Ord. 20, r.13(5)(e)). The trial judge retains power to refuse to admit evidence taken at the examination if in the interests of justice he thinks fit to do so (FPR, r.2.28(2)).

(ii)   County court procedure

6.23   Applications for evidence to be by way of deposition under CCR Ord. 20, r.13 are limited to examination at any place in England and Wales. Application is made to the District Judge by notice of application. Form D11 can be used. The form of order is CCR, Form N21. An application should be supported by affidavit stating the grounds of the application, *e.g.* why the witness cannot attend the hearing. A fee of £30 will be payable if the application is made with the consent of the other parties, otherwise the fee will be £60.

The examination must take place before an officer of the court making the order or of the court for the district in which the witness resides or carries on business or such other person as the court may appoint.

A copy of the order allowing examination on oath of any person must be **6.24** sent to every party to the action. Of course the order needs to be served on the person to be examined. The order will contain details of the day and place specified for the examination and must be served a reasonable time before the day appointed. When served monies should be paid to the person to be examined in accordance with CPR, r.34.7).

As for examinations outside of England and Wales in a cause pending in a county court, the County Courts Act 1984, s.56 applies. The application should be made in the High Court by originating summons and RSC Ord. 107, r.3 applies.

(iii)   High court procedure

Applications under RSC Ord. 39, r.1 are not limited to examination in **6.25** England and Wales. Ord. 39, r.2 applies to examinations out of the jurisdiction. RSC Ord. 38, r.9 and RSC Ord. 39, rr.1–14 regulate the procedure with appropriate modifications. The procedure is set out in the notes to RSC Ord. 39, r.1. The examination takes place before a judge, an officer or examiner of the court or some other person (RSC Ord. 39, r.1(1)).

Forms of summons and order for examination are contained in RSC, App.A, Forms 31–37. The fee is £30.

7   Exchange of witness statements

The court may under RSC, Ord. 38, r.2A or CCR, Ord. 20, r.12A direct any **6.26** party at any stage of the proceedings to serve on the other parties written statements of the oral evidence which the party intends to rely on when the court considers issues of fact at the trial. The purpose is to achieve expedition, save costs, promote fair settlements and identify the real issues. Such a direction may also serve to reduce the number of pre-trial applications, such as for further and better particulars of pleadings or for further discovery or for interrogatories. A direction for the exchange of witness statements might be sought, for example, in a defended cause.

Statements should be dated, be signed by the intended witness and shall include a statement that the contents are true to the best of his knowledge and belief. The statement should sufficiently identify any documents referred to and, where statements are filed and are served by one or more party, they should be mutually exchanged (RSC Ord. 38 2A, r.3).

The application for evidence by way of witness statement may be made on notice by summons in the High Court or by way of application on notice in the county court to the District Judge or when directions are given in a defended cause under FPR, r.2.24(4).

8   Discovery and inspection

See para. 9.79.   **6.27**

6.28   9   Interrogatories

6.29   See para. 4.41 *et seq.*

10   Subpoenas and witness summonses

(i)   Applications

6.30   Where a party to proceedings wishes for a person to be summoned as a witness to provide oral evidence at trial or to produce a document in his possession, power or custody at trial, the court can, upon application, issue a *subpoena* (High Court RSC Ord. 38, r.14), or witness summons (county court CCR Ord. 20, r.12).

A witness summons or *subpoena ad testificandum* enforces the attendance of a witness to provide testimony at a hearing, whereas a witness summons to produce documents or *subpoena duces tecum* compels the production of documents at the hearing.

A witness summons in a cause pending in a divorce county court may be issued in that court or in the court of trial at which the cause is to be tried (FPR, r.2.30(1)).

6.31   A writ of subpoena in a cause pending in the High Court may issue out of:

(*a*) the registry in which the cause is proceeding; or

(*b*) if the cause is to be tried at the Royal Courts of Justice, the principal registry; or

(*c*) if the cause is to be tried at a divorce town, the registry for that town (FPR, r.2.30(2)).

6.32   As an alternative to an inspection appointment (FPR, r.2.62 (7)–(9) a party to divorce proceedings can apply to the court to fix a date for a *subpoena duces tecum* or witness summons to be heard in advance of the main hearing. This is now referred to as a *Khanna* hearing (*Khanna v Lovell White Durrant (a Firm)* [1995] 1 W.L.R. 121). This avoids the initial hearing under the inspection appointment procedure for an order that the document(s) be produced.

A witness who is served with a witness summons or *subpoena* can apply to the court for it to be set aside. Such application may succeed if it can be shown that the order is oppressive or too speculative.

(ii)   County court procedure

6.33   A witness summons in a divorce county court may be issued as of right. No leave is required (CCR Ord. 20, r.12(1); *Senior v Holdsworth* [1975] 2 All E.R. 1009).

A request in Form N286 (supplied by the court) must be used for the issue of a witness summons. No fee is payable.

Conduct money, which must be paid or tendered to the witness at the time of service, consists of a sum to cover costs of travelling each way plus a sum of £7.50 (minimum) as compensation for loss of time. The summons and copy are drawn by the court in Form D39 (oral evidence) and Form D40 (to produce documents). The summons must contain the name of one witness only but may in this regard be issued in blank (CCR Ord. 20, r.12 (3)). The summons must be served personally a reasonable time before the return day, unless a certificate for postal service has been given (N219). In this latter case, the court serves by first class post and the deemed date of service is seven days after the posting date.

If a witness fails to attend without good reason having been served he can be fined by the court.

(iii) Procedure in the High Court

RSC Ord. 32, r.7 and Ord. 38, rr.14–19 apply. Forms of *subpoena* are con- **6.34** tained in RSC, App.A, Forms 28–30. The requirements for an application for a subpoena are:

    (*a*) praecipe;

    (*b*) writ of *subpoena.*

No fee is payable.

A *subpoena* for attendance at trial before a judge may be issued as of right without leave. However, a *subpoena* for attendance for a hearing in chambers (whether before a judge or district judge) may not be issued without leave by a note from a judge or district judge (RSC Ord. 32, r.7).

The praecipe is completed and filed and the writ of *subpoena* is sealed and handed back. Two or more persons may be included within one writ of *subpoena ad testificandum* (RSC Ord. 38, r.15). Only one person may be named on a writ of *subpoena duces tecum.*

A *subpoena* must be served personally and the service is not valid unless effected within twelve weeks after issue and not less than four days or such other period as the court may fix before the day on which attendance is required (RSC Ord. 38, r.17). Substituted service may be ordered.

(iv) Subpoenas in Scotland or Northern Ireland

Where a witness is in Scotland or Northern Ireland (not the Irish Republic) a **6.35** *subpoena* may be issued with leave of the district judge upon filing an affidavit explaining the facts (Supreme Court Act 1981, s.36). No fee is payable.

The order providing leave is not drawn up, but leave granted is marked on the affidavit. The necessary additional words to be added to the subpoena are contained in a note to Form 28 in RSC, App.A. The words are as follows: after "We command you", insert "wherever you shall be within the United Kingdom", and at the foot of the *subpoena* add, "Take notice that this writ is issued by the special order of the High Court of Justice in England dated the day of [ ] ,200[ ], pursuant to Supreme Court Act 1981, s.36.

11 Hearsay and expert evidence

(i) Hearsay evidence

The Civil Evidence Act 1995 came into force on January 31, 1997. Section 1 **6.36** of the Civil Evidence Act 1995 (CEA) makes clear that evidence should not be excluded on the ground that it is hearsay. The general rule is that, if to be relied upon in proceedings, hearsay evidence must be either agreed or notice of intention to rely on that evidence should be given.

The Act provides that "hearsay" is a statement made otherwise than by a person while giving oral evidence in the proceedings which is tendered as evidence of the matters stated. References to hearsay include hearsay of whatever degree (CEA, s.1 (2)(a–b)).

(a)   Family Proceedings

6.37   The rules for adducing hearsay evidence are RSC Ord. 38, rr.20–34 and CCR Ord. 20, rr.14–26. R.2.31 of the FPR applies RSC Ord. 38, r.21 to a defended cause in the High Court with modifications.
Practice Direction (Family Proceedings: Case Management) [1995] 1 F.L.R. 456 attempts to exercise more control over evidence to be adduced. At para.(3) it directs that "if hearsay evidence is to be adduced, the source of the information must be declared or good reason given for not doing so."

A party proposing to adduce hearsay evidence must provide notice to the other party to the proceedings of the fact that he intends to do so and upon request must provide particulars of, or relating to, the evidence as is reasonable and practicable in the circumstances (CEA, s.2(1)). This enables the other party to deal with any matters arising from its being hearsay. It is possible for the other party to waive the necessity for notice of hearsay to be given (CEA, s.2(3)).

6.38   If a party fails to give notice this may not be fatal to the admissibility of the hearsay evidence, but may be taken into account by the court either when consideration is given to exercise of the court's powers, weight to be given to the evidence and/or costs.

In considering what weight is to be attached to hearsay evidence the court must have regard to any circumstances from which any inference could reasonably be drawn as to the reliability or otherwise of the evidence (CEA. s.4(1)). In particular the court may have regard to matters set out in section 4(2) of the CEA;

(a) whether it would have been reasonable and practicable for the party by whom the evidence was adduced to have produced the maker of the original statement as a witness;

(b) whether the original statement was made contemporaneously with the occurrence or existence of matters stated;

(c) whether the evidence involves multiple hearsay;

(d) whether any person involved had any motive to conceal or misrepresent matters;

(e) whether the original statement was an edited account, or was made in collaboration with another or for a particular purpose;

(f) whether the circumstances in which the evidence is adduced as hearsay are such as to suggest an attempt to prevent proper evaluation of its weight.

6.39   It has been held that the admission of hearsay evidence in civil proceedings without the possibility of cross examination does not automatically result in an unfair trial within Article 6(1) of the European Convention on Human Rights (*R. v Marylebone Magistrates' Court*, ex p. *Andrew Clingham* T.L.R. February 20, 2001).

Hearsay evidence will not be admitted if the maker of the statement was not competent at the time of making it (CEA, s.5). This may relate to mental or physical infirmity, or lack of understanding as would render a person incompetent generally as a witness within civil proceedings.

Where a party wishes to adduce hearsay evidence and does not call the maker of the statement, any other party to the proceedings may, with leave of the court, call that person and cross examine him (CEA, s.3).

The CEA preserves the common law rule which was specifically preserved by the Civil Evidence Act 1968. The common law rule provides that any rule of law continues to have effect whereby in civil proceedings:

(i) published works dealing with matters of a public nature (*e.g.* histories, scientific works, dictionaries, maps) are admissible as evidence of the facts of a public nature stated in them;

(ii) public documents (*e.g.* public registers, returns made under public authority relating to matters of public interest) are admissible as evidence of the facts stated in them; and

(iii) records (*e.g.* records of certain courts, treaties, Crown grants, pardons and commissions) are admissible as evidence of facts stated in them.

(b) Proceedings relating to children

The rules relating to hearsay evidence in proceedings relating to children, whether in the High Court, county court or family proceedings court, or in relation to civil proceedings under the Child Support Act 1991 in a magistrates' court, adopt a different approach. **6.40**

The rules, contained within The Children (Admissibility of Hearsay Evidence) Order 1993 (SI 1993/621), made under the Children Act 1989, s.96(3), are not affected by the CEA. The Order provides that evidence given in connection with the upbringing, maintenance or welfare of a child is admissible, notwithstanding any rule of law relating to hearsay evidence.

It is recognised that the more relaxed approach to hearsay evidence is adopted in children proceedings to allow the wishes and feelings of the child to be represented to the court by third parties such as officers of Cafcass.

Careful consideration should be given to whether the hearsay evidence contemplated to be placed before the court is to be given in the type of proceedings covered by the Order and/or whether the evidence relates to the upbringing, maintenance or welfare of a child. Both tests as to type of proceedings and content of evidence must be satisfied – (*C v C (Contempt: Evidence)* [1993] 1 F.L.R. 220). **6.41**

In all children proceedings the weight to be given to hearsay evidence is a matter for the discretion of the court (*Re W (Minors) (Wardship: Evidence)* [1990] 1 F.L.R. 203). It is submitted that to a certain extent the court will have consideration of those factors set out at s.4(2) CEA listed above.

(ii) Expert evidence

The court may be assisted in the exercise of its discretion in proceedings by the use of expert evidence. Expert evidence should be relevant to the issues within **6.42** the case. If expert evidence is conflicting, it is for the court to decide the case on the evidence (*Re J (a minor)(Expert Evidence: Hearsay)Re, (Fam Div)* [1999] 2 F.L.R. 661).

(a)   Family proceedings

6.43   RSC Ord. 38, rr.35–44, CCR Ord. 20, rr.27–28 and the Civil Evidence Act 1972, s.2 apply.

Section 2(3) of the 1972 Act provides that experts reports prepared for pending or contemplated civil proceedings, or for the purpose of obtaining or giving legal advice, are in certain circumstances privileged from disclosure. In other words, if they are not to be relied upon, there is generally no duty to disclose the report.

Section 2(3)(a)provides for the court to direct that, with respect to medical matters or matters of other class of expert reports, a report must be disclosed to the other parties to the proceedings if it is intended that one party will adduce such report as part of his case at trial.

6.44   If such direction for prior disclosure is not complied with, the party will be prohibited from adducing such report in evidence except without leave of the court (CEA, 1972, s.2(3)(c)).

Oral expert evidence may be given in civil proceedings in certain circumstances (CEA, 1972, s.2 (4)). It is considered that prior disclosure of such evidence should still be given.

Furthermore, FPR, r.2.28(3)(*c*) provides that the court may order that not more than a specified number of expert witnesses may be called. FPR, r.4.17 requires the filing and service of any expert's report that a party intends to rely on.

In publicly funded cases prior authority from the Legal Services Commission may be required before instructing an expert.

Whilst the Civil Procedure Rules 1998 (CPR) do not specifically apply to all types of family proceedings, it should be borne in mind the court may adopt a similar approach to expert evidence in family proceedings as it is now obliged to adopt in other civil proceedings. CPR, Pt 35 covers the provisions relating to expert evidence. Part 35 covers the court's power to restrict expert evidence, direct the use of single joint experts, and the consequences of failure to disclose expert's reports.

(b)   Proceedings relating to children

6.45   Many different types of expert reports may be utilised in children proceedings. Such evidence may relate to factual issues, opinion evidence or both. There are various guidelines for the use of experts in such proceedings including those produced by the Children Act Advisory Committee (see *The Family Court Practice* [2002] p.2487).

Leave of the court must be sought, by application on notice unless the court directs otherwise, for any child to be medically or psychiatrically examined or otherwise assessed for the purpose of the preparation of expert evidence for use in proceedings under the Children Act 1989 (FPR, r.4.18). *Re G* [1994] 2 F.L.R. 291 provides useful guidelines on obtaining leave, and directions for experts generally. If leave is not granted in advance, the evidence may not be adduced without subsequent leave of the court. Breach of the provision to obtain leave of the court in advance of any examination will be considered most seriously by the court and this approach should not be adopted without serious reason.

Oxfordshire CC v M [1994] 1 F.L.R. 175 stressed that the wardship jurisdiction and the Children Act 1989 operate on the principle that the welfare of the child is paramount, and that therefore all expert's reports, whether in favour of or adverse to the party, must be disclosed.

The court will strenuously attempt to limit examinations and assessment of a child possibly by encouraging the parties to agree on the use of one single expert.

In *Re G (Minors) (Expert Witnesses)* [1994] 2 F.L.R. 291, Wall J provided comprehensive indication on the granting of leave and subsequent directions when dealing with expert evidence in children cases.

(c)   Other family proceedings

The Maintenance Orders (Reciprocal Enforcement) Act 1972, s.13 deals with the admissibility of evidence given in reciprocating countries in proceedings relating to maintenance orders. **6.46**

12   Scientific tests

(i)   Issues of parentage

The obtaining of evidence relating to issues of parentage is governed by the Family Law Reform Act 1969 (FLRA 1969), ss.20–25 (as slightly amended by the Child Support, Pension and Social Security Act 2000). RSC Order 112 and CCR, Ord. 47, r.5 (as amended) also apply. The CPR do not apply to applications for scientific tests under the Family Law Reform Act 1969. **6.47**

S.12(1)(b) of the Civil Evidence Act 1968 provides that if in any civil proceedings a person has been found to be the father of a child, this shall be admissible in evidence for the purpose of proving that he has committed adultery.

(ii)   Direction for bodily samples

In the past, the court had power to direct blood tests in those cases where there was an issue of paternity in court proceedings. However, scientific advances mean that the use of scientific tests rather than blood tests now provide almost conclusive evidence as to parentage. *Genetic* or *DNA* (deoxyribonucleic acid) *fingerprinting* are the tests most likely to be used. Legislation has therefore been amended to allow the court power in certain instances to direct scientific tests (FLRA 1969, s.20). **6.48**

Section 20 of the FLRA 1969 provides that in any civil proceedings in which the parentage of any person falls to be determined, the court may, either of its own motion or on an application by any party to the proceedings, give direction for the use of scientific tests to ascertain whether such tests show that a party to the proceedings is or is not the father or mother of that person; and for the taking, within a period specified in the direction, of bodily samples from all or any of the following, namely any party who is alleged to be the father or mother of that person and any other party to the proceedings.

The provisions of FLRA 1969 do not prevent scientific tests from being carried out if all parties, from whom samples are to be taken, provide consent. The results can be submitted in evidence without any former court direction.

(iii)   Consent to taking of samples

6.49   It is unlikely that a direction under section 20 of the FLRA 1969 will be made if no issue of parentage arises within proceedings. Even if the court provides a direction for scientific tests such appropriate bodily sample cannot be taken from a person without his or her consent (FLRA 1969, s.21). Bodily samples include blood, semen, saliva, or hair.

Minors of aged 16 years and over can provide the necessary consent to sample(s) being taken. For a minor below the age of 16 years, consent must be given by the person who has care and control of the child. In *Re O and J (Paternity: Blood Tests)* [2000] 1 F.L.R. 418, it was held that the person having care and control of a child had an absolute right to refuse to allow a sample of blood to be taken from a child for the purpose of determining paternity. However, The Child Support, Pensions and Social Security Act 2000 (CSPSSA) amends FLRA 1969, s.21 relating to consent so that the court may now decide it is in the best interests of the child for the sample to be taken, allowing a sample to be taken even though the person with care and control does not consent. This amendment was made against a background of thinking that a child has a right to know who its parents are. In *Re T (PATERNITY:ORDERING BLOOD TESTS)*[2001]2 F.L.R. 1190, it was held that for the purpose of an application for blood tests the welfare of the child was not paramount under the Children Act 1989, s.1 but that the applicable test was of the child's best interests under FLRA 1969, s.21 as amended by the CSPSSA. In that case, the interests of the child to have certainty as to parentage outweighed the possibility of tests upsetting the stability and privacy of the family. The position has been confirmed by *Re (1)H(2)A(CHILDREN)* (2002) not yet fully reported.

6.50   When scientific tests are likely to be directed, it is not necessary for the court in the first instance to make an order appointing the Official Solicitor to represent the minor, unless either the minor is ten years old or more, or there are special circumstances making such an appointment immediately desirable. Where separate representation for the minor is not appointed, the direction for scientific tests should include a provision that the proceedings be restored for further directions by the District Judge when the report by the tester has been filed (*Practice Direction* December 20, 1974 [1975] 1 All E.R. 223).

Where a child may be HIV positive, application for leave to have the child tested should be made to a High Court judge (*Re HIV Test* [1994] 2 F.L.R. 116).

(iv)   Failure to comply with a direction

6.51   When a court provides a direction pursuant to FLRA, s.20 for scientific tests and any person fails to take any step required of him for the purpose of giving effect to that direction, the court may draw such inferences as may appear proper in the circumstances FLRA 1969, s.23(1). In *Re A (A Minor) (Paternity: Refusal of Blood Test)* (1994) 2 F.L.R. 463 and *Re G (Parentage: Blood Sample)* (1997) 1 F.L.R. 360, the court drew adverse inferences against the person who refused to take a test/obstructed a test.

Similarly, if a person fails to consent to the taking of a bodily sample from himself or any person of whom he has care and control, he shall be deemed to have failed to take a step required of him for the purpose of giving effect to a direction (FLRA, s.23(3)).

In certain circumstances if a person claiming relief fails to take a step required he or she may have their claim for relief dismissed notwithstanding that there is no evidence to rebut the presumption of legitimacy (FLRA, s.23(2)).

(v)   Jurisdiction of the court

The court must be satisfied that it has, in the particular circumstances, juris-   **6.52** diction to direct scientific tests. Where there is no issue as to parentage to be decided within proceedings the power to direct tests under s.20 of the FLRA 1969 does not arise; (*Hodgkiss v Hodgkiss* [1984] F.L.R. 563 *sub nom H v H* (1984) 128 Sol. Jo. 332).

The principles upon which the court should determine whether or not to direct tests were fully discussed in *Re H (Paternity: Blood Test)* (1996) 2 F.L.R. 65 and by the House of Lords in *S v S and W v Official Solicitor* [1972] A.C. 24. Those cases were considered guiding authorities in *Re T* [2001] 2 F.L.R. 1190.

The doctrine of *res judicata* does not apply in affiliation proceedings. Consequently, previous paternity cases involving inconclusive blood tests can be reopened to take advantage of the further scientific testing (*H v O* [1992] 1 F.L.R. 282).

(vi)   Standard of proof

There is a general presumption of law that a person is legitimate. FLRA 1969,   **6.53** s.26, provides that the presumption of legitimacy may be rebutted where it is more probable than not that the child is illegitimate. This is a fairly heavy standard of proof and, although not as heavy as in criminal proceedings, is more than the ordinary civil standard of a balance of probabilities (*W v K* [1988] 1 F.L.R. 86).

(vii)   Applications

The normal rules as to making applications to court apply, except that any   **6.54** notice or summons required to be served on a person who is not a party to the proceedings must be served personally on him. An affidavit in support of the application would be expected.

District registries and divorce county courts have copies of the Notes for the Guidance of Samplers and a list of testers.

(viii)   Other relevant legislation

(a)   Blood Tests (Evidence of Paternity) (Amendment) Regulations 1971

The current levels of charges for blood testing are contained in the Blood Tests   **6.55** (Evidence of Paternity) (Amendment) Regulations 1971 as amended by the 1992 and 2001 regulations of the same title. The provisions within those reg-ulations also include details of the sampling procedure together with the forms to be adopted within the procedure. The regulations provide that tests must be carried out by an accredited body and the conditions to be met for accreditation are again set out within the regulations.

(b)   Child Support Act 1991 (as amended)

When an application for a maintenance calculation has been made to the   **6.56** Child Support Agency, the Secretary of State (or person with care) may apply to the court for a declaration of parentage (Child Support Act 1991, s.27A). In such cases the declaration only has effect for the limited purposes set out in section 27(3) of that Act.

The Child Support (Pensions and Social Security) Act 2000 extended certain presumptions as to parentage contained in the Child Support Act 1991 (CSA 1991) solely for the purposes of that Act.

(c)   Human Fertilisation and Embryology Act 1990

6.57   A court also has the power to decide issues of paternity under the Human Fertilisation and Embryology Act 1990, s.28.

For scientific tests see *Rayden and Jackson* (17th ed.) ss.26.56, 35.19 – 35.30 and 55.25 and *Butterworth's Family Law*, Service Binder 3.

13   Medical inspection (nullity) (FPR, rr.2.22 and 2.23)

6.58   As to the evidence of medical inspectors in nullity suits, see Chapter 2.

14   Documents handed in at the hearing

6.59   The *Practice Direction:(Family Division);(Family Proceedings:Court Bundles)(2000)FAM (Dame Butler-Sloss P)* March 10, 2000, provides clear guidance as to the correct preparation, content and presentation of court bundles in all hearings in family proceedings in the High Court and Royal Courts of Justice and for hearing with a time estimate of over half a day in care centres, family hearing centres and divorce county courts.

A Bundle for use by the court should be prepared by the Applicant in proceedings and should contain documents relevant to the hearing in chronological order. The bundle should be paginated and divided into separate sections for applications and orders, statements and affidavits, experts reports and other reports, and other documents (subdivided if necessary).

6.60   At the commencement of the bundle there should be a summary of the background to the hearing limited to one page of A4 if possible, a statement of issues or issues to be determined, and a summary of the order sought. In certain hearings a chronology and skeleton arguments should be included with copies of any authorities to be relied upon.

Exhibits, photographs and other documents placed in evidence during divorce proceedings are generally retained by the court until after decree absolute, or, in the case of final decrees, until after time for appeal has expired. Otherwise the applicant is responsible for retrieving the bundle of documents.

In undefended causes, exhibits will be handed back by leave of the District Judge and on copies being left, if so directed. In defended causes, the consent of the other party must also be lodged. A receipt must be given for documents returned. Marriage certificates are not, as a rule, returned; however an application may be made to the District Judge, in certain circumstances, for instance where the suit has been dismissed following a reconciliation. An explanatory letter will usually suffice.

Chapter 7

Trial

1 Hearing

It is the duty of the court to enquire, so far as it reasonably can, into the facts **7.01** alleged by the petitioner and respondent. If the court is satisfied of any such fact mentioned in MCA 1973, s.1(2), then, unless it is satisfied on all the evidence that the marriage has not broken down irretrievably, it must grant a decree of divorce (MCA 1973, s.1(3), (4)). In the case of a petition for judicial separation, the court is not concerned to consider whether the marriage has broken down irretrievably (MCA 1973, s.17(2)) and, subject to being satisfied as to considerations regarding arrangements for children (MCA 1973, s.41), must grant a decree. In the case of five years' separation (MCA 1973, s.1(2)(*e*)), if the petition is opposed under the statutory defence contained in MCA 1973, s.5, the court must, inter alia, consider the question of grave financial or other hardship to the respondent.

2 Shorthand note of proceedings

R.10.15 of FPR provides for the use of shorthand writers or for the recording **7.02** of the trial by mechanical means. Unless the judge otherwise directs, a shorthand note (or recording) must be taken of the proceedings at the trial of every cause in open court pending *in the High Court*. Arrangements are made by the court. *Practice Direction* July 17, 1973 [1973] 3 All E.R. 224 provides for there to be a system of mechanical recording of county court matrimonial causes heard at the Royal Courts of Justice, but indicates no shorthand note is normally taken of such causes tried elsewhere. In such a cause in which for some special reason it is considered that the taking of a shorthand note would be advisable, early notice (if possible when applying for directions for trial) must be given by the petitioner's solicitor to the district judge of the court in which the cause is proceeding. Early notice must also be given if, for some special reason, it is thought advisable that a shorthand note should be taken of ancillary proceedings before a judge (whether in the High Court or a divorce county court) for hearing elsewhere than at the Royal Courts of Justice. The court refers the matter to the Court's Administrator when a shorthand writer is required (*Departmental Direction*, September 15, 1976).

CCR Ord. 50, r.9B provides for there to be an official shorthand note of all **7.03** trials in the County Court and this provision has led to there being installed, in fact, mechanical recording equipment at trial centres and all District Judges have recording equipment in their chambers.

Any party, any person who has intervened, the Queen's Proctor or, where a declaration of parentage has been made under FLA 1986, s.56(1)(*a*), the Registrar General is entitled to require a transcript from the shorthand writer on payment of the fixed fee. The shorthand writer may not, without the permission of the court, furnish a transcript to any other person (FPR, r.10.15 (5), (6)).

3 Right to be heard on ancillary matters

7.04 A respondent may, without filing an answer, be heard on any question of ancillary relief (FPR, r.2.52).

A respondent, co-respondent or party cited may, without filing an answer, be heard on any question as to costs but the court may at any time order any party objecting to a claim for costs to file and serve a written statement setting out the reasons for his objection (FPR, r.2.37(1)).

The above parties may be heard on either of the above questions even though they have not returned to the court office an acknowledgment of service stating their wish to be heard on that question (FPR, rr.2.37(2) and 2.52).

In proceedings after a decree nisi of divorce or a decree of judicial separation, no order which would make a co-respondent or a party cited liable for costs which are not directly referable to the decree may be made, unless the co-respondent or party cited is a party to such proceedings or has been given notice of the intention to apply for such an order (FPR, r.2.37(3)).

4 Ancillary matters adjourned at the hearing

7.05 Where at the trial of a cause any application is adjourned by the court for hearing in chambers, it may be restored:

> (*a*) in the High Court, by notice without a summons;
>
> (*b*) in a divorce county court, on notice under *t*he general provisions of CCR Ord. 13, r.1 (which deals with applications during the course of proceedings);
>
> (*c*) in the High Court or a divorce county court, by notice given by the district judge when in his opinion the matter ought to be further considered (FPR, r.2.41));

The notice states the place, date and time for hearing the restored application and must be served on every party concerned. Such applications will normally relate to children (FPR, r.2.40) and to ancillary relief (FPR, r.2.59).

5 Decrees and orders

7.06 *Preparation and service*: All decrees and orders made in open court and every other order which is required to be drawn must be drawn up by the court except in a case to which FPR, r.2.61 (consent orders) applies. The decree or order is drawn up by the court at the place where it is made (FPR, r.2.43(1), (2)).

A copy of every *decree* must be sent by the court to every party to the cause (FPR, r.10.16(1)). A sealed or other copy of a decree or *order* made in open court can be issued to any person requiring it on payment of the prescribed fee (FPR, r.10.16(2)). The fee payable is prescribed in the Family Proceedings Fees Ord. 1999 Sch.1, s.7, at £1 for the first page and 20p for each subsequent page.

Where an order made in family proceedings has been drawn up, the court **7.07** where the order was made must, unless otherwise directed, send a copy of the order to every party affected by it. Where a party against whom the order is made is acting by a solicitor, a copy may, if the district judge thinks fit, be sent to that party as if he were acting in person, as well as to his solicitor. It is not necessary for the person in whose favour the order was made to prove that a copy of the order has reached any other party to whom it is required to be sent (FPR, r.10.17(1)-(3)). However, where the order requires a person to do, or refrain from doing, some act and is to be enforced by committal (CPR Sch.1 (RSC Ord. 45, r.5) and Sch.2 (CCR Ord. 29, r.1)), the order must be served in accordance with the rules applicable and also with any other rule or enactment which requires an order to be served in a particular way (FPR, r.10.17(4); *B v B (Contempt: Committal)* [1991] 2 F.L.R. 588.) The court may, however, in some circumstances dispense with service and enforce by committal (CPR Sch.1 (RSC Ord. 45, r.7(7)); CPR Sch.2 (CCR Ord. 29, r.1(7))). For affidavits of service of orders, see Appendix 2.

Decrees nisi: Every decree of divorce or of nullity must in the first instance **7.08** be a decree nisi (MCA 1973, ss.1(5) and 15). Other decrees are final, *e.g.* for judicial separation (MCA 1973, ss.17(2)) and the court sends a copy of the decree to all parties (FPR, r.10.16(1)). A copy of a decree may be issued to any person on payment of the prescribed fee (see above) (FPR, r.10.16(2)).

If a supplementary order is made at the same time as the decree is pronounced, such an order for ancillary relief or an order for costs, a separate order is drawn.

Restriction on decrees where there are children: Section 41 of the MCA 1973 **7.09** (as substituted by CA 1989, s.108(4), Sch.12, para.31) provides for certain restrictions on the making of decrees where there are children.

In any proceedings for divorce, nullity or judicial separation the court *must* consider whether there are any children of the family to whom the section applies (see below) and, if so, whether (in the light of the arrangements which have been or are proposed to be made for their upbringing and welfare) it should exercise any of its powers under CA 1989 with respect to any of them (MCA 1973, s.41(1)).

The court may direct that a decree of divorce or nullity is not to be made **7.10** absolute or that a decree of judicial separation is not to be granted, until the court orders otherwise, where it appears that:

(*a*) the circumstances of the case require, or are likely to require, the court to exercise any of its powers under CA 1989 with respect to any such child;

(*b*) it is not in a position to exercise that power or (as the case may be) those powers without giving further consideration to the case; and (*c*) there are exceptional circumstances which make it desirable in the interests of the child that the court should give such a direction (MCA 1973, s.41(2)).

The parties must be notified of any such direction made by the court (FPR, r.2.39(4)). The section applies to any child of the family who:

(*a*) has not reached the age of 16 at the date when the court considers the case; and

(*b*) has reached that age at that date but in relation to whom the court directs that it shall apply (MCA 1973, s.41(3)).

7.11   Once the district judge has made his certificate that he is satisfied that the petitioner has sufficiently proved the content of the petition and is entitled to a decree (FPR, r.2.36(1)) or after the provision of any evidence as to the arrangements for the children of the family directed to be produced in a defended cause (FPR, r.2.24(4)) and, providing there is no application pending under CA 1989, Pts I or II, he *must* then consider the matters specified in MCA 1973, s.41(1) (FPR, r.2.39(1)). The district judge will consider all the relevant evidence including the statement of arrangements in Form M4 and any statement filed by the respondent pursuant to FPR, r.2.38.

If the district judge is satisfied that there are no children of the family to whom MCA 1973, s.41 applies or there are such children but that the court need not exercise its powers under CA 1989 or make a direction under MCA, s.41(2), he will certify accordingly. The court sends the petitioner and the respondent a copy of the certificate made by the district judge (FPR, r.2.39(2)).

7.12   If the district judge is not satisfied as mentioned in FPR, r.2.39(2), he may make one or more of the following directions:

(*a*) that the parties, or any of them, *must* file further evidence relating to the arrangements for the children (specifying the matters to be dealt with in the further evidence);

(*b*) that a welfare report on the children, or any of them, be prepared;

(*c*) that the parties, or any of them, *must* attend before him at the date, time and place as specified in the direction.

7.13   The parties must be notified accordingly (FPR, r.2.39(3)).

In FPR, r.2.39, "parties" means the petitioner, the respondent and any person who appears to the court to have care of the child (FPR, r.2.39(5)).

It follows that the district judge is not required to consider the arrangements for the children of the family where an application is pending under CA 1989, Pts I or II as the court will have the opportunity of doing so on disposing of that application (FPR, r.2.39(1)).

A certificate should not be refused on the basis that a child is being maintained by welfare benefits, as the arrangements may be the best available in the circumstances (*Cook v Cook* [1978] 3 All E.R. 1009). A nominal order may be appropriate where the respondent is unemployed. The issue of the certificate should not be withheld pending the determination of a financial provision application (*Hughes v Hughes* [1984] F.L.R. 70). The omission of the name of a child of the family from a certificate under MCA 1973, s. 41 does not preclude later ancillary relief proceedings in respect of that child (*Healey v Healey* [1984] 3 All E.R. 1040).

A certificate under MCA 1973, s.41 need not be withheld because residence, **7.14** education or the distribution of family assets are contested issues. The court may still certify that, whilst it does, or may, need to exercise its powers under CA 1989 with respect to some or all of the children of the family, there are no exceptional circumstances which make it desirable for a direction to be given under MCA 1973, s.41 (2).

In the case of divorce or nullity, the decree nisi cannot be made absolute unless the court has complied with MCA 1973, s.41(1) and has not given any direction under MCA 1973, s.41(2) (FPR, r.2.49(2)). If a decree is made absolute or a decree of judicial separation granted without complying with MCA, s.41(2) or where the court has given a direction under MCA 1973, s.41(2), the decree is void (*Scott v Scott* (1977) 121 S.J. 391). However, if a certificate is given under MCA, s.41(1), then no person is entitled to challenge the validity of the decree on the ground that the conditions prescribed were not fulfilled (for instance where a child of the family has been omitted from the certificate): (*Healey v Healey* [1991] 3 All E.R. 1040).

Rectification: A clerical error in a decree (*e.g.* as to the date or place of mar- **7.15** riage: *Thynne v Thynne* [1955] 2 All E.R. 377) or in an order may be corrected by the court under the "slip rule" (CPR 40.12 & 40.12[1]; *Rayden and Jackson*, 17th ed., pp. 433 & 1120). Additionally, the court has an inherent power to vary its own orders so as to carry out its own meaning and to make its meaning plain. An order made without jurisdiction cannot be saved by the slip rule or the court's inherent jurisdiction (*Munks v Munks* [1985] F.L.R. 576; *Board (Board Intervening) v Checkland* [1987] 2 F.L.R. 257 and *Pounds v Pounds* [1994] 1 F.L.R. 775). If the order as drawn correctly expresses the intention of the court, it cannot be corrected under the slip rule or the inherent jurisdiction, even if procured by fraud or misrepresentation. The power to correct clerical errors extends not only to those made by court staff but also to those made by a party or his advisers. Any party can apply; a letter by way of ex parte application to the district judge will usually suffice.

For further discussion see Butterworth's *Family Law Service*, 4A [765].

6 Application for rehearing (FPR, r.2.42)

An application for rehearing of a cause tried by a judge alone (whether in the **7.16** High Court or a divorce county court), where *no error of the court at the hearing* is alleged, must be made to a judge. This is to be interpreted restrictively in the High Court so as to exclude from a rehearing all cases which would ordinarily go to the Court of Appeal. The county court is not so restricted. (*B-T v B-T* [1990] 2 F.L.R. 1; *Re C* [1993] 2 F.L.R. 799 and *Benson v Benson* [1996] 1 F.L.R. 692). Where a party wishes to review a consent order made in the county court, this may be achieved by the following methods:

(*a*) an application to set aside the consent order;

(*b*) a rehearing under CCR, Ord. 37 r.1, where no error of the court is alleged;

(*c*) appeal from the district judge to a circuit judge (but only where the consent order was not induced by fraud, mistake or material non-disclosure);

(*d*) the issue of a summons;

(*e*) where the terms of the order are executory, notice can be given to the original court.

7.17　　Unless otherwise directed, the application must be made to the judge by whom the cause was tried and must be heard in open court (FPR, r.2.42(1), (2)). This rule applies to a cause disposed of in the special procedure list except that in cases where the decree was pronounced by a district judge, the application is made to a district judge (FPR, r.2.42(10)).

The application is made:

(*a*) in the High Court, by notice to attend before the judge on a day specified in the notice; and

(*b*) in the county court, by notice in accordance with CCR Ord. 13, r.1 FPR, r.2.42(3)).

The fee is £60.

The notice must state the grounds of the application.

7.18　　Unless otherwise directed, the notice must be issued within six weeks after the judgment and served on every other party to the cause not less than fourteen days before the day fixed for the hearing of the application. The applicant must file a certificate that the notice has been duly served on each party required to be served (FPR, r.2.42(4), (5)).

The application must be supported by affidavit setting out the allegations on which the applicant relies or exhibiting a copy of any pleading which he proposes to file if the application is granted, and a copy of the affidavit must be served on every other party (FPR, r.2.42(6)).

The applicant must file a copy of a transcript or so much as is relevant of any official shorthand note not less than seven days before the hearing of the application (FPR, r.2.42(7)).

Where a party wishes to appeal against a decree absolute of divorce or nullity, the question whether he has had the time and opportunity to appeal from the decree nisi on which the absolute was founded must be determined on an application for a rehearing (FPR, r.2.42(8); *Clark v Clark* [1995] 2 F.L.R. 487). No appeal lies from a decree absolute in favour of any party who, having had time and opportunity to appeal from the decree nisi on which it was founded, has not done so (SCA 1981, s.18(1)(*d*); *Krenge v Krenge* [1999] 1 F.L.R. 969).

Any other application for rehearing must be by appeal to the Court of Appeal (FPR, r.2.42(9)).

7　Rescission of decree nisi by consent

7.19　　The court has an inherent jurisdiction to rescind a decree as a matter of discretion on the application of the party to whom it was granted or on the application of the other party with the consent of the party to whom it was granted. This power may be used to rescind a decree nisi of divorce and substitute a decree of judicial separation (*Griffiths v Griffiths* (1912) 106 L.T. 646) or to rescind, by consent, a decree nisi which was made in divorce proceedings issued prior to December 1, 2000 in order to clear the way for fresh proceedings in which a pension sharing order would be available (SvS(Rescission of decree nisi:pension sharing provision) (2002) L.T.L. 22/1/2002) . However the power should not be used where this rescission is objected to by the respondent and serves an ulterior purpose by allowing the petitioner to gain financial advantage by putting pressure on the Respondent *(Jeffrey v Jeffrey* [1947–51] C.L.Y. 2897). The power should not be used where the decree is one of nullity because of some procedural defect. In such circumstances, the appropriate application is to set the decree aside and have the petition reheard (*Roberts v Roberts and Peters* [1959] 2 All E.R. 209).

Only the High Court has this inherent jurisdiction, since the county court's jurisdiction is statute based. Therefore, when it is sought to rely upon the inherent jurisdiction, it will be necessary to seek a transfer to the High Court (Matrimonial and Family Proceedings Act 1984, s.39) and to make an application to a judge in open court.

Where a reconciliation has been effected between the petitioner and the **7.20** respondent, after a decree nisi has been pronounced but before it has been made absolute, or after the pronouncement of a decree of judicial separation, either party may apply for an order rescinding the decree by consent. The notice of application, if the cause is pending in a divorce county court, or a copy of the summons, if pending in the High Court, must be served on the other spouse and any other party against whom costs have been awarded or who is otherwise affected by the decree. The application must be made to a district judge and may be heard in chambers (FPR, r.2.48). A fee of £30 is payable. The application is made in the proceedings and should be supported by affidavit.

8 Rescission of decree nisi under MCA 1973, s.10(1)

Where the court has granted a decree of divorce on the basis of the fact of two **7.21** years' separation coupled with the respondent's consent (MCA 1973, s.1(2)(*d*)) and has made no finding as to any other fact in MCA 1973, s.1(2), the respondent may apply to the court before the decree is made absolute to rescind the decree on the ground that the petitioner misled the respondent (whether intentionally or unintentionally) about any matter which the respondent took into account in deciding to consent (MCA 1973, s.10(1)). The requirements are as follows:

(*a*) in High Court, notice to attend before the judge on a specified day and copy for service; or, in county court, notice of application and copy for service (for forms, see Appendix 2);

(*b*) affidavit in support and copy for service;

(*c*) a fee of £60.

In the county court, the application is on notice in accordance with CCR, Ord. 13, r.1, subject to the provisions of FPR, r.2.44. The application must be made to a judge and must be heard in open court except where the decree was pronounced by a district judge when the application is made to a district judge (FPR, r.2.44(1)).

The notice must state the grounds of the application. It must be served on **7.22** the petitioner not less than 14 days before the day fixed for the hearing, unless otherwise directed. The respondent must file a certificate that the notice has been duly served on the petitioner (FPR, r.2.44(2), (3)).

The affidavit in support must set out the allegations on which the respondent relies and a copy must be served on the petitioner (FPR, r.2.44(4)).

Other circumstances giving rise to the rescission of a decree nisi are discussed in Butterworth's *Family Law Service*, 2A [685–688]. In particular, it should be noted that where fraud, mistake or misrepresentation is alleged and the decree has been granted other than under MCA 1973, s.1(2)(*d*), an application may be made to set the decree aside (*Parkes v Parkes* [1971] 3 All E.R. 870).

9   Effect of final decree

7.23   *Decree absolute of divorce*: The marriage ceases to subsist and either party is free to remarry from the moment the decree nisi is made absolute. Upon remarriage, the right of the party who has remarried to apply for a financial provision order or a property adjustment order for himself ceases (MCA 1973, s.28(3)). However, a pending application (which includes a prayer in a petition) may still be entertained (*Jackson v Jackson* [1973] 2 All E.R. 395). An order for periodical payments (secured or otherwise) in favour of a former spouse terminates automatically on his or her remarriage (MCA 1973, s.28(1)). The doctrine of relation back does not apply; the decree absolute is effective only from the moment it is made and is not related back to the beginning of the day on which it was made (*Re Seaford, Seaford v Seifert* [1968] 1 All E.R. 482).

Periodical payments, lump-sum and property adjustment orders for a party and property adjustment orders in favour of a child of the family take effect upon the grant of the decree absolute (MCA 1973, ss.23(5) and 24(3)).

A decree absolute is a judgment *in rem* on the status of the parties which binds third parties, including a trustee in bankruptcy (*Bater v Bater* [1906] P. 209).

7.24   A former wife remains entitled to use her former husband's name and title as an alternative to reverting to her former surname.

Any devise or bequest to a former spouse contained in the will of a testator dying after December 31, 1983 lapses and any appointment of a former spouse as executor or as executor and trustee of a testator's will *is* of no effect, except so far as a contrary intention appears, if the marriage was dissolved, or annulled, or declared to be void after the will was made (Wills Act 1837, s.18A (added by Administration of Justice Act 1882, s.18(2)). By section 3 of the Law Reform (Succession) Act 1995, s.18A has been further amended and where the testator dies on or after January 1, 1996, regardless of the dates of the will and dissolution or annulment of the marriage, the gift to or appointment of a former spouse will take effect as if he or she had died on the date when the marriage was dissolved or annulled. Thus, where the will directs that the gift or appointment should pass to a third party if the former spouse was dead, the third party will now take the gift on appointment.

An injunction may be expressed to continue after decree absolute in certain circumstances (*Lucas v Lucas* [1992] 2 F.L.R. 53).

7.25   *Decree absolute of nullity: void marriages*: The decree is declaratory only.

Orders for ancillary relief take effect on decree absolute as above in the case of divorce. The effect of remarriage is also the same.

The effect of the annulment of a void marriage on a will is as in the case of divorce as above.

Decree absolute of nullity: voidable marriage: A decree of nullity granted after **7.26** July 31, 1971 operates to annul the marriage only with effect from the date it is made absolute. The marriage is treated as if it had existed up to that time (MCA 1973, s.16).

Orders for ancillary relief take effect on decree absolute as above in the case of divorce. The effect of remarriage is also the same.

The effect of the annulment of a voidable marriage on a will is as in the case of divorce as above.

Decree of judicial separation: The decree ends the duty to cohabit and there- **7.27** fore terminates desertion. However, a period of desertion immediately preceding the presentation of a petition for judicial separation is deemed immediately to precede a subsequent petition for divorce if the decree of judicial separation has been continuously in force (MCA 1973, s.4(3)).

A decree of judicial separation does not prevent a subsequent divorce on the same or substantially the same facts and may be treated as sufficient proof of the relevant fact. Evidence will, however, still be required from the petitioner (MCA 1973, s.4(1), (2)).

As to the limited effect of a decree of judicial separation where there is a **7.28** subsequent foreign decree of dissolution or nullity, see *Rayden and Jackson*, 17th ed., p.448.

If, while a decree of judicial separation is in force and the separation is continuing, either of the parties dies intestate on or after August 1, 1970, all his real or personal property devolves as if the other party to the marriage had then been dead (MCA 1973, s.18(2)).

As to the effect of a decree of judicial separation on an application for an order under I(PFD)A 1975, s.2, see s.3(2) of that Act.

Chapter 8

Conclusion of Proceedings

1 Decree absolute

Application by spouse to whom decree nisi has been pronounced

8.01 (FPR, rr.2.49–2.51) A decree nisi may not be made absolute before the expiration of six weeks from the date of its grant unless the court by general or special order from time to time fixes a shorter period (MCA 1973, s.1(5) and Matrimonial Causes (Decree Absolute) General Order 1972). The period of six weeks is calculated from the day *after* the decree nisi is pronounced. Thus, a decree pronounced on a Monday may not be made absolute before a Tuesday six weeks later. Where the six weeks' period expires on a day on which the office or registry of the court is closed, the period is extended until the end of the first day thereafter on which the office or registry is open (Matrimonial Causes (Decree Absolute) General Orders 1972 and 1973).

An application by a spouse to make absolute a decree pronounced in his favour may be made by lodging with the district judge a notice in Form M8 (supplied by the court as Form D36 (county court) or Form D136 (High Court)) (FPR, r.2.49(1)), which should be signed by the solicitor acting for the petitioner, unless the petitioner is acting in person or fee exempt. The fee is £30, unless exempt from payment of fees. It is not possible to avoid this fee by both parties making a consent application for the decree absolute as the application is not for an *order* by consent (Family Proceedings Fees Order 1999, Sch.1, Fee 4).

8.02 On lodging the notice, the district judge causes the records of the court to be searched and if he is satisfied of the following matters as set out in FPR, r.2.49(2) he *must* make the decree absolute:

(*a*) that no application for rescission of the decree or for rehearing of the cause and no appeal against the decree or the dismissal of an application for re-hearing of the cause is pending;

(*b*) that no order has been made by the court extending the time for making an application for rehearing of the cause or by the Court of Appeal extending the time for appealing against the decree or the dismissal of an application for rehearing of the cause or, if any such order has been made, that the time so extended has expired;

(*c*) that no application for such an order to extend is pending;

(*d*) that no intervention under FPR, r.2.46 (by the Queen's Proctor) or FPR, r.2.47 (by any other person) is pending;

(*e*) that the district judge has complied with MCA 1973, s.41(1) and has not given any direction under MCA 1973 s.41(2);

(*f*) where a certificate has been granted under the Administration of Justice Act 1969, s.12 in respect of the decree (certificate by trial judge permitting leapfrog appeal directly to House of Lords):

    (i) that no application for leave to appeal directly to the House of Lords is pending;

    (ii) that no extension of the time to apply for leave to appeal to the House of Lords has been granted or, if any such extension has been granted, that the time so extended has expired; and

    (iii) that the time for any appeal to the Court of Appeal has expired; and

(*g*) that the provisions of MCA 1973, s.10(2)-(4) do not apply or have been complied with (financial protection of the respondent in certain cases where petition is based on MCA 1973, s.1 (2)(*d*) (two years' separation and consent) and section 1(2)(*e*) (five years' separation)).

The requirements of FPR, r.2.49(2) are mandatory and, if they are not carried out, the decree absolute will be void (*Dackham v Dackham* [1987] 2 F.L.R. 358).   **8.03**

If the notice is lodged more than twelve months after the decree nisi, an explanation in writing must be lodged with the notice containing the following:

(*a*) reasons for the delay;

(*b*) a statement as to whether the parties have lived together with each other since the decree nisi and, if so, between what dates; and

(*c*) a statement as to whether the applicant, being the wife, has or, being the husband, has reason to believe that his wife has, given birth to any child since the decree nisi and, if so, stating the relevant facts and whether or not it is alleged the child is or may be a child of the family.

The district judge *may* require the applicant to file an affidavit verifying the explanation, although he may be prepared to accept a letter. The district judge may make such order on the application as he thinks fit or refer the application to a judge. If the application is referred to a judge, it should be heard in open court and oral evidence may be given (*Biggs v Biggs and Wheatley* [1977] 1 All E.R. 20). In *Savage v Savage* [1983] 4 F.L.R. 126, a decree absolute was refused and the decree nisi rescinded, where the decree nisi was pronounced some four years previously and the parties had cohabited for a period of three years on the principle that such a long period of cohabitation led to the conclusion that the marriage had not, in the first instance, broken down. The court may require notice to be given to the respondent. The application will be determined in the same way as when deciding whether to grant a decree nisi, *e.g.* where there has been a resumption of cohabitation after the granting of a decree nisi based upon a petition under MCA 1973, s.1(2)(*b*) (*Court v Court* [1982] 2 All E.R. 531). It may be appropriate to incorporate an application in the alternative for leave to present a second petition.   **8.04**

If a decree nisi is pronounced on May 30, an application to make it absolute is in time if it is made on May 30 of the following year. (FPR, r.1.5(3)). If the court office is closed, FPR, r.1.5(5) applies and an application would be in time if made on the next day the office is open.

Where a decree nisi is made absolute, the court makes an endorsement to that effect on the decree, stating the precise time at which it was made absolute (FPR, r.2.51).

8.05   On a decree nisi being made absolute, the court sends to the petitioner and the respondent spouse (or their solicitors) a certificate in Form M9 (divorce) or Form M10 (nullity), whichever is appropriate, authenticated by the seal of the court from which it is issued (FPR, r.2.5(2)). The certificate in Form M9 or M10 contains a note of the effect of a decree of divorce or nullity upon inheritance under a will.

If the cause is proceeding in a district registry or divorce county court an index card is sent to the principal registry, where a central index of decrees absolute is kept. A search may be made there or at the court where the cause was pending. A fee of £20 is payable for a search in the central index in London (Family Proceedings Fees Order 1999 Sch.1, Fee 6). Any person is entitled to require a search to be made in the central index.

8.06   A certificate in Form M9 or M10 that a decree nisi has been made absolute must be issued to any person requiring it on a payment of the appropriate fee. The fee is £1 for both postal and personal applications. A certificate is obtained from the court office where the cause is proceeding. For the purpose of remarriage an office copy of the certificate is sufficient. For use abroad, a signed and sealed copy of Form M9 or M10 will usually be required. It should be endorsed with a certificate signed by the district judge:

> I certify that this is a true copy of the decree of this court relating to the proceedings above mentioned.

8.07 *Application to a judge (FPR, rr.2.50(1), 2.51(4))*: An application for a decree nisi to be made absolute *must* be made to a judge in the following cases:

> (*a*) where the Queen's Proctor gives notice to the court and to the party in whose favour the decree was pronounced that he requires more time to decide whether to show cause against a decree being made absolute and the notice has not been withdrawn; or
>
> (*b*) where there are other circumstances which ought to be brought to the attention of the court before the decree nisi is made absolute.

8.08   The circumstances which ought to be brought to the attention of the court are not defined. The powers of the court are set out in MCA 1973, s.9(1). In the absence of an appeal, it would appear that any steps taken by the district judge when considering the exercise of his powers under MCA 1973, s.41 cannot be reopened. It is submitted therefore, that any changes in the arrangements for the children would not constitute circumstances which ought to be brought to the attention of the court under FPR, r.2.50(1). There is a duty upon the person who has obtained the decree nisi to disclose circumstances which would affect the decision whether or not to make the decree absolute and the court has the discretion whether to treat any such failure as an irregularity or to allow the decree nisi to be made absolute (*Terry-Smith v Terry-Smith* (1981) 11 Fam. Law. 121). In *Biggs v Biggs and Wheatley* [1977] 1 All E.R. 20 cohabitation exceeding six months after a decree nisi based on adultery was held to be a bar to the granting of the decree absolute and the decree nisi was rescinded.

Unless otherwise directed, the summons by which the application is made (or, where the cause is pending in a divorce county court, notice of the application) must be served on every party to the cause (other than the applicant) and, where (*a*) above applies, on the Queen's Proctor (FPR, r.2.50(1)).

Application by spouse against whom decree nisi has been pronounced (FPR, **8.09** *r.2.50(2))*: Where no application has been made by the party who has obtained a decree nisi to make the decree absolute, then at any time after the expiration of three months from the earliest date on which that party could have made such application, the party against whom it was granted may make an application (MCA 1973, ss.9(2), 15). The court may make the decree absolute, rescind the decree, require further enquiry or otherwise deal with the case as it thinks fit (MCA 1973, ss.9(1), 15).

An application by a spouse for a decree nisi pronounced against him to be made absolute may be made to a judge or district judge (see note to Appendix 2, form), and the summons by which the application is made (or notice of application in a county court) must be served on the other spouse not less than four clear days before the day on which the application is heard (FPR, r.2.50(2)). The district judge (by his clerk) must search the court minutes and satisfy himself as to the matters set out in FPR, r.2.49(2) in the usual way before the order granting the application takes effect. The district judge has *the discretion* to refuse to make the decree absolute even if he is satisfied as to the matters set out in FPR, r.2.50(2). In *Smith v Smith* [1990] 1 F.L.R. 438 the district judge refused to make the decree absolute on the grounds that there were still ancillary proceedings in course and to be heard (FPR, r.2.50(3)). The decree nisi will not be made absolute if the refusal to do so is the only way of ensuring that a party complies with an ancillary relief order (*Wickler v Wickler* [1998] 2 F.L.R. 326). This principle was followed in *O v O* [2000] 2 F.L.R. 147, where it was held to be within the court's powers to refuse to make the decree nisi absolute upon the application of the respondent husband on the basis of his refusal to obtain a Get under Jewish law. The discretion, in this case, being used to ensure that no gross injustice was done to either party. The power under MCA 1973, s.9 gives wide powers under ss.1(d) to consider matters not limited to the MCA 1973. The application should be supported by affidavit. The fee payable is £60.

Application to expedite decree absolute: Section 1(5) of the MCA 1973 applies. **8.10** Whenever it is possible, there should be an application to expedite a hearing of the suit in preference to an application at or after trial to expedite the decree absolute. Such an application should rarely be necessary due to the special procedure (*Practice Direction* June 15, 1977 [1977] 2 All E.R. 714).

Where an application to expedite a decree absolute is necessary, it should normally be made to the trial judge at the hearing of the suit. The petitioner (or respondent, as the case may be) should then have available all such evidence (including where appropriate, a medical certificate as to the expected date of birth of a child) as is necessary to enable the judge to rule whether the decree absolute should be expedited. If some matter arises after decree nisi making it desirable that the decree absolute should be expedited, a party may apply to a judge in chambers for an order to that effect or for directions (*Practice Direction* November 19, 1964 [1964] 3 All E.R. 775).

In Special procedure cases, the application for an order to expedite decree **8.11** absolute is made to a district judge by summons in the High Court, or by notice of application in the county court. A fee of £60 is payable. For form, see Appendix 2, form . The application should be supported by affidavit and the summons or notice of application served on the other parties. The

application will be listed for hearing as soon as convenient after pronouncement of the decree nisi. (*Practice Direction* June 15, 1977 [1977] 2 All E.R.
714).

8.12 *Defective decrees absolute*: A decree absolute may be set aside as being void or
voidable because of a defect in procedure as shown in the table below.

8.13

Defective procedure		
Defect	*Consequence*	*Authority*
Failure to comply with MCA 1973, s.10(2)	Voidable	*Wright v Wright* [1976] 1 All E.R. 796 *Dryden v Dryden* [1973] 3 All E.R. 526
Application for decree absolute inadvertently made after death of either party	Void	*Re Seaford, Seaford v Seaford* [1968] 1 All E.R. 482
Failure to comply with FPR, r.2.49(2)	Void	*Dackham v Dackham* [1987] 2 F.L.R. 358
Application for decree absolute made prematurely	Void	*Woolfenden v Woolfenden* [1947] 2 All E.R. 673
Failure to comply with FPR, r.2.50(2)	Voidable	*Batchelor v Batchelor* [1983] 3 All E.R. 618
Failure to comply with MCA 1973, s.9(2) and FPR, r.2.50(2)	Void	*Manchanda v Manchanda* [1995] 2 F.L.R. 590 *Dennis v Dennis [2000] 2 F.L.R. 231 (see below)*
Order for substituted service or dispensing with service wrongfully made	Voidable	*Wiseman v Wiseman* [1953 1 All E.R. 601 *Purse v Purse* [1981] 2 All E.R. 465 *Clifford v Clifford* [1985] F.L.R. 732
Total lack of service	Void	*Everitt v Everitt* [1948] 2 All E.R. 545 *Ebrahim v Ali* [1983] 3 All E.R. 615
Petition Presented in breach of MCA 1973, s.3(1)	Void	*Butler v Butler* [1990] 1 F.L.R. 114

8.14 In *Dennis v Dennis* [2000] 2 F.L.R. 231, the court had to consider the impact
of the European Convention on Human Rights 1950 (the Human Rights Act
1998 having retrospective effect). The court was asked to consider whether rendering a decree absolute void, and thus invalidating a subsequent marriage,
breached Articles 8 and 12 of the Act which provide for a right to family life
and a right to marry. The court ruled that, although the court was acting as a

public body under the Act, the proceedings rendering the decree void were not new ones instigated by the court. Accordingly, the HRA 1998 did not apply. Furthermore, it specifically referred to the fact that, even had the HRA 1998 applied, it had not been breached as Article 12 provides for a right to marriage according to national law, which was, in the absence of a valid decree absolute, not the case.

Where no question arises as to the jurisdiction of the court pronouncing a decree absolute, or as to the procedural regularity which led to its being made, the decree is unimpeachable (*Callaghan v Hanson—Fox and Another* [1991] 2 F.L.R. 319).

For appeals from decree absolute, see Chapter 14.

2   Intervention to show cause

Intervention by Queen's Proctor: If the Queen's Proctor wishes to show cause   **8.15**
against a decree nisi being made absolute, he must give notice to that effect to the district judge and to the party in whose favour it was pronounced. FPR, r.2.46 sets out the procedure.

Sections 8, 9 and 15 of the MCA 1973 set out the powers of the court and the Queen's Proctor.

Intervention by person other than Queen's Proctor: If any person other than the   **8.16**
Queen's Proctor wishes to show cause under MCA 1973, ss.9(1) and 15 against a decree nisi being made absolute, he must file an affidavit stating the facts on which he relies and a copy must be served on the party in whose favour the decree was pronounced. R.2.47 of the FPR sets out the procedure.

3   Judicial separation

In suits for judicial separation the decree is a final decree (MCA 1973, s.17(2)). Section 1(5) of the MCA 1973 does not apply.

4   Dismissal and striking out

Before a petition is served on any person, the petitioner may file a notice of   **8.17**
discontinuance and the cause thereupon stands dismissed (FPR, r.2.8). Service by post is not for this purpose deemed to have been effective until an acknowledgment of service in form M6 is returned (FPR, r.2.9(5)). Otherwise, once a petition has been filed, it may not be removed or withdrawn. If a petitioner wishes to abandon the proceedings, application must be made to the district judge to have the petition dismissed, and a copy of the application must be served on the other party or parties (FPR, r.10.9). Where, for instance, the application is on the ground that the parties have become reconciled, or that the petitioner wishes to file a further petition, the application may also seek the return of the marriage certificate. Where a petition is dismissed on the petitioner's application or by consent, there is no estoppel preventing the petitioner from presenting a further petition based on the same facts as there has

been no adjudication, unless the previous charges have been withdrawn (*Goldblum v Goldblum* [1938] 4 All E.R. 477).

A respondent or co-respondent may apply in similar manner to dismiss a petition for want of prosecution. A respondent may be precluded from obtaining ancillary relief claimed in the answer if the petition is dismissed; a stay may therefore be preferable.

8.18   Application is made by summons if the proceedings are in the High Court, or if the proceedings are in a divorce county court, by notice of application. The other parties must be served at least two clear days before the hearing. A fee of £60 is payable. It is submitted that an affidavit should be filed in anything other than a simple case unless the application is by consent.

Section 23(2)(*b*) of the MCA 1973 provides that where proceedings for divorce, nullity or judicial separation are dismissed after the beginning of the trial, the court may make provision for the maintenance of any child of the family either forthwith or within a reasonable time after the dismissal. 'After beginning of trial' includes when the suit has been called (*P(JM) v P(LE)* [1971] 2 All E.R. 728). Any other issues concerning the welfare of any such child should be dealt with by means of an application under the CA 1989.

8.19   Non-compliance with the FPR or an order of the court may be a ground for an application by a respondent to strike out the proceedings, but only if the non-compliance has caused a serious risk that a fair trial is no longer possible wholly due to the party's refusal to comply (*Evans v Evans* (1859) 29 L.J.P.M. & A. 53 and *Landaver Ltd v Cummins & Co (A Firm)* (1991) *The Times* August 7).

If nobody appears to support a petition, other than one in the special procedure list, it may be struck out (and subsequently reinstated). At the Royal Courts of Justice hearing numbers run from 1 to 9999 with a prefix letter. The lists are periodically cleared by the striking out of cases which have been set down for some time and the hearing date has been vacated. They may be restored by filing a notice to restore in the principal registry.

5   Abatement of suit

8.20   On the death of a *petitioner* at any time before decree absolute is made, the suit abates and nobody can apply to make a decree nisi (if already pronounced) absolute. On the death of a *respondent*, a suit will abate except perhaps where the decree sought was a declaratory decree of nullity in the case of a void marriage. This does not, however, mean that no further proceedings can be taken in relation to the suit (MCA 1973, s.31(6), (7), (8) and (9); *Barder v Barder (Caluori intervening)* [1987] 2 F.L.R. 480). The matter will depend upon:

(*a*) the nature of the relief claimed by the surviving spouse;

(*b*) the construction of the relevant statutory provisions or of the orders made under them; and

(*c*) the applicability of the Law Reform (Miscellaneous Provisions) Act 1934, s.1(1), where appropriate.

8.21   Thus, certain action may be taken in relation to ancillary relief by:

(*a*) Variation (MCA 1973, s.31(6), (7), (8) and (9)).

(*b*) Orders for repayment in certain cases of sums paid under certain orders (MCA 1973, s.33).

(*c*) Enforcement of accrued rights or liabilities as at the date of death. The personal representatives of a deceased party are entitled to enforce the terms of the consent order for financial relief against the surviving wife (*Warren-Gash v Lane* (1984) 14 Fam. Law. 184 and *Smith v Smith* [1991] 2 F.L.R. 432). An order for costs against the co-respondent can be enforced by the petitioner's personal representatives (*Kelly v Kelly and Brown* [1960] 3 All E.R. 232). A surviving party may enforce an order for costs already obtained against the deceased party's estate.

(*d*) Appeals to vary or set aside an existing order. The death of a party before a consent order was executed, but after the expiry of the time limit for appeal may justify the court granting leave to appeal out of time (*Barder v Barder (Caluori intervening)* [1987] 2 F.L.R. 480).

However, a claim for ancillary relief pending at the date of death cannot be **8.22** continued by or against personal representatives under the Law Reform (Miscellaneous Provisions) Act 1934, s.1. Note, however, the rights of a former spouse and children of the deceased to apply under the Inheritance (Provision for Family and Dependants) Act 1975.

There is no abatement on the death of a co-respondent or party cited. If he dies during the suit, application should be made for an order that his name be struck out of the title of the suit (*Delahunty v Delahunty* [1961] 1 All E.R. 923).

The court has power to set aside a decree nisi and a decree absolute granted **8.23** to a party who has since died (*Purse v Purse* [1981] 2 All E.R. 465).

When a cause has abated, a notice of abatement must be filed by the petitioner's solicitor and notice given to the other parties. No fee is payable. If a decree nisi is made absolute inadvertently after the death of either party, the decree absolute is void (*Seaford, Seaford v Seaford* [1968] 1 All E.R. 482). A notice of abatement should be filed and the decree absolute on the court file endorsed as ineffective (*Practice Direction* October 12, 1953).

6 Stay of proceedings

The court has a discretionary power to stay proceedings (Supreme Court Act **8.24** 1981, s.49(3) (High Court); County Courts Act 1984, s.38 (county court)). This power may be used to prevent a party who is not complying with an order of the court from taking further steps in the proceedings or in lieu of dismissal of a petition which would prevent a respondent from proceeding on his answer.

In a defended suit, a stay may be used to allow one party to proceed to trial undefended. If the suit is to proceed on the prayer of the petition, the petitioner may apply to the district judge by summons if the cause is pending in the High Court or on notice if the cause is still pending in a divorce county court for an order:

(*a*) if the answer does not claim ancillary relief, dismissing the answer;

(*b*) if the answer claims ancillary relief, striking out denials contained in the answer, staying any prayer for matrimonial relief and allowing the respondent to proceed with any prayer for ancillary relief; or

(*c*) if the answer claims ancillary relief, dismissing the answer with leave to the respondent to apply for ancillary relief under FPR, r.2.53(2).

8.25   Stay of proceedings where concurrent proceedings exist outside England and Wales is discussed on p.[ ] *et seq.*

Where a respondent to a petition alleging two years' separation coupled with the respondent's consent to a decree being granted (MCA 1973, s.1(2)(*d*)) gives notice to the court that he does not consent to a decree being granted, or that he withdraws any consent which he has already given, the proceedings on the petition must be stayed, if none of the other facts mentioned in MCA 1973, s.1(2) is alleged. The district judge must give notice of the stay to all parties (FPR, r.2.10(2)).

In exceptional circumstances, the court may order an application to make a decree nisi absolute to be stayed (*England v England* (1979) 10 Fam. Law. 86; *O v O* [2000] 2 F.L.R. 147).

Chapter 9

Ancillary Relief

Part II of MCA 1973 (ss.21 to 40) and FPR, rr.2.52 to 2.68 contain provisions inter alia for ancillary relief.

1 Definitions

Definitions (although not all of them) are contained in FPR, r.1(2). **9.01**
Financial relief has the same meaning as in MCA 1973, s.37, *i.e.* the following reliefs:

(*a*) order for maintenance pending suit in proceedings for divorce, nullity and judicial separation (MCA 1973, s.22);

(*b*) financial provision order in proceedings for divorce, nullity and judicial separation (MCA 1973, s.23);

(*c*) property adjustment order in proceedings for divorce, nullity and judicial separation (MCA 1973, s.24);

(*d*) pension sharing order in proceedings for divorce and nullity (not judicial separation) (MCA 1973, s.21(A) and s.24B);

(*e*) variation order (MCA 1973, s.31) (except where the person liable to make secured periodical payments has died: s.31(6));

(*f*) financial provision order in proceedings for having failed to provide reasonable maintenance (MCA 1973, s.27);

(*g*) alteration by the court of an agreement during the lives of the parties to a marriage (MCA 1973, s.35).

Financial provision order means an order mentioned in MCA 1973, s.21(1) (except (for the purpose of FPR) an order under MCA 1973, s.27(6) (failure to provide reasonable maintenance)), *i.e.*:

(*a*) order for periodical payments in favour of a party to the marriage;

(*b*) order for secured periodical payments in favour of a party to the marriage;

(*c*) order for lump sum provision in favour of a party to the marriage;

(*d*) order for periodical payments in favour of a child of the family;

(*e*) order for secured periodical payments in favour of a child of the family;

(*f*) order for lump sum in favour of a child of the family (MCA 1973, s.23).

9.02   In MCA 1973, a financial provision order includes orders made under MCA 1973, s.27(6).

Where the petition for divorce, nullity of marriage or judicial separation is presented on or after 1 July 1996, a financial provision order may include a *pension attachment order* under MCA 1973, s.25B or s.25C (as amended by Pensions Act 1995, s.166) as follows:

(*a*) an order directing the trustees or managers of a pension scheme to pay the benefits of that scheme in favour of a party to the marriage;

(*b*) order that pension rights be commuted and paid in whole or part in favour of a party to the marriage;

(*c*) order a lump sum payable on death under a pension scheme in favour of a party to the marriage.

Pension sharing order means an order as defined under MCA 1973, s.21A transferring a percentage of sharable rights under a pension arrangement or second state scheme (SERPS 152P) under MCA 1973, s.24B, where a petition for divorce or nullity (but not judicial separation) has been filed on or after the December 1, 2000. These sections are inserted by Welfare Reform and Pensions Act 1999, s.19, Sch. Ch. 3, para.2 and para.4.

Property adjustment order means any of the orders mentioned in MCA 1973, s.21(2), *i.e.*:

(*a*) order for transfer of property (MCA 1973, s.24(1)(*a*));

(*b*) order for settlement of property (MCA 1973, s.24(1)(*b*));

(*c*) order for variation of settlement (MCA 1973, s.24(1)(*c*), (*d*)).

Avoidance of disposition order means an order under MCA 1973, s.37(2)(6) or (*c*), *i.e.*:

(*a*) order setting aside a disposition made in anticipation of the granting of financial relief;

(*b*) order setting aside a disposition made after an order granting financial relief.

Such an order may be obtained in proceedings for divorce, nullity, judicial separation, failure to provide reasonable maintenance (MCA 1973, s.27) and alteration of an agreement during the lives of the parties (MCA 1973, s.35).

Ancillary relief (FPR r.1.2) means:

(*a*) avoidance of disposition order;

(*b*) financial provision order;

(*c*) order for maintenance pending suit;

(*d*) property adjustment order;

(*e*) variation order.

2 Maintenance pending suit

This is an order requiring either party to the marriage to make to the other **9.03** periodical payments for his or her maintenance for a term beginning not earlier than the presentation of the petition and ending with the date of the determination of the suit (MCA 1973, s.22).

The overriding consideration will be the needs of the parties pending suit. There should be an empirical approach and the court should take a broad view. The order should meet the immediate and temporary situation. Although the MCA 1973, s.22 makes no reference to the MCA 1973, ss.25 or 25A, the principles governing an application for maintenance pending suit are the same as those governing an application for a final order (*F v F (Maintenance Pending Suit)* (1983) 4 FLR 382; *Peacock v Peacock* [1984] 1 All E.R. 1069; *T v T* [1989] Fam Law 438). (As to the court's approach, see *Rayden and Jackson*, 17th ed, ss.21.3 – 21.16; Butterworth's *Family Law Service* Volume 4A [708 – 750].)

For a guide to the procedural requirements, see *Interim Orders* at para.9.57 below.

In certain circumstances, maintenance pending suit may include provision for the legal fees of the recipient (*A v A (Maintenance Pending suit: Payment of Legal Fees*) [2001] 1 W.L.R. 605; *G v G (Maintenance Pending Suit: Legal Costs)* [2002] All E.R.(D) 306).

3 Financial provision order

This is an order for the purpose of adjusting the financial position of the **9.04** parties to a marriage and any children of the family (MCA 1973, s.21(1)).

In the case of periodical payments, secured periodical payments or a lump sum in favour of a *party* to the marriage, the court may make an order on or after the granting of a decree nisi of divorce or nullity, but the order does not take effect unless the decree has been made absolute (MCA 1973, s.23(5)). An order made before decree nisi is without jurisdiction, even if made by consent and expressed only to come into effect on decree nisi (*Board v Checkland* [1987] 2 FLR 257; *Pounds v Pounds* [1994] 1 FLR 775). There is, however, no statute of limitation in this jurisdiction (*Twiname v Twiname* [1992] 1 FLR 29).

In the case of periodical payments, secured periodical payments or lump sum in favour of a *child of the family*, the court may make an order before the granting of a decree subject to what is said below with regard to the Child Support Act 1991 (paras 9.29–9.37). Where proceedings are dismissed after the beginning of the trial, it may still (subject as above) make a financial provision order in favour of a child of the family, either forthwith or within a reasonable period after the dismissal (MCA 1973, s.23(2)).

Subject to these modifications, a financial provision order may be made on the granting of a decree of divorce, nullity or judicial separation or at any time thereafter, whether in the case of divorce or nullity before or after a decree is made absolute (MCA 1973, s.23(1)).

Order for periodical payments in favour of a party (MCA 1973, s.23(1)(a)) **9.05** This is an order that either party to the marriage shall make to the other such periodical payments for such term as may be specified in the order. The term may not begin earlier than the date of the making of an application and must be so defined as not to extend beyond the death of *either* of the parties to the marriage or, in the case of divorce or nullity, the remarriage of the payee (MCA 1973, s.28(1)(*a*)).

Order for secured periodical payments in favour of a party (MCA 1973, s.23(1)(b)) This is an order that either party to the marriage shall secure to the other such periodical payments for such term as may be specified in the order. Secured periodical payments are commonly referred to as "secured provision" although this term is not defined in MCA 1973 or FPR.

The term may begin not earlier than the date of the making of the application and must be so defined as not to extend beyond the death or, in the case of divorce or nullity, the remarriage of the payee (MCA 1973, s.28(1)(*b*)). For form of order, see Registrar's Circular, 8 March 1989.

Under an order for secured periodical payments, the party against whom the order is made is required to set aside a fund, usually land or securities, from which the periodical payments are made. An order to *secure* is not an order to *pay* periodical payments. Therefore the party against whom the order is made cannot be called upon to make good any deficiency, if the security does not yield what was anticipated under the order (*Shearn v Shearn* [1931] P 1; *Barker v Barker* [1952] 1 All E.R. 1128). The secured assets remain the property of the person against whom the order is made; he resumes control of them when the order terminates as indicated above.

Order for lump sum provision in favour of a party (MCA 1973, s.23(1)(c)) This is an order that either party to the marriage shall pay to the other such lump sum or sums as may be specified in the order. The words "or sums" do not allow the court to make more than one lump sum order. Only one lump sum order may be made, which may provide for payment by instalments (*Coleman v Coleman* [1972] 3 All E.R. 886; *Banyard v Banyard* [1984] FLR 643). The court does not have jurisdiction to make an interim lump sum order (*Bolsom v Bolsom* [1983] FLR 21; *Wicks v Wicks* [1998] 1 FLR 470), except to enable the other party to meet any liabilities or expenses reasonably incurred by him or her in maintaining himself or herself or any child of the family before the making of any financial provision order (MCA 1973, s.23(3)(*a*)). An order may be made for payment by instalments, which may be secured (MCA 1973, s.23(3)(*c*)). In certain limited circumstances, the time limit within which such a payment must be made can be extended (*Masefield v Alexander* [1995] 1 FLR 100).

9.06   The existence of a prior arrangement by a party not to claim a lump sum requires the party to adduce prima facie evidence to relieve her or him from the effect of this agreement (*Edgar v Edgar* [1980] 3 All E.R. 887; cf *Camm v Camm* [1983] 4 FLR 577 and *B v B* [1995] 1 FLR 9. For pre-existing arrangements generally, see *N v N* [1993] 2 FLR 868 and *Benson v Benson (deed)* [1996] 1 FLR 692; *G v G (Financial Provision: Separation Agreement)* [2000] 2 FLR 18; *Smith v Smith* [2000] 3 FCR 374). The important case of *Xydhias v Xydhias* [1999] 2 All E.R. 386 sets out the principles the court will apply when considering whether or not to uphold an agreement reached between the parties which has been negotiated in the shadow of an impending court fixture. See also *Rose v Rose* [2022] 1 FLR 978, where the parties reached an agreement at the FDR hearing which was approved by the court; this was held to be an unperfected order.

Where the court makes a lump sum order which is to be deferred or paid by instalments, the court may order that the amount deferred or the instalments shall carry interest at such rate as the order specifies from a date not earlier than the date of the order until the date when payment is due (MCA 1973, s.23(6) added by Administration of Justice Act 1982, s.16; *L v L (Lump Sum: Interest)* [1994] 2 FLR 324)). If payment is not made on the due date, the order (if made in the High Court) will carry interest at the rate set under the Judgements Act 1838 or (in the case of a county court order for £5,000 or more) under the County Court (Interest on Judgment Debts) Order 1991 (SI No 1184).

Pension Attachment Order directing the trustees or managers of a pension scheme to pay the benefits of that scheme in favour of a party to the marriage (MCA, s.25B(4)) This is an order that can be made where the relevant petition for divorce, nullity of marriage, or judicial separation has been presented to the court on or after July 1, 1996. This follows an amendment of MCA 1973 by the Pensions Act 1995, s.166 (and further amended by Welfare Reform and Pensions Act 1999, ss.21, 88, Sch.4, para.1, Sch.13, Pt II). The order may be made against the pension provider in respect of a pension scheme in which a party to the marriage has a benefit. The pension is "attached" so that a percentage of the pension income ". . .can be made directly out of the pension to a spouse without pension rights". This type of order was formerly called "earmarking". Regarding commencement, see the Pensions Act 1995 (Commencement) (Number 5) Order 1996 (SI No 1675); for general procedure see FPR 1991, r.2.70. For a review of this section, see *T v T* (Financial Relief: Pensions) [1998] 1 FLR 1072; *Burrow and Burrow* [1999] 1 FLR 508. For the relationship between pension attachment orders and pension sharing orders, see para.9.16 below.

Pension Attachment Order that pension rights be commuted and paid in whole or part in favour of a party to the marriage (MCA 1973, s.25B(4) and (7) This is also an order introduced by the Pensions Act 1995, s.166 amending MCA 1973 by inserting section 25B(4) and (7). Again, such an order can only be made where the relevant petition for divorce, nullity of marriage, or judicial separation has been presented to the court on or after 1 July 1996. A court may order the party to the marriage who is a pension scheme member to commute all (or part of) the benefits under the pension scheme subject to the rules of the scheme and Inland Revenue requirements. The commuted lump sum can be paid in whole or in part to the other party to the marriage. The order can be made direct against the trustees or ". . . managers of the pension scheme in question for the benefit of the other party". The order must be expressed as a percentage of the commutable lump sum. Regarding commencement, see the Pensions Act 1995 (Commencement) (Number 5) Order 1996 (SI No 1675); for general procedure see FPR 1991, r.2.70. For a review of this section, see *T v T* (Financial Relief: Pensions) [1998] 1 FLR 1072. For the relationship between pension attachment orders and pension sharing orders, see para.9.16 below.

9.07

Pension Attachment Order that a lump sum be payable on death under a pension scheme in favour of a party to the marriage (MCA 1973, s.25C) This provision has also been inserted by the Pensions Act 1995. Such an order can be made provided the petition for divorce, nullity of marriage or judicial separation has been presented to the court on or after July 1, 1996. The trustees or managers of a pension scheme in which one party has an interest can be ordered to pay any lump sum death benefit arising under that pension scheme to the other party to the marriage but not to a child of the family. The order can be for any proportion of, or the whole, of the benefit, and must be expressed as a percentage of it. The order under this section can be made where the trustees or managers have the power to determine to whom any sum is paid or where the party to the marriage has the power to ". . . nominate the person to whom the sum is paid". Regarding commencement, see the Pensions

Act 1995 (Commencement) (Number 5) Order 1996 (SI No 1675); for general procedure see FPR 1991, r.2.70. For a review of this section, see *T v T (Financial Relief: Pensions)* [1998] 1 FLR 1072. For the relationship between pension attachment orders and pension sharing orders, see para.9.16 below.

9.08   *Order for periodical payments in favour of a child of the family (MCA 1973, s.23(1)(d))* This is an order that a party to the marriage shall make to such person as may be specified in the order for the benefit of a child of the family, or to such child, such periodical payments for such term as may be so specified. As to the effect of the Child Support Act 1991, see paras 9.29–9.37.

Order for secured periodical payments in favour of a child of the family (MCA 1973, s.23(1)(e)) This is an order that a party to the marriage shall secure to such person as may be specified in the order for the benefit of a child of the family, or to such child, such periodical payments for such terms as may be so specified. As to the effect of the Child Support Act 1991, see pp 167–174.

Order for lump sum provision in favour of a child of the family (MCA 1973, s.23(1)(f)) This is an order that a party to the marriage shall pay to such person as may be specified in the order for the benefit of such a child, or to such a child, such lump sum as may be so specified. Such an order may be made for the purpose of enabling any liabilities or expenses incurred by or for the benefit of that child before the making of an application for the order to be met. The order may provide for payment by instalments and may require them to be secured (MCA 1973, s.23(3)(6), (c)).

The order may make provision for interest (MCA 1973, s.23(6)) (see above).

The court's powers to order lump sum provision in favour of a child are unaffected by the Child Support Act 1991 (*Phillips v Peace* [1996] 2 FLR 230; *V v V (Child Maintenance)* [2001] 2 FLR 799).

9.09   *Duration of financial provision orders in favour of a party to marriage and effect of remarriage (MCA 1973, s.28)* The duration of a periodical payments or secured periodical payments order in favour of a party to a marriage has been indicated above. This is subject to the overriding power of the court to specify a term during which the order will operate within the limits indicated (MCA 1973, s.28(1)).

Where a periodical payments or secured payments order is made in favour of a party to a marriage in divorce or nullity, the court may direct that no variation application may be made under MCA 1973, s.31 for an extension of the term specified in the order (MCA 1973, s.28(1A); *N v N* (1993) 2 FLR 868; *Richardson v Richardson* [1994] 1 FLR 286). However, such direction may be inappropriate where there are young children; *C v C* [1997] 2 FLR 26 and *Flavell v Flavell* [1997] 1 FLR 353. Where the order for a specific term does not contain a direction under MCA 1973, s.28(1A), it is possible to apply by way of variation to extend not only the amount payable by way of periodical payments, but also to extend the term for which they might be paid; on variation, a court may also substitute such a term order with an order for open ended maintenance, i.e. on the basis of joint lives etc (*Flavell v Flavell* above). Such an application has to be filed before the expiry of the term original specified; see *Jones v Jones* [2000] 2 FLR 307.

If an order for periodical payments or secured periodical payments is made in favour of a party to a marriage otherwise than on or after the granting of a decree of divorce or nullity and the marriage is subsequently dissolved or annulled leaving the order in force, the order will cease to have effect on the remarriage of that party, except in relation to any arrears due on the date of the remarriage (MCA 1973, s.28(2)).

Section 28(3) of MCA 1973 bars an application for a financial provision order or property adjustment order by a spouse who has remarried. As to what constitutes an application for this purpose, see para.9.47. Applications for children are unaffected.

Duration and age limit in respect of financial provision orders in favour of child   **9.10**
of family (MCA 1973, s.29) Under (*d*), (*e*) and (*f*) above, ie, financial provision orders for a child of the family, an order may not be made in favour of a child who has attained the age of eighteen (MCA 1973, s.29(1)), nor may an order extend beyond the date of a child's eighteenth birthday (MCA 1973, s.29(2)(*b*)). The restrictions as to age do not apply:

(*a*) where it appears that the child is, or will be, or if an order were made would be, receiving instruction at an educational establishment or undergoing training for a trade, profession or vocation, whether or not he is also, or will be, in gainful employment; or

(*b*) where there are special circumstances which justify the making of an order (MCA 1973, s.29(3)).

An order in favour of a child ceases to have effect on the death of the person liable to make payments under the order except in relation to any arrears (MCA 1973, s.29(4)).

The term specified in a periodical payments order or a secured periodical payments order in favour of a child of the family may begin with the date of the making of an application for the order or at any later date or a date ascertained in accordance with MCA, s.29(5) or (6) (backdating of orders to the date of a maintenance assessment under the Child Support Act 1991: see p.173). However, the order may not in the first instance extend beyond the date of the birthday of the child next following the upper limit of compulsory school age, unless the court considers that in the circumstances of the case, the welfare of the child requires that it should extend to a later date (MCA 1973, s.29(2)).

An order expressed "until the child attains the age of 17 years or ceases full-time [school]/[tertiary] education or further order" will be treated by the Inland Revenue as ceasing when the first event occurs. Therefore, the words "(whichever shall be the [later]/[earlier])" should be added after "education", as appropriate. See *Practice Direction*, July 10, 1987 [1987] 2 All E.R. 1084, which sets out the procedure for correcting an old order.

4   Property adjustment order

Meaning This is an order dealing with property rights available for the purpose   **9.11**
of adjusting the financial position of the parties to a marriage and any children of the family on or after the grant of a decree of divorce, nullity or judicial separation (MCA 1973, s.21(2)). Such an order will not take effect in the case of divorce or nullity, unless the decree nisi has been made absolute (MCA 1973, s.24(3); *Board v Checkland* [1987] 2 FLR 257).

Order for transfer of property (MCA 1973, s.24(1)(a)) This is an order that a party to the marriage transfers to the other party, or to any child of the family or to such person as may be specified in the order for the benefit of such a child, such property as may be so specified, being property to which the first-mentioned party is entitled, either in possession or reversion.

Such an order may not be made in favour of a child who has attained the age of eighteen except in the same cases as in a financial provision order, eg where the child continues education (see above; *A v A* [1994] 1 FLR 657).

Order for settlement of property (MCA 1973, s24(1)(b)) This is an order that a settlement of such property as may be specified in the order, being property to which a party to the marriage is entitled, either in possession or reversion, be made to the satisfaction of the court for the benefit of the other party to the marriage and of the children of the family, or either or any of them.

Order for variation of settlement (MCA 1973, s.24(1)(c) and (d)) This is an order varying for the benefit of the parties to the marriage and of the children of the family, or either or any of them, any ante-nuptial or post-nuptial settlement (including such a settlement by will or codicil) made on the parties to the marriage. It can also encompass an order extinguishing or reducing the interest of either party to the marriage under such a settlement.

The court's powers to make property adjustment orders for the benefit of children are unaffected by the Child Support Act 1991.

Scope of "property" "Property", which is not defined in MCA 1973, extends beyond real property to any asset to which a party is entitled in possession or reversion, *e.g.* shares or life assurance policies.

9.12   A weekly or any other tenancy is property within the meaning of MCA 1973, s.24(1) (*Hale v Hale* [1975] 2 All E.R. 1090). A council tenancy is also property within the meaning of MCA 1973, s.24(1) (*Newton Housing Trust v Alsulaiman* [1998] 2 FLR 690), but the court should not exercise its discretion where there is a covenant against assignment or where it would interfere with the statutory duties and discretion of the local authority (*Thompson v Thompson* [1975] 2 All E.R. 208; *Regan v Regan* [1977] 1 All E.R. 428). The definition includes overseas property (*Hamlin v Hamlin* [1986] 1 FLR 61). (As to the transfer of statutory tenancies under the FLA 1996, 553 and Sched. 7.

Powers of the court An order under one subparagraph of MCA 1973, s.24(1) will not preclude a later application under another subparagraph (*Carson v Carson* [1983] 1 All E.R. 478). However, on any subsequent application, any earlier order will be examined to determine its true intent. Only if a final settlement of *any* further claim under MCA 1973, s.24(1) was intended will a second application in respect of another property be precluded (*Dinch v Dinch* [1987] 2 FLR 162).

The court's powers on a property adjustment application relating to the matrimonial home fall broadly into two methods of approach:

Sale A judge or district judge has power to order the sale of property under MCA 1973, s.24A (see p.150). An order for sale under the MCA 1973, s.24 A may be made at the time of the corresponding order under the MCA 1973, ss.23 or 24 *or at any time thereafter*. However, a subsequent order for sale may only be made if it does not vary a final order in breach of MCA 1973, s.31, but amounts simply to a working out of the original order (*Thompson v Thompson* [1986] 2 ALL E.R. 243, CA; *Burton v Burton* [1986] 2 FLR 419; *Taylor v Taylor* [1987] 1 FLR 142; *cf. R v Rushmoor Borough Council* [1988] 2 FLR 252; *Omielan v Omielan* [1996] 2 FLR 306).

The order will deal with the division of the proceeds of sale and may contain supplementary provisions as to the conduct of the sale (MCA 1973, s.24A(2)). Such provisions must be consequential or supplementary to the order for sale, including the method of sale, costs of sale and payments to third parties having a beneficial interest. As to estate agents' and auctioneers' fees, see *Practice Direction* December 22, 1982 [1983] 1 All E.R. 160. The court cannot order payments to creditors unconnected with an interest in the property (*Burton v Burton* [1986] 2 FLR 419). The court now has power to order any party bound by the order for sale and in possession of the land or any part of it or in receipt of the rents and profits thereof to deliver up such possession or receipt to the purchaser or to such other person as the court may direct (FPR, r.2.64(3)).

An order for sale cannot take effect until the decree has been made absolute **9.13** in the case of divorce or nullity (MCA 1973, s.24A(3)).

The court may direct that the order for sale will not take effect until the occurrence of a specified event (MCA 1973, s.24A(4)).

Where some person other than a party to the marriage also has a beneficial interest in a property, the court must give that other person an opportunity to make representations before deciding whether to make an order under MCA 1973, s.24A. Any representations so made are included among the circumstances to which the court must have regard under MCA 1973, s.25(1) (MCA 1973, s.24A(6)).

For form of order, see Appendix 2, Form 37.

Transfer of legal and/or beneficial interest. Examples of how the court may approach transfer of property are:

(a) An *outright transfer* to the other party.

(b) A *transfer to one party with a lump sum* payment to the other party. The lump sum should be expressed to be payable on the completion of the transfer (*Potter v Potter* [1990] 2 FLR 27). Difficulties can, however, arise where there is a delay in paying the lump sum: see *Hope-Smith v Hope-Smith* [1989] 2 FLR 56.

(c) A *Mesher order* whereby the property is settled on the parties on trust for sale in defined shares with one party having exclusive rights of occupation. The trust for sale will become exercisable only on the happening of specified events, eg remarriage or cohabitation of the occupying spouse; upon the youngest child reaching a specified age or ceasing full-time education; death or voluntary removal of the occupying spouse (*Mesher v Mesher* [1980] 1 All E.R. 126).
For form of order, see Appendix 2, form 38.

(d) A *Martin order* under which the wife is given a right to occupy the property during her lifetime (*Martin v Martin* [1977] 3 All E.R. 762). In such circumstances, the wife may be ordered to pay an occupational rent to the husband (*Harvey v Harvey* [1982] 1 All E.R. 693).

As the order for sale is to be postponed in the case of either a *Mesher* or a *Martin* order, consideration must be given to factors such as mortgage repayments, repairs, maintenance and improvements pending sale. Such matters should be dealt with by way of undertakings in the order in view of the limitation placed upon MCA 1973, s.24A(2) by *Burton v Burton* [1986] 2 FLR 419.

(e) *A deferred charge.* A transfer of property order in favour of one spouse giving to the other a charge for a proportion of the equity or a fixed sum with sale postponed until the happening of certain specified events as above (*Hector v Hector* [1973] 3 All E.R. 1070; *Browne v Pritchard* [1975] 3 All E.R. 721). In *Leate v Leate* (1982) 12 Fam Law 121 the charge was deferred until the wife's death or remarriage. (As to the problems arising out of an early redemption of the charge, see *Knibb v Knibb* [1987] 2 FLR 396; *Kiely v Kiely* [1988] 1 FLR 248; *Ross v Ross* [1989] 2 FLR 257; *Popat v Popat* [1991] 2 FLR 163.)

Where the charge is for a proportion of the equity, as will normally be the case (see *Hope-Smith v Hope-Smith above*), the order will again need to deal with matters such as repairs, renewals and improvements.

For form of order, see Appendix 2, Form 39.

9.14   An application for a transfer of property (whether or not specified) is a pending land action which is registerable under the Land Charges Act 1972, s.5(1)(a) (*Whittingham v whittingham* [1978] 3 All E.R. 805; *Perez-Adamson v Perez-Rivas* [1987] 3 All E.R. 20). In the case of registered land, a pending land action can be registered by lodging a caution in the Proprietorship Register (Land Registration Act 1925, s.59(1). Practitioners should be aware that the Land Registration Act 1925 is to be repealed in whole by the Land Registration Act 2002 which is currently due to come into force in October 2003).

See also *A Practical Approach to Family Law*, (6th ed.) Jill Black, Jane Bridge and Tine Bond, p.338.

5   Pension sharing order

9.15   *Meaning* A pension sharing order is an order which provides that one party's shareable rights under a specified arrangement or shareable state scheme rights be subject to pension sharing for the benefit of the other party. The order specifies the percentage value to be transferred. (MCA 1973, s.21A, as inserted by Welfare Reform and Pensions Act 1999, s.19, Sch.3, para.2).

"Shareable rights under a pension arrangement" are widely defined in Welfare Reform and Pensions Act 1999, ss.19 – 46 to include all pension arrangements and unfunded public service pensions except for the great offices of state and those arising from being the widow, widower or other dependant of a deceased person (Pension Sharing (Valuation) Regulations 2000(SI No 2000/1052)).

"Shareable State Scheme rights" are defined by Welfare Reform and Pensions Act 1999, s.47 as earnings related additional pension and shared additional pension, *i.e.* SERPS 152P; but note the Basic State Retirement Pension is excluded from the scope of pension sharing.

Pension sharing order in connection with divorce proceedings (MCA 1973, s.24B, as inserted by Welfare Reform and Pensions Act 1999, s.19, Sch 3, para.4). The Court may on the granting of a decree of divorce or nullity of marriage, or at any time thereafter, make one or more pension sharing orders in relation to the marriage. A pension sharing order cannot be made after a decree of judicial separation.

When a pension sharing order is made, a pension debit is transferred from the relevant pension arrangement. The transferor spouse's shareable rights under the relevant pension arrangement become subject to a debit of an equivalent percentage amount. The transferee spouse becomes entitled to a credit of that amount as against the person responsible for the relevant pension arrangement. The transferee spouse gains an indefeasible right to the pension credit, which is unaffected by remarriage or death. Different rules apply to different pension schemes as to whether an internal transfer or an external transfer is offered to the transferee spouse. An internal transfer confers rights on the transferee spouse within the pension member's scheme. An external transfer occurs when the pension credit is transferred to an external pension scheme or personal pension policy (see Welfare Reform and Pensions Act 1999, Sch.5, para.1(2) and the Pension Sharing (Implementation and Discharge of Liability) Regulations 2000, Reg 7 (SI No 2000/1053)). The client should receive advice from an independent financial advisor about the respective benefits of internal and external transfers. If there is an internal transfer, the rights gained by the transferee spouse may differ from those of the transferor spouse who was the original pension member, and the rules of the relevant pension arrangement should be checked.

Scope of provision a pension sharing order is only available if the petition   **9.16** for divorce or nullity was filed on or after December 1, 2000. (The Welfare Reform and Pension Act 1999 (Commencement No 5) Order 2000 (SI No 2000/1116)). Pension sharing is not retrospective.

Unless the proceedings were begun before December 1, 2000, it is no longer possible to issue and have heard an application for a *Brooks* order after that date (*Brooks v Brooks* [1995] 2 FLR 13; Welfare Reform and Pension Act 1999, s.85(4)).

Relationship with pension attachment orders a pension sharing order may not be made where there is in force a pension attachment order in relation to a particular pension arrangement (MCA 1973, s.24B(5)). A pension attachment order arising from a previous divorce would also preclude a pension sharing order being made. Significantly, therefore, it is not possible to have a pension sharing order and at the same time apply to the court under the MCA 1973, s.25C for a pension attachment order against death benefits, which might otherwise be used as security for ongoing periodical payments.

Similarly, a pension attachment order may not be made in relation to a pension arrangement which is subject already of a pension sharing order (MCA 1973, ss.25B(7) and 25C(4)). However, because of the wording of the statute ("in relation to the marriage") this restriction only applies to a pension sharing order relating to the marriage in question.

Variation of pension sharing order there is only very narrow scope within which to apply for a variation of a pension sharing order. An application can only be made if the decree nisi has not been made absolute, and if the pension sharing order has not taken effect (MCA 1973, ss.31(2)(g) and (4)(A)). This is in marked contrast with the ability of the Court to vary pension attachment orders.

See generally *"Pensions and Insurance on Family Breakdown"* Jordans (Ed Salter).

6   Order for sale of property (MCA 1973, s.24A)

Where the court makes a secured periodical payments order, a lump sum   **9.17** order or a property adjustment order under the MCA 1973, ss.23 or 24, it may make a further order for the sale of property of the parties. The order for sale may be made at the time of the secured periodical payments order etc *or at any time thereafter* (MCA 1973, s.24A(1); *Omielan v Omielan* [1996] 2 FLR 306).

7   Avoidance of disposition order/injunction under the MCA 1973, s.37

An avoidance of disposition order is an order under the MCA 1973, s.37(2)(*b*)   **9.18** or (*c*) (FPR, r.1.2) to set aside a disposition already made. Additionally, the court may restrain by injunction a disposition about to be made under MCA 1973, s.37(2)(*a*).

Where proceedings for financial relief are brought by one person against another, MCA 1973, s.37(2) gives power to the court to make an order in the following circumstances:

(1) If the court is satisfied that the other party to the proceedings is, with the intention of defeating a claim for financial relief, about to make any disposition or to transfer out of the jurisdiction or otherwise deal with any property, it may make an order restraining the other party from so doing or otherwise for protecting the claim (MCA 1973, s37(2)(*a*)).

(2) If the court is satisfied that the other party has, with the intention mentioned above, made a reviewable disposition and different financial relief would be granted if the disposition were set aside, it may make an order setting aside the disposition (MCA 1973, s.37(2)00).

(3) If the court is satisfied that the other party has, with the intention mentioned above, made a reviewable disposition where an order for financial relief has been made, the court may make an order setting aside the disposition (MCA 1973, s.37(2)(*c*)). An application for the purposes of (2) must be made in the proceedings for the financial relief in question (MCA 1973, s.37(2)).

Any disposition is a reviewable disposition unless it was made for valuable consideration (other than marriage) to a person who, at the time of the disposition, acted in relation to it in good faith and without notice of any intention on the part of the other party to defeat the applicant's claim for financial relief (MCA 1973, s.37(4)). As to the position of third parties, see *Sherry v Sherry* [1991] 1 FLR 307 and *McGladdery v McGladdery* [1999] 2 FLR 1102. Where a disposition is a clear and obvious sham it may not be necessary to go to the expense of formally setting it aside (*Purba v Purba* [2000] 1 FLR 444). "Disposition" does not include any provision contained in a will or codicil but, with that exception, includes any conveyance, assurance or gift of property (MCA 1973, s.37(6)). As to the need to ensure that the injunction is for an appropriate duration, see *Langley v Langley* [1994] 1 FLR 383.

Where a disposition took place less than three years before the date of the application for an avoidance of disposition order or where a disposition is about to take place, then, if the court is satisfied that the disposition would have or has had the consequence of defeating the applicant's claim for financial relief, there is a rebuttable presumption that the person who disposed of or who is about to dispose of the property did so with the intention of defeating the applicant's claim for financial relief (MCA 1973, s.37(5)).

The powers of the court under MCA 1973, s.37 are in addition to the powers of the court to make an order under the Supreme Court Act 1981, s.37(3) and the County Courts Act 1984, s.52 for the preservation or detention of property which may become the subject matter of subsequent proceedings or under the inherent jurisdiction to grant a freezing injunction, formerly called a Mareva order (Supreme Court Act 1981, s.37(3) and County Courts Act 1984, s.38). In contrast to an order made under MCA 1973, s.37, an order made under the inherent jurisdiction is not dependent upon proof of an intention to defeat claims for ancillary relief (*Shipman v Shipman* [1991] 1 FLR 250; *Khreino v Khreino (No 2) (Court's Power to Grant Injunctions)* [2000] 1 FLR

578). Such an order is also available against assets not yet in existence, *e.g.* prospective civil damages, a redundancy payment or an inheritance (*Roche v Roche* [1981] 11 Fam. Law 243). See also *Ghoth v Ghoth* [1992] 2 FLR 300. An application may also be made (in the High Court only) for a writ *ne exeat regno*, the purpose of which is to prevent a respondent leaving the jurisdiction before an order is obtained against him (*Thaha v Thaha* [1987] 2 FLR 142). As to search orders(formerly called Anton Piller orders), see p.below.

An application under MCA 1973, s.37(2)(*a*) for an order restraining any   **9.19** person from attempting to defeat a claim for financial provision or otherwise for protecting the claim may be made to a district judge (FPR, r.2.68(1)).

The requirements for an application under MCA 1973, s.37(2)(*a*) are:

(*a*) in the county court, notice of application or in the High Court, summons, with copy;

(*b*) affidavit in support;

(*c*) draft injunction;

(*d*) fee of £60 (on notice) or £30 (*ex parte*).

An application under MCA 1973, s.37(2)(*a*) may be made ex parte when urgent.

Applications made under MCA 1973, s.37(2)(*b*) or(*c*), as applications for an avoidance of disposition order, fall within the definition of ancillary relief (FPR, r.1.2). The applicable procedure is therefore FPR, rr.2.52–2.67.

An order for a payment into court may be made under MCA 1973, s.37 (*Graham v Graham* [1993] 1 FCR 339).

8   Variation order

This is an order under MCA 1973, s.31 (FPR, r.1(2)).   **9.20**

Section 31 gives power to the court to vary or discharge certain financial provision orders, or to suspend any provision of them temporarily and to revive the operation of any provision so suspended, unless the court has directed under MCA 1973, s.28(1 A) that there must be no extension of a limited term order for periodical payments or secured periodical payments (MCA 1973, s31(1), and see *Richardson v Richardson* [1994] 1 FLR 286 and *B v B* [1995] 1 FLR 9). The application to vary must be made in the lifetime of the order (*Jones v Jones* [2000] 2 FLR 307) The relevant financial provision orders are any order for maintenance pending suit, any interim order for maintenance, any periodical payments order, any secured periodical payments order, any order for the payment of a lump sum by instalments, any order made on or after the grant of a decree of judicial separation for a settlement of property or a variation of settlement and any order under the MCA 1973, s.24A(1) for the sale of property (MCA 1973, s.31 (2)). The court can only exercise its powers under the MCA 1973, s.31 in relation to a settlement of property order or a variation of settlement order in proceedings for the rescission of a decree of judicial separation by reference to which the order was made, or in proceedings for dissolution of marriage (MCA 1973, s.31(4)). Where an order for a lump sum by instalments or a deferred order is made by virtue of MCA 1973, s.23(1)(c), including an order made under the MCA 1973, s.25B(4) or s.25C (inserted by the Pensions Act 1995 s.166), the court may vary such an order (even as to quantum) (MCA 1973, s.31(2)(d) and (dd)). However the power to vary such an order ceases on the death of either of the parties to the marriage (s.31(2B), MCA).

The court has power to remit arrears when considering, under MCA 1973, s.31, an order for maintenance pending suit, any interim order for mainte-nance, any periodical payments order or any secured periodical payments order (MCA 1973, s.31(2A)). The powers of the court under MCA 1973, s.31 also extend to any instrument executed in pursuance of an order (MCA 1973, s.31(3)).

Further capital orders are now possible on the application of either party for a clean break on a variation application. Although s.31(5) prohibits the court from making a property adjustment or lump sum order on an applica-tion for variation of maintenance, there are two exceptions to this rule. Firstly, as from 1 November 1998 the court has power, on an application made by either party for an immediate or deferred clean break, to order a lump sum or make a further property adjustment order (MCA 1973, s.31(7A - 7G). This power applies to all petitions including those filed before November 1, 1998 and therefore means that the provision has retrospective effect (*Harris v Harris* [2001] 1 FCR 68). Secondly, as from December 1, 2000 the court has power to make a pension sharing order in the course of an application for variation, also on an application for an immediate or deferred clean break. This power applies only to those petitions filed on or after December 1, 2000 (Welfare Reform and Pensions Act 1999, s.85(3)(b)).

9.21 The principles to be applied by the court in exercising the powers conferred by MCA 1973, s.31 are contained in MCA 1973, s.31(7). The court must con-sider all the circumstances of the case, including any change in the matters to which the court was to have regard when making the original order, the first consideration being the welfare, while a minor, of any child of the family under eighteen. The court is under a duty to consider, in the case of a period-ical payments or secured periodical payments order made on or after the grant of a decree of divorce or nullity, whether they should be made only for such further period as will enable the recipient to adjust without undue hardship to the termination of the payments (MCA 1973, s.31(7)(*a*);*S v S, supra; Boylan v Boylan* [1988] 1 FLR 282; *Ashley v Blackman* [1988] 1 WLR 222; *Whiting v Whiting* [1988] 2 All E.R. 275; *Peacock v Peacock* [1991] 1 FLR 324; *H v H* [1993] 2 FLR 35; *Cornick v Cornick (No 3)* [2001] 2 FLR 1240). The case of *Cornick v Cornick (No 3)* (above) makes it clear that the court has a virtually unfettered discretion as to the orders which it can make when determining an application for variation.

Where the party against whom the order was made has died, the circum-stances of the case include the changed circumstances resulting from his death (MCA 1973, s.31(7)(*b*)).

The court has power to direct that the variation or discharge of an order for periodical payments or secured periodical payments shall not take effect until the expiration of a period specified in the order, subject to MCA 1973, s.28(1) and (2) (MCA 1973, s.31(10)). As to the backdating of a variation order fol-lowing a maintenance assessment under the Child Support Act 1991, see MCA 1973, s.31(11)-(14) and para.9.35.

The court is not confined when considering a variation application to looking at changes in the means of the parties which have occurred since the original order was made. The court can regard the assessment of maintenance as being at large and consider all the circumstances *de novo* unless some estoppel arises (*Lewis v Lewis* [1977] 3 All E.R. 992; *Garner v Garner* [1992] 1 FLR 573; *Cornick v Cornick (No 3)* [2001] 2 FLR 1240).

As to an application for a variation order following the payee's cohabitation, *see Atkinson v Atkinson* [1987] 3 All E.R. 849; *Atkinson v Atkinson* [1995] 2 FLR 356 *and Atkinson v Atkinson (No. 2)* [1996] 1 FLR 51.

An application for a variation order is an application for ancillary relief (FPR, r.1.2). FPR, rr.2.52–2.68 apply.

9   Repayment order (MCA 1973, ss.33 and 38)

In the case of any order for maintenance pending suit, any interim order for   **9.22**
maintenance, any periodical payments order and any secured periodical payments order, the court may order the repayment of a sum not exceeding the amount of the excess paid by reason of:

    (*a*) a change in the circumstances of the person entitled to, or liable to make, payments under the order since the order was made, or

    (*b*) the changed circumstances resulting from the death of the person so liable (MCA 1973, s.33).

A similar order for repayment may be made when an order for periodical payments or secured periodical payments has ceased to have effect by reason of the remarriage of the person entitled to payments under the order; but the person liable to make payments under the order, or his personal representatives, has made payments in respect of a period after the date of the remarriage in the mistaken belief that the order was still subsisting (MCA 1973, s.38).

10   Principles to be applied: statutory criteria

A new MCA 1973, s.25 was substituted by MFPA 1984, s.3. The section sets   **9.23**
out the matters to which the court is to have regard in deciding whether, and how, to exercise its powers under MCA 1973, ss.23, 24 and 24A. There is no rule that any one consideration should be given greater weight than any other (*Piglowska v Piglowski* [1999] 2 FLR 763). The court must have regard to all the circumstances of the case, the *first consideration* being given to the welfare while a minor of any child of the family who has not attained the age of eighteen (MCA 1973, s.25(1)).

Party to the marriage. In particular, when the court is deciding whether to exercise its powers under the MCA 1973, ss.23(1)(*a*), (*b*) or (*c*), 24 or 24A (periodical payments order, secured periodical payments order, lump sum order, property adjustment order and order for sale), it must have regard to the following matters in relation to a party to the marriage (MCA 1973, ss.25(2)):

    (*a*) the income, earning capacity, property and other financial resources which each of the parties to the marriage has or is likely to have in the foreseeable future, including in the case of earning capacity any increase in that capacity which in the opinion of the court it would be reasonable to expect a party to the marriage to take steps to acquire;

(*b*) the financial needs, obligations and responsibilities which each of the parties to the marriage has or is likely to have in the foreseeable future;

(*c*) the standard of living enjoyed by the family before the breakdown of the marriage;

(*d*) the age of each party to the marriage and the duration of the marriage;

(*e*) any physical or mental disability of either of the parties to the marriage;

(*f*) the contributions made or likely to be made in the foreseeable future by each of the parties to the welfare of the family, including any contribution made by looking after the home or caring for the family;

(*g*) the conduct of each of the parties, if that conduct is such that it would in the opinion of the court be inequitable to disregard it;

(*h*) in the case of proceedings for divorce or nullity of marriage, the value to each of the parties to the marriage of any benefit (*e.g.*, a pension) which, by reason of the dissolution or annulment of the marriage, that party will lose the chance of acquiring.

9.24 Where the petition for divorce, nullity of marriage or judicial separation is presented on or after July 1, 1996, the court is to have regard specifically to any benefits under a pension scheme which a party to a marriage has or is likely to have, and any benefit under a pension scheme which, by reason of the dissolution or annulment of the marriage, a party to the marriage will lose the chance of acquiring (MCA 1973, s.25B, inserted by the Pensions Act 1995, s.166). Importantly, when the court considers the benefits under a pension scheme which a party to the marriage has or is likely to have, such consideration by the court is not restricted by the words "in the foreseeable future" as is the case with any other financial resources. The court is able to consider all pension benefits, not merely those arising in the foreseeable future (*cf. Milne v Milne* [1981] FLR 286).

Child of the family In particular, when the court is deciding whether to exercise its powers under MCA 1973, ss.23(1)(*d*), (*e*) or (*f*), (2) or (4), 24 or 24A (periodical payments order, secured periodical payments order, lump sum order, property adjustment order and order for sale), it must have regard to the following matters in relation to a child of the family (MCA 1973, s.25(3)):

(*a*) the financial needs of the child;

(*b*) the income, earning capacity (if any), property and other financial resources of the child;

(*c*) any physical or mental disability of the child;

(*d*) the manner in which he was being and in which the parties to the marriage expected him to be educated or trained;

(*e*) the considerations mentioned in relation to the parties to the marriage in paras (*a*), (*b*), (*c*) and (*e*) of MCA 1973, s.25(2).

In deciding whether to exercise its powers to make an order as above against **9.25**
a party to a marriage in favour of a child of the family *who is not a child of*
that party, the court must also have regard to, inter alia, the following circumstances (MCA 1973, s.25(4)):

(1) Whether that party assumed any responsibility for the child's maintenance, and, if so, the extent to which, and the basis upon which,
that party assumed responsibility and the length of time for which
that party discharged such responsibility.

(2) Whether in assuming and discharging such responsibility that party
did so knowing that the child was not his or her own.

(3) The liability of any other person to maintain the child.

Termination of financial obligations Section 25A of the MCA 1973, inserted by
the MFPA 1984, s.3, imposes upon the court, when granting a decree of
divorce or nullity (but *not* judicial separation), a duty to consider whether it
would be appropriate to exercise its powers under the MCA 1973, ss.23(1)(*a*),
(*b*) or (*c*), 24 or 24A in favour of a party to the marriage (periodical payments
order, secured periodical payments order, lump sum order, property adjustment order or order for sale) so that the financial obligations of each party
towards the other will be terminated as soon after the grant of the decree as
the court considers just and reasonable (MCA 1973, s.25A(1)). This may be
achieved by the following means.

Limited term order. Where the court decides to make a periodical payments
or secured periodical payments order in favour of a party to the marriage, it
must in particular consider whether it would be appropriate to require those
payments to be made or secured only for such term as would in the opinion of
the court be sufficient to enable the recipient to adjust without undue hardship to the termination of his or her financial dependence on the other party
(MCA 1973, s.25A(2)). Unless a direction has been made under MCA 1973,
s.28(1 A) that no application may be made under MCA 1973, s.31 for an extension of the term specified in the order, the court may extend the term, *e.g.* if it
has not proved possible for the recipient of the periodical payments to find
work within the original term. Care should be taken in drafting an order by
consent, so that a direction under MCA 1973, s.28(1 A) is expressly included,
where that is the intention of the parties (*Richardson v Richardson* [1994] 1
FLR 286; *B v B* [1995] 1 FLR 9).

For form of order, see Appendix 2, Form 42.

Imposed clean break. When a party to the marriage makes application for a **9.26**
periodical payments or secured periodical payments order in his or her favour
on or after the grant of a decree of divorce or nullity, the court may dismiss
the application with a direction that the applicant shall not be entitled to make
any further application in relation to their marriage for a periodical payments
or secured periodical payments order (MCA 1973, s.25A(3)). The court must
consider whether any continuing obligation should be imposed on either party
to make or secure periodical payments in favour of the other. The wording of
the subsection is such as to suggest that both dismissal of the application and
a direction in the terms indicated above are necessary to effect a clean break.
The consent of the applicant is not required (*Dipper* v *Dipper* [1980] 2 All E.R.
722 overruled).

For form of order, see Appendix 2, Form 44.

Inheritance (Provision for Family and Dependants Act 1975, s.15 Section

8 of MFPA 1984 substituted a new s.15(1) which enables the court on granting a decree of divorce, nullity *or judicial separation* (or at any time thereafter) to order on the application of either party to the marriage that the other party shall not, on the death of the applicant, be entitled to apply for an order under I(PFD))A 1975, s.2, if it considers it just to do so. The order may be made without the consent of the other party. As to the procedural considerations involved in obtaining an order under I(PFD)A 1975, s.15.

For form of order, see Appendix 2, Form 45.

There are essentially four ways of dealing with applications for periodical payments:

(*a*) to make a substantive order including a limited term order (see above);

(*b*) to make a nominal order (to enable a party subsequently to obtain a variation order);

(*c*) to adjourn the application generally if the court does not wish to make any order at that time;

(*d*) to dismiss the application, the consent of the applicant not being required (MCA 1973, s.25A).

It is not safe for the court to make "no order".

11   Principles to be applied: approach adopted by the courts

9.27   A detailed discussion of the case law relating to ancillary relief is outside the scope of this book and the reader is referred to *Rayden and Jackson*, 17th ed, Chapter Part XII, Butterworth's *Family Law Service*, Volume 4A and Duckworth, *Matrimonial Property and Finance* (Jordans).

In the case of *White v White* [2000] 2 FLR 981, the House of Lords reviewed the approach of the courts to ancillary relief cases, and in particular of the interpretation of MCA 1973, s.25. The *White* case marks a watershed in the judicial approach to this area, and pre-existing case law relating to MCA 1973, s.25 must be reconsidered in the light of their Lordships' opinions.

The previous approach of the courts, which applied a *Duxbury* calculation in determining the level of need or "reasonable requirement" in big money cases was rejected.

The House of Lords directed that in every case the approach should be to look at each of the s.25 considerations, and then to apply the "yardstick of equality", to ensure that there is no discrimination to the respective roles of the spouses. The role of the "home maker" and "child rearer" should not be regarded differently as a contribution to the family to that of the "bread-winner".

For interpretation of the *White* case see in particular the Court of Appeal judgments in *L v L* and *Cowan v Cowan* [2001] 3 WLR 684, CA, and also *D v D (lump sum: adjournment of application)* [2001] 1 FLR 633, *Dharamshi v Dharamshi* [2001] 1 FLR 736, CA, *Elliott v Elliott* [2001] 1 FCR 477, CA, *N v N (financial provision: sale of company)* [2001] 2 FLR 69, *L v L (financial provision: contributions)* [2002] 1 FLR 642, and *H-J v H-J (financial provision: equality)* [2002] 1 FLR 415.

(1) *Needs in small and middle money cases* — although the House of Lords in the White case made clear that the artificial limit of "reasonable requirements" is no longer appropriate, for the majority of cases where resources are limited, meeting the needs — and in particular the housing needs — of the parties is likely to be use up the available financial resources. In *Elliott v Elliott* (above) Thorpe LJ stated that the yardstick of equality should not apply merely to cases where the assets exceeded the needs of the parties; he went on to reinstate a charge in favour of the husband realisable of *Mesher* terms (see para.9.13 above for the possible approaches of the Court when dealing with the matrimonial home). The effect of this approach may be to make *Mesher* orders or charge back arrangements more frequent in cases where the majority or all of the equity in the home is transferred to or used by a wife with children.

(2) *Contributions and surplus assets* — in cases where the financial resources of the family are more substantial, greater emphasis has been given in the post *White* cases to the contributions of the parties. Whilst reinforcing the view in *White* that the contribution of the "homemaker" and "child- rearer" should be treated as equal to that of the "bread winner", the courts post-*White* have allowed a greater proportion of the financial assets to be given to a spouse whose contribution is seen to have been significantly greater. In *Cowan v Cowan* (above) it was felt that the husband should receive more by virtue of his contribution as an outstanding entrepreneur who had shown exceptional vision and application in building up the family's wealth. In contrast, see *H-J v H-J* (above) where the court felt it wrong to depart from an equal approach. In *L v L* the Court of Appeal preferred the approach in *HJ v HJ* to that of the court below. It was held that, having found the husband's contribution to be special but not equivalent to that of a genius, and that the wife could not have done more, the judge at first instance should not have elevated one contribution above the other. In *White*, the inheritance and contribution from the husband's family was noted, and such resources from an original family can also be considered as a significant contribution. See in particular the judgement of Mance LJ in *Cowan v Cowan* (above), at paragraphs 155 to 160.

(3) *Family businesses and companies* — the case of *White* brought about a fundamental change in the approach of the courts to family businesses. In *N v N* (above), Coleridge J stated that before the *White* decision "the court would have strained to prevent a disruption of the husband's business and professional activities except the minimum extent necessary to meet the wife's needs". However, he went on to say that the old taboo against "selling the goose that lays the golden egg" had largely been laid to rest. Courts may therefore take a more intrusive role in analysing whether a business can raise capital to meet the needs of the parties, or even consider selling the business in whole or in part. However, even where there is liquidity within a business or company, or even proceeds of sale of a business, the requirements of future business needs will also need to be considered (see *Cowan v Cowan* above). Although the pre-*White* case law cautioning against obtaining expensive valuations cannot be ignored (*e.g. P v P* [1989] 2 FLR 241; *Evans v Evans* [1990] 1 FLR 319), it is submitted that practitioners may need to give greater consideration to the value of com-

panies and businesses, and the assets contained within them, because of the greater tendency on the part of the courts to allocate assets and resources on a proportional basis. See Family Businesses and Accountants' Reports in para.9.80 below.

9.28

(4) *Pensions* — the introduction of new remedies dealing specifically with pensions has radically improved the powers of the courts for dealing with such assets. Before the introduction of pension attachment orders and, more importantly, pension sharing orders, the court's powers were limited because of the illiquid nature of pension benefits; if there were sufficient liquid resources, the courts could make adjustments by "off setting" the value of the pension benefits, or as a last resort by enabling maintenance rights to be kept open. As noted above (paras 9.06–9.07) where a petition was filed after the July 1, 1996, the court is able to make pension attachment orders, dealing with the income arising from pensions, or the commutable lump sums arising on retirement, or the death benefits arising from pension schemes or policies. Where a petition has been filed after the December 1, 2000 (see para.9.15 above) the court is may make a pension sharing order. By enabling pension benefits to be reallocated, the prospect of a clean break being made is thereby extended to many more cases. Practitioners will need to pay particular attention to the valuation evidence (see para.9.83 below). A distinction has been drawn between liquid and illiquid assets when re-allocating resources on divorce (see *Cowan v Cowan* above, per Thorpe LJ at para.69; *Maskell v Maskell* [2001] 3 FCR 296, CA). It is important that clients receive advice from independent financial advisors as to the choice of internal or external transfers, and as to the future yields of pension benefits and other financial resources. See further Salter (Ed, "Pensions and Insurance on Family Breakdown" (Jordans).

(5) *Conduct* Section 25(2)(g) of the MCA 1973 redefines the relevance of conduct. It is submitted that the intention of the change brought about by the MFPA 1984 in this respect was not to make any radical alteration to the pre-existing test under *Wachtel v Watchel* [1973] 1 All E.R. 829, under which conduct would be disregarded unless it was "gross and obvious" (*Kyte v Kyte* [1987] 3 All E.R. 1041; *Evans v Evans* [1988] 1 FLR 351; *K v K* [1990] 2 FLR 225; *cf. Leadbeater v Leadbeater* [1985] FLR 789). Whilst conduct will usually, where appropriate, be a discounting factor, it may also increase the provision made for a party (*Kokosinski v Kokosinski* [1980] 1 All E.R. 1106; *H v H* [1994] 2 FLR 801; *A v A* [1995] 1 FLR 345). Relevant conduct may take the form of financial misconduct, *e.g.* dissipation of assets (*Martin v Martin* [1976] 3 All E.R. 625; *cf. Primavera v Primavera* [1992] 1 FLR 16) or misconduct within the proceedings (*M v M* [1995] 3 FLR 323; but see *P v P* [1994] 2 FLR 381 and *T v T* [1994] 2 FLR 1083). However, the consequent misconduct within proceedings is more likely to be dealt within by way of a punitive costs order than by a different allocation of financial resources; as to the distinction between marital misconduct and misconduct in the litigation see *Tavoulareas v Tavoulareas* [1998] 2 FLR 418, CA.

(6) *Children.* The Child Support Act 1991 does not repeal the court's powers to make secured or unsecured periodical payments orders for

the benefit of children. It does, however, severely restrict the circumstances in which those powers may be exercised (see para.9.29 et seq). The case law which pre-dates the Act, including those cases referred to below, may be relevant in circumstances where the court's powers are still available. Where the court retains jurisdiction, it is submitted that the court may still have regard to the Child Support Act formula as a yardstick in the assessment of the level of maintenance payable (*E v C* [1996] 1 FLR 472). Section 25(1) of MCA 1973 makes the children's welfare the first, but not the paramount, consideration in determining the level of periodical payments to be awarded to a wife (*Suter v Suter* [1987] 2 All E.R. 336). A child's interest under a discretionary trust is a financial resource within MCA 1973, s.25(3) (*J v J* [1989] 1 FLR 453). The means of those caring for children may be relevant (*S v X and X* [1990] 2 FLR 187).

As to lump sum orders for children, see *Kiely v Kiely* [1988] 1 FLR 248. As to property adjustment orders for children, see *A v A* [1994] 1 FLR 657.

(7) *Cohabitation* Cohabitation should not be equated to remarriage or disentitle a wife from anything other than nominal maintenance. Cohabitation and a decision not to remarry are conduct to be considered under MCA 1973, s.25(2)(*g*). The court must, however, look at all the circumstances of the cohabitation and in particular financial dependency upon a cohabitee (*Duxbury v Duxbury* [1987] 1 FLR 7; *Suter v Suter* [1987] 2 FLR 232; *Atkinson v Atkinson* [1988] 2 FLR 353; *Hepburn v Hepburn* [1989] 1 FLR 373; *Clutton v Clutton* [1991] 1 FLR 242); *Atkinson v Atkinson* [1995] 2 FLR 356 *and Atkinson v Atkinson (No 2)* [1996] 1 FLR 51).

(8) *Short marriages* Section 25(2)(*d*) MCA 1973 directs the court to have regard, *inter alia*, to the duration of the marriage. The approach of the court will depend upon whether or not there are children and the exact length of the marriage. The court may decide to discount the level of provision for the wife or to make a fixed term order for periodical payments by way of rehabilitative maintenance. For a summary of the relevant case law, see Duckworth, *Matrimonial Property and Finance* (Jordans).

(9) *Low income cases* The court may adopt the "subsistence level" approach (*Shallow v Shallow* [1978] 2 All E.R. 483). (For further discussion of welfare benefits generally, see pp 213 et seq. It must, however, be borne in mind that where maintenance is also payable in respect of children assessed under the formula in the Child Support Act 1991, Sch.1, that the assessment will contain an element attributable to the mother as carer. (See also *Delaney v Delaney* [1992] FLR 457).

(10) *Clean break* Section 25A of MCA 1973 does not create a presumption that periodical payments should be terminated as soon as possible, unless the wife can show some good reason to the contrary (*M v M* [1987] 2 FLR 1; *Barren v Barren* [1988] 2 FLR 516). However, where a young or young middle-aged wife is in possession of substantial capital the idea of periodical payments for life is largely obsolescent (*C v C* [1989] 1 FLR 11). A "one-sided clean break", ie where one party continues to make financial provision, is possible

(*Thompson v Thompson* [1988] 2 All E.R. 376). "Undue hardship" has to be considered in relation to the standard of living previously enjoyed by the wife (*Boylan v Boylan* [1988] 1 FLR 282). Where there are young children (*C v C, Flavell v Flavell, Suter v Suter* [1987] 2 All E.R. 336; *Waterman v Waterman* [1989] 1 FLR 380; *Mawson v Mawson* [1994] 2 FLR 985) or where the parties' resources are small and/or welfare benefits are involved (*Ashley v Blackman* [1988] 3 WLR 562; *Tandy v Tandy* [1988] FCR 561; *Seaton v Seaton* [1986] 2 FLR 398). However, these decisions must now be viewed against the background of the Social Security Administration Act 1992 ss.105 and 106 and the Child Support Acts 1991 and 1995. The Tax Credits Act 1999 relating to Working Families Tax Credit should also be considered.

As to the approach to a clean break on variation applications, see para.9.21 above. For an analysis of the post-*White* approach to capitalization of periodical payments see in particular *Cornick v Cornick (No 3)* [2001] 2 FLR 1240.

(11) *Future interests and potential inheritances* Section 25(2)(*a*) of MCA 1973 directs the court to have regard to resources which the parties are likely to have in the foreseeable future. Such future prospects may include an entitlement under a family settlement (*Calder v Calder* (1976) 6 Fam Law 242). It will, however, be rare for an interest which a person might inherit under a will to constitute property which a person is likely to have in the foreseeable future (*Michael v Michael* [1986] 2 FLR 389; *H v H* [1993] 2 FLR 335; but see *MT v MT* [1992] 1 FLR 362; *Thomas v Thomas* [1995] 2 FLR 668).

The court may take account of future changes of circumstances which are foreseeable as being likely to occur, rather than those which are merely speculative (*Archibald v Archibald* [1989] 1 All E.R. 257). This approach may avoid a further variation application within a short period (*Furlong-Taylor v Furlong-Taylor* (1982) 13 Fam Law 143).

(12) *Trusts* Assets held on discretionary trusts in favour of a party are financial resources which can properly be taken into account where a party has effective control over them. The court will look at the reality of the situation (*Browne v Browne* [1989] 1 FLR 291; *E v E* [1990] 2 FLR 233; *Thomas v Thomas* [1995] 2 FLR 668). The court may also have regard to the financial interests of a child under a discretionary trust when assessing the amount of maintenance to be paid to the child (*J v J* [1989] 1 All E.R. 1121). See also *Surplus Assets and Contributions* above regarding inheritances.

12　Child Support Act 1991

(*a*)　Introduction

9.29　The Child Support Act 1991 ("CSA 1991") came into effect on April 5, 1993. It places the responsibility for the assessment, collection and enforcement of child support maintenance on the Child Support Agency ("CSA"). It applies to all cases irrespective of whether welfare benefits are involved. It has subsequently been amended by the Child Support Act 1995 ("CSA 1995") and Child Support, Pensions and Social Security Act 2000 ("CSA 2000"). Given that one of the objectives of CSA 1991 is to remove issues of child maintenance from the court's jurisdiction, a detailed discussion of the workings of the CSA 1991 as amended is outside the scope of this work. This section reviews briefly the ways in which CSA 1991 and CSA 1995 impact upon the court's residual jurisdiction. The substantive changes to the CSA 1991 that are to be introduced by the CSA 2000 were expected to come into effect in April 2002 but implementation has been delayed and it looks unlikely that they will come into effect before Summer 2003 (see Appendix 5 for changes that will be introduced by CSA 2000). Certain parts of the CSA Act 2000 came into force in 2001 and these are referred to at paragraph (f) below.

The fundamental restriction on the court's role is contained in CSA 1991, s.8(3), which provides that, where the CSA has jurisdiction, no court shall exercise any power which it would otherwise have to make, vary or revive any maintenance order in relation to the child and non resident parent ("NRP") concerned. This restriction is subject to certain exceptions which are discussed in (b) below. The restriction does, however, still apply even though an assessment would not be made if one were applied for (CSA 1991, s.8(2)).

The Child Support Act 1991, s.9(3) ensures that the existence of a maintenance agreement does not prevent an application for a maintenance assessment. "Maintenance agreement" is defined by CSA 1991, s9(1) as "any agreement for the making, or for securing the making, of periodical payments by way of maintenance . . . to or for the benefit of any child" (*AMS v Child Support Officer* [1998] 1 FLR 955,CA). The definition is therefore wide enough to encompass an oral agreement. The Act does not prevent the making of maintenance agreements (CSA 1991, s.9(2)), which may then be converted into a court order under CSA 1991, s.8(5) (see (b) below). However, CSA 1991, s.9(4) makes void any provision in an agreement which purports to restrict the right of any person to apply for a maintenance assessment. The court may not use its jurisdiction to vary maintenance agreements under MCA 1973, s.35, where CSA 1991, s.8, would prevent the court from making a maintenance order (CSA 1991, s.9(5)).

The Family Proceedings Rules, rr.10.24–10.25 (inserted by Family Proceedings (Amendment) Rules 1993 (SI No 295), r.6) place upon the court a duty to notify the parties where a district judge considers that an application to the court is precluded by CSA 1991, s.8 (FPR, r.10.24(1)). The applicant may allow his application to be treated as withdrawn (FPR, r.10.24(7)) or seek a hearing before the district judge on the issue of whether or not his application is precluded (FPR, r.10.24(4)). The Family Proceedings Rules, r.10.25 allows the balance of an application to proceed as if the application in relation to a qualifying child had not been contained in it.

(*b*) The residual role of the court

(i)   Until implementation of section 2 of CSA 2000 the CSA's jurisdiction   **9.30**
can be ousted indefinitely except in benefits cases

When the CSA 1991 was enacted, it was envisaged that by April 1997 the CSA would be dealing with child maintenance on a universal basis, including where court orders had previously been in existence. However, pressure upon the Agency has meant that the timetable has been revised. Section 18 of the CSA 1995 has amended the CSA 1991, s.4 so that where:

(*a*) there is in force a written maintenance agreement made before April 5, 1993 or a maintenance order (whenever made) in respect of that child or children and the absent parent; or

(*b*) benefit (as prescribed) is being paid to, or in respect of, a Parent With Care ("PWC");

9.31   no application may be made for a maintenance assessment. However, see Appendix 5 for significant amendments to section 4 of the CSA 1991 to be implemented by CSA 2000.

It means that provided the consent order is approved by the court prior to the implementation of CSA 2000 the jurisdiction of the CSA can be ousted indefinitely where the parties are not on, and do not go on to, welfare benefits (as prescribed in CSA 1991 and subsequent regulations). Where the parent with care is being paid income support, an income-based jobseeker's allowance or any other benefit of a prescribed kind the Secretary of State may require her to authorise him to take action under the CSA 1991 to recover child support maintenance from the NRP (CSA 1991, s.6, *R v Secretary of state for Social Security exp. Harris* [1999] 1 FLR 837).

A further amendment has been made to CSA 1991 s.8(3) by the addition of s.8(3A) under CSA 1995 so that, where benefit is being paid to, or in respect of, a PWC and a maintenance order is in force, the court can exercise its power to vary such an order until a maintenance assessment has been made. This recognises that maintenance assessments have not been and are not yet being carried out in every benefits case despite the CSA's jurisdiction, due to delays and pressure of workload upon the CSA. In such circumstances an application to vary an existing order can therefore be made to the court. The CSA has also specifically deferred taking on benefits cases in certain circumstances as a policy decision.

Where a decision has been made by a court either that it has no power to vary or that it has no power to enforce a maintenance order in a particular case, Child Support (Maintenance Arrangements and Jurisdiction) Regulations 1992, reg.9 provides that CSA 1991 s.4(10) shall not apply so that an application may then be made to the CSA (as inserted by Child Support (Miscellaneous Amendments) (No 2) Regulations 1995 (SI No 3261)).

Whilst revocation of an existing order would mean that the CSA then has jurisdiction to carry out an assessment, the courts will only revoke an order where appropriate in all the circumstances, applying the criteria set out in MCA 1973, s.31(7) (*B v M* [1994] 1 FLR 342).

9.32   Given the changes that shall be introduced by section 2 CSA 2000 to section 4 CSA 1991 practitioners must warn their client that, from implementation of section 2 CSA 2000, it is open to either party to apply for a child maintenance assessment under CSA 1991 after the order has been in operation for twelve months (see Appendix 5). In circumstances where it is unlikely that the order will be approved by the court prior to section 2 CSA 2000 being implemented, consideration should be given to the following:

(1) "*Segal* Orders"

The purpose of these orders is to enable any changes in child maintenance provision to be compensated for by way of a reduction in spousal maintenance. Any such order has to include a substantial element of spousal support to be legitimate. If the PWC has no entitlement to spousal maintenance any form of order that is not an agreed order circumvents the statutory prohibition in s.8 (3) CSA 1991. (*Dorney-Kingdom v Dorney-Kingdom* [2000] 2 FLR 855,CA, *V v V (Child Maintenance)* [2001] 2 FLR 799 *and* see *SFLA Precedents for Consent Orders,* (6th ed.) precedent 75).

(2) Charge back provision

This provides for a charge that is secured on the property transferred to the PWC whereby, any excess of the subsequent maintenance calculation made by the CSA over the maintenance order made by the court, is clawed back in favour of the NRP *(Smith v McInerney* [1994] 2 FLR 1077, *Precedents for Consent Orders* (6th ed.), precedent 46).

(3) School fees adjustment

A school fees order by the NRP against the PWC made by consent could be expressed only to be operative where the maintenance calculation exceeds a certain figure (s.23 (1)(d) of MCA 1973 and s8(7) of CSA 1991).

(4) Compensating periodical payments for the NRP

The PWC would be required to pay periodical payments equal to the excess of maintenance calculation over the maintenance order (see, *Precedents for Consent Orders* (6th ed.), precedent 78).

(5) Declaration by the PWC

Declaration by the PWC not to seek a discharge of a child maintenance order *(see Precedents for Consent Orders* (6th ed.), precedent 9).

(6) Recital as to child maintenance

A recital could be incorporated in the order recording (a) the level of the child maintenance and that the order is made on this basis or (b)as to the circumstances that would alter the child maintenance payments *(see Precedents for Consent Orders* (6th ed.), precedent 40 and 41).

(ii)   The court retains jurisdiction in certain circumstances

Despite the restriction on the court's jurisdiction contained in CSA 1991, **9.33** s.8(3), the court retains a residual role in respect of new cases in the following circumstances.

(1) *Jurisdiction*: where the CSA does not have jurisdiction because one or more of the NRP's, the PWC or the child are not habitually resident in the United Kingdom (CSA 1991, s.44(1), see also paragraph (f) (3) below) or where the parents remain living in the same household the court may make an order.

(2) *Revocation of orders*: a court may still make an order revoking a maintenance order (CSA 1991, s.8(4) but see *B v M* [1994] 1 FLR 342).

(3) *Stepchildren*: The CSA can only levy its assessment against a natural parent or adoptive parent, so CSA 1991 has no application to stepchildren. The court retains its power to make periodical payments orders for stepchildren as children of the family under section 23 of the MCA 1973.

(4) *Older children*: A person is a "qualifying child" and potentially subject to the CSA jurisdiction if they are under the age of 16, or over 16 and under 19 and in full time non-advanced education, or under 18 and undergoing certain types of training in accordance with certain conditions and unmarried (CSA 1991, s.55 and Child Support (Maintenance Assessment Procedure) Regulations 1992 (SI No 1813)). Where an agency assessment cannot be made in respect of a child because of his age or his occupation, it is still possible for the child or his carer, if the child is in education or training or there are special circumstances, to make an application for periodical payments under Schedule 1 of the Children Act 1989. If there has been a periodical payments order in respect of the child under section 23 of the MCA 1973 which has expired then the application will need to made in those proceedings and not under the Children Act 1989 (see *"Maintenance Liability for Students"* [1999] Fam Law 45, and *"Children – The Continuing Duty to Maintain"* [2001] Fam Law 839).

(5) *Capital orders*: the court retains its power to make capital orders under MCA 1973, ss.23 and 24 and CA 1989, Sch.1. Such orders are, however, rarely made in practice (*Kiely v Kiely* [1988] 1 FLR 248; *cf. K v K* [1992] 2 FLR 220, *V v V (Child Maintenance)* [2001] 2 FLR 799 but see *Philips v Peace* [1996] 2 FLR 230)).

(6) *Additional payments*: the court is able to make a periodical payments order by way of topping-up maintenance in respect of a qualifying child where a maintenance assessment has been made in accordance with the alternative additional element formula contained in CSA 1991, Sch.1, para.4(3) (CSA 1991, s.8(6)).

(7) *Educational and training expenses*: the court is still able to make a periodical payments order in relation to a child if:

    (*a*) the child is, or will be or (if an order were to be made) would be receiving instruction at an educational establishment or undergoing training for a trade, profession or vocation (whether or not while in gainful employment); and

    (*b*) the order is made solely for the purposes of requiring the person making or securing the making of periodical payments fixed by the order to meet some or all of the expenses incurred in connection with the provision of the instruction or training (CSA 1991, s.8(7)). The CSA has no jurisdiction over responsibility for school fees and therefore the court has retained jurisdiction to make orders concerning those, as well as all other educational and training expenses (*Secretary of State for Social Security v Foster*) [2001] 1 FCR 376 FCA).

(8) *Disabled children*: the court is not prevented from making a periodical payments order in relation to a child if:

  (*a*) a disability living allowance is paid to or in respect of him; or

  (*b*) no such allowance is paid but he is disabled, and the order is made solely for the purpose of requiring the person making or securing the making of periodical payments fixed by the order to meet some or all of any expenses attributable to the child's disability (CSA 1991, s.8(8)).

  "Disabled" is defined for the purposes of CSA 1991, s.8(8) by CSA 1991, s.8(9).

(9) *Orders against the PWC*: the court is not prevented from making a periodical payments order in relation to a child if the order is made against a PWC of the child (CSA 1991 s.8(10), see, eg *Sherdley v Sherdley* [1987] 2 FLR 242; *Simister v Simister (No 1)* [1987] 1 FLR 189).

(10) *Inheritance (Provision for Family and Dependents) Act 1975*: children (of whatever age) may still apply for an order under the I(PFD)A 1975, s.2 for provision from their parents' estates.

(11) *Conversion of written agreements*: until implementation of CSA 2000 the court may still convert a written agreement into an order for periodical payments in relation to a child (CSA 1991, s.8(5); Child Maintenance (Written Agreements) Order 1993 (SI No 620), but see (b)(i)above). The written agreement (whether or not enforceable) must provide for the making, or securing, by an NRP of the child, of periodical payments to or for the benefit of the child and the maintenance order which the court makes must be, in all material respects, in the same terms as the agreement. The Child Maintenance (Written Agreements) Order 1993 does not require that the written agreement should be in any particular form nor that the agreement should predate 5 April 1993 when CSA 1991 came into effect. Practice may differ from area to area, but most courts accept an agreement recited in the preamble to a notice of application for a consent order. An order under CSA 1991, s.8(5) may be made by consent (with a statement under FPR, r.2.61 or (in the case of proceedings under CA 1989, Sch.1) under FPR, r.4.4(6) or after a contested hearing, provided there is a written agreement in respect of child maintenance as defined above. The district judge cannot make an order save for in the terms and amount as agreed therein. However, the court retains its power to make lump sum orders for the benefit of the children in certain circumstances (MCA 1973 (s.23(1)(f) see para.9.33 (5) above). Once a court order has been made under this provision, prior to implementation of CSA 2000, the jurisdiction of the CSA is ousted indefinitely (see paras 9.30–9.32 above).

(c) Calculation of child maintenance—the Child Support Agency and the courts

Maintenance payable under CSA 1991 as amended is calculated in accordance with formulae set out in CSA 1991, Sch.1, Part I. Component parts of   **9.33** the formulae have been defined and amended by attendant and subsequent legislation and a detailed analysis is not the subject of this book. However, CSA 1995 has provided for a departure direction system, where either the PWC or the NRP may apply for a direction under Child Support Act 1991, s.28F. For the cases in which such a departure direction will be considered, see further CSA 1995, Sch.2, Part 1. In such cases discretion may be applied to vary the amount of child support payable under the formulae in CSA 1991, Sch.1.

E v C [1996] 1 FLR 472 provides judicial guidance indicating that where a court is considering the question of child maintenance, it should consider (but the court is not bound to) what the CSA assessment would be in the circumstances. When dealing with negotiations to agree or vary child maintenance, therefore, practitioners should also consider that calculation. If a court is asked to consider the matter, such a calculation should be provided to it (see paragraph 1.13 of the Form E).

The court's overall approach to ancillary relief applications will be greatly influenced by the CSA 1991 as amended because of the duty imposed upon the court by MCA 1973, s.25 to have regard inter alia to:

(i) all the circumstances of the case, first consideration being given to the welfare while a minor of any child of the family who has not attained the age of 18 (MCA 1973, s.25(1));

(ii) the financial obligations which each of the parties to the marriage has or is likely to have in the foreseeable future (MCA 1973, s.25(2)(i));

(iii) the contributions which each of the parties has made or is likely in the foreseeable future to make to the welfare of the family (MCA 1973, s.25(2)f).

(*d*)   The clean break—inter-spousal/child maintenance

9.34   Whereas the formulae in CSA 1991, Sch.1, includes in the assessment of the maintenance requirement amounts attributable to the income support allowances for the PWC, MCA 1973, s.25A (see p.163) requires the court to consider exercising its powers in such a way that the financial duties of the parties to a marriage one to the other are terminated and a "clean break" effected. These allowances in the formulae may be regarded as a form of inter-spousal maintenance and therefore appear to conflict with the self-sufficiency principle embodied in MCA 1973, s.25A. This may be used to support an argument for a dismissal of inter-spousal claims, given the element included in a calculation of child maintenance under CS A 1991. Contrary to that, CSA 1991 makes it clear that there can be no clean break in respect of child maintenance and any such attempt is void (CS A 1991, s.9(4)). This equally applies to pre-1993 cases, before CSA 1991 was in operation, as confirmed in *Crozier v Crozier* [1994] 1 FLR 126 (but see also *Smith v McInerney* [1994] 2 FLR 1077, *AMS v Child Support Officer* [1998] 1 FLR 955,CA). However, in a limited sense the impact of this has been ameliorated by the insertion of Sch.3A into the Child Support (Maintenance Assessment and Special Cases) Regulations 1992, providing in certain instances for pre-1993 capital settlements to be taken into account in CSA calculations. The departure direction system referred to at (*c*) in para.9.33 above may also take into account such settlements.

Where little or no child maintenance is being paid, the courts may reflect that in spousal maintenance, perhaps for a fixed term until child maintenance is increased or to take account of the amount assessed (see for instance *Mawson v Mawson* [1994] 2 FLR 985).

(e) Backdating of court orders

The Maintenance Orders (Backdating) Order 1993 (SI No 623) enables **9.35** maintenance orders made by the court under MCA 1973 or CA 1989 to be backdated to the effective date of a maintenance assessment (*i.e.* beyond the date which the court would ordinarily have jurisdiction to backdate). This power caters for the situation where the applicant is only able to apply to the court for an order when a maintenance assessment has been carried out. The "effective date" for payments under an assessment is either the date on which the maintenance enquiry form is sent to the absent parent, or in certain circumstances eight weeks after that date (Child Support (Maintenance Assessment Procedures) Regulations 1992, reg.30 as amended by Child Support and Income Support (Amendment) Regulations 1995, reg.36). Applications for backdating must be made within six months of the date on which the assessment was made. The power to backdate is discretionary and the court may backdate to the effective date of the maintenance assessment or a later date.

The power to backdate arises in the following situations:

(1) *Additional payments*: an application for additional payments (see p.170) under CSA 1991, s.8(6) can be backdated to the effective date of the maintenance assessment covering the period up to the making of the order (MCA 1973, s.29(5); CA 1989, Sch.1, para.3(5)).

(2) *Loss of spousal maintenance*: where a maintenance assessment cancels an existing order which contained a high level of child maintenance but a lower level of spousal maintenance, the maintenance assessment may reduce the total level of maintenance payable. In this situation, the wife may apply to the court for her periodical payments order to be varied backdating the variation order to the effective date of the maintenance assessment which cancels the original order (MCA 1973, s.31(12)).

(3) *Loss of jurisdiction*: where one or more of the PWC's, the NRP or the qualifying child cease to be habitually resident within the United Kingdom so that the CSA no longer has jurisdiction, the maintenance assessment is cancelled (CSA 1991, s44(3); Child Support (Maintenance Arrangements and Jurisdiction) Regulations 1992 (SI No 2645), reg.7, see paragraph (f) (3) below). However, until the CSA loses jurisdiction, no application to the court may be made. The court may therefore backdate a periodical payments order in respect of a child to the date of the cancellation under CSA 1991, s.44(3) (MCA 1973, s.29(7); CA 1989, Sch.1, para.3(7)).

(4) *Unapportioned orders*: if there is a periodical payments order for two or more children for an amount which is not apportioned between them and there is then a maintenance assessment which does not cover all of the children named in the order, the NRP must pay the

maintenance assessment and the whole of the amount of the existing order. An application may therefore be made by the absent parent for variation of such an order backdated to the effective date of the maintenance assessment (MCA 1973, s.31 (12); CA 1989, Sch.1, para.6(9)).

(*f*)   Provisions of CSA 2000 that came into force on 31 January 2001 (CSA 2000 (Commencement Order No 5) Order 2000 (SI 2000 No 3354)

9.36   (1) Section 13 of CSA 2000 which inserted section 14A which makes it a criminal offence to fail to provide information for child support purposes or to provide false information.

(2) Parentage

Section 26 of CSA 1991 as amended by section 15 of CSA 2000 sets out grounds upon which the Secretary of State is entitled to proceed on the assumption that the man is the child's father and to make a maintenance calculation. There are various grounds and the main ones are:

(*a*) alleged NRP was married to the PWC at any time between conception and birth of the child and the child has not subsequently been adopted;

(*b*) alleged NRP is named as the child's father on the birth certificate and the child has not subsequently been adopted;

(*c*) alleged NRP has refused to take a DNA test or he has submitted to such a test, which shows "no reasonable doubt" that he is the child's parent and he refuses to accept it (see also *F v Child Support Agency* [1999] 2 FLR 244);

(*d*) where the alleged NRP has adopted the child;

(*e*) the courts have already decided on parentage and the child has not subsequently been adopted.

The NRP or the Secretary of State can apply to the court for a declaration of parentage in the event of a dispute concerning parentage.

(3) Section 22 of the CSA 2000 amends section 44 of CSA 1991 to extend the jurisdiction of the CSA to include certain NRP's based abroad (*e.g.* NRP employed in civil service, member of the naval, military or air forces).

(4) The term "absent parent" in the CSA 1991 is replaced by "non-resident parent"("NRP") (CSA 2000, Sch.3 para.11 (2)).

(*g*)   Provision of CSA 2000 that came into force on 2 April 2001 (CSA 2000 (Commencement Order No 5) Order 2000 (SI 2000 No 3354)

9.37   These provisions give power to magistrates courts in England and Wales, and the sheriff in Scotland, where there has been wilful refusal or culpable neglect to pay child support maintenance, to commit the liable person to prison, or make an order for him to be disqualified from holding or obtaining a driving licence for a maximum of two years (new section 39A, 40A and 40B of CSA 1991 inserted by section 16 of CSA 2000, came into force on April 2, 2001 (The Child Support, Pensions and Social Security Act 2000 (Commencement No.5) Order 2000 (SI No.3354)).

13   Applications for financial protection of respondent

MCA 1973, s.5. Section 5 provides a statutory defence allowing a respondent **9.38**
to a petition alleging five years' separation (MCA 1973, s.1(2)(*e*)) to oppose
the grant of a decree on the ground that the dissolution of the marriage will
result in *grave financial or other hardship* and that it would in all the circumstances be wrong to dissolve the marriage (MCA 1973, s.5(1)). The defence
only applies to petitions for divorce.
Where the grant of a decree is opposed under MCA 1973, s.5, then:

(*a*) if the court finds that the petitioner is entitled to rely in support of
his petition on the fact of five years' separation and makes no such
finding as to any other fact mentioned in MCA 1973, s.1(2); and

(*b*) if apart from MCA 1973, s.5 the court would grant a decree on the
petition,

then the court must consider all the circumstances, including the conduct of
the parties to the marriage and interests of those parties and of any children
or other persons concerned. If it is of the opinion that the dissolution of the
marriage will result in grave financial or other hardship to the respondent and
that it would in all the circumstances be wrong to dissolve the marriage, the
petition must be dismissed (MCA 1973, s.5(2)).
"Hardship" for the purposes of MCA 1973, s.5 includes the loss of the chance
of acquiring any benefit which the respondent might acquire if the marriage
were not dissolved (MCA 1973, s.5(3)), *e.g.* loss of widow's pension rights.
The hardship must result from the dissolution of the marriage and not
simply its breakdown (*Talbot v Talbot* (1971) 115 SJ 870).
"Conduct" in MCA 1973, s.5(2) does not have the restricted meaning used
in MCA 1973, s.25. It can include matters constituting the old concept of the
matrimonial offence, eg desertion (*Brickell v Brickell* [1973] 3 All E.R. 508).
It should be noted that there are two limbs to the defence. Even if grave
financial or other hardship is proved, the court still has a discretion under the
second limb of the defence as to whether or not it finds that it would in all the
circumstances be wrong to dissolve the marriage. An application in the alternative under MCA 1973, s.10(2) may be desirable (see below).
"Grave financial hardship" has usually involved the loss of pension rights
both under occupational pension schemes and state retirement benefit (*Mathias
v Mathias* [1972] 3 All E.R. 1; *Reiterbund v Reiterbund* [1975] 1 All E.R. 280; *cf.
Johnson v Johnson* (1982) 12 Fam Law 116; *Jackson v Jackson* [1993] 2 FLR 848;
Archer v Archer [1999] 1 FLR 327). The Respondent should identify the benefits lost and their value.
"Grave" also applies to "other hardship" and may consist of social
ostracism resulting from divorce (*Rukat v Rukat* [1975] 1 All E.R. 343; *Balraj
v Balraj* [1980] 11 Fam. Law 110).
The problems caused by contingent loss of pension rights are now less difficult to overcome. Since sections 25B and 25C MCA 1973 have come into
force, the powers of the court have been enhanced in cases where the petition
for divorce, nullity of marriage or judicial separation was filed on or after July
1, 1996. The courts are able by way of pension attachment orders to order the
benefits which a party with pension rights has or is likely to have under a
pension scheme, including any lump sum payable in respect of his or her

death, to be paid to the other party to the marriage. See paras 9.06 and 9.07 above.

9.39   Perhaps more importantly, the introduction of pension sharing (MCA 1973, s.24B) for petitions filed on or after December 1, 2000 enables Respondents to obtain pension benefits in their own names at the time of divorce, in appropriate cases (see para. 9.15).

In the absence of pension attachment or pension sharing remedies, an insurance-based solution may be found as an alternative to (further) capital provision from non-pension assets. The husband might take out a whole life policy sufficient to fund a deferred annuity for the former wife. This can be written in trust so that should the former wife remarry the proceeds pass, eg, to the children. A term policy may also be appropriate to cover loss of death in service benefits. A husband cannot be ordered to take out a life policy (*Milne v Milne*) (1981) 2 FLR 286). Where a conciliated solution cannot be found, a lump sum order or property adjustment order may be the course open to the court (see, also para. 9.11 et seq above).

See further *Pensions and Insurance on Family Breakdown* (Jordans) (ed Salter).

A respondent who wishes to oppose the granting of a decree under MCA 1973, s.5 should say so in the acknowledgement of service (Form M6) in the answer to question 7. The respondent must then file an answer specifically pleading the statutory defence. If the answer raises a prima facie case of grave financial hardship, the petitioner should file a reply putting forward financial proposals. The procedure is discussed in *Parker v Parker* [1972] 1 All E.R. 410 and *Le Marchant v Le Marchant* [1977] 3 All E.R. 610.

MCA 1973, s.10(2)-(4) Where a petition for divorce alleges two years' separation coupled with the respondent's consent to a decree being granted or five years' separation (MCA 1973, s.1(2)(*d*) or (*e*)) and a *decree has been granted* on the basis of these facts and the court has made no finding on any other fact mentioned in MCA 1973, s.1(2), the respondent may make an application for consideration of his or her financial position (MCA 1973, s.10(2)).

9.40   On the hearing of such an application, the court must consider all the circumstances, including the age, health, conduct, earning capacity, financial resources and financial obligations of each of the parties, and the financial position of the respondent as, having regard to the divorce, it is likely to be after the death of the petitioner should the petitioner die first (MCA 1973, s.10(3)). The notice of proceedings (Form M5) which is served on the respondent sets out in para.5 the consequences of a decree being made absolute, and in para.7 a respondent's rights under MCA 1973, s.10(2)-(4).

The court may not make the decree absolute unless it is satisfied:

> (*a*) that the petitioner should not be required to make any financial provision for the respondent; or

> (*b*) that the financial provision made by the petitioner for the respondent is reasonable and fair or the best that can be made in the circumstances (MCA 1973, s.10(3)).

If a decree is made absolute in contravention of the section, it is voidable, not void (*Wright v Wright* [1976] 1 All E.R. 796).

The court may make a decree absolute notwithstanding these requirements if:

> (*a*) it appears that there are circumstances making it desirable that the decree should be made absolute without delay; *and*

(*b*) the court has obtained a satisfactory undertaking from the petitioner that he will make such financial provision for the respondent as the court may approve (MCA 1973, s.10(4)).

To enable the court to decide whether an undertaking is satisfactory, the petitioner should outline his specific financial proposals supported by evidence of his financial position (*Grigson v Grigson* [1974] 1 All E.R. 478).

The procedure provided by MCA 1973, s.10(2) may be applied where there is breach of a pre-existing obligation, eg to pay child maintenance under a separation agreement (*Garcia v Garcia* [1992] 1 FLR 256). It would be negligent of a solicitor not to make an application under MCA 1973, s.10(2) to hold up the decree absolute in order to protect a wife from losing her right to a widow's pension until investigations had been made, unless he had received instructions to the contrary (*Griffiths v Dawson & Co* [1993] 2 FLR 315).

Applications for ancillary relief and applications under MCA 1973, s.10(2) **9.41** which were commenced by Form M11 or M 12 before June 5, 2000, are governed by the pre-June 5, 2000 procedure, as to which see the 19th edition of this work. For the purposes of this edition it is assumed that the proceedings are to be commenced after June 5, 2000. The new procedure is governed by FPR 1991, rr.2.51B — 2.70. The date of filing Form M11/M12 or Form A/B is the factor which determines whether the proceedings are pre or post-June 5, 2000, rather than the date of filing the petition.

If the respondent wishes to apply under this section, he should say so in the acknowledgement of service (Form M6) in answer to question 8. The notice of proceedings (Form M5) informs the respondent at para.8 that he must make application to the court by filing and serving on the petitioner a notice in Form B, which may be obtained from the court. Form B is reproduced in para.A4.03.

Rule 2.45 of FPR applies. The requirements are:

(*a*) Form B and a copy for service;

(*b*) fee of £80.

The court must serve a copy of Form B within four days of the filing of the notice (FPR, r.2.61A(4)(b)). The application will normally be made at the same time as the respondent's application for ancillary relief under MCA 1973, ss.23 and 24. The same considerations apply whether the application is made under MCA 1973, s.10(2) or ss.23 and 24 (*Lombardi v Lombardi* [1973] 3 All E.R. 625; *Robertson v Robertson* (1983) 4 FLR 387).

The procedure to be followed is the same as that which applies for ancillary relief (see paragraph 13 below). The considerations taken into account by the court are very similar to those in an application under s.25, MCA 1973. The respondent will usually make the s.10(2) application together with an application for ancillary relief under ss.23, 24, 25B and C, MCA 1973 and normally the applications will be heard together. Generally speaking, one Form E (statement of financial information: see paragraph 9.46) will be filed in support of both applications. Once the court has heard the applications it will make ancillary relief orders but will also be asked to make an order under section 10(3) approving the financial provision so that the petitioner can proceed to apply for decree absolute.

A statement that the court is satisfied under MCA 1973,s 10(3) or that the court has obtained a satisfactory undertaking or that the decree should be made absolute without delay (MCA 1973, s.10(4)) must be entered in the court records (FPR, r.2.45(6)).

Where a respondent, who has applied under the MCA 1973, s.10(2) for the court to consider his or her financial position, elects not to proceed with the application, a notice of withdrawal of the application signed by the respondent or his or her solicitor may be filed and served on the petitioner's solicitor without leave. A formal order dismissing or striking out the application is not necessary. Notice of withdrawal should be given to the petitioner or his or her solicitor (Registrar's Direction November 7, 1973 (1973) *Family Court Practice* (Jordans) (2002) p.2413).

14   Procedure

9.42   Applications for ancillary relief which were commenced by Form M11 before June 5, 2000, are governed by the pre-June 5, 2000 procedure, as to which see the 19th edition of this work. For the purposes of this edition it is assumed that the proceedings are to be commenced after June 5, 2000. The new procedure is governed by FPR 1991, rr.2.51B — 2.70. The date of filing Form M11 or Form A is the factor which determines whether the proceedings are pre or post-June 5, 2000, rather than the date of filing the petition.

Pre-Action Protocol

9.43   A pre-action Protocol applies to all applications for ancillary relief. This is based on the recommendations of Lord Wolf in his Access to Justice Report in July 1996 The object is to promote early settlement wherever possible and appropriate. Non-compliance with the Protocol may result in a costs penalty for the defaulting party. Making an application to court should not be regarded as a hostile step or last resort but rather as a way of starting the court timetable, controlling disclosure and endeavouring to avoid the costly final hearing and the preparation for it (paragraph 2.4, Protocol).

The Protocol contains guidance as to what should be contained in the first letter (paragraph 3.7, Protocol). Consideration should be given to the impact of any correspondence on the reader and in particular the parties. Irrelevant issues should be avoided, as should contents which could cause the reader to adopt an entrenched or hostile position. The client should approve the first letter in advance. Where the solicitor writes to an unrepresented party he should recommend that he seeks independent legal advice and enclose a second copy to be passed to any solicitor instructed. All correspondence should focus on the clarification of claims and protracted correspondence should be avoided (paragraph 3.6, Protocol).

It is crucial that there is full and frank disclosure of all material facts, documents and other relevant information (paragraph 3.4, Protocol). This must be explained to the client and the solicitor should emphasise that the duty to disclose is ongoing throughout the existence of the proceedings. If parties carry out voluntary disclosure before the issue of proceedings, they should provide the information and documents using Form E as a guide (paragraph 5.4, Protocol). Documents should only be disclosed to the extent required by Form E and disproportionate costs should not be incurred.

The Protocol also gives guidance on expert valuation evidence; see *Expert Evidence* at para. 9.56 below.

Application for ancillary relief

Application for the following ancillary reliefs should be made in the petition,   **9.44**
or in the answer where a respondent spouse files an answer seeking a decree:

(*a*) order for maintenance pending suit;

(*b*) financial provision order (periodical payments, secured periodical payments and lump sum orders in favour of a party to the marriage or a child of the family: see paras 9.04–9.10);

(*c*) property adjustment order (transfer of property, settlement of property and variation of settlement orders: see paras 9.11–9.14) (FPR, r.2.53(1)).

(*d*) pension sharing and pension attachment orders: see paras 9.15–9.16 and 9.06–9.07 respectively.

Care should be taken to ensure that the prayer is accurately worded. Although a notice asking for a transfer of property enables the court to order a lump sum (*Doherty v Doherty* [1975] 2 All E.R. 635; cf *Robin v Robin* (1983) 4 FLR 632), a petition asking for a periodical payments order does not entitle the court to make a lump sum order (*Wilson v Wilson* [1975] 3 All E.R. 464).

An omission of an application for ancillary relief which should have been made in a petition or answer may subsequently be remedied:

(1) if the main suit has been determined:

    (*a*) with leave of the court, either by notice in Form A or at the trial (FPR, r.2.53(2)(b));

    (*b*) where the parties are agreed upon the terms of the proposed order, without leave, by notice in Form A;

(2) prior to determination of the main suit, by an application to amend the petition or answer and by then pursuing the application by notice in Form A. Leave to amend may be refused if the respondent has been misled by the omission of a prayer, where there has been unjustifiable delay (*S v S* [1989] FCR 570) or if it would be unjust or oppressive to make an order against the respondent (*Powys v Powys* [1971] 1 All E.R. 116; *Marsden v Marsden* [1973] 2 All E.R. 851). The application for leave may be treated as the substantive application which will save time and expense (*Chaterjee v Chaterjee* [1976] 1 All E.R. 719). Leave will be refused if the court has no power to make the order sought (*Sandford v Sandford* [1986] 1 FLR 412). Reservice of the petition or answer will normally be ordered (*Practice Direction* 5 March 1957 [1957] 1 All E.R. 860).

Where a prayer for ancillary relief is made in a petition or answer, it is not usually dealt with at the trial (if any) of the cause, but is adjourned to be dealt with in chambers before the district judge. If there is an agreement between the parties as to the terms, the order may be made at the same time as the pronouncement of the decree by the district judge. The order for ancillary relief is a supplementary order, which is drawn up separately from the decree. Consent orders are discussed at paras 9.64–9.65 *et seq.*

An application for ancillary relief which is not required to be made in the petition or answer (such as when an answer is filed not seeking a decree or where no answer has been filed) must be made by notice in Form A (FPR, r.2.53(3)) (see p.183 for requirements). Leave is not required. An acknowledgement of service (Form M6), stating that a party wishes to apply for ancillary relief, can only be at most an expression of an intention or wish to apply for such relief, and does not amount to the formal initiation of the application itself as required by FPR, r.2.53(3) (*Jenkins v Hargood* [1918] 3 All E.R. 1001).

It is particularly important, where a remarriage is contemplated, to bear in mind the effect of MCA 1973, s.28(3) (see para.9.09). It is the prayer in a petition or answer and not the notice of intention to proceed, which constitutes the application for ancillary relief (*Jackson v Jackson*) [1973] 2 All E.R. 395). An application for a property adjustment order or a lump sum order made prior to remarriage may be heard after remarriage (*Jackson v Jackson*, supra). Remarriage may, however, affect the quantum of the lump sum awarded (*H v H* [1975] 1 All E.R. 367). If a wife has previously filed an application for ancillary relief for the children of the family but not for herself, the court has no jurisdiction to allow her to amend the application after her remarriage so as to include an application on her own behalf (*Nixon v Fox* [1978] 3 All E.R. 995).

Where a petition for divorce or nullity is issued on or after July 1, 1996 the prayer may include an application for a pension attachment order under MCA 1973, ss.25B — D. Where a petition for divorce or nullity is issued on or after December 1, 2000, the prayer may also include an application for pension sharing order pursuant to s.24B and 25B or 25C, MCA 1973. Where a petition was issued prior to December 1, 2000 and decree nisi has already been pronounced it may still be possible to make an application to the court for rescission of the decree nisi to enable a fresh petition to be issued. The effect of this would be to enable the parties to take advantage of the pension-sharing provisions. It can only be done by agreement and where there are no legal arguments to the contrary (*S v S (Rescission of Decree Nisi: Pension Sharing Provisions)* [2002] 1 FLR 457 and *H v H (Pension Sharing: Rescission of Decree Nisi)* [2002] 2 FLR 116).

9.45   In addition to the spouse, the following may apply for an order for ancillary relief in respect of a *child of the family* by notice in Form A:

(*a*) the parent or guardian of a child of the family;

(*b*) any person in whose favour a residence order has been made with respect to a child of the family, and any applicant for such an order;

(*c*) any other person who is entitled to apply for a residence order with respect to a child;

(*d*) a local authority, where an order has been made under CA 1989, s.30(1)(*a*) placing a child in its care;

(*e*) the Official Solicitor, if appointed the guardian ad litem of the child of the family under FPR, r.9.5;

(*f*) a child of the family who has been given leave to intervene in the cause for the purpose of applying for ancillary relief (*Downing v Downing* [1976] 3 All E.R. 474) (FPR, r.2.54(1)).

In the case of an application for a *variation of settlement order*, the court *must*, unless it is satisfied that the proposed variation does not adversely affect the rights or interests of any children concerned, direct that the children be separately represented on the application, either by a solicitor or by a solicitor and counsel. The Official Solicitor or other fit person may be appointed to be guardian ad litem of the children for the purpose of the application (FPR, r.2.57(1)). In the case of any other application for ancillary relief, the court *may* give a similar direction or make a similar appointment of a guardian ad litem (FPR, r.2.57(2)). Before a person other than the Official Solicitor is appointed guardian ad litem, there must be filed a certificate by the solicitor acting for the children that the person proposed as guardian has no interest in the matter adverse to that of the children and that he is a proper person to be guardian (FPR, r.2.57(3)).

The new procedure for ancillary relief

The overriding objective

The new procedure for ancillary relief is governed by the overriding objective in r.2.51B, FPR 1991 which is to enable the court to deal with cases "justly" by ensuring, so far as is practicable, that the parties are on an equal footing, that costs are not unreasonably incurred and that cases are dealt with in ways which are proportionate to the amount of money involved, the importance of the case, the complexity of the issues and the financial position of each party. The court is obliged to actively manage cases by encouraging the parties to co-operate with each other in the conduct of the proceedings; identifying the issues at an early point; regulating disclosure of documents and expert evidence; helping the parties to settle the whole or part of the case; fixing timetables and controlling the progress of the case; making use of technology and giving directions to ensure that the case proceeds quickly and efficiently.

9.46

Making the application for ancillary relief

Where a petition for divorce, nullity or judicial separation has been presented then proceedings for maintenance pending suit, a financial provision order, a property adjustment order or a pension sharing or pension attachment order may be begun at any time after the presentation of the petition (s.26, MCA 1973). Any application by the petitioner for these forms of relief should be made in the petition The application is then activated by filing Form A with the court (r.2.53, FPR 1991). It is usually advisable to make the fullest possible claim for ancillary relief at the outset as circumstances can change between the initiation of the proceedings and the hearing, it protects the client from falling into the re-marriage trap (paras 9.09 and 9.44) and it avoids the need to apply later to the court for permission to include an application for additional forms of relief that were omitted originally.

9.47

Where the respondent wishes to apply for ancillary relief he may do this either when he files an answer or, where no answer is filed (which will be the usual case), by filing Form A. See para.A4.02 for a copy of Form A. Rule 2.53, FPR 1991 applies to an application for ancillary relief by a respondent in exactly the same way as an application by a petitioner. It is not sufficient for a respondent to indicate in the acknowledgement of service (Form M6) that he intends to apply for ancillary relief (*Hargood v Jenkins* [1978] 3 All E.R. 1001).

Where no application for ancillary relief has been made in the petition or answer, it may be made at a later stage by leave of the court or without leave if the parties are agreed upon the terms (r.2.53(2), FPR 1991).

Form A – the notice of application for ancillary relief

The procedure where the application for ancillary relief is made comprehensively in the prayer or answer to the petition is set out in rules 2.61A – 2.61F, FPR 1991.

9.48

The notice of intention to proceed is made by filing Form A in the county court or registry of the High Court in which the petition was lodged (r.2.61A). Where there is an application for a property adjustment order relating to land, Form A should identify the land and state whether it is registered or unregistered. If it is registered, the Land Registry title number should be included, together with details of any mortgage of the land or an interest in it (r.2.59(2), FPR 1991).Where an application is made for a pension sharing or pension attachment order under ss.24B, 25B or 25C, MCA 1973, the terms of the order requested must be specified in Form A (r.2.61A(3), FPR 1991). Where the applicant is seeking periodical payments or secured periodical payments for children, Form A must state whether the application is for payments for a step-child, for "top up" maintenance over and above a CSA assessment, to meet expenses arising from a child's disability, to meet educational or training expenses for a child, to cover a situation where the CSA does not apply or for any other reason (eg to reflect a written agreement pursuant to the Child Maintenance (Written Agreement) Order 1993).

Other documents to be filed

9.49   The documents to be filed with the court are:

    (*a*) Form A, with a copy for service on the other party;

    (*b*) Where the party is publicly funded, a copy of the certificate for General Family Help and a notice of issue of the certificate;

    (*c*) Notice of acting, if the solicitor is not already on the court record;

    (*d*) A fee, currently £80.

Notice of First Appointment

9.50   When Form A has been filed with the court, the court must:

    (*a*) fix a first appointment not less than 12 weeks and not more than 16 weeks after the date of filing Form A and give notice of the date to the applicant;

    (*b*) serve a copy of Form A on the respondent within four days of the filing of Form A (r.2.61A(4)).

    (*c*) The Notice of First Appointment (see para.A4.04 for a copy of the Notice) also sets out the date (which will be at least 35 days before the first appointment) by which the parties must file with court and exchange with each other their respective financial statements in Form E (see Appendix 2, form 48). It also sets out the date by which each party is to file with the court their respective chronologies, statements of issues, any proposed request from the other party for further information and documentation and Form G (see below).

Form E – the financial statement

9.51   Both parties to the application must exchange with one another simultaneously a copy statement of their financial circumstances contained in Form E and file the original with the court on or before the date specified in the Notice of First Appointment (r.2.61B(1)). See para. A4.06 for a copy of Form E. The parties must attach to Form E the documents specified by the form, for example, payslips for the last three months and a form P60, bank statements for the last 12 months, a mortgage statement and any property valuation. The parties are not entitled to the disclosure of any further information prior to the first appointment. Form E must be signed by the person who has made the statement and sworn it to be true (r.2.61B(1)).

Service of Form A and Form E on other parties

Where an application is made for a variation of an ante-nuptial or post- **9.52**
nuptial settlement a copy of Form A and Form E must be served on the trustees of the settlement and the settlor if living (r.2.59(3), FPR 1991). If served the trustees and the settlor may file a statement in answer within 14 days of service or receipt as the case may be. Where the property in the proceedings is subject to a mortgage, a copy of Form A must be served on the mortgagee, who may apply to the court for a copy of Form E. The mortgagee may also file a statement in answer to the application within 14 days of being served with Form A, although it is rare for this to happen.

Where Form A includes an application for a pension sharing or a pension attachment order, the applicant must serve a copy of Form A on the trustees or managers of the scheme. As the provisions for such orders are complex they merit separate consideration: for the procedure regarding pension sharing applications see paras 9.61–9.68 below. For the procedure regarding pension attachment applications see paras 9.69–9.72 below.

In the case of an application for a *variation of settlement* order, copies of Forms A and E must be served on the trustees of the settlement and the settlor if living as well as the respondent (FPR, r.2.59(3)(*a*)).In the case of an application for an *avoidance of disposition* order, copies of Forms A and E must be served on the person in whose favour the disposition is alleged to have been made as well as on the respondent (FPR, r.2.59(3)(b)).

Where a form or other document filed with the court contains an allegation of adultery or of an improper association with a named person the court may direct that the party who filed the relevant form or document serve a copy of all or part of that form or document on the named person, together with Form F (see para.A4.07 for a copy of Form F) which sets out the statement and gives the third party the opportunity to apply for directions within a week of receiving the notice (FPR 1991, r.2.60(1)). If the court makes such a direction, the named person may file a sworn statement in answer to the allegations (FPR 1991, r.2.60(2)). The district judge has a general power to direct that other persons be served with a copy of Form A together with a copy of Form E (FPR, r.2.59(3)).

Preparing for the first appointment

At least 14 days before the first appointment (on or before the date specified **9.53**
in the Notice of First Appointment) each party must file with the court and serve on the other party (r.2.61B(7), FPR 1991):

  (*a*) a concise statement of the issues involved;

  (*b*) a chronology;

  (*c*) a questionnaire setting out any further information and documentation requested from the other party or a statement that no such information is required (r.2.61B(7), FPR 1991);

(*d*) a notice in Form G (Appendix 2, form 50) stating whether or not he will be in a position to use the first appointment as a Financial Dispute Resolution meeting and giving reasons if he is not able to do so.

Estimate of costs

9.54   At every court hearing or appointment, including the first appointment, each party should file with the court and with the other party an estimate of the costs incurred to date in Form H (see Appendix 2, form 51) (r.2.61F(1), FPR 1991). Where a party wishes to claim the costs of the hearing or appointment he must, at least 24 hours in advance of the hearing, file with the court and serve on the other parties a written statement of costs. Failure to do so may affect his entitlement to claim costs *MacDonald v Taree Holdings Ltd* (2000) *The Times*, December 28).

The court no longer has the power to reserve costs and must, at each appointment or hearing, deal with the question of costs. The court may:

(*a*) specify that there be no order as to costs; or

(*b*) determine that one party be responsible for the costs of the other, indicating the amount of the costs so awarded where a summary assessment of costs is possible.

The first appointment

9.55

The object of the first appointment is to define the issues between the parties and to save costs where possible. Both parties must attend unless the court orders otherwise (r.2.61D(5), FPR 1991). The district judge will have read the documents filed and has a number of duties to carry out at the first appointment, as follows:

(*a*) to determine the extent to which the requests for information and documentation contained in the parties' Questionnaires must be answered, giving directions as necessary, ordering the disclosure and inspection of documents or requiring further statements (r.2.62(4), FPR 1991);

(*b*) to order the attendance of any person for the purpose of being examined or cross-examined, see further under *Discovery and inspection*, at para.9.79 below;

(*c*) to order where necessary that any person attend an inspection appointment (formerly called a "production appointment") before the court and produce documents specified in the order (r.2.62(7), FPR 1991 and see *D v D (Production Appointment)* [1995] 2 FLR 497);

(*d*) to require a valuation of a pension scheme from the trustees or managers of the scheme where the application seeks a pension sharing or pension attachment order (r.2.61D(2)(f)). See para.9.83 below;

(*e*) to give directions about the valuation of assets, the obtaining and exchanging of expert evidence, if required (see under *Expert evidence*, at para.9.56 below);

(*f*) to give such other directions as are necessary for the efficient disposal of the case, for example the filing of further statements or schedules by the parties. See under *Further directions*, at para.9.82 below;

(*g*) to direct that the case be referred for a Financial Dispute Resolution appointment (FDR), unless this is inappropriate;

(*h*) if an FDR is inappropriate then the district judge must direct one of the following:

(*i*) that a further directions appointment be fixed;

(ii) that an appointment be fixed for the making of a further interim order

(iii) that a final hearing be fixed, giving directions as to the appropriate judicial level for the hearing;

(iv) that the case be adjourned for mediation, private negotiation or generally (although this would be exceptional).

(*i*) to make an interim order (see *Interim orders*, at para.9.57 below) where an application has been made within the proceedings, returnable at the first appointment;

(*j*) to treat the first appointment as an FDR, where the parties have indicated in their Form G that they are in a position to do this;

(*k*) to consider whether an order for costs is appropriate, bearing in mind all the circumstances and the extent to which each party has complied with the Rules, particularly the requirements for disclosure in Form E.

Practitioners should make a careful note of the directions made at the hearing and deal with the requirements of the order within the time-scale set down by the court; it is not uncommon for the court offices to delay in supplying the confirmation of the order, by which time the deadlines may be imminent. Replies to Questionnaires should not be filed at the court, but will form part of the bundle as necessary; see para.9.59 below.

Expert evidence

The Pre-Action Protocol contains important guidance as to the use of experts; **9.56** these should be followed even after proceedings have been issued (see the Law Society's Family Law Protocol – Protocols for Ancillary Relief, para.7.1).

Expert valuation evidence is only necessary where the parties cannot agree or do not know the value of some significant asset. Where possible, parties should jointly instruct a single expert in order to save costs. Where one party wishes to instruct an expert, he should give the other a list of names of one or more experts in the relevant speciality whom he considers suitable. Within 14 days the other party may indicate an objection to one or more of the named experts and if so should supply the names of one or more experts whom he considers suitable (para 3.8, Protocol).The parties should disclose whether they have already consulted that expert about the assets in issue (paragraphs 3.9 and 3.13, Protocol).

The parties should agree a joint letter of instruction. If the expert is commissioned prior to the issue of proceedings, it should be made clear that he should consider himself bound by the guidance as to expert witnesses in CPR 1998, Part 35 (see below). For specimen letter of instruction, see Appendix 2, form 64 below.

If, however, the parties are unable to agree as to the identity of a suitable expert, they should consider the costs implications of instructing their own expert. Where a party instructs his own expert, he should be encouraged to disclose the report to the other side so that areas of agreement and disagreement may be identified as soon as possible (paragraph 3.14, Protocol). If, however, the parties are unable to agree as to the identity of a suitable expert, they should consider the costs implications of instructing their own expert. If those implications are significant it may be better for the court to decide the issue in the context of ancillary relief proceedings (paragraph 3.10, Protocol).

From June 5, 2000, by virtue of FPR 1991, r2.61C, the rules governing the use of expert evidence in ancillary relief proceedings are to be found in Civil Procedure Rules 1998, rr35.1 to 35.14 (except for rr.35.5(2) and 35.8(4)(b) which relate to fast-track claims and payments into court). The important points are as follows:

(a) expert evidence may only be called with the permission of the court (r35.4, CPR 1998);

(b) parties should agree where possible on a single expert, to be instructed by them jointly (*President's Direction of May 25, 2000*, para.4.1); if the parties are unable to agree on an expert, the court has power under Part 35, CPR 1998, to direct that evidence be given by one expert only;

(c) the expert has a duty to help the court on the matters within his expertise, which overrides his duties to the person who instructs and/or pays him (r.35.3, CPR 1998);

(d) the expert's report, which will usually be in writing, must be addressed to the court (see r.35.5, CPR 1998 and paragraph 3.12, Protocol);

(e) where the expert has been instructed by one party, other parties may put written questions to the expert, however, they may only do this once and within 28 days of receiving service of the report (r.35.6, CPR 1998);

(f) the expert may seek directions from the court, without notice to the parties, at any stage (r.35.14, CPR 1998);

(g) the court may direct that the experts meet together, indicating the issues to be discussed and requiring them to prepare a statement to identify those issues on which they are agreed and those on which they are not, detailing their reasons for any disagreement (r.35.12, CPR 1998);

(h) the court may exercise its power to restrict the unnecessary use of experts, particularly bearing in mind the costs implications (r.35.1, CPR 1998);

(i) oral evidence may only be given with the permission of the court (see *Daniels v Walker* [2001] 1 WLR 1382, in particular the remarks of Woolf LJ)).

For guidance on the specific content of experts' reports, see *Practice Direction – Experts and Assessors* which supplements CPR Part 35(PD35). On the duties of an expert witness, see *The Ikarian Reefer* [1993] 2 Lloyd's Rep 69, and in particular the summary of Cresswell J at 81.

Interim orders

Once Form A has been filed, either party may at any stage of the proceedings **9.57** apply for maintenance pending suit, interim periodical payments or an interim variation order (r.2.69F(1), FPR 1991). Where a party wishes to apply for an interim order, he should file a notice of application at the court, and if this is done before a Form E has been filed the notice should be filed with a draft of the order requested and a short sworn statement explaining the reasons for the application and summarising his or her financial means (r.2.69F(4), FPR 1991).

The date fixed for the hearing must be not less than 14 days after the date of issue of the application (r.2.69F(2), FPR 1991). A copy of the notice of application must be served on the respondent forthwith (r.2.69F(3), FPR 1991). Not less than seven days before the hearing, the other party must file with the court and serve on the other party a short sworn statement of his means, unless he has already filed Form E (r.2.69F(5), FPR 1991).

Where the order is not expressed as continuing after decree absolute as an order for periodical payments, it is possible under FPR 1991, r.2.67 to request the court to provide for payments to continue at the same rate. Such an order, called a corresponding order, should be requested in writing by the recipient of the maintenance, whereupon the proper officer of the court shall serve the paying party under Form I requiring him if he objects to give notice to that effect to the court and the other party within 14 days. If no such objection is made, the district judge may make the corresponding order without the need for either party to attend court.

The Financial Dispute Resolution (FDR) appointment

The FDR appointment usually takes place when all of the evidence has been **9.58** exchanged, so that the court and the parties are in a position properly to identify the issues. At least seven days before the FDR appointment the applicant must file with the court details of all offers and proposals and responses to them (FPR 1991, r2.61E(3)). The purpose of the FDR is for discussion, negotiation and conciliation (FPR, r.2.61E(1)). It is conducted on a privileged basis so that none of the discussions can be disclosed at a later date (*Re D* [1993] Fam 231).

Legal representatives who attend are expected to have full knowledge of the case so that the best possible use can be made of the appointment (Protocol, paragraph 3.4). The parties must attend unless the court orders otherwise (FPR 1991, r.2.61E(9)). They are under a duty to use their best endeavours to reach agreement on the matters at issue between them (FPR 1991, r.2.61E(6)). The parties have the opportunity to put their fundamental positions to the district judge who may make such comments as he considers helpful to enable the parties to achieve a settlement. The district judge hearing the FDR is disqualified from further participation in the case if it proceeds to a full hearing at a later date, so that the privileged nature of the discussions is protected. Given this protection, the parties are expected to approach the appointment "openly and without reserve" and to make and give proper consideration to offers and proposals (Protocol, paragraphs 3.2, 3.3).

If the FDR produces a settlement the court can make a consent order accordingly. If it fails to produce a settlement, the district judge may direct a further FDR appointment or give further directions, for example for the filing of further evidence, such as the filing of statements as to contribution, and fixing a date for the final hearing (FPR 1991, r.2.61E(2),(7),(8)). In this event, all offers, proposals and responses to them must at the request of the party who filed them be returned to him and not retained on the court file (FPR 1991, r.2.61E(5)).

Preparing for the final hearing

9.59   Where the FDR has failed to produce a settlement the legal representatives will need to prepare for the final hearing.

In accordance with *Practice Direction (Family Proceedings: Court Bundles)* [2000] 1 FLR 536 the applicant or his legal representative should prepare the court bundles. The bundle should be agreed between the parties, if possible, and must be paginated and indexed. A copy of the index must be provided to all other parties before the hearing. The bundle must normally be lodged two clear days before the hearing.

The applicant should file with the court and serve on the respondent, not less than 14 days before the final hearing, an open statement setting out concise details, including the amounts involved, of the orders he proposes to ask the court to make (FPR 1991, r.2.69E(1)). Not more than 7 days after receiving service of the statement, the respondent must file with the court and serve on the applicant a similar statement in relation to the orders he seeks (FPR 1991, r.2.69E(2));

Both parties should prepare an estimate of the likely costs of the hearing and the divorce generally in respect of his client (*Practice Direction* [1988] 2 All E.R. 63; FPR 1991, r.2.61F(1)); these should be filed on or before the date directed by the court, or in any event 24 hours before the hearing.

Those representing the parties should also consider the following practical points:

(*a*) identify the issues to be resolved at a final hearing and ensure that the appropriate evidence has been gathered to establish any disputed factual matters; if possible a schedule of issues and chronology should be agreed and prepared for the court;

(*b*) prepare a concise schedule of the parties' respective financial information so that a convenient summary is to hand for the court;

(*c*) prepare a calculation of his client's tax position with copies for the other parties and the district judge, showing the impact of taxation on each party, in particular any capital gains tax implications;

(*d*) include in the court bundle information as to the likely level of any Child Support Agency calculation, where there are children of the family in relation to whom the CSA is likely to carry out an assessment to determine the level of maintenance to be paid by the absent parent, since it is likely to have an impact on the outcome of the ancillary relief application;

(*e*) check that any further directions given by the district judge at the conclusion of the unsuccessful FDR have been carried out in full, for example as to the filing of any further evidence;

(*f*) consider whether to send a further *Calderbank* letter containing proposals for settlement to the other side, in order to preserve the client's position in relation to the costs of the hearing (see under *Costs and offers of settlement*, at para.9.86 below);

(*g*) where accommodation for the parties is an issue, obtain details from estate agents as to the likely cost of such accommodation, letters from the housing authority giving details of waiting lists, indications from mortgagees as to their willingness or otherwise to arrange a mortgage for the party in question;

(*h*) continue to negotiate with the other side until the commencement of the final hearing, in an effort to save the substantial costs of a contested hearing.

The final hearing

The hearing will usually be before a district judge. The district judge has power **9.60** to transfer the application for hearing by a High Court judge where appropriate (FPR 1991, rr.2.65, 2.66). The hearing is conducted in chambers and in private. The usual format for the hearing is for the applicant to open the case and call his evidence, the respondent to call his evidence, the respondent to make submissions and then the applicant to make submissions. Finally, the district judge will give his judgment either immediately or reserve it to a future date to give him time for further consideration.

At the conclusion of the hearing there are a number of practical points that should not be overlooked:

(*a*) there is power to back-date periodical payments to the date when the application was made (*see para. 9.35*);

(*b*) an order for periodical payments may be registered in the family proceedings court, so that the order is paid and enforced through that court and any variation application is made to that court;

(*c*) seek an order for costs, where appropriate (*see para. 9.86*);

(*d*) seek a certificate from the district judge that the case is fit for counsel, where counsel has appeared on behalf of a party; if this is not done, the cost of instructing counsel will not be recoverable from the other party in the event that he is ordered to pay costs or from the Community Legal Service fund (where the client is publicly funded);

(*e*) request a direction for a detailed assessment of costs where a client is publicly funded, to enable costs to be recovered from the Community Legal Service fund;

(*f*) seek the inclusion of a provision for "liberty to apply" in the order, so that either party may seek guidance from the court as to the implementation and/or interpretation of the order in the event of future difficulties; this provision does not, however, enable the parties to seek variation of any substantive parts of the order.

Procedure on application for Pension Sharing Order

The procedural complexities following an application for a pension sharing **9.61** order justify separate consideration. However, it should be remembered that this procedure is within the overriding requirements of the ancillary relief procedure, as set out above. The main procedural requirements are set out in FPR, r.2.70; practitioners should note that FPR, rr.2.70(7)–(12) only apply to applications for pension attachment orders.

The Form A application should specify the terms of the order requested (FPR, r.2.61A (3)). If the details of the relevant pension are known, then those should be inserted into the Form A.

The Applicant shall send to the person responsible for each pension arrangement concerned a copy of the Form A, either upon giving notice to proceed with an application which includes a pension sharing order, or later upon adding a request for such a provision to a pre-existing application for ancillary relief (FPR, r.2.70(6)). If the details of the Respondent's pension arrangements are not available when the Form A is to be served, so preventing service of the pension arrangement, it is recommended that the Applicant's solicitor should write to the Respondent or his legal representative requesting such information, and putting them on notice as to costs, if as a consequence the First Appointment cannot also be dealt with as an FDR appointment.

Within seven days after receiving notification of the First Appointment, each party, if they have pension rights, must request the person responsible for each pension arrangement the information required under the Pensions on Divorce etc. (Provision of Information) Regulations, reg.2(2) and (3) (b) – (f) (FPR, r.2.70 (2)). This information includes the following:

(a) a valuation of the pension rights or benefits accrued;

(b) a statement summarizing the way in which the valuation is calculated;

(c) the pension benefits included in the valuation;

(d) whether an internal transfer will be offered to the potential transferee, and if so the types of benefits available to the pension credit member;

(e) whether the pension provider intends to discharge his liability for a pension credit other than by offering membership;

(f) a schedule of charges and how these are required to be paid.

The duty to apply for this information exists whether or not the application includes a claim for a pension sharing order. However, under FPR, r.2.70(4) the above request for information does not need to be made where the party concerned has, or has requested, a "relevant valuation" of the pension rights or benefits accrued under the pension arrangement in question. "Relevant valuation" means the valuation of pension rights or benefits as at a date "not more than twelve months earlier than the date fixed for the first appointment" (FPR, r.2.70(5)).

Because Form E requires additional information to be included, it is recommended that those further details should be included in the request for information at the same time. See Appendix 2, form 63; the draft letter sets out the information in full. These additional details will include the lump sums available on death, and whether Additional Voluntary Contributions (AVCs) have been paid. Because of the delay in getting replies from pension providers, see below, it is further recommended that practitioners may consider applying for this information at the earliest opportunity, perhaps in advance of the issue of proceedings.

9.62 The person responsible for the pension arrangement has to supply a valuation:

(a) within three months from receipt of the request or order to provide the information; or

(b) within six weeks of receiving the request or order for providing the information which is expressly in connection with ancillary relief; or

(c) within such shorter period as is specified by the court;

(d) other information (*i.e.* everything except the valuation evidence) shall be furnished within one month of the request for that information from the member, his spouse or the court (Pensions on Divorce etc. (Provision of Information) Regulations 2000, reg.2(5)).

The court in addition can demand any other information it considers relevant by virtue of Pensions on Divorce etc. (Provision of Information) Regulations 2000, reg.2(1)(c) and (4).

When the pension arrangement receives notification that a pension sharing order may be made it shall furnish the information set out in the Pensions on Divorce etc. (Provision of Information) Regulations 2000 reg.4(2) within twenty one days of receiving notification, or within such additional time-scale as the court orders. This information includes full details of the pension arrangement and, broadly, whether there are any factors which might prevent a Pension Sharing Order being made.

A pension provider may charge for supplying the information and for administering the pension sharing arrangement. These aspects are regulated by WRPA 1999, s.41 and The Pensions on Divorce etc (Charging) Regulations 2000 (SI 2000/1049). A Schedule of charges giving full details has to be given otherwise the pension provider will not be able to recover those charges.

Preparing Form E

As noted above, the Form E requires additional information about pensions **9.63** over and above that required under the procedure under FPR, r.2.70. This information has to be supplied by both parties if they have pension benefits, whether or not an application for a pension sharing order is made.

Section 2.16 of the Form E should also include information about SERPS and the State Second Pension (S2P), which was introduced on 6 April 2002 to replace SERPS. It is recommended that each party should make an application under BR20 to the Department for Work and Pensions to obtain the lump sum valuation of SERPS and S2P, which should then be included in the From E.

All other information about State pensions, including forecasts of future benefits can be obtained by making an application under form BR19. When acting for a wife, this form should be completed in the alternative, with a request that the recipient's calculation should also assume that a final decree of divorce will occur at a putative date in the future so that the full benefits available to a divorced wife can be calculated based on the husband's contributions during the marriage.

Any documents furnished to the party producing the Form E by a person responsible for a pension arrangement, either following a request under FPR, r.2.70(2) or as part of a relevant valuation as defined in FPR, r.2.70(4), should be attached to the Form E. The information supplied under the Pensions on Divorce etc. (Provision of Information) Regulations 2000, r.4(2) together with the response to any form BR19 or BR20 should also be attached to the Form E.

Drafting the Court Order

9.64 Where an order includes a pension sharing order, an annex should be attached in respect of each pension arrangement, under Form P1, setting out the information required under FPR, r.2.70(14) – see Appendix 2, form 61.

Drafting the Form P1 requires care, and attention should be given to the following points:

(*a*) the pension sharing order cannot be expressed as a particular figure, but only as a percentage of the CETV;

(*b*) the annex has to state the date of the valuation, being not earlier than one year before the date of the Petition and not later than the date on which the court is exercising its power – (The Divorce etc.) Pensions Regulations 2000, reg.3(1)(a)) – see *"Floating Target" syndrome* below at para.9.85 below;

(*c*) the annex should state how the pension sharing charges are to be apportioned, and in the absence of any such statement, they fall to be paid by the pension member/ transferor (WRPA, s.43(3)(b));

(*d*) the date of implementation has to be inserted in the annex (see *Implementation* para.9.67 below), and it is recommended that the following wording is used "upon the later of twenty one days from the date of this Order or decree nisi being made absolute" (thirty five days if in the High Court); such wording allows for the expiry of the period within which an appeal can be applied for.

For a form of pension sharing order, see Appendix 2, form 60.

Before an Order can be made, the court requires evidence that the information required under the Pensions on Divorce etc. (Revision of Information) Regulations 2000, reg.4 has been supplied and that it appears from the information that there is power to make an order under MCA, s.24(B). If this information has not been attached to the Form E, then it should be filed at the court by the applicant's solicitor.

Consent Orders

9.65 Under FPR r.2.61(1)(dd), the Statement of Information (Form M1) shall, where the order includes provision under MCA s.24B (pension sharing), include a statement confirming that the person responsible for the pension arrangement in question has been served with the documents set out below, and that no objection to such an order has been made by that person within 14 days from such service. The pension provider must have been served with the following documents:

(*a*) the (full) Notice of Consent Application for a Consent Order under FPR, r.2.61(1);

(*b*) a draft of the proposed Order under FPR r.2.61(1), together with the annex (Form P1);

(*c*) the address to which any notice which the person responsible for the pension is required to serve on the applicant under the Divorce etc. (Pensions) Regulations 2000 is to be sent;

(*d*) an address to which any payment which the person responsible is required to make to the applicant is to be sent; and

(*e*) where the address at (d) is that of a bank, a building society or the Department of National Savings, sufficient details to enable payment to be made into the account of the Applicant (FPR, r.2.70(11))

As noted above, the court must also have from the person responsible for the pension arrangement the information required by Pensions on Divorce, etc. (Provision of Information) Regulations 2000, reg.4. This should be attached to the Form M1. It is anticipated at the time of writing that the need to file this actual information may be removed by an amendment to Form M1 whereby the applicant's solicitor certifies that the regulation for information has been provided and that the court is empowered to make the pension sharing order.

After the court order

FPR 1991, rule 2.70(16) and (17) states that the court shall send to the pension arrangement, a copy of the decree nisi, a copy of the decree absolute, and a copy of the order (including the annex relevant for each pension arrangement) within seven days of the making of the relevant order, or seven days after the Decree Absolute, whichever is the later. It is recommended that the Applicant checks that service has taken place, or alternatively duplicates it at the appropriate point. The pension provider has also to be given the extensive list of information set out in the Pensions on Divorce etc (Provision of Information) Regulations 2000, reg.5, which includes the following: **9.66**

(*a*) in relation to the transferor, all names by which the Transferor has been known, date of birth, address, National Insurance Number, name of the pension arrangement to which the pension sharing order relates and the Transferor's membership or policy number;

(*b*) in relation to the transferee, all names by which the transferee has been known, date of birth, address, National Insurance Number, and he transferee is a member of the pension arrangement from which the pension credit is derived, the membership or policy number;

(*c*) where the transferee has given consent to the transfer to a qualifying scheme, the full name of that qualifying arrangements, its address, if known, the transferee's membership or policy number in that arrangement and the name or title, business address, business telephone number, and where available, the business facsimile number and e-mail address of the person who may be contacted in respect of the discharge of liability for the pension credit;

(*d*) where the rights from which the pension credit is derived are held in an occupational scheme which is being wound up, whether the transferee has given an indication whether he/she wishes to transfer his/her pension credit rights which may have been reduced in accordance with the provisions of regulations 16(1) of the Implementation and Discharge of Liability Regulations 2000;

(*e*) any information requested by the person responsible for the pension arrangements as to the member's state of health or generally in order to implement the pension sharing order.

Implementation of the order

9.67   Under WRPA 1999 s.34(1), the relevant pension arrangement has 4 months
within which to implement the order, from the receipt of the Decree Nisi, the
Decree Absolute, the court order, the Regulation 5 information above
(PoD(PoI)R 2000, reg.5) or from the date the order takes effect, if later. Failure
to implement the pension sharing order or to advise OPRA of this within the
prescribed time scales may result in a fine of up to £1,000 for an individual
trustee, and up to £10,000 for a corporate trustee (WRPA, s33(2)(b)).
   There are a number of factors that can delay implementation:

   (*a*) non payment of charges;

   (*b*) information not being supplied under PoD(PoI)R, reg.5;

   (*c*) orders and decrees not being served on pension arrangement;

   (*d*) decree Absolute not being applied for;

   (*e*) external arrangement not being chosen for pension credit;

   (*f*) postponement can be agreed by OPRA (WRPA, s33(4));

   (*g*) an appeal being made in relation to the order.

The pension arrangement, when asked to implement the order, must serve one
of two notices upon the parties.
   Under PoD(PoI)R, reg.7(1) the pension provider must either supply to both
transferor and transferee within 21 days of receiving the pension sharing
order:

   (*a*) a notice of what charges need to be paid before implementation can
        take place (Pensions on Divorce etc (Charging) Regulations 2000,
        reg.7(1);

   (*b*) a list of the information which has been requested, is needed and
        remains outstanding (e.g. PoD(PoI)R, regulation 5 information);

   (*c*) a statement as to why the PSO cannot be implemented.

Otherwise, if the order can be implemented, then in place of the above statement the pension provider must send to both transferor and transferee notice
of implementation within 21 days of the beginning of the implementation
period (WRPA, s.34(i)):

Notice of discharge
9.68   Under PoD(PoI)R 2000, regulation 8, the pension arrangement shall issue to
both transferor and transferee a notice of discharge within 21 days from completion of the pension credit. The information which the notice of discharge
shall contain differs, depending upon the party and the circumstances of the
party concerned.

Procedure on Application for Pension Attachment Order

9.69   The procedure for applications for pension attachment orders (formerly called
earmarking orders) is set out below for cases where the petition and the notice
of application were filed on or after December 1, 2000. Where an application

under Form A is made before 1 December 2000, see the nineteenth edition of this work and in particular the Family Proceedings (Amendment) Rules 2000 (SI 2000 no 2267), rule 2(1)-(3). As emphasised above in relation to pension sharing, this procedure does not stand separate to the main ancillary relief procedure set out above, but is dealt with as a separate part of such proceedings purely for the sake of clarity.

The Form A should specifically refer to ss.25B-D, and "the terms of the order requested must be specified in the notice in Form A" – FPR, rule 2.61A(3). Upon giving notice of intention to proceed with an application which includes pension attachment, or upon adding a request for such provision, the Applicant shall send to the pension arrangement: **9.70**

(a) a copy of Form A;

(b) an address to which any notice which the pension arrangement is required to serve on the Applicant under the Divorce, etc (Pensions) Regulations 2000 is to be sent (see regulation 4(4) regarding the transfer of pension rights);

(c) an address to which any payment which the pension arrangement is required to make to the Applicant is to be sent; and

(d) where the above address is that of a bank, a building society or the Department of National Savings, sufficient details to enable payment to be made into the account of the Applicant. (FPR, rule 2.70(7)).

When served with the Form A and other information, the pension arrangement may, within 21 days, require the Applicant to provide a copy of paragraph 2.16 of Form E. The Applicant has to supply the information either not less than 35 days before the date of the First Appointment, or 21 days after being required to do so — whichever is the later (FPR, rule 2.70(8) and 2.61B(2).) Having received a copy of paragraph 2.16 of Form E, the pension provider may within 21 days file a statement in answer – which has to be served on both the Applicant and the Respondent (FPR, rule 2.70(9)). If the pension provider files such a statement, then it shall be entitled to be represented at the First Appointment. The court, having received the statement in answer, has to give notice of the date of the First Appointment within 4 days (FPR, rule 2.70(10)).

The same rules as set out at paras 9.61–9.63 above, relating to the requirements to give disclosure regarding pension sharing, apply where an application is made for a pension attachment.

Consent Orders

Unless the pension provider has already been served with the information and documents under FPR, r2.70(7), FPR, the parties must, where the terms are agreed, serve the person responsible for the pension arrangement with: **9.71**

(a) a notice of application for a consent order;

(b) a draft of the consent order with the appropriate annex (Form P2; see Appendix 2, for 62) under rule 2.70(15);

(c) an address to which any notice which the pension arrangement is required to serve on the Applicant under the Divorce etc (Pensions) Regulations 2000 is to be sent;

(*d*) an address to which any payment which the pension arrangement is required to make to the Applicant is to be sent;

(*e*) where the address above is that of a bank, a building society or the Department of National Savings, sufficient details to enable payment to be made into the account of the Applicant (FPR, rule 2.70(11)).

A consent order can not be made unless the pension arrangement has had an opportunity to raise an objection within 21 days after service of a notice under FPR, rule 2.70(11), or the court has considered any such objection. In such circumstances, the court may make such direction as it sees fit for the person responsible for the pension to attend before it or to furnish written details of his objection (FPR 2.70(12)).

Preparing and Serving Court Orders

9.72   In the body of the order, whether by consent or not, the wording shall refer to the annex or annexes. The following wording may be used by way of precedent: "Provision is made in favour of the Applicant/Respondent by way of pension attachment in accordance with the annex(es) to this order". The information to be contained in the annex is set out in FPR, rule 2.70(15) relating specifically to pension attachment orders, see Form P2 in Appendix 2, form 62 below.

Under FPR, rule 2.70(16) the court is responsible, within 7 days of making the relevant order or within 7 days after the decree absolute if later, for serving the pension arrangement with the following documents:

(*a*) a copy of the Decree Nisi or Decree of Judicial Separation;

(*b*) a copy of the Decree Absolute;

(*c*) a copy of the order together with the relevant annex (Form P2).

After a pension attachment order, there is likely to be a long delay between the order and its being implemented. The practitioner should consider writing to the client emphasising the need to send details of any change of address, change of banking arrangements or remarriage (if the pension attachment order is against pension income under s.25B(4)), see in particular The Divorce etc (Pensions) Regulations 2000, regulation 6(2).

15   Consent Orders — Application for ancillary relief where terms are agreed

9.73   On an application for a consent order for financial relief the court may, unless it has reason to think that there are other circumstances into which it ought to inquire, make an order in the terms agreed on the basis only of the pre-scribed information furnished with the application (MCA 1973, s.33A(1)). Section 33A(1) applies to an application for a consent order varying or dis-charging an order for financial relief as it applies to an application for an order for financial relief (MCA 1973, s.33A(2)). See generally *Xydhias v Xydhias* [1999] 1 FLR 683.

"Prescribed information" means the information required by FPR, r.2.61(1). A statement of information must be lodged with every application for a consent order for financial relief or for a consent order varying or discharging an order for financial relief. The statement, which may be in more than one document, must include:

(a) the duration of the marriage and the age of each party and of any minor or dependent child of the family;

(b) an estimate in summary form of the approximate amount or value of the capital resources and net income of each party and of any minor child of the family;

(c) what arrangements are intended for the accommodation of each of the parties and of any minor child of the family;

(d) whether either party has remarried or has any present intention to marry or cohabit with another person;

(dd) where the order includes provision to be made under section 24B, 25B or 25C of the MCA 1973, a statement confirming that the person responsible for the pension arrangement in question has been served with the documents required by r.2.70(11) and that no objection to such an order has been made by that person within 14 days from such service;

(e) where the terms of the order provide for the transfer of property, a statement confirming that any mortgagee of that property has been served with notice of the application and that no objection to such a transfer has been made by the mortgagee within fourteen days from such service;

(f) any other especially significant matters (FPR, r.2.61(1)).

A specimen form of statement under FPR, r2.61 based upon the suggested **9.74** form scheduled to the *Practice Direction 5 January 1990* [1990] 1 FLR 234 is at Appendix 2, Form [ ]. The details of capital and net incomes should be stated as they are at the date of the statement (and not as they will be following implementation of the order). Additionally, the statement should give the net equity of any property concerned and the effect of its proposed distribution. Where the order includes a pension sharing or pension attachment order, see paras 9.71 and 9.65 respectively.

Where the application is for an interim periodical payments order pending the final determination of an application for ancillary relief or for a consent order varying an order for periodical payments, the statement of information need only deal with net income mentioned in (b) above omitting information about capital resources (FPR, r.2.61(2)). If the application is for an order for maintenance pending suit, a statement of information does not need to be lodged, as FPR, r.2.61 does not apply to the MCA 1973, s.22.

Where all or any of the parties attend the hearing of an application for financial relief, the court may dispense with the lodging of a statement of information in accordance with FPR, r.2.61(1) and give directions for the information which would otherwise be required to be given in such a statement to be given in such a manner as it sees fit (FPR, r.2.63(3)).

Although FPR, r.2.61 does not require the statement of information to be signed by either party, it may be appropriate for the form to be signed by or on behalf of both parties as a means of establishing the accuracy of the information given (para 5 of *Practice Direction* 17 February 1986 [1986] 1 All E.R. 704).

The following should be filed at the court:

9.75   (*a*) two copies of a draft of the order in the terms sought, one of which must be endorsed with a statement signed by the respondent to the application signifying his agreement;

(*b*) both parties' statements of information under FPR, r.2.61 (whether jointly in one document or in separate documents);

(*c*) a notice of application in Form A (unless already filed)on behalf of the respondent is required in many, but not all, courts including the Principal Registry;

(*d*) fee currently of £30.

Two copies of the proposed order are required so that the unsigned copy can be used by the court as the sealed order without the need for retyping. Although it is not a requirement for both parties to sign the draft minute of order, as a matter of good practice it may be sensible to require them to sign it, as well as their solicitors, to indicate that they understand the terms of the order and agree its terms. It is also important for the parties to sign the draft order if either or both have given undertakings, and where the order includes provision for child maintenance outside the CSA 1991, since CSA 1991, s.8(5) requires such an order to have arisen out of an agreement.

There is no formal requirement in FPR, r.2.61 that the statements of information (where contained in separate documents) be served on the other party. This is, however, required as part of the duty of full and frank disclosure.

The courses open to a district judge on considering consent applications are:

(*a*) to make an order in the terms agreed between the parties;

(*b*) to make further enquiry by listing the application for a short appointment or seek further information or clarification from the parties or their solicitors by letter;

(*c*) to reject the application in its entirety (MCA 1973, s.33A(1)).

9.76 The district judge should not make an order which varies or omits some of the terms agreed between the parties without their consent.

Where a respondent is acting in person, the district judge may require the respondent's signature to be identified. A direction may be given that the parties attend before the district judge to enable him to satisfy himself that they understand the effect of the order and consent to its terms, particularly when one or both parties are acting in person or where the order imposes a clean break.

A useful and comprehensive set of precedents for consent orders can be obtained through the Solicitors Family Law Association, PO Box 320, Orpington, Kent BR6 8QX or DX 86853 Locksbottom (Tel: 01689 850227). See also D Salter and S Bruce *Matrimonial Consent Orders and Agreements* (FT Law and Tax) 3rd Edition.

Great care should be taken when drafting consent orders to ensure that:

(*a*) the agreement reached between the parties is accurately reflected in the order;

(*b*) all claims intended to be disposed of are so disposed of in such a way as to leave no room for any future doubt or misunderstanding;

(*c*) the court has the power to make an order in the terms sought by the parties.

The primary duty in this regard lies with the practitioners concerned with the **9.77** negotiation and drafting of the terms of the order. Although it is also the duty of the court, when called upon to make a consent order, to consider for itself the jurisdiction which it is being called upon to exercise and to make clear what claims for ancillary relief are being disposed of, the primary duty lies with the practitioners. When that duty is breached by practitioners, they cannot be excused by the fact that the court may also have overlooked any inaccuracy or ambiguity in the order (*Dinch v Dinch* [1987] 1 All E.R. 818).

It should be indicated in the order under which of the various provisions of MCA 1973, ss.23 and 24 the order is being made (*Burton v Burton* [1986] 2 FLR 419).

Obligations which are not within the court's powers (eg to discharge a debt due to a third party or to take out a life insurance policy) should be incorporated by way of undertakings given to the court (*Livesey v Jenkins [1985]* 1 All E.R. 106).

When drafting an order for periodical payments in favour of a child which is to continue beyond the age of seventeen years, and the child is to continue full-time education beyond that age, it should be made clear that it is the later date, if the order is expressed in the alternative, which is the operative date on which the order will cease (*Practice Direction* July 10, 1987 [1987] 2 All E.R. 1084).

A common form of consent order, the clean break order, whereby one spouse relinquishes all claims which he or she may have against the other, was firmly established in *Minton v Minton* [1979] 1 All E.R. 79. A clean break order can be made without the parties' consent (MCA 1973, s.25A). The court has power to dismiss one party's claim for ancillary relief while making an order for ancillary relief in favour of the other party (*Thompson v Thompson* [1988] 2 FLR 170). For further discussion of the principles to be applied when considering whether a clean break is appropriate, see paras 9.27(10) and 9.20 (on variation).

Once the agreed terms have been incorporated into a consent order, they derive their legal effect from the court order rather than the underlying agreement of the parties (*Thwaite v Thwaite* [1981] 2 All E.R. 789; *Xydhias v Xydhias* above). A party may therefore apply to the court for a consent order for maintenance pending suit, periodical payments or secured periodical payments made by consent to be varied under MCA 1973, s.31 (*Gregory v Wainwright* (1984) 14 Fam Law 86). It is, however, important that a consent order should be marked "By consent" so that the order cannot be appealed on its merits as there has been no adjudication on the merits.

It is possible to challenge a consent order in exceptional circumstances. The **9.78** grounds upon which an order may be set aside include:

(*a*) failure by the parties to make *full and frank disclosure* which, if made, would have resulted in the court making a substantially different order (*Robinson v Robinson* [1982] 2 All E.R. 699; *Livesey v Jenkins* [1985] 1 All E.R. 106));

(b) if it can be shown that the parties' agreement was reached on the basis of a serious mistake by one of the parties, or as a result of fraud or serious misrepresentation (*Vicary v Vicary* [1992] 2 FLR 271,CA);

(c) if events subsequent to the making of the order destroy the fundamental basis on which the order was made (*Border v Caluori* [1987] 2 All E.R. 440; *Benson v Benson* [1996] 1 FLR 692).

Challenging such orders is by way of a rehearing, by an action to set aside or by way of appeal. If the order was made in a county court then the aggrieved party should apply for a re-hearing. If the order was made in the High Court then he could apply to set aside the order, but see *Benson v Benson* above. In most cases, the practical route is to apply under CCR 1981, Order 37 r.1 (*T v T (Consent Order: Procedure to Set Aside)* [1997] 1 FCR 282; *Middleton v Middleton* [1998] 2 FLR 821,CA). Under this provision the judge has power on an application made within 14 days (or later with permission) to order a rehearing where no error of the court at the hearing is alleged. The rehearing will be on the basis of a consideration of the documents only. In the High Court where the application would be to set aside the original order, there is no specific time limit for the application to be made, but two weeks would normally be regarded as appropriate.

The party who wishes to set aside an order (in relation to a High Court order) or apply for a rehearing (in relation to a county court order) is likely to have to appeal out of time. Four conditions are to be satisfied if such leave to appeal out of time is to be granted:

(1) New events have occurred since the making of the order which invalidate the basis upon which the order was made so that an appeal is certain or likely to succeed.

(2) The new events have occurred in a relatively short time after the making of the order.

(3) The application for leave to appeal out of time has been made reasonably promptly in the circumstances.

(4) The grant of leave will not prejudice third parties who have acquired, in good faith and for valuable consideration, interests in the property which is the subject of the order (*Barder v Barder (Caluori intervening)* [1988] 2 WLR 1350).

For examples as to how the courts have interpreted these conditions, see *Heard v Heard* [1995] 1 FLR 970; *Benson v Benson (deed)* [1996] 1 FLR 692; *Ritchie v Ritchie* [1996] 1 FLR 898; *Middleton v Middleton* [1998] 2 FLR 821); *P v P(Consent Order: Appeal Out of Time)* [2002]1 FLR 743. See Chapter 14 below on the law relating to appeals.

For a review of the procedural complexities see *Jackson's Matrimonial Finance and Taxation* seventh edition (Butterworths), especially Chapter 13, and D Salter and S Bruce, *Matrimonial Consent Orders and Agreements* above.

16 Discovery and inspection

Balancing the duty of care with the need to control costs

9.79 There is a duty on both parties to make full and frank disclosure of their respective financial circumstances both when an application has been made to the court for ancillary relief and where the parties are exchanging information with a view to making a consent order (*Livesey v Jenkins* [1985] 1 All E.R. 106).

The full and frank disclosure must include all the circumstances of the case, including the particular matters specified in MCA, s.25 (*Robinson v Robinson* [1982] 2 All E.R. 699). Where there is doubt as to whether disclosure of any particular matter is required, it is safer to resolve the doubt by disclosure rather than risk a consent order being set aside.

The duty exists at all times up to the making of the order and continues after initial disclosure has been made. It applies to both contested and consent proceedings and whether or not the parties are legally represented. It is not open to the parties to contract out of the requirement of full and frank disclosure.

A legal advisor who fails to obtain proper disclosure may risk a claim of negligence (for example *Dickinson v Jones Alexander & Co* [1993] 2 FLR 521; *Westbury v Sampson* [2001] 2 FCR 210). Under the Supreme Court Act 1981 (as amended by the Courts and Legal Services Act 1990, s4) the courts have power to make a wasted costs order against counsel or solicitor where such costs have been incurred by a party as a result of any improper, unreasonable or negligent act or omission (*Ridehalgh v Horsefield and Watson v Watson (Wasted Costs Orders)*[1994] 2 FLR 194,CA). The practitioner has a fine line to take between doing too little in pursuing questions of disclosure and being over-keen. At the same time the parties and their advisors must be aware of the need to keep costs proportionate; see *The overriding objective* at para.9.46 above.

Such difficulties can be placed before the court at the first appointment. The court has a duty to manage actively all cases (FPR, r.2.51B). The new procedure governing the way in which the court deals with issues of disclosure has already been outlined above under the section headed *The first appointment* at para.9.55 above.

Where the district judge considers that to answer any questions would entail considerable expense and that there is doubt whether the answer would provide any information of value, he may make the order for the question to be answered at the questioner's risk as to costs. The district judge may refuse to order an answer to a question if he considers that its value would be small in relation to the property or income of the party to whom the question is addressed (*Practice Direction 4* June 1981 [1981] 2 All E.R. 642). A party can request information which does not at the time exist in written form and, in appropriate cases, the court may order the production of a document corroborating that information (*G v G* [1992] 1 FLR 40).

If the court is satisfied that discovery is not necessary for disposing fairly of the matter or for saving costs, it must in any case refuse to make such an order (RCS Ord 24, r.8; CCR Ord 14, r.8). The standard for discovery is anything which is reasonably necessary for the purpose of performing the balancing exercise which is required to be performed under MCA 1973, s.25.

Family Businesses and Accountants' Reports

As to disclosure of documents of a company in which a party has an interest, see B v B [1979] 1 All E.R. 801 and *Nicholas v Nicholas* [1984] 5 FLR 285. Form E , see above, requires that two years' accounts shall be attached. If these reveal the existence of loan accounts or other hidden benefits then additional documentation may need to be requested in the Questionnaire. Similarly, if the company owns property, then further evidence of the proprietary interests **9.80** may be necessary to enable valuations to be carried out, *e.g.* details of leases and current rent payable.

Care should be taken when instructing accountants to ensure that the cost of the accountants' investigations is not out of proportion to the value of the business to be investigated or is a meaningless exercise because the business is the family's income-producing asset which will not in any event be sold (*Potter v Potter* [1988] 3 All E.R. 321; *B v B* [1988] 1 All E.R. 652; *P v P* [1989] 2 FLR 241; *Evans v Evans* [1990] 1 FLR 319). However given the change of approach by the courts to family companies and businesses following the case of *White v White* above, the need for such evidence may be more prevalent; see pp above and in particular *N v N (financial provision: sale of company)* [2001] 2 FLR 69. See especially para.9.56 above, *Expert Evidence.* The need to obtain valuation evidence may be may be more compelling in the following cases:

(*a*) where the value of the company is likely to be substantial relative to the other assets of the parties;

(*b*) where there is likely to be a sale of the business in the near future;

(*c*) where the business contains substantial assets which could be sold or used as security for borrowing, without damaging the viability of the core business;

(*d*) where the parties are approaching retirement age at which point a disposal of the business is anticipated;

(*e*) where there are other good reasons for the business to be sold either in whole or in part.

In many such cases, the report should focus not only upon the value of the company, but also upon the liquidity within the business, and the ability of the party to raise capital with which to pay a lump sum. The court will also require evidence about any capital gains tax payable upon the disposal of assets or shares, whose net values should be given.

Inspection appointments and search orders

9.81   Any party may apply to the court for an order that any person do attend an appointment, an "inspection appointment"(formerly a "production appointment"), before the court and produce any documents to be specified or described in the order, the production of which appears to the court to be necessary for disposing fairly of the application for ancillary relief or for saving costs (FPR, r.2.62(7)). Usually such applications are made against third parties, such as cohabitants or some person or institution (like a bank or accountancy firm) with whom the other party has a financial relationship. It is important to establish on a prima facie basis that the evidence is necessary.

No-one can be compelled by such an order to produce any document at an inspection appointment which he could not be compelled to produce at the hearing of the application for ancillary relief (FPR, r.2.62(8)). The court must permit any person attending an inspection appointment pursuant to an order made under FPR, r.2.62(7) to be represented (FPR, r.2.62(9)). The court has no power to require the person producing the document to give oral evidence at the inspection appointment. However, by so doing, the necessity for a subpoena or witness summons being taken out in relation to the substantive hearing may be avoided. The court must balance the interests of the parties to the suit with the interests of privacy of the third party (*Morgan v Morgan* [1977] 2 WLR 712).

In *Frary v Frary* [1993] 2 FLR 696, the Court of Appeal determined that the new FPR 1991, r.2.62(7) did not change the law but merely brought forward the time at which a witness might be required to attend the court. In this case, the respondent's cohabitee appealed successfully against a request that she attend court and produce a wide range of documents. However, it may be that the decision was influenced by the fact that the petitioner had no intention of calling the appellant to give evidence at the final hearing. For a broader inter-pretation of the procedure, see *D v D (Production Appointment)* [1995] 2 FLR 497, where there was "manifest evidence of an avoidance of the duty of full and frank disclosure".

The correct procedure for obtaining an order for an inspection appointment was confirmed in *B v B (Production Appointment: Procedure)* [1995] 1 FLR 913. The process involves two separate stages, the first being where the appli-cation is made to the court and the second being the inspection appointment itself. The application for the order should be made on notice to the other party, not on notice to the person who is being asked to produce the docu-ments. It is likely in practice that such applications will be made at the first appointment or perhaps at the end of an unsuccessful FDR appointment. The application should be supported by a sworn statement, except where there is a legitimate anxiety that notice might lead to the destruction or invasion of a document, when an ex parte application might be justified. The statement should set out:

(*a*) the nature of the proceedings;

(*b*) why the documents are needed;

(*c*) an exact description of the documents sought;

(*d*) whether the applicant intends to call the witness at the hearing.

In exceptional circumstances, a judge may grant a search order (formerly called an Anton Piller order) (*Emanuel v Emanuel* [1982] 2 All E.R. 342; *Kepa v Kepa* [1983] 4 FLR 515; *Burgess v Burgess* [1996] 2 FLR 34). This is an order permitting the applicant's representatives to enter the premises of the respon-dent to look for and inspect specified documents and to take them into the custody of the applicant's solicitors and to make copies thereof (Civil Procedure Act 1997, s7 and CPR 1998, Part 25.1).A party who obtains such an order which turns out to be unjustified may be ordered to pay the costs of the other party on an indemnity basis (*Araghchinchi v Araghchinchi* [1997] 2 FLR 142,CA). Such an application which by its nature is likely to be made without notice should where such a pre-emptive strike is fully justified to prevent a denial of justice.

As to the steps which a party can take in securing or photocopying the doc-uments belonging to the other party ("self-help"), see *T v T* [1994] 2 FLR 1083.

Further directions

The district judge may at any stage of the proceedings, whether before or during the hearing, order the attendance of any person for the purpose of being examined or cross-examined (FPR, r.2.62(4)). The same result can be achieved by the issue of a subpoena or witness summons (see para.6.30). The

9.82

court does not have power under FPR, r.2.62(4) to order a non-party to file a sworn statement (see further *Butterworths Family Law Service*, volume 4A, Chapter 4; *Wynne v Wynne* [1980] 3 All E.R. 659; *W v W* [1981] 1 WLR 69). However, if a party wishes to call a witness to give oral evidence, it is essential that the witness should have filed a sworn statement and done so well in advance of the final hearing(*Krywald v Krywald* [1988] 2 FLR 401). The district judge may also at any stage of the proceedings order the discovery and production of any document or require further sworn statements (FPR, r.2.62(4)). He may also at any stage of the proceedings give directions as to the filing and service of sworn statements (FPR, r.2.62(4A)).

There is power under the Bankers' Book Evidence Act 1879 as amended by the Banking Act 1979 to obtain copies of bank accounts but banks are not under a duty to produce paid cheques or paying-in slips (*Williams v Williams* [1987] 1 All E.R. 257). Of particular help to practitioners is the Data Protection Act 1998, s7 whereby data controllers (*i.e.* banks, building societies, charge or credit card companies) can be required in writing to produce statements for maximum fee, currently of £10.

17   Valuation of pension benefits

9.83   In any case where the court has fixed a First Appointment, whether or not an application has been made for a pension sharing order or a pension attachment order, either party if they have pension rights or benefits must within seven days after receiving notification of that appointment request the person responsible for each pension arrangement to supply a relevant valuation (FPR, r2.70)(2) and (4). See procedure on application for pension sharing order above at paras 9.61–9.63. Under FPR, Rule 270(5) a "relevant valuation" is defined as a valuation of pension rights or benefits as at a date not more than twelve months earlier than the date fixed for the First Appointment which has been furnished or requested for the purposes of any of the following provisions:

> (*a*) the Pensions on divorce etc (Provision of Information) Regulations 2000;
>
> (*b*) regulation 5 of and Schedule 2 to the Occupational Pension Schemes (Disclosure of Information) Regulations 1996 and regulation 11 of and Schedule 1 to the Occupation or Pension Schemes) transfer value regulations 1996;
>
> (*c*) pension schemes at 1993, s.93A or 94(1)(A) or (aa);
>
> (*d*) Pension Schemes Act 1993, s.94(1)(b) or para.2(a) of Schedule 2 to the personal pension schemes Disclosure of Information Regulations 1987.

Broadly, this is the Cash Equivalent Transfer Value (the CETV). This is the relevant methodology which is required by the court in every application involving pensions. For judicial comment upon this methodology for pension attachment orders, see *T v T (financial relief: pensions* [1998] 1FLR 1072. The CETV, however, does not include a valuation of all pension benefits; death in service benefits are excluded, and discretionary benefits may also be excluded. Importantly, the CETV does not take into account future expectations.

Instructing an Actuary

Although the CETV will be needed in each case (*e.g.* to be inserted in the Form   **9.84**
E and so that the order can be expressed as a percentage of it), in certain circumstances the petitioner may wish to instruct an actuary to supply a further
valuation of the pension benefits concerned. If there are doubts about the valuation, these could be raised at the First Appointment. In all cases, practitioners should be careful to ensure that the costs of re-valuing the pension
benefits are not disproportionate. In particular, a re-valuation may be helpful
in the following circumstances:

> (*a*) uniformed services — if the relevant party is a member of the armed
>   services or the police, etc, it is likely that he or she will be entitled to
>   retire at an earlier age than exists under most occupational schemes,
>   and therefore the benefits may be worth more than would be given
>   under the standard CETV calculation supplied in such cases;
>
> (*b*) if the scheme is over funded or under funded;
>
> (*c*) where the CETV excludes marital status in calculating the CETV (*e.g.*
>   the NHS pension scheme);
>
> (*d*) where the member is in poor health (which may mean that the CETV
>   is over valued).

Where the benefits concerned relate to a private pension policy or Retirement
Annuity Contract it may be more cost effective to direct any enquiries about
valuation to an independent financial advisor. In any case, as noted above, the
parties will need advice from an independent financial advisor as to the
amount of any future benefits, and as to retirement planning generally.

"Floating Target" syndrome

When negotiating the terms of a pension sharing order, or at the time a court   **9.85**
makes such an order, the CETV figure may already be several months old. The
valuation to be inserted in the Form P1 (for a pension sharing order) or Form
P2 (for a pension attachment order) is that defined in The Divorce etc
(Regulations 2000, reg.3: this is the valuation referred to in the court order
which shall be "not earlier than one year before the date of the petition and
not later than the date on which the court is exercising its power".

   However, when the pension provider implements the pension sharing order,
it deals with the pension debit and pension credit on the "valuation day",
which is defined by WRPA, section 29 (7) as being "such day within the implementation period . . . as the person responsible for the relevant arrangement
may specify by notice in writing to the transferor and transferee". This therefore is a separate and later date for implementation purposes which will necessarily be different to the earlier valuation in the order.

   Practitioners, and their clients, should be aware that this difference in valuation dates between that which was used in negotiations or appears in the court
order on the one hand, and that which is used for implementation on the other
hand, may give different results to that which had been anticipated. For
example, in some occupational schemes, the valuation at implementation may
be higher, so giving the transferee benefits which are more valuable. Conversely,
in a money purchase scheme the value on the investments may have

depreciated, so that the transferee would have less valuable benefits. See in particular the article *The Pitfalls of Pension Sharing – Part One, David Salter* [2002] Fam Law 598–603. For a comprehensive guide to this complex area, see *Pensions and Insurance on Matrimonial Breakdown ed D Salter* (Jordans), 3rd Ed.

18   Costs and offers of settlement

9.86   Costs in civil proceedings are now governed by Part 44, Civil Procedure Rules 1998, the majority of which applies to family proceedings pursuant to the Family Proceedings (Miscellaneous Amendments) Rules 1999.

Once the district judge has announced his decision in ancillary relief proceedings he must then consider the question of costs. The court has a discretion to decide (CPR 1998, r.44.3):

(*a*) whether costs are payable by one party to another;

(*b*) the amount of those costs;

(*c*) when they are to be paid.

The general principle in r.44.3(2) that the unsuccessful party will be ordered to pay the costs of the successful party is disallowed in family proceedings. This is because it is often impossible in ancillary relief proceedings to say who has won and who has lost, there are restrictions on making costs orders against publicly funded litigants and in any event the district judge may well have taken into account the question of costs in making his substantive order. Nevertheless, the starting point should be that costs follow the event (*Gojkovic v Gojkovic (no 2)* [1991] 2 FLR 233). It is quite usual for the judge to say that "there be no order as to costs", the effect of which is that each party pays their own costs. On the other hand, if it can be shown that one party made a reasonable offer of settlement from the outset and the other party has been resisting an appropriate settlement the court may well be persuaded to make an order for costs against him. The factors which the court must take into account when exercising its discretion are set out in CPR 1998, r.44.3(5). These include all the circumstances of the case and the conduct of the parties both before and during the proceedings. In particular, the court will consider the extent to which the parties complied with the Pre-Action Protocol (see para.9.43) and were prepared to engage in the Financial Dispute Resolution process (see para.9.48) or mediation (see para.9.89).

Where a party wishes to make an offer in settlement of an ancillary relief claim he may do so in various ways, for example:

(*a*) by sending an open letter to the other side incorporating the offer, on the basis that it can be referred to at the hearing both in relation to the question of costs and to the substantive order;

(*b*) by including his offer in Form E or his open proposal, so that it can be referred to throughout the hearing;

(*c*) by way of a *Calderbank* offer, in writing and expressed to be without prejudice but which reserves the right to refer to the terms of the offer at the hearing in relation to the issue of costs only (*Calderbank v Calderbank* [1975] 3 All E.R. 333).

Since it is not possible in ancillary relief proceedings for a party to make a **9.87** payment into court, the *Calderbank* procedure referred to in (c) above was developed instead.

The Family Proceedings (Amendment No 2) Rules 1999 set out the various restrictions which apply to such offers. Either party to the application may make a written offer to the other at any time which is expressed to be "without prejudice except as to costs" and which relates to any issue in the proceedings relating to the application (r.2.69(1)). The fact that such an offer has been made must not be drawn to the attention of the court, except for the purposes of the FDR appointment, until the question of costs falls to be decided (r.2.69(2)). If one party rejects the offer and in the event is awarded no more than the *Calderbank* offer, it is then open to the other party to produce the letter containing the offer and ask for costs. However, the offer cannot affect the position on costs until a period of 28 days has elapsed. This gives the other party a proper opportunity to consider the offer and respond to it.

If the court makes an order which is more advantageous to one party than the offer made by the other party, the court must, unless it considers it unjust to do so, order that other party to pay any costs incurred after the date beginning 28 days after the offer was made (r.2.69B (1) and (2)).

Where both parties have made offers under r.2.69(1) but the judgment in favour of the successful party is more advantageous than either of the offers, the court may, where it considers it just, order interest on the whole or part of any sum of money to be awarded to the successful party (r.2.69C(2)).

In deciding whether it would be unjust or not to make the orders referred to in r.2.69B and r.2.69C, the court must take into account all the circumstances of the case, including (r.2.69D):

(*a*) the terms of any r.2.69(1) offers;

(*b*) the stage in the proceedings at which any offer was made;

(*c*) the information available to the parties at the time when the offer was made;

(*d*) the conduct of the parties in relation to giving or refusing to give information for the purpose of enabling the offer to be made or evaluated; and

(*e*) the respective means of the parties.

In exercising its discretion as to liability for costs, the court may consider pre-application offers to settle and the conduct of disclosure (Pre-Action Protocol, para.3.3). It will be recalled that at every court hearing or appointment, including the first appointment, each party should file with the court and with the other party an estimate of the costs incurred to date in Form H (r.2.61F(1), FPR 1991; see further under *Estimate of costs*, at para.9.54 above). For orders for costs against parties who are publicly funded, see Chapter 17 at para.17.32 below.

19 Transfer of application for ancillary relief to another registry or divorce county court

Rule 10.10 of FPR applies to the transfer of an *application* to another registry **9.88** or divorce county court.

Where an application for ancillary relief is pending in the High Court, the district judge of the registry in which the application is proceeding or a judge may order that the application be transferred *to another registry*. Before making such an order the court must consider whether it would be more convenient to transfer the cause under FPR, r.10.10(1) (FPR, r.10.10(3)).

Where an application for ancillary relief is pending in a divorce county court, the court may order that the application be transferred to *another divorce county court*. Before making such an order the court must consider whether it would be more convenient to transfer the cause under FPR, r.10.10(2) (FPR, r.10.10(3)).

When the court is considering an order for transfer of the application under FPR, r.10.10(1), (2) or (3) it must not, either of its own motion or on the application of any party, make an order for transfer unless the parties have either had an opportunity of being heard on the question or consented to such an order (FPR, r.10.10(4)). When any one or more of the parties desires to be heard on the question of a transfer, the court must give the parties notice of a date, time and place at which the question will be considered (FPR, r.10.10(5)).

The criteria for determining whether an application for ancillary relief should be dealt with in the High Court or a county court are set out in *Practice Direction* June 5, 1992 [1992] 2 FLR 87 and discussed at para.2.52.

Rule 10.10(4) and (5) of FPR apply with the necessary modifications to an order for the transfer of family proceedings under MFPA 1984, ss.38 or 39 (see pp.80–81) as they apply to an order under FPR, r.10.10(1) or (2) (FPR, r.10.10(6)).

Rule 10.10(4) and (5) of FPR do not apply where the court makes an order for transfer under FPR, r.10.10(1), (2) or (3) in compliance with the provisions of any order made under CA 1989, Sch 11, Pt I (FPR, r.10.10(7)).

20 Mediation

9.89 Mediation is a form of alternative dispute resolution. It is now widely available to deal with all issues relating to divorce, including disputes over property, finance and children. It can help divorcing or separating couples to make their own arrangements for the future and to move forward. It can help to reduce the need for court proceedings and the consequential legal costs.

The UK College of Family Mediators was set up in 1996 by the Family Mediators Association, National Family Mediation and Family Mediation Scotland. It is the professional body for all family mediators in England, Scotland, Wales and Northern Ireland. It provides training and accreditation standards for family mediators and makes available details of registered UK College mediators. It is based at 24–32 Stephenson Way, London NW1 2HX. Publicly funded mediation is available for those who are eligible.

There are many court-based mediation schemes available in a number of areas and judges and district judges are encouraged, before ordering a court welfare report in child-related disputes, to be prepared to consider referring the matter to any local mediation service (see *Practice Direction* July 28, 1986 [1986] 2 FLR 171). The new ancillary relief procedure which is described above provides for a financial dispute resolution appointment (see para.9.89), in the course of which the district judge plays a mediation-type role in assisting the parties to reach an agreed settlement wherever possible and appropriate, thus avoiding the need for a contested hearing. In addition, there is a scheme run by the Family Law Bar Association (FLBA) which enables solicitors to submit agreed facts to a member of the FLBA for an opinion as to the likely outcome of a case if it were to be contested.

21   The New Child Support Regime

Child Support, Pensions and Social Security Act 2000 ("CSA 2000")

1.   Change in terminology

The CSA 2000 introduces new terminology. For example, the term "absent parent" in CSA 1991 is replaced by "non-resident parent"("NRP") (CSA 2000, Sch.3 para.11 (2) came into force on 31 January 2001 (The Child Support, Pensions and Social Security Act 2000 (Commencement No.5) Order 2000 (SI No 3354))), the term "assessment" is replaced by "maintenance calculation" (CSA 2000 Sch.1), "departure directions" are replaced by "application for variation" (CSA 2000, s.5 (2)).   **9.90**

The meaning of "child" for the purposes of CSA 1991 is defined in CSA 1991, s.3(1) and s.55 (1) and in the Child Support (Maintenance Calculation Procedure) Regulations 2000, Sch.1.

2.   The residual role of the court

The effect of a court order on the ability of the CSA to make a maintenance calculation   **9.91**

Section 2 of the CSA 2000 has amended CSA 1991, s.4 so that no application may be made for a child support maintenance calculation where:

(i)   there is in force a written maintenance agreement made before April 5, 1993, or a maintenance order made before a prescribed date, in respect of that child or those children and the NRP; or

(ii)   a maintenance order made on or after the date prescribed for the purposes of paragraph (i) is in force in respect of them, but has been so for less than the period of one year beginning with the date on which it was made.

Therefore, from the implementation of CSA 2000 child maintenance can still be agreed between the NRP and the parent with care ("PWC") and incorporated into a consent order. However, the court will only have exclusive jurisdiction for 1 year (plus the two months notification of the intention to apply for a calculation that has to been given to the other party). Thereafter either parent can invoke the jurisdiction of the CSA. The order ceases to have effect two days after a CSA assessment is made until the end of CSA jurisdiction (Child Support (Maintenance Assessment and Jurisdiction Regulations) S.I. No.1992, reg. 3(5)).

Parents with maintenance orders in force at the time when the new rules come into force, and those with written maintenance agreements made on or before April 5, 1993 will, as now, use the courts for enforcement and variation of child maintenance liability.

Note, however, that the CSA could still gain jurisdiction even in relation to "pre-prescribed date orders" if one of the parents claims benefits (CSA 1991, s.6 (1)).

3.   Calculation of child support maintenance (CSA 2000)

9.92   Maintenance payable under CSA 1991 as amended is calculated in accordance with rates set out in Child Support (Maintenance Calculations & Special Cases) Regulations 2000 (S.I. 2001 No. 155) ("MCSC Regs 2000"). When it comes into force it will replace the existing formula with a simpler system of rates and will clarify the responsibilities of parents.

4.   The Maintenance Calculation (MCSC Regs 2000)

9.93   (1) Net income
For the purposes of the calculation the net income of the PWC is not taken into account. The net income of the NRP is defined according to whether the NRP is an employed or self employed earner by virtue of the Schedule to MCSC Regs 2000.

(*a*) Employed earners
For employed earners net income means gross pay including bonuses, commission and overtime less income tax, Class 1 National Insurance contributions and full pension contributions (although in the case of pension mortgages only 75% of the payment can be deducted from net income).

(*b*) Self employed earners
For self employed earners net income means taxable profits as submitted to the Inland Revenue or gross receipts less income tax, Class 1 National Insurance contributions and full pension contributions (although in the case of pension mortgages only 75 per cent of the payment can be deducted from net income).

(*c*) Other income
Pension payments are included as income for the purposes of calculating net income (MCSC Regs, Sch.Part V para.15).

Working Families Tax Credit (WFTC) is included as income for the purposes of calculating net income (MCSC Regs, Sch.Part IV para.11). Where WFTC is payable and the NRP and their new partner are earning exactly the same, only half of the WFTC will be included as income for these purposes. In cases where the NRP's new partner is the principal earner, WFTC is not included as net income.

Income that is not included as net income is investment income, dividend income and benefits in kind although variation provisions may apply (see paragraph 5 below).

(*d*) Net income cap
The NRP's net income is capped at £2,000 per week net income (CSA 2000, Sch.1, para.10(3)). This means that the maximum child maintenance payable for three children is £26,000 per annum. However, this is not an absolute ceiling because the court has jurisdiction to make "top-up" orders (CSA 1991, s.8(6) as amended by CSA 2000, Sch.3 para.11(5)) in suitable cases, school fees orders and the CSA can make a variation in certain circumstances (see paragraph 5 below).

(2) Rates
The calculation is based on one of four rates: basic rate, reduced rate, **9.94** flat rate or nil rate.

(*a*) Basic Rate (CSA 2000, Sch.1 para.2)
The general rule is that the basic rate is paid by the NRP unless one of the other rates applies. The calculation is based on a percentage of the NRP's net weekly income and will depend on whether the NRP is liable to pay for one, two, three or more children. Where the NRP is liable for maintenance for one child, the basic rate is 15 per cent, for two children, the basic rate is 20 per cent and for three or more children, the basic rate is 25 per cent.

If the NRP is also responsible for other children living in his household (referred to as "relevant other children") *e.g.* step-children his net income is reduced by 15 per cent if there is one relevant other child, 20 per cent if two relevant other children and 25 per cent if three relevant other children before the basic rate percentages are applied.

(*b*) Reduced rate (CSA 2000, Sch.1 para.3, MCSC Regs 2000, reg. 3)
The reduced rate (£5 plus a percentage of income falling in £100–£200 bracket) applies where the NRP's weekly income is more than £100 but less than £200.

(*c*) Flat rate (CSA 2000, Sch.1 para.4, MCSC Regs 2000, reg.4)
The flat rate of £5 per week is payable when the NRP's net weekly income is £100 or less, or the NRP receives a prescribed benefit including income support, jobseeker's allowance, incapacity benefit or retirement pension or the NRP's partner receives income support or jobseeker's allowance.

(*d*) Nil rate (CSA 2000, Sch.1 paragraph 5, MCSC Regs 2000, reg.5)
Certain categories of NRP will have a nil rate liability eg. full-time students, children under 16 years, Income Support claimants aged 16 or 17 years, those hospitalised for more than a year and prisoners.

(3) Apportionment (CSA 2000, Sch.1 para.6 and MCSC Regs 2000, reg.6)
If the NRP has more than one qualifying child and in relation to them there is more than one PWC, then the maintenance liability will be apportioned between the carers. The NRP's liability is divided by

the number of qualifying children and then shared between the carers in proportion to the number of qualifying children in each family. For example, if H was married and divorced twice and has two children by W1 and one child by W2 (W1 and W2 having care of the respective children) the rate will be apportioned between W1 and W2 so that W1 gets two-thirds of the rate and W2 gets one-third.

There may be difficulties if the PWC's are not all within the CSA system. This is because the CSA maintenance calculation can only be shared between those qualifying children which are the subject of CSA maintenance calculations.

(4) Shared care and its effect on the payment (CSA 2000, Sch.1 para.7, MCSC Regs 2000, reg. 7–9)

NRP's who have children to stay overnight can have the level of maintenance reduced if they look after the qualifying child for at least one night per week. The amount payable will reduce proportionately to the number of overnight stays as follows:

Number of nights	Fraction to subtract
52–103	1/7
104–155	2/7
156–174	3/7
175 or more	1/2

If the qualifying children stay for varying lengths of time, the applicable decrease is the sum of the appropriate fractions divided by the number of qualifying children *e.g.* where the NRP has contact with two children, one for an average of one night per week and the other for an average of 2 nights per week, his liability will be reduced by 3/14 (1/7 + 2/7) × 0.5 = 3/14 (CSA 2000, Sch.1 para.7 (5)).

If the fraction is one half in relation to any qualifying child then the total payable to the PWC is to be further reduced by £7 per week for each such child (CSA 2000, Sch.1 para.7 (6)).

Where a child is a boarder at a boarding school, or in hospital, the person who, but for those circumstances, would otherwise have care of the child overnight shall be treated as providing that care during the relevant periods (MCSC Regs 2000, reg. 7 (6)).

The maintenance will never be reduced below £5 per week, except where the flat rate applies ((CSA 2000, Sch.1 para.7 (7)). If the flat rate does apply, the NRP who has at least 52 nights staying contact during a prescribed 12 month period may have his liability reduced to nil (CSA 2000, Schedule 1 para.7 (8)).

9.95   **5.   Application for a Variation**
(CSA 1991, s.28A to 28G (amended or replaced by CSA 2000, s.5 to 7), CSA 1991, Sch.4A and 4B (replaced by CSA 2000, s.6 and CSA 2000, Sch.2), Child Support (Variations) Regulations 2000 (S.I. 2001 No. 156))

Variations can only be made in a limited number of clearly defined and exceptional circumstances. An application for a variation can be made at the same time as the application for a maintenance calculation. A NRP can apply for a variation from the usual rules for calculating maintenance when "special expenses" are incurred. A PWC can apply for a variation in some circumstances ("additional cases").

(1) A NRP can apply for a variation where he has the following special expenses:

    (a) costs incurred by the NRP or child in maintaining contact with the child to whom the application for the maintenance calculation has been made, including travel costs and accommodation costs of essential overnight stays;

    (b) costs attributable to a long term illness or disability of a relevant other child;

    (c) repayment of some debts incurred at a time when both parents were living together (credit cards and business debts are specifically excluded);

    (d) maintenance element of ongoing boarding school fees for the qualifying child (ie. tuition costs do not count);

    (e) mortgage payments by the NRP on the home he and the PWC shared, if he no longer has an interest in it and the PWC and qualifying child still live there;

    (f) property and capital transfers made before April 5, 1993.

(2) A PWC can apply for a variation in the following cases (known as "additional cases"):

    (a) the NRP has "assets" (means money, land, shares and choses in action but excludes business and home) together worth over £65,000;

    (b) a person's lifestyle is inconsistent with his income for the purposes of the calculation;

    (c) a person has income which is not taken into account in such a calculation, for example, dividends and investment income;

    (d) a person has unreasonably reduced the income which is taken into account in such a calculation.

(3) Special expenses will only be considered if they exceed a certain threshold level (Child Support (Variations) Regulations (SI 2001 No. 156), reg. 15(1)). The threshold is £15 a week for NRP's with net income of £200 a week or more and £10 a week for NRP's with net earnings below that level.

(4) Applicants must show that making a variation would be just and equitable. Factors that will not be taken into account in assessing "just and equitable" circumstances (Child Support (Variations) Regulations (SI 2001 No. 156), reg. 21(2)) are the fact that the conception of the child concerned in the calculation was unplanned, apportionment of responsibility for the breakdown of the relationship and any new relationship of either of the parents. The outcome of variation applications is hard to predict (see article "Child Support Update, Part 1" [2002] Fam Law 195).

6.   Child maintenance premiums

Applicants on income support (or income-based jobseeker's allowance) can **9.96** keep up to £10 per week of any child maintenance paid. If child maintenance is less than £10 a week the premium will equal the amount of maintenance received. The premium will only apply where a case has actually been assessed under the formula in CSA 2000. (See Explanatory Note to CSA 2000, s.23, The Social Security (Child Maintenance Premium and Miscellaneous Amendments) Regulations (S.I. 2000 No. 3176)).

7. Transitional provisions

9.97 The new formula provided for by CSA 2000 will only be applied to existing cases when the system is operating properly. This is unlikely to be before April 2003.

> (1) Old child maintenance scheme to new child maintenance scheme
>
>> Under the CSA 2000 rules child maintenance may be higher or lower than in the existing scheme. The new rules will be phased in by fixed annual steps.
>>
>> There will be three phasing bands when converting a case from the old scheme to the new scheme. For example, the child maintenance payable by a NRP with a net income of over £400 per week will be adjusted by £10 a week (*i.e.* a maximum of £520 per annum), whether up or down, every year for a maximum of five years ((Child Support (Transitional Provisions) Regulations (S.I. 2000 No. 3186, Part III).
>
> (2) Maintenance calculation follows a court order
>
>> There are separate phasing provisions where a maintenance calculation follows a court order which provided for child maintenance. These provisions provide for the amount payable to be phased by reference to the following transitional amounts (years ((Child Support (Transitional Provisions) Regulations (S.I. 2000 No. 3186), reg. 31):
>>
>> (*a*) during the first 26 weeks of the transitional period, the old amount plus either 25 per cent of the excess or £20, whichever is the greater;
>> (*b*) during the next 26 weeks of the transitional period, the old amount plus either 50 per cent of the excess or £40, whichever is the greater; and
>> (*c*) during the last 26 weeks of the transitional period, the old amount plus either 75 per cent of the excess or £60, whichever is the greater.

If the transitional provisions would result in an amount of child support maintenance becoming payable which is greater than the calculation amount then the child maintenance calculation shall become payable.

8. Sanctions

> (1) Within the child support framework

9.98 >> (*a*) Default and interim maintenance decisions (CSA 2000, s.4 inserts a new section 12 into CSA 1991)

In circumstances where a final maintenance calculation cannot be made straight away, for example, when sufficient details are not made available or need to be verified a system of default rates will apply. The Government intends to provide by regulations that default rates will be £30 per week for one qualifying child, £40 for two children and £50 for three or more children (see explanatory notes to CSA 2000). For a non-co-operative NRP, maintenance liability for the past will only be recalculated if the full rate is higher than the default maintenance rate.

Where the calculation cannot be completed because an application for a variation is outstanding an interim rate will be applied. The interim rate will be set at the same level as the normal maintenance calculation pending a decision on the variation application.

(b) Penalty payments (CSA 2000, s.18 inserts a new section 41A into CSA 1991)

The full details of the scheme are to be set out in regulations. It provides the CSA with the power to make provision for penalty payments to be incurred by NRP's who are in arrears with payments of child support maintenance. The penalty payment may not exceed 25% of the amount of child support maintenance payable in any given week. The penalty payment does not affect his liability to pay the arrears of child support maintenance.

(c) Applications by those claiming or receiving income support or income-based jobseeker's allowance.

Applicants receiving income support or income-based jobseeker's allowance will be treated as having applied for a maintenance calculation unless the PWC specifically asks the Secretary of State not to act (CSA 2000, s.3 substitutes a new section 6 into CSA 1991). The PWC will have four weeks to provide reasons why the NRP should not be pursued by the CSA for maintenance. The Secretary of State will then consider whether the PWC has shown good cause. In the event that the PWC has not shown good cause there is a reduced benefit penalty (CSA 2000, s.19 substitutes a new section 46 into CSA 1991).

(2) Court imposed sanctions

Child support maintenance can be enforced by way of a deduction from earnings order or a liability order (which can be enforced by distress, garnishee proceedings or a charging order) (CSA 1991, s.31 to 39). As a last resort the NRP can be sent to prison for a maximum of 6 weeks (CSA 1991, s.40) or be disqualified from driving for a maximum of 2 years (new section 39A and 40B of CSA 1991 inserted by section 16 of CSA 2000, came into force on 2 April 2001 (The Child Support, Pensions and Social Security Act 2000 (Commencement No.5) Order 2000 (S.I. No.3354)).

9. Appeals

The PWC or NRP can appeal against a review or refusal to review or against **9.99** a refusal to make a calculation. The PWC can appeal against a reduced benefit direction. The NRP can appeal against a requirement to make penalty payments, the amount of those payments and any fees imposed (section 10 of CSA 2000 substitutes a new section 20 CSA 1991, section 11 of CSA 2000 inserts a new section 23A, came into force on February 15, 2001 (The Child Support, Pensions and Social Security Act 2000 (Commencement No.5) Order 2000 (SI No.3354))).

Chapter 10

Taxation and welfare benefits

1 Taxation

(a) Introduction

The purpose of this section is to give a concise resume of those taxation con- **10.01**
siderations which impact on an application for ancillary relief. For a fuller
treatment of this subject, reference should be made to Butterworth's *Family
Law Service*, Vol.4, Chap.10. At the time of going to print a Tax Credits Bill
was before parliament which, if implemented, would affect certain of the benefits referred to below.

(b) Tax relief on maintenance payments

Tax relief on maintenance payments has undergone fundamental change in **10.02**
recent years.

Prior to the implementation of the Finance Act 1988 on March 15, 1988,
maintenance payments due under court orders or agreements were taxable
income of the recipient and tax deductible to the payer. The maximum
amount on which a payer could claim relief was "capped" at the total maintenance on which the payer obtained relief in 1988/9, and the amount on
which the recipient was taxable was similarly limited to the taxable amount
received in 1988/9. Maintenance orders or agreements made or entered into
before March 15, 1988 are referred to as old arrangements.

Maintenance orders or agreements entered into after 15th March 1988
("new arrangements") are governed by sections 347A and 347B of the Taxes
Act 1988 which provide that:

(*a*) the recipient of maintenance is exempt from income tax on the maintenance. This applies whether the recipient is a spouse or a child;

(*b*) with a single limited exception, a payer of maintenance gets no tax
relief for maintenance. All maintenance is paid gross whether or not
it qualifies for tax relief.

The exception is that a payer of "qualifying maintenance payments" is enti- **10.03**
tled to tax relief on the payment or on £2,000, whichever is the less. The relief is
a tax credit of 10 per cent of this amount or £200 if the maintenance is £2,000
or greater. The conditions which must be satisfied for a payment to be a qualifying maintenance payment are contained in section 347B of the Taxes Act 1988:

• One or both of the parties to the marriage in respect of which tax
relief is claimed for maintenance must have been over 65 before April
6, 2000.

- The maintenance is payable under a binding written legal obligation for which the proper law is the law of the United Kingdom or (from April 6, 1992) another European Community country.

- The legal obligation must require payment of maintenance by a spouse to or for the benefit and for the maintenance of a former or separated spouse, or to a former or separated spouse for the maintenance of a "child of the family".

- The recipient spouse must not have remarried.

- The payer and the recipient must not be a married couple.

- Maintenance must not qualify for tax relief (under any other provision in taxation legislation).

In summary, the only tax relief now available for maintenance payments, whether made under new or old arrangements, is the limited relief referred to above from which most individuals will be excluded by reason of being less than 65 years of age on April 6, 2000.

(c)   Income tax treatment on separation

10.04   Change of status for income tax purposes occurs in the year in which the parties permanently separate and not the year of divorce. Treatment of the married couples allowance was until April 5, 2000 a significant consideration in most cases. From April 6, 2000, however, this allowance was abolished except in for married couples where one spouse was 65 before that date. For the year ended April 5, 2002 the allowance is £5,365 if neither spouse was 75 or more in the year and £5,435 if one of them was. The tax relief is a credit of 10 per cent of the allowance.

For separating couples, where one of the spouses was 65 before April 6, 2000, in the year of separation, the husband remains entitled to the full married couple's allowance. If the husband has insufficient income to cover that allowance, he may transfer the unused allowance to his wife.

In the year of separation, the wife is entitled to her personal allowance and prior to the year ended April 5, 2000 might additionally have been entitled to claim an additional personal allowance if she had a qualifying child residing with her during part of the year she separated from her husband. In the year to April 5, 2002 this allowance has been replaced by the children's tax credit which is dealt with at para. 10.14 below.

(d)   Capital gains tax

10.05   A disposal between husband and wife is treated as producing no gain or loss (Taxation of Chargeable Gains Act 1992, s.58(1)). This provision therefore postpones the charge to tax until the asset is disposed of by the transferee. Only transfers within the fiscal year of separation qualify, unless they take place after decree absolute. Where a married couple are separated or are divorced and one partner ceases to occupy the matrimonial home and subsequently, as part of a financial settlement, disposes of the home, or an interest in it, within 36 months of leaving, to the other partner, the private residence exemption under the Taxation of Chargeable Gains Act 1992, ss.222 and 223 applies. The exemption will apply whether the transfer takes place before or after decree absolute. Further, the exemption will continue to apply where the transfer takes place more than thirty-six months after the husband's departure by virtue of Extra-Statutory Concession D6. By this Concession, the home is deemed to continue to be the transferring spouse's only or main residence if the transferor has not elected to treat some other property as his main residence and the transferee has remained in occupation of the property as his or her only or main residence.

(e) Inheritance tax

Most transfers between spouses on divorce or nullity will not give rise to inheritance tax problems. Whilst the marriage subsists, transfers are exempt whether or not the spouses are living together (Inheritance Tax Act 1984, s.18). After decree absolute of divorce or nullity, most transfers will be exempt as transactions at arm's length not intended to confer any gratuitous benefit (Inheritance Tax Act 1984, s.10(1) and Senior Registrar's Statement (1975) 119 S.J. 596) or because the transfer was made for the maintenance of the other party or a child under eighteen or over 18 but in full-time education (Inheritance Tax Act 1984, s.11). **10.06**

(f) Stamp duty

A transfer of property in consideration of marriage or in connection with divorce executed after May 1, 1987 either by virtue of a separation deed or a court order is exempt from the payment of stamp duty by virtue of the Stamp Duty (Exempt Instruments) Regulations 1987 made under the Finance Act 1988, s.87. A certificate of the category listed in the Schedule to the Regulations within which the instrument falls must be included in, endorsed on or physically attached to the instrument. Without the appropriate certificate the document is not duly stamped. The certificate must be signed by the transferor or grantor or by his solicitor or authorised agent. Transfers in connection with divorce come within category H. **10.07**

Voluntary dispositions are also exempt from stamp duty although it should be noted that where property subject to a mortgage is transferred by way of gift, the mortgage debt outstanding is treated as consideration under the Stamp Act 1891, s.57, even if the transfer takes place between spouses. A voluntary disposition *inter vivos* comes within category L if there is no consideration in money or money's worth nor any consideration referred to in the Stamp Act 1891, s.57.

2   Welfare benefits

It is important for practitioners to advise clients of available welfare benefits and equally to consider whether welfare benefits being received by the other spouse should be regarded as resources when assessing the quantum of periodical payments. The main welfare benefits to be considered are given below. **10.08**

(a) Income support

Income Support (General) Regulations 1987 (as amended) apply. Income support (formerly supplementary benefit) is one of the main "income-related benefits" governed by the Social Security Contributions and Benefits Act 1992 and the Social Security Administration Act 1992, the other most important being Job Seekers Allowance, Working Families' Tax Credit, Housing Benefit and Council Tax Benefit (see below). The term "applicable amount" is used in relation to the income-related benefits and signifies the level of income which has been prescribed as the particular amount of income that is appropriate for an individual and his family.

To be entitled to income support, a person has to be aged 18 or over (exceptionally 16 or 17-year-olds may be eligible), be in Great Britain and have an income that does not exceed his applicable amount. Neither he nor his partner (whether married or not) must be in remunerative work which is defined as being 16 hours or more a week of paid employment. Income support is not generally available to those in full-time remunerative work or who have a partner who is so engaged, to those who are required to register for work and who are eligible to receive income-based job seekers allowance. The level of income support payable is determined by the difference between a person's income and his applicable amount.

10.09   The availability of, and the extent of entitlement to, income support of the prospective payee under any order can be taken into account as a resource when assessing the quantum of any financial provision order (*Peacock v Peacock* [1984] F.L.R. 263; *Delaney v Delaney* [1990] 2 F.L.R. 457). This, however, does not entitle a payee to throw on to the state a burden which he ought to bear (*Barnes v Barnes* [1972] 3 All E.R. 872). Even if the maintenance level is less than the payee's applicable amount and would thus require a topping-up payment from income support, this would be no reason for a maintenance order not to be made. However, in some cases, a clean break order may be appropriate when the payee is in receipt of state benefit (*Ashley v Blackman* [1988] 2 F.L.R. 278). Regard must also be had to the needs of the husband in assessing the level of financial provision to be paid. His income should not be reduced below subsistence level, *i.e.* the husband's applicable amount for income support (*Shallow v Shallow* [1978] 2 All E.R. 483). These decisions must now be viewed in the light of the Child Support Act 1991 and the Social Security Administration Act 1992, ss.105 and 106 (as amended).

In deciding whether there is grave financial hardship within MCA 1973, s.5, the court should consider the availability of income support (*Jackson v Jackson* [1993] 2 F.L.R. 848).

(b)   Working Families' Tax Credit (WFTC)

10.10   The WFTC is the replacement for the Family Credit system. One major difference is that spousal maintenance, child maintenance and child benefit are not taken into account when assessing eligibility for WFTC. This means that many divorcing or separating parents are eligible to receive WFTC, even if they are in receipt of significant maintenance payments.

The WFTC is administered directly by the Inland Revenue and is paid through the PAYE system for those in employment. It is available to families, being couples or lone parents, who:

- have one or more children;

- work at least 16 hours a week on an employed or self-employed basis (for couples at least one spouse or partner must work 16 hours or more);

- are UK residents and are entitled to work in the UK;
- have savings of £8,000 or less.

The WFTC comprises four elements: **10.11**

- a basic credit of £53.15 per week; and
- a further credit for those working over 30 hours per week of £11.25; and
- a further credit of £25.60 per week for each child of the family aged between 0 and 15 years and £26.35 per week for those aged between 16 and 18; and
- a "Childcare Tax Credit" if applicable (see below) of up to 70 per cent of eligible costs of childcare subject to a total of £100 per week for one child and £150 per week for two or more children.

The credits are aggregated. If the family income exceeds £91.45 per week after deduction of Income Tax and National Insurance, the WFTC is reduced by 55p for every £1 over £91.45. Claims are payable for 26 weeks before reassessment.

Clearly those at the lower income levels are the target and will benefit most. However, the tapered nature of the WFTC means that families with two or more children and a total income of around £30,000 will still benefit.

(c)   Childcare Tax Credit (CCTC)

The CCTC is claimed as an element of WFTC, where the claimant has child   **10.12**
care costs. The maximum credit is 70 per cent of the cost of eligible childcare up to a ceiling of £100 per week for one child or £150 per week for two or more children.

In order to qualify, the basic criteria for WFTC must be met, and:

- the children must be of qualifying age (see below)
- in "eligible" childcare (see below)
- for couples, both claimant and partner must each be working 16 hours or more or the non-working partner must be incapacitated.

All children will qualify up to the September following their 15th birthday (or following their 16th birthday if they are registered blind or in receipt of disability living allowance).

Eligible childcare qualifying for the tax credit includes: **10.13**

- childcare for the under eight year-olds registered under the Children Act 1989 with Local Authorities (registered childminders and nurseries)
- out of school childcare for the over eight year-olds which is provided by or at schools or by the local authority (breakfast clubs, after-school clubs).

Nannies and grandparents will not qualify, unless they are registered childminders.

(d) Children's Tax Credit (CTC)

10.14 The CTC differs from the WFTC in that it is not an actual payment, but reduces the claimant's overall income tax bill. CTC is aimed at those who have a child or children (aged under 16 at the start of the tax year) living with them for at least part of that tax year. It is payable irrespective of capital and savings, but will reduce by £1 for every £15 the claimant earns over the higher rate band of income tax. Therefore, it is unlikely to provide any benefit to claimants earning over £41,000 per year.

  The CTC may reduce income tax payable by up to £520 per year, and may be claimed by single parents or couples. The higher earner of a couple must make the claim.

  If children spend time with separated parents, the CTC is shared between the parents either 50/50 or in accordance with the proportion of time spent with each.

  Each of the available credits should be treated as a resource when calculating a party's entitlement to maintenance.

(e) Disability living allowance

10.15 Disability living allowance (DLA) is a tax-free benefit for individuals aged three or over with severe difficulty in walking or aged five or over and needing help in getting around. DLA is available if the individual has needed help for three months and is likely to need it for at least another six months. DLA is not affected by savings, is not usually affected by other income and is usually ignored as income when calculating an individual's entitlement to Income Support and Jobseeker's Allowance.

(f) Housing benefit

10.16 Housing benefit is a government scheme administered by local authorities. It is only payable to an individual on a low income who is liable to make payments (but not mortgage payments) in respect of a dwelling in Great Britain which he occupies as his home.

  If an individual has savings of over £16,000, Housing Benefit will not ordinarily be available and income will be considered when evaluating eligibility.

  Prior to the introduction of housing benefit, rent and rate rebates were taken into consideration in assessing the wife's resources, where the husband was living at or near subsistence level (*Walker v Walker* [1978] 3 All E.R. 141). The same principle applies to housing benefit as the amount of benefit payable will be dependant on the level of maintenance payments.

(g) Council tax benefit

10.17 Council Tax Benefit (General) Regulations 1992 apply.

  Council Tax Benefit is a government scheme administered by local authorities and operates in a similar way to housing benefit. It is paid as a rebate in the amount of council tax payable up to a maximum of one hundred per cent. Deductions from benefit are made in respect of non-dependant adults.

  It is suggested that, since maintenance payments are taken into account in assessing the level of council tax benefit payable, council tax benefit should be taken into account as a resource.

(h) Child benefit

Child benefit is payable to a person responsible for one or more children, a **10.18** child being defined as a person under the age of 16 or under the age of 19 and receiving full-time non-advanced education at school or some other recognised educational establishment (Social Security Contributions and Benefits Act 1992, s.141).

Child benefit should be taken into account as a resource within ancillary relief proceedings (*Walker v Walker* (1982) 4 F.L.R. 44).

The lone parent rate of child benefit, which replaced the former one parent benefit in April 1997, was abolished from July 6, 1998. The lone parent rate of child benefit is still available to individuals who satisfy certain conditions. The first such condition is that the individual must have been receiving the lone parent rate of child benefit since at least July 5, 1998.

(i) Jobseeker's *Allowance (JSA)*

The statutory basis for Job Seeker's Allowance is the Jobseekers Act 1995. **10.19** Where a person under pensionable age has made the requisite national insurance contributions, he is entitled to Jobseeker's Allowance if he:

- is not working or working on average less than 16 hours a week

- is capable of working

- is available for work

- is actively seeking work

- normally, is 18 or over

There are two types of JSA, contribution-based JSA and income-based JSA.

Contribution-based JSA is paid where the applicant has paid a certain number of NI contributions. JSA cannot be obtained if NI contributions have been paid for self-employment only. In those circumstances, income-based JSA may be available.

Contribution-based JSA is paid at a fixed rate based on the applicant's age for up to 182 days and is reduced if the applicant has an occupational or personal pension over a certain amount.

A recipient of contribution-based JSA with income below a certain level may be able to receive income-based JSA in addition.

Income-based JSA is payable to those on a low income even if the NI contributions required to secure contribution-based JSA have not been paid. Savings over £3,000 usually affect how much income-based JSA is paid. Savings over £8,000 usually mean that income-based JSA is not available.

(j) State retirement pension

Eligibility for state retirement pensions is based upon a person attaining pen- **10.20** sionable age and having fulfilled the contribution conditions. Where a person has fulfilled only the minimum contribution requirement he will be entitled to the Category A Basic Pension. Where a person has not contracted out to pay into an occupational pension scheme or personal pension and he has fulfilled the contribution requirements, he will be entitled to the Category B State Earnings Related Pension (SERPS) which includes in addition to the flat rate an earnings-related component based upon his contributions and earnings. Where a woman has been out of work caring for her children or an elderly relative, the "home responsibilities' provision will apply. Provided that such time amounts to no more than 20 years, she will potentially be able to achieve the same level of pension as if she had had no time out from paid employment. Where there is a shortfall in the minimum contribution requirement, a wife can normally make this good by reference to her husband's contributions. Upon the granting of a decree absolute, a non-working spouse will no longer be able to rely upon her husband's contributions record to make up a SERPS pension, unless the divorce occurs after she is 60. It may, therefore, be critical for a wife who is about to divorce at the time of her 60th birthday to ensure that the decree absolute is delayed until after that birthday. This will ensure that the wife's position under SERPS is not prejudiced and that she will obtain a full pension without having to pay national insurance contributions in the period between decree absolute and her 60th birthday. With regard to the Basic Pension, a wife may rely upon her former husband's contribution record during the years of marriage as well as her own contributions before and after marriage. A loss of a SERPS pension entitlement may be taken into consideration when assessing financial provision and may be considered sufficient grounds for refusing to grant a divorce owing to grave financial hardship which might ensue (but see *Reiterbund v Reiterbund* [1975] 1 All E.R. 280).

An enquiry may be made by form BR19 to the Benefits Agency, Pensions and Overseas Benefits Directorate, RPFA Unit, Newcastle upon Tyne, NE98 1YX to ascertain whether an individual's state pension entitlement will be adversely affected by divorce.

10.21   SERPS is excluded from the valuation methodology of the Divorce, etc. (Pensions) Regulations 2000 but may be the subject of a pension sharing order. A lump sum valuation of an individual's SERPS entitlement may be obtained by submitting form BR 20 to the Benefits Agency, Pensions and Overseas Benefits Directorate, RPFA Unit, Newcastle upon Tyne, NE98 1YX.

SERPs was replaced on April 6, 2002 by the State Second Pension (S2P) pursuant to the Child Support, Pensions and Social Security Act 2000. S2P can be the subject of a pension sharing order (Child Support, Pensions and Social Security Act 2000, s.41).

(k)   Minimum Income Guarantee

10.22   The minimum income gurantee (MIG) is a safety net for pensioners who fail to make sufficient contributions. It is a form of income support for retired people awarded on a means-tested basis that takes into account additional income and savings.

Current rates are £92.15 for a single person and £140.55 for couples from April 6, 2001.

It has been argued that MIG penalises those who have saved for their retirement. To address this, the government has increased the savings limit affecting MIG entitlement with effect from April 6, 2001 so that MIG entitlement is reduced by £1 per week for every £250 worth of savings above £6,000 and up to £12,000 where it ceases. The savings limit will be abolished in 2002.

(l)   Council Tax – Single Person Discount

10.23   Pursuant to section 11 of the Local Government Finance Act 1992 where only a single adult lives in a property, a 25 per cent discount is available, upon application, on the full rate of Council Tax payable. This discount is not means-tested and, therefore, available to all eligible people, irrespective of income and savings.

In addition, some people may be disregarded when counting the number of adult residents of a property. These people include, but are not limited to:

- severely mentally impaired people

- persons for whom child benefit is payable

- student nurses

- school or college leavers who are under 20 years of age and left a course of full-time education after April 30 in any given year — in these circumstances they are disregarded until either their 20th birthday or the November 1, of the year in which they left the course, whichever is the earliest.

Full details of people who can be disregarded in this way can be obtained from the Council Advice and Benefits Office.

(m)   Council Tax Benefit

Pursuant to section 131 of the Social Security Contributions and Benefits Act **10.24** 1992 people who are on a low income and have savings of less than £16,000 can claim Council Tax Benefit. The benefit is means tested and, therefore, the amount received depends upon levels of household income, savings and personal circumstances.

(n)   Second Adult Rebate

If Council Tax Benefit is not available and the presence of a second adult in **10.25** the household prevents the Single Person Discount from applying, then a Second Adult Rebate may be available pursuant to Council Tax Benefit (General) Regulations 1992 if a member of the household is on a low income. For this to apply, the person making the claim must:

- not have a partner; and

- have someone living with them (*e.g.* a grown up son or daughter or a parent) who fits the means testing criteria applicable from time to time.

Applications for the Single Person Discount, Council Tax Benefit and Second Adult Rebate should be made to the Council Advice & Benefits Office.

Significant changes to the benefit system are anticipated in 2003. Further information may be obtained from the Department of Work and Pensions on 0845 609 5000 or by visiting the website at *www.dss.gov.uk*. A further useful point of reference with regard to welfare benefits is Butterworth's *Family Law Service* A[21]-[245] and D[l 151]-[1168].

Chapter 11

Children

1 Introduction

11.01 This chapter deals primarily with private law applications under the Children Act 1989 (CA 1989). It does not attempt to discuss applications to the family proceedings courts (formerly magistrates' courts) nor does it deal with public law applications. Wardship, financial applications relating to children and the issue of child abduction are discussed at Chapter 12.

2 Jurisdiction

11.02 Jurisdiction is governed by CA 1989, s.92 and FPR, rr.4.1 to 4.28. The Act confers concurrent jurisdiction on the family proceedings courts, the county courts and the High Court, although the Children (Allocation of Proceedings) Order 1991 (as amended) ('the Allocation Order') specifically states where certain applications should be commenced or transferred (see paras 11.23–11.25).

   The Allocation Order defines three classes of county court, namely:

   (1) *Divorce County Courts* — which may hear private law applications except contested applications under CA 1989, s.8.

   (2) *Family Hearing Centres* — which may hear private law applications, whether contested or not.

   (3) *Care Centres* — which may hear both parties and public law applications.

   A list of the divorce county courts, family hearing centres and care centres is set out at Appendix 1. The principal registry has jurisdiction as a divorce county court, family hearing centre and care centre (art.19). Lambeth County Court and Woolwich County Court may both hear applications under CA 1989, s.8 despite the fact that they are neither divorce county courts nor family hearing centres (art.20).

11.03 In the county court, specific classes of judicial officers have been nominated to hear family proceedings (defined below) by virtue of the Family Proceedings (Allocation to the Judiciary) (Amendment) Directions 2002. The Directions apply, inter alia, to private law proceedings pending in a county court or in county court proceedings in the principal registry.

   'Family proceedings' are defined by CA 1989, s.8(3) and (4) as meaning any proceedings under the inherent jurisdiction of the High Court and any proceedings under the following enactments:

(*a*) CA 1989, Pts I, II and IV.

(*b*) MCA 1973

(*c*) Adoption Act 1976

(*d*) Domestic Proceedings and Magistrates' Court Act 1978.

(*e*) MFPA 1984, P III.

(*f*) the Family Law Act 1996.

(*g*) sections 11 and 12 of the Crime and Disorder Act 1998.

This differs from the definition of 'family proceedings' provided by MFPA **11.04**
1984, s.32 (see para.1.02). Although not included within CA 1989, s.8, proceedings under the Human Fertilisation and Embryology Act 1990, s.30 are
also family proceedings (section 30(8) of the 1990 Act). The section, which
only applies to married couples, deals with cases where a child is genetically
the son or daughter of the husband or wife, or both, but is carried by a sur-
rogate. Applications for a 'parental order' must be made within six months of
the birth of the child (s.30(2)).

Section 41 of the MCA 1973 provides that in any proceedings for divorce,
nullity or judicial separation, the court must consider whether it should exercise any of its powers under CA 1989 in respect of any child of the family (as
defined) to whom the section applies.

3 Section 8 orders

One or more of the following orders may be made under CA 1989, s.8 in *any* **11.05**
family proceedings:

(1) *A Contact Order* — An order requiring the person with whom a child
    lives, to allow the child to visit or stay with the person named in the
    order, or for that person and the child otherwise to have contact with
    each other. Contact does not need to be physical and may, for
    instance, be made by letter or telephone. Provision may be made for
    contact to be supervised. A child may be the subject of more than one
    contact order at the same time.

(2) *A Prohibited Steps Order* — An order that no step which could be
    taken by a parent in meeting his parental responsibility (defined
    below) for a child, and which is of a kind specified in the order, must
    be taken by *any* person without the consent of the court. The step to
    be prohibited must be specific and relate to an act which falls within
    the concept of parental responsibility. An order forbidding a child's
    parents from having contact with each other cannot, therefore, form
    the basis of a prohibited steps order (*Croydon London Borough
    Council v A* [1992] 2 F.L.R. 341). In contrast, an order could be made
    against someone who is neither a parent nor a party to the proceed-
    ings requiring him not to have contact with a child (*Re H* [1995] 1
    F.L.R. 638).

(3) *A Residence Order* — An order settling the arrangements to be made **11.06**
    as to the person with whom a child is to live. A child cannot be the

subject of more than one residence order at the same time although an order may be made in favour of two or more persons who do not themselves all live together. In such circumstances, the order for shared residence may specify the periods during which the child is to live in the different households (CA 1989, s.11(4)). Contrary to earlier case law it is no longer necessary to show that exceptional circumstances exist before a shared residence order may be granted, nor is it necessary to show a positive benefit to the child. What is needed is to show that the order is in the interests of the child in accordance with CA 1989, s.1(1) (*D v D (Shared Residence Orders)* [2001] 1 F.L.R. 495).

(4) *A Specific Issue Order* — An order giving directions for the purpose of determining a specific question which has arisen, or which may arise, in connection with any aspect of parental responsibility for a child. Specific issues include matters of education, religion and medical treatment.

The court cannot make a specific issue order or a prohibited steps order with a view to achieving by the "back door" a result which could be achieved by making a residence or contact order (CA 1989, s.9(5) (a); *Nottingham County Council v P* [1993] 2 F.L.R. 134).

11.07   Reference to 'a section 8 order' means any of the above orders together with any order varying or discharging them (CA 1989, s.8(2)). An application may be made at any time during the course of *any* family proceedings in which a question arises with respect to the welfare of *any* child or may be made as a free-standing application (CA 1989, s.10(1) and (2)). A section 8 order may be made by the court of its own motion even though no application has been made, if the courts considers that one should be made (CA 1989, s.10(1)(*b*)) or even though the court is not in a position to dispose finally of the proceedings (CA 1989, s.11(3)). The court may order that no application for any order under CA 1989 is to be made without leave (CA 1989, s.91(14)). The power to make such an order should, however, be exercised sparingly. In *Re P (section 91(14) Guidelines) (Residence and Religious Heritage)* [1999] 2 F.L.R. 573, the Court of Appeal laid down a number of useful guidelines drawn from the reported cases, whilst indicating that the court always has to carry out a balancing exercise between the welfare of the child and the right of unrestricted access of the litigant to the court.

11.08   A section 8 order may contain directions as to how it is to be carried into effect (CA 1989, s.11(7)(*a*)). It may also impose conditions which must be complied with by any person (a) in whose favour the order is made; (b) who is the parent of the child concerned; (c) who is not a parent of the child but who has parental responsibility for him, or (d) with whom the child is living, and to whom the conditions are expressed to apply (CA 1989, s.11(7)(*b*)). For a discussion as to the conditions which can be attached to a contact order, see *Re O* [1995] 2 F.L.R. 124.

A section 8 order may be made to have effect for a specified period or contain provisions which are to have effect for a specified period (CA 1989, s.11(7)(*c*)). The court may also make such incidental, supplemental or consequential provision as it thinks fit (CA 1989, s.11(7)(*d*)). Where, however, a local authority is required to supervise contact, a Family Assistance Order should be sought under CA 1989, s.16 (see p.238) and not a direction under CA 1989, s.11(7) (*Leeds County Council v C* [1993] 1 F.L.R. 269; *Re E (Family Assistance Order* [1999] 2 F.L.R. s.12).

Unless the court is satisfied that the circumstances of the case are exceptional, it cannot make any section 8 order which will have effect for a period which will end after the child has reached the age of 16 nor can it make any section 8 order in respect of a child who has reached that age other than varying or discharging such an order (CA 1989, s.9(6) and (7)). A child is a person under the age of 18 (CA 1989, s.105(1)).

A residence order ceases to have effect where as a result of the order, the child lives, or is to live, with one or two parents who each have parental responsibility for him and the parents live together for a continuous period of more than six months (CA 1989, s.11(5)). **11.09**

A contact order which requires the parent with whom the child thereafter lives to allow the child to visit, or otherwise have contact with, his other parent ceases to have effect if the parents live together for a continuous period of more than six months (CA 1989, s.11(6)). There is no similar automatic consequence where the parties are not both the child's parents, so that if, for example, the mother of the child remarries and then separates from her second husband (H2), resulting in H2 applying for and obtaining a contact order in relation to his stepchild, where the couple then reconcile and resume cohabitation, the contact order will not lapse automatically and an application would have to be made to the court to discharge the order.

A section 8 order, other than a residence order, cannot be made with respect to a child who is in the care of a local authority (CA 1989, s.9(1)). If a residence order is made, the care order is automatically discharged (CA 1989, s.91(1)). Any section 8 order is automatically discharged if a care order is *subsequently* made in respect of the same child (CA 1989, s.92(2)). An application for contact may, however, still be made under public law proceedings by virtue of CA 1989, s.34.

4   Parental responsibility

Parental responsibility is defined by CA 1989, s.3(1) as 'all the rights, duties, powers, responsibilities and authority which by law a parent of a child has in relation to the child and his property'. **11.10**

It also includes the rights, powers and duties which a guardian of the child's estate (appointed before February 1, 1992) would have had in relation to the child and his property (CA 1989, s.3(2)).

The fact that a person has, or does not have, parental responsibility for a child does not affect any obligation which he may have in relation to the child (such as the statutory duty to maintain the child) or any rights which, in the event of the child's death, he (or any other person) may have in relation to the child's property (CA 1989, s.3(4)). A person who does not have parental responsibility for a particular child but has care of the child may (subject to the provisions of the Act) do what is reasonable in all the circumstances for the purpose of safeguarding or promoting the child's welfare (CA 1989, s.3(5)). This would include friends, relatives or persons in authority temporarily caring for a child.

Section 2 of the Act specifies those persons who automatically have parental responsibility for a child. Where a child's father and mother were married to each other at the time of his birth, they *each* have parental responsibility for the child (CA 1989, s.2(1)). Where the child's father and mother were not so married, only the mother will automatically have parental responsibility for **11.11** the child and the father will not unless he acquires it by one of the means discussed below (CA 1989, s.2(2)). The rule of law that a father is the natural guardian of his legitimate child has been abolished (CA 1989, s.2(4)). An adoption order extinguishes the parental responsibility which *any* person had the child immediately before the order was made (Adoption Act 1976, s.12(3)).

More than one person may have parental responsibility for the same child at the same time and a person who does have parental responsibility for the child usually does not cease to do so solely because some other person subsequently acquires parental responsibility for the child (CA 1989, s.2(5) and (6)). Where more than one person does have parental responsibility for a child, each of them may act alone in meeting that responsibility unless the consent of more than one person is specifically required elsewhere (CA 1989, s.2(7)). If the other parent or another person with parental responsibility wishes to challenge any such acts, he should seek a prohibited steps order or a specific issue order as appropriate. The fact that a person has parental responsibility for a child does not, however, entitle him to act in any way which could be incompatible with any existing order or any order made under the Act (CA 1989, s.2(8)). Parental responsibility can be delegated but cannot be transferred or surrendered (CA 1989, s.2(9)–(11)).

11.12   A father not married to the child's mother at the time of his birth (and who does not subsequently marry the mother) may acquire parental responsibility in one of five ways:

(1) by order of the court following an application by the father ('a parental responsibility order') (CA 1989, s.4(1)(*a*)). Application is made on Form C1 where there are no family proceedings and on Form C2 where such proceedings do exist. A fee of £80 is payable.

(2) by agreement with the mother providing for the father to have parental responsibility for the child ('a parental responsibility agreement') (CA 1989, s.4(1)(*b*)).

(3) by order of the court which *must* be made whenever the court makes a residence order in favour of a father who would not otherwise have parental responsibility (CA 1989, s.12(1)).

(4) by appointment as the child's guardian in the event of the mother's death (CA 1989, s.5(6); see below).

(5) by adopting the child (Adoption Act 1976, s.12).

Separate consideration must be given to a free-standing application for a parental responsibility order independent of any other applications (*Re CB* [1993] 1 F.L.R. 920). There is, however, no obligation to apply for another order, such as a contact order, at the same time.

11.13   When deciding whether to make a parental responsibility order, the court will take a number of factors into consideration including the degree of commitment shown by the father to the child, the degree of attachment between them and the father's reasons for applying for the order (*re H* (Parental Responsibility) [1998] 1 F.L.R. 855; *Re S* (Parental Responsibility) [1995] 2 F.L.R. 648). A parental responsibility order may be appropriate even where a contact order is not (*Re H* [1993] 1 F.L.R. 484) and notwithstanding the mother's resistance (*Re A* [1993] Fam. Law. 464) or inability to enforce it (*Re C* [1992] 1 F.L.R. 1).

A parental responsibility agreement will not have effect unless it is made in the prescribed form and recorded in the prescribed manner provided by the Parental Responsibility Agreement Regulations 1991 (as amended). An agreement is recorded by filing it, together with two copies, at the principal registry.

A parental responsibility order made at the same time as a residence order in favour of a father under CA 1989, s.12 (1) may not be brought to an end whilst the residence order remains in force (CA 1989, s.12(4)). Where a residence order no longer remains in force, the parental responsibility order will still do so unless and until it is terminated.

A person who is not the natural parent or existing guardian of a child will acquire parental responsibility in the event that the court makes a residence order in their favour. In such circumstances, the parental responsibility continues so long as the residence order remains in force (s.12(2)). A residence order *may* be appropriate even where the child's actual residence is not in dispute in order to bestow parental responsibility on the child's carer and provide the child with greater security (*B v B* [1992] 2 F.L.R. 327 where a residence order was made in favour of a grandmother). **11.14**

A person appointed as a child's guardian under CA 1989, s.5 also acquires parental responsibility (CA 1989, s.5(6)). The appointment will, however, only prove to be effective in certain circumstances and it is then that the guardian will acquire parental responsibility (see below).

5   Guardians

A guardian may only be appointed in accordance with the provisions of CA 1989, s.5 (CA 1989, s.5(13)). Appointment may be by the court, by a parent having parental responsibility for the child or by an existing guardian of the child (CA 1989, s.5(1)–(4)). An appointment by a parent or guardian may be made by two or more persons acting jointly (CA 1989, s.5(10)). A person appointed as a child's guardian automatically acquires parental responsibility for the child once the appointment becomes effective (CA 1989, s.5(6)). **11.15**

Where the appointment is by a parent (who must have parental responsibility) or an existing guardian, it will only take effect on the appointor's death where there is no parent with parental responsibility for the child or, immediately before the death of the appointor, a residence order in his favour was in force (CA 1989, s.5(7)). The residence order must *not* also have been made in favour of a surviving parent if the appointment is to take immediate effect (CA 1989, s.5(9)). Where no such residence order is in force and there is a parent with parental responsibility for the child, the appointment will not take effect until the child no longer has such a parent (CA 1989, s.5(8)). This will usually occur on the death of the surviving parent although if he is an unmarried father the appointment could take effect in the event that his parental responsibility is terminated.

The court may make an appointment either upon the application of any person seeking to be the child's guardian or in *any* family proceedings if the court considers that the order should be made even though no application has been made. The court may, however, only exercise the power where there is no parent with parental responsibility for the child or a residence order has been made in favour of a parent or guardian who has died whilst the order was in force (CA 1989, ss.5(1) and (2)). **11.16**

Once effective, an appointment as a guardian can be terminated by the guardian himself or by the court (CA 1989, s.6). In addition, unless an express intention to the contrary is shown, the appointment of a former spouse as guardian, where the appointor dies on or after January 1, 1996, will automatically be revoked by the parties' marriage either being dissolved or annulled (Law Reform (Succession) Act 1995, s.4).

6   Principles to be applied

11.17   The welfare of the child is the court's paramount consideration when determining any question with respect to his or her upbringing (CA 1989, s.1(1)). The court must also have regard to the general principle that *any* delay in determining any such question is likely to prejudice that welfare (CA 1989, s.1(2)). The court must draw up a timetable with a view to determining any application without delay and give appropriate directions to ensure that such timetable is adhered to so far as reasonably practicable (CA 1989, s.11(1)). The court may, however, consider that planned and purposeful delay may be beneficial in certain circumstances (see, for instance, *C v Solihull Metropolitan Borough Council* [1993] 1 F.L.R. 290 and *Re B* [1994] 2 F.L.R. 269). The practical procedure for arranging the timing of proceedings is contained in FPR, r.4.15 and the rules governing the giving of directions are in FPR, r.4.14.

CA 1989, s.1(3) sets out particular factors to which the court must have regard when considering whether to make, vary or discharge a section 8 order *which is opposed* by any party to the proceedings. The guidance provided by the checklist may nevertheless be adopted by the court in other proceedings. The factors are:

(1) the ascertainable wishes and feelings of the child concerned (considered in the light of his age and understanding).

(2) his physical, emotional and educational needs.

(3) the likely effect on him of any change in circumstances.

(4) his age, sex, background and any characteristics of his which the court considers relevant.

(5) any harm which he has suffered or is at risk of suffering.

(6) how capable each of his parents, and any other person in relation to whom the court considers the question to be relevant, is of meeting his needs.

(7) the range of powers available to the court under CA 1989 in the proceedings in question.

The child's wishes and feelings do not take priority over the other factors listed and will be disregarded if they appear to diverge from the child's welfare (see for instance, *Re B* [1996] 1 F.L.R. 791). However, the greater the age and maturity of the child, the more likely it is that the court will give weight to their wishes (*e.g. Re S (Change of Surname)* [1999] 1 F.L.R. 672).

Where the court is considering whether or not to make one or more orders under CA 1989, it must not make an order unless it considers that doing so would be better for the child than making no order at all (section 1(5)). The court will need to be satisfied that it is in the child's interests that an order be made before intervening. Where the parties are in agreement there will usually be no need for the court to exercise its powers under CA 1989.

7   Applicants

Additional parties to proceedings, such as grandparents, should not intervene unless they have a separate point of view to put forward (*Re M (Minors)* [1993] 1 F.L.R. 822). Where competing applications do exist, they should be heard together (*G v G (Children: Concurrent Applications)* [1993] 2 F.L.R. 306).   **11.18**
S.8 orders: The following persons are entitled to apply to the court for any section 8 order with respect to a child:

> (1) any parent or guardian (appointed in accordance with CA 1989, s.5) of the child;

> (2) any person in whose favour a residence order is in force with respect to the child (CA 1989, s.10(4)).

A natural parent of a child who is either freed for adoption or actually adopted is no longer a 'parent' for the purposes of CA 1989, s.10(4) (*M v C and Calderdale Metropolitan Borough Council* [1993] 1 F.L.R. 505; *Re C* [1993] 2 F.L.R. 431). Persons with the benefit of old style custody or care and control orders, who are not a parent or guardian of the child, are nevertheless entitled to apply to the court for a section 8 order as of right (CA 1989, Sch.14, para.7(3)).
Residence and contact orders: The following persons are entitled to apply for a residence or contact order with respect to a child: **11.19**

> (1) any party to a marriage (whether or not subsisting) in relation to whom the child is a child of the family (*e.g.* step-parents).

> (2) any person with whom the child has lived for a period of at least three years (which need not be continuous but must not have begun more than five years before, or ended more than three months before, the application is made (CA 1989, s.10(10)).

> (3) any person who:
>
>> (*a*) in any case where a residence order (or an existing order for care and control) is in force with respect to the child, has the consent of each of the persons in whose favour the order was made;
>>
>> (*b*) in any case where the child is in the care of a local authority has the consent of that authority (although a contact order cannot be made under section 8 where a child is in care: see para.11.09; or
>>
>> (*c*) in any other case, has the consent of each of those (if any) who have parental responsibility for the child (CA 1989, s.10(5)).

Variation and discharge: A person who would not otherwise be entitled under the above provisions to apply for the variation or discharge of a section 8 order is nevertheless entitled to do so if: **11.20** (*a*) the order was made on his application; or

(*b*) in case of a contact order, he is named in the order (CA 1989, s.10(6)).

11.21 *Rules of court*: Any person who falls within a category of person prescribed by rules of court is entitled to apply for any such section 8 order as may be prescribed in relation to that category of person (CA 1989, s.10(7)). No such rules of court have yet been made.

11.22 *Leave to apply*: Any person who has obtained the leave of court to make an application for a s.8 order may do so (CA 1989, s.10(1)(*a*)(ii)). If the person apply for leave is the child concerned, the court may only grant leave if it is satisfied that he has sufficient understanding to make the proposed application for the s.8 order (CA 1989, s.10(8)). In certain circumstances a child may participate in proceedings without a next friend or guardian ad litem (FPR, r.9.2A, discussed at para.3.29 *et seq*. Where any other person applies for leave the court must, in deciding whether or not to grant leave, have particular regard to:

(1) the nature of the proposed application for the s.8 order.

(2) the applicant's connection with the child.

(3) any risk there might be of that proposed application disrupting the child's life to such an extent that he would be harmed by it.

(4) where the child is being looked after by the local authority, the authority's plans for the child's future and the wishes and feelings of the child's parents (CA 1989, s.10(9)).

The child's welfare is *not* the paramount consideration when the court is considering whether to grant leave to anyone other than the child concerned to apply for a section 8 order (*Re A and W (Minors) (Residence Order: Leave to Apply*.) [1992] 2 F.L.R. 154. However, there is a divergence of opinion as to whether it is paramount where the applicant for leave is the child himself (*Re SC* [1994] 1 F.L.R. 96; *Re C* [1995] 1 F.L.R. 927; held that it is not, whereas *Re C* [1994] 1 F.L.R. 26 held that it is). Where a child makes an application for leave, this should be dealt with in the High Court (Practice Direction of February 22, 1993) [1993] 1 F.L.R. 668. The court may have regard to matters other than those set out in CA 1989, s.10(9) above (*Re A (A Minor) (Residence Order: Leave to Apply)* [1993] 1 F.L.R. 425). The merits of the substantive application itself should be considered. (*Re M (Care: Contact: Grandmother's Application for Leave)* [1995] 2 F.L.R. 86, although a public law case relating to leave, contains the most authoritative guidance on this topic. There is, however, no presumption that a party who has obtained leave to apply for a contact order is entitled to such an order unless there are cogent reasons for denying contact (*Re A* [1995] 2 F.L.R. 153).

8   Allocation and transfer of proceedings

11.23 Private law applications may be made to the High Court, county courts or family proceedings courts. In some cases, the choice of court will be determined by other proceedings (see below).

The Allocation Order (see para.11.02) provides that, generally, an application for a section 8 order which is made to a county court must be made to a divorce county court, the principal registry or Lambeth and Woolwich

County Court (art.14). An application for a section 8 order which is opposed must, however, be commenced in or transferred to a family hearing centre (art.16).

Where a matrimonial cause (see para.1.04) is pending, an application by a **11.24** party to the cause or by any other person for a section 8 order in relation to a child of the family, *must* be made in the cause. Where the applicant is not a party but has obtained leave to make the application, leave is not necessary to intervene in the cause (FPR, r.2.40(1)). If, while a cause is pending, proceedings relating to any child of the family are begun in any other court, a concise statement of the nature of the proceedings must immediately be filed by the person commencing the proceedings or, if he is not a party to the cause, by the petitioner (FPR, r.2.40(2)). A cause begun by petition is pending even if a final decree or order has been made (FPR r.1.2(2)). As to who constitutes a child of the family, see paras 2.07–2.09.

An application to extend, vary or discharge, or the determination of which may have the same effect, must usually be made to the court which made the original order (art.4(1)). However, if a section 8 order is sought which would have the effect of varying or discharging an existing county court order which was originally made by the court of its own motion, the application must be made to a divorce county court (art.4(2)). If the effect of a successful application would be to vary an earlier order or direction of the court made prior to the enactment of CA 1989, then the application should be made to the court which made that earlier order (*Sunderland Borough Council v A* [1993] 1 F.C.R. 396).

Applications made by a child for a section 8 order should be commenced or transferred to the High Court (President's Direction February 22, 1993 [1993] 1 F.L.R. 668).

The Allocation Order also provides for the transfer of proceedings from one **11.25** court to another. Transfer from one county court to another is dealt with by art.10, from the county court to the High Court by art.12 and from the High Court to a county court by art.13. In each instance consideration must be given to the principle set out at s.1(2) of the CA 1989 (delay may be prejudicial to the welfare of the child) and whether the transfer would be in the interests of the child. Following any transfer from the magistrates' court, the county court must consider whether the proceedings should be further transferred to the High Court (FPR, r.4.6(4)).

Proceedings under CA 1989 are not made invalid if commenced or transferred in contravention of the provisions of the Allocation Order. Nor does any appeal lie against the determination of the proceedings on the basis of any contravention alone (art.21).

9 Procedure (section 8 orders)

A district judge who is not of the principal registry and not nominated for **11.26** public law proceedings may hear unopposed applications for any section 8 order and may also give directions in opposed applications. Likewise, applications for a contact order where the principle of contact is unopposed may be heard. It is not clear whether an ex parte order counts as an order limited in time until the next hearing. If it does not the district judge would have to transfer the case to a nominated circuit judge, a district judge of the principal registry or a district judge nominated for public law proceedings. Deputy district judges may hear interlocutory matters and unopposed trials in applications under CA 1989, s.10 for a section 8 order. A district judge of the principal registry or who is nominated for public law proceedings is not so restricted (see further the Family Proceedings (Allocation to Judiciary) (Amendment) Directions 2002). An application may be made at any time during the course of *any* family proceedings in which a question arises with respect to the welfare of *any* child or may be made as a free-standing application (CA 1989, s.10(1) and (2)).

11.27   *Leave required*: The person seeking leave must file:

> (*a*) a written request in Form C2 setting out the reasons for the application; and

> (*b*) a draft of the application in Form C1 (free-standing) or Form C2 (existing family proceedings) for the making of which leave is sought, together with sufficient copies for one to be served on each proposed respondent (FPR, r.4.3(1)). A fee of £80 is payable.

The court will consider the request and either grant it or direct that a date be fixed for the hearing of the request. In such cases, the court clerk will fix a date and give such notice as the court directs to the applicant and to such other persons as the court requires to be notified (FPR, r.4.3(2)).

If the request for leave is successful, the application proceeds in accordance with FPR, r.4.4 below save that an actual application is not required (FPR, r.4.3(3)).

Leave not required

Ex parte: Application may be made ex parte for any section 8 order (FPR, r.4.4(4)). An application in Form C1 (free-standing) or in Form C2 (existing family proceedings) must be filed:

> (*a*) within twenty-four hours where the application is made by telephone; or

> (*b*) in any other case, at the time the ex parte application is made (FPR, r.4.4(4)(i)).

> A fee of £80 per application is payable.

Where exceptional circumstances require an application to be made by telephone an approach should first be made to the court office where it is intended that the application will ultimately be filed. If the office is closed or a hearing cannot be arranged, the Urgent Business Officer at the Royal Courts of Justice should be contacted on 020 7947 6000.

The applicant must serve a copy of the application on each respondent within forty-eight hours after the making of the order (FPR, r.4.4(4)(ii)). The applicant must also serve a copy of the ex parte order on each party and any person who has actual care of the child or who had such care immediately prior to the making of the order within forty-eight hours (FPR, r.4.21(7)). If a difficulty with service is anticipated or encountered recourse to FPR, r.4.8(8) should be made (see para.11.31–11.32).

Where the court refuses to make an order ex parte it may direct that the application be made inter partes (FPR, r.4.4(5)).

11.28   An ex parte residence order altering the care of a child will only be made in

cases of extreme urgency or exceptional circumstances (*e.g.* where there is an issue of child abduction). Consideration should be given as to whether an application to abridge time for service under FPR, r.4.8(8) is more appropriate (*Re B (A Minor) (Residence Order: Ex Parte)* [1992] 2 F.L.R. 1; *Re G (Ex Parte Interim Residence Order)* [1993] 1 F.L.R. 910). An ex parte order in any event will normally only be made for a short duration until an inter partes hearing can be arranged. Important guidance as to the way in which ex parte applications are to be conducted is to be found in *Re J (Children) (Ex Parte Orders)* [1997] 1 F.L.R. 606 and in *Re S (Ex Parte Orders)* [2001] Fam. Law 21.
Inter Partes: Requirements are as follows (FPR, r.4.4(1)(a) and (1)(A)):

(1) application in Form C1 (free-standing) or in Form C2 (existing family proceedings). Some courts insist on the use of Form C1 even in pending proceedings, but it is suggested that the practitioner follow the general rules unless the court concerned rejects that course. Where the application is made in respect of more than one child of a particular family, all the children should be included in one application.

(2) sufficient copies of the application for one to be served on each respondent.

(3) public funding certificate, if any, and notice of issue of legal aid certificate and copy for service.

(4) fee of £80.

On receipt of the application, the court clerk will fix a date for the hearing **11.29** of the application or, more usually, a directions appointment. The court will seal the copies of the application and return them to the applicant together with Form C6, and Form C6A if appropriate (notice of proceedings to persons who are parties and non-parties respectively) and Form C7 (acknowledgment) duly completed by the court. Details of the first court appointment are endorsed by the court on the notice of proceedings (FPR, r.4.4(2)). The applicant must then serve a copy of the application, Form C6 and Form C7 on each respondent within fourteen days prior to the date fixed for the hearing or directions appointment (FPR, r.4.4(1)(*b*)). At the same time, the applicant must give written notice of the proceedings and the hearing or directions appointment in Form C6A, to the persons set out at FPR, Appendix 3, column (iv) (FPR, r.4.4(3)).

Each respondent must file, and serve on the other parties, the acknowledgment of the application in Form C7 within 14 days of service (FPR, r.4.9(1)). *Parties*: The respondents to an application for a s.8 order are set out in FPR, **11.30** Appendix 3, column (iii) (FPR, r.4.7(1)). Any other person may file a request in Form C2 that he or another person be joined as a party or cease to be a party (FPR, r.4.7(2)). Where a person with parental responsibility requests that he be joined as a party, the court *must* grant his request (FPR, r.4.7(4)).

The court has a discretion to direct that a person who would not otherwise be a respondent be joined as a party or that any party to the proceedings ceases to be a party (FPR, r.4.7(5)). The court will consider the matters set out at CA 1989, s.10(9) (see para.11.22) and the merits of the application itself should the party be joined to the proceedings (*G v Kirkless Metropolitan Borough Council* [1993] 1 F.L.R. 805). The welfare of the child is not, however, the court's paramount consideration (*North Yorkshire County Council v G* [1993] 2 F.L.R. 732).

11.31   *Service*: Service of any document in connection with an application for a s.8 order is dealt with by FPR, r.4.8.

In summary, service may be effected either personally, by delivery to the relevant address or by first class post where the applicant is not aware whether the person to be served has a solicitor acting for him (FPR, r.4.8(1)(*a*)) or to a solicitor by first class post, delivery to the relevant address, document exchange or fax where the applicant is aware that the person to be served does have a solicitor acting for him (FPR, r.4.8(1)(*b*)). Service is deemed to have been effected on the second business day (see FPR, r.1.5(6)) after posting the document first class or leaving it at the document exchange, unless the contrary is proved (FPR, r.4.8(6)). Where the document is sent by fax before 4 pm on a business day, it is deemed to have been served on the date of transmission and otherwise on the next business day (RSC Ord. 65, r.5(2B)).

The court has the power to direct that the requirements as to service do not apply, the time for service be abridged or service be effected in a particular manner (FPR, rr.4.8(8)). In urgent cases, the request for such a direction may, with leave of the court, be made orally and/or without notice to the other parties (FPR, r.4.14(4)). In all other cases, the request should be made in writing in Form C2 and served on the other parties (FPR, r.4.14(3)(*b*)) when the court clerk will fix a date for the hearing of the request giving not less than two days' notice to the parties (FPR, r.4.14(5)).

11.32   Where a child is required to serve a document as a party to proceedings, service is effected by the solicitor acting for the child, or the children's guardian where there is no such solicitor, or if there is neither, the court (FPR, r.4.8(3)). Where a child is to be served with a document, subject to any direction of the court, service may be effected on the solicitor acting for the child, the children's guardian where there is no solicitor acting, or where there is neither, and with leave of the court, the child himself (FPR, r.4.8(4)). If leave is refused, the court must make a direction under FPR, r.4.8(8) (FPR, r.4.8(5)).

At or before the first directions appointment or before the hearing of the proceedings, the applicant must file a statement in Form C9 that service of a copy of the application together with Forms C6 and C7 has been effected on each respondent and that notice of the proceedings in Form C6A has been given in accordance with FPR, r.4.4(3). The statement must indicate the manner, date, time and place of service or where service has been effected by post, the date, time and place of posting (FPR, r.4.8(7)).

Where, in proceedings for a section 8 order (other than an order varying or discharging such an order) in respect of a child, the court does not have available to it adequate information as to the child's whereabouts, the court may order any person who it has reason to believe may have relevant information to disclose it to the court (FLA 1986, s.33(1)). For the procedure to obtain from a Government Department the address of a child or the person with whom the child is believed to be, see paras 3.43–3.50 *et seq.*

10   Conduct of proceedings

11.33   Recent years have seen a growing emphasis on court control over the conduct of children cases. During a case, early and careful consideration should be given to the *Practice Direction*, January 31, 1995, [1995] 1 F.L.R. 456 which concerns the preparation for, and conduct of, substantive hearings. Reference should also be made to:

(*a*) the *Best Practice Note of January 1996*, taken from the *Children Act Advisory Committee Annual Report 1994/95* dealing with the *Joint Instruction of Experts in Children Act Cases* (reproduced in Pt IV of the *Family Court Practice 2002*);

(*b*) the *Best Practice Guidance of June 1997*, taken from the *Children Act Advisory Committee Handbook of Best Practice in Children Act cases* (s.4 — private law cases; s.5 — experts and the courts) (reproduced in Pt IV of the *Family Court Practice 2002*);

(*c*) the *President's Direction (Family Proceedings: Court Bundles)* March 10, 2002 [2000] 1 F.L.R. 536;

(*d*) the *President's Direction (Human Rights Act 1998)*, July 24, 2000 [2000] 2 F.L.R. 429.

The court must draw up a timetable with a view to determining any application without delay and give appropriate directions to ensure that such timetable is adhered to so far as reasonably practicable (CA 1989, s.11(1)). The court may give, vary or revoke directions for the conduct of the proceedings including:

(*a*) the timetable for the proceedings:

(*b*) varying the time within which or by which an act is required to be done;

(*c*) the attendance of the child;

(*d*) the appointment of a children's guardian;

(*e*) the service of documents;

(*f*) the submission of evidence including expert's reports;

(*g*) the preparation of welfare reports under CA 1989, s.7;

(*h*) the transfer of proceedings to another court;

(*i*) consolidation with other proceedings (FPR, r.4.14(2)).

11.34 Directions may be made by the court of its own motion or on the written request of a party in Form C2. Where the other parties to the proceedings consent to the direction sought by another party, the form should be signed by either the party concerned or his representative (FPR, r.4.14(3)). In urgent cases, a request for a direction may, with leave of the court, be made orally and/or without notice to the other parties (FPR, r.4.14(4)). In all other cases, the request should be made in Form C2 and served on the other parties (FPR, r.4.14(3)(*b*)) when the court clerk will fix a date for the hearing of the request giving not less than two days' notice to the parties (FPR, r.4.14(5)).

Notice of any directions made, varied or revoked must be served by the court, as soon as practicable, on any party who was not present at the hearing (FPR, r.4.14(10)).

A period of time within which or by which a certain act is to be performed, as provided for by the FPR or any other rules of court, may not be extended otherwise than by direction of the court (FPR, r.4.15(1)). Similarly, the court retains control over the conduct of proceedings, by fixing dates upon which the proceedings must come back before the court for such purposes as the court directs, whenever proceedings are transferred or a hearing or directions appointment is postponed or adjourned or upon the conclusion of any hearing or directions appointment other than one at which the proceedings are determined (FPR, r.4.15(2)). Cases cannot therefore be adjourned to the 'next available date'.

11.35   The parties must attend a directions appointment arranged following a written request from one of the parties of which they have been given notice unless the court otherwise directs (FPR, r.4.16(1)). The FPR do not, however, place any obligation upon the parties to attend a directions appointment which is arranged at the court's own motion. The court will often direct a further appointment to take place without actually specifying that the parties should attend. It is, nevertheless, submitted that a party should always attend an appointment of which he has received notice unless, perhaps, agreement has been reached over procedural directions to be made and the parties' legal representatives are to be present.

Proceedings or any part of them may take place in the absence of any party, including a child, if the court considers it in the interests of the child, having regard to the matters to be discussed or the evidence likely to be given, and the party to be excluded is represented by a children's guardian or solicitor. When considering the interests of the child, the court must give the children's guardian, solicitor for the child and, if he is of sufficient understanding, the child himself an opportunity to make representations (FPR, r.4.16(2)). It follows that a party cannot be excluded where he is acting in person.

11.36   Where the applicant appears but one or more of the respondents do not, the court may still proceed with the hearing or directions appointment (FPR, r.4.16(3)). But the court must not begin to hear an application in the absence of the respondent unless it proved to the satisfaction of the court that he received reasonable notice of the date of the hearing or the court is satisfied that the circumstances of the case justify proceeding with the hearing (FPR, r.4.16(4)). Where the applicant does not appear but one or more of the respondents do, the court may refuse the application or, if sufficient evidence has previously been received, may proceed in his absence (FPR, r.4.16(5)). Where neither the applicant nor any respondent appear, the court may refuse the application (FPR, r.4.16(6)). The court may alternatively decide to adjourn the appointment where a particular party fails to attend.

Unless the court orders otherwise, a hearing or directions appointment takes place in chambers (FPR, r.4.16(7)).

R.4.21(1) and (2) of the FPR provide for the order of speeches and evidence at a hearing or directions appointment. After the final hearing the court must deliver its judgment as soon as practicable and a copy must be served by the court, again as soon as practicable, on the parties and on any person with whom the child is living (FPR, r.4.21(3) and (6).) When making an order, or when refusing an application, the court must

(a) where it makes a finding of fact, state such finding and complete Form C22; and

(b) state the reasons for the court's decision (FPR, r.4.21(4)).

An application may be withdrawn only with leave of the court in accordance with the procedure set out in FPR, r.4.5.

11 Evidence

The FPR provide for written statements comprising the substance of the oral **11.37** evidence which a party intends to adduce at a directions appointment or hearing to be filed. These replace affidavits. Unless otherwise directed, every witness statement in family proceedings will stand as the evidence in chief of the witness concerned. The substance of the evidence must be sufficiently detailed but without prolixity and confined to material matters of fact and not opinion (except in the case of expert witnesses). The source of any hearsay evidence must be declared or a good reason given for not doing so (*Practice Direction*, January 31, 1995 [1995] 1 F.L.R. 456). A child who is the subject of an application before the court should not generally be asked to make a statement (*Re M* [1995] 2 F.L.R. 100).

In proceedings for a s.8 order, a party cannot file any statement or copy of any document, including an expert's report, upon which he intends to rely until such time as the court directs (FPR, r.4.17(5)). Likewise, a party cannot file or serve any document, other than as required or authorised by the FPR, and in completing a prescribed form must not give any information or make a statement, which is not required by or authorised by that form, without leave of the court (FPR, r.4.17(4)). The emphasis is on court control over both documentation and procedure.

Written statements must be dated, signed by the maker and contain a declaration that the maker believes it to be true and understands that it may be placed before the court. The top right hand corner of the first page of the statement must show the initials and surname of the maker, the number of the statement for that particular person, the date on which it was made and the party on whose behalf it is filed (FPR, r.4.17(1)(*a*)).

In proceedings other than those for a section 8 order, statements, together **11.38** with copies of any documents, including experts' reports, upon which a party intends to rely at a directions appointment or hearing must be filed and served on the other parties, any children and family reporter and any children's guardian in accordance with any direction of the court or, if none, before the hearing or appointment (FPR, r.4.17(1)).

A party may not adduce evidence or seek to rely on a document in respect of which he has failed to comply with the requirements of FPR, r.4.17, without leave of the court (FPR, r.4.17(3)).

Supplementary statements may be made without leave of the court unless a specific restriction has been imposed. Such statements are, however still subject to any direction of the court as to timing (FPR, r.4.17(2)). Leave of the court is required to amend any document which has been filed or served (FPR, r.4.19(1)). A copy of the statement with the proposed amendments identified should accompany the request.

Once any document (whether statement, expert's report, children and family reporter's report or otherwise) has been filed at court, leave is required before it can be disclosed to any person other than a party to the proceedings, his legal representatives, a children and family reporter or the Legal Services Commission. The only exception is a record of a court order (FPR 1991, r.4.23(1)).

Hearsay evidence in family proceedings is admissible pursuant to the **11.39** Children (Admissibility of Hearsay Evidence) Order 1993 providing that it is given in connection with the upbringing, maintenance or welfare of a child. The proposed evidence must, however, show a substantial connection with the upbringing, maintenance or welfare of a child and will not be admissible where the proceedings primarily affect the child's parents (*C v C (Contempt: Evidence)* [1993] 1 F.L.R. 220). The weight given to hearsay evidence is entirely a matter for the court (*F v Child Support Agency* [1998] 2 F.L.r. 444).

A child may not be medically or psychiatrically examined or otherwise assessed for the purpose of expert evidence without leave of the court (FPR, r.4.18(1)). Where leave has not been obtained, no evidence arising out of an examination or assessment may be adduced without leave (FPR, R. 4.18(3)).

11.40   There is now a wealth of case law concerning the involvement of experts in children cases. The need to instruct a particular expert will need to be demonstrated to the court which deals with the leave applications. Extensive guidance is to be derived from the case law (see *Re G* [1994] 2 F.L.R. 291; *Re C* [1995] 1 F.L.R. 204) and from the *Best Practice Guidance of June 1997*, taken from the *Children Act Advisory Committee Handbook of Best Practice in Children Act cases* (s.5 — experts and the courts) (reproduced in Pt IV of the *Family Court Practice 2002*). Wherever possible the examination of a child should be conducted by one expert agreed upon by parties or there should be a single examination which the parties' experts are all invited to attend. It should be a condition of appointment of any expert that he should be required to hold discussions with other experts instructed, in advance of the hearing, to identify areas of agreement and dispute, which should then be incorporated into a schedule for the court. Once leave has been granted, the letter of instruction should be disclosed to the other parties. The letter should identify the papers disclosed to the expert. Experts on each side should meet to discuss their reports in advance of the hearing in an attempt to reach agreement or at least limit the issues. Careful co-operative planning between the parties' legal advisers at an early stage in the preparation for the hearing should be undertaken to ensure the experts availability and so that they can be called in a logical sequence (*Re M* [1994] 1 F.L.R. 749).

There has been extensive debate as to the court's power to order disclosure of experts' medical reports in proceedings relating to children where leave of the court has been given to obtain them. It would appear that in family proceedings a party can be ordered to disclose all such experts' reports, whether or not they are favourable and despite having no intention to rely upon them (*Re L* [1996] 1 F.L.R. 731; but see also *R. v Derby Magistrates' Court*, ex p. B [1996] 1 F.L.R. 513). The court does, however, retain a discretion to direct that certain material should not be disclosed to another party if to do so may be damaging to the child (*Re B (A Minor)* [1993] 1 F.L.R. 191; *Re M* [1994] 1 F.L.R. 760; *Re D* [1995] 2 F.L.R. 687). Where there are doubts as to what the proper course should be concerning disclosure, it may be appropriate to seek the court's direction by means of a directions appointment (FPR, r.4.14). Questions of relevance and admissibility should normally be referred to the judge, who will be conducting the final hearing (*Re CB and JB* [1998] 2 F.L.R. 211)

12   Welfare reports

11.41 In September 1994 the Home Office issued its *National Standards for Probation Service Family Court Welfare Work*, which were implemented in January 1995. The objective is to ensure that family court welfare work is carried out consistently and fairly. To that end they set out basic standards of good practice which are expected to be followed.

Since April 1, 2001, the Children and Family Court Advisory and Support

Service (CAFCASS) has had responsibility for the services previously provided by GALRO Panels and the probation-run Family Court Welfare Services, together with much of the work of the Official Solicitor in the field of child law (Criminal Justice and Court Services Act 2000).

The introduction of CAFCASS has led to a renaming of the roles to which "Officers of the Service" may be appointed by the court: "guardian ad litem" becomes "children's guardian"; "welfare officer" becomes "children and family reporter" for the purposes of a report commissioned by the court and directed to a CAFCASS officer pursuant to CA 1989, s.7(1)(a), but the title "welfare officer" remains in existence for the purposes of a report commissioned by the court and directed to a local authority officer pursuant to CA 1989, s.7(1)(b). There are two new practice directions which govern the involvement of CAFCASS and the Official Solicitor in family proceedings concerning children (*CAFCASS Practice Note (Officer of CAFCASS Legal Services and Special Casework: Appointment in Family Proceedings*) March 2001 [2001] 2 F.L.R. 151, and *Practice Note (Official Solicitor: Appointment in Family Proceedings*) April 2, 2001 [2001] 2 F.L.R. 155).

A court considering any question with respect to a child may ask a children and family reporter to report to the court on such matters relating to the welfare of that child as are required to be dealt with in the report (CA 1989, s.7(1)). The request will be directed to either the CAFCASS or the local authority. In private law proceedings it will most frequently be the CAFCASS. The request is entirely at the court's discretion and it is, therefore, inappropriate to appeal against the court's decision (*Re W* [1995] 2 F.L.R. 142).

11.42 A direction may be made by the court of its own motion or on the request of a party (FPR, r.4.14(3)). The court may specify those matters on which the report is to be made without preventing the reporting officer from bringing to the notice of the court any other matters which he considers the court should have in mind (*Practice Direction*, 16 July, 1981 [1981] 2 All E.R. 1056). The court should not, however, direct that a court welfare report be made where a children's guardian has already prepared a report for the court concerning the child, unless there are exceptional circumstances (*Re S (A Minor)* [1993] 1 F.L.R. 110 although in a difficult case where a childrens' and family reporter has already commenced his investigations prior to the appointment of a children's guardian, it might be beneficial in certain circumstances for the children and family report to remain involved (*L v L* [1994] 1 F.L.R. 156).

11.43 The combination of the requirement for the court to draw up a timetable (CA 1989, s.11) and the ability to make directions for the conduct of the proceedings (FPR, r.4.14) should facilitate the general principle that any delay in determining the application is likely to prejudice the welfare of the child. To minimise delay, the court will arrange a hearing date for when the report is *likely* to be available (*B v B* [1994] 2 F.L.R. 489). However, if a welfare report is unduly delayed, the court may proceed to hear the application if a further delay is likely to cause any harm to the child (*Re H (Minors)* [1990] 2 F.L.R. 172).

The report may be written or oral, as the court requires (CA 1989, s.7(3)). In practice, it is usually made in writing. The court may take account of any statement contained in the report and any evidence given in respect of the matters to which it refers to the extent that, in the opinion of the court, it is relevant to the question which is under consideration (CA 1989, s.7(4)). The reporting officer should ensure that the court is provided with all relevant information. The *National Standards* offer children and family reporters guidance on the preparation and content of reports. The children and family reporter's duty is not to act as a conciliator in preparing his report but to investigate and assist the court to resolve disputes (*Registrar's Direction* [1986] 2 F.L.R. 171; *National Standards*, 4.3). A person who has already been involved in conciliation should not subsequently act as a children and family reporter in the same case (Relt [1986] 1 F.L.R. 476). A children and family reporter cannot guarantee confidentiality to persons whose comments are incorporated into a report (*Re G* [1993] 2 F.L.R. 293).

11.44   Where the court has given a direction for the preparation of a welfare report, it must be filed at or by such time as the court directs or, in the absence of any such direction, at least 14 days before the hearing at which the officer has been notified his report will be considered. The filing of the report should form part of the overall timetable for the case (*Re A and B (No. 2)* [1995] 1 F.L.R. 351). The court clerk must, as soon as practicable, serve a copy of the report on the parties and any children's guardian (FPR, R. 4.13(1)). Once filed, the court may direct that the children and family reporter attend any hearing at which the report is to be considered. Any party may question the children and family reporter at the hearing about his report (FPR, r.4.13(3)) and should, therefore, ensure that an appropriate direction is made by the court for the children and family reporter's attendance. A judge should only see a children and family reporter privately in exceptional circumstances (*Re C (A Minor)* [1991] 2 F.L.R. 438).

Reasons should be given by the court for not following the recommendations of the children and family reporter (*Re J (Children) (Residence: Experts Evidence)* [2001] 2 F.L.R. 751). The requirement is that the judgment as a whole discloses the reasons for departing from the recommendations; its precise format and phraseology are a matter for the court (*Re V* [1995] 2 F.L.R. 1010). In certain circumstances a court may depart from recommendations without hearing oral evidence from the children and family reporter concerned (*Re C* [1995] 1 F.L.R. 617 and *Re L* [1995] 2 F.L.R. 445; compare *CB* [1995] 1 F.L.R. 622).

11.45   A notice must be boldly endorsed on all reports indicating that it has been prepared for the court and should be treated as confidential. Reports must not be shown nor their contents revealed to any person other than a party or a legal adviser to such a party. Such legal advisers may make use of a report in connection with an application for public funding (*Practice Direction*, February, 24, 1984 [1984] F.L.R. 356). Once the report has been filed at court, leave of the court must be obtained before it may be disclosed to anyone other than a party, legal representative, children's guardian or the Legal Services Commission (FPR 1991, r.4.23(1)).

The role of an independent reporter, such as a social worker, is strictly limited and the other party to the proceedings is not under any duty to be interviewed in the preparation of independent reports (*Practice Direction*, 24 March, 1983 (1983) F.L.R. 450).

13   Family assistance orders

11.46   In any family proceedings, the court may make an order (whether or not it makes a section 8 order) requiring a children and family reporter to be made available or a local authority to make an officer available to advise, assist and (where appropriate) befriend any person named in the order (CA 1989, s.16(1)). The only persons who may be named in such an order are any parent, guardian of the child, any person with whom the child is living or in whose favour a contact order or existing access order is in force with respect to the child and the child himself (CA 1989, s.16(2)). A family assistance order cannot be made unless the court is satisfied that the circumstances of the case are exceptional and it has obtained the consent of every person to be named in the order other than the child (CA 1989, s.16(3)). The order has effect for a period of six months unless a shorter period is specified (CA 1989, s.16(5)). Where a s.8 order is also in force, the officer concerned may refer to the court the question as to whether the s.8 order should be varied or discharged (CA 1989, s.16(6)).

14   Care and supervision orders

The court can only make a care or supervision order in accordance with Pt IV   **11.47**
of the Children Act. However, section 37 of the Act provides that where, in *any* family proceedings in which a question arises with respect to the welfare of *any* child, it appears to be the court that it may be appropriate for a care or supervision order to be made with respect to him, the court may direct the appropriate local authority to undertake an investigation of the child's circumstances (CA 1989, s.37(1)). The local authority is then required to consider whether an application should be made for a care or supervision order under s.31 of the Act (CA 1989, s.37(2)). Where the local authority, having undertaken their investigation, decide not to make such an application, they must inform the court of their reasons for so deciding together with any service or assistance which they have provided, or intend to provide, for the child or his family and any other action which they have taken, or propose to take, with respect to the child (CA 1989, s.37(3)). In such circumstances, the local authority must also consider whether it would be appropriate to review the case at a later date and, if so, set the appropriate date (CA 1989, s.37(6)). R. 4.26 of the FPR applies.

15   Change of name

Where a residence order is in force, no person may cause a child to be known   **11.48**
by a new surname without either the written consent of every person who has parental responsibility for the child or the leave of the court (CA 1989, s.13(1)). Where no residence order is in force, no restrictions are imposed and therefore a person with parental responsibility who opposes a change of name should seek a prohibited steps order and/or a specific issue order. The procedure to be followed where a person seeks to enrol a deed poll to change the surname of a child is set out in *Practice Direction*, December 20, 1994 [1995] 1 F.L.R. 458.

The child's welfare remains the court's paramount consideration (CA 1989, s.1(1); *Re W, Re A, Re B (Change of Name)* [1999] 2 F.L.R. 930; *Dawson v. Wearmouth* [1999] 1 F.L.R. 1167). The case of *Re W, Re A, Re B* (above) sets out useful guidelines for such applications.) Case law demonstrates that leave will not readily be granted (see, for instance, *Re F* [1993] 2 F.L.R. 837; and *Re B* [1996] 1 F.L.R. 791 where an application was refused contrary to the wishes of three adolescent children). Parents and courts should be much more prepared to contemplate the use of the surnames of both parents (for example, by hyphenation) in appropriate cases as this recognises the importance of both parents (*Re R (Surname: Using Both Parents')* [2001] 2 FLR 1358).

11.49 A district judge not of the principal registry and who is not nominated for public law proceedings may only hear an unopposed application to change a child's surname or give directions in an opposed application.

16 Removal of children from the United Kingdom

11.50 Where a residence order is in force, no-one may remove a child from the United Kingdom (note that the UK includes Scotland: *Re T (A Child)*, June 28, 2001 (unreported), CA (The President, Thorpe L.J.) where it was held that if a residence order is in place the removal of a child from England and Wales to Scotland does not require an application for leave to remove the child from the jurisdiction as Scotland is part of the UK), without either the written consent of every person who has parental responsibility for the child or the leave of the court (CA 1989, s.13(1)). This does not, however, prevent the removal of a child, for a period of less than one month, by the person in whose favour the residence order is made (CA 1989, s.13(2)). Where a person with parental responsibility wishes to oppose a visit abroad for a period of less than one month, a prohibited steps order should be sought or a variation to the residence order so as to impose an appropriate condition under CA 1989, s.11(7).

Where no residence order is in force, there remain restrictions on the removal of a child by virtue of the Child Abduction Act 1984. Any person connected with the child who removes him from the United Kingdom without the appropriate consent may commit a criminal offence under section 1 of the 1984 Act. However, a defence exists where the person believes that the other party had consented or would consent, the other party unreasonably refused to consent or all reasonable steps have been taken to communicate with the other party but these have been unsuccessful. However, any existing order restricting the removal of the child, such as a prohibited steps order, must still be complied with

11.51 Leave to remove a child from the United Kingdom may be granted either generally or for specified purposes (CA 1989, s.13(3)). A residence order states that any person with parental responsibility may obtain advice on what can be done to prevent the issue of a passport to the child by contacting the United Kingdom Passport Agency, Clive House, Petty France, London SW1H 9HD.

Useful guidelines to such an application are set out in *Payne v. Payne* [2001] 1 F.L.R. 1052, which include the following:

(*a*) The welfare of the child is always paramount;

(*b*) There is no presumption in favour of the applicant parent;

(*c*) The reasonable proposals of the parent with a residence order wishing to live abroad carry great weight;

(*d*) The proposals must be carefully scrutinised and the court must be satisfied there is a genuine need for the move and not the intention to bring contact between the child and the other parent to an end;

(*e*) The effect upon the applicant and parent and the new family of the child of a refusal of leave is very important;

(f) The effect upon the child of the denial of contact with the other parent and in some cases his family is very important;

(g) The opportunity for continuing contact between the child and the parent left behind may be very significant.

A district judge not of the principal registry and who is not nominated for public law proceedings may only hear an unopposed application to remove a child from the United Kingdom, whether temporarily or permanently, or give directions in opposed applications. Applications to permanently remove a child should be made either to the county court or the High Court, depending upon the complexity and difficulty of the decision (*MH v GP* [1995] 2 F.L.R. 106).

Any order made prohibiting the removal of a child out of the United Kingdom or any specified part of it has effect in other parts of the United Kingdom as if it had been made by the appropriate court in that other part (FLA 1986, s.36(1) and (2)(*a*)).

Where a child has been taken to another part of the United Kingdom in **11.52** contravention of an order prohibiting removal to that other part, the order automatically has effect in that other part as if including a provision prohibiting further removal except one which is consistent with the order (FLA 1986, s.36(2)(*b*)).

Section 36 of the FLA 1986 only applies to children under the age of 16.

Where there is in force an order prohibiting or restricting the removal of a child from the United Kingdom or from any specified part of it, the court which made the order, or by which it is treated under FLA 1986, s.36 as having been made, may require any person to surrender any United Kingdom passport which has been issued to the child or which contains particulars of the child (FLA 1986, s.37).

17 Proceedings in other courts

If, while a cause is pending, proceedings relating to any child of the family are **11.53** begun in any other court, a concise statement of the nature of the proceedings must immediately be filed by the person beginning the proceedings, or, if he is not a party to that cause, by the petitioner (FPR, r.2.40(2)).

R. 7.14 of the FPR provides that a party to proceedings for or relating to a section 8 order or an existing custody order who knows of other proceedings (including proceedings out of the jurisdiction and concluded proceedings) which relate to the child concerned must file an affidavit stating:

(a) in which jurisdiction and court the other proceedings were instituted;

(b) the nature and current state of such proceedings and the relief claimed or granted;

(c) the names of the parties to such proceedings and their relationship to the child;

(d) if applicable, and if known, the reasons why the relief claimed in the proceedings for or relating to the section 8 or custody order was not claimed in the other proceedings.

A court in England and Wales which has jurisdiction to make a section 8 order may refuse an application such such an order in any case where the matter in question has already been determined in proceedings outside England and Wales (FLA 1986, s.5(1)). The court has a discretion to stay proceedings for a section 8 order at any stage where it appears to the court that proceedings with respect to the matters to which the application relates are continuing outside England and Wales or that, although no such proceedings have been commenced, it would be more appropriate for those matters to be determined in proceedings to be taken outside England and Wales (FLA 1986, s.5(2)).

If there is unreasonable delay in taking other proceedings, or those proceedings have been stayed, sisted or concluded, the court has the power to remove the stay (FLA 1986, s.5(3)).

11.54   If a custody order made by a court in Scotland or Northern Ireland (or a variation of such an order) comes into force with respect to a child at a time when a section 8 order made by a court in England and Wales has effect with respect to the same child, the latter order should cease to have effect so far as it makes provision for any matter for which the same or different provision is made by the order made by the court in Scotland or Northern Ireland (FLA 1986, s.6(1)). Thereafter, the English court does not have power to vary its own order so as to make provision for the matters covered by the later order (FLA 1986, s.6(2)).

English court does not have power to vary a section 8 order, whilst proceedings for divorce, nullity or judicial separation between the child's parents are continuing in Scotland or Northern Ireland unless; (a) the section 8 order was made in, or in connection with, proceedings for divorce or nullity in England and Wales which are continuing; (b) the s.8 order was made in connection with proceedings for judicial separation in England and Wales which are continuing and the decree has not yet been granted; or (c) the court in Scotland or Northern Ireland has made an order for the purpose of enabling the section 8 proceedings with respect to the child concerned to be taken in England and Wales and that order is in force (FLA 1986, s.6(3A) (3B) and (4)).

18   Mediation and conciliation

11.55   Neither conciliation nor mediation is mandatory in proceedings affecting children but most courts do now operate such schemes in contested applications in children proceedings. The two terms are now regarded as being interchangeable, although the current rend is such that mediation is much the more popular.

The conciliation scheme which has operated in the principal registry since January 1, 1983 was modified from October 14, 1991, to reflect the changes brought about by CA 1989. A district judge may, at any time whilst considering arrangements for children under MCA 1973, s.41, direct a conciliation appointment. Where an application is made for a residence or contact order, it must be referred to conciliation. An application for a prohibited steps or specific issue order may be referred where the applicant so requests. The appointment takes place before a district judge with the attendance of a children and family reporter. All discussions are privileged and are not disclosed on any subsequent application. If the conciliation proves to be unsuccessful, the district judge and children and family reporter are not further involved in that application (*Practice Direction*, October 18, 1991 [1992] 1 F.L.R. 228).

Other courts operate a scheme whereby a 'family meeting', usually with a children and family reporter, is arranged prior to the first directions appointment in the proceedings. If the meeting proves to be successful, the district judge will consider whether an order needs to be made having regard to the non-intervention principle (CA 1989, s.1(5)). If no agreement is reached, the court will make the appropriate directions for the application to proceed. The children and family reporter who conducted the family meeting is not prohibited from preparing any welfare report.

There are also a variety of hybrid schemes in existence which, although operating under the auspices of the probation services, are not formally part of the CAFCASS. Where a local conciliation service exists, the court should consider before ordering a report by a children and family reporter whether the case is suitable for conciliation and, if so, a direction to this effect should be made. If conciliation fails, any welfare report which is ordered must be prepared by an officer who did not act as the conciliator (*Registrar's Direction* [1986] 2 F.L.R. 171; *Re H* [1986] 1 F.L.R. 476). **11.56**

In addition, mediation schemes exist which are entirely independent of the courts both in terms of finance and manpower. The main organisations to which such services are affiliated are National Family Mediation (NFM) and the Family Mediators' Association (FMA), the United Kingdom College of Family Mediators, Family Mediation Scotland and the Solicitors' Family Law Association.

Statements made by any party in connection with conciliation meetings, whether operated in court or on a voluntary basis, are not admissible as evidence in proceedings under the CA 1989, except in the exceptional case where the statement indicates that the maker has or is likely to cause serious harm to the child. Even then, it is still the court's discretion as to whether or not to admit the evidence (*Re D* [1993] 1 F.L.R. 932).

19   Human Rights Act 1998

The Human Rights Act 1998 came into force on October 2, 2000. It incorporates the majority of the provisions of the Convention for the Protection of Human Rights and Fundamental Freedoms 1950 into our domestic law. This means that in future domestic law will be enacted, interpreted and amended so that it is compatible with the Convention. **11.57**

There are a number of fundamental rights guaranteed by the Convention which relate to family law. These include:

(*a*) the right to life (Art.2);

(*b*) the right to liberty (Art.5);

(*c*) the right to a fair trial (Art.6);

(*d*) the right to respect for private and family life (Art.8);

(*e*) the right to freedom of expression (Art.10);

(*f*) the right to marry and found a family (Art.12).

In practice, Articles 6 and 8 are the ones most commonly raised in the course of family law cases. The President of the Family Division has made it clear that all Human Rights Act 1998 points must be dealt with as and when **11.58**

they arise and in the court in which they arise, whether that be a family proceedings court, a county court or the High Court. Examples of important
family law cases which have considered human rights points to date are:

(*a*) Change of surname—change of child's surname was not an infringe-
ment of the father's rights under Art.6 (*Dawson v Wearmouth* [1999]
1 F.L.R. 1167);

(*b*) Relationships of unmarried fathers with their children—no breach of
Art.8 and no discrimination against unmarried fathers as compared
with married fathers in relation to the protection given by the UK
courts to their relationships with their children (*B v UK* [2000] 1
F.L.R. 1);

(*c*) Leave to remove a child permanently from the jurisdiction—no
breach of Art.8 rights of the parent who is "left behind" in the
approach taken by UK courts in relation to applications to remove a
child permanently from the jurisdiction (*Payne v Payne* [2001] 1
F.L.R. 425; *Re A* [2000] 2 F.L.R. 225);

(*d*) Holding CA 1989 hearings in private and not making judgments generally available to the public—no breach of Article 6 by UK in
holding residence order proceedings in private and not making judgments generally available to the public (*B and another v UK* [2001] 2
F.C.R. 221);

(*e*) S.91(14) restrictions on bringing proceedings—no breach of Art.6
when an order under CA 1989, s.91(14) is made because it does not
deny access to the court, but merely creates an extra filter whereby the
person subject to the order must apply for leave before he can bring
further applications (*Re P (s.91(14) Guidelines)* [1999] 2 F.L.R. 573).

Chapter 12

Other Originating Proceedings Relating to Children

1   Scope

This chapter deals with the following issues: child abduction, wardship and   **12.01**
financial applications relating to children. Chapter 11 deals with private law
applications under CA 1989.

2   Child abduction: recognition and enforcement of rights

Section 1(5)) of the CA 1989 provides that the court, when considering   **12.02**
whether or not to make one or more orders under the Act, must not make an
order unless it considers that doing so would be better for the child than
making no order at all. The existence of a court order will be invaluable if not
essential to a party seeking recognition or enforcement of their rights. Where
a section 8 order has not been made, consideration should be given as to
whether an order should be sought and, in cases of urgency, whether an ex
parte application should be made (see paras 11.27 to 11.32 *et seq.*). A court in
England and Wales may still be able to make a section 8 order even where a
child has already left the country providing that the provisions of FLA 1986,
ss.2A or 3 are satisfied. An order may be made if, although not capable of direct
enforcement, it may nevertheless prove to be of assistance to a party in proceedings outside England and Wales (*Re D (A Minor)* [1992] 1 All E.R. 892).

A   Within the UK

Preliminary considerations

The failure of a party to obey a section 8 order is punishable by committal   **12.03**
(RSC, Ord. 45, r.5; CCR, Ord. 29, r.1; FPR r.4.21A). Such orders are, however,
only enforceable by committal where they require a person to do, within a
specified time, or to abstain from doing, an act and will therefore depend on
the precise terms of the order (*Re H (Contact) (Enforcement)* [1996] 1 F.L.R.
614). The magistrate's court has the specific power to enforce a residence order
by fine or committal under the Magistrates Courts Act 1980, s.63(3) (CA 1989,
s.14). Sequestration and emergency protection orders are further alternatives,
although are generally not to be encouraged.

   Where a person is required by a section 8 order or existing custody order (as
defined under the FLA 1986, s.1), or an order for the enforcement of such an

order, to give up a child to another person and the court which made the order imposing the requirement is satisfied that the child has not been given up in accordance with the order, it may make an order authorising an officer of the court or a constable to take charge of the child and deliver him to the other person (FLA 1986, s.34(1)). Such application can be made on an ex parte basis (FPR 1991, r.6.17). The authority given includes authority to enter and search any premises where the person acting in pursuance of the order has reason to believe the child may be found and to use such force as may be necessary to give effect to the purpose of the order (FLA 1986, s.34(2)). Under FLA 1986, s.33 as amended, the court also has power to order disclosure of a child's whereabouts. (For consideration of such issues generally, including where the child is taken overseas, see *Re B* [1994] 2 F.L.R. 479.)

The Family Law Act 1986 (Dependent Territories) Order 1991 (SI 1991 No. 1723) modifies the FLA 1986, Pt I, so as to bring orders made by courts in dependent territories within the scheme and to provide for their recognition and enforcement in the United Kingdom. So far, only the Isle of Man has been listed as a dependent territory.

Recognition

12.04   A section 8 or existing custody order relating to a child under the age of sixteen made in one of the parts of the UK is recognised in any other part of the UK as having the same effect as if it had been made in that other part of the UK by the appropriate court and as if that court had jurisdiction to make it (FLA 1986, s.25(1)). Recognition does not, however, extend to the means by which rights conferred by the order are to be enforced (FLA 1986, s.25(2)). In order to enforce a s.8 or existing custody order in another part of the UK *registration* of the order and *enforcement* proceedings must take place (FLA 1986, s.25(3)).

Registration

12.05   Any person on whom any rights are conferred by a section 8 or existing custody order may apply to the court which made the order for it to be registered in another part of the UK (FLA 1986, s.27).

The application for registration is made by lodging in the principal or district registry or county court where the order was made:

(1) a certified copy of the order and any order varying its terms;

(2) an affidavit by the applicant, and copy, which must state:

   (*a*) the name and address of the applicant and his interest under the order;
   (*b*) the name and date of birth of the child in respect of whom the order was made, his whereabouts or suspected whereabouts and the name of any person with whom he is alleged to be;
   (*c*) the name and address of any person who has an interest under the order and whether it has been served on him;
   (*d*) whether the order is to be registered in Scotland or in Northern Ireland or in both jurisdictions;
   (*e*) that, to the best of the applicant's information and belief, the order is in force;
   (*f*) whether, and if so where, the order is already registered; and

    (*g*) details of any order known to the applicant which affects the child and is in force in the jurisdiction in which the section 8 or existing custody order is to be registered;

(3) a fee of £60.

Any document relevant to the application should be exhibited to the affidavit (FPR, r.7.8(1)–(3)).

On receiving an application for registration, the court which made the section 8 or existing custody order must, unless it appears to the court that the order is no longer in force, cause the following documents to be sent to the appropriate court in the part of the UK specified in the application: **12.06**

    (*a*) a certified copy of the order;

    (*b*) where the order has been varied, prescribed particulars of any variation which is in force; and

    (*c*) a copy of the application and of any accompanying documents (FLA 1986, s.27(3)).

When the prescribed officer of an appropriate court receives a certified copy of a section 8 or custody order under FLA 1986, s.27(3), he *must* register the order in that court together with particulars of any variation (FLA 1986, s.27(4)). The appropriate court in England and Wales is the Family Division of the High Court (FLA 1986, s.32(1)).

Registration is not allowed if the child has already attained the age of sixteen. If registration has already taken place, it will cease when the child reaches that age (FLA 1986, s.27(5)). **12.07**

Where a registered order is revoked or varied, notice is given to the court in which it is registered by the court making the revocation or variation. On receipt of a notice of revocation, the registration is cancelled (FLA 1986, s.28(1)(*a*)). On receipt of a notice of variation, particulars of the variation are registered.

Where the order ceases to have effect other than by means of a revocation, the receiving court may, of its own motion, or on the application of any person who appears to the court to have an interest in the matter, cancel the registration (FLA 1986, s.28(2)(*a*), (*b*)).

Enforcement

Where a section 8 or custody order has been registered, the court in which it is registered has the same powers for the purpose of enforcing the order as it would have had if it had itself made the order and had jurisdiction to make it. Proceedings for or with respect to enforcement may be taken accordingly (FLA 1986, s.29(1)). **12.08**

Before an application for enforcement has been determined, the court to which such an application has been made may give such interim directions for the purpose of securing the welfare of a child or preventing changes in the circumstances relevant to the determination of the application (FLA 1986, s.29(2)). Any order available under the court's inherent jurisdiction may be made as necessary.

Any person who appears to have an interest in the matter may apply for the enforcement proceedings to be stayed or sisted on the ground that he has taken or intends to take other proceedings (in the UK or elsewhere) as a result of which the order may cease to have effect or may have a different effect in the part of the UK in which it is registered (FLA 1986, s.30(1)).

The court may remove a stay or recall a sist if it appears that there has been unreasonable delay in taking or prosecuting the other proceedings or those other proceedings are concluded and the registered order is still in force (FLA 1986, s.30(3)(*a*), (*b*)).

Where a registered order has ceased to have effect, the court must dismiss the proceedings for enforcement (FLA 1986, s.31(3)).

The detailed procedure is set out at FPR, r.7.7–7.15, as amended by the Family Proceedings (Amendment) (No. 3) Rules 1994 which joined the Isle of Man to the scheme.

B   Outside the UK

12.09   In addition to the Child Abduction Unit at the Lord Chancellor's Department (tel: 020 7210 8500) which can offer essential advice when dealing with an issue of child abduction, Reunite (the National Council for Abducted Children, PO Box 24875, London E1 6FR, tel: 020 7375 3440) is a charitable organisation which aims to co-operate with other agencies in preventing child abduction and offers advice on recovery of such children.

HAGUE CONVENTION

Preliminary considerations

12.10   Pt I of the Child Abduction and Custody Act (CACA) 1985 implements the Hague Convention of 1980 on the civil aspects of international child abduction. By CACA 1985, s.1(2), the provisions of the Convention as set out in Sch.1 of the Act have force of law in the UK, subject to the provisions of Pt I of the Act.

Although there will be some cases in which the Hague Convention and the European Convention (see below) are equally applicable, their format and underlying purpose are not the same. The Hague Convention is concerned with abduction of children and their speedy return to the person who previously had custody. Although it may be convenient in some cases to have a court order, the order is not the conclusive factor. The rights of custody which are being recognised and enforced are those which are in fact currently being exercised. The use of the Hague Convention may not necessarily involve court proceedings at all if the central authority is able to carry out its duties without resorting to them. In contrast, the European Convention's aim is the enforcement of custody orders (for the meaning of which, see para.12.12) of one jurisdiction in another. The existence of an order is essential and matters concerning the validity of the order may be relevant in the decision as to whether it should be registered and enforced in another jurisdiction. In cases where the two conventions are equally applicable, the Hague Convention takes precedence. The central authority in England and Wales for both conventions is the Lord Chancellor's Department, from which advice may be sought in cases of doubt.

12.11   The contracting states to the Hague Convention are set out in Sch.1 of the Child Abduction and Custody (Parties to Convention) Order 1986, to which further contracting states are periodically added.

The Convention applies to the *wrongful removal or retention* of a child under sixteen who immediately *before* the removal or retention was habitually resident in a contracting state.

The habitual residence of a child is a question of fact (*Re M* [1996] 1 F.L.R. 887). A child cannot be concurrently resident in two places (*Re V* [1995] 2 F.L.R. 992); his residence will focus upon that of the parents and must have a degree of settled purpose (*Re A* [1996] 1 F.L.R. 1). For a further consideration of the meaning of habitual residence, see for instance *C v S* [1990] 2 All E.R. 961; *V v B* [1991] 1 F.L.R. 266; *Re R* [1993] 1 F.L.R. 249; *Re B* [1993] 1 F.L.R. 993; *Re N* [1993] 2 F.L.R. 224; *Re K* [1995] 3 F.L.R. 697; *Nessa v Chief Adjudication Officer* [1999] 2 F.L.R. 1116; *Al-Habtoor v Fotheringham* [2001] 1 F.L.R. 951. For further discussion of the meaning of habitual residenece, see paras 1.17–1.19.

A removal or retention is wrongful where:

(*a*) it is in breach of rights of custody attributed to a person, an institution or any other body under the law of the state in which the child was habitually resident; and

(*b*) at the time of removal or retention those rights were actually exercised, either jointly or alone, or would have been so exercised but for the removal or retention (CACA 1985, Sch.1, art.3).

For discussion as to what acts constitute wrongful removal or retention see **12.12** Butterworth's *Family Law Service* 5A [2118]–[2153] *C v S* [1990] 2 F.L.R. 442 and *Re H, Re S* [1991] 3 All E.R. 230 and *Re S* [1998] 1 F.L.R. 122. Where the court becomes aware of a wrongful removal or retention when no application under the Convention has been made, the court should refrain from making an interim or full residence order but not other CA 1989, s.8 orders, unless a reasonable time has elapsed since the court first received notice of the removal or retention (*R v R* [1996] 1 F.C.R. 480).

The Convention applies to any child who was habitually resident in a contracting state immediately before any breach of custody or access rights. The Convention ceases to apply when the child attains 16 (CACA 1985, Sch.1, art.4; *Re H* [2000] 2 F.L.R. 51).

Rights of custody include rights relating to the care of the person of the child and, in particular, the right to determine the child's place of residence (CACA 1985, Sch.1, art 5(*a*)). Rights of custody include the rights conferred upon a person in whose favour a residence order is made, or where no order is made, the rights conferred upon a person who has parental responsibility for a child (see paras 11.10–11.14). For further consideration of what constitutes rights of custody see for instance *Re R* [1994] 1 F.L.R. 190; *Re B* [1994] 2 F.L.R. 249; *Re F* [1995] 2 F.L.R. 31; *Re H* [2000] 1 F.L.R. 374; *Re W, Re B* [1998] 2 F.L.R. 146. See also *Practice Note*, October 14, 1997 [1998] 1 F.L.R. 496.

Rights of access include the right to take a child for a limited period of time to a place other than the child's habitual residence (CACA 1985, Sch.1, art.5(*b*)). Rights of access in England and Wales means a decision as to the contact which a child may, or may not, have with any person (CACA 1985, s.27(4)). However, mere rights of access are insufficient to establish a right of custody (*S v H* [1997] 1 F.L.R.; *Re V-B* [1999] 2 F.L.R. 192).

Procedure

An application for the return of a child may be made either to the Lord **12.13** Chancellor or to the central authority of the requested state, that is, the foreign contracting state to which the child has been removed (CACA 1985, Sch.1, art.8). Where a court becomes aware of a wrongful removal (see para.12.11

above) and hence receives notices of the same where no application under the Convention has been made, it is the duty of the court to consider taking steps to ensure that the parent in the state from where the children had been removed was able to be informed of rights under the Convention (*R v R* [1995] 2 F.L.R. 625).

12.14   If application is made to the Lord Chancellor's Department, a questionnaire will be sent to the applicant or his solicitor to elicit the relevant information. In cases of particular urgency, this may be completed for the applicant over the telephone. A form of authority authorising the overseas central authority to act on the applicant's behalf will also be required and is available from the Lord Chancellor's Department. The applicant is responsible for supplying copies of any relevant orders. R. 10.20 of the FPR allows for the provision of authenticated copies of court decisions relating to the child. The Lord Chancellor's Department will then check the validity of the application, translate the request where necessary and then transmit the relevant information about the child to the appropriate overseas central authority.

The application to the overseas authority must contain the following matters:

(a) information concerning the identify of the applicant, of the child and of the person alleged to have removed or retained the child;

(*b*) where available, the date of birth of the child;

(*c*) the grounds upon which the applicant's claim for return of the child is based;

(*d*) all available information relating to the whereabouts of the child and the identity of the person with whom the child is presumed to be (CACA 1985, Sch.1, art.8).

The application may be accompanied or supplemented by:

(*a*) an authenticated copy of any relevant decision or agreement;

(*b*) a certificate or an affidavit emanating from a central authority, or other competent authority of a state of the child's habitual residence, or from a qualified person, concerning the relevant law of that state;

(*c*) any other relevant document (CACA 1985, Sch.1, art.8).

The central authority of the state where the child is must take or cause to be taken all appropriate measures in order to obtain voluntary return of the child (CACA 1985, Sch.1, art.10).

12.15   If the central authority which receives an application has reason to believe that the child is in another contracting state, it must directly and without delay transmit the application to the central authority of that contracting state and inform the requesting central authority or the applicant that it has done so (CACA 1985, Sch.1, art.9). Where a child is expected to arrive in a contracting state, it is open to the court in that state under CACA 1985, s.5 to make such orders as necessary to be enforced upon his arrival (*A v A* [1995] 1 F.L.R. 341).

On receiving an incoming application in England and Wales, the Lord Chancellor's Department, if satisfied that the application complies with the Convention, will grant public funding without the need for a means or merit test and instruct a firm of solicitors under the public funding certificate. Applicants will not be required to make a contribution (The Community Legal Service (Financial) Regulations 2000, reg. 3(1)(f)). The relevant documents will be passed to the solicitors who will thereafter have carriage of the case with the normal solicitor and client relationships between them and the applicant. If court proceedings are found to be necessary, then the court will be the Family Division of the High Court. The procedure is set out in FPR, r.6.2–6.12. As to the presentation of cases to the court, guidance has been given in *Re B* [1994] 2 F.L.R. 915 and *Re W* [1995] 1 F.L.R. 1021. Any written statements should be succinct and confined to the issues, which must be identified (*Re S* [2000] 1 F.L.R. 454).

The judicial or administrative authorities of contracting states must act **12.16** expeditiously in proceedings for the return of children. If such authorities have not reached a decision within six weeks from the date of commencement of the proceedings, the applicant or the central authority of the requested state, on its own initiative or if asked by the central authority of the requesting state, may request a statement of the reasons for the delay (CACA 1985, Sch.1, art.11). In *Re P* [1995] 1 F.L.R. 831 where delays were experienced from the requested state, it was held to be possible and appropriate to obtain a declaration by the court in the requesting state that the removal had been wrongful, pursuant to CACA 1985, s.8. If there is a delay in prosecuting proceedings by the applicant, they may be struck out (*Re G* [1995] 2 F.L.R. 410). The reason for the delay in bringing the proceedings, and the parties' conduct, are relevant factors (*Re H* [2000] 2 F.L.R. 51). The Convention comprises a summary procedure which should be operated only once; second or subsequent applications will not be allowed unless fresh issues are raised (*Re O* [1997] 2 F.L.R. 712; *Re L* [1999] 1 F.L.R. 433).

If a child has been wrongfully removed or retained and, at the date of the **12.17** commencement of the proceedings in the contracting state where the child is, a period of less than one year has elapsed from the date of wrongful removal or retention, the judicial or administrative authority concerned must order the return of the child forthwith subject to the three exceptions set out in the CACA 1985, Sch.1, art.13. Even where proceedings have been commenced after the expiration of one year, the judicial or administrative authority must order the return of the child, unless it is demonstrated that the child is now settled in its new environment (CACA 1985, Sch.1, art.12; *Re M* [1996] 1 F.L.R. 315; *Re H* [2000] 2 F.L.R. 51).

The court is not obliged to adjourn proceedings for the summary return of a child under CACA 1985 in order to obtain further information from the authorities of the other state, nor is it obliged to admit oral evidence on the application (*Re E* [1989] 1 F.L.R. 135). (As to the value of oral evidence, see for instance *Re C* [1996] 1 F.L.R. 414).

The court does not have power to compel a defendant to a summons under CACA 1985 to give evidence *after* a child has been found and surrendered to the court (*Re D* [1989] 1 F.L.R. 97).

An order to return or not to return a child in Hague Convention proceedings is final and any application to set aside has to be made to the Court of Appeal (*Re M* [1995] 1 F.L.R. 1021). When disposing of Hague Convention proceedings, the court may also make orders in respect of the continuation and appropriateness of domestic proceedings (*H v H* [1994] 1 F.L.R. 530).

Refusal to return

Notwithstanding article 12 above, the judicial or administrative authority of **12.18** the requested state is not bound to order the return of a child if the person,

institution or other body which opposes its return establishes one of the following:

(1) The person, institution or other body having the care of the person
of the child was not actually exercising the custody rights at the time
of removal or retention, or had consented to or subsequently acqui-
esced in the removal or retention. (For discussion as to what amounts
to acquiescence see, for example, *Re H* [1997] 1 F.L.R. 872; *Re B*
[1999] 2 F.L.R. 818.)

(2) There is a grave risk that his or her return would expose the child to
physical or psychological harm or otherwise place the child in an
intolerable situation (CACA 1985, Sch.1, art.13). The risk must be
weighty, of substantial and not trivial psychological harm. For a discussion of what constitutes psychological harm, see for example *Re
F* [1995] 2 F.L.R. 31; *Re C* [1999] 1 F.L.R. 1145; *Re C* [1999] 2 F.L.R.
478; *Re S* [2000] 1 F.L.R. 454.

The judicial or administrative authority may also refuse to order the return
of the child if it finds that the child objects to being returned and has obtained
an age and degree of maturity at which it is appropriate to take account of his
views (CACA 1985, Sch.1, art.13; *Re M* [1994] 2 F.L.R. 126; *Re R* [1995] 1
F.L.R. 716; *Re HB* [1997] 1 F.L.R. 392; *The Ontario Court v M and M* [1997]
1 F.L.R. 475; *Re M* [1997] 2 F.L.R. 690; *Re B* [1998] 1 F.L.R. 667). The provisions of CACA 1985, Sch.1, art.13 do not, however, limit the power of the
judicial or administrative authority to order the return of the child at *any* time
(CACA 1985, Sch.1, art.18).

Contact

12.19   An application to make arrangements for organizing or securing the effective
exercise or rights of access or contact may be made in the same way as an
application for the return of a child (CACA 1985, Sch.1 art.21). The court has
power to make fresh orders for access and contact under the Convention,
where, for instance, an order for the return of the child is not sought (see *C v
C* [1992] 1 F.L.R. 163) and the children are to remain in this jurisdiction.
However, the spirit behind the Convention in respect of foreign access orders
is one of executive co-operation and therefore it will not be appropriate for
art.21 of the Convention to be used to seek such access orders (see *Re G* [1993]
1 F.L.R. 669 and *Re T* [1993] 2 F.L.R. 617).

The central authorities must take steps to remove, as far as possible, all
obstacles to the exercise of the peaceful enjoyment of access or contact rights
and the fulfilment of any conditions to which the exercise of those rights may
be subject (CACA 1985, Sch.1, art.21). The duty of the Lord Chancellor's
Department, as central authority for England and Wales, is set out at *Practice
Note*, 5 March, 1993 [1993] 1 F.L.R. 804. The appropriate application is for a
contact order under CA 1989, s.8.

When dealing with breaches of access rights, as opposed to custody rights,
the Convention does not prevent the court from exercising its own independent judgment of the merits of the case. The court does not, however, have
power to enforce access rights which arose in a state before that state became
a party to the Convention (*B v B* [1988] 2 F.L.R. 6).

Use of undertakings

The use of undertakings is increasingly featured in child abduction cases as a **12.20** means of managing the process of a child's return and attaching specified conditions. These may operate to ensure return in circumstances where otherwise the art.13(b) defence would be found to apply (see *Re O* [1994] 2 F.L.R. 349; *Re M* [1995] 1 F.L.R. 89; *Re M* [1995] 1 F.L.R. 1021; *Re M* [1996] 1 F.L.R. 478; *Re M* [2000] 1 F.L.R. 930; and the article at [1997] Fam. Law. 384).

Costs and expenses

A central authority and other public services of the contracting state cannot **12.21** impose any charges in relation to an application and may not require an applicant to pay towards the costs and expenses of the proceedings or, where applicable, those arising from the participation of legal counsel or advisers, whatever the means of the applicant may be (CACA 1985, Sch.1, art.26).

The person who removed the child or prevented the exercise of rights of access may be ordered to pay necessary expenses incurred by or on behalf of the applicant, including travelling expenses, any costs incurred or payments made for locating the child, the costs of legal representation of the child and those of returning the child. The applicant, too, may have to meet some or all of the expenses incurred in implementing the child's return (CACA 1985, Sch.1, art.26).

The detailed procedure is set out at FPR, r.6.1–6.16.

Application to non-Convention cases

The underlying philosophy of the Convention will be applied even though a **12.22** particular country is not a party thereto (see, for example, *Re F* [1991] 1 F.L.R. 1; *Re S* [1994] 1 F.L.R. 297; *D v D* [1994] 1 F.L.R. 137; *Re M* [1995] 1 F.L.R. 89; *Re E* [1998] 2 F.L.R. 647; and the article at [1999] Fam. Law. 611. However, how it is to be applied has been clarified in *Re P* [1997] 1 F.L.R. 780, which also stated that in such cases the welfare of the child is the paramount consideration.

EUROPEAN CONVENTION

Preliminary considerations

Pt II of the Child Abduction and Custody Act 1985 ratifies and implements **12.23** the European Convention of 1980 on the recognition and enforcement of custody decisions and the restoration of custody of children. In England and Wales, 'custody' includes both existing custody orders and residence orders (CACA 1985, s.27 and Sch.3). By CACA 1985, s.12(2) the provisions of the Convention as set out in Sch.2 of the Act have force of law in the UK, subject to the provisions of Pt II of the Act.

For a discussion of the differences between the European Convention and the Hague Convention see para.12.10. The basic purpose of the Convention is to enable a person who has obtained a decision relating to the custody of a child, to have that decision recognised or enforced in any state which is a party to the Convention. Where EC regulations 1347/2000 ("Brussels II") applies, the provisions of the 1980 European Convention are subject to the provisions of Brussels II (see further in chap.1, paras 1.10–1.13 and paras 1.20–1.55).

It should be noted that Brussells II, in so far as it relates to decisions concerning children, is limited to issues relating to the "parental responsibility" for the children of both spouses arising in proceedings relating to divorce, separation and annulment (mantrimonial proceedings) (see Art 1(1)(b)). It has no application to issues arising in non-matrimonial proceedings concerning children. The jurisdiction under Brussells II only applies to proceedings commenced after March 1, 2001 and it only continues until the making of a final order within those proceedings (see Art 3(3)). Brussells II only applies where the children concerned are those of both spouses. This means that it does not apply to step-children or non-marital children, even if they would be regarded as 'children of the family' under UK domestic law (see chapter 2, paras 2.07–2.09 for the meaning of 'child of the family'). Furthermore, 'parental responsibility' is not defined in Brussells II and it is not clear how far it extends to issues ancillary to determining with whom the child should live and with whom he can have contact. Although UK domestic law describes these aspects as "residence" and "contact" respectively, some other countries use the terms "custody" and "access" which may have a wider meaning. This means that it is not clear, for example, whether the concept of "parental responsibility' under Brussells II would include specific issues and prohibited steps orders. The question of how to define "parental responsibility" is for the domestic court of each state to decide. In doubtful cases a reference must be made to the European Court of Justice unde Article 234 of the EC Treaty. For further information see also the article at [2002] Fam. Law 674.

The contracting states to the Convention are set out in Sch.2 of the Child Abduction and Custody (Parties to Convention) Order 1986 (SI No. 479) to which further contracting states are periodically added. Any person who has obtained in a contracting state a decision relating to the custody of a child and who wishes to have that decision recognised or enforced in another contracting state may submit an application for that purpose to the central authority in any contracting state (CACA 1985, Sch.2, art.4).

A decision relating to custody is a decision of an authority insofar as it relates to the care of the person of the child, including the right to decide on the place of his residence or to the right of access to him (CACA 1985, Sch.2, art.1). A decision relating to rights of access in England and Wales means a decision as to the contact which a child may, or may not, have with any person (CACA 1985, s.27(4)).

Procedure

12.24   In order to process an application for recognition or enforcement, the Lord Chancellor's Department requires completion of a form of authority which will be supplied on request from Lord Chancellor's Department, 81 Chancery Lane, London WC2A 1DD, tel: 020 7911 7047. It is also necessary to provide proof of service of the proceedings in which the relevant order was made.

When acting as a requesting authority, the Lord Chancellor's Department has a duty to ensure that the documentation is complete and in the correct form. Unless it is clear that the application is outside the terms of the Convention, in which case the application should be rejected, the application must be sent directly and without delay to the central authority of the state addressed.

12.25   The requirements are set out in CACA 1985, Sch.2, art.13. A request for recognition or enforcement must be accompanied by the following documents:

(1) a document authorising the central authority of the state addressed to act on behalf of the applicant or to designate another representative for that purpose;

(2) an authenticated copy of the decision; usually a certified copy of the court order;

(3) where the decision was given in the absence of the defendant or his legal representative, a document which establishes that the defendant was duly served with the document which instituted the proceedings;

(4) if applicable, any document which establishes that, in accordance with the law of state of origin, the decision is enforceable;

(5) if possible, a statement indicating the whereabouts or likely whereabouts of the child in the state addressed (this may well be the most difficult document to complete);

(6) proposals as to how the custody of the child should be restored (CACA 1985, Sch.2, art.13).

Enforcement: The central authority receiving the application may refuse to intervene where it is manifestly clear that the conditions laid down by the Convention are not satisfied (CACA 1985, Sch.2, art.4(4)). **12.26**

Upon receiving an incoming application in England and Wales, the Lord Chancellor's Department will verify that the application is in order and then instruct solicitors to act on behalf of the applicant. The applicant will automatically be entitled to public funding without any means or merits tests and will not be required to make any contribution (The Community Legal Service (Financial) Regulations 2000, reg. 3(1)(f)). The solicitor will then assume sole conduct of the case.

The central authority in the state addressed must take without delay all steps which it considers to be appropriate, if necessary by instituting proceedings in order:

(*a*) to discover the whereabouts of the child;

(*b*) to avoid, in particular by any necessary provisional measures, prejudice to the interests of the child or the applicant;

(*c*) to secure the recognition or enforcement of the decision;

(*d*) to secure the delivery of the child to the applicant where enforcement is granted;

(*e*) to inform the requesting authority of the measures taken and their results (CACA 1985, Sch.2, art.5(1)).

The court may request the disclosure of addresses by government departments in order to assist in tracing the whereabouts of a child or person with whom the child is said to be (*Practice Direction* February 13, 1989 [1989] 1 All E.R. 765; see paras 3.43 to 3.50). Where adequate information about the whereabouts of the child is not available to the court, it may order any person who it has reason to believe may have relevant information to disclose it to the court. A person will not be excused from complying with such an order by reason that to do so may incriminate him or his spouse of an offence. However, any incriminating statement will not be admissible in evidence against either of them in proceedings for **12.27** any offence other than perjury (CACA 1985, s.24A inserted by FLA 1986, s.67(4)).

Refusal of recognition and enforcement

12.28 Recognition and enforcement may be *refused* in the following cases (per CACA 1985, Sch.2, arts 9 and 10):

(1) A decision was given in the absence of the defendant or his legal representative and either:

    (*a*) the defendant was not duly served with the document instituting the proceedings in sufficient time to enable him to arrange his defence providing that the failure to serve him was not due to the defendant's own concealment of his whereabouts; or

    (*b*) the competence of the court or other authority giving the decision was not founded on the habitual residence of the defendant, or on the last common habitual residence of the child's parents, or at least one parent being habitually resident there, or on the habitual residence of the child. For interpretation, see *Re S* [1996] 1 F.L.R. 660.

(2) The decision is incompatible with a decision relating to custody which will become enforceable in the state addressed before the removal of the child, unless the child has had his habitual residence in the territory of the requesting state for one year before his removal.

(3) The effects of the decision are manifestly incompatible with the fundamental principles of the law relating to the family and children in the state addressed (see for instance *Re M* [1994] 1 F.L.R. 551).

(4) By a change in circumstances including the passage of time but not including a mere change in the residence of the child after improper removal, the effects of the original decision are manifestly no longer in accordance with the welfare of the child (see for instance the facts of *Re H* [1994] 1 F.L.R. 512). An unexplained delay in seeking to enforce the decision may result in enforcement being refused (*F v F* [1988] 3 W.L.R. 959). The exception is, however, to be interpreted strictly (*Re G* [1990] 2 F.L.R. 325; *Re A* [1996] 1 F.L.R. 561).

(5) At the time when the proceedings were instituted in the state of origin:

    (*a*) the child was a national of the state addressed or was habitually resident there and no such connection existed with the state of origin;

    (*b*) the child was a national both of the state of origin and of the state addressed and was habitually resident in the state addressed.

(6) The decision is incompatible with the decision given in the state addressed or enforceable in that state after being given in a third state, pursuant to proceedings begun before the submission of the request for recognition or enforcement, and if the refusal is in accordance with the welfare of the child.

Recognition and enforcement are to be interpreted disjunctively (*Re H* [1994] 1 F.L.R. 512 as above).

If recognition or enforcement is refused the central authority of the state **12.29** addressed may comply with a request by the applicant to bring in that state proceedings concerning the substance of the case. If such proceedings are brought, that authority must use its best endeavours to secure the representation of the applicant in the proceedings under conditions no less favourable than those available to a person who is resident and a natural of that state (CACA 1985, Sch.2, art.5(4)).

Adjournment of proceedings for recognition and enforcement

Proceedings for recognition or enforcement may be adjourned if: **12.30**

(*a*) an ordinary form of review of the original decision has been commenced;

(*b*) proceedings relating to the custody of the child, commenced before the proceedings in the state of origin were instituted, are pending in the state addressed;

(*c*) another decision concerning the custody of the child is the subject to proceedings for enforcement or of any other proceedings concerning the recognition of the decision (CACA 1985, Sch.2, art.10(2)).

Contact

Decisions on rights of access and contact and provisions dealing with such **12.31** rights contained in decisions relating to custody are recognised and enforced subject to the same conditions as other decisions relating to custody (CACA 1985, Sch.2, art.11(1)).

The competent authority of the state addressed may fix the conditions for the implementation and exercise of the right of access or contact taking into account, in particular, undertakings given by the parties on this matter (CACA 1985, Sch.2, art.11 (2)).

Where no decision on the right of access or contact has been taken or where recognition or enforcement of a decision relating to custody is refused, the central authority of the state addressed may apply to its competent authorities for a decision on such rights if the person claiming a right of access or contact so requests (CACA 1985, Sch.2, art.11(3)).

The detailed procedure is set out at FPR, r.6.1–6.16.

C   Criminal liability

Where there is no court order preventing the removal of a child out of the **12.32** jurisdiction, a parent (see *R. v D* [1984] 3 W.L.R. 186) or a non-parent may be criminally liable for the common law offence of kidnapping. The offence should not be pleaded where an action under the Child Abduction Act 1984 is available (*R. v C* [1991] 2 F.L.R. 252). A parent or a non-parent may additionally be criminally liable under the Child Protection Act 1984 for the offence of child abduction. Under the Act, a distinction between abduction by persons connected with the child and abduction by persons no so connected is made. The distinction is made in order to emphasise the policy that normally family obligations should be enforced by civil and not criminal remedies. As to what amounts to abduction, see *R. v Leather* [1993] 2 F.L.R. 770.

Where there is a real threat that a child is about to be removed unlawfully from the country, a 'port alert' may be instituted (*Practice Direction*, 14 April 1986 [1986] 2 F.L.R. 89; see also Home Office Circular No. 21/1986).

Other provisions

12.33 The provisions set out in the Family Law Act 1986 as amended, ss.33 and 34, to order disclosure of a child's whereabouts and to order recovery of a child may be used (*e.g. Re B* [1995] 1 F.L.R. 774; *Re H* [2000] 1 F.L.R. 766). Sequestration may also be considered, but only where there is knowing and deliberate frustration of a court order (*Re S* [1995] 1 F.L.R. 858).

3 Wardship

Introduction

12.34 The inherent wardship jurisdiction of the court is used to protect the interests of children. Custody of a child who is a ward vests in the court, and although day to day care and control of the ward is given to an individual, or to a local authority, no important step can be taken in the child's life without the court's consent. The reforms of the private and public law relating to children introduced by the CA 1989 imposed major restrictions upon the use of the High Court's inherent jurisdiction, particularly in wardship, and especially when used by local authorities. Wardship cannot now be used by local authorities to circumvent the statutory criteria. It is also far less likely to be used in private proceedings in view of the powers available to the court under the CA 1989 which should be invoked in favour of wardship, unless conferring on the child the status of a ward will provide a more effective remedy to the matter to be determined by the court (*Re CT* [1993] 2 F.L.R. 278). As to the continuing role of wardship, see for instance *Re G* [1999] 1 F.L.R. 409 (restricting publicity); *Re M* [1999] 2 F.C.R. 577 (medical treatment); *Re HG* [1993] 1 F.L.R. 587 (sterilisation); *Re KR* [1999] 2 F.L.R. 542 (kidnapping).

Where the High Court's inherent jurisdiction has been invoked there is no difference between its powers under its inherent and wardship jurisdictions (*Re W* [1993] 1 F.L.R. 1).

Jurisdiction

12.35 A child will only become a ward of court if an order is made to that effect by the High Court (SCA 1981, s.41(1)).

The court's jurisdiction in wardship depends upon the basis upon which the jurisdiction is exercised. If it is exercised for the purpose of making a Pt I order, as defined by s.1(1) FLA 1986, the court's jurisdiction will be governed by FLA 1986 (*Re E* [1993] Fam. Law. 15). An order which does not come within the FLA 1986 definition of a Pt I order is governed by common law rules of jurisdiction.

Jurisdiction to make a Pt I order under FLA 1986

12.36 The High Court has jurisdiction under sections 2(2); 2(3); 3(1) and (2) of the FLA 1986 to make a Pt I order in wardship proceedings only if on the relevant date the child concerned:

(*a*) is habitually resident in England and Wales; or

(*b*) is present in England and Wales and is not habitually resident in any part of the United Kingdom; and

(*c*) in the case of either (*a*) or (*b*), on the relevant date proceedings for divorce, nullity, or judicial separation are not continuing in a court in Scotland or Northern Ireland in respect of the marriage of the parents of the child concerned; or

(*d*) is present in England and Wales and the court considers that the immediate exercise of its powers is necessary for the child's protection.

Thus, a situation may arise where the child is not present in England or Wales, but is habitually resident within either country. In such a circumstance, the court will have jurisdiction to make the child a ward (*Re B-M* [1993] 1 F.L.R. 979).

Section 7 of the FLA 1986 defines the relevant date as follows:

(*a*) where an application is made for an order to be made or varied, the date of the application (or first application, if two or more are determined together); and

(*b*) where no such application is made, the date on which the court is considering whether to make or, as the case may be, vary the order.

When a child who is under the age of 16, and is habitually resident in a part **12.37** of the United Kingdom, becomes habitually resident outside that part of the United Kingdom, without the agreement of the person or all of the persons having, under the law of that part of the United Kingdom, the right to determine where he is to reside, or in contravention of an order made by a court in any part of the United Kingdom, he is treated as habitually resident in the country of his previous habitual residence for a period of one year. If during that period, the child attains the age of 16 or becomes habitually resident outside that part of the United Kingdom with the agreement of all the persons who have the right to determine where he shall live, and not in contravention of an order made by a court in any part of the United Kingdom, the child ceases to be habitually resident in the country of his previous habitual residence (FLA 1986, s.41). There is no statutory definition of "habitual residence" and its meaning is a question of fact to be determined by reference to all the circumstances of the case (*Al-Habtoor v Fotheringham* [2001] 1 F.L.R. 951; see also chapter 1, paras 1.17–1.19).

A court which has jurisdiction to make a Pt I order under the FLA 1986 in wardship proceedings has a discretion to refuse an application where the matter has already been determined in proceedings outside England and Wales. The court also, at any stage of the proceedings, has a discretion to stay the proceedings if:

(*a*) proceedings with respect to the matters to which the application relates are continuing outside England and Wales; or

(*b*) it would be more appropriate for those matters to be determined in proceedings to be taken outside England and Wales.

If it appears that there has been unreasonable delay in the taking or prosecution of the proceedings outside England and Wales, or that those proceedings are stayed, sisted or concluded, the court may remove the stay (FLA, 1986, s.5(3)).

Jurisdiction to make an order other than a Part I order under FLA 1986

12.38 The court has the power to exercise its wardship jurisdiction other than under FLA 1986 over any child who is:

(*a*) living (not unborn) (*Re F (in utero)* [1988] 2 F.L.R. 307);

(*b*) under the age of 18; and

(*c*) a British subject,

irrespective of whether or not the child is physically within the jurisdiction and regardless of his place of birth, domicile, habitual residence or ordinary residence.

An application that a minor be made, or cease to be, a ward of court may be heard and determined in the High Court alone (MFPA 1984, s.38(2)(*b*)). Providing that the requirements of *President's Direction*, July 23, 1987, [1988] 1 F.L.R. 540 are satisfied, the court has power at any stage in wardship proceedings, either of its own motion, or on an application of any party to the proceedings, to order the transfer of the whole or any part of the proceedings to such county court as the High Court directs (MFPA 1984, ss.32 and 38). The circumstances in which such a transfer may be made are discussed at paras 4.43–4.55.

Who can apply?

12.39 Any person with a genuine interest in the person who is to be the subject of wardship proceedings may commence such proceedings (FPR, r.5.1(6)). S.100 of the CA 1989 imposes restrictions upon local authorities to commence wardship proceedings., For further interpretation and consideration of s.100, see *Nottingham C C v P* [1993] 2 F.L.R. 134; *C v K* [1996] 2 F.L.R. 506; *Re T* [1997] 1 F.L.R. 502; *Devon CC v B* [1997] 1 F.L.R. 591; *Re P* [2000] 2 F.L.R. 385. If the application is considered by the court to be an abuse of the process of the court, it will be dismissed (*Re Dunhill* [1967] 111 S.J. 113).

Although an applicant is required to state his interest in, or relationship to, the ward in the originating summons (FPR, r.5.1(6)), the relationship between the applicant and the ward does not have to be a blood tie providing that it gives the applicant sufficient personal interest in the child. Examples of applicants who are not related to the child, but who have sufficient personal interest, include foster parents and step-parents.

If a child wishes to apply to have himself made a ward of court, he may do so without a next friend or guardian ad litem either with leave of the court or if a solicitor considers that the child is able, having regard to his understanding, to give instructions in relation to the proceedings and the solicitor has accepted instructions from the child to act (FPR r.9.2(A)) (*Re CT* [1993] 2 F.L.R. 278; *Re H* [1993] 2 F.L.R. 552; *Re S* [1993] 2 F.L.R. 437).

If the court is not already seized of jurisdiction, there is no authority to support it acting on its own initiative, even when the child lacks a next friend (*Re AW* [1993] 1 F.L.R. 62).

Against whom the application is made

The defendant to the proceedings is the person or persons against whom the **12.40** order is sought. Where the dispute is between parents, the parents will be named as plaintiff and defendant respectively. One or both of the parents may make the application where the minor is in the care of a third party, *e.g.* a local authority. The local authority and not one of its officers should be made a defendant (*Re L (An Infant) (Practice Note)* [1963] 1 All E.R. 176). If the child has recently been removed from care it may be advisable to join the local authority as a defendant, although there is no requirement to do so.

If the parents wish to prevent a minor from entering into an undesirable association with another person, that other person should not be named as a defendant, but should be made a defendant to any summons in the wardship proceedings for an injunction or committal, and not be allowed to see any documents other than those relating to the summons. In such a case, where there is no parental conflict of interest, it is inappropriate for either parent to be named as defendant (*Practice Direction* [1983] 2 All E.R. 672).

The child is not normally a defendant to the proceedings. However, where there is no-one who is a suitable defendant, an ex parte application may be made for leave to name the child as defendant providing that special reasons can be shown for taking this step (FPR, r.5.1(3)). If the child is joined as a defendant the reasons for doing so should be noted and sent to CAFCASS Legal. Once the child becomes a party, he must act by a next friend or guardian ad litem, who must act by a solicitor. The first port of call when seeking representation for a child should be CAFCASS Legal (see *Practice Note*, March 2001 [2001] 2 FLR 151). In cases where for some reason CAFCASS Legal is unable to or declines to act then the Official Solicitor may be invited to represent the child, but his will be the exception rather than the rule (see *Practice Note*, April 2, 2001 [2001] 2 F.L.R. 155; *Re JD* [1984] F.L.R. 359; *Re C* [1984] F.L.R. 419). Any child who is a party to proceedings under the inherent jurisdiction may rely on the provisions of FPR 1991, r.9.2A if they wish to instruct a solicitor without the intervention of a next friend or guardian ad litem (see *Practice Note* (above), para.6).

Consideration should also be given to joining anyone who is likely to have **12.41** a close interest in the application in addition to joining all persons against whom an order is sought. Anyone who wishes to be joined as a party may apply ex parte to the district judge for leave to be joined.

Where in wardship proceedings there are or will be two parties requiring the appointment of guardians ad litem, *e.g.* where there is a child whom the court has ordered to be joined and the parent of the child is also a minor or is incapable of managing his or her affairs, consideration should be given to the appointment of the Official Solicitor as guardian ad litem of the child party. This would not normally be suitable if the Official Solicitor has acted for the parent in other proceedings and would of course be impossible if the Official Solicitor is already guardian ad litem of the other minor or incapable party. In such a case the child party's guardian at litem should normally be a suitable near relative who is willing to act, or a children and family reporter from an area outside the area of the court making the order; such a guardian ad litem would also be suitable for the other minor or disabled party if the Official Solicitor is already guardian ad litem of the child party (*Practice Direction*, December 8, 1983).

Procedure

12.42 FPR, rr.5.1–5.6 apply.

A minor becomes a ward of court on the issue of an originating summons (SCA 1981, s.41(2)). An application to make a minor a ward of court is assigned to the Family Division and may be made in the principal registry or in a district registry (SCA 1981, Sch.I).

A minor ceases to be a ward of court:

> (*a*) at the expiration of 21 days from the issue of the originating summons if an application for an appointment for the hearing of the summons is not made within that period (FPR, r.5.3(1)(*a*) (it is not necessary, however, for the hearing of the application to take place within that time); or

> (*b*) if an application is made for an appointment within that time, then on determination of the application made by the summons, unless the court hearing it orders that the minor be made a ward of court (FPR, r.5.3(1)(*b*)); or

> (*c*) when the court so orders (FPR, r.5.3(2)) (SCA 1981, s.41(3)).

The requirements are:

> (*a*) originating summons in RSC, Appendix A, Form 8 adapted appropriately and copy (one signed in margin, both to be 'top copies'), and a copy for each person to be served;

> (*b*) certificate as to existence of other proceedings (see Appendix 2, Form 53);

> (*c*) acknowledgement of service in RSC, Appendix A, Form 15 adapted appropriately for each person to be served;

> (*d*) the minor's birth certificate or entry in the adopted children's register;

> (*e*) public funding certificate, if any, and notice of issue of public funding certificate and copy for service;

> (*f*) a fee of £120.

12.43 If (*d*) above is not available at the time the proceedings are issued, it must be lodged by the plaintiff's solicitors before or at the first hearing. If no birth certificate is available, directions as to proof of birth should be sought at the first hearing (FPR, r.5.1(5)).

In accordance with FPR r.5.1(5)–(7) the following information, *inter alia*, must be included in the originating summons:

> (*a*) the date of the minor's birth;

> (*b*) the name of each party to the proceedings qualified by a brief description, in the body of the summons, of his interest in, or relationship to, the minor;

> (*c*) unless the court otherwise directs, the whereabouts of the minor or, as the case may be, that the plaintiff is unaware of his whereabouts.

The originating summons must contain a notice to every defendant other **12.44** than the minor, informing him that he must forthwith after being served with the summons:

(*a*) lodge in the registry out of which the summons was issued a notice stating the address of the defendant and the whereabouts of the minor or, as the case may be, that the defendant is unaware of his whereabouts; and

(*b*) unless the court otherwise directs, serve a copy of the notice on the plaintiff.

The notice must also inform the defendant that where any party other than the minor changes his address or become aware of any change in the whereabouts of the minor after the issue or, as the case may be, service of the summons, he shall, unless the court otherwise directs, forthwith lodge notice of the change in the registry out of which the summons was issued and serve a copy of the notice on every other party (FPR, r.5.1(9)); *Practice Direction*, December 18, 1972 [1973] 1 All E.R. 144).

The originating summons must also contain an endorsement informing the parties that it is a contempt of court, which may be punished by imprisonment, to take any child named in the summons out of England and Wales without leave of the court (*Practice Direction*, July, 20 1977 [1977] 3 All E.R. 122).

It is customary to include in the title to the proceedings a reference to the CA 1989 since the plaintiff may wish to invoke the court's powers under that Act even if the wardship does not continue.

Such applications may be made on an ex parte basis only exceptionally in respect of care and control. The proper procedure for challenging such an order is considered in *Re H* [1994] 2 F.L.R. 981.

Powers of the court

The court has a wide and special jurisdiction and control over its wards. **12.45** Although the welfare of the child is the paramount consideration (CA 1989, s.1) the jurisdiction must be exercised with due regard to the rights of outside parties, whether such rights arise at common law or by contract or otherwise. Because the court's paramount concern is the welfare of its ward, it will sometimes have a duty to look beyond the submissions of the parties and to adopt a course not advocated by any party to the proceedings.

4 Applications for financial relief for a child under CA 1989, Sch.I

Introduction

The provisions for financial relief for children previously contained in the **12.46** Guardianship of Minors Act 1971, the Guardianship Act 1973 and the Children Act 1975 were repealed and re-enacted with amendments and minor modifications by CA 1989, s.15 and Sch.I. If the child's parents are, or have been, married, it will generally be more appropriate to invoke the greater procedural powers available under the MCA 1973 which are not affected by CA 1989, Sch.I. However, when considering whether to make an application for financial provision for a child under CA 1989, Sch.I, or indeed under the MCA 1973, it must be borne in mind that the CSA 1991 has very greatly curtailed the power of the court to make, vary and revive orders made under CA 1989, s.15, Sch.I (see chapter 9).

Relief available

12.47   Sch. I of the CA 1989 provides three forms of financial relief for a child:

> (1) *Sch.I, para.1* enables periodical payments, secured periodical payments, lump sum, settlement and transfer of property orders to be made in favour of a child against either or both of its parents.

> (2) *Sch. I, para.2* enables periodical payments and lump sum orders to be made in favour of a child who has reached 18 where

>> (*a*) the child's parents are not living with each other (Sch. I, para.2(4)); and
>> (*b*) there was not in force a periodical payment order for the child immediately before he reached the age of 16 (Sch. I, para.2(3)); and
>> (*c*) the child is, or will be if an order were made, undergoing education or training or there are special circumstances which justify the making of an order (Sch. I, para.2(1)(*a*) and (*b*)).

> (3) *Sch.I, paras 10 and 11* enable a maintenance agreement continuing financial arrangements for the child to be varied either during the life time of the parent or after the death of one of them.

Sch.I, para.6 enables orders for the making or securing of periodical payments made under Sch.I, paras 1 and 2 to be varied or extended. Under Sch.I, para.1, more than one application may be made for periodical payments, secured periodical payments or a lump sum if the child concerned has not yet reached the age of 18. Only one settlement of property and transfer of property order may be made against the same person in respect of the same child (CA 1989, Sch.1, para.1(5)).

Provision for periodical payments may also be made where the child is resident in a country outside England and Wales (CA 1989, Sch.1, para.14).

Who can apply?

12.48   *Sch. I, para.1*: A parent or guardian of a child, or any person in whose favour a residence order is in force (Sch. I Para. 1(1));

Sch. I, para.2: The child who is over 18 (Sch. I Para. 2(1));

Sch. I, paras 10 & 11: Either party to the agreement or a person representative (Sch. I, paras 10(2) and 11(1)).

Even where there is no application under Sch.1 before the court, the court may exercise any of its powers under the Schedule of its own motion upon the making, varying or discharging of a residence order or where the child is a ward of court (CA 1989, Sch.1, paras 1(6) and 1(7)), although an opportunity to make representations should be given (*Re C* [1995] 1 F.L.R. 925).

12.49   The definition of a parent for the purposes of the Schedule, save for paras 2 and 15, includes any party to a marriage (whether or not subsisting) in relation to whom the child concerned is a child of the family (CA 1989, Sch.1, para.16(2)) and hence applies in such cases to step-parents as well as natural and adoptive parents, whether or not married. Para. 4(2) sets out the additional points to which the court must have regard if considering an order against a person who is not the mother or father of the child.

The court has jurisdiction to make an order under Sch.1 notwithstanding the bankruptcy of the person against whom the application is made (*Re G* [1996] 2 F.L.R. 171).

Procedure

FPR r.4.4 as amended applies.   **12.50**

Application can made to the High Court, county court or magistrates' court, but the magistrate's powers are restricted (see Sch.1, paras (1(1)(*b*), 5(2), 5(4), 10(6)). The requirements for filing are:

(*a*) form C1 and C10 with copies for service;

(*b*) statement of means on form C10A with copies for service;

(*c*) fee of £80.

Where the application is made in respect of more than one child, all the children must be included in one application (FPR, r.3 4.4(1A)).

The persons to be served are:

(*a*) every person whom the applicant believes to have parental responsibility;

(*b*) where the child is a subject of a care order, every person whom the applicant believes to have had parental responsibility immediately before the making of the care order;

(*c*) in the case of an application to extend, vary or discharge an order, the parties to the proceedings leading to the order;

(*d*) those persons whom the applicant believes to be interested in or affected by the proceedings (FPR, r.4.4(1(*b*)) and Appendix 3).

All applications may be withdrawn only with leave of the court (FPR, r.4.5(1)).

General

The no order presumption (see p.225) is not applicable to an application for   **12.51**
financial relief under CA 1989. Such orders may be useful for tax purposes and give security in case of future difficulties (*K v H* [1993] 2 F.L.R. 61).

When deciding whether to exercise its powers under paras 1 or 2 of the CA 1989, the court must apply the guidelines laid down by Sch.I, para.4 of the CA 1989. In this context, the child's welfare is not paramount, the financial provisions of the CA 1989 being largely self-contained (*K v K* [1992] 2 F.L.R. 220; *H v P* (1993) Fam. Law. 515).

The court has power to order to transfer property, including a secure tenancy, to an applicant for the child's benefit, for example in order to preserve the family home for children after the breakdown of the parental relationship (*J v J* [1993] 2 F.L.R. 56; *K v K* [1992] 2 All E.R. 727; *Pearson v Franklin* [1994] 1 F.L.R. 246; *J v L* [1999] 1 F.L.R. 152).

Para. 5 of Sch.1 details the provisions relating to lump sums. The court has stated that the power to make a lump sum order is not to be exercised in such a way as to provide for the regular support of a child; it should only be used to meet the need of a child in respect of a particular item of capital expenditure (*Phillips v Peace* [1996] 2 F.L.R. 230).

When considering making capital provision, the court has interpreted Sch.1 restrictively (*A v A* [1994] 1 F.L.R. 657 and *T v S* [1994] 2 F.L.R. 883). The court emphasised that the aim of the provisions is to provide financially for children, as children or dependants, and hence in normal circumstances only during their minority. Therefore the usual provisions, where appropriate, would provide accommodation during the minority to revert thereafter to the settlor. As to duration of Sch.1 orders generally, see Sch.1, para.3 as amended.

Chapter 13

Other Originating Proceedings

1 Declarations as to legal status

Declaratory relief in family matters is governed by FLA 1986, Pt III, ss.55–60. **13.01** These provisions replace the declaratory relief previously available under MCA 1973, s.45.

Declarations as to marital status (FLA 1986, s.55)

Jurisdiction: A court has jurisdiction to entertain an application for a declaration as to marital status only if either of the parties to the marriage to which the application relates:

(*a*) is domiciled in England and Wales on the date of the application;

(*b*) has been habitually resident in England and Wales throughout the period of one year ending with that date; or

(*c*) died before that date and either was at death domiciled in England and Wales or had been habitually resident in England and Wales throughout the period of one year ending with the date of death (FLA 1986, s.55(2)).

Relief: Any person may apply to the court for one or more of the following declarations:

(*a*) that the marriage was at its inception a valid marriage; **13.02**

(*b*) that the marriage subsisted or did not subsist on a specified date;

(*c*) that the validity of a divorce, annulment or legal separation obtained in any country outside England and Wales in respect of the marriage is, or is not, entitled to recognition in England and Wales (FLA 1986, s.55(1)).

Where an application for a declaration as to marital status is made by any person other than a party to the marriage to which the application relates, the court must refuse to hear the application if it considers that the applicant does not have a sufficient interest in the determination of that application (FLA 1986, s.55(3)).

Declarations of parentage (FLA 1986, s.55A)

Jurisdiction: A court has jurisdiction to entertain an application for a declaration of parentage only if either of the persons named in it: **13.03** (*a*) is domiciled in England and Wales on the date of the application;

(*b*) has been habitually resident in England and Wales throughout the period of one year ending with that date; or

(*c*) died before that date and either was at death domiciled in England and Wales or had been habitually resident in England and Wales throughout the period of one year ending with the date of death (FLA 1986, s.55A(2)).

13.04 *Relief*: Any person may apply to the court for a declaration as to whether or not a person named in the application is or was the parent of another person so named (FLA 1986, s.55A(1)).

Unless the declaration sought is as to whether or not the applicant is the parent of a named person, a named person is the parent of the applicant or a named person is the other parent of a named child of the applicant, the court must refuse to hear the application unless it considers that the applicant has a sufficient personal interest in the determination of the application subject to the Child Support Act 1991, s.27 (FLA 1986, s.55A(3) and (4)).

Where one of the persons named in the application is a child, the court may refuse to hear the application if it considers that the determination of the application would not be in the best interests of the child (FLA 1986, s.55A(5)).

Where a court refuses to hear an application, it may order that the applicant may not apply again for the same declaration without leave of the court (FLA 1986, s.55A(6)).

Where a declaration is made, the court must notify the Registrar General of the making of that declaration (FLA 1986, s.55A(7)).

Declarations as to legitimacy or legitimation (FLA 1986, s.56)

13.05 *Jurisdiction*: A court has jurisdiction to entertain an application for a declaration as to legitimacy or legitimation only if the applicant:

(*a*) is domiciled in England and Wales on the date of the application; or

(*b*) has been habitually resident in England and Wales throughout the period of one year ending with that date (FLA 1986, s.56(3)).

13.06 *Relief*: Any person may apply to the court for one of the following declarations:

(*a*) that he is the legitimate child of his parents:

(*b*) that he has become or has not become a legitimated person (FLA 1986, s.56(1) and (2)).

Where a declaration is made that the applicant is the legitimate child of his parents, the court must notify the Registrar General of the making of that declaration (FLA 1986, s.55(4)).

A legitimated person is a person legitimated or recognised as legitimated:

(*a*) under Legitimacy Act 1976, ss.2 or 3:

(*b*) under Legitimacy Act 1926, ss.1 or 8; or

(c) by a legitimation (whether or not by virtue of the subsequent marriage of his parents) recognised by the law of England and Wales and effected under the law of another country (FLA 1986, s.56(5)(a)-(c)).

Declarations as to adoption effected overseas (FLA 1986, s.57)

Jurisdiction: A court has jurisdiction to entertain an application for a declaration as to adoption effected overseas only if the applicant: **13.07**

(a) is domiciled in England and Wales on the date of the application; or

(b) has been habitually resident in England and Wales throughout the period of one year ending with that date (FLA 1986, s.57(3)).

Relief: Any person whose status as an adopted child of any person depends on whether he has been adopted by that person by either: **13.08**

(a) an overseas adoption as defined by the Adoption Act 1976, s.72(2); or

(b) an adoption recognised by the law of England and Wales and effected under the law of any country outside the British Isles,

may apply to the court for a declaration that the applicant is or is not for the purposes of the Adoption Act 1976, s.39 the adopted child of that person (FLA 1986, s.57(1), (2)).

Procedure: The procedure for making an application under FLA 1986, ss.55–57 is contained in FPR, rr.3.12–3.16. All applications are commenced by petition supported by an affidavit verifying the petition and giving particulars of every person whose interest may be affected by the proceedings and his relationship to the petitioner (FPR, r.3.16(1)). **13.09**

The application may be made to the Family Division of the High Court or to any county court whether or not it is a divorce county court (see p.000) (FLA 1986, s.63). The contents of the petition are prescribed in FPR, r.3.12 (application for a declaration as to marital status), FPR, r.3.13 (application for a declaration of parentage), FPR, r.3.14 (application for a declaration of legitimacy or legitimation), FPR, r.3.15 (application for a declaration as to an adoption effected overseas).

A copy of the petition and every document accompanying it must be sent to the Attorney General at least one month before the petition is filed (FPR, r.3.16(4)).

The subsequent procedure after a petition has been filed at court is contained in FPR, r.3.16.

See further Butterworth's *Family Law Service* 3A[490]-[512].

General provisions: Where, on an application for a declaration, the truth of the proposition to be declared is proved to the satisfaction of the court, the court must make that declaration unless to do so would manifestly be contrary to public policy (FLA 1986, s.58(1)). **13.10**

Any declaration made is binding upon Her Majesty and all other persons (FLA 1986, s.58(2)).

Where an application for a declaration has been dismissed, the court does not have power to make any declaration for which an application has not been made (FLA 1986, s.58(3)).

A court may not make a declaration as to marital status, parentage, legitimacy, legitimation or adoption effected overseas otherwise than under FLA 1986, ss.55–57.

No declaration may be made by any court whether under FLA 1986, ss.55–57 or otherwise that a marriage was at its inception void. This does not, however, prevent the court from granting a decree of nullity of marriage (FLA 1986, s.58(5) and (6)).

Provisions relating to the Attorney General (FLA 1986, s.59)

13.11 Section 59 of the FLA 1986 provides that the court may at any stage of the proceedings, of its own motion or on the application of any party to the proceedings, direct that the matter be sent to the Attorney General. It is also provided that the Attorney General may intervene in the proceedings in such manner as he thinks necessary or expedient and argue before the court any question in relation to the application which the court considers it necessary to have fully argued.

2   Failure to provide reasonable maintenance (MCA 1973, s.27)

13.12 Either party to a marriage may apply to the court for an order for financial relief on the ground that the other party has failed to provide reasonable maintenance (whether or not such failure is wilful) for the applicant or a child of the marriage (MCA 1973, s.27(1)).

Jurisdiction: An application may not be made unless:

(*a*) the applicant or the respondent is domiciled in England and Wales on the date of the application; or

(*b*) the applicant has been habitually resident in England and Wales throughout the period of one year ending with the date of the application; or

(*c*) the respondent is resident in England and Wales at the date of the application (MCA 1973, s.27(2)).

13.13 *Procedure*: R.3.1 of the FPR applies. The procedure is similar to that in a claim for financial relief in divorce proceedings. The application may be made in any divorce county court (FPR, r.3.1(2)). The requirements are:

(*a*) originating application in Form M19 and copy;

(*b*) affidavit in support and copy;

(*c*) public funding certificate, if any, and notice of issue of public funding certificate for service and copy;

(*d*) fee of £120.

The affidavit in support must state:

13.14 (*a*) the same particulars regarding the marriage, the court's jurisdiction, the children and the previous proceedings as are required in the case of a petition by FPR, App.2, para.1, sub-paras (*a*), (*c*),(*d*),(*f*) and (*i*) (see Appendix 1, Form 1);

(*b*) particulars of the respondent's failure to provide reasonable maintenance for the applicant, or, as the case may be, of the respondent's
failure to provide or to make a proper contribution towards, reasonable maintenance for the children of the family;

and

(*c*) full particulars of the applicant's property and income, and of the
respondent's property and income, so far as may be known to the
applicant (FPR r.3.1(3).

If it is not practicable to fix a day for the hearing at the time of issue, it may
be fixed subsequently. In this case the district judge must send notice of the
appointment to every party on fixing the day (FPR, rr.3.1(10) and 2.62(3).

A copy of the application and of the affidavit in support of the application,
together with a notice in Form M20 and M6 must be served on the respondent
(FPR, r.3.1(4)).

If the respondent's address is unknown, it may be possible to obtain it
from a Government department (*Practice Direction*, February 13, 1989
[1989] 1 All E.R. 765 as amended by *Practice Direction*, July 20, 1995 [1995]
2 F.L.R. 813).

The respondent must acknowledge service on Form M6, which must be   **13.15**
received by the court within 14 days of receipt by the respondent inclusive of
the day of receipt (FPR, r.10.8(2)(6)).

Unless the respondent challenges the jurisdiction of the court to hear the
application, he must file an affidavit, with copy, so as to reach the court within
fourteen days after the time allowed for acknowledging service, The affidavit
must state:

(*a*) whether the alleged failure to provide, or to make a proper contribution towards, reasonable maintenance is admitted or denied, and, if
denied, the grounds on which he relies;

(*b*) any allegations which he wishes to make against the applicant; and

(*c*) full particulars of his property and income, unless otherwise directed
(FPR, r.3.1(5)).

Where the respondent challenges the jurisdiction, for example because the   **13.16**
requirements of MCA 1973, s.27(2) are not fulfilled, he must within fourteen
days after the time allowed for acknowledging service, file an affidavit setting
out the grounds of the challenge. The court will then determine jurisdiction as
a preliminary issue. If it is decided by the court that jurisdiction does exist, the
respondent has fourteen days as from the date of the court's decision to file an
affidavit in answer to the application containing the information prescribed by
FPR, r.3.1(5).

Where the respondent's affidavit contains an allegation of adultery or
improper association with a person named, a further copy of the affidavit
must be supplied for service by the court. R.2.60 of FPR, which deals with
service on, and intervention by, a named person, applies (FPR, r.3.1(7)).

If the respondent does not file an affidavit and copy, the court may order
him to do so and in that case the respondent must serve a copy of any such
affidavit on the applicant (FPR, r.3.1(8)).

The applicant may file a further affidavit with copy within 14 days after   **13.17**
being served with a copy of any affidavit filed by the respondent, the affidavit

being as to means and as to any fact in the respondent's affidavit which is disputed. In that case the respondent must serve a copy of any such affidavit on the applicant. (FPR, r.3.1(9)).

No further affidavit may be filed without leave (FPR, r.3.1(9)).

The application is heard by a district judge (FPR, rr.3.1 (10) and 2.62(1)). FPR, rr.2.61–2.66 and 10.10, regarding the investigation by the district judge of an application for ancillary relief, the making of an interim order, reference to the judge, transfer of the application and the arrangements for the application to be heard, apply to applications under MCA 1973, s.27 with such modifications as may be appropriate (FPR, r.3.1(10)).

The application may be transferred to the High Court if it comes within the requirements laid down in *Practice Direction*, June 5, 1992 [1992] 2 F.L.R. 87.

13.18   The matters to which the court is to have regard in considering what order should be made under MCA 1973, s.27 are set out in MCA 1973, s.27(3), (3A) and (3B). The court must have regard to the same criteria as if it were considering an application for financial relief following a decree of divorce, nullity or judicial separation, although there is no power under MCA 1973, s.27 to make a property adjustment order. For the circumstances in which interest is payable upon a lump sum order which is to be deferred or paid by instalments. If an application is made in respect of the applicant *and* a minor child of the family, first consideration must be given to the welfare of the child while a minor. If the application is only in respect of the applicant, the welfare of any minor child does not need to be given first consideration (MCA 1973, s.27(3)). It must, however, be remembered that in most cases the court is prevented by the Child Support Act 1991 from making orders for periodical payments, secured or unsecured, for children. It may only do so under section 27 if the case falls within one of the exceptions to this general principle, *e.g.* the child is not a "child" for the purpose of the Child Support Act 1991. Conduct is treated in the same way as in an application for ancillary financial relief, *i.e.* it must be taken into account if it is such that in the opinion of the court it would be inequitable to disregard it.

An interim order may be made in favour of the applicant or any child of the family where there is immediate need of financial assistance (MCA 1973, s.27(5)). The orders which the court may make are set out in MCA 1973, s.27(6).

See further Butterworth's *Family Law Service* 4A[526]-[559].

3   Financial relief in England and Wales after overseas divorce, nullity or legal separation (MFPA 1984, Pt III)

Introduction

13.19   Hardship could result from the recognition of an overseas decree because the jurisdiction of the English court to grant financial relief under MCA 1973 is limited to decrees granted in England and Wales. There were limited exceptions, *e.g.* where a foreign decree had not been made final, the English court granted a decree nisi and directed that it be made absolute forthwith (*Torok v Torok* [1973] 3 All E.R. 101). However, Pt III of the MFPA 1984 enables the court to grant orders for financial relief after an overseas divorce, nullity or legal separation.

13.20   *Who may apply*: Either party may apply in the following circumstances:

(*a*) the decree of divorce, nullity or legal separation must have been obtained in an overseas country by means of judicial or other proceedings (MFPA 1984, s.12(1)(*a*)). The decree may have been obtained before MFPA 1984, Pt III came into force on September 16, 1985 (*Chebaro v Chebaro* [1987] 1 All E.R. 999);

(*b*) the decree must be entitled to be recognised as valid in England and Wales (MFPA 1984, s.12(1)(*b*)). If the decree is not recognised, the parties will remain married and an application may be made under MCA 1973 for financial relief;

(*c*) the applicant must not have remarried (even if remarriage is void or voidable) (MFPA 1984, s.12(2), (3)); and

(*d*) no application may be made under Pt III of the MFPA 1984, unless the leave of the court, which may be granted subject to conditions, has been obtained. A substantial ground for the making of an application must be shown (MFPA 1984, s.13). The court must at this stage consider the appropriateness of the application under MFPA 1984, s.16 (see below). An order granting leave may be set aside in the absence of full and frank disclosure (*W v W* [1989] 1 F.L.R. 22). The burden of establishing that leave should be granted rests upon the applicant (*Z v Z* [1992] 2 F.L.R. 291).

Jurisdiction: The court has jurisdiction if any of the following requirements are satisfied: **13.21**

(*a*) either party was domiciled in England and Wales on the date of the application for leave under MFPA 1984, s.13, or was so domiciled on the date on which the overseas decree took effect in that country (MFPA 1984, s.15(1)(*a*));

(*b*) either party was habitually resident in England and Wales throughout the period of one year ending with the date referred to in (*a*) above (MFPA 1984, s.15(1)(*b*)); or

(*c*) either or both parties had at the date of the application for leave under MFPA 1984, s.13 a beneficial interest in possession in a dwelling house situated in England or Wales, which was at some time during the marriage the matrimonial home of the parties (MFPA 1984, s.15(1)(*c*)).

The court means the High Court or any county court which has jurisdiction   **13.22**
by virtue of MFPA 1984, Pt V (MFPA 1984, s.27). Pt V of the MFPA 1984 (s.33(4)) enables the Lord Chancellor by order to designate a divorce county court as a court for the exercise of jurisdiction under MFPA 1984, Pt III. No such order has as yet been made and for the time being all applications under MFPA 1984, Pt III must be commenced in the High Court out of the principal registry (FPR, r.3.18(1)).

Pt I of the Civil Jurisdiction and Judgments Act 1982 (implementation of certain European Conventions) is to prevail, if jurisdictional requirements fail to be determined by that Act (MFPA 1984, s.15(2)).

Appropriateness of England and Wales as venue: The court must be satisfied that   **13.23**
England and Wales is an appropriate venue for an application. If the court is

not satisfied, it must dismiss the application (MFPA 1984, s.16(1)). The burden of establishing that it would be appropriate for the English court to make an order under section 16 is upon the applicant (*Z v Z* [1992] 2 F.L.R. 291).

In particular, the court is directed by MFPA 1984, s.16(2) to have regard to the following matters:

(*a*) the connection which the parties have with England and Wales;

(*b*) the connection which the parties have with the country in which the overseas decree was pronounced;

(*c*) the connection which the parties have with any other country outside England and Wales;

(*d*) any financial benefit which the applicant or a child of the family has received, or is likely to receive, in consequence of the overseas decree by virtue of any agreement or the operation of the law of an overseas country;

(*e*) where an order has been made for financial relief by an overseas court for the benefit of the applicant or a child of the family, the financial relief given by the order and the extent to which it has been complied with or is likely to be complied with;

(*f*) any right which the applicant has, or has had, to apply for financial relief under the law of any overseas country and, if the applicant has omitted to exercise that right, the reason for that omission;

(*g*) the availability in England and Wales of any property in respect of which an order under MFPA 1984, Pt III could be made;

(*h*) the extent to which any order made is likely to be enforceable;

(*i*) the length of time which has elapsed since the date of the overseas decree.

13.24   As to appropriateness, see *Holmes v Holmes* [1989] 3 W.L.R. 302; *Z v Z* [1992] 2 F.L.R. 291; *M v M* [1994] 1 F.L.R. 399; *N v N* [1997] 1 F.L.R. 900; *E v E* [1997] Fam. Law. 637; *Jordan v Jordan* [1999] 2 F.L.R. 1069. The scope of the Act is narrow and not to be extended to cover, for example, a wife making a claim following a clean break order abroad on the basis that she had resumed cohabitation with her former husband for a time (*Hewitson v Hewitson* [1995] 1 F.L.R. 241).

13.25   *Powers of the court*: Where leave is granted under MFPA 1984, s.13, the court may grant an interim order for periodical payments to the applicant or any child of the family if either is in immediate need of financial assistance (MFPA 1984, s.14(1)). An interim order may not be made where jurisdiction is based solely upon a matrimonial home having been in England and Wales (MFPA 1984, s.14(2)).

The court may make financial provision orders, pension sharing and property adjustment orders as on divorce (MFPA 1984, s.17), except where jurisdiction depends solely upon a matrimonial home having been in England or Wales. In this latter situation, the powers of the court are restricted by MFPA 1984, ss.20 and 21(2).

13.26   The other powers of the court in making orders for financial relief are similar to its powers in divorce proceedings in the following respects:

(*a*) the matters to which the court is to have regard in exercising its powers; the court is specifically directed where an order has been made by an overseas court to have regard to the extent to which the order has been complied with or is likely to be complied with (MFPA 1984, s.18);

(*b*) consent orders (MFPA 1984, s.19);

(*c*) provisions as to lump sums (MCA 1973, s.23(3); MFPA 1984, s.21);

(*d*) provisions as to orders for sale (MCA 1973, s.24A(2), (4), (5), (6); MFPA 1984, s.21);

(*e*) provisions about pension sharing orders; duty to stay pension sharing orders; apportionment of pension sharing charges; power, by financial provision order, to attach payments under a pension arrangement, or to require the exercise of a right of commutation under such an arrangement; extension of lump sum powers in relation to death benefits under a pension arrangement (MCA 1973, ss.24B(3) to (5), 24C, 24D, 25B(3) to (7B) and 25C; MFPA 1984, s.21);

(*f*) duration of financial provision orders (MCA 1973, ss.28(1), (2), 29; MFPA 1984, s.21);

(*g*) direction for settlement of instrument for securing payments or effecting property adjustment (MCA 1973, s.30 (except para.(*b*); MFPA 1984, s.21);

(*h*) variation, discharge, etc. of certain orders for financial relief (MCA 1973, s.31 (except subs 2(*e*) and subs (4); MFPA 1984, s.21);

(*i*) payment of certain arrears unenforceable without leave of the court (MCA 1973, s.32; MFPA 1984, s.21);

(*j*) orders for repayment of sums paid under certain orders (MCA 1973, s.33; MFPA 1984, s.21);

(*k*) orders for repayment of sums paid after cessation of order by reason of remarriage (MCA 1973, s.38; MFPA 1984, s.21); **13.27**

(*l*) settlements, etc. made in compliance with a property adjustment order may be avoided on bankruptcy of settlor (MCA 1973, s.39; MFPA 1984, s.21);

(*m*) payments, etc. under order made in favour of person suffering from mental disorder (MCA 1973, s.40; MFPA 1984, s.21);

(*n*) appeals relating to pension sharing orders which have taken effect (MCA 1973, s.40A; MFPA 1984, s.21);

(*o*) orders for transfer of certain tenancies (MFPA 1984, s.22);

(*p*) avoidance of transactions intended to defeat applications for financial relief (MFPA 1984, s.23);

(*q*) in addition to the court's powers to grant freezing injunctions under Supreme Court Act 1981, s.37 (and the Civil Procedure Act 1997, s.7), the court may, where there has been an overseas decree, restrain a party who is about to make any disposition or to transfer out of the jurisdiction or otherwise deal with any property with the intention of defeating a claim for maintenance, where the applicant intends to apply for leave to apply for an order under MFPA 1984, s.17 as soon as he or she has been habitually resident in England and Wales for one year (MFPA 1984, s.24); **13.28** (*r*) Inheritance (Provision for Family and Dependants) Act 1975; "former wife" and "former husband" in section 25(1) of the 1975 Act are redefined to enable a spouse whose marriage with the deceased was dissolved or annulled during the lifetime of the deceased under the law of any part of the British Islands, or outside the British Islands by a decree which is entitled to be recognised as valid by the law of England and Wales, to apply for reasonable financial provision from the estate of a deceased former spouse (MFPA 1984, s.25(1), (2)). An application under MFPA 1984, s.12 is not a prerequisite to such an application under the 1975 Act. Section 25(3) of the MFPA 1984 inserts a new section 15A into the 1975 Act whereby, when making an order under MFPA 1984, section 17, the court may make an order in terms similar to section 15 of the 1975 Act precluding the making of an order under section 2 of the 1975 Act.

Procedure: Rr.3.17–3.19 of FPR apply.

13.29   For leave under MFPA 1984, s.13 (FPR, r.3.17) the requirements are:

(*a*) an application made ex parte by originating summons in Form M25 out of the principal registry;

(*b*) affidavit in support from the applicant stating the facts relied on with particular reference to MFPA 1984, s.16(2) and particulars required by FPR, r.3.17(2);

(*c*) fee of £120 (except where fee already paid on an application for an order under MFPA 1984, s.24).

The application is heard by a judge in chambers (FPR, r.3.17(3).

13.30   For financial relief (including an interim order) or an avoidance of transaction order (FPR, r.3.18) the requirements are:

(*a*) an originating summons in Form M26 issued out of the principal registry;

(*b*) affidavit in support giving full particulars of property and income (unless otherwise directed);

No fee is payable.

13.31   An application for an interim order or an avoidance of transaction order may alternatively be made by summons under FPR, r.10.9(1) (FPR, r.3.18(4)).

The application is heard by a judge (FPR, r.3.18(8)).

For an order preventing a transaction under MFPA 1984, s.24 (FPR, r.3.19) the requirements are:

(*a*) an originating summons in Form M27 out of the principal registry;

(*b*) affidavit in support;

(*c*) fee of £120.

The application is heard by a judge in chambers (FPR, r.3.19(4)).

See further Butterworths' *Family Law Service* 4A[3101]-[3200].

4 Alteration of maintenance agreement during lives of parties (MCA 1973, s.35 and CA 1989 Sch.1, para.10)

Section 35 of the MCA 1973 empowers the court to alter financial arrangements **13.32**
contained in a subsisting agreement between the parties. Para.10 of Sch.1 to the
CA 1989, which replaced section 15 of the FLRA 1987, empowers the court,
subject to the restrictions imposed by the CSA 1991, to alter a subsisting maintenance agreement made in respect of a child. Except where used to express a
relationship, a "child" is a person who has not attained the age of eighteen (CA
1989, s.105). Section 15 was introduced to enable agreements relating to the
maintenance of a child of unmarried parents to be amended by the court. Prior
to FLRA 1987, s.15 coming into force on April 1, 1989, although a maintenance
agreement containing provision for a child could be altered by the court under
MCA 1973, s.35, the parties to the agreement had to be parties to a marriage.
Therefore, if an agreement has been made between parties to a marriage, which
contains provision for a child, application could be made to amend the agreement insofar as it relates to maintenance for the child either under MCA 1973,
s.35 or under CA 1989, Sch.1, para.10. These provisions do not affect any power
of the court under any other enactment to make an order containing financial
arrangements or any other right of either party to the agreement or any child
concerned (MCA 1973, s.35(6) and of CA 1989, Sch.1, para.10(7)).

Jurisdiction: The court has jurisdiction to consider an application for altera- **13.33**
tion of an agreement providing that:

(*a*) a maintenance agreement is for the time being subsisting; and

(*b*) each of the parties to the agreement is for the time being either dom-
     iciled or resident in England and Wales (MCA 1973, s.35(1) and CA
     1989, Sch.1, para.10(2)).

Definition of maintenance agreements: A "maintenance agreement" under **13.34**
MCA 1973, s.35 is any agreement in writing made, whether before or after the
commencement of MCA 1973, between the parties to a marriage being:

(*a*) an agreement containing financial arrangements, whether made
     during the continuance or after the dissolution or annulment of the
     marriage; or

(*b*) a separation agreement which contains no financial arrangements in
     a case where no other agreement in writing between the parties con-
     tains such arrangements (MCA 1973 s.34(2)).

"Financial arrangements" are provisions governing the rights and liabilities
towards one another of the parties to a marriage (including a marriage which
has been dissolved or annulled) when living separately in respect of the
making or securing of payments or the disposition or use of any property,
including such rights and liabilities with respect to the maintenance or education of any child, whether or not a child of the family (MCA 1973, s.34(2)).

A "maintenance agreement" under CA 1989, Sch.1, para.10(1) is any agree- **13.35**
ment in writing made in respect of a child, whether before or after the commencement of CA 1989, Sch.1, para.10 (October 14, 1991), being an
agreement which:

(*a*) is or was made between the father and mother of the child; and

(*b*) contains provision in respect of the making or securing of payments, or the disposition or use of any property, for the maintenance or education of the child.

Such provisions are "financial arrangements" (CA 1989, Sch.1, para.1).

A provision purporting to restrict any right to apply for an order containing financial arrangements in a maintenance agreement is void, but this does not itself render any other financial arrangements void or unenforceable (MCA 1975, s.34(1)). Whilst the jurisdiction of the court cannot be ousted in subsequent proceedings, the court will be reluctant to interfere with an agreement properly arrived at where the parties have been legally advised (*Edgar v Edgar* [1980] 3 All E.R. 887; *Cook v Cook* [1984] F.L.R. 446; *Peacock v Peacock* [1991] 1 F.L.R. 324; *Xyhdias v Xyhdias* [1999] 1 F.L.R. 683. *Rose v Rose* [2002] 1 F.L.R. 978).

Procedure

13.36 *Application under MCA 1973, s.35*: R.3.2 FPR applies. Proceedings are commenced in any divorce county court (FPR, r.3.2(2)). Proceedings may be commenced in a magistrate's court, although greater restrictions on jurisdiction and range of orders then apply (MCA 1973, s.35(3)).

The requirements in the county court are:

(*a*) originating application containing the information required by Form M21, unless otherwise directed, and copy;

(*b*) affidavit exhibiting copy of agreement in support and copy of affidavit;

(*c*) public funding certificate, if any, and notice of issue of public funding certificate and copy for service;

(*d*) fee of £120.

13.37 Form M20 with Form M6 attached and copy of affidavit are annexed to the copy of application for service (FPR, r.3.2(4)).

The respondent must send an acknowledgment of service to reach the court within 14 days after service inclusive of the day of service (FPR, r.10.8(2)(*b*)). He must file, within 14 days after the time for acknowledging service, an affidavit with copy, containing full particulars of his property and income and setting out any grounds on which he intends to contest the application (FPR, r.3.2(5)). The court serves a copy of the affidavit on the applicant (FPR, r.3.2(6)).

Subject to modifications, rules applicable to petitions apply (FPR, r.3.5(2)). In general, rules relating to ancillary relief apply (FPR, r.3.5(1)).

The application is heard by a district judge (FPR, r.3.2(2)).

13.38 *Applications under CA 1989, Sch.1, para.10*: FPR, r.4.4 applies.

Proceedings are commenced in the High Court or any county court.

The requirements are:

(*a*) application in writing and copy. There is no prescribed form. Form C1 could be used;

(*b*) statement of means and copy;

(*c*) public funding certificate, if any, and notice of issue of public funding certificate and copy for service;

(*d*) fee of £80.

A separate application and fee for each child may be required. The procedure is the standard procedure for applications under CA 1989, Sch.1 (see para. 12.50).

General matters: The court may alter the arrangement if satisfied either that **13.39** there has been a change (whether foreseen or not) in the circumstances on which financial arrangements were based, or that an agreement does not contain proper financial arrangements with respect to any child (of the family where the application is under MCA 1973, s.35). The court may make such alterations in the agreement by varying or revoking any financial arrangements contained in it or by inserting in it financial arrangement for the benefit of one of the parties or of a child of the family, as may appear to be just (MCA 1973, s.35(2)).

The duration of provisions inserted by the court in an agreement are governed by MCA 1973, s.35(4), (5) and CA 1989, Sch.10, para.10(5).

The court making an order to vary a maintenance agreement may antedate the order to meet the justice of the case (*Warden v Warden* [1981] 3 All E.R. 193), although only to a limited extent (*S v S* [1987] 1 W.L.R. 382).

See further Butterworth's *Family Law Service* 4A[511]-[514].

5 Alteration of maintenance agreement after death of one party (MCA 1973, s.36 as amended by Inheritance (Provision for Family and Dependants) Act 1975, s.26(1) and CA 1989, Sch.1, para.11)

Where a maintenance agreement as defined by MCA 1973, s.34 and CA 1989, **13.40** Sch.1, para.11 provides for the continuation of payments after the death of one of the parties, and that party dies domiciled in England and Wales, the surviving party or the personal representatives of the deceased party may apply as set out below for an order altering the maintenance agreement under MCA 1973, s.36 and CA 1989, Sch.1, para.11.

Jurisdiction: The court has jurisdiction to consider an application for altera- **13.41** tion of an agreement after the death of one party providing that the deceased died domiciled on England and Wales.

Procedure

Application under MCA 1973, s.36: R.3.3 of FPR applies. Proceedings are **13.42** commenced in the High Court or in the county court for the district in which the deceased resided (FPR, r.3.3(1) and CCR, Ord. 48 r.3(1)).

The requirements are:

(*a*) originating summons or application in Form M22 and copies for service on every respondent;

(*b*) affidavit in support exhibiting a copy of the agreement, an official copy of the grant of representation to the deceased's estate and of every testamentary document admitted to proof containing the information required by FPR r.3.3(2)(*a*)-(*i*); and copies of affidavit;

(*c*) public funding certificate, if any, and notice of issue of public funding certificate and copies;

(*d*) fee of £120.

Service is effected in the same manner as a petition (FPR, r.3.5(2)).

13.43   A respondent must send an acknowledgment of service to reach the court within 14 days after service inclusive of the day of service (FPR, r.10.8(2)(*b*)). A respondent who is a personal representative of the deceased *must* file, within 14 days after time for acknowledging service, an affidavit in answer with a copy for service by the court on the applicant. Contents of the affidavit are set out in FPR, r.3.4(4) (*d*)-(*c*). A respondent who is not a personal representative of the deceased *may* file, within fourteen days after the time for acknowledging service, an affidavit in answer with a copy for service by the court on the applicant (FPR, r.3.4(6)).

Subject to modifications, rules applicable to petitions apply (FPR, r.3.5(2)) and in general, rules relating to ancillary relief (FPR, r.3.5(1)). The application may be heard by a judge or a district judge (FPR, rr.3.5(1) and 2.64).

In the county court, CCR, Ord. 48 applies.

13.44   *Applications under CA 1989, Sch.1, para.11*: FPR, r.4.4 applies.

Proceedings are commenced in the High Court or any county court. The procedure is the same as for an application under CA 1989, Sch.1, para.10.

13.45   *General matters*: An application may not, except with the permission of the court, be made after the end of the period of six months from the date on which representation in regard to the estate of the deceased was first taken out (MCA 1973, s.36(2) and CA 1989, Sch.1, para.11(3)).

If a maintenance agreement is altered by the court the like consequences ensue as if the alteration had been made immediately before the death by agreement between the parties and for valuable consideration (MCA 1973, s.36(4) and CA 1989, Sch.1, para.11(2)).

Where an application is made under MCA 1973, s.36, the court is empowered to make an order under the I(PFD)A 1975, s.21 (I(PFD)A 1975, s.18).

See further Butterworth's *Family Law Service* 4A[515]-[520].

6   Married Women's Property Act 1882, s.17

13.46   *General principles*: Section 17 of the MWPA 1882 (as amended by Matrimonial Causes (Property and Maintenance) Act 1958, ss.7 and 8 (assets already disposed of), Married Women's Property Act 1964, s.1 (money and property derived from housekeeping allowance), Law Reform (Miscellaneous Provisions) Act 1970, s.2 (engaged couples), Matrimonial Proceedings and Property Act 1970, s.37 (contributions to improvements of property) and MFPA 1984, s.43 (jurisdiction)) enables the court to decide in the case of spouses, former spouses, engaged or formerly engaged couples any question as to the title to or possession of property.

The powers of MWPA 1882, s.17 extend to afford relief in a case where the promise to marry was not enforceable because the promisor was already married (*Shaw v Fitzgerald* [1992] 1 F.L.R. 357).

13.47   The court can only give effect to existing property rights and cannot vary those rights (*Pettitt v Pettitt* [1969] 2 All E.R. 385). The court does not therefore have the discretionary powers given to it under MCA 1973, where it is unnecessary for the court to determine precisely the respective interests of the parties (*Mossop v Mossop* [1988] 2 All E.R. 202). The court's powers under MCA 1973, ss.24 and 25, if available, should normally be used in preference to proceedings under MWPA 1882, s.17 (*Kowalczuk v Kowalczuk* [1973] 2 All E.R. 1042; *Fielding v Fielding* [1978] 1 All E.R. 267). This is particularly so given that the court may make an order for sale under MCA 1973, s.24A.

The court in which the application has been issued will seek to ensure that all applications relating to the same matrimonial property are dealt with by the same court. It may therefore be necessary to transfer proceedings from or to the High Court or county court, or to the principal registry. The order for transfer may be made by the court of its own motion or on the application of one of the parties (*Practice Direction* [1992], June 5, 1992 2 F.L.R. 87 and *H v M* [1992] 1 F.L.R. 229). The court may stand over an application under MWPA 1882, s.17 pending determination of a pending application under MCA 1973.

There may still, however, be situations in which MWPA 1882, s.17 is still of use to engaged couples (see paras 13.60–13.63) or to determine a spouse's precise interest, *e.g.* to protect a spouse from a claim by a creditor, trustee in bankruptcy or the personal representatives of the other spouse. The court has jurisdiction to assess the monetary value of a party's interest and to order the other party to pay a lump sum in that amount (*Bothe v Amos* [1975] 2 W.L.R. 838). **13.48**

Where the occupying spouse makes the mortgage repayments after the date of separation, that spouse is entitled to a credit equal to half of the capital element of the mortgage repayments made after separation. The interest element of the mortgage repayments can be regarded as a rent or payment for use and occupation (*Leake v Bruzzi* [1974] 2 All E.R. 1196; *Suttill v Graham* [1977] 3 All E.R. 1117).

An application may be made under this section by either party to a marriage, notwithstanding that the marriage has been dissolved or annulled, so long as the application is made within the period of three years beginning with the date on which the marriage was dissolved or annulled (Matrimonial Proceedings and Property Act 1970; s.39).

See further *Rayden and Jackson*, (17th ed., pp. 997–1006) and Butterworths' *Family Law Service* 4A[90]-[114].

Procedure

No existing ancillary relief proceedings: Rules 3.6 and 3.7 of FPR apply. **13.49**

Originating summons may be issued out of the principal registry or a district registry (FPR, r.3.6(1)). County court proceedings must be issued in the divorce county court in which any matrimonial cause is proceeding or is intended to be commenced, or the court for the district in which either the applicant or the respondent resides where no such proceedings have been, or are intended to be commenced (FPR, r.3.6(3)). If a matrimonial cause has been commenced, or is about to be commenced, in the principal registry and treated as if in the county court, the applicant has the option of issuing the proceedings in the principal registry as if in a county court. If no such proceedings have been, or are to be, commenced, the application should be issued in the principal registry as High Court proceedings (FPR, r.3.7).

The requirements are:

(*a*) originating summons or application in Form M23 and copies for service;

(*b*) affidavit in support and copies for service;

(*c*) public funding certificate, if any, and notice of issue of public funding certificate and copy for service;

(*d*) fee of £120.

13.50   Form M23 is set out in Appendix 2 as Form 54.

Where the application concerns the title to or possession of land, Form M23 must:

(*a*) state whether the title to the land is registered or unregistered, and, if registered, the Land Registry title number; and

(*b*) give particulars, so far as known to the applicant, of any mortgage of the land or any interest therein (FPR, r.3.6(4)).

13.51   A copy of Form M23 with Form M6 (acknowledgment of service) and a copy of affidavit annexed are served on the respondent in the same way as a petition (FPR, r.3.6(5)). A copy of Form M23 is served by the court on any mortgagee named in Form M23. It is unnecessary for a copy of the affidavit in support to be served on the mortgagee, but the mortgagee may apply to the court in writing within fourteen days after service of Form M23 for a copy of the affidavit in support, within fourteen days after receiving such an affidavit may file an affidavit in answer and is entitled to be heard on the application (FPR, r.3.6(6)). The applicant or solicitor must provide the address for service of the mortgagee, if it does not appear in Form M23.

The application may be heard by a judge or district judge (FPR, r.2.62(4)). The first appointment is usually a preliminary hearing for directions.

13.52   The respondent must send an acknowledgment of service to reach the court within 14 days after service, inclusive of the day of service (FPR, r.10.8(2)(*b*)). If the respondent intends to contest the application, he must, within 14 days after the time limited for giving notice to defend, file an affidavit in answer with a copy for service on the applicant (FPR, r.3.6(7)). The respondent may be ordered to file an affidavit and, in default, may be debarred from defending (FPR, r.3.6(8)).

Subject to modifications, rules applicable to petitions apply (FPR, r.3.6(11)), as do rules relating to ancillary relief (FPR, r.3.6(10)).

A district judge may grant an injunction so far as it is ancillary or incidental to any relief sought in the proceedings (FPR, r.3.6(9); *Lee v Lee* [1952] 1 All E.R. 1299; *Halden v Halden* [1966] 3 All E.R. 412).

Existing ancillary relief proceedings

13.53   Where proceedings for ancillary relief are already in existence, the application for an order under MWPA 1882, s.17 is made in Form Mil by notice of application or summons (FPR, r.3.6(2)).

7   Trusts of Land and Appointment of Trustees Act 1996, s.14

13.54   *General principles*: A family home which is vested in a husband and wife (or cohabitants) jointly was formerly usually held by them on statutory trusts for sale. The dual system of trusts for sale and strict settlements was abolished and replaced with a single trust of land by the Trusts of Land and Appointment of Trustees Act 1996 (TOLATA 1996) with effect from January 1, 1997. All implied trusts for sale were converted on January 1, 1997 into trusts of land without a duty to sell. In future, the new trust of land will apply whenever there is a conveyance to co-owners. The trustees will hold the property on a trust of land whether the beneficial owners are tenants in common or joint tenants. There will again be no duty to sell. Minor amendments have been made to TOLATA 1996 by the Trustee Act 2000 with effect from February 1, 2001.

Prior to January 1, 1997, it was open to either party, where agreement could not be reached, to apply under the Law of Property Act 1925, s.30 for the trust for sale to be put into effect and for the property to be sold. TOLATA 1996 has repealed the Law of Property Act 1925, s.30. Under the old law, the court was constrained to look for a collateral purpose to the trust in order to mitigate the effect of the duty to sell. Under the new law, where there is no duty to sell, the court is able to take a more flexible approach. However, as under the old law, the new powers of the court remain declaratory and do not permit established property rights to be varied (*Lowson v Coombes* [1999] 2 W.L.R. 720).

A trustee (*Oke v Rideout* [1998] C.L.Y.B. 4876) or a beneficiary may make **13.55** an application to the court under TOLATA 1996, s.14. As well as ordering an immediate or postponed sale (as under the old law), an order may be made, for example, preventing a sale or relieving the trustees of an obligation to obtain the consent of, or to consult, any person in the exercise of their function. An application may also be made to the court in relation to the powers conferred on trustees by TOLATA 1996, s.13 to exclude or restrict a beneficiary's entitlement to occupy land.

The new powers of the court are exercisable where an application was made under the Law of Property Act 1925, s.30 before January 1, 1997, which falls to be dealt with after that date (TOLATA 1996, s.14(4)).

A new statutory checklist found in TOLATA 1996, s.15 sets out the matters **13.56** to which the court must have regard in determining an application for an order under TOLATA 1996, s.14. These include the intentions of the person who created the trust, the purposes for which the property subject to the trust is held (*Oke v Rideout* [1998] C.L.Y.B. 4876), the welfare of any minor who occupies or might reasonably be expected to occupy any land subject to the trust as his home and the interests of any secured creditor of any beneficiary (TOLATA 1996, s.15(1)). The established case law has effectively been given statutory force and is not made redundant (*TSB Bank plc v Marshall* [1998] 2 F.L.R. 769; *Oke v Rideout* [1998] C.L.Y.B. 4876). Where there is a conflict between a secured creditor's interest in a matrimonial home and the interest of an innocent spouse, the interest of the secured creditor will prevail except where there are exceptional circumstances. TOLATA 1996, s.15(1)(c) confines consideration of the welfare of any children to minors (*TSB Bank plc v Marshall* [1998] 2 F.L.R. 769). The interest of secured creditors are just one factor to be considered and are not distinguished as priority interests (*The Mortgage Corporation Limited v Shaire* [2000] 1 F.L.R. 973; *Bank of Ireland Home Mortgages Limited v Bell* [2001] 2 F.L.R. 809).

Where the application to the court is made under TOLATA 1996, s.13 to exclude or restrict a beneficiary's right to occupy, the court must also have regard to the circumstances and wishes of each of the beneficiaries who is, or apart from any previous exercise by the trustees of their powers would be, entitled to occupy the trust land (TOLATA 1996, s.15(2)). In the case of any other application, the court must also have regard to the circumstances and wishes of any beneficiary of full age who is entitled to an interest in possession in the trust property or, where there is a dispute, the majority of the beneficiaries according to the value of their combined interest. Where there is a question of the trustees conveying land to beneficiaries who are absolutely entitled, their circumstances and wishes are irrelevant (TOLATA 1996, s.15(3)). These provisions do not apply where an application is made by a trustee in bankruptcy; the rules contained in the Insolvency Act 1986, s.335A apply (TOLATA 1996, s.15(4)).

13.57   Where possible, the court will prefer to use its wider discretionary powers under MCA 1973, s.24 in the absence of some genuine third party interest (*Brown v Pritchard* [1975] 3 All E.R. 721; *Laird v Laird* [1999] 1 F.L.R. 791; *Tee v Tee and Hillman* [1999] 2 F.L.R. 613). However, such powers are only available on granting a decree of divorce, nullity or judicial separation to take effect upon the decree. TOLATA, s.14 (or MWPA 1882, s.17) may be the only means of obtaining a sale where one party refuses to sell or to commence proceedings for divorce, nullity or judicial separation. TOLATA 1996, s.14 may be the only available remedy if proceedings under the MCA 1973 are barred by remarriage and/or under MWPA 1882, s.17 by limitation.

If the title deeds quantify the beneficial interests of the parties that is conclusive, unless one party can show evidence of fraud or mistake (*Goodman v Gallant* [1986] Fam.106). Where the title deeds do not quantify the respective beneficiarial interests of the parties, the court must determine their shares. The respective interests are determined by applying trust law. There is no discretion to make an order that meets the judge's view of what is "fair" in all the circumstances (*Bernard v Josephs* [1982] Ch.391 at 402). Much of the case law under the Law of Property Act 1925, s.30 and under TOLATA 1996, s.14 arises from disputes between cohabitants; the "legal principles to be applied are the same whether the dispute is between married or unmarried couples" (per Griffiths L.J. in *Bernard v Josephs* at 402).

13.58   There is a substantial body of case law dealing with the doctrine of constructive trusts which involves looking at the conduct of the parties to see if an intention to share beneficial ownership can be inferred (*e.g.* contributions by the non-owner: *e.g. Grant v Edwards* [1987] 1 F.L.R. 87; *Cooke v Head* [1972] 1 W.L.R. 518) together with some form of detriment to one party as a result of reliance in the belief of shared ownership (*e.g. Lloyds Bank plc v Rosset* [1990] 1 All E.R. 1111; *Midland Bank v Cooke* [1995] 2 F.L.R. 915). Resulting trusts arise where no common intent is established and when there is a presumption as to shares based on contribution (*e.g. Springette v Defoe* [1992] 2 F.L.R. 388; *Evans v Hayward* [1995] 2 F.L.R. 511). Issues of proprietary estoppel may also arise where a party is encouraged to act on a mistaken belief (*e.g. Pascoe v Turner* [1979] 1 W.L.R. 431; *Greaseley v Cooke* [1980] 3 All E.R. 710; *Matharu v Matharu* [1994] 2 F.L.R. 597; *Wayling v Jones* [1995] 2 W.L.R. 1029; *Yaxley v Gotts* [1999] 2 F.L.R. 941) rather than on an alleged common intention.

13.59   *Procedure*: In the High Court, proceedings may be issued in the Chancery Division or the Family Division (*Bernard v Josephs* [1982] Ch 391).

The requirements are (High Court or county court):

(*a*) claim form in Form 208;

(*b*) witness statement in support of claim;

(*c*) public funding certificate, if any, and notice of issue of public funding certificate and copy for service;

(*d*) fee of £120.

A county court has jurisdiction whatever the value of the land (High Court and County Courts Jurisdiction Order 1991, art.2(1)(a)). District judges (including district judges of the Principal Registry) have jurisdiction to hear and dispose of proceedings under TOLATA 1996, s.14 (*Practice Direction (Family Proceedings: Allocation and Costs)* April 22, 1999 [1999] 1 W.L.R. 1128).

See further Butterworth's *Family Law Service* 4A[115]-[123].

8   Disputes between engaged couples

Property: Section 2(2) of the Law Reform (Miscellaneous Provisions) Act 1970 extends MWPA 1882, s.17 (as amended) to any property in which either or both of the parties has a beneficial interest. An application by either party to the engagement under MWPA 1882, s.17 must be made within three years of the termination of the engagement. The law and practice under MWPA 1882, s.17 (as amended) is discussed at paras 13.46–13.53.   **13.60**

Gifts between engaged couples: A party to an engagement who makes a gift to the other party on condition that it shall be returned if the engagement is terminated is not prevented from recovering the gift by reason only of his having terminated the engagement (Law Reform (Miscellaneous Provisions) Act 1970, s.3(1)). The gift of an engagement ring is presumed to be an absolute gift. The presumption may be rebutted by proving that the ring was given on condition that it should be returned if the marriage did not take place for any reason (Law Reform (Miscellaneous Provisions) Act 1970, s.3(2)).   **13.61**

Gifts to engaged couples: Where an engagement is terminated, any rule of law concerning the rights of husbands and wives in relation to property in which either or both has or have a beneficial interest, including Matrimonial Proceedings and Property Act 1970, s.37, applies to property in which either or both parties to the engagement had a beneficial interest whilst the engagement was in force (Law Reform (Miscellaneous Provisions) Act 1970, s.2(1)). See, however, *Mossop v Mossop* [1988] 2 All E.R. 202.   **13.62**

So far as gifts to engaged couples are concerned, the court will attempt to ascertain the intention of the donor. The court may hold that gifts belong to the party from whose relations or friends they came (*Samson v Samson* [1960] 2 All E.R. 653).

Procedure: Engaged couples are unable to avail themselves of the court's wide powers under MCA 1973, ss.24 and 25, as a result of which a stricter application of the relevant rules of law may result (*Mossop v Mossop* [1988] 2 All E.R. 202).   **13.63**

The procedures for resolving disputes between engaged couples are:

(*a*) MWPA 1882, s.17 as amended (paras 13.46–13.53);

(*b*) TOLATA 1996, s.14 (paras 13.54–13.59).

9 Application for provision from deceased's estate under Inheritance (Provision for Family and Dependants) Act 1975

13.64 *Introduction*: S.1 of the I(PFD)A 1975 provides that where a person dies on or after April 1, 1976 certain persons may apply for provision out of the deceased's estate on the ground that the disposition of the deceased's estate effected by his will, or the law of intestacy, or the combination of his will and that law, is not such as to make reasonable financial provision for the applicant.

13.65 *Jurisdiction*: An application can be made under the I(PFD)A 1975, providing that the deceased died domiciled in England and Wales (I(PFD)A 1975, s.1(1)). *Who may apply?*: The following may make an application under the I(PFD)A 1975:

(*a*) the wife or husband of the deceased;

(*b*) a former wife or former husband of the deceased who has not remarried;

(*ba*) any person not included in (a) or (b) above who, where the deceased died on or after January 1, 1996, was living in the same household as the deceased and as the husband or wife of the deceased for the whole of the period of two years ending immediately before the date of the deceased's death (I(PFD)A 1975, s.1(1A));

(*c*) a child of the deceased;

(*d*) any person (not being a child of the deceased) who, in the case of any marriage to which the deceased was at any time a party, was treated by the deceased as a child of the family in relation to the marriage;

(*e*) any other person who immediately before the death of the deceased was being maintained, either wholly or partly, by the deceased (I(PFD)A 1975, s.1(1)(*a*)–(*e*).

13.66 A child includes an illegitimate child, an adopted child or a child *en venire sa mère* at the date of death of the deceased (I(PFD)A 1975, s.25(1); *Re McC* (1978) 9 Fam. Law. 26; *Williams v Johns* [1988] 2 F.L.R. 475). The child does not need to be still in its minority (*Re Debenham* [1986] 1 F.L.R. 404: successful application by 58 year-old daughter of deceased). However, an adult child is not entitled to make a claim where he is in comfortable circumstances in order to maintain his standard of living (*Re Jennings* [1994] 1 F.L.R. 536; *Re Hancock* [1998] 2 F.L.R. 346).

In contrast to the meaning of a child of the family in MCA 1973, for the purposes of I(PFD)A 1975, a child can become a child of the family after the marriage has ceased to exist (*Re Leach* [1985] 2 All E.R. 754). A child of the family may include a grandchild (*Re A* [1998] 1 F.L.R. 347). However, a child of the deceased who has been adopted may not claim against the deceased's estate even if the adoption took place after the death but before the application (*Re Collins* [1990] 2 F.L.R. 72).

13.67 A cohabitant of the deceased no longer has to surmount the hurdle of proving "dependency" within category (e) above if such a person falls within category (ba) above. The question whether a person falls within I(PFD)A

1975, s.1(1A) is determined by asking whether, in the opinion of a reasonable person with normal perceptions, it could be said that the two people in question were living together as husband and wife (*Re Watson* [1999] 1 F.L.R. 878).

A person is treated as being maintained either wholly or partly by the deceased if the deceased (for the purposes of category (e)), otherwise than for full valuable consideration, was making a substantial contribution in money or money's worth towards the reasonable needs of that person (I(PFD)A 1975, s.1(3)). Valuable consideration does not include marriage or a promise of marriage (I(PFD)A 1976, s.25(1)). Full valuable consideration is not further defined in the Act. Section 1(3) operates so as to qualify the right of a person being maintained to apply to the court under section 1(1)(*e*) and not so as to provide an alternative to it (*Re Beaumont* [1980] 1 All E.R. 266). The fact of maintenance raises a presumption of the assumption of financial responsibility (*Jelley v Iliffe* [1981] 2 All E.R. 29). The fact that the applicant looked after the deceased with extra-devoted care and attention, particularly when the deceased was in ill-health, does not constitute full valuable consideration so as to debar the applicant from claiming (*Bishop v Plumley* [1991] 1 F.L.R. 121).

Applications under the Act are personal actions which abate on the death of the applicant and do not survive for the benefit of his estate (*Whytte v Tilehurst* [1986] 2 All E.R. 158; *Re Bramwell* [1988] 2 F.L.R. 263; *Re R* [1986] Fam. Law. 58).

Reasonable financial provision

Reasonable financial provision means: **13.68**

(1) Where the applicant is the surviving spouse (except in a case where there has been a judicial separation and, at the date of death, the decree is still in force and the separation continuing), such financial provision as it would be reasonable in all the circumstances of the case for a husband or wife to receive, whether or not that provision is required for his or her maintenance (I(PFD)A 1975, s.1(2)(*a*)). The fact that an applicant widow is a person of means will not necessarily preclude a successful claim (*Re Bunning* [1984] 3 All E.R. 1; *Re Besterman* [1984] Ch.458). See, further, *Jessop v Jessop* [1992] 1 F.L.R. 591; *Davis v Davis* [1993] 1 F.L.R. 54; *Adams v Adams* [2001] W.T.L.R. 493 (application of principles established in *White v White* [2000] 2 F.L.R. 981).

(2) In the case of any other applicant (including a surviving spouse who has been judicially separated provided that the decree is in force and the separation continuing at the date of death), such financial provision as it would be reasonable in all the circumstances for the applicant to receive for his maintenance (I(PFD)A 1975, s.1(2)(*b*)). As to adult children, see p.000. As to former spouses, see *Re Abram* [1996] 2 F.L.R. 379; *Barrass v Harding and Newman* [2001] 1 F.L.R. 138. A former spouse needs to establish exceptional circumstances to succeed (*Re Fullard* [1981] 2 All E.R. 796). As to cohabitants, see p.000 and *Graham v Murphy* [1997] 1 F.L.R. 860.

In *Moody v Stevenson* [1992] 1 F.L.R. 494 the Court of Appeal gave guidance as to the approach to be adopted when considering whether reasonable financial provision has been made. The court must apply a two-stage test. First, whether under I(PFD)A 1975, s.2(1), the disposition failed to make **13.69** reasonable financial provision for the applicant. Secondly, whether, and how financial provision should be made for the applicant. Authorities prior to the 1975 Act should be approached with caution because of the substantial changes made in the legislation itself (*Moody v Stevenson*, above).

In order for the court to find that there has not been reasonable provision for maintenance, the court has to find that it was unreasonable on the part of the testator to make no provision for the person in question, or that it was unreasonable not to make a larger provision.

Where, within 12 months of the date of the making absolute of a decree of nullity or divorce, or the granting of a decree of judicial separation, a party to a marriage dies, and either no application for provision under MCA 1973, s.23 or 24 has been made by the surviving spouse, or such application has been made but has not been determined at the date of death, if that surviving spouse should then apply for an order under I(PFD)A 1975, s.2 the court may, if it thinks it just to do so, treat the applicant as if the decree of divorce or nullity had not been made absolute or a decree of judicial separation had not been granted (I(PFD)A 1975, s.14).

13.70   *Procedure*: An application may be made to the High Court or to a county court. The previous county court jurisdictional limit no longer applies (The High Court and County Courts Jurisdiction Order 1991, art.2). Ordinarily, the action will be tried in the High Court if the value of the action is £50,000 or more, and in the county court if less than £25,000, unless there are exceptional circumstances (The High Court and County Court Jurisdiction Order 1991, art.7).

Proceedings under I(PFD)A 1975 have been governed since April 26, 1999 by CPR 1998, Sch.1, RSC Ord. 99 irrespective of whether the proceedings are in the High Court or a county court (RSC Ord. 99, r.A1). References below are to RSC Ord. 99 as appearing in CPR 1998, Sch.1.

13.71   *High Court*: Proceedings are assigned to the Chancery Division or to the Family Division and may be commenced in the Central Office, the Principal Registry of the Family Division or any district registry (RSC, Ord. 99, r.2). An application to the Chancery Division will usually be appropriate where the application will involve the taking of complicated accounts.

County court

13.72   As to the jurisdiction of a county court, see County Courts Act 1984, s.25. *Requirements* (High Court or county court):

(a) claim form (Form N208);

(b) witness statement/affidavit by applicant exhibiting an official copy of the grant of representation to the deceased's estate and of every testamentary document admitted to proof;

(c) public funding certificate, if any, and copy of notice of issue of public funding certificate;

(d) fee of £120.

See RSC Ord. 99, r.3. See *Hannigan v Hannigan* [2000] 2 F.C.R. 650 as to the need to ensure that the proper procedures are followed.

13.73   The rules do not prescribe the contents of the witness statement/affidavit in support but the statement/affidavit must set out the facts which establish the right to apply. In the case of a spouse, the marriage certificate should be exhibited; where there has been a divorce, nullity or judicial separation, a certified copy of the decree should be exhibited. A certified copy of the death certificate should in all cases be exhibited.

An application may not be made after six months from the date on which representation is first taken out except with permission of the court (I(PFD)A 1975, s.4). In order to gain protection against the possibility that a grant may be issued without its existence coming to the attention of an interested party, facilities are available for a standing search to be made at the principal registry or sub-registry (*Practice Direction* [1975] 3 All E.R. 403). The application for permission may be made in claim form and the grounds of the application set out in the statement/affidavit in support. The court's power to extend time is discretionary. In exercising its discretion the court will look at all the circumstances and consider whether such an extension is required in the interests of justice (*Re Salmon, Coard v National Westminster Bank Ltd* [1980] 3 W.L.R. 760; *Re C* [1995] 2 F.L.R. 24; *Re W* [1995] 2 F.L.R. 689).

13.74 A defendant who is a personal representative must and any other defendant may, within 21 days after service of the claim form on him, inclusive of the day of service, file with the court a witness statement or affidavit in answer to the application (RSC, Ord. 99, r.5(1)). The contents of the witness statement or affidavit to be filed by a personal representative are prescribed by RSC, Ord. 99, r.5(2). Every defendant who lodges a witness statement or affidavit must at the same time serve a copy on the claimant and on every other defendant who is not represented by the same solicitor (RSC, Ord. 99, r.5(3)).

The court may at any stage direct that any person be added as a party to the proceedings or that notice of the proceedings be served on any person (RSC, Ord. 99, r.4(1)).

The proceedings may be heard and disposed of by a district judge including a district judge of the Principal Registry (*President's Direction*, April 22, 1999 [1999] 1 F.L.R. 1295).

13.75 On the hearing, the personal representative must produce the grant of representation and, if an order is made under the Act, the grant must remain in the custody of the court until a memorandum of the order has been endorsed on or permanently annexed to the grant in accordance with I(PFD)A 1975, s.19(3) (RSC, Ord., 99, r.7).

Where an application is made jointly by two or more applicants and the claim form is accordingly issued by one solicitor on behalf of all of them, they may, if they have conflicting interests, appear on any hearing of the claim by separate solicitors or counsel or in person, and where at any stage in the proceedings it appears that one of the applicants is not but ought to be separately represented, the court may adjourn the proceedings until he is (RSC, Ord. 99, r.6).

13.76 *Orders which can be made*: If the court is satisfied that the applicant has substantiated the ground of his application it may make any one or more of the following orders under s.2(1)(*a*)-(*f*) of the I(PFD)A 1975:

(*a*) an order for periodical payments for the applicant out of the deceased's net estate;

(*b*) an order for the payment to the applicant of a lump sum out of the net estate;

(*c*) an order transferring to the applicant specified property comprised in the net estate;

(*d*) an order settling for the applicant's benefit specified property comprised in the net estate;

(*e*) an order for the acquisition out of property comprised in the net estate of specified property and for the transfer to the applicant, or the settlement for his benefit, of that property;

(*f*) an order varying any ante or post-nuptial settlement (including such a settlement made by will) made on the parties to a marriage to which the deceased was a party. In this case, the variation can only be for the benefit of the surviving party to that marriage or any child of the marriage or any person treated by the deceased as a child of the family in relation to that marriage.

13.77 *The net estate of the deceased*: Section 25(1) of the I(PFD)A 1975 defines the net estate of the deceased as:

(*a*) all property, including any chose in action, of which the deceased had power to dispose by his will (other than by virtue of a special power of appointment) less the amount of his funeral, testamentary and administration expenses, debts and liabilities including any inheritance tax payable out of the estate;

(*b*) any property in respect of which the deceased held a general power of appointment, not exercisable by will, which had not been exercised;

(*c*) any sum of money or other property which is treated by virtue of the I(PFD)A 1975, s.8(1) or (2), or by virtue of any order made under I(PFD)A 1975, s.9 as part of the net estate;

(*d*) any sum of money or other property which is ordered under I(PFD)A 1975, ss.10 or 11 to be provided for the purpose of making financial provision under the Act.

The deceased's net estate is further defined in I(PFD)A 1975, ss.8 and 9 (see *Re Crawford* (1982) 4 F.L.R. 273; *Jessop v Jessop* [1992] 1 F.L.R. 591; *Powell v Osbourne* [1993] 1 F.L.R. 1001).

13.78 *General matters*: When exercising its powers to make orders under I(PFD)A 1975, s.2, the court must have regard to the matters set out in I(PFD)A 1975, s.3. (See *Malone v Harrison* [1979] 1 W.L.R. 1353; *Williams v Johns* [1988] 2 F.L.R. 475; *Espinosa v Bourke* [1999] 1 F.L.R. 747). It is not necessary in every case for the applicant to establish a moral obligation (*Re Coventry* [1980] Ch.461; *Re Pearce* [1998] 2 F.L.R. 705).

In the case of a surviving spouse, the court must also have regard to the provision which the applicant might reasonably have expected to receive if on the day on which the deceased died the marriage, instead of being terminated by death, had been terminated by a decree of divorce: I(PFD)A 1975, s.3*(2)(b)*. This is one of the section 3 factors and not to be treated as the starting-point (*Re Krubert* [1997] 1 F.L.R. 42).

The court has power to make interim orders under I(PFD) A 1975, s.5 and to vary, discharge, suspend and revive orders under I(PFD)A 1975, s.6.

I(PFD)A 1975, ss.10 and 11 contain provisions intended to prevent a person intentionally evading the consequences of the Act by disposing of his assets before his death or contracting to do so after his death.

The rights conferred by I(PFD)A 1975, s.1 to apply for an order under **13.79** section 2 cannot be overridden or excluded by an agreement between the parties (*Re Fullard* [1981] 2 All E.R. 796). By virtue of section 15(1) of the Act, where a court in England and Wales grants a decree of judicial separation, divorce or nullity, it may at that time or at any time thereafter, if it considers it just to do so, and on the application of either party to the marriage, order that the other party shall not on the death of the applicant be entitled to apply for an order under s.2. It appears that the court must be given some indication of what the applicant's estate is likely to consist of, and some details of the persons whom the applicant considers to have a prior claim on his estate in the event of his decease, in order to enable the court to conclude that it is just to make the order (*Whiting v Whiting* [1988] 2 F.L.R. 189).

On making an order under MFPA 1984, s.17 (applications for financial relief in England and Wales by a person whose marriage has been dissolved or annulled, or who has been legally separated from his spouse by reasons of judicial or other proceedings in an overseas country), the court, if it considers it just, may, on the application of either party to the marriage, order that, on the death of the applicant, the other party shall not be entitled to apply for an order under I(PFD)A 1975, s.2 (I(PFD)A 1975, s.15A).

Chapter 14

Appeals

1 General considerations

14.01 The legal position in relation to appeals has been reviewed substantially by the introduction of the Access to Justice Act 1999, the new CPR Pt 52 and supplemental Practice Direction 52, and judicial efforts to rationalise the process and reduce the number of disproportionately costly appeals.

The Access to Justice Act 1999, s.55 and CPR r.52.13(2) provide that now there should be no appeal to the Court of Appeal from the decision of a county court or High Court unless the appeal would raise an important point of principle or there is some other compelling reason for the Court of Appeal to hear it.

In *Piglowska v Piglowski* [1999] 1 W.L.R. 1360, the House of Lords granted permission to appeal partly in the hope expressed by Lord Hoffman of reducing the chances of such disasters (a reference to the fact that the then Legal Aid Board expenditure exceeded the value of the assets in dispute) happening in the future. In his judgment following the appeal, Lord Hoffman emphasised:

(1) the advantage that the first instance judge has in seeing the parties and any other witnesses both in relation to issues of fact and credibility;

(2) that the judge's reasons should be read on the assumption that the judge knew how to perform his functions and what matters should be taken into account (unless he demonstrated the contrary);

(3) that diversity of values amongst the judiciary is an acceptable price for the flexibility of the discretionary jurisdiction; and

(4) the principle of proportionality should operate to prevent successive appeals in cases where the amount at issue and the resources available do not justify it.

14.02 In *Re W, Re A, Re B (Change of Name)* [1999] 2 F.L.R. 930, the Court of Appeal indicated that the test that should be applied on appeal to the Court of Appeal in children cases in accordance with the principles in *G v G (Minors: Custody Appeal)* [1985] 1 W.L.R. 647, HL, should be applied equally in the county court and the High Court (see further at para. 14.26 below).

In *Cordle v Cordle* [2002] 1 F.L.R. 207, the Court of Appeal indicated that appeals in ancillary relief proceedings from a district judge's decision should be brought into line with appeals in other civil, non-family proceedings (see further p.83 below). In *English v Emery Reimbold & Strick Ltd* [2002]

E.W.C.A. Civ. 605, the Court of Appeal gave guidance on how and when to appeal on the ground that the trial judge's reasons were inadequate.

As well as considering whether an appeal is justified in the light of the tests to be applied and the issue of proportionality, the practitioner should also ensure that an appeal is the correct course of action, rather than an application to set aside the order, for a re-hearing, variation of relevant provisions of the order or amendment under the "slip" rule (CCR, Ord. 15, r.5). "Hopeless" appeals should not be made (*Grepe v Loam* (1887) 37 Ch.168, *B v B (Unmeritorious Applications)* [1999] 1 F.L.R. 505), and the Court of Appeal has held that it is an abuse of process to appeal on a point of no significance to the parties (*Re S* [1994] 2 F.C.R. 18).

2   From a district judge in the county court

Categorisation and nature of appeals: Appeals from a district judge in the **14.03** county court may be categorised as follows:

(1) Appeals in proceedings which are *not* "family proceedings", by reference to the Matrimonial and Family Proceedings Act 1984 (MFPA 1984), s.32 and Supreme Court Act 1981 (SCA 1981), s.61 (see further paras 1.02–1.04 above), to which the Civil Procedure Rules 1998 (CPR) Pt 52, and supplementary Practice Direction (PD52) apply. Such appeals would embrace, for example, proceedings under the Trusts of Land and Appointment of Trustees Act 1996, s.14.

"Family proceedings" are defined by FPR, r.1.2(1). Within this category, a distinction must be drawn between "final decisions" and decisions which are not final decisions. A final decision is a decision of a court that would finally determine (subject to any possible appeal or detailed assessment of costs) the entire proceedings whichever way the court decided the issues before it (PD52, para.2A.3). An appeal from a final decision in relation to claims referred to in PD52 para.2A.2 is to the Court of Appeal. Appeals from non-final decisions and other final decisions by a district judge not within PD52 para.2A.2 are to a circuit judge (PD52, para.2A.1). Detailed consideration of this category of appeals is outside the scope of this book.

(2) Appeals in family proceedings to which the County Court Rules 1981 (CCR) and Family Proceedings Rules 1991 (FPR) r.8.1(2) or r.8.1A(6) apply.

FPR r.8.1 applies to any order or decision granting or varying an **14.04** order (or refusing to do so) on an application for ancillary relief or in proceedings to which FPR rr.3.1, 3.2, 3.3 or 3.6 apply; and such an order or decision is defined as a "final order" for the purposes of CCR, Ord. 37, r.6 (FPR r.8.1(2)). FPR r.3.1 relates to applications under the Matrimonial Causes Act 1973 (MCA 1973) s.27 for financial provision in the case of neglect by a party to a marriage to maintain the other party or a child of the family. FPR rr.3.2 and 3.3 relate to applications under MCA 1973 ss.35 and 36 for the alteration of maintenance agreements during the lifetime of the parties or after the death of one party respectively. FPR r.3.6 relates to applications under the Married Women's Property Act 1882 s.17. FPR r.8.1A(6)

applies to orders or decisions granting or refusing to grant occupation orders under the Family Law Act 1996 (FLA 1996) ss.33(3) and
(4) and transfers of tenancies (s.53)

This category embraces the majority of orders made in family proceedings. CCR, Ord. 37 r.6 provides that the judge may set aside or
vary the order, make another order in substitution, remit the matter
for re-hearing by the district judge or for further consideration, or
order a new trial to take place before him, or another circuit judge.
The circuit judge may exercise his own discretion in substitution for
that of the district judge (FPR, r.8.1(3)). Until recently, it was clear
that in exercising his own discretion, the circuit judge might give such
weight as he thought fit to the manner in which the district judge exercised his discretion and might, in his discretion, admit such further
oral evidence as he thought relevant and just upon such terms as he
thought fit (*Marsh v Marsh* [1993] 1 F.L.R. 467). There was not,
however, a right or a requirement of the judge to begin *de novo*. Such
an appeal was a hybrid between a vetrial and an appeal. This exercise
of discretion also applied to appeals from costs orders in the relevant
proceedings (*A v A* [1996] 1 F.L.R. 14).

14.05   However, the Court of Appeal has now advocated reform of the basis
on which an appeal from a district judge's decision in ancillary relief
proceedings should be allowed in *Cordle v Cordle*. Dame Elizabeth
Butler-Sloss P and Thorpe L.J. reviewed the decision in *Marsh v Marsh*
[1993] 1 F.L.R. 467 and indicated that appeals should only be allowed
if there was a procedural irregularity, if the district judge failed to take
account of relevant matters or took account of irrelevant matters, or
was plainly wrong. Fresh evidence should not usually be allowed on
appeal and appeals should not be re-hearings. *Cordle* was endorsed by
a differently constituted Court of Appeal in *Shaw v Shaw* (2002)
Lawtel, 31st July. It is unclear how this approach may be reconciled with
FPR, r.8.1(3), which was not considered by the Court of Appeal.

The new approach brings appeals from ancillary relief orders sub-
stantively in line with the approach in appeals in other civil cases.

In this category of appeals, no appeal will lie from an order to
which a party has consented (CCR, Ord. 37, r.6(1)), and instead an
application to set the order aside or for a re-hearing (see p. 284 below)
should be made (see further para. 9.79 above).

(3) Appeals in family proceedings to which the CCR and FPR r.8.1(1)
apply.

14.06   FPR r.8.1(1) applies to any order or decision in family proceedings
except those orders and decisions covered by FPR r.8.1(2) or
r.8.1A(6). FPR r.8.1(1) disapplies CCR, Ord. 13, r.1(10) (which
enables the circuit judge to vary or rescind an order made by a district judge in the course of proceedings) and CCR, Ord. 37, r.6
described above. It is unclear, in the absence of any express statutory
provision prescribing the powers of the circuit judge on such an
appeal, what those powers are. It seems that an appeal will require the
decision of the district judge to be established as "plainly wrong" in
a similar manner as appeals to the Court of Appeal, and now category (2) appeals following *Cordle*.

Such appeals embrace orders made in family proceedings not
within category (2) (for example, orders or decisions to which FPR

r.3.11 (proceedings in respect of polygamous marriage) or r.3.12 (applications for declaration as to marital status) apply, or interlocutory orders in category (2) proceedings). This category also includes appeals against a decree nisi (*Marya v Marya* [1995] 2 F.L.R. 911).

(4) Appeals from orders or decisions in proceedings under the CA 1989 to which FPR Pt IV and r.4.22 apply.

FPR r.4.1(2) sets out the applications to which FPR Pt IV (and therefore FPR r.4.22 on appeals) applies. As indicated above, the test to be applied should be the same whether the appeal is heard by the county court, High Court or Court of Appeal; in accordance with the principles in *G v G (Minors: Custody Appeal)* [1985] 1 W.L.R. 647, HL (*Re W, Re A, Re B (Change of Name)* [1999] 2 F.L.R. 930, CA) (see further at para. 14.26 below).

Re-hearing: As an alternative to an appeal, a district judge (or judge) in the **14.07** county court has power to order a rehearing under CCR, Ord. 37, r.1. An application for a re-hearing rather than an appeal is appropriate where no error of the court at the hearing is alleged (CCR, Ord. 37, r.1(1)); for example, where there is an allegation of material non-disclosure (or where the factual basis on which the original order was made has proven to be incorrect; *Fournier v Fournier* [1998] 2 F.L.R. 990, CA). If an error of the court is alleged, the appropriate course of action is to appeal.

Procedure on appeals: Any party may appeal from an order or decision within **14.08** categories (2) to (4) referred to above to a circuit judge of the county court on notice. Leave to appeal is not required (FPR, rr.4.22, 8.1, and see also the judgment of the Court of Appeal in *Egbaiyelo v Egbaiyelo* [2002] E.W.C.A. Civ. 454. However, leave may be ordered to be required where one party makes frequent unsuccessful and unmeritorious appeals; *B v B (Unmeritous Applications)* [1999] 1 F.L.R. 505). "Permission to appeal" to use the correct CPR terminology, is required for category (1) appeals (CPR, r.52.3(1)).

In the case of category (1) appeals, the notice of appeal must request permission to appeal and must be filed at the appeal court within such period as directed by the lower court, or within 14 days after the date of the decision of the lower court if no direction was made (CPR, r.52.4(2)). It must be served on the Respondent as soon as practicable and, in any event, not later than seven days after it is filed (CPR, r.52.4(3)). PD52 para.5.6 sets out the documents that must be filed with the notice of appeal, and CPR r.52.3(6) sets out the criteria to be met before permission will be given. CPR rr.52.10 and 52.11 and PD52 para.6.1 define the powers of the appeal court and the procedure for the hearing of appeals.

In the case of most category (2) or (3) appeals (FPR, r.8.1 appeals), unless **14.09** the court otherwise directs, the notice of appeal must be issued within fourteen days of the order appealed against and served not less than fourteen days before the date fixed for the hearing of the appeal (FPR, r.8.1(4)). Appeals under FPR, r.8.1 are heard in chambers, unless the judge otherwise directs (FPR, r.8.1(5)). Unless the court otherwise orders, an appeal under FPR, r.8.1 does not operate as a stay (FPR, r.8.1(6)).

The requirements for those appeals in categories (2)-(3) are as follows:

(*a*) notice and copy (stating briefly the grounds of the application) (for form, see Appendix 2, para. A2.55);

(*b*) the bundle of documentation which was before the district judge;

(c) notes of evidence and judgment (see below);

(d) fee of £80 (FPFO para.5.1);

(e) bundle in accordance with the *President's Direction (Family Proceedings: Court Bundles)*, March 10, 2000 [2001] 1 W.L.R. 737 if the appeal falls within para.1 of the Direction.

14.10   Appeals in category (2) to which FPR r.8.1A applies are hybrid in nature in that FPR rr.8.1(5) and (6) apply, but r.8.1(4) does not. Instead, FPR rr.4.22(2), (3), (4), (5), (7) and (8) apply, but subject to the provisos of FPR r.8.1A (see the procedure for category (4) appeals below), and FPR rr.8.2(4)(e) and (6) also apply (FPR r.8.1A(1)).

In the case of a category (4) appeal, the notice of appeal must be filed and served on the parties to the proceedings and on any children's guardian, in the case of an appeal against an order under CA 1989, s.38(1) (interim orders), within seven days, or, in any other case, within 14 days after the determination against which the appeal is brought (FPR, r.4.22(3)).

14.11   The requirements for a category (4) appeal are as follows:

(a) notice and copies (setting out the grounds relied upon) (for form, see Appendix 2, para. A2.55);

(b) a certified copy of the summons or application and of the order appealed against, and of any order staying its execution;

(c) a copy of any notes of the evidence;

(d) a copy of any reasons given for the decision (FPR, r.4.22(2));

(e) a bundle of evidence filed for the original hearing (*Re U(T) (A Minor) (Care Order: Contact)* [1993] 2 F.L.R. 565);

(f) fee of £80 (FPFO, para.5.1);

(g) bundle in accordance with the *President's Direction (Family Proceedings: Court Bundles)* March 10, 2000 [2001] 1 W.L.R. 737 if the appeal falls within para.1 of the Direction.

The documents required under (b)-(d) must be filed and served as soon as practicable after the filing and service of the notice of appeal (FPR, r.4.22(4)).

14.12   Save in respect of an appeal against an order under CA 1989, s.38 (interim care or supervision orders), where the respondent wishes:

(a) to contend on the appeal that the decision of the court below should be varied, either in any event or in the event of the appeal being allowed in whole or in part; or

(b) to contend that the decision of the court below should be affirmed on grounds other than those relied upon by that court; or

(c) to contend by way of cross-appeal that the decision of the court below was wrong in whole or in part. (FPR 1991, r.4.22(5) and (6))

he must within fourteen days of receipt of notice of the appeal, file and serve on all other parties to the appeal a notice in writing setting out the grounds upon which he wishes to rely.

In relation to appeals in categories (2)-(4), *Practice Direction*, February 21, 1985 [1985] 1 W.L.R. 361 sets out the requirements in relation to notes of evidence and judgment.

Where the appellant is represented by a solicitor, and either party wishes to **14.13**
obtain a copy of the district judge's notes of evidence, the appellant's solicitor
must:

(*a*) within 21 days from the date upon which the appeal is lodged, certify
that either the appellant or the respondent considers that notes of evidence taken before the district judge are necessary for the purpose of
appeal and that notes of evidence will be lodged; and

(*b*) if he has so certified, unless otherwise directed, not less than 21 days
prior to the hearing of the appeal lodge a copy of the notes of evidence (which can be bespoken from the district judge) and of judgment (being notes prepared by the appellant's solicitor, and where the
respondent is represented by his legal advisers, and approved by the
district judge).

Where the appellant is acting in person and the respondent is represented, **14.14**
the respondent's solicitor must, after service of the notice of appeal, comply
with obligations imposed by paras (1) and (2) above (save as to the agreement
as to notes of judgment) as if he were acting for the appellant, and inform the
appellant of the lodging of such notes and (if so required) supply to him a
copy thereof on payment of the usual copying charge.

Where either party is represented but neither party wishes to bespeak a copy
of the district judge's notes of evidence, a copy of the notes of judgment must be:

(*a*) prepared by the appellant's solicitor and, if the respondent is represented, agreed by his solicitor; or

(*b*) prepared by the respondent's solicitor if the appellant is not represented,

and in any case shall be approved by the district judge, and not less than 21
days prior to the hearing a copy of the notes must be lodged by the solicitor
who prepared them.

It may be more economic to obtain a transcript of the tape-recording of the
hearing and judgment.

Where both parties to the appeal are acting in person, the appellant must **14.15**
notify the district judge of the appeal and the district judge must, where possible, make a note for the assistance of the judge hearing the appeal and
furnish each party with a copy of that note or certify that no note can be made.

Where it appears to a district judge that an appeal from his decision in an
ancillary relief application raises a difficult or important question, whether of
law or otherwise, he must transfer the appeal to the High Court (*Practice
Direction*, June 5, 1992 [1992] 3 All E.R. 151).

Permission to appeal out of time: In category (2)-(4) appeals where the appeal **14.16**
is not lodged in time, the judge may be asked for leave (or to use CPR terminology, although strictly it does not apply, "permission") to extend the time
for appealing. An extension should generally be given where no hardship
would be caused to the other party or where there would be a denial of justice
to the applicant if permission were refused (*Johnson v Johnson* [1978] 1 F.L.R.
331). However, in relation to category (4) appeals where young children are
concerned, justifiable reasons may be hard to establish, and delay itself may
be a determining factor (*SM v E County Council and CM (by his guardian ad
litem J G)* (2002) Lawtel, January 10, at the time of writing unreported fully

elsewhere). Permission to appeal out of time is inappropriate where the court considers the appeal to be hopeless (*Re F-B (Leave to Appeal)* [1999] Fam. Law. 451, CA). If the application for leave is made ex parte, the judge should confine himself as to whether it should be dismissed. If he is not minded to dismiss it, he should adjourn so that notice may be given to the other party (*Aveyard v Aveyard* [1984] 1 All E.R. 159). The Court of Appeal has jurisdiction to hear an appeal from a county court judge's refusal under CCR, Ord. 13, r.4(1) to extend the time for appealing to the judge from an order of the district judge (*Rickards v Rickards* [1989] 3 All E.R. 193).

As to the challenging of consent orders, see further para. 9.79 above.

3   From a district judge in the High Court

14.17   *Procedure*: An appeal from a district judge of the principal registry of the Family Division (other than in proceedings treated as pending in a county court) and from a district judge of a district registry is to a judge of the same court in chambers (RSC Ord. 58, r.1). The appeal is as of right.

For an appeal from a district judge in proceedings under the CA 1989 and the FLA 1996 Pt IV, the procedure is governed by RSC Ord. 58 as modified by FPR, r.4.22 and FPR r.8.1A(1) respectively (see above).

In cases other than under the CA 1989 or FLA 1996 Pt IV, an appeal to a judge in chambers must be brought by serving on every other party to the proceedings a notice to attend before the judge on a day specified in the notice (RSC Ord. 58, r.1(3)). Unless otherwise ordered, the notice must be issued within five days after the order or decision was made or given in the case of a district judge in the principal registry, and within seven days in the case of a district judge of a district registry. The notice must be served not less than two clear days before the day fixed for the hearing of the appeal in the case of an order of a district judge in the principal registry, and not less than three days in the case of an order of a district judge of a district registry (RSC Ord. 58, rr.1(3), 3(2)). The notice is issued in the registry where the cause is proceeding. Enquiries can be made of the court manager for the appropriate divorce town whether a judge will hear an appeal locally.

14.18   The requirements are as follows:

> (*a*) summons and copy for service;
>
> (*b*) notes of evidence and judgment as in the case of an appeal in county court proceedings (*Practice Direction*, February 21, 1985 [1985] 1 W.L.R. 361 applies, see above);
>
> (*c*) fee of £80 (FPFO, para.5.1).

Prior to the Court of Appeal decision in *Cordle v Cordle* [2001] 1 F.L.R. 207, the appeal was dealt with by way of a re-hearing, although on the basis of the notes of evidence from the previous hearing. The evidence was not heard afresh. It remains to be seen what impact the decision in *Cordle* (see p. 83 above) will have on this approach, if any.

Where, in an appeal from a district judge to a judge, questions of law of considerable magnitude are involved, a skeleton argument might be prepared in the same manner as is required in the Court of Appeal (*Marsh v Von Sternberg* [1986] 1 F.L.R. 526).

Leave to appeal out of time: Where the time to appeal from a district judge of   **14.19**
a district registry in High Court proceedings has not expired, an extension of
time can be made by the district judge. Where the time has expired, leave to
appeal out of time can be given by the judge.

As to the challenging of consent orders, see para. 9.79 above.

4   To the Court of Appeal

Applicable rules: The Civil Procedure (Amendment) Rules 2000 (SI 2000/221)
introduced a new Pt 52 to the CPR dealing with appeals. It applies to all appeals
to the Court of Appeal from judgments or orders made on or after May 2, 2000,
but not (at first sight) to appeals in family proceedings (see paras 1.02–1.04
above). However, the Practice Direction which supplements Pt 52 expressly provides that it also applies to appeals to the Court of Appeal from cases in family
proceedings (whether from the county court in accordance with the County
Courts Act 1984, s.77, or from the High Court (RSC, Ord. 59)) with such modifications as are required (PD52, para.2.2). It is assumed, therefore, that Pt 52
will be applied in family proceedings, despite the fact that it is not itself expressly
applied to appeals in family proceedings. Clearly PD52 is intended to be read
together with Pt 52. Strictly RSC, Ord. 59 still applies to appeals to the Court
of Appeal in family proceedings where in other civil proceedings it has been
superceded by CPR, r.52.

Requirement of permission to appeal: PD52 para.4.2 provides that permission   **14.20**
for all appeals to the Court of Appeal is required, save as provided for by
statute, or in CPR r.52.3. CPR r.52.3 provides that permission is required as
provided by the relevant practice direction, or for an appeal from a High Court
or county court judge except where the appeal is against committal, refusal to
grant habeas corpus or a secure accommodation order (CA 1989, s.25). See
further in relation to appeals against the decision of a circuit judge to punish
contempt, the Court of Appeal's decision in *Barnet LBC v Hurst* [2002] 4 All
E.R. 457. Such permission should be applied for either orally at the hearing at
which the order to be appealed against was made (para.4.6) or, if no such
application was made, or if it was refused, to the appeal court (para 4.7).
Permission to appeal will only be given where the court considers the appeal
would have a real prospect of success, or there is some other compelling reason
why the appeal should be heard (CPR, r.52.3(6)). See *English v Reimbold &
Strick Ltd* [2002] E.W.C.A. Civ. 605 for Court of Appeal guidelines on how
and when to appeal on the ground that the trial judge's reasons for his decisions were inadequate.

If the appeal is a second appeal, permission is required from the Court of
Appeal, not the lower court (CPR, r.52.13(1)) and the Court of Appeal will
only give permission if the appeal would raise an important point of principle or practice, or there is some other compelling reason for the appeal to be
heard (Access to Justice Act 1999, s.55 and CPR r.52.13(2)).

The application for permission may be considered by the Court of Appeal
without a hearing (para 4.11). If permission is refused, the appellant has the
right to have that decision reconsidered at an oral hearing (para 4.13). The
hearing on paper may be refused by a single Lord Justice and then listed before
the same Lord Justice (either sitting alone or with another) for oral hearing
(*Khreino v Khreino* [2000] 1 F.L.R. 578, where the appellant unsuccessfully
argued that the involvement of the same judge at the oral hearing would be a

breach of art.6 of the European Convention on Human Rights 1950 and the principle of procedural fairness). See *Jolly v Jay and Jay* [2002] E.W.C.A. Civ. 277 for guidance on the circumstances in which a respondent to an application for permission to appeal might make written or oral representations and awarded costs if successful.

14.21   *Procedure on appeals*: The appellant must file a notice of appeal (form N161) at the Court of Appeal within such period directed by the lower court (which should not normally exceed 28 days; PD52 para.5.19), or otherwise within 14 days after the date of the decision (CPR, r.52.4(2)). The appeal notice must then be served as soon as practicable (and in any event within 7 days) of being filed (CPR, r.52.4(3)). If a human rights issue is raised for the first time (whether by the appellant or the respondent), PD52 paras 5.1A and 5.1B should be followed, and note also the provisions of the *President's Direction (Human Rights Act 1998)* July 24, 2000 [2000] 2 F.L.R. 429.

Filing a notice of appeal does not stay the decision of the lower court, unless the Court of Appeal or the lower court orders otherwise (CPR, r.52.7). Any application for a stay should be made at the same time as the application for permission to appeal if not immediately after the decision of the lower court.

14.22   If permission to appeal has been given by the lower court, then with the notice of appeal, the appellant must file the following documents (see PD52, para.5.6):

(*a*) notice of appeal (and copies for the court and each respondent);

(*b*) skeleton argument in accordance with PD 52 paras 5.10 and 5.11 (although this may be lodged and served within 14 days of filing the notice if is impractical to produce it with, or contained as part of, the notice of appeal; PD52, para.5.9);

(*c*) sealed copy order;

(*d*) order giving/refusing permission to appeal, with a copy of the reasons for that decision;

(*e*) any witness statements or affidavits in support of any application included in the appellant's notice;

(*f*) bundle of documents containing the above and any others which are necessary to enable the Court of Appeal to reach its decision. These should include the documents referred to in PD52, para.5.6(7) (and see also PD52, paras 5.12 to 5.18) subject to PD52, para.5.8. PD52, para.5.8 provides that the bundle should be limited to 150 pages (excluding transcripts of judgments and proceedings in the lower court) containing the documents which the court might reasonably be expected to pre-read, with a full set being brought to court for reference. The bundle should comply with the *President's Direction (Family Proceedings: Court Bundles)* [2001] 1 F.L.R. 536, all documents should be filed in the Civil Appeals Office Registry, Room E307, Royal Courts of Justice, Strand, London WC2A 2LL and, where service of documents on others is required, it should be effected by the parties (PD52, para.15.1).

(*g*) Fee of £100 where permission to appeal and/or an extension of time for appealing is sought, or £200 where permission is not sought or has been granted (Supreme Court Fees Order 1999, Sch. 1, para.9.1).

If, for any reason, it is not possible to file all the documents, the appellant must indicate which have not been filed and why (PD52, para.5.7).

If permission to appeal has not yet been granted and the notice of appeal includes an application for permission, the documents required to be filed by PD52 para.5.6 need to be filed within seven days of the grant of permission (PD52, para.6.2).

If permission is obtained, the Court of Appeal will notify the parties of the **14.23** listing window during which the appeal is likely to be heard and the long-stop "hear by date", together with a copy of the order giving permission and any other directions order (PD52, para.6.3), and will send the appellant an appeal questionnaire to be completed and returned within 14 days (see PD52, paras 6.4, 6.5 and 15.7–15.9). On filing the appeal questionnaire, a fee of £200 is payable, unless the appellant has already paid a £200 fee (*i.e.* a fee of £200 will be payable where permission to appeal or an extension of time has been sought and therefore a fee of only £100 paid previously). The appeal questionnaire requires a time estimate to be given, and if the respondent disagrees with it, he must inform the court within seven days (PD52, para.6.6).

The respondent need not take any action until he receives notification that permission to appeal has been given (PD52, para.5.22). However, if he wishes to ask the Court of Appeal to vary the order, he must appeal and obtain permission on the same basis as the appellant (PD52, para.7.1) or if he wishes to ask the Court of Appeal to uphold the order but for different or additional reasons, he must file a respondent's notice (PD52 para. 7.3, in which case he is not appealing and therefore does not require permission; (PD52 para.7.2), and see also PD52, para.7.11).

A respondent's notice must be filed within such period directed by the lower **14.24** court, or otherwise within 14 days after being served with the appellant's notice (if permission was given by the lower court or is not required), or being served with notification that permission has been granted, or with notification that the application for permission and the appeal itself are to be heard together (CPR, rr.52.5(4) and (5)). The respondent's notice must then be served on the appellant and any other respondent as soon as practicable and at least within 7 days (CPR, r.52.5(6)). The fee payable is £100 when the respondent is seeking permission to appeal or an extension of time for appealing, £200 when permission is not sought, and £100 if the respondent is asking the Court of Appeal to uphold the decision of the lower court for different or additional reasons (Supreme Court Fees Order 1999, Sch. 1 paras 9.1 and 9.2).

The respondent must provide a skeleton argument either with the respondent's notice, or lodge and serve such a skeleton argument no later than 21 days after the respondent receives the appellant's skeleton argument (PD52, paras 7.6 to 7.8). Additional documents must be lodged in accordance with PD52, paras 7.10 and 7.12. An appeal questionnaire will need to be completed and a further fee may be payable (see above for the procedure as described in relation to the appellant).

Prior to the appeal hearing, lists of authorities must be filed in accordance with PD52, para.15.11.

The appeal hearing: At the appeal hearing itself, the Court of Appeal will not **14.25** usually receive oral evidence or new evidence unless it orders otherwise (CPR, r.52.11(2)). In cases involving the welfare of a child, fresh evidence may more readily be introduced (*M v M* [1987] 2 F.L.R. 146, *Re B* [1991] 1 F.L.R. 137). Evidence of events prior to the hearing of the lower court should only be admitted if the conditions in *Ladd v Marshall* [1954] 3 All E.R. 745 are satisfied.

The appeal will be allowed where the decision of the lower court was wrong or unjust because of a serious procedural or other irregularity in the proceedings in the lower court (CPR, r.52.11(3)). Where the factual basis on which the judge made the original order has proven to be incorrect, and where a relatively limited period of time has elapsed, the matter should not form the basis of an appeal to the Court of Appeal, but be referred back to the judge (*Fournier v Fournier* [1998] 2 F.L.R. 990, CA). Permission of the court is required before a party may rely on a matter not detailed in the appeal notice.

14.26 The Court of Appeal should only intervene when reviewing a judge's exercise of discretion in cases involving the welfare of children when it considers that the judge has exceeded the generous ambit within which judicial disagreement is reasonably possible. The Court of Appeal must be satisfied that the judge erred in principle or was in fact plainly wrong and not merely that the Court of Appeal itself, had it carried out the balancing exercise of weighing the various facts for and against each party, would have preferred a solution which the judge did not choose (*Re W, Re A, Re B (Change of Name)* [1999] 2 F.L.R. 930 in which the Court of Appeal endorsed the decision in *G v G* [1985] 1 W.L.R. 647 and *Re M* [1995] 1 F.L.R. 546).

Costs are likely to be assessed summarily where PD52 para. 14.1 applies (but see also *Practice Note (Civil Procedure Rules 1998: Court of Appeal: Summary Assessment of Costs)* [1999] T.L.R. 309). The Court of Appeal has power to set aside or vary the order or judgment made by the lower court, refer any issue for determination by the lower court, order a new hearing and make orders for interest and costs in relation to the whole or part of the order made by the lower court (CPR, r.52.10). If judgment is not give orally, and unless the court orders otherwise, copies of written judgments will be made available in accordance with PD52, paras 15.12 to 15.14.

14.27 *Restrictions on appeals to the Court of Appeal*: Restrictions on appeals are set out in the Supreme Court Act 1981, s.18, as amended. No appeal *at all* lies from:

(*a*) an order allowing an extension of time for appealing from a judgment or order (SCA 1981, s.18(1)(b)), although the Court of Appeal does have jurisdiction to hear an appeal against a refusal to extend time (*Rickards v Rickards* [1989] 3 W.L.R. 748).

(*b*) any order, judgment or decision which is expressed to be final by virtue of the SCA 1981, s.18(1)(*c*)) or any other Act. Although at first reading this provision appears to prohibit all appeals, SCA 1981 s.60 states that rules of court may provide for orders to be treated as final for the purposes of appeals to the Court of Appeal, which in effect means that CPR r.52 and PD52 determine when appeals may be made against final orders.

(*c*) a decree absolute of divorce or nullity of marriage, by a party who, having had time and opportunity to appeal from the decree nisi on which that decree was founded, has not appealed from the decree nisi (Supreme Court Act 1981, s.18(1)(*d*)). Where a party wishes to appeal against a decree absolute of divorce or nullity, the question whether he has had the time and opportunity to appeal from the decree nisi on which the decree absolute was founded must be determined on an application for a rehearing under FPR, r.2.42 (FPR, r.2.42(8)). A rehearing may be ordered provided that an error on the part of the court is not alleged (FPR, r.2.42(1)). Such an application will be heard by the court which heard the divorce cause (*Clark v*

Clark [1995] 2 F.L.R. 487). Any other application for a rehearing (*e.g.* where an error *is* alleged) must be made by way of appeal to the Court of Appeal (FPR, r.2.42(9)).

No appeal lies *without permission* either of the court below or of the Court **14.28** of Appeal from an order made with the consent of the parties or relating only to costs which are by law left to the discretion of the court, unless the judge failed to exercise that discretion (RSC, Ord. 59, r.1B(1)(*b*) and (3)); *Hird v Hird* (1981) 11 Fam. Law 244). See also *Re R* [1995] 1 W.L.R. 184, concerning appeals from consent orders relating to children.

In the case of a decree nisi in a matrimonial cause, an appeal appears to lie as of right (PD52, paras 2.1 and 21.1).). *Marya v Marya* [1995] 2 F.L.R. 911 has confirmed that, where a decree nisi has been pronounced by a district judge in the county court, an appeal can only be made to a judge of the county court (see also FPR, r.8.1). Therefore, appeals will only be made to the Court of Appeal in the first instance in the small number of cases where a judge of the county court or High Court deals with the divorce or nullity itself.

PD52 para.21.1 contains the following specific procedural provisions for appeals against a decree nisi of divorce or nullity of marriage.

The appellant must file a notice of appeal at the Court of Appeal within 28 days after the date of pronouncement of the decree, together with the decree and a certificate of service of the notice. The notice must be served on the respondent and the "appropriate district judge" as defined in para.21.1(6) and, where the appellant intends to apply for an extension of time for serving or filing the notice, he must give notice of that intention also to the "appropriate district judge".

Permission to appeal out of time: An extension of time for appealing should be **14.29** applied for in the notice of appeal, stating the reasons for the delay and the steps taken prior to the application being made (PD52, para.5.2; and see PD52, para.7.4 for applications by respondents for an extension of time for filing a respondent's notice).

The respondent has the right to be heard on the application (if permission to appeal has been given or is not required) and must be served with the appellant's bundle. Otherwise, presumably, the matter will be dealt with on paper. Costs may be awarded against the respondent if opposition to the application is unreasonable (PD52, para.5.3). If the appellant's application is successful, then the same procedure which applies following the grant of permission to appeal is followed, as set out in PD52, paras 6.1 to 6.5 (PD52, para.5.4).

As to the criteria applied on an application for an extension of time under **14.30** the old rules (RSC Ord. 59; length of delay and reason for it, prejudice to the respondent if permission was granted, and the appellant's prospect of success), see *Norwich and Peterborough Building Society v Steel* [1991] 2 All E.R. 880; *Jordan v Jordan* [1993] 1 F.L.R. 169.

As to the challenging of consent orders, see para. 9.79 above.

Applications made for incidental remedies (*e.g.* interim orders) should be made in accordance with PD52, para.5.5, and if not contained in the notice of appeal, a further fee of £100 is payable (Supreme Court Fees Order 1999 para.9.3).

5   To the House of Lords

An appeal to the House of Lords is made by way of petition lodged within **14.31** three months of the order of the Court of Appeal (or the High Court, if a certificate has been issued under the Administration of Justice Act 1969 (AJA 1969), ss.12 and 13, permitting a "leapfrog" appeal direct to the House of Lords). The appeal may be made with permission of the Court of Appeal (in the case of an appeal from that court) or of the House of Lords (in the case of an appeal from the High Court, or from the Court of Appeal where that court has refused permission) (Appellate Jurisdiction Act 1876, s.3; Administration of Justice (Appeals) Act 1934, s.1). The procedure and relevant precedents are contained in the House of Lords Practice Directions and Standing Orders Applicable to Civil Appeals (HLPD) and at time of writing the most recent edition is dated June 2001. It may be accessed via the website *www.parliament.uk* (judicial work, practice directions).

Permission to appeal must be sought within one month from the order of the Court of Appeal (HLPD Dir.2.1) or one month from the grant of the certificate under AJA 1969 s.12, unless extended by the House of Lords (on appeals from the High Court), or one month from the determination of an application for public funding (HLPD Dir.1.8). If such an application has been made, the Judicial Office must be informed in writing within that timescale and see further Dir.4 in relation to the procedure on presentation of a petition for "leave" to appeal (the CPR terminology does not apply, so strictly the petition is for "leave" not "permission".

The respondent may cross-appeal within six weeks of the appeal if permission of the Court of Appeal (or, if refused, the House of Lords) is granted (Dir.26).

14.32   The appellant must prepare a statement of facts and issues and submit it to the respondent for discussion. The statement should be agreed and lodged within six weeks of the presentation of the appeal together with an appendix and application to set the appeal down for hearing (Dirs 13.1 and 14). Any disputed material should be included in each party's case (Dirs 11, 13 and 30). The appendix should contain documents used in evidence or recording proceedings in the courts below and must be agreed (Dirs 12 and 30). Within seven days of the setting down of the appeal, each party should notify the Judicial Office of the time estimate for their address (Dir.14.3).

The appellant must lodge and serve his case no later than five weeks before the proposed hearing date. The respondent (or cross-appellant) must lodge his reply (or case for cross-appeal) three weeks before the proposed hearing date (Dirs 15.13 and 30).

Then, not later than two weeks before the proposed hearing date, the appellant must lodge bound volumes of documents and copy authorities in accordance with Dirs 16, 17 and 30.

The fee payable for presenting a petition applying for permission to appeal is £570, and for entering appearance is £115. The fee for presenting a petition of appeal following the grant of permission is £570, save where permission was granted by the Court of Appeal, when the fee is £1,140. The fee for entering appearance is £230. The fee for setting down and lodging the statement of facts and issues and appendix of documents is £3,420. Details of the fees payable may be found at the end of the HLPD.

6   From a family proceedings court

14.33   There are three modes of appeal from magistrates sitting as a family proceedings court to the Family Division of the High Court in family proceedings:

(1) by notice of motion. FPR, r.8.2 applies in respect of appeals under the Domestic Proceedings and Magistrates' Courts Act 1978. RSC, Ord. 55 as varied by FPR, r.8.2 and *Practice Directions* December 1, 1972 [1973] 1 All E.R. 64 and May 11, 1977 [1977] 2 All E.R. 543 apply in relation to adoption appeals and in the case of an appeal against fine or committal under the Administration of Justice Act 1960, s.13, FPR, r.8.3 applies.

(2) by case stated. Magistrates' Courts Act 1980, s.111, RSC, Ord. 56 and *Practice Direction* January 22, 1981 [1981] 1 All E.R. 400 apply. Such an appeal will be heard by a single judge unless the court directs that it should be heard by a Divisional Court.

(3) by notice under FPR, r.4.22 in respect of appeals under Children Act 1989, s.94. *Practice Direction* January 31, 1992 [1992] 1 F.L.R. 463 and *Procedural Directive: Lord Chancellor's Department: Children Act 1989–Appeals* [1992] 2 F.L.R. 503 apply, and see further *Re M* [1995] 1 F.L.R. 546.

The rule is that every appeal should be by way of notice of motion except where it may be brought by case stated under statute or RSC, Ord. 55 or by notice under FPR, r.4.22. For further discussion of the three routes, see *P v P* [1995] 1 F.L.R. 563.

The procedure is discussed further in *Butterworth's Family Law Service* 2A [1121]-[1164].

Chapter 15

Enforcement

1 Introduction

15.01 This Chapter provides an overview of methods of enforcement and procedures to assist with enforcement. The less common means of enforcement (for example, the appointment of a receiver by way of equitable execution) are not considered. For a more detailed text on enforcement see Smith and Bishop, "Enforcing Financial Orders" in *Family Proceedings* (Butterworths). Bear in mind also the likelihood of future change to the enforcement regime in family proceedings in light of the proposals put forward by the Enforcement Sub-Group of the President of the Family Division's Ancillary Relief Advisory Group for informal consultation in September 2002, and see also para. (b) below.

Before the specific methods and procedures are considered there are matters of general application which require consideration.

(*a*) Human Rights Act 1998

The introduction of the Human Rights Act 1998 (HRA) has had a considerable impact on the courts' approach to enforcement, especially in relation to judgment summons (see paras 15.59–15.68 below).

(*b*) The Civil Procedure Rules 1998

As explained further at paras 1.02–1.04 above, family proceedings are largely unaffected by the Civil Procedure Rules 1998 (CPR 1998) (Family Proceedings Rules 1991 (FPR 1991), r.1.3, Matrimonial and Family Proceedings Act 1984 (MFPA 1984), s.32 and Supreme Court Act 1981 (SCA 1981), s.61 and Sch.1, para.3). The enforcement of orders made in family proceedings is also unaffected currently. There was suggestion that the Civil Procedure (Amendment No.4) Rules 2001 (CP(A No.4)R 2001) would be applied to family proceedings, presumably by statutory instrument (The Family Court Practice 2001 (Jordans)). As yet, this has not happened, but they may be applied in the future. The CP(A No.4)R 2001 introduce four new Parts to the CPR 1998 covering general rules about enforcement (Pt 70), orders to obtain information from judgment debtors (formerly oral examination) (Pt 71), third party debt orders (formerly garnishee orders) (Pt 72) and charging orders, stop orders and stop notices (Pt 73) from March 25, 2002. The previous rules are revoked for the purposes of civil proceedings. The Civil Procedure (Amendment No.5) Rules 2001 make amendments to the judgment summons procedure in CCR, Ord. 28 (contained within Sch.2 to the CPR 1998) which likewise do not yet apply to family proceedings. Practitioners should keep under review whether the CPR 1998 Pts 70–73 and the amendments to

CCR, Ord. 28 within Sch.2 to the CPR 1998 are subsequently applied to family proceedings.

The CPR 1998 (as amended) will apply to the enforcement of orders which were not made in family proceedings, including free-standing applications made in connection with, although not within, family proceedings. Detailed consideration of those rules is outside the scope of this book.

(*c*) Requirement for affidavits

Before any process is issued for the enforcement of an order in family **15.02** proceedings for *the payment of money to any person*, an affidavit must be filed verifying the amount due and showing how that amount is arrived at (FPR, r.7.1(1)).

(*d*) Interest

The County Courts (Interest on Judgment Debts) Order 1991 provides for certain county court orders made on or after July 1, 1991 to carry interest at the same rate as that payable on High Court judgments, in relation to which interest automatically accrues from the date of the judgment under the Judgments Act 1838. The rate of interest currently payable is 8 per cent. Interest is payable in family proceedings in the county court in respect of costs and lump sum orders where the judgment (which seems to include costs for the purpose of determining whether interest is payable) is of £5,000 or more, and in the High Court in respect of any lump sum and costs order. It is not, therefore, applicable to arrears of maintenance. Where an application is made to enforce payment of the order (other than by way of charging order), interest will cease to accrue where the enforcement proceedings are wholly or partially successful. A certificate of interest (plus copy) should be filed with any application for enforcement giving the details specified by CCR, Ord. 25, r.5A. The complementary power of the court to award interest under the Matrimonial Causes Act 1973 (MCA 1973), s.23(6) up to the date due for payment is discussed at para. 9.06.

(*e*) Restrictions on writs of fi fa and warrants of execution.

Except with leave of the district judge, no writ of fi fa or warrant of execution may be issued to enforce payment of any sum due under an order for ancillary relief or an order made under MCA 1973, s.27 (failure to provide reasonable maintenance) where an application for a variation order is pending (FPR, r.7.1(2)).

(*f*) Service of the order to be enforced

It is not necessary to prove that a copy of an order has reached the other party. However, this is without prejudice to the Rules of the Supreme Court 1965 (RSC) Ord. 45, r.7 and the County Court Rules 1981 (CCR) Ord. 29 r.1 which relate to orders which, *inter alia*, may be enforced by committal, and to any other rule or enactment which requires service in a particular way (FPR, r.10.17(3) and (4)).

(*g*) Transfer of proceedings and extent of jurisdiction

Any person desiring the transfer to the High Court of any order made **15.03** in family proceedings by a divorce county court (except for periodical payments or for the recovery of arrears of periodical payments) applies to the court ex parte by affidavit stating the amount which remains due. The transfer takes effect on the filing of the application. Where an order is so transferred, it has the same force and effect and the same proceedings may be taken on it as if it were an order of the High Court (FPR, r.7.3). In relation to periodical payments orders (to which r.7.3 does not apply), it will be necessary to transfer the entire proceedings (not just the order) under MFPA 1984, s.38 (from High Court) or s.39 (to High Court). The wide powers available to transfer judgments or orders to and from the High Court provided by the County Courts Act 1984, ss.40 and 42 (as substituted by the Courts and Legal Services Act 1990) do not apply to family proceedings (for definition of "family proceedings' see para. 1.04).

In any proceedings in a county court, the court may now make any order which could have been made by the High Court if proceedings were in the High Court (except to order mandamus, certiorari, prohibition or orders prescribed by subsequent regulations) (County Courts Act 1984, s.38 as substituted by Courts and Legal Services Act 1990, s.3). So far, "prescribed orders' have only been specified by the County Courts Remedies Regulations 1991 (as amended by the County Court Remedies (Amendment) Regulations 1995). There should, therefore, be only limited occasions when it will prove necessary to transfer proceedings to the High Court for enforcement.

In the High Court, "writ of execution" includes a writ of fi fa, writ of possession, writ of delivery, writ of sequestration and any further writ in aid of any of these writs (RSC, Ord. 46, r.1). In the county court, "warrant of execution" is the equivalent of a writ of fi fa only (County Courts Act 1984, s.85).

(*h*) The court's power to order payment by instalments

The court may make an order for payment of a money judgment forthwith or by instalments and may suspend or stay the order (County Courts Act 1984, s.71). The court's power to vary or discharge certain financial provision orders under MCA 1973, s.31 is discussed at paras 9.20–9.21.

(*i*) Arrears of maintenance

15.04   Leave is required to enforce the payment of arrears under an order for maintenance pending suit, an interim order for maintenance or a financial provision order, if those arrears became due more than twelve months before the proceedings to enforce payment are begun (MCA 1973, s.32(1)). Leave may be granted subject to restrictions and conditions and the arrears (or part) may be remitted (MCA 1973, s.32(2)). The general rule is that more than a year's arrears will not be enforced unless there are special circumstances (*B v C* [1995] 1 F.L.R. 467; *Ross v Pearson* [1976] 1 All E.R. 790; *Bernstein v O'Neill* [1989] 2 F.L.R. 1; *cf. Russell v Russell* [1986] 1 F.L.R. 465). No rules have been prescribed for applying for leave except in the case of attachment of earnings. In this case, leave is applied for in the application for an attachment of earnings order (CCR, Ord. 27, r.17(3)). Otherwise an application for leave is made to a district judge by summons in the High Court and by notice in Form N244 in the county court (FPR, r.10.9). An affidavit in support should be filed.

If the order sought to be enforced was made more than six years previously, then even if the arrears only started to accrue less than 12 months ago, RSC, Ord. 46, r.2 and CCR, Ord. 26, r.5(1)(*a*) provide that leave will be required to enforce by the issue of a writ of fi fa, possession, delivery or sequestration or a warrant of execution.

(*j*) Contempt of court

There is a pre-HRA principle of general application that a person who has disobeyed a court order and is, therefore, in contempt of court, may not have any application made by him entertained by the court (save for an application to purge his contempt) (*Hadkinson v Hadkinson* [1952] 2 All E.R. 567, CA, applied in *Baker v Baker (No.2)* [1997] 1 F.L.R. 148). See further an article by T.J. Wilson, "Contempt in Ancillary Relief Proceedings — The Principle of Denial" [1999] Fam. Law. 254. The effect of the HRA and, in particular, the right to a fair trial on this principle remains to be seen.

2 Child Support Agency

The scope of the enforcement powers of the Child Support Agency (CSA) **15.05** under the Child Support Act 1991 (CSA 1991) lies outside the scope of this book. In addition, the regime of the CSA is due to change significantly when the relevant provisions of the Child Support Pensions and Social Security Act 2000 are brought into force fully. At time of writing, no date has been set for this. The Child Support Agency does, however, have extensive powers of enforcement in relation to child support maintenance which have already been extended by the new Act, notably by section 16 (inserting a new section 39A CSA 1991 from April 2, 2001) introducing the penalty of disqualification from holding or obtaining a driving licence in certain circumstances.

Where the Secretary of State is arranging for collection of any payments of child support maintenance, by virtue of CSA 1991, s.30, he may also arrange for the collection and enforcement of periodical payments under an order made:

(*a*) to a child in accordance with the provisions of CSA 1991, s.8(6)-(8) ("top-up" orders, orders for expenses in connection with instruction or training, and orders to meet expenses attributable to a child's disability);

(*b*) to or for the benefit of a spouse or former spouse who is the person with care of a child who is a qualifying child in respect of whom a child support maintenance assessment is in force and where payments are being collected by the Secretary of State; and

(*c*) for any periodical payments under a maintenance order payable to or for the benefit of a former child of the family of the person against whom the order is made and who lives with the person with care.

(Child Support (Collection and Enforcement of Other Forms of Maintenance) Regulations 1992, SI No. 2643, as amended).

3 Oral examination

Where an order for payment of money is made in a county court or High **15.06** Court, and where the extent of a defaulting payer's assets or his ability to pay the money due under an order is unknown, an application can be made for an order that the payer attend at court to be orally examined as to his means and/or to produce relevant books or documents (RSC, Ord. 48 r.1, CCR, Ord. 25 r.3). A similar application may be made in respect of orders other than for payment of money, which may be useful for example in relation to disputes about the whereabouts of specific chattels (RSC, Ord. 48 r.2, CCR, Ord. 25, r.4). It is a procedure to assist with enforcement rather than a method of enforcement.

15.07   *County court*: Oral examination is governed by CCR, Ord. 25, r.3 and FPR, r.7.1(5). The application is made to such divorce county court as in the opinion of the applicant is nearest to the place where the debtor resides or carries on business (FPR, r.7.1(5)(*a*)). There is no need to transfer the cause to the relevant divorce county court (notwithstanding CCR, Ord. 25 r.2).

The requirements are as follows:

(*a*) application on CCR, Form N316;

(*b*) affidavit verifying amount due and showing how that amount was arrived at (FPR, r.7.1(1) and (5));

(*c*) if order to be enforced was made in a court other than that to which the application for oral examination is made, a copy of order should be exhibited to affidavit (FPR, r.7.1(5));

(*d*) certificate of interest, if appropriate (CCR, Ord. 25, r.5A);

(*e*) fee in family proceedings: £40 (Family Proceedings Fees Order 1999 (FPFO) Sch.1 para.12.3)

An appointment is given by the court for oral examination to take place, usually before an officer of the court (CCR, Ord. 20, r.13(2)). The creditor's attendance may be required, and in any event would be advisable so that the creditor (or his solicitor) may cross examine the debtor. The court may, however, give the debtor an opportunity to make a statement in writing or affidavit as to his means before deciding whether to make an order for oral examination (CCR, Ord. 25, r.3(7)).

15.08   The order for examination (CCR, Form N37) is drawn by the court and is served in the same manner as a default summons under CCR, Ord. 7, r.10 (CCR, Ord. 25, r.3(3)) that is, by post (unless the creditor or his solicitor requests personal service — CCR, Ord. 7, r.10(1)(a) and (2)). Travelling expenses should be paid in accordance with CCR, Ord. 20, r.12(7) (CCR, Ord. 20, r.13(3) and Ord. 25, r.3(6)).

If personal service is effected by a solicitor, an affidavit of service exhibiting a copy of the order should be filed before the examination (CCR, Ord. 7, r.6(1)(b).

15.09   If the debtor fails to attend to be examined on the first occasion, the court may adjourn the examination and order him to attend on another day. Any payments made thereafter are to be paid into court, not to the judgment creditor(CCR, Ord. 25, r.3(4)). This order (CCR, Form N39) should be returnable before the judge and must be served *personally* on the debtor at least 10 days before the adjourned hearing (CCR, Ord. 25, r.3(5)). Travelling expenses should be paid, if requested, not less than seven days before the adjourned hearing, unless already paid at the time of service of the original order for an oral examination (CCR, Ord. 25, r.3(5A)). No more than four days before the adjourned hearing, a certificate must be filed stating either that no request for travelling expenses has been made or that a sum has been paid (CCR, Ord. 25, r.3(5B)). If the debtor fails to attend the adjourned hearing where he was personally served he may be committed for contempt (CCR, Ord. 25 r.3(5) and Ord. 27, r.7B), and see further below paras 15.37–15.52). An order such as this would usually be suspended to allow the debtor to attend an oral examination in any event. No committal order may be made, if the debtor has requested travelling expenses, unless these have been paid before the adjourned hearing (CCR, Ord. 25, r.3(5C).

If the hearing has taken place at a court other than that in which the original order was made, after the examination the papers are returned to the original county court.

High Court: Oral examination in the High Court is governed by RSC, Ord. 48. **15.10**

Unlike the county court, the application must be made by summons to the district registry in which the order was made and the supporting affidavit should request that the examination be conducted at the nearest registry , be it the divorce registry, a district registry or a county court.

Examination may be ordered to take place before the district judge or nominated officer (not lower than the grade of higher executive officer) of any county court or district registry, as the court may appoint (RSC, Ord. 48, r.1(1) and (4)). If the court appoints a district judge without specifying him personally, the examination may be conducted before a nominated officer of the court (RSC, Ord. 48, r.1(1)).

The requirements are as follows: **15.11**

(*a*) affidavit (Form PF 98) verifying the amount due and showing how that amount is arrived at (FPR, r.7.1(1));

(*b*) order in Form PF99 and copy;

(*c*) fee in family proceedings: £40 (FPFO, Sch.1, para.14.2)

The order for the examination and copy are taken or sent to the court where the examination is to take place for an appointment to be given. The appointment is set out at the foot of the order:

"The District Judge of County Court (*or as the case may be*) appoints day the of 19 , at o'clock at (*state address*) for the above examination." This endorsement is sealed. The order should be endorsed with the customary penal notice. The order must be served personally a reasonable time before the appointment.

A debtor is entitled to his travelling expenses. If the debtor having been personally served fails to attend the appointment, the creditor may immediately apply for his committal. Where the examination is adjourned to a further appointed date, the debtor must be personally served with an amended order indorsed with the new date and a fresh penal notice. **15.12**

4 Execution against goods

In the High Court a writ of fieri facias, and in the county court a warrant of execution, can be issued requiring the seizure and sale of the debtor's goods (by a Sheriff in the High Court, or a bailiff in the county court) to provide monies to satisfy the sum due under an order, interest (if accruing) and costs **15.13** of execution. The types of order which may be enforced in this way include lump sum orders (plus any interest), arrears of periodical payments, and costs orders (if the specified sum due has been ascertained, plus any interest). Separate warrants (or writs as applicable) may be issued in respect of orders for payment of money and subsequently in respect of costs orders if the specific amount of the costs due has yet to be ascertained (CCR, Ord. 26, r.1(5), RSC, Ord. 47, r.3(1)).

Leave to enforce is required in certain circumstances (MCA 1973 s.32, RSC, Ord. 46, r.2, CCR, Ord. 26, r.5).

Rule 7.1(1)-(3) of FPR apply.

15.14 *County court*: This is governed by CCR, Ord. 25, rr.5–8 and Ord. 26, rr.1–15. The requirements are as follows:

  (*a*) request (CCR Form N323);

  (*b*) affidavit (FPR, r.7.1(1));

  (*c*) certificate of interest, if appropriate (CCR, Ord. 25, r.5A)

  (*d*) fee in family proceedings of £25 (if the amount for which the warrant issues does not exceed £125) or £45 (if the amount exceeds £125) (FPFO Sch.1, para.12.1).

Solicitors' allowable fixed costs are £2 if the amount in respect of which the warrant issued exceeds £25 and unless the court otherwise orders (CCR, Ord. 38, r.18 — although most of the CPR costs rules apply to family proceedings, Pt 45 does not, so the CCR apply) plus the court fee.

The proper officer (court manager) issues the warrant (CCR, Ord. 26, r.1(1A)), and it is then forwarded to the bailiff for the relevant area.

To issue execution in the High Court to enforce an order of the county court, CCR, Ord. 25, r.13 applies. The order must be for a sum in excess of £2,000 (Transfer of County Court Judgments (Specified Amount) Order 1984). The High Court and County Courts Jurisdiction Order 1991 does not apply to family proceedings.

15.15 *High Court*: Orders 45, 46 and 47 of RSC apply. The requirements are as follows

  (*a*) praecipe (Form PF86);

  (*b*) affidavit (FPR, r.7.1(1));

  (*c*) production of the order or office copy;

  (*d*) writ of fi fa (Form 53);

  (*e*) fee in family proceedings of £20 (FPFO Sch.1 para.14.1).

The costs to be allowed on the writ are £66.50 (if the order is in excess of £600 or the creditor has been awarded costs — RSC, Ord. 62, App.3).

The court may, however, stay execution by writ of fi fa absolutely or subject to conditions (RSC, Ord. 47, r.1), and may (for example) continue such stay for so long as the debtor makes payments by instalments. This power mitigates the fact that the High Court (unlike the county court) otherwise has no power to order payment by instalments.

The writ of fi fa is sealed and returned to the creditor for delivery to the under-sheriff for the relevant area.

To issue execution in the county court to enforce an order of the High Court, CCR, Ord. 25, r.11 and Ord. 26, r.2 apply. The warrant may be issued in any county court in the district of which execution is to be levied.

The requirements are as follows: **15.16**

(*a*) an order for transfer of the proceedings to the county court (CCR, Ord. 25, r.11(1)(d));

(*b*) request (praecipe) (CCR Form N323);

(c) affidavit (FPR, r.7.1(1)) (CCR Form N321 but showing how the amount is arrived at);

(*d*) order or office copy for filing in county court;

(*e*) where a writ of fi fa has been issued, copy of the sheriff's return;

(*f*) fee of £25 or £45.

Notice in CCR Form N327 of the issue of the warrant is sent by the county court to the registry where the cause is pending (CCR, Ord. 26, r.2(3)).

5 Attachment of earnings

On an application by a creditor (or in specified circumstances the justices' **15.17** chief executive ("justices' chief executive" was substituted for "court clerk" by the Access to Justice Act 1999 s.90(1), sch.13, paras 72 and 77) for the magistrates' court or the debtor — Attachment of Earnings Act 1971 (AEA 1971), s.3), the court may order an employer to deduct specified sums from an employee's "earnings" (as defined in AEA 1971, s.24, and including certain pensions and statutory sick pay) and pay them to the court in satisfaction of money due under an order. The AEA 1971, Maintenance Enforcement Act 1991 (MEA 1991) and CCR, Ord. 27 apply. CCR, Ord. 27, r.17 specifically applies to maintenance orders. The procedure governing applications in the High Court was previously governed by RSC, Ord. 105, rr.13–20, which were revoked with effect from October 14, 1991 and not replaced. Since the High Court retains jurisdiction to make attachment of earnings orders (AEA 1971, s.1(1)), the county court procedure should therefore be adapted.

"Maintenance order" is defined in the AEA 1971, s.2(*a*) and Sch.1 and includes "periodical or other payments" under Pt II of the MCA 1973. Lump sum orders as well as periodical payments orders seem to be included therefore (see *Graham v Graham* [1992] 2 F.L.R. 406, CA). In any event, if lump sum orders were not included within the definition of maintenance orders, they would be subject to the Act by virtue of s.2(c) (although the extent of the jurisdiction would differ — AEA 1971, s.1).

The High Court may only make an attachment of earnings order to secure payments under a High Court maintenance order (Attachment of Earnings Act 1971, s.1(1)).

A county court may make an attachment of earnings order to secure pay- **15.18** ments under a High Court or a county court maintenance order or the payment of a judgment debt for £50 or more or the balance of a judgment debt for £50 or more (AEA 1971, s.1 (2) and CCR, Ord. 27, r.7(9)).

The magistrates' court also has jurisdiction to make attachment of earnings orders (Magistrates' Courts (Attachment of Earnings) Rules 1971), although the procedure will not be detailed here.

Any reference in the AEA 1971 to sums payable under a judgment or order, or to the payment of such sums, includes a reference to costs and the payment of them (AEA 1971, s.25(2)).

15.19   It is not necessary to show that the debtor has failed to make one or more payments required by a maintenance order before an attachment of earnings order can be made (AEA 1971 s.3(3A)) and it is no longer necessary to prove that the debtor's failure to make the payments is due to his wilful refusal or culpable neglect (MEA 1991, s.11 and Sch.2, para.1, repealing AEA 1971, s.3(5)). It seems unlikely, however, that that court will make an attachment of earnings order if there has been no default.

Where the court makes a *qualifying periodical maintenance order* it may at the same time, or on any subsequent hearing of the matter, whether of its own motion or on application by an interested party, make an attachment of earnings order to secure payments under the qualifying periodical maintenance order in question (MEA 1991, s.1(1) and (4)).

A periodical maintenance order is one which:

(*a*) requires money to be paid periodically by one person (the debtor) to another (a creditor); and

(*b*) is a maintenance order (as specified in the Administration of Justice Act 1970 (AJA 1970) Sch.8, and MEA 1991 s.1(10)),

and becomes a "qualifying periodical maintenance order" where the debtor is ordinarily resident in England and Wales at the time it is made (MEA 1991, s.1(2)). It includes lump sums payable by instalments (MEA 1991, s.1(10)) and "other payments" made under Pt II of the MCA 1973 (AJA 1970, Sch.8, para.2A) but not lump sum payments (*Ranson v Ranson* [2001] E.W.C.A. Civ. 1929, CA).

Any interested party must, if practicable, be given the opportunity to make representations to the court (MEA 1991, s.1(8)).

An application under MCA 1973, s.32 for leave to enforce payment of arrears which became due more than 12 months before the application for an attachment of earnings order must be incorporated in that application (CCR, Ord. 27, r.17(3)).

15.20   *Procedure*: In the case of a county court maintenance order, an application for an attachment of earnings order to secure payments under the order must be made to the county court which made the order (CCR, Ord. 27, r.17(2)). Otherwise, in the case of all other orders (*e.g.* High Court maintenance order, costs of the petition), the application is made in the county court for the district in which the debtor resides, or, if the debtor does not reside within England and Wales, or if the applicant does not know where he resides, in the court in which or for the district in which, the judgment or order sought to be enforced was obtained (CCR, Ord. 27, r.3(1) and (2)).

If a county court order for costs is to be enforced, not being the costs of a maintenance order (see AEA 1971, s.25(2)), it would seem that a transfer is required under CCR, Ord. 25, r.2, where the judgment debtor's address is within the district of another county court.

15.21   The requirements for an application to enforce a maintenance order (CCR, Ord. 27, r.4) are:

(*a*) application (CCR Form N337);

(*b*) affidavit (FPR, r.7.1(1));

(*c*) certificate of interest, if appropriate (CCR, Ord. 25, r.5A).

(*d*) office copy of the order in the case of a High Court order or certified copy of the order in the case of a magistrates' court order;

(*e*) fee of £50: in addition, if service by bailiff is required (if available) £10.

Service: The court prepares CCR Forms N55 (debt) or N55(A) (maintenance) **15.22** and N56 which are served with the application on Form N337. A date for the hearing of the application to enforce a maintenance order is fixed immediately before a district judge in chambers (CCR, Ord. 27, rr.4(2) and 17(5)). The application must be served in the manner prescribed for a fixed date summons, *i.e.* not less than 21 clear days before the return day (CCR, Ord. 27, rr.5(1) and 17(3A), Ord. 7, r.10(5)). In all other cases the application is served in the manner prescribed for a default summons (where no return day is automatically fixed) (CCR, Ord. 27, r.5(1), Ord. 7, r.10).

Form N56 requires the debtor to give details of his employer, and his earnings and liabilities and provides the opportunity to make an offer for payment. If this form is not completed, he may be ordered to attend court. If he does not do so when the order has been served upon him personally, he may be committed to prison for up to 14 days (AEA 1971, s.23(1)). (See further paras 15.37–15.52 below).

Order: The order is in CCR Form N60 (judgment debt) or Form N65 (main- **15.23** tenance order).

If the court makes an order, it will specify the *normal deduction rate* and the *protected earnings rate* (AEA 1971, s.6). If the "normal deduction rate" would result in the debtor's wage falling below the "protected earnings rate", only the element of earnings exceeding the protected earnings rate will be deducted from the wage in that week.

6   Maintenance Enforcement Act 1991

The provisions of the MEA 1991 were originally seen as interim measures **15.24** pending implementation of the CSA 1991. Its provisions, however, remain of assistance where the CSA 1991 does not apply.

High Court and county courts: When making a "qualifying periodical mainte- **15.25** nance order" (see para.15.19 above), or at any time thereafter, the court may order payment to be made by standing order or some other similar method (*a means of payment order*) (MEA 1991, s.1(4) and s.1(5)). In addition, a defaulting party may be ordered to open a bank account for this purpose (MEA 1991, s.1 (6)). Any interested party must be given the opportunity to make representations (MEA 1991, s.1(8)). There is no prescribed procedure.

Magistrates' court: The MEA 1991 substituted a new section 59 of the Magistrates' **15.26** Courts Act 1980 which sets out the means of payment available on making an order for periodical payments. Where the order is not a maintenance order, then the court shall order payment direct to the creditor or via the justices' chief executive for the court (s.59(3)(*a*) and (*b*)). Where the order is a "qualifying maintenance order" (defined in similar terms as a "qualifying periodical maintenance order" in the

higher courts), the court may order alternatively payment to the creditor by standing order or equivalent means (section 59(3)(*c*)) or payment by attachment of earnings (section 59(3)(*d*)). The other provisions under the new section 59 also reflect
the changes relating to the higher courts' powers; *i.e.* the ability to order the debtor
to open a bank account (section 59(4)) and allowing the parties the opportunity to
make representations (section 59(5)). For the avoidance of doubt, section 59(12)
clarifies that lump sum orders payable by instalments are included in the definition
of orders requiring money to be paid periodically by one person to another. Lump
sums are not (*Ranson v Ranson* [2001] E.W.C.A. Civ. 1929, CA).

7   Garnishee proceedings

15.27   Garnishee proceedings aim to obtain payment of the sum due from monies
owed by a third party to the debtor or held by a third party on the debtor's
behalf (*e.g.* in a bank account).

   If a cause is pending in a county court, see CCR, Ord. 30; if pending in High
Court, see RSC, Ord. 49.

   In both the High Court and a county court, the application is made ex parte
by affidavit to a district judge for a temporary order (a garnishee order nisi)
which binds the debt in the hands of the garnishee, and a return date is given
for the court to consider whether the garnishee order nisi should be made
absolute. The garnishee order absolute requires the garnishee to make
payment direct to the creditor. For the contents of the affidavit, see RSC, Ord.
49, r.2 or CCR, Ord. 30, r.2. A garnishee order is an equitable remedy, and the
power to make such an order is discretionary.

15.28   The garnishee order nisi is served on the garnishee by the court by post in
the county court and personally in the High Court, and in either case at least
15 days before the hearing, and on the judgment debtor at least seven days
after service on the garnishee but at least seven days before the hearing (RSC,
Ord. 49, r.3; CCR 1981, Ord. 30, r.3).

   A garnishee order cannot be obtained in the High Court or county court
for less than £50.

   The fees in family proceedings are £50 (for every party against whom the
order is sought), and in addition for every garnishee or judgment debtor to be
served by bailiff, £10 (if available).

   On the return date in the county court the hearing may be before a judge or
a district judge (CCR, Ord. 30, r.15). In the High Court, the hearing is before
a district judge.

   Garnishee proceedings may be used to enforce lump sum orders plus
accrued interest, arrears of periodical payments, and costs orders (if the
amount is ascertained) plus accrued interest. An undertaking may also be
enforced by way of garnishee proceedings (*Gandolfo v Gandolfo* [1981] Q.B.
359: undertaking to pay school fees enforced by garnishee order against
husband's bank account).

8   Charging orders on land and securities

15.29   A charging order may be made by either the High Court or a county court to
enforce the payment of maintenance (as defined in AEA 1971, s.2(a) and Sch.1),

outstanding lump sum orders, or orders for costs (provided the amount is ascertained) over land or securities (see Charging Orders Act 1979 (COA 1979), s.1). Arguably financial undertakings may be enforceable also. The court will not grant a charging order where payment has been ordered by instalments which are not in arrears (or presumably in relation to maintenance which is not in arrears) (*Mercantile Credit Co Ltd v Ellis* [1987] C.L.Y. 2917). The property which may be charged is defined in the COA 1979, s.2. A charging order may be obtained against a beneficial interest under a trust of land as well as against a property of which the debtor is the sole beneficial owner. It is a means of securing a debt rather than directly enforcing payment. A further application to enforce the charging order by ordering a sale is necessary to achieve payment for the debt.

If the cause is pending in county court, CCR, Ord. 31 applies and incorporates significant parts of RSC, Ord. 50, which applies to causes pending in the High Court.

The requirements for an application for a charging order are:

(*a*) on application ex parte by affidavit;

(*b*) fee in family proceedings: £50 in the High Court and county court for each party against whom the order is sought.

Application is made to the "appropriate court" (COA 1979, s.1(2)): **15.30**

(*a*) in the case of a maintenance order of the High Court: the High Court or a county court;

(*b*) if the application does not relate to arrears of maintenance and the order to be enforced is of the High Court and is for a sum in excess of £5,000: the High Court or a county court; and

(*c*) in any other case: a county court (see CCR, Ord. 31, r.1(1) as to the county court to which application should be made).

In both the High Court and a county court, the application is made ex parte by affidavit to a district judge for a charging order nisi. For the contents of the affidavit, see RSC, Ord. 50, r.1 (3) or CCR, Ord. 31, r.1 (2).

The charging order nisi is an order to the debtor to show cause why the **15.31** charging order should not be made absolute. The charging order nisi and affidavit is served by post by the creditor upon the debtor and such others as the district judge may direct at least seven days before the hearing of the application to show cause (RSC, Ord. 50, r.2; CCR, Ord. 31, r.1(6) and (8)). The hearing of the application to show cause is normally before a district judge in chambers and either a charging order absolute (with or without modifications) is made or the order nisi is discharged.

The charging order nisi should be protected by a land charge registered under the Land Charges Act 1972 or a notice or caution registered under the Land Registration Act 1925 (COA 1979, s.3, or in due course under the Land Registration Act 2002 when that Act is brought into force – see the Act for details of the changes to the land registration regime). A charging order made on an undivided share is not capable of registration under the Land Charges Act 1972 — but pre-TLATA see *Perry v Phoenix Assurance PLC* [1988] 3 All E.R. 60. The court may grant an injunction preventing the property being dealt with before the hearing of the application. In the High Court, the application is to a district judge (RSC, Ord. 50, r.9), but in the county court usually to the judge (CCR, Ord. 13, r.6).

A charging order is a discretionary remedy. In deciding whether to make a charging order, the court must consider all the circumstances of the case and in particular:

(*a*) the personal circumstances of the debtor; and

(*b*) whether any other creditor of the debtor would be likely to be unduly prejudiced by the making of the order (COA 1979, s.1(5) and see *Roberts Petroleum Ltd v Bernard Kenny Limited* [1982] 1 All E.R. 685 (CA) and [1985] 1 All E.R. 564 (HL) for more detailed guidance).

15.32   The court will take into account the size of the debt in relation to the asset to be charged (*Robinson v Bailey* [1942] Ch.268, [1942] 1 All E.R. 498).

In High Court proceedings, RSC, Ord. 50, r.2 provides for the order and affidavit in support to be served on the judgment debtor, and for the court to direct, if appropriate, for service on any other creditor or interested person. In county court proceedings, CCR, Ord. 31, r.1(6) provides slightly differently for the order and affidavit to be served on the debtor and other creditors named on the affidavit, *unless* the court otherwise directs.

15.33   The costs of obtaining a charging order are fixed (CPR 1998 Sch.2 – incorporating the CCR, Ord. 38, Appendix B schedule of fixed costs – the CPR costs provisions apply in family proceedings by virtue of the FP(MA)R 1999 r.4 (see para.1.02 above)). Some district judges will readily exercise their discretion in the county court by adding disbursements incurred, *e.g.* HM Land Registry fees.

A charging order may be enforced by sale of the property. RSC, Ord. 88, r.5A(1) and CCR, Ord. 31 r.4 govern the procedure where the chargor(s) own the whole of the beneficial interest in the property. Where the charging order relates to part only of the beneficial interest, an application for sale must be made under s.14 of the TLATA 1996. The chargee is not limited to applying for the sale of the beneficial interest only, or to the appointment of a receiver (*Midland Bank Plc v Pike* [1988] 2 ALL E.R. 434).

15.34   Views differ over the application of RSC, Ord. 88, r.5A and CCR, Ord. 31, r.4. The rules provide for an originating application to commence the proceedings (r.5A(2) and r.4(1)). One view is that such an application will be freestanding and therefore outside the definition of "family proceedings", and so the CPR will apply. The other view regards that application as being within the family proceedings, to which the CCR continue to apply. Certainly, the CPR will apply to any application under section 14 of the TLATA.

When deciding whether to apply for a charging order and subsequent order for sale, consideration should also be given to the possibility of applying for an order for sale under section 24A of the MCA 1973. Such an order may be made at any time after the making of a secured periodical payments order, lump sum order or property adjustment order (section 24A(1)). Although an application under section 24A of the MCA 1973 will not provide security in relation to the debt, it should be a more straightforward and cost effective method of enforcement (to which the RSC/CCR will apply).

9   Sequestration

15.35   Sequestration is a process for punishing contempt of court. Assets of the contemnor are seized and retained until the order is complied with. The court can authorise realisation of such assets so as to fund other steps to secure compliance (*Richardson v Richardson* [1990] 1 F.L.R. 186; *Mir v Mir* [1992] 1 F.L.R. 624; *Re S (Abduction: Sequestration)* [1995]1 F.L.R. 858).

Application is made in the High Court under RSC, Ord. 46, r.5 or in the county court under County Courts Act 1984, s.38 (*Rose v Laskington Ltd and others* [1989] 3 All E.R. 306). No specific procedure is laid down in the county court and the procedure in RSC, Ord. 45 and 46 must therefore be followed.

Application for leave to issue a warrant for sequestration in the county court **15.36** or a writ of sequestration in the High Court is made to a judge by notice of motion in the High Court and by notice of application in the county court, stating the grounds of application and supported by affidavit. Personal service is required unless dispensed with.

Sequestration is a costly process and therefore consideration should be given as to whether it is appropriate in the particular circumstances of the case and whether another more appropriate remedy is available (*Clark v Clark* [1988] 1 F.L.R. 174; *Clark v Clark (No. 2)* [1991] 1 F.L.R. 179).

As an example of the application of the process to family proceedings see *Re S* [1995] 1 F.L.R. 858. For further discussion and detailed procedure see Smith and Bishop, *Enforcing Financial Orders in Family Proceedings*, pp.181–189.

10 Committal

General principles: The practical use of committal as a means of enforcement **15.37** has been affected by the introduction of the HRA, especially on applications by judgment summons. This was demonstrated by the Court of Appeal decision in *Mubarak v Mubarak* [2001] 1 F.L.R. 698 when, on an application for judgment summons, the procedures under the Debtors Act 1869 and the FPR were found not to be compliant with Art.6 of the European Convention for the Protection of Human Rights and Fundamental Freedoms 1950 (right to a fair trial). The Court of Appeal found that proceedings which subject the Respondent to the risk of the criminal sanction of imprisonment are properly characterised as criminal proceedings, even when originating in family proceedings. The Respondent, therefore, has the right to:

(*a*) a presumption of innocence throughout (the standard of proof is of the criminal standard, and the burden is on the applicant),

(*b*) a clear and detailed explanation of the nature and cause of the accusation,

(*c*) adequate time to prepare a defence, and

(*d*) examine the supporting evidence and witnesses.

Although the decision in *Mubarak* involved judgment summons procedure (which comprised the incompatible elements of an enquiry as to the debtor's means, requiring potentially self-incrimination by cross-examination under oath, and then committal proceedings) it has resulted in more scrutiny of committal applications generally to ensure HRA compliance.

Following *Mubarak*, the President issued a Direction ([2001] 1 F.L.R. 949) **15.38** on "Committal applications and proceedings in which a committal order may be made", which requires compliance with the Civil Procedure Practice

Direction (supplemental to the RSC, Ord. 52 and CCR, Ord. 29 and incorporated into Scheds 1 and 2 of the CPR respectively) subject to necessary specified modifications. Any attempt therefore to use committal as a means of enforcement must comply with the President's Direction and the Practice Direction, and the existing rules must be applied to give full effect to the HRA.

Subject to the above, where a person is required by order to do an act within a time specified in the order and refuses or neglects to do it, or where a person disobeys an order requiring him to abstain from doing an act, the order may be enforced by committal (RSC, Ord. 45, r.5 and CCR, Ord. 29, r.1). Committal can be used for breach of or non-observance of a procedural step, such as failure to give discovery or file an affidavit when ordered to do so, or for breach of an injunction (or undertaking which is in the nature of an injunction). However, it is not available as a remedy for failure to pay a sum of money ordered under the Family Law Act 1996 s.40(1)(a)(ii) – *Nwogbe v Nwogbe* [2000] 2 F.L.R. 744. The purpose of committal in family proceedings is to bring the matter back to the court in order to seek future compliance with the order and not generally to punish (*Thomason v Thomason* [1985] F.L.R. 214).

15.39   Committal orders have always been remedies of last resort; in family proceedings, they have traditionally been viewed as the *very* last resort (*Ansah v Ansah* [1977] 2 All E.R. 638, *Re M (Contact Order: Committal)* [1999] 1 F.L.R. 810, CA). Committal should be used particularly sparingly in the context of matters relating to children (*Re N* [1992] 1 F.L.R. 134). Committal should only be ordered when every other effort to bring the situation under control has failed or is almost certain to fail, and should never be used where some other method of achieving compliance exists (*Danchevsky v Danchevsky* [1984] 3 All E.R. 934; *George v George* [1986] 2 F.L.R. 347). Not every breach of an order of the court justifies the making of a committal order, whether suspended or otherwise. The breach must be serious and real and not minor or technical (*Marshall v Marshall* (1966) 110 S.J. 112; *Smith v Smith* [1988] 1 F.L.R. 179). The breach must also have been deliberately and wilfully made (*P v W* [1984] 1 All E.R. 866).

15.40   *Procedure*: RSC, Ord. 45, rr.5 and 7 and Ord. 52 (as modified by FPR, r.7.2(1)), CCR, Ord. 29, rr.1–3 and FPR, r.7.2, all as modified by the President's Direction and Civil Procedure Practice Direction, govern procedure.

Great care should be taken by practitioners and the courts to ensure that all documentation relating to an application for an order for committal is strictly in accordance with the procedural requirements. Although para.10 of the Civil Procedure Practice Direction provides that procedural defects may be waived if no injustice has been caused, pre-HRA case law contains many examples of defects being regarded as fundamental and so preventing a committal order being made, or causing the order to be set aside and the sentence quashed. (*Nguyen v Phung* [1984] F.L.R. 773; *B v B (Contempt: Committal)* [1991] 2 F.L.R. 588; *Smith v Smith (Contempt: Committal)* [1992] 2 F.L.R. 40). This seems even more likely post-HRA. Alternatively, the court may order a re-hearing (*Duo v Osborne (formerly Duo)* [1992] 2 F.L.R. 425). On an application to commit, the court will not exercise its powers to cure defects in the procedure which affect the essential rights of the respondent (*Clarke v Clarke* [1990] 2 F.L.R. 115).

15.41   Any application for committal must comply with the provisions of para.2.6 of the Civil Procedure Practice Direction and therefore must:

> (*a*) set out in full the grounds for the application and details of each alleged contempt,

(*b*) contain a notice of the possible consequences of a committal order being made and of the respondent not attending the hearing (see annex to the Practice Direction),

(*c*) be personally served on the respondent together with all written evidence in support (unless the court otherwise directs), and

(*d*) not be disposed of without a hearing.

The application should be made in the county court in the existing proceedings if it relates to a breach of a county court order made in those proceedings (or in the other circumstances described in para.1.2 of the Civil Procedure Practice Direction (CPPD)) and otherwise in the High Court.

If an order is to be enforced by committal, the order should be endorsed with **15.42** a "penal notice" (although the omission of a penal notice was not critical in the pre-HRA case of *Jolly v Hull* [2000] 2 F.L.R. 69, CA). If the order is an injunction, a penal notice should be indorsed on the order at the time it is drawn up. A penal notice should be indorsed on any other order enforceable by committal on the request of the judgment creditor (CCR, Ord. 29, r.1(3)). In High Court proceedings, the form of notice is set out in the notes to RSC, Ord. 45, r.7 in the Supreme Court Practice. It must be prominently displayed on the front of the order. In county court proceedings, the notice is on CCR Form N77. When the court has accepted an undertaking, an order reciting the undertaking in Form N117 must be issued (CCR, Ord. 29 r.1A). Form N117 contains a penal notice and a statement for signature by the person giving the undertaking recording that a breach may result in a prison sentence for contempt.

To be enforced, the order must be served personally within the time limit for **15.43** the performance of the act unless that is to run from the time of service. Substituted service may be allowed, for example, when there is evidence that the defendant is seeking to evade service (RSC, Ord. 65, r.4; CCR, Ord. 7, r.8). Service of the order may be dispensed where the court deems it just to do so (RSC, Ord. 45, r.7(7); CCR, Ord. 29, r.1(7)), although it is anticipated that the courts will be even more reluctant to deem service to ensure HRA compliance. Pre-HRA cases in relation to this issue include *Lewis v Lewis* [1991] 3 All E.R. 251, *Hussain v Hussain* [1986] 1 All E.R. 961, and *Turner v Turner* (1978) 122 S.J. 696. Service may not be required if the court is satisfied that the person against whom or against whose property it is sought to enforce the order, has had notice thereof either by being present when the order was made, or by being notified of the terms of the order, whether by telephone, telegram or otherwise (RSC, Ord. 45, r.7(6); CCR, Ord. 29, r.1 (6)), and see also *Anthony Francis Rion Benson v Samantha Jane Richards* (2002) L.T.L. 11/10/02, CA as yet unreported elsewhere.

Application for committal: An application for committal requires the follow- **15.44** ing:

(*a*) summons in the High Court (FPR, r.7.2), or notice to show good reason why a committal order should not be made in the county court (Form N78; CCR, Ord. 29, r.1(4))(although the court may initiate a committal hearing of its own motion; *Re M (Contact Order: Committal)* [1999] 1 F.L.R. 810, CA);

(*b*) affidavit in support which complies with the President's Direction and Civil Procedure Practice Direction;

(*c*) proof of service of order;

(*d*) fee of £60 (FPFO, Sch.1 para.4.3 High Court and county court).

If the court decides that the summons or notice is defective, an adjournment can be granted to allow an amended notice to be prepared. Permission of the court is required for an amendment to be made (para 2.6(3) CPPD). The respondent may then be given further time to prepare his case (*Bluffield v Curtis* [1988] 1 F.L.R. 170).

15.45   The summons or notice accompanied by a copy of the affidavit in support and any other written evidence in support must be served personally not less than two clear days before the hearing (RSC, Ord. 52, r.4(2), CCR, Ord. 13, r.1(2), Civil Procedure Practice Direction, para.2.6). Although the court has power to abridge time for service (RSC, Ord. 3, r.5; CCR, Ord. 13, r.4), only in very rare circumstances is this power exercised, and a request for time for service to be abridged may be less likely to be granted post-HRA given that the Respondent must have adequate time to prepare a response (HRA, Sch.1 Art.6). If the hearing of an application to commit is adjourned, unless the alleged contemnor is present in court and heard the date, time and place when the adjourned hearing is to take place, notice of the adjourned hearing must also be served personally.

Subject to compliance with the HRA, the court has power to order substituted service of the summons or notice which will authorise future service in a manner approved by the court (RSC, Ord. 65, r.4; CCR, Ord. 7, r.8). Service may be dispensed with (RSC, Ord. 45, r.7(7); CCR, Ord. 29, r.1(7)) and committal ordered ex parte provided that the court is satisfied that the alleged contemnor has been adequately informed of the terms of the injunction or order, warned of the consequences of a breach and has flagrantly disobeyed the order and continues or threatens further serious disobedience (*Lamb v Lamb* [1984] F.L.R. 278; *Wright v Jess* [1987] 2 F.L.R. 373). An ex parte committal order must only be made if no other course is open to uphold the authority of the court. The circumstances would need to be sufficiently extreme for such an order to be made without a breach of the HRA. Where service is dispensed with in county court proceedings and an ex parte committal order made, the judge may of his own motion fix a date and time when the person to be committed is to be brought before him or before the court (CCR, Ord. 29, r.1(8)), and if an application for an ex parte committal order to be set aside is successful, the whole matter must be reheard (*Aslam v Singh* [1987] 1 F.L.R. 122).

15.46   *Committal hearing*: The hearing is before the High Court or a circuit judge and usually held in open court. In wardship and proceedings relating wholly or mainly to children, an application may be heard in private. If the hearing is in private, the judge should state in open court the general nature of the contempt and the period of committal (Para.9, Civil Procedure Practice Direction, RSC, Ord. 52, r.6).

Since imprisonment is a possible result of the hearing, the alleged contemnor should be legally represented, or invited to consider whether he wants legal representation in the light of the possible penalty if the contempt is proved (*Re K (Children)* (2002) L.T.L. 22/10/02 as yet unreported elsewhere). This is critical to ensure HRA compliance. If the alleged contemnor remains unrepresented, the court should ensure that he understands his right to give evidence and to call other witnesses (*Shoreditch County Court Bailiffs v de Maderios* (1988) *The Times*, February 24; *Bowen v Bowen* [1990] 2 F.L.R. 93 – pre-HRA). Whether represented or not, a person who is liable to be committed should be given a proper opportunity to mitigate (*Taylor v Persico* (1992) *The Times*, February 12). Sufficient care must be taken to ensure that the facts are established, adequate time is allowed for the disposal of the matter and a judgment is given (*Manchester City Council v Worthington* [2000] 1 F.L.R. 411, CA — pre-HRA).

An alleged contemnor is not a compellable witness since proceedings for **15.47** committal are criminal proceedings (*Mubarak v Mubarak*, paras 6 and 7 CPPD). A subpoena can be issued by the court to a person who has witnessed an alleged contempt even if no application has been made for a subpoena by a party (*Yianni v Yianni* [1966] 1 W.L.R. 120).

Committal proceedings *may* be heard and a sentence imposed even though separate criminal proceedings are pending arising out of the same facts (*Szczepanski v Szczepanski* [1985] F.L.R. 468). However, the court has a discretion to decide on the particular facts of the case whether or not serious prejudice would be caused by going ahead with the hearing of committal proceedings before the conclusion of criminal proceedings arising out of the same incident, and may therefore adjourn the committal proceedings (*H v C* [1993] 1 F.L.R. 787; see also *London Borough of Southwark v B* [1993] 2 F.L.R. 559 and *Keeber v Keeber* [1995] 2 F.L.R. 748). Of course, the court should only punish for the contempt and not the crime (*Smith v Smith* [1991] 2 F.L.R. 55).

Committal order: Once the court has found a contempt of court proved, the **15.48** contemnor should be allowed to make representations as to why he should not be committed or fined, and to purge, *i.e.* apologise for, his contempt (*Stilwell v Williamson* (1986) *The Times*, September 1).

Committal to prison is not an automatic result of a breach of an order of the court; that depends on all the circumstances (*Smith v Smith* [1988] 1 F.L.R. 179). Neither is it the inevitable consequence of a breach of an order committed at a time when a party is subject to a suspended committal order (*Banton v Banton* [1990] 2 F.L.R. 465).

If the court finds that there are other methods of achieving justice available to it, they will be used (*Danchevsky v Danchevsky* [1974] 3 All E.R. 934).

Consideration should always be given to suspending execution of the order on such terms or conditions as directed by the court (RSC, Ord. 52, r.7, FPR, r.7.4(10), *McIntosh v McIntosh* [1990] F.C.R. 351). Normally, where there is no history of criminal violence and it is not a case of exceptional gravity and threat to the other party, if there is no other way of dealing with the default, a suspended order should be made. If the contemnor shows contrition, the case for the committal order to be suspended is strengthened (*Goff v Goff* [1989] 1 F.L.R. 436; *Brewer v Brewer* [1989] 2 F.L.R. 251). The suspension ought only to be for a specified time (*Pidduck v Molloy* [1992] 2 F.L.R. 202), unless no injustice would be caused (*Griffin v Griffin* [2000] 2 F.L.R. 44, CA).

If a suspended committal order is made, an order for committal on a judg- **15.49** ment summons shall not be issued until the judgment creditor has filed an affidavit of default on the part of the debtor (FPR, r.7.4(10)(c)) and, in the county court, a request for the issue of a committal warrant has been filed (CCR, Ord. 28, r.11(1)). In applications other than judgment summons, the court may direct that, on an affidavit being lodged deposing as to the defaulting party's further default, the warrant for arrest and committal be issued. If the contemnor is not present at court on the committal hearing, an affidavit of service of the suspended committal order should be filed and will usually be required before the warrant is issued.

Where there is no specific limit to the period of imprisonment for a particular contempt, the maximum term is two years (Contempt of Court Act 1981, ss.14(1) and 14(4A), or a fine. The length of imprisonment imposed depends upon the facts of each individual case and is not subject to any guidelines laid down by the court (*Re H (A Minor) (Injunction: Breach)* [1986] 1 F.L.R. 558).

For an indication for the length of sentences imposed for various types of breach, see *George v George* [1986] 2 F.L.R. 347; *Wright v Jess* [1987] 2 F.L.R. 373; *Smith v Smith* [1988] 1 F.L.R. 179; *Lightfoot v Lightfoot* [1989] 1 F.L.R. 414; *G v G* [1993] Fam. Law. 335, *G v C* (Residence Order: Committal) [1998] 1 F.L.R. 43, *Cambridgeshire CC v D* [1999] 2 F.L.R. 42, *Thorpe v Thorpe* [1998] 2 F.L.R. 127, *Neil v Ryan* [1998] 2 F.L.R. 1068, *Wilson v Webster* [1998] 1 F.L.R. 1097, *Rafiq v Muse* [2000] 1 F.L.R. 820, CA, *Hale v Tanner* [2000] 2 F.L.R. 879, CA).

15.50   If a committal or a suspended committal order is made, it is drawn up by the solicitor in High Court proceedings in Form 85 in Appendix A to RSC and by the court in county court proceedings in CCR Form N79. It must specify exact details of each contempt found proved and specify the disposal ordered (*Nguyen v Phung* [1984] F.L.R. 773, *Re C (A Minor)* [1986] 1 F.L.R. 578). Failure to draw up an order on Form N79 is a fundamental defect not capable of cure (Couzens v Couzens [2001] E.W.C.A. Civ. 992, [2001] 2 F.L.R. 701, CA).

If the order is not suspended, a warrant of committal is issued in Form PF103 (High Court) and N80 (county court).

Although it is necessary to recite in the order whether the defendant appeared or how service was effected or that service of the notice to show cause was dispensed with, defects in such recitals before the HRA came into force were not necessarily fatal (*Wright v Jess* [1987] 2 F.L.R. 373). That may not be the case now.

15.51   Unless the court orders otherwise, a copy of an order in the county court must be served on the contemnor before or at the time of the execution of the warrant or, where the warrant has been signed by the judge, within 36 hours of the execution of the warrant of committal (CCR, Ord. 29, r.1(5)).

In proceedings pending in the High Court, warrants of arrest are executed by the tipstaff, or if there is none, by the usher or some other official to whom the order is addressed on the authority of the judge's signature. Where the person to be arrested is in court, the tipstaff will take him to prison. Where the person to be arrested is not in court the tipstaff will travel to arrest him, or communicate with the local police who will arrest him and hold him until the tipstaff arrives (see notes to RSC, Ord. 52, r.7 in The Supreme Court Practice).

In proceedings pending in a divorce county court, warrants of arrest are executed by a county court bailiff. A bailiff executes process normally only within a distance of not more than 500 yards beyond the boundary of his county court district (CCR, Ord. 7, r.4(1)). It sometimes occurs, when it is expedient to arrest without delay a person who may be violent, that his precise whereabouts are not known, and that he might be met in more than one of several county court districts. In such a case, consideration should be given to the exercise of the power of the judge under CCR, Ord. 7, r.4(2) to direct that the county court bailiff execute the warrant within the district of another county court.

15.52   *Release of person committed*: In family proceedings, an application for discharge may be made to a district judge, where no judge is conveniently available to hear the application. The district judge may make an order if satisfied of the urgency of the matter and that it is expedient to do so (FPR, r.7.2(2)). An order for release on terms that the remaining part of the sentence be suspended was overturned by the Court of Appeal in *Harris v Harris* [2001] 3 W.L.R. 765.

R.7.2(2) of the FPR and RSC, Ord. 52, r.8 apply in the High Court.

R.7.2(2), (3) and (4) of the FPR and CCR, Ord. 29, r.3 apply in the county court. The application should be in writing and served on the other party (CCR, Ord. 29, r.3 and see notes to this rule in The County Court Practice for a form of notice of application).

The contemnor should be present in court to hear the outcome of an application for his release, except where the provisions of the Mental Health Act 1983 apply and it is considered by the solicitor conducting the application that in the particular circumstances it would not be desirable for the contemnor to attend (*Practice Direction* [1983] 2 All E.R. 1066).

11 Bankruptcy

Outstanding obligations to a spouse arising by virtue of an order made in any **15.53** family proceedings or under a CSA assessment are not provable against a bankrupt (Insolvency Rules 1986, r.12.3). This covers maintenance arrears, any balance of a lump sum payment and outstanding costs. Arrears of maintenance or outstanding lump sums due under a deed of separation as distinct from a court order, are provable within bankruptcy proceedings. The minimum debt to support a bankruptcy petition is presently £750.

Following the making of a bankruptcy order the bankrupt's assets vest in the trustee in bankruptcy who must then apply them in payment of provable debts. Since maintenance arrears, unpaid lump sums and outstanding costs under a court order (*Levy v Legal Services Commission* [2001]1 F.L.R. 435, *Wehmeyer v Wehmeyer* [2001] 2 F.L.R. 84) are not provable within bankruptcy proceedings the trustee in bankruptcy would have no obligation to pay them out of the bankrupt's assets (but see *Cartwright v Cartwright* [2002] F.L.R. 610, CA in relation to maintenance arrears under a Hong Kong order). Thus, although it would be open to a party who had not received payment of maintenance, a lump sum or costs due under an order to petition for bankruptcy, there would usually be little point in doing so since it would not result in payment of the debt, and as a matter of discretion it will not usually be appropriate to make a bankruptcy order (*Russell v Russell* [1998] 1 F.L.R. 937, *Wheatley v Wheatley* [1999] 2 F.L.R. 205).

The fact that a defaulting party has been made bankrupt does not prevent the **15.54** party to whom the payment should have been made taking steps to enforce the liability. However, the difficulty they will face is that once the husband's assets have vested in the trustee in bankruptcy, the defaulting party will have no capital assets left with which to satisfy the liability. Theoretically in circumstances where the debtor has, or has had, the means to pay, the defaulting party could still be punished for failing to pay by committal to prison if the payee obtains a judgment summons (*Woodley v Woodley* [1992] 2 F.L.R. 417; *Woodley v Woodley (No. 2)* [1993] 2 F.L.R. 477), see further paras 15.59–15.73 below and paras 15.37–15.52 above in relation to judgment summonses and committal. This course of action is only advisable if the bankrupt has sufficient income (free from any income payments order) to satisfy the liability, or if there will be a surplus in the bankrupt's estate. It should be remembered that the bankruptcy court may stay any enforcement proceedings. Alternatively, the creditor could apply for an attachment of earnings order, to have the bankruptcy order annulled (under IA 1986, s.282; and see *Couvaras v Wolf* [2002] 2 F.L.R. 107 by way of example) if the creditor believes the bankruptcy was a device to frustrate the enforcement of the ancillary relief order, or rescinded (under IA 1986 s.375).

Subsequent discharge from bankruptcy does not release the bankrupt from **15.55** obligations under an order made in family proceedings unless the court otherwise directs (IA 1986, s.281(5)), and thus such obligations remain enforceable after the bankrupt's discharge. In many cases therefore the creditor will be advised to wait for the bankrupt's discharge before enforcing the order. Discharge will be effective however in relation to liabilities due under a deed of separation.

It is possible for an individual to seek to enter into an arrangement with his creditors in the hope of avoiding bankruptcy proceedings. These are known as individual voluntary arrangements under which a debtor puts forward proposals for the payment of his debts in whole or in part. Unpaid liabilities arising under an order made in family proceedings, whilst not provable within bankruptcy proceedings, would enable a spouse or former spouse to participate in such a voluntary arrangement (*Re Bradley-Hole (a bankrupt)* [1995] 1 W.L.R. 1097 and *M (A Debtor), Re; J (A Debtor), Re; JP (A Debtor)* [1999] 1 F.L.R. 926) and hence rank alongside the other creditors for payment out of the debtor's assets.

12   Settlement of instrument

15.56   Where the court decides to make a financial provision order requiring any payments to be secured or a property adjustment order, it may direct that the matter be referred to one of the conveyancing counsel of the court for him to settle a proper instrument to be executed by all necessary parties. Where the order is to be made in proceedings for divorce, nullity or judicial separation, the court may defer the granting of the decree until the instrument has been executed (MCA 1973, s.30).

Where the necessary document is a common form transfer, assignment, conveyance or simple settlement, it is usual for it to be prepared by the solicitor for the party concerned. Conveyancing counsel should only be involved where cases are of exceptional complexity.

13   Execution by nominee

15.57   If any party neglects or refuses to comply with an order directing him to execute a transfer, contract or other document, the court may order it to be executed by such other person as it may nominate, usually a district judge (Supreme Court Act 1981, s.39 (High Court) and County Courts Act 1984, s.38 (county court)).

A common use of this power of the court is on the sale or transfer of property pursuant to a property adjustment order and/or order for sale. There must be an express order of the court requiring the person to execute the document, so in the usual case it may be necessary to apply under the "liberty to apply" jurisdiction for a suitable direction and, in default, an order for execution by nominee. Whether an undertaking may be enforced in this way remains unclear.

15.58   A document so executed operates as if executed by the party originally directed to execute it (SCA 1981, s.39(2)). Usually, the court will require that the order should first be served on the party and that he should have had an opportunity to consider the proposed document and to execute it or make a reasonable objection to it. A copy of the document should be sent by post to the party's solicitor, or by recorded delivery to the party if he has no solicitor, with a letter giving a time and place where the party can attend to execute the document. Personal service is not necessary.

There is no prescribed procedure in the High Court or county court, and so the application should be by summons (High Court) or notice of application (county court) with an affidavit in support. There is no power for the magistrates court to make such an order. Consideration should be given to whether it is necessary also to seek a possession order under RSC, Ord. 31, r.1, CCR, Ord. 22, r.12, and whether the proceedings should be served on any third parties (see FPR 1991 r.2.59 in relation to applications for property adjustment orders).

14   Judgment summons

A judgment summons is a summons under section 5 of the Debtors Act 1869 **15.59** (DA 1869) requiring a debtor to appear in court and be examined on oath as to his means (FPR, r.7.4(1)) and providing that the debtor has, or has had, the means the pay the debt and refuses or neglects to pay, and that he may be committed to prison for up to six weeks and until he pays.

As indicated above (see para.15.37) this procedure was found to be non-HRA compliant by the Court of Appeal in *Mubarak v Mubarak* [2001] 1 F.L.R. 698, to the extent that Thorpe L.J. considered that the necessary re-evaluation of the procedure was likely to render it a largely obsolete means of enforcement. Certainly the procedure has been significantly revised by the President's Direction ([2001] 1 F.L.R. 949) requiring compliance with the Civil Procedure Practice Direction on Committal Applications (supplemental to RSC, Ord. 52 and CCR, Ord. 29 and incorporated into Schs 1 and 2 of the CPR respectively). CCR, Ord. 28 (in Sch.2 to the CPR 1998) has also amended procedure post-*Mubarak* with effect from March 25, 2002 to ensure HRA-compliance. Although the CPR 1998 do not apply to family proceedings in this context yet, practitioners would be well advised to take account of the provisions of the amended CCR, Ord. 28.

It remains to be seen whether Thorpe L.J.'s prediction will prove to be **15.60** correct, but in any event it is clear that considerable care must now be taken to ensure that any application by judgment summons and the proceedings themselves are HRA compliant.

One major difficulty is that reliance cannot be placed on findings of fact made at the ancillary relief hearing resulting in the order which the judgment creditor seeks to enforce, because the more onerous criminal standard of proof applies in relation to a committal application and the burden of that proof lies with the applicant. In effect, therefore, a retrial of relevant issues is required.

Another major difficulty is that the wording of section 5 of the DA 1869 (and judgment summons Form M17) provides that the debtor may be summoned to attend at court to be cross-examined as to his means and therefore to potentially incriminate himself in direct breach of the HRA.

As a result, Jacob J. in *Mubarak* suggested that alternative remedies such as freezing orders and orders requiring disclosure should be used.

FPR, rr.7.4–7.6 and (subject thereto) CCR, Ord. 28 contain the rules which **15.61** apply to the issue of judgment summonses in family proceedings. No rule in RSC specifically applies to judgment summonses, but FPR, r.7.5(1) applies

RSC, Ord. 38, r.2(3) (which enables evidence to be given by affidavit in certain cases) to judgment summonses issued in the High Court as if they were originating summonses.

The Administration of Justice Act 1970 (AJA 1970), s.11 provides that a judgment summons may be issued in the High Court in respect of a High Court maintenance order, and in a county court in respect of a High Court or county court maintenance order. "Maintenance order" is defined in Sch.8 to the Act and has the same meaning as in relation to attachment of earnings orders (see para.15.17 above); including orders for lump sums. School fees orders may also be enforced by judgment summons, where the order provides for a non-specified sum equivalent to the fees to be paid to the school direct (*L v L (School fees: maintenance: enforcement)* [1997] 2 F.L.R. 252). It is unclear whether orders for costs may be enforced by judgment summons (they are not referred to in the AJA 1970, but are referred to in FPR L, r.7.4(9)(a). If arrears are more than 12 months old at the date of issue of the judgment summons, application should be made at the hearing of the judgment summons to enforce those arrears (s.32 of the MCA 1973). A financial undertaking in the nature of a maintenance order may also be enforced by way of judgment summons (*Symmons v Symmons* [1993] 1 F.L.R. 317), as may an undertaking to pay an unquantified sum (*M v M* [1993] Fam. Law. 469).

A judgment summons may be issued to enforce a maintenance order for the benefit of a minor child without the need to seek leave to act as the child's next friend in the circumstances provided for in FPR, r.7.4(8).

For the principles to be applied where the debtor is bankrupt see paras 15.53–15.55 above.

15.62 *Procedure*: An application for the issue of a judgment summons may be made:

(1) in the case of an order of the *High Court*, to the principal registry, a district registry or a divorce county court, whichever in the opinion of the judgment creditor is most convenient;

(2) in the case of an order of a *divorce county court*, to whichever divorce county court is in the opinion of the judgment creditor most convenient,

in either case having regard to the place where the debtor resides or carries on business and irrespective of the court or registry in which the order was made (FPR, r.7.4(2); CCR, Ord. 28 applies only as amended by FPR r.7.6).

15.63 The requirements are:

(*a*) request (Form M16 (FPR, r.7.4(3) and App.1));

(*b*) affidavit (FPR, rr.7.1(1) and 7.4(3));

(*c*) certificate of interest, if appropriate (CCR, Ord. 25, r.5A);

(*d*) copy of order exhibited to affidavit where order made in another registry or divorce county court (FPR r.7.4(3));

(*e*) fee in family proceedings of £80 in High Court or county court; if issued in county court and service is by bailiff (if available), an additional £10 (FPFO Sch.1 paras 12.5, 14.4, 11.1);

(*f*) conduct money to cover travelling expenses, where service is by bailiff (FPR, r.7.5);

(g) draft Form M17 amended to ensure HRA compliance (although this is not required by the rules, it should avoid an unamended form being issued).

The creditor must prove beyond all reasonable doubt that the debtor has, or **15.64** has had since the due date, sufficient means to meet the debt (section 5(2) of the DA 1869), and a clear and detailed explanation of the nature and cause of the accusation is required (HRA 1998, Sch.1, Art.6). Relevant information should be included in the supporting affidavit, and the supporting evidence should be disclosed in advance to enable the debtor to have adequate time to prepare a defence (HRA 1998, Sch.1, art.6).

A judgment summons may not be issued without leave of a judge if the debtor is in default under an order of commitment made on a previous judgment summons in respect of the same order (FPR, r.7.4(4)).

The judgment summons in Form M17 must be served on the debtor person- **15.65** ally not less than 10 (or 14) clear days before the hearing (r 7.4(5) provides for 10 days, but CCR, Ord. 38, r.3 provides for 14 days notice and is applied by r.7.4(6); it would seem advisable to allow 14 days). At the time of service there must be paid or tendered to him a sum reasonably sufficient to cover his expenses to and from the court where he has to appear (FPR, r.7.4(5)). The provisions for postal service under CCR, Ord. 28, r.2 do not apply (FPR, r.7.6(1)).

Whether issued in the High Court or a divorce county court, a successive judgment summons may be issued in the case of non-service, within 4 months of the date of the original judgment summons (FPR, r.7.4(6) applying CCR, Ord. 28, r.3 and CCR, Ord. 7, r.19–20) notwithstanding that the debtor has since ceased to reside or carry on business at the address stated at the time of the original application (FPR, r.7.4(7)). A fee of £10 is payable (County Court Fees Order 1982 Sch.1, Fee No 1(iv)). The period of service of a summons may be extended on application by up to 12 months (CCR, Ord. 7, r.20(3)).

Hearing: The hearing of a judgment summons takes place at the principal reg- **15.66** istry or in a district registry of the High Court or in a divorce county court in open court and before a High Court and circuit judge respectively.

If the debtor fails to attend the hearing, the judge in a divorce county court will adjourn the hearing and make an *order to attend* (Form N69), which must be served personally not less than five clear days before the date fixed (Ords 28 r.4(1), 27, r.8(1)). If he fails to do so or refuses to give evidence, he may be committed to prison for a period not exceeding 14 days (County Courts Act 1984, s.110). In the High Court, a bench order is issued.

The remedy is discretionary and the orders the court may make include a means of payment order (see para.15.25 above), attachment of earnings order (see paras 15.17–15.23 above), an order adjourning the application on terms, or a suspended committal order (r.7.4(10) and (12)). An immediate committal order is unusual (see further paras 15.37–15.52 above in relation to committal). Committal does not extinguish the debtor's liability (DA 1869, s.5).

The court may make a *new order for payment of the amount* due under the **15.67** original order, together with the costs of the judgment summons, either at a specified time or by instalments where:

(a) the order is for the payment of a lump sum or costs (although it is unclear whether an order for costs can be enforced by judgment summons, see para.15.61 above); or (*b*) the order is for maintenance pending suit or other periodical payments and it appears to him that the order would have been varied or suspended if the debtor had made an application for that purpose (FPR, r.7.4(9)).

All payments must be made to the judgment creditor, unless the judge otherwise directs (FPR, r.7.4(11)).

Costs are fixed and governed by CPR 1998, Sch.1 and RSC, Ord. 62, app.3 (High Court) and Sch.2 and CCR, Ord. 38, r.18, app.B (county court) and are only allowed where a (suspended or immediate) committal order is made or the debtor pays the sum the judgment summons seeks to enforce before the hearing.

15.68   *After hearing*: Notice of the order made is sent by the court to the debtor and, if the original order was made in another registry or court, to that registry or court (FPR, r.7.5(4)).

Where an order of committal is suspended, all payments thereafter made under the order are deemed to be made, first, in or towards the discharge of any sums from time to time accruing due under the original order and, secondly, in or towards the discharge of the debt in respect of which the judgment summons was issued and the costs of the summons (FPR, r.7.4(12)(*a*)).

A judgment debtor, whether in the High Court or a divorce county court, may apply for further suspension under CCR, Ord. 28, r.7(4) and (5) (FPR, r.7.4(12)(*b*)).

For the procedure where a committal order is made, see paras 15.48–15.52 above, and see further *Smith and Bishop*, pp.137–160.

15   Registration of maintenance

15.69   *In magistrates' court*: Applications are made under the Maintenance Orders Act 1958 (MOA 1958), Pt I. FPR, rr.7.22–7.29 and the Magistrate's Courts (Maintenance Orders Act 1958) Rules 1959 apply.

Applications for leave to register orders for nominal amounts in favour of spouses only should not be allowed, and except in special circumstances, leave to register should not be granted in respect of orders for maintenance pending suit and interim orders (*Practice Direction*, March 10, 1980 [1980] 1 All E.R. 1007).

Application may be made for the registration of a "maintenance order" (defined widely in the MOA 1958, s.1(1A) as any order specified in Sch.8 of the AJA 1970) in a magistrates' court for the petty sessions area in which the person liable appears to be (MOA 1958, s.2(2)(b)).

15.70   Application for registration of an order must be the subject of a separate subsequent application (FPR, r.7.23(1)), although the original order may direct that the order be registered upon compliance with FPR, r.7.23(1).

The application is to the court which made the order.

The requirements are:

(*a*) application in Form M33 in duplicate;

(*b*) a certified copy of the maintenance order (certified by the proper officer of the court; FPR r.1.2(1) MOA 1958 s.2(7);

(*c*) fee of £30 plus copying charges (FPFO 1999, Sch.1 paras 7.1 and 9.1)

If there are no pending proceedings for enforcement, the justices' chief executive sends a certified copy of the maintenance order, endorsed with a note that the application for registration has been granted, and a copy of the application to the justices' chief executive for the appropriate magistrates' court (MOA 1958, s.2(2)(*b*); FPR, r.7.23(3)). In cases where it is difficult to determine the appropriate court, the justices' chief executive makes inquiry of the Lord Chancellor's Department. Where an application for registration is granted, no enforcement proceedings may be issued before the order is registered in the magistrates' court or the expiration of 14 days from the grant of the application, whichever first occurs (MOA 1958, s.2(2)(*a*); FPR, r.7.23 (2)). **15.71**

Payments under a maintenance order registered in the magistrates' court are made not to the payee direct but to the magistrates' court, thus enabling the regularity of payments to be monitored, unless there is an existing *means of payment order* (see para.15.25) in force which will continue to have effect after registration unless subsequently varied or revoked (MOA 1958, s.2(6ZA)). An attachment of earnings order ceases to have effect on registration (AEA 1971, s.11(1)(a). The general principle is that once a maintenance order has been registered in the magistrates' court, it is enforceable by the magistrates' court. No proceedings may be taken for the enforcement of the order in the High Court or a divorce county court after registration (MOA 1958, s.3(4)). An application to vary a registered maintenance order may only be made to the magistrates' court where the variation relates solely to the rate of payment specified in the order, unless a party to the order is not present in England (MOA 1958, s.4(2) and (5)). However, on hearing an application for variation, the powers of the magistrates' court to vary the order include requiring payment to be made by standing order, directly to the creditor or the justices' chief executive for the court, or making an attachment of earnings order. The magistrates' court may vary a registered order made by a different court as if it were an order which it had made (MOA 1958, s.4(5A) and s.4(5B)). The original court still has power to hear an application to vary provisions other than the rate of payment (*e.g.* duration of the order) and upon hearing such an application the original court may vary the rate of payment (MOA 1958, s.4(5)). Upon hearing a variation application, the magistrates' court may remit the application to the original court if it appears appropriate (MOA 1958, s.4(4)) (*e.g.* where an order for discovery is required: see *Goodall v Jolly* [1984] F.L.R. 143). On any application to vary or enforce a registered maintenance order, the magistrates' court now has the additional powers conferred by MEA 1991 (see para.15.26). **15.72**

As to cancellation of registration, see FPR, r.7.29, the Magistrates' Courts (Maintenance Orders Act 1958) Rules 1959, rr.7 and 8A and the MOA 1958, s.5.

In the High Court of a magistrates' court order: The MOA 1958, ss.1–3, 4A and 5, FPR, r.7.25 and the Magistrates' Courts (Maintenance Orders Act 1958) Rules 1959 apply. An order may be registered in a district registry. **15.73**

16   Enforcement out of England and Wales and of overseas orders

(a)   Maintenance Orders Act 1950

Pt II of the Maintenance Orders Act 1950 (MOA 1950) enables a maintenance order made in one part of the United Kingdom to be registered for enforcement in any other part of the United Kingdom. **15.74**

Rr.7.18–7.21 of the FPR apply.

Where a maintenance order has been made in England, an application to register the order in Scotland or Northern Ireland may be made by lodging with the court which made the order a certified copy of the order and an affidavit (and copy of that affidavit) in support of the application (FPR, r.7.19(1)). The affidavit should include the information required by FPR r.7.19(1). The district judge (in the county court, and presumably a High Court judge in the High Court — although not expressly referred to in r.7.19) will then consider whether the person by whom the maintenance is payable is resident in Scotland or Northern Ireland and, if so, whether it is convenient that the order be enforceable there. If he concludes that it would be convenient, he sends a certified copy of the order and the applicant's affidavit to the deputy principal clerk in charge of the petition department of the court of session (in Scotland) or the chief registrar of the Queen's Bench Division (Matrimonial) of the High Court of Justice (FPR, r.7.19(2)).

15.75   A maintenance order made in Scotland or Northern Ireland is registered in the principal registry. If a person wishes to take proceedings for enforcement in a district registry, he may apply by letter to the senior district judge in the principal registry for an order accordingly (FPR, r.7.20(6)). An order so registered may be re-registered in a magistrates' court under the MOA 1958.

A fee of £30 (plus copying charges if certified copy of the maintenance order required) applies (FPFO 1999 Sch.1, paras 7.1 and 9.1).

See, generally, *Rayden and Jackson*, (16th ed.), pp.992–998.

(b)   Maintenance Orders (Facilities for Enforcement) Act 1920

15.76   This Act provides for the reciprocal enforcement in this country of maintenance orders made in certain Commonwealth countries which are not designated as reciprocating countries under the Maintenance Orders (Reciprocal Enforcement) Act 1972 (see further below at paras 15.77–15.84, and for a list of the relevant countries see *The Family Court Practice 2001* (Jordans) p.106/5 in the note to s.1 of the 1920 Act), and vice versa. The Act also enables a person resident in this country to obtain a provisional maintenance order against a person resident in certain Commonwealth countries and vice versa. The Act is to be superseded by the Maintenance Orders (Reciprocal Enforcement) Act 1972, but remains in force for the time being in relation to those countries not yet affected by the 1972 Act.

FPR, r.7.17 applies.

See further *Rayden and Jackson*, (16th ed.), pp.968 *et seq.*

(c)   Maintenance Orders (Reciprocal Enforcement) Act 1972

15.77   The Maintenance Orders (Reciprocal Enforcement) Act 1992 amended both the Maintenance Orders (Facilities for Enforcement) Act 1920 and the 1972 Act to enable the forms of procedure which now apply in proceedings in magistrates' courts under the Domestic Proceedings and Magistrates' Courts Act 1978 and Children Act 1989 (CA 1989) to be used for the purposes of reciprocal enforcement of maintenance orders and of claims for the recovery of maintenance.

15.78   *Pt I*: This replaces the 1920 Act and deals with the reciprocal enforcement of maintenance *orders* already made in the United Kingdom or in a *reciprocating country*. Reciprocating countries are designated in Orders in Council (s.1(1)) under the Reciprocal Enforcement of Maintenance Orders (Designation of Reciprocating Countries) Orders 1974 and 2001. The relevant countries are noted in Butterworth's *Family Law Service* 5A [1009].

The provisions of Part I for the reciprocal enforcement of maintenance orders have been applied in an amended form to various countries by the Reciprocal Enforcement of Maintenance Orders (Hague Convention Countries) Order 1993, the Reciprocal Enforcement of Maintenance Orders (Hague Convention Countries) (Variation) Orders 1994, 1999 and 2001, the Reciprocal Enforcement of Maintenance Orders (United States of America) Order 1995, the Reciprocal Enforcement of Maintenance Orders (Republic of Ireland) Order 1993 and the Reciprocal Enforcement of Maintenance Orders (Variation) Order 2001 (See further Butterworth's *Family Law Service* 5A [1008] – [1020]; *Rayden and Jackson*, (16th ed.), pp.983, *et seq.*, and *K v M, M and L (Financial Relief: Foreign Order)* [1998] 2 F.L.R. 59).

"Maintenance order" means an order which provides for the payment of a **15.79** lump sum or the making of periodical payments towards the maintenance of any person for whom the payer is liable to maintain (according to the law applied in the place where the order was made). It also means, in the case of a maintenance order which has been varied, that order as varied (Maintenance Orders (Reciprocal Enforcement) Act 1972, s.21(1) as amended by the Civil Jurisdiction and Judgments Act 1982). The Act does not therefore apply to an order for costs only or property adjustment orders.

Rr.7.30–7.36 of the FPR apply (with modifications as regards the Republic of Ireland, in r.7.37, and the Hague Convention countries, in r.7.38).

Applications in a magistrates' court under the 1972 Act are not covered in this.

Under Pt I, where a certified copy of a *maintenance order which has been made abroad* in a reciprocating country is received by the Lord Chancellor, he sends it to the prescribed officer of the appropriate court for registration (section 6). The appropriate court in relation to a person residing in England and Wales is a magistrates' court (section 21(1)). The prescribed officer is the justices' chief executive for that court.

Pt I also deals with the transmission of a *maintenance order made in the United Kingdom* to a reciprocating country for enforcement there (section 2), and also with the taking of evidence for the purposes of a maintenance application in a court in a reciprocating country (section 14).

An application for a maintenance order to be sent to a reciprocating **15.80** country should be made by lodging the following with the court where the order was made (FPR r.7.31):

(*a*) affidavit by the applicant stating:

    (i) the applicant's reasons for believing that the payer under the maintenance order is residing in the reciprocating country; and

    (ii) the amount of any arrears due to the applicant under the order, the date to which the arrears have been calculated, and the date on which the next payment falls due;

(*b*) certified copy of the maintenance order (in practice a certified copy of the order will be prepared by the court office, whether in the High Court or a county court);

(*c*) statement giving such information as the applicant possesses as to the whereabouts of the payer;

(*d*) statement giving such information as the applicant possesses for facilitating the identification of the payer (including, if known, the name and address of any employer of the payer, his occupation and the date and place of issue of any passport of the payer);

(*e*) photograph of the payer, if available;

(*f*) fee of £30 plus copying charges for certified copy of the order (FPFO 1999 Sch.1, paras 7.1 and 9.2).

15.81   Inquiries may be made through the court to trace a payer under a maintenance order in Australia, Canada, New Zealand and South Africa; see *Practice Note*, February 10, 1976. An applicant who does not know the payer's address in those countries should, on or before making an application for transmission of a maintenance order or for a provisional maintenance order, complete and lodge with the court a questionnaire together with a written undertaking from the solicitor (or applicant in person) that any address of the payer received in response to the inquiries will not be disclosed or used except for the purpose of the proceedings.

On receipt of an application for transmission and pursuant to the requirements of section 2(4), copies of the documents listed above are sent by the court manager or justices' chief executive (as applicable), if he is satisfied that the payer is resident in the reciprocating country, to the Lord Chancellor, together with the following certificate for forwarding to the reciprocating country:

I,   ,   of the   [County Court] certify that:

(1) (*Name, address and occupation of payee*) is entitled to enforce payment of the attached certified order in the United Kingdom against (*name of payee*);

(2) arrears due up to and including the *(insert date)*   of amount to £   ;

(3) the information given in the copy affidavit attached is, to the best of my knowledge, an accurate statement of facts.

Dated

(*Signed*)

Court Officer

15.82   Section 5 applies to a variation or revocation of a maintenance order which has been sent to a reciprocating country for enforcement and to a provisional maintenance order under section 3 against a person residing in a reciprocating country and confirmed by a competent court in that country. Where the rate of payments under the order is increased, unless the parties appear in the proceedings, or the applicant appears and the appropriate process has been served on the other party, the order is varied by a provisional order (section 5(3)).

Where a provisional order varying or revoking a maintenance order made in the United Kingdom is *received from* a reciprocating country, section 5(5)-(8) and FPR, r.7.33 apply.

15.83   A court in a reciprocating country may request evidence to be taken of a person residing in England and Wales for the purpose of any proceedings relating to a maintenance order (section 14(1)). Rr.7.34(1) and (2) of the FPR apply where the request for evidence relates to a maintenance order made by a superior court in the United Kingdom and the witness resides in England and Wales. Rr.7.34(3) and (4) of the FPR apply where the evidence relates to a maintenance order made by a county court which order is not for the time being registered in a magistrates' court. The Magistrates' Courts (Reciprocal Enforcement of Maintenance Orders) Rules 1974 (as amended), r.10 applies in other cases. A court in England and Wales may make a similar request of a court in a reciprocating country (section 14(5)).

Pt II: This deals with an application for a maintenance order to be transmit-**15.84** ted to and made in another country, termed a *convention* country and gives effect to the United Nations Convention on the Recovery Abroad of Maintenance 1956. Convention countries are declared by Orders in Council (section 25) (Recovery Abroad of Maintenance (Convention Countries) Order 1975 (SI No 423) (as amended); and the relevant countries are noted in Butterworth's *Family Law Service* 5A [1022]). Pt II has been extended to certain states of the United States of America by Recovery of Maintenance (United States of America) Order 1993 (SI 1993/591).

Pt II allows a person in the United Kingdom to apply to the Secretary of State to have a claim for maintenance transmitted to a convention country or specified state. An application to the Lord Chancellor is made through the appropriate officer. Where the applicant resides in England and Wales, the appropriate officer is the justices' chief executive for the local magistrates' court (section 26(6)). A similar application may be made by a person in a convention country or specified state. When such an application is received by the Lord Chancellor it is treated as an application for a maintenance order under the Domestic Proceedings and Magistrates' Courts Act 1978 or CA 1989 as appropriate (section 27 A) and forwarded to the justices' chief executive for the local magistrates' court (section 27B).

Some countries are both convention countries under Pt II and reciprocating countries (or other countries to which the Part applies) under Pt I. In such circumstances there is therefore a choice to be made as to which jurisdiction should be used.

(d)   Civil Jurisdiction and Judgments Acts 1982 and 1991

The 1982 Act as amended by the 1991 Act provides for the recognition and **15.85** enforcement of maintenance orders within the European Union by giving effect to the Brussels and Lugano Conventions of 1968 and 1988 respectively on Jurisdiction and Enforcement of Judgments in Civil and Commercial Matters. The Lugano Convention extends the rules within the Brussels Convention to the members of the European Free Trade Association (EFTA) Act, who ratify it. The Act does not apply to the enforcement of maintenance orders in other parts of the United Kingdom to which Pt II of the MOA 1950 applies (section 18(5)(*a*) of the Act).

A "maintenance order" is defined by section 15(1) of the Act as having the same meaning as "maintenance judgment" in the Brussels Convention. The Brussels Convention does not, however, define this term and it has been suggested that the definition in the Maintenance Orders (Reciprocal Enforcement) Act 1972, s.21 should be used, although it may be that the definition extends to costs orders only. Authentic instruments and court settlements which are maintenance orders may also be enforced (Civil Jurisdiction and Judgments (Authentic Instruments and Court Settlements) Order 1993 (SI No. 604)).

The grounds upon which a maintenance order may be refused recognition are set out in Sch.1, art.27 of the Act.

For enforcement in contracting states s.12 of the Act, RSC, Ord. 71, r.36 and CCR, Ord. 35, r.3 apply.

For enforcement in United Kingdom s.5(1)-(3) of the Act and Magistrates' Courts (Civil Jurisdiction and Judgments Act 1982) Rules 1986 (as amended) apply. An application for enforcement is transmitted by the Lord Chancellor to the justices' chief executive the magistrates' court having jurisdiction where the person liable to make payments is domiciled.

(e)   Administration of Justice Act 1920 and Foreign Judgments (Reciprocal Enforcement) Act 1933 (FJ(RE)A 1933)

15.86   Pt II of the AJA 1920 provides for the registration, for enforcement in the UK, of judgments obtained in a superior court in Her Majesty's dominions abroad, provided that reciprocal provisions for enforcement of the orders of the High Court in England, Court of Session in Scotland, and High Court in Ireland, are in place in those dominions, and an Order in Council has been made applying the Act to those dominion. The FJ(RE)A 1933 extends this principle to any foreign country where substantial reciprocity will be assured in relation to similar judgments in similar courts in the UK, and provides also for Orders in Council to be made to bring appropriate countries within the scope of the Act.

The 1920 Act therefore applies to High Court orders only whereby "any sum of money is made payable" (section 12(1)). The 1933 Act extends to county court orders, but section 1(2)(a) of the Act requires that the judgment be final and conclusive as between the parties. It seems, therefore, that periodical payment orders may not be enforced under this Act (or under the reciprocal provisions in the relevant foreign country, unless they do not require the order to be final and conclusive). RSC, Ord. 71 and CCR, Ord. 35 apply, provided that the order sought to be enforced comes within the definition of "family proceedings' (see para.1.04 above). Otherwise, the CPR will apply.

Chapter 16

Injunctions and Undertakings

1 Introduction

Pt IV of the Family Law Act 1996 ("The Act") came into force on October 1 **16.01**
1997. The effect of this was to repeal the Domestic Violence and Matrimonial
Proceedings Act 1976 and the Domestic Proceedings and Magistrates' Courts
Act 1978 ss.16 – 18. The Act also substantially amended the Matrimonial
Homes Act 1983 and removed certain sections, namely, section 8(4) (c) and (f),
from the Children Act 1989. The result is a unified set of remedies available in
all courts (having jurisdiction in family matters, whether the High Court,
county courts or magistrates' courts [known as family proceedings courts] to
provide protection in certain violence- related circumstances. Two forms of
injunction order are provided by Pt IV of the Act being "occupation orders"
and "non-molestation orders".

   Pt IV of the Act places greater emphasis upon enforcement of the orders
than the previous provisions. The Act introduces the facility for the person
with the benefit of the order to apply for the issue of a warrant of arrest. The
provisions of the Act also make it more likely that the court will attach a power
of arrest to orders. The Act provides for a wide class of potential applicants
and gives detailed guidelines to direct the court in the exercise of its jurisdiction with the aim of achieving a unified approach to applications in whichever
court the application is made.

2. Applications for injunctions

An injunction is an instruction by the court for a person to take, or not to take, **16.02**
certain action often within a specified period of time, the breach of which is
an offence by virtue of the contempt of court provisions.

   Care should be taken before any application is made for an injunction.
Consideration should be given to the consequences of what is often considered a hostile step. Further consideration should be undertaken to ensure the
applicant is entitled to make such an application and that the order is available against the intended Respondent. A court will be unlikely to grant an
order where service cannot be effected or where enforcement is unavailable, for
instance where the Respondent is under the age of 17 years (*Re S* [1991] 2
F.L.R. 319; *R v Selby Justices* ex p. *Frame*[1991]2 All E.R. 344; *Mawson v
Lawton* [1991] 2 F.L.R. 50).

   Pt IV of the Act makes specific provision that applicants must satisfy a
balance of harm test. The practitioner must assess whether there is sufficient
evidence to satisfy this test if an application is to be successful. Furthermore,

there may be steps to be taken prior to an application in order to ensure the applicant has complied with any requirements of the Legal Services Commission before issue of any application. For instance, a pre-action letter may be necessary in appropriate circumstances. Such a step may also impact upon the outcome of any later costs application.

3   Persons entitled to apply for an order — Family Law Act 1996

16.03   The Act makes clear who is entitled to apply for an order under Pt IV and against whom any such application can be made. The list of possible applicants varies depending upon the order sought — an occupation order or a non-molestation order.

a   Applicants for occupation orders

16.04   It is important to be clear as to the exact nature of an applicant's interest in the property in question in order to ascertain whether he/she is entitled to apply for an occupation order. In some cases, it must also be clear whether or not the respondent is entitled to occupy the property which is the subject of the application. Furthermore, an occupation order cannot be made in respect of a property which is not, nor has ever been or was intended to be the home of the possible applicant and respondent.

Potential applicants for an occupation order are divided by the Act into those persons "entitled" and those "non-entitled". The phrases refer to whether an applicant has a legal right to occupy the property which is the subject of the application.

(i)   Entitled applicants

16.05   An entitled applicant is defined within section 33 (1) (a) of the Act as one who:

> (i) is entitled to occupy a dwelling house by virtue of a beneficial estate or interest or contract or by virtue of any enactment giving him the right to remain in occupation; or
>
> (ii) has matrimonial home rights in relation to a dwelling house.

Entitled applicants must show that the applicant and the respondent were associated. The concept of associated persons is discussed below. If it can be established that they were associated, then it will be possible for an application to be made for an occupation order under section 33 of the Act.

(ii)   Non-entitled applicants

16.06   Non-entitled applicants may be former spouses or cohabitants who have no existing right to occupy the property. A further distinction is then drawn within the Act as to whether the respondent is himself/herself entitled or non-entitled. By virtue of these provisions, there are at least three classes of potential non-entitled applicants.

If an applicant is able to show that he/she is the former spouse who is not entitled to occupy the property which is the subject of the application, that the respondent is entitled to occupy and the property in question is (or was intended to be) at some time their matrimonial home, he/she may apply for an order under section 35 of the Act.

If an applicant does not meet these criteria, it may be possible to apply for an order under sections 36, 37 or 38 of the Act.

A former spouse not entitled to occupy who does not meet the criteria for an order under section 35 of the Act because the respondent is similarly not entitled to occupy the property (such property being, or was intended to be, the matrimonial home) would need to apply for an order under section 37 of the Act.

Cohabitants have the choice of applying for an occupation order under sections 36 or 38 of the Act depending upon whether or not the applicant and the respondent are entitled to occupy the property the subject of the application. Such property must be the dwelling-house in which they live together, have lived together or intended to live in together.

If one cohabitant is entitled to occupy the property and the other cohabitant is not, then an application would be made under section 36. In the case of an occupation order sought under section 38 of the Act neither the applicant nor the respondent will be entitled to occupy the property which is the subject of the application.

b Applicants for non-molestation orders

An applicant who is associated with the respondent may apply for a non-molestation order. For details as to who is associated with whom, see below. **16.07**

Additionally, the court may make a non-molestation order within any family proceedings to which the respondent is party for the benefit of any party to the proceedings or any relevant child if it considers an order should be made. Family proceedings are defined within section 63 (2) of the Act and includes the Matrimonial Causes Act 1973 and certain parts of the Children Act 1989.

c Associated persons

The Act introduces a new concept of associated persons. The concept is applicable to both applicants for occupation orders and applicants for non-molestations orders. Applicants need to be able to show that he/she was associated with the potential respondent. **16.08**

Associated persons are defined by section 62 (3) of the Act. A person is associated with another person if;

(*a*) they are or have been married to each other,

(*b*) they are cohabitants or former cohabitants,

(*c*) they live, or have lived in the same household otherwise than by reason of being the other's employee, tenant, lodger or boarder,

(*d*) they are relatives,

(*e*) they have agreed to marry each other (although that agreement may have been terminated),

(*f*) they are parties in other family proceedings.

If parties can be shown to be associated there is no reason, provided they meet the required provisions of the Act and the court decides to exercise its discretion to grant an order, why they should not obtain relief under the Family Law Act. The range of associated persons is drafted widely to include family disputes of various natures (*Chechi v Bashier* [1999] F.L.R. 489 CA).

16.09   "Cohabitants" are defined by section 62(1) of the Act as a man and a woman who, although not married to each other, are living together as husband and wife. *G v G (Non-molestation: Jurisdiction)* [2000] 2 F.L.R. 532 considered whether or not a couple could be cohabitants for the purpose of the Act. The court holding that the evidence should be viewed as a whole. In this decision three of the "signposts" for cohabitation referred to in an earlier decision of *Crake v Supplementary Benefits Commission* [1982]1 All E.R. 498 were present — sexual relations, living in the same household and a joint bank account.

Reference to same household would require a degree of shared living arrangements, although there is no definition of this within the Act. This would therefore include a same sex couple who were living together but did not come within the definition of cohabitants.

Relative is defined within section 63 (1) of the Act as the father, mother, stepfather, stepmother, son, daughter, stepson, stepdaughter, grandfather, grandmother, grandson or granddaughter of the applicant/respondent or of the applicant/respondent's spouse or former spouse. Relative can also mean a brother, sister, uncle, aunt, niece or nephew (whether of the whole blood or half blood) of the applicant/respondent or of the applicant/respondent's spouse or former spouse.

If it cannot be shown that the applicant and respondent are associated persons, there can be no valid application for either an occupation order or a non-molestation order by a person entitled.

d   Child applicants

16.10   A child under the age of 16 years may not apply for an occupation order or a non-molestation order without leave of the court. It is anticipated that the child should have sufficient understanding of the application being made before such leave would be granted.

4   Types of orders available — Family Law Act 1996

a   Occupation orders

16.11   Occupation orders regulate who may occupy, and on what terms, certain property. Technically occupation orders are defined by section s.39 of the Act as being those orders made under sections 33, 35, 36, 37 and 38 of the Act. It will be seen from s.3 of the Act that the difference between these five orders relates essentially to the different categories of applicant and respondent, and the property which is the subject of the application.

An occupation order may be applied for within other family proceedings (defined in section 63 (2) of the Act) or as a free-standing application in the absence of other family proceedings.

Section 39 (4) of the Act confirms that the application for an occupation order does not affect any third parties right to claim a legal or equitable interest in property the subject of the application.

S.33 Occupation orders

16.12   Where an applicant is entitled to apply under section 33 (see section 3 above) the order may contain the following provisions, set out within s.33 (3) of the Act;

(a) enforce the applicant's entitlement to remain in occupation as against the other person ("the respondent");

(b) require the respondent to permit the applicant to enter and remain in the dwelling-house or part of the dwelling-house;

(c) regulate the occupation of the dwelling-house by either or both parties;

(d) if the respondent is entitled as mentioned in subsection (1) (a) prohibit, suspend, or restrict the exercise by him of his right to occupy the dwelling-house;

(e) if the respondent has matrimonial home rights in relation to the dwelling-house and the applicant is the other spouse, restrict or terminate those rights;

(f) require the respondent to leave the dwelling-house or part of the dwelling-house; or

(g) exclude the respondent from a defined area in which the dwelling-house is included.

The court's approach to orders under section 33

The Act provides detailed criteria for guidance for the exercise of the court's **16.13** discretion. The approach of the court will vary depending upon the type of order applied for whether under sections 33, 35, 36, 37 or 38 of the Act.

Section 33 (6) of the Act provides that in exercising its discretion whether to make an occupation order under section 33 of the Act, the court shall have regard to all the circumstances including;

(a) the housing needs and resources of the parties and of any relevant child;

(b) the financial resources of each of the parties;

(c) the likely effect of any order, or of any decision by the court not to exercise its powers under section 33 (3) of the Act, on the health, safety or well-being of the parties and of any relevant child;

(d) the conduct of the parties in relation to each other and otherwise.

It can be seen that the factors to be considered by the court are wider than **16.14** merely the financial positions of either party. Similarly, there is no presumption that conduct should be given undue weight as against other relevant considerations. However the court must make an order (section 33 (7) of the Act) if it considers that the applicant or any relevant child is likely to suffer significant harm attributable to the conduct of the respondent if an order is not made unless it appears that:

(a) the respondent or any relevant child is likely to suffer significant harm if the order is made, and

(b) that harm is as great as, or greater than, the harm attributable to conduct of the respondent which is likely to be suffered by the applicant or child if the order is not made.

This is known as the "balance of harm test". Harm is defined by section 63 (1) of the Act as ill-treatment or impairment of health (and for a child includes impairment of development).

16.15 Essentially, where there is no question of significant harm, the court has the power to make an order taking into account the four factors set out above. However, in cases where there is the possibility of significant harm, that power becomes a duty. The court must make an order after balancing the harm likely to be suffered by both parties and by any children. For consideration of the court's approach to applications under section 33 and the balance of harm test, see *Chalmers v Johns* [1999] 1 F.L.R. 392 CA; and *B v B (Occupation Order)* [1999] 1 F.L.R. 715.

Clearly, it will be essential to set out within the evidence provided to the court in support of any application sufficient information to show the applicant is entitled to apply for an order under s.33 of the Act, and to provide details so as the court can consider the factors set out within s.33 (6) of the Act and, if appropriate, information to allow the court to carry out the balance of harm test effectively.

Duration of section 33 orders

16.16 An occupation order under section 33 of the Act may be made for a specified period, until the occurrence of a specified event, or until further order.

Court's approach to orders under section 35 of the Act

16.17 Orders under s.35 are those where the applicant is a former spouse non-entitled to occupy the property and the respondent is so entitled.

If the court is inclined to grant an order under s.35 of the Act there are certain provisions which the court could provide in the order and certain provisions that it must provide in the order.

S.35 (5) of the Act sets out the regulatory provisions that the court may include within an order;

(*a*) regulate the occupation of the dwelling-house by either or both parties;

(*b*) prohibit, suspend or restrict the exercise by the respondent of his right to occupy the dwelling-house;

(*c*) require the respondent to leave the dwelling-house or part of the dwelling-house;

(*d*) exclude the respondent from a defined area in which the dwelling-house is included.

16.18 Because the applicant is non-entitled to occupy the property, the court must make certain provisions within a section 35 order (section 35 (3) and (4)). If the applicant is in occupation, the order must give the applicant the right not to be evicted or excluded from the property by the respondent for the period specified in the order. If the applicant is not in occupation at the time of the application, the order must give the applicant the right to enter into and occupy the property for the period specified in the order, and for the respondent to permit the exercise of that right.

In deciding whether to make an occupation order and the terms of it, the court must have regard to the same matters set out within section 33 (6) of the

Act. Section 35 (6) of the Act provides certain additional factors to be considered. The following additional factors will also be taken into account in considering whether to grant an order under section 35 of the Act;

(e) the length of time that has elapsed since the parties ceased to live together;

(f) the length of time that has elapsed since the marriage was dissolved or annulled;

(g) whether there are any proceedings pending between them for financial provision, or relating to the legal or beneficial ownership of the dwelling-house.

Again there will be a need to ensure that sufficient evidence is provided to the court to enable the court to consider all relevant factors when exercising its discretion.   **16.19**

As with orders made under section 33 of the Act, the court must make an order if it appears likely that the applicant or any relevant child will suffer significant harm attributable to the conduct of the respondent if an order is not made unless the harm caused to the respondent or to any relevant child will be as great as, or greater than, the harm attributable to conduct of the respondent which is likely to be suffered by the applicant or any relevant child if the order is not made (section 35 (8) of the Act).

Duration of section 35 order

The duration of orders made under section 35 of the Act is different to those orders made under s.33 of the Act for entitled applicants.   **16.20**

The order must be granted for a specified period not exceeding six months. However, such an order may be extended (on one or more occasion) for a further specified period not exceeding six months.

Orders for cohabitants and court's approach

When only one cohabitant is entitled to occupy a dwelling (the other being non-entitled) and the dwelling is the home in which they live together (or lived together or intended to live together) as husband and wife, an application for an occupation order will be made under section 36 of the Act.   **16.21**

In deciding whether to exercise its discretion, the court must again consider the factors set out within section 33 (6) of the Act. Section 36 (6) extends this list to include additional factors to be considered where the applicant is a cohabitee;

(e) the nature of the parties relationship;

(f) the length of time during which they have lived together as husband and wife;

(g) whether there are or have been any children who are children of both parties or for whom both parties have or have had parental responsibility;

(h) the length of time that has elapsed since the parties ceased to live together.

If the court decides to make the occupation order under section 36 of the Act the regulatory provisions included within section 33 (3) are available to the court (section 35 (5)). Again, there are certain provisions which the court must include in view of the fact that the applicant has no legal entitlement to occupy the property. These are set out within section 36 (3) of the Act and are identical to those provisions set out above for sections 35 (3) and (4) of the Act.

The balance of harm test for a s.36 application is slightly different. The wording of section 36 (8) of the Act shifts the onus to the respondent to show why the court should not make regulatory provisions. There is no obligation upon the court to exercise its discretion in any particular way once it has considered the question of harm.

Duration of section 36 order

16.22   As with orders made under s.35, a s.36 order may not be made for a period exceeding six months. A section 36 order can only be extended on one occasion. The order cannot be made after the death of one party and will cease to have effect on the death of either of them.

Occupations orders made where neither party is entitled to occupy

16.23   Unlike the other type of orders available, the parties to such an application must still be in occupation. The property will either be the matrimonial home in the case of non-entitled former spouses, or the property in which non-entitled cohabitants live together as husband and wife. It is likely that such applicants will be either squatters or bare licensees where their right to occupy has terminated.

The court may make similar regulatory provisions as with the previous orders (section 37 (3) and section 38 (3)).

The Act sets out at section 38 (4) the factors the court must give consideration to when exercising its discretion in relation to cohabitants. The factors to be taken into account when a non-entitled spouse is applying section 37 (4) are identical to those set out at section 33 (6). These are set out above.

The balance of harm test is treated as a question with no requirement for the court to exercise it's discretion if the test is made out.

Duration of s.37 and s.38 orders

16.24   By the nature of the circumstances, it is anticipated that any order made under section 37 or section 38 of the Act for these parties will be of only very short duration. The Act does, however, provide for an order for a specified period not exceeding six months with the possibility of one further extension.

Enforcement of occupation orders

16.25   Occupation orders may be made on an ex parte basis. This will usually only occur in exceptional circumstances (see below).

A power of arrest may be attached to an occupation order (see below).

Section 46 (1) of the Act provides the court with the power to accept an undertaking from a party to an application for an occupation order (see below).

b   Non-molestation orders

16.26   A non-molestation order is defined by section 42 (1) of the Act as an order containing either or both of the following provisions;

(*a*) provision prohibiting a person ("the respondent") from molesting another person who is associated with the respondent;

(*b*) provision prohibiting the respondent from molesting a relevant child.

The order can be made upon application (in family proceedings or free-standing) or by the court of its own motion in family proceedings where it considers that the order should be made for the benefit of any other party to the proceedings or any relevant child. "Relevant child" is defined by section 62 (2) of the Act as:

(*a*) any child who is living with or might reasonably be expected to live with either party to the proceedings; or

(*b*) any child in relation to whom an order under the Adoption Act 1976 or the Children Act 1989 is in question in the proceedings; and

(*c*) any other child whose interests the court considers relevant.

Associated persons

If the parties to an application are not already parties within existing family proceedings, then the applicant and the respondent must be associated persons. Section 62 (3) of the Act sets out the list of associated persons. This has been considered above at para.16.08.   **16.27**

Additionally, a party may be a relevant child provided he/she has sufficient understanding of the application. The issue of sufficiency of a child's understanding was considered in *Gillick v West Norfolk & Wisbech Area Health Authority and Another* [1986] A.C. 112, HL.

Molestation

There is no statutory definition of molestation within the Act. It was established in *Davis v Johnson* [1979] A.C. 264, HL that molestation includes, but is not limited to, violence. The test, referred to below, for the court to consider when deciding whether to exercise its discretion would also seem to suggest that molestation must be considered a far wider concept than violence itself.   **16.28**

Court's approach to non-molestation orders

The court must have regard to all the circumstances of the case in deciding whether to exercise its powers and grant a non-molestation order including the need to secure the health, safety and well-being of the applicant or the person for whose benefit the order would be made, and of any relevant child section 42 (5).   **16.29**

Health is defined at section 63 of the Act as being both physical and mental health.

Duration of non-molestation orders

The order may be made for a specified period or until further order. The order may subsequently be varied or revoked. This was confirmed by the Court of Appeal in *Re B-J (A Child) (Non-Molestation Order; Power of Arrest)* [2000] 2 F.L.R. 443.   **16.30**

c Ex Parte orders

Power of the court to make ex parte orders

16.31 Section 45 of the Act provides for the making of both occupation orders and non-molestation orders without first giving notice to the respondent (ex parte orders).

Ex parte applications for an order should not be made, or granted, unless there is a real immediate danger of serious injury or irreparable damage (*Practice Direction* June 26, 1978 [1978] 2 All E.R. 919), and it is not reasonably practicable to give notice, even informally, or giving notice would give the respondent time to defeat the purpose of the application and it is likely that he would do so *(Re First Express Ltd* (1991) *The Times,* October 10 and *Loseby v Newman* [1995] 2 F.L.R. 754).

The court may only make ex parte orders where it considers it just and convenient to do so. Section 45 (2) of the Act prescribes the factors which the court must take into account in addition to all the circumstances of the case:

(*a*) any risk of significant harm to the applicant or a relevant child, attributable to the conduct of the respondent, if the order is not made immediately;

(*b*) whether it is likely that the applicant will be deterred or prevented from pursuing the application if an order is not made immediately; and

(*c*) whether there is reason to believe that the respondent is aware of the proceedings but is deliberately evading service and that the applicant or a relevant child will be seriously prejudiced by the delay involved —
    (i) where the court is a magistrates' court, in effecting service of proceedings; or
   (ii) in any other case, in effecting substituted service.

Content of an ex parte order

16.32 An ex parte order must clearly state its terms. There must be no ambiguity which might leave the respondent in any doubt as to its requirements. It should contain a return date, the time and place of the hearing and must expressly state the date upon which the order expires. Notice of the hearing of the return date should include notice of the orders which will be sought at the *inter partes* hearing.

An ex parte order should contain notification to the respondent that he may change or cancel the order upon notice. Where the respondent seeks to vary, discharge or otherwise challenge the order the proper course is to go back to the court which made the order and not to the Court of Appeal unless no judge is available to hear the application (*WEA Records Ltd v Vision Channel 4 Ltd* [1983] 1 W.L.R. 721; *Re A ((Minor: Wardship)(Challenging ex parte order)* (1993) *The Times,* 5 October). If no judge is available during normal court hours, the decision as to whether to arrange a late sitting should be made by a District Judge where possible (*G v G,* above at para.16.08).

In *Re W (Ex Parte Orders)* [2000] 2 F.L.R. 927 (*Family Division;* Munby J; 12 July 2000) it was stated that an ex parte order ought to contain on its face a list of all affidavits, statements and other evidential materials read by the judge.

No delay in making the application

In making an application for an ex parte order there should be a minimum period of time, ideally of less than a day, between the last incident referred to and the application to the court for the order. If it is shown that the applicant has delayed with full knowledge of the facts, then the application should be refused (*Bates v Lord Hailsham and Others* [1972] 1 W.L.R. 1373).   **16.33**

An application to exclude a spouse from the matrimonial home should seldom, if ever, be made ex parte *(Masich v Masich* (1977) 7 Fam. Law. 245; *Shipp v Shipp* [1988] 1 F.L.R. 345), and not without a proper cross-examination of the parties' evidence *(Whitlock v Whitlock* [1989] 1 F.L.R. 208; *Harris v Harris* [1986] 1 F.L.R. 12). An application on notice is thought to be more appropriate for all types of occupation order.

Evidence in support of ex parte application

The statement sworn in support of an ex parte application must contain an explanation of why the application is made ex parte (CCR, Ord. 13, r.6(3A)).   **16.34**

It is good practice when making application for an order, whether for an occupation order or non-molestation order, to provide the court with three copies of the perfected order sought. This is particularly important with an ex parte order when time is short.

d   Duration of ex parte order

An ex parte order, whether an occupation or non-molestation order should be limited for the shortest period until an *inter partes* hearing can be arranged. Section 45 (3) of the Act provides that upon the making of an ex parte order the court must afford the respondent an opportunity to make representations to the court as soon as is just and convenient at a full hearing. In *G v G* [1990] 1 F.L.R. 395 a period of seven weeks between the ex parte order being made and a full hearing was said to be completely unjustifiable.   **16.35**

For calculating the maximum period for which an occupation order (subsequently obtained on notice) may subsist, the term should run from the date of the ex parte order.

5   Procedure for application

Choice of court

Section 57 of the Act sets out the jurisdiction of the courts to hear applications under the Act.   **16.36**

In essence, applications can be made in a magistrates' court, a county court or the High Court. However, not all county courts or magistrates' courts have jurisdiction to consider applications and reference should be made to the Family Law Act 1996 (Pt IV) (Allocation of Proceedings) Order 1997 (SI 1997/1896). Usually a county court will have jurisdiction if it is a divorce county court, family hearing centre or a care centre. A magistrates' court will have jurisdiction if it is a family proceedings court.

Any minor applicants must seek leave pursuant to section 43 of the Act in the High Court prior to any application being made (FPR, 3.8(2)).

There is wide provision for transfer of application from one court to another. In particular, the magistrates' court must consider whether to transfer the hearing to another court when an application for an occupation order or non-molestation order is pending (FPR, r.3.8(9)). Transfer would be particularly likely if the application involved a conflict with the law of another jurisdiction, some novel or difficult point of law, some issue of public interest or the proceedings were exceptionally complex.

The magistrates' court must transfer proceedings to a county court if a child under 18 years is the respondent or becomes a party to the proceedings or where one party is a mental patient incapable of managing his affairs.

Procedure for application

16.37   Procedures for orders under the Family Law Act 1996 are governed by the Family Proceedings Rules 1991 (FPR).

In the county court the requirements of an originating application are;

> (*a*) application for either an occupation order or a non-molestation order is made on Form FL401 (whether or not the application is free-standing or made within existing family proceedings).
>
> (*b*) application to vary, extend or discharge an occupation order or non-molestation order is made on Form FL403. It is necessary to establish within those forms that the Applicant is "associated" with the Respondent.
>
> (*c*) application by a child under the age of 16 years must be made on Form FL401 and must be treated in the first instance as an application for leave to the High Court.
>
> (*d*) Evidence by way of a sworn statement must be filed in support of the application (FPR, r.3.8(4)).
>
> (*e*) Notice of legal services commission certificate
>
> (*f*) Notice of acting
>
> (*g*) Fee of £40
>
> (*h*) If an applicant wishes to omit his/her address from the form, he/she must complete Form C8 and file this with the application.

Applications will be heard in chambers in the county court unless the court otherwise directs (FPR, r.3.9(1)). Although unlikely, it is therefore possible for the application to be heard in open court. The court has a duty to keep a record of the hearing. Representations can be made at the hearing by interested third parties such as mortgagees or landlords.

The court must consider certain factors when deciding to exercise its discretion to make an order. These factors are set out above. Similarly if an order is made certain requirements are made in relation to service of the order. These are set out below.

6   Service of proceedings

Service of the application

16.38   The application, together with the affidavit in support and notice of proceedings, must be served personally on the respondent not less than two days before the date of the hearing (FPR, 1991 r.3.8(6)). Where the applicant acts in person, service may be effected by the court.

The court has the power to order substituted service (FPR, r.3.8(8)) or may abridge time for service of the application (FPR, r.3.8(7)). Abridged service may form an alternative to an ex parte application.

Where an application is made for an occupation order under sections 33, 35 or 36 of the Act a copy of the application must be served by the applicant upon the mortgagee or landlord of the property which is the subject of the application. Service is effected by first class post. He must be informed of his right to make representations at the hearing (FPR r.3.8(11)).

The applicant should file proof of service in Form FL415 following service of the application.

Service of the Order

A copy of any order obtained ex parte should be served on the respondent personally together with a copy of the application, affidavit in support and notice of proceedings (FPR, r.3.9(2)).   **16.39**

Similarly an order obtained on notice should be served personally upon the respondent (FPR, r.3.9(4)).

If an occupation order has been granted, a copy of the order should be served by first class post upon any interested third party such as a mortgagee.

7   Enforcement of orders

Sections 47 and 48, and Sch.5 to the Act cover the provisions for enforcement of occupation orders and non-molestation orders made pursuant to the Act in the event of a breach.   **16.40**

Power of arrest

When the court makes a "relevant order", section 47 (2) provides that where it appears to the court that the respondent has used or threatened violence against the applicant or a relevant child, it shall attach a power of arrest to one or more provisions of the order unless the court is satisfied that in all the circumstances of the case the applicant or child will be adequately protected without such a power of arrest.   **16.41**

S.47 (1) defines a relevant order as an occupation order or a non-molestation order.

Where the court believes the respondent has used or threatened violence, it is under an obligation to attach a power of arrest unless it is satisfied the applicant is protected without such power being attached. It is not a matter of discretion; In *H v H (Occupation Order: Power of Arrest)* [2001] 1 F.L.R. 641 it was held that a power of arrest could be attached to an occupation order, even though the respondent was under 18 years and therefore not liable to detention. The mandatory nature of the court's obligation required the power of arrest to be attached.

The court must therefore first make a finding of fact when considering any application as to whether the respondent has used or threatened violence. It is reasonable to assume such violence or threat must have occurred within a reasonable timeframe prior to the application being made.   **16.42**

In deciding whether the applicant or child will be adequately protected without a power of arrest, the court must look to evidence provided by the parties to the proceedings. If the court cannot be satisfied upon the evidence produced, it must attach a power of arrest.

If the court attaches a power of arrest, it must state the period for which the power will exist. This may be for a shorter period than the duration of the order itself.

Ex parte orders and power of arrest

16.43   The mandatory obligation referred to above is to be used by the court when the application is made on notice to the respondent. Section 47 (3) provides that section 47 (2) does not apply to ex parte orders.

S.47 (3) provides a discretionary approach to powers of arrest when the application is made ex parte. The court may attach a power of arrest to specified provisions within an ex parte order if it appears to the court that;

  (*a*) the respondent has used or threatened violence against the applicant or a relevant child; and

  (*b*) there is a risk of significant harm to the applicant or child, attributable to conduct of respondent, if the power of arrest is not attached to those provisions immediately.

Even if both (*a*) and (*b*) above are found by the court, it is still a matter for the court's discretion as to whether or not to attach a power of arrest to the ex parte order.

The effect of a power of arrest

16.44   Where a power of arrest is attached to specific provisions of the order a Police constable may arrest without warrant a person whom he has reasonable cause for suspecting to be in breach of any such provision (s.47 (6)).

Form FL406 must be completed with details of those provisions of the order to which the power of arrest is attached and delivered to the officer for the area in which the applicant resides. This form is usually accompanied by a letter from the applicant's solicitor confirming the respondent has been served with a copy of the order.

When an order is varied or discharged the court, or the applicant, must deliver a copy of the new order to the officer in question.

16.45   If arrested for breach of the order, the respondent must be brought before the relevant judicial authority within 24 hours beginning at the time of his arrest. In calculating the time no account is taken of Christmas Day, Good Friday or Sunday (*Practice Direction: Family Law Act 1996 — Attendance of Arresting Officer*, 9 December 1999 [2000] 1 F.L.R. 270). The relevant judicial authority will depend upon the court which granted the order. If the order was made in the county court, the relevant judicial authority will be the judge or district judge in that or any county court. All courts have the power to remand the respondent on bail or in custody if the matter is not disposed of forthwith. Sch.5 of the Act (Powers of the High Court and county court to remand) sets out in detail the provisions the court has in relation to remand.

When the respondent is brought before the court, the attendance of the arresting officer is not necessary unless the arrest itself is in issue. A written statement of the circumstances of the arrest should be sufficient. If, however, the arresting officer is able to provide details of breach leading up to the arrest his attendance would be beneficial.

The court will conduct a full hearing in open court to determine whether the facts, and the circumstances which led to arrest, amount to disobedience of the order. Such hearing must take place within 14 days of the arrest and the respondent must be given at least two clear days notice of the hearing. Where the respondent is remanded on bail or in custody, the hearing should take place within 8 clear days of the arrest.

Warrant for arrest

On those occasions when it is not appropriate to attach a power of arrest, it is **16.46** possible for the court to issue a warrant for arrest upon application. S.47 (8) of the Act provides, where a court has made a relevant order but has not attached a power of arrest to any provisions or has attached that power only to certain provisions, that if at any time the applicant considers the respondent has failed to comply with the order he/she may apply to the relevant judicial authority for the issue of a warrant for the arrest of the respondent.

Application for a warrant for arrest is made on Form FL407 and the warrant is issued in Form FL408. The procedure is set out in section 47 (9). The application must be substantiated on oath and the court must have reasonable grounds for believing that the respondent has failed to comply with the order. The warrant will be executed by the bailiffs attached to the county court.

The provisions upon arrest are set out within Sch.5 to the Act and are the same as those for the exercise of the power of arrest.

Committal

In the event of a person being arrested the court will need to determine **16.47** whether or not he has breached the terms of the order (or undertaking); this is a matter of evidence. The court will, if it finds there has been a breach, need to consider the penalty to punish such breach; this is a matter of discretion.

The President's Practice Direction (Family Law Act 1996, Pt IV), 17 December 1997 [1998] 1 F.L.R. 496 contains various procedural matters.

A further practice direction, *Practice Direction: Family Division: Committal Applications and Proceedings in which a Committal Order may be made* March 16, 2001, has been made concerning the application of the CPR committal procedure to family proceedings subject to the Family Proceedings Rules 1991 with appropriate modifications.

FPR, r.3.9A (6) provides that a court can adjourn consideration of the penalty **16.48** and such consideration may be restored if certain conditions imposed by the court are not met. This provides a means to impose a suspended sentence. In *Griffin v Griffin* [2000] 2 F.L.R. 44 CA, the county court judge made an order committing the respondent to prison for 2 months but suspended this for so long as he complied with the terms of a non-molestation and occupation orders. The non-molestation and occupation orders were expressed to last "until further order". The respondent breached the orders and the suspended order was activated, the respondent being committed to prison for the original 2 months plus a further 4 months for the breaches. The respondent appealed on the basis that an order suspended on terms that he complied with other orders of indefinite duration was invalid. The appeal was dismissed. The order was held to be valid even though it effectively suspended the imprisonment indefinitely.

A range of penalties are possible including no order, adjournment, fines, sequestration of assets, and a mental health order. Sentencing to a term of imprisonment is also available.

The Court of Appeal set out some guidelines for imprisonment on breach in *Hale v Tanner* (2000) 2 F.L.R. 879, CA. There is no automatic consequence that imprisonment should follow a breach, nor was there any principle that imprisonment was not an available penalty on the first breach. The maximum period of committal to prison is 2 years. In this case the court indicated that consideration should be given to any concurrent proceedings, whether the breach had occurred in the context of mitigating or aggravating circumstances and whether any child was involved. The Court of Appeal held that the seriousness of the contempt had to be judged not only for its intrinsic gravity but also in the light of the court's objective both to mark its disapproval of the disobedience of the order and to secure compliance in the future.

Whilst the Act does not specifically state that the provision for arrest and remand is intended to replace the previous procedure for applications for committal for breach it is felt that there will be little, if any, need for the previous procedure.

8   Undertakings

16.49   Section 46 (1) of the Act provides that in any case where the court has power to make an occupation order or a non-molestation order, the court may accept an undertaking from any party to the proceedings. An undertaking is a promise which the respondent makes to the court to do, or not to do, something.

When may an undertaking be appropriate?

16.50   No power of arrest may be attached to an undertaking given pursuant to s.45 (1) of the Act. For this reason, a court may not accept an undertaking where a power of arrest would be attached to the order. S.47 (as above) imposes upon the court an obligation to attach a power of arrest in all cases where it appears to the court that the respondent has used or threatened violence against the applicant or a relevant child unless it is satisfied that in all the circumstances of the case the applicant or child will be adequately protected without one.

If the parties agree that there should be an undertaking this should be given prior to the court hearing evidence and making any finding of fact as to the level of violence. Otherwise the court, if it makes a finding that there has been use or threat of violence, has no choice than to attach a power of arrest to an order.

It frequently happens that an application for an order is compromised at the full hearing by the respondent to the application giving an undertaking to the court. The advantage to the respondent is that he will feel that he has made no admissions as to the truth of the allegations made in the application. The advantage to the applicant is that the trauma and uncertainty that a full hearing is likely to cause will be avoided. Costs of both parties can be limited by proceeding in this way. Undertakings can assist to lessen the conflict between the parties.

Content of an undertaking

16.51   The undertaking ought to state its duration and, if it requires the respondent to take some action, it should be clear as to the time by which the action should be taken. If the action is to be carried out at a particular place, the place should also be stated.

An undertaking should not be in terms too wide to be practicable and so careful thought should be given to drafting the wording of the undertaking.

When an undertaking is given, the judge should explain the content of the undertaking and possible consequences of a breach to the respondent. In the county court, a general form of undertaking has been devised (Form N117). The respondent should sign the undertaking in the presence of the judge.

Service can be effected by a sealed photocopy being handed to the respondent before he leaves the court building. Where delivery cannot be effected in this way the court must deliver a copy to the party for whose benefit the undertaking is given for that person to serve personally upon the respondent as soon as practicable.

Although this section assumes the undertaking has been given by the respondent, there is no reason why in theory the court could not accept any undertaking from the applicant if appropriate.

Enforcement of an Undertaking

Although it is not essential for an undertaking to be recorded in an order, it is **16.52** desirable that it be so recorded, and that the order draws attention to the consequences of any breach of the undertaking.

Section 46 (4) provides for an undertaking to be enforced as if it were an order of the court. It seems that although it is open to an applicant to apply for a warrant for arrest under s.47 (8) it is more usual for a notice to show cause to be issued.

9   Children Act 1989

In exceptional circumstances, a residence order can be granted ex parte with **16.53** an attached injunctive direction that the child be returned forthwith to the parent given residence (*Re B* [1992] 2 F.L.R. 1). The direction is attached under the Children Act 1989, s.11(7).

A prohibited steps order under section 8 of the Children Act 1989 can be issued to prevent someone taking a step which could be taken by a parent in meeting his parental responsibility for a child which is not in the child's best interest.

A prohibited steps order should not be used to obtain a type of non-molestation order (*M v M* [1994] Fam Law 440); neither should an application for a specific issue order be used as a backdoor means of achieving an occupation order (*Pearson v Franklin* [1994] 1 F.L.R. 246).

Any judge, including any district judge, can exercise the power conferred by the Children Act 1989, s.10(1)(*b*), to make an order under the Children Act 1989, s.8, even though no specific application has been made. The court may therefore be prepared to make a s.8 order upon an application for a non-molestation order. A temporary s.8 order can be made by a district judge *(Family Proceedings (Allocation to Judiciary) Directions 1993)*.

10   Protection from Harassment Act 1997

The Protection from Harassment Act 1997 came fully into force in September **16.54** 1998.

Pt IV of the Family Law Act 1996 entitles those associated persons to make application for the available orders. Any relationships which do not come within the definition of associated persons under section 62 (3) of the Family Law Act 1996 will have to rely upon the Protection from Harassment Act 1997. Of course, the 1997 Act is still open to associated persons for the purposes of the FLA 1996 who may wish to pursue remedies under this Act, particularly given the criminal and tortuous remedies available.

There is therefore a degree of overlap between this Act and Pt IV of the Family Law Act 1996. This Chapter would not be complete without reference to the 1997 Act. However, it is not intended to provide more than a broad outline in order to make the practitioner aware of available remedies in addition to the Family Law Act 1996.

Criminal and civil remedies

16.55   Section 1 of the 1997 Act provides that a person must not pursue a course of conduct which amounts to harassment of another, and which he knows or ought to know amounts to harassment of that other.

The test used as to whether or not a person ought to know his/her conduct amounted to harassment of a reasonable person is that of *R v Colohan* [2001] 2 F.L.R. 757. In that case the defendant was suffering from schizophrenia and appealed his conviction under the Act saying his conduct was outside the 1997 Act. The Court of Appeal confirmed that the objective test was what a reasonable person would think, and no account had to be taken of the defendants' standards or characteristics.

The 1997 Act creates two criminal offences. Section 2 provides for the summary offence of criminal harassment whilst s.4 provides for aggravated indictable offence involving the fear of violence. The section 2 offence is committed if a person pursues a course of conduct in breach of section 1. Somewhat graver, the section 4 offence is committed if a person's course of conduct causes another to fear, on at least two occasions, that violence will be used against him, and he knows or ought to know that his conduct will cause the other fear on each of those occasions.

The civil remedy of the statutory tort of harassment is created by section 3 of the 1997 Act. This remedy relates to sections 1 and 2 of the Act. Breach of an injunction order made under this section is a criminal offence and the criminal courts are given the power to deal with the breach. Furthermore, a breach of the civil remedy will give rise to an action for damages.

The 1997 Act provides remedies where there has been a course of conduct which, according to an objective test, amounts to harassment (section 1). A course of conduct is defined under section 7 (3) as "conduct on at least two occasions" (*R v Hills* [2001]1 F.L.R. 580, CA: *Kevin Malcolm Pratt v DPP* TLR 22/8/2001). Here, two assaults six months apart punctuated by a period of reconciliation was not sufficient to amount to a course of conduct.

Conduct likely to amount to harassment is referred to at s.7(2) as including that which is alarming or likely to cause distress. No specific definition of harassment is provided by the 1997 Act.

Enforcement

16.56   Enforcement is covered by section 3 of the 1997 Act. There is no provision for a power of arrest to be attached. Enforcement is similar to the provisions of the Family Law Act 1997 for issue of a warrant for arrest.

The criminal penalties which can be invoked may again persuade an applicant to apply under the 1997 Act rather than the Family Law Act 1996. On an indictable offence, (section 4), a penalty of up to five years' imprisonment can be imposed, or a fine, or both.

On summary conviction, a person in breach of an order can be imprisoned for up to six months, or fined, or both.

A person cannot be found guilty of both a contempt of court and a criminal offence – it must be one or the other.

11   Court's inherent jurisdiction

The High Court by virtue of the Supreme Court Act 1981, s.37, and the **16.57** County Court by virtue of the County Courts Act 1984, s.38, has jurisdiction to grant injunctive relief in support of legal and equitable rights.

For an example of where the powers exercisable by the court under such jurisdiction extended to the grant of injunctions against third parties see *C v K (INHERENT POWERS: EXCLUSION ORDER)* [1996] 2 F.L.R. 506.

12   Conclusion

There are various reasons why consideration should be given to the provisions **16.58** of both the Family Law Act 1996 and the Protection from Harassment Act 1997 before deciding which application should be made.

Clearly, if a person can allow the police to take action against a potential respondent for a criminal offence it may save the anguish of bringing an application under the Family Law Act 1996. The remedies set out in brief under the 1997 Act can clearly be quite different from those available under the 1996 Act.

The High court, county court and magistrates' court all have jurisdiction to consider applications under both Acts. Whilst it has been suggested there is no reason why a combined application should not be made at the same time, it should be noted that the Family Proceedings Rules 1991 apply to the Family Law Act whereas the Civil Procedure Rules 1998 apply to The Protection from Harassment Act 1997.

Chapter 17

Costs and Public Funding

1 The Community Legal Service (CLS)

17.01 The passing of the Access to Justice Act 1999 heralded a fundamental change to the system of public funding originally set up as the Legal Aid Scheme under the Legal Aid Act 1998. The Act provides for a transitional phase which is scheduled to last until 2003 and during which the new LSC scheme will systematically replace former legal aid. In particular, the scope of services for which public funding may be granted was very considerably reduced by the AJA 1999 (see Sch.2 to the Act) and, through the Funding Code which was published pursuant to sections 8 and 9 of the AJA 1999, the criteria for CLS Funding and the administrative procedures relating to it revised legal services to be available under the CLS were established. On the April 1, 2000, the Legal Services Commission (LSC) formally replaced the Legal Aid Board.

The various levels of legal services under the Funding Code are as follows:

Legal Help

Help at Court

Approved Family Help:

(a) General Family Help; or
(b) Help with Mediation

Legal Representation

Support Funding:

(a) Investigative Support; or
(b) Litigation Support

Family Mediation

17.02 Along with these changes, the basis of authority to provide public funding legal assistance of the various sorts defined above were made subject to General Civil Contracts. In general terms, these contracts covers the exclusive provision of Legal Help, Help at Court and Approved Family Help. It also includes some forms of Legal Representation, which corresponds broadly to the old Civil Legal Aid and ABWOR ("Assistance by way of representation") and as such the contract covers family proceedings in a magistrates court. All other forms of Legal Representation, however, are subject to individual applications to be made by those acting for the publicly-funded client and these have to be made to the Commission as indeed was the case with Civil Legal Aid prior to the changes. Under the General Civil Contract, payment is made in respect of Controlled Work (*i.e.* Legal Help, Help at Court and Controlled Legal Representation) by means of a regular payment on account on a monthly basis which is subject to a ceiling over the term of the contract schedule. All other licensed work is assessed and paid for on a case by case basis as was the case with Assessment of Costs under the old Civil Legal Aid Certificates. Controlled Work and Licensed Work are together generally referred to as "Contract Work" and since April 2001 all such CLS Funded Legal Services are delivered exclusively through contracted suppliers.

2 The Franchise Scheme

Franchising came into operation on the August 1, 1994 and originally was the means by which the then Legal Aid Board sought to improve the quality of services provided by solicitors to the public. Under the current reformed CLS system, only franchised firms are able to undertake legal aid work in future. During the transitional stage some work may be undertaken by non-franchised firms; this is not dealt with in details here nor are the provisions of the old system of legal aid and reference should be made to the Legal Aid Handbook for further guidance on these matters. **17.03**

3 The Regulations

The details of the new scheme may be found in the following regulations: **17.04**

> Community Legal Service (Financial) Regulations 2000
>
> Community Legal Service (Costs Protection) Regulations 2000
>
> Community Legal Service (Costs) Regulations 2000
>
> Community Legal Service (Funding) Order 2000

As already mentioned, a significant publication is the "Funding Code" and much useful material will be found in the "Legal Services Commission Manual" a four volume loose-leaf work, which is published by the LSC and which is updated on a frequent basis. This in effect replaces the old Legal Aid Handbook.

4 The Scope of Public Funding

Over the years, what commenced as a relatively simple and straightforward Public Funding Scheme (Legal Aid) has seen modifications, additions, amendments and sub-divisions to such an extent that the whole system long before the introduction of the LSC had become something of a complex mass. Unfortunately, the new system appears to do little to unravel the situation even though the number of different legal services available for public funding has been severely reduced. **17.05**

Legal Help

17.06 The first level of service prescribed under the new system is intended to cover those services set out in the Access to Justice Act 1999, s.4 (2) with the exception of:

(*a*) The provision of general information about the law and the availability of legal services.

(*b*) Issuing or conducting court proceedings.

(*c*) Advocacy.

(*d*) Mediation or Arbitration. Legal Help is always provided as "Controlled Work" under contracts.

Help at Court

17.07 This authorises help and advocacy for a client in relation to a particular hearing. It is not necessary for the solicitor to have been formally acting as the client's legal representative in the proceedings. Once again, this is always provided as Controlled Work under contracts.

Legal Representation

17.08 This grants legal representation for a party to proceedings or for a party who is contemplating taking proceedings including:

(*a*) Litigation Services.

(*b*) Advocacy Services.

(*c*) All such help as is usually given by a person providing representation in proceedings, including steps preliminary or incidental to those proceedings.

(*d*) All such help as is usually given by such a person in arriving at or giving effect to a compromise to avoid or bring to an end any proceedings.

It does not include the provision of mediation or arbitration.

17.09 In the case of family proceedings, firms can only carry out work if they have a franchise in the relevant category. Legal Representation may be sub-divided into two sections:

1. Investigative Help which does not apply in family proceedings (see para.17.13 and 17.18) which means that the representation is limited to investigation of the strength of a proposed claim, but does include the issue and conduct of the proceedings only so far as necessary to obtain disclosure of relevant information or to protect the client's position in relation to any urgent hearing or time limit for the issue of proceedings;

2. Full representation means a grant of Legal Representation other than Investigative Help.

Legal Representation itself is also described as "Controlled" or "Authorised". Licensed Work under the General Civil Contract covers certificated representation in relation to Court proceedings in family and immigration matters from the January 1, 2000. An application to the CLS is required for a Funding Certificate in such cases but in the case of "Authorised Legal Representation", which involves representation in family proceedings in a Magistrates Court, firms authorised may grant cover themselves under their contract and no formal application to the CLS is required for each individual matter.

Support Funding

This authorises the same service as Legal Representation, but it is limited to partial funding of proceedings which are otherwise being pursued privately under or with a view to a Conditional Fee Agreement (in family proceedings CFAs cannot be used — see the Access to Justice Act, s.58A (1) (*b*)).   **17.10**

Investigative Support means support funding limited to investigation of the strength of a proposed claim with a view to a Conditional Fee Agreement.

Litigation Support means a grant of Support Funding other than Investigative Support and it covers the partial funding of high cost litigation proceeding under a Conditional Fee Agreement. Support Funding in high costs cases may be provided under a multi-party action or a high cost case contract at the discretion of the Commission's Special Cases Unit. Otherwise it is funded as Licensed Work under certificates issued by the LSC.

Approved Family Help

The grant of this authorises help in relation to a family dispute including assistance in resolving that dispute through negotiation or otherwise. This includes the services covered by Legal Help (see above) as well as issuing proceedings and representation in proceedings where necessary to obtain disclosure information from another party or to obtain a Consent Order following settlement of part or all of the dispute and related conveyancing work.   **17.11**

"Help with Mediation" means Approved Family Help limited to advice to a client in support of family mediation and help in drawing up any agreement reached in mediation and, where appropriate, help in confirming such an agreement in a Court Order and related coneyancing work.

"General Family Help" means a grant of Approved Family Help other than help with mediation.

Family Mediation

This is a level of service the grant of which authorises mediation of a family dispute including assessing whether mediation appears suitable to the dispute and to the parties and all the circumstances.   **17.12**

Particular reference is made to the provision of family services for which initial Legal Help is distinguished from "Approved Family Help". Approved Family Help itself is sub-divided into "Help with Mediation" and "General Family Help". Approved Family Help generally is remunerated at the higher prescribed rates (as opposed to the rates for "Legal Help") although Help with Mediation is at civil contract rates rather than the full prescribed family rates as for legal representation.

Help with Mediation is limited to advice to a client in support of Family

Mediation including help in drawing up any agreement reached as a result of mediation and in certain circumstances where help in confirming such an agreement in a Court Order is needed.

17.13   General Family Help relates to all other Approved Family Help. This includes issuing proceedings and initial representation to obtain disclosure from another party to the proceedings or for the obtaining of a consent order following settlement of the dispute. It can also cover interim applications. It is not a full authority as with a certificate for legal representation but it is similar and is remunerated at the same rates as for legal representation but it has specific limitations as set out above. For family cases, legal representation may only take the form of full representation and "Investigative Help" is not available. Instead the category "General Family Help" is designed to cover disclosure, initial steps in Ancillary Relief Proceedings and negotiations between the parties. It is possible therefore for an application for "Legal Representation in Family Proceedings" to result in the limited grant of a certificate covering only General Family Help rather than full representation. If it becomes necessary to issue an application for a full certificate because proceedings must be continued and cover is not provided by the level of service represented by "General Family Help", an application to amend the certificate to cover full representation may be made. In this connection it should be noted that in family cases help with mediation may not be provided under the same certificate as either General Family Help of Legal Representation. The reason for this is that the costs associated with Help with Mediation have to be recorded separately since they do not attract the statutory charge. It is still possible to obtain a certificate for Approved Family Help which includes the provision of conveyancing services (generally excluded from the CLS system) in order to give effect to a court order or to an agreement reached in family proceedings. Specific application must be made for this cover however.

The above is intended to be an introduction to the modern day complex world of public funding for family proceedings. However the Funding Code, which is volume three in the Legal Services Commission Manual, has a complete section devoted to Family Proceedings and Public Funding. A summary of its provisions is set out below but for a more detailed guidance reference should be made to the LSC Manual itself.

5   Definition of Family Proceedings and Scope of Family Work

17.14   The scope of cover for family proceedings is set out in section 11 of the Funding Code. It applies to applications for Approved Family Help, Family Mediation or Legal Representation in Family Proceedings. The categories and the criteria relating to each are set out below:

Criteria for Help with Mediation

17.15   This may only be granted if the client is participating in family mediation or has reached an agreement or settlement. Legal Help may be more appropriate in which case help with mediation could be refused. Furthermore Help with Mediation may only be provided where there is sufficient benefit to the client to justify work or further work being carried out.

Criteria for General Family Help

General Family Help will be refused if the cases must first be referred to a **17.16**
Mediator for determination as to whether mediation is suitable. It may be
refused if mediation, supported as necessary by help with mediation, is a more
appropriate avenue to follow. General Family Help may also be refused if it is
more appropriate for the client to be assisted by way of Legal Help and it may
only be provided where there is sufficient benefit to the client having regard to
all the circumstances including the personal circumstances of the client to
justify work or further work being carried out.

Criteria for Family Mediation

An assessment of whether mediation is suitable to the dispute and to the **17.17**
parties and to all the circumstances may only be provided if the standard criteria contained in section 4 of Pt A of the Funding Code are satisfied. This is
known as "Intake Assessment". Mediation beyond the Intake Assessment can
only be provided where the Mediator is satisfied that mediation is suitable to
the dispute and the parties and all the circumstances.

Criteria for Full Representation

(a) Investigative Help.   **17.18**
   This is not available in family proceedings.
(b) Legal Representation in Family Proceedings
   This must take the form only of full representation and the criteria contained in the General Funding Code relating to Conditional Fee Agreements
do not apply to family proceedings nor does the criterion under 5.4.6 of the
Code relating to small claims.

Criteria for Special Children Act Proceedings

Providing the criteria in section 4 of the Funding Code is satisfied Legal **17.19**
Representation for these proceedings will be granted. The standard criteria in
s.5.4 of the General Funding Code do not apply to these proceedings. In addition where Legal Representation had been granted in Special Children Act
Proceedings (see para.12.27), it may also be granted to the same person in
related proceedings which are being heard together with the Special Children
Act Proceedings.

Public Law Children Cases

The standard criteria for Legal Representation in section 5.4 of the General **17.20**
Funding Code do not apply in other public law children cases except for the
following:

> 5.42 relating to refusal on the ground of the availability of alternative
> sources of funding and 5.4.5 relating to refusal on the ground that repre-
> sentation is not necessary.

Where Legal Representation is sought on behalf of a client who is making
or supporting an Application or Appeal, Legal Representation will be
refused if the prospects of the application or appeal being successful are

poor. It may also be refused if it appears unreasonable for funding to be granted having regard to the importance of the case to the client and all other circumstances.

Domestic Violence Cases

17.21 These criteria apply to proceedings seeking an injunction, committal order or other orders for the protection of a person from harm, other than public law children proceedings. Legal Representation will be refused if the prospects of obtaining the order sought in the proceedings are poor and it will also be refused unless the likely benefits to be gained from the proceedings for the client justify the likely costs.

Private Law Children Cases

17.22 These criteria apply to proceedings concerning residents, contact and other private law issues concerning children other than the issues of financial provision. Legal Representation will be refused if in accordance with code procedures there must first be a referral to a mediator for determination as to whether mediation is suitable to the dispute. If mediation is more appropriate to the case than Legal Representation, the latter may be refused. Legal Representation may also be refused unless reasonable attempts have been made to resolve the dispute without recourse to proceedings. It will also be refused if prospects of success are poor and if the likely benefits to be gained from the proceedings for the client do not justify the likely costs. In this context, the test is whether a reasonable private paying client would be prepared to take or defend the proceedings in all the circumstances.

Financial Provision and Other Proceedings

17.23 These apply to ancillary relief and other family proceedings relating to financial provision and to all other family proceedings which are not covered above. Once again Legal Representation will be refused if the case must first be referred to a Mediator to determine whether mediation is suitable to the dispute. Legal Representation may then be refused if mediation appears to be more appropriate to the case. Similarly Legal Representation may be refused unless reasonable attempts have been made to resolve the dispute without recourse to proceedings. Prospects of success are important in determination of Legal Representation in financial matters. It will be refused if prospects of success are either borderline or unclear except where the case has overwhelming importance to the client or a significant wider public interest or where the prospects of success are poor. It will also be refused unless the likely benefits to be gained from the proceedings justify the likely costs so that a reasonable private paying client would be prepared to take or defend the proceedings in all the circumstances.

Child Abduction Cases

17.24 Legal Representation must be granted to a person whose application under the Hague Convention or European Convention has been submitted to the Central Authority in England and Wales pursuant to section 3 (2) or section 14 (2) of the Child Abduction and Custody Act 1985.

Registration of Foreign Orders and Judgments

This category applies to someone who appeals to a magistrates court against **17.25** the registration of or the refusal to register a maintenance order made in a Hague Convention Country or who applies for the registration of a Judgement under the Civil Jurisdiction and Judgments Act 1982, s.4 or satisfies the following criterion:

> Legal Representation shall be granted if the standard criteria in Section 4 of the Funding Code are satisfied and if the client benefited from complete or partial legal aid or other public funding or exemption from costs or expenses in the country in which the Maintenance Order was made or the Judgment was given.

6 Definitions

"Family Proceedings"

This is defined in section 2.2 of the Funding Code and means proceedings which **17.26** arise out of family relationships, including proceedings in which the welfare of children is determined other than Judicial Review Proceedings. Family proceedings also includes all proceedings under any one or more of the following:

(*a*) the Matrimonial Causes Act 1973;

(*b*) the Inheritance (Provision for Family and Dependants) Act 1975;

(*c*) the Adoption Act 1976;

(*d*) the Domestic Proceedings and Magistrates' Courts Act 1978;

(*e*) Pt III of the Matrimonial in Family Proceedings Act 1984;

(*f*) Pts I, II & IV of the Children Act 1989;

(*g*) Pt IV of the Family Law Act 1996;

(*h*) The inherent jurisdiction of the High Court in relation to children.

Only those members of the Family Franchise Panel, *i.e.* those authorised litigators who from time to time are authorised under a contract with the LSC to provide representation and assistance by way of representation in relation to family proceedings can act with the benefit of public funding.

"Special Children Act Proceedings" means proceedings under the Children **17.27** Act 1989, other than appeal proceedings, where Legal Representation is applied for on behalf of:

(*a*) A child in respect of whom an application is made for an order under

    (i) Section 31 (Care or Supervision Order)
    (ii) Section 43 (A Child Assessment Order)
    (iii) Section 44 (An Emergency Protection Order) and
    (iv) Section 45 (Extension or Discharge of an Emergency Protection Order).

(*b*) Any parent of such a child or person with parental responsibility for the child within the meaning of the 1989 Act.

(c) A child who is brought before a Court under section 25 (Use of Accommodation for Restricting Liberty) who is not legally represented before the Court but who wishes to be so represented.

17.28   *"Other Public Law Children Cases"* means Public Law Proceedings concerning the welfare of children other than Special Children Act Proceedings or related proceedings. These include:

(1) Appeals (whether interim or final) from orders made in Special Children Act Proceedings

(2) Other proceedings under Pt IV or V of the 1989 Act

(3) Adoption Proceedings, including freeing for adoption and

(4) Proceedings under the inherent jurisdiction of the High Court in relation to Children.

7   Franchise Category Definitions

17.29   The definitions given below explain what falls into this category and it applies to all levels of service in relation to matters falling within that definition. Originally the franchise category relating to Family Proceedings was previously known as Family/Matrimonial but the title has now been changed to "Family". It is defined as follows:

1. Legal Help on matters and all proceedings which arise out of family relationships, including proceedings in which the welfare of children is determined.

2. Also included are Legal Help on matters and all proceedings under any one or more of the following:
   - (a) the Matrimonial Causes Act 1973;
   - (b) the Inheritance (Provision for Family Dependants) Act 1975;
   - (c) the Adoption Act 1976;
   - (d) the Domestic Proceedings and Magistrates' Courts Act 1978;
   - (e) Part III of the Matrimonial and Family Proceedings Act 1984;
   - (f) Parts I to V of the Children Act 1989;
   - (g) Part IV of the Family Law Act 1996;
   - (h) the inherent jurisdiction of the High Court in relation to children.

3. For the avoidance of doubt. the following matters/proceedings are also included within the franchise category:
   - (a) Legal Help in making a will where the client is the parent or guardian of a disabled person who wishes to provide for that person in a will, or of a minor living with a client but not with the other parent, and the client wishes to appoint a guardian for the minor in a will;
   - (b) Proceedings to enforce any order made within family proceedings;
   - (c) Proceedings under the Child Support Act 1991 s.20 or s.27;

(*d*) Proceedings under the Family Law Act 1986;
(*e*) Proceedings under the Child Abduction and Custody Act 1985 (but note that devolved powers do not extend to take such proceedings);
(*f*) Proceedings under the Protection from Harassment Act 1997 or in assault and trespass where the proceedings are family proceedings and only an injunction and either no or only nominal damages are sought or where an application is made to vary or discharge an order made under section 5, and the proceedings are family proceedings;
(*g*) Proceedings for an order under the Social Security Administration Act 1992, s.106, or under the National Assistance Act 1948, s.43;
(*h*) Applications to enforce orders made in family/matrimonial proceedings under the Civil Jurisdiction and Judgments Act 1983 and 1991;
(*i*) Proceedings under the Trusts of Land and Appointment of Trustees Act 1996, s.14 where the proceedings are family proceedings;
(*j*) Proceedings for or in relation to an affiliation order within the meaning of the Affiliation Proceedings Act 1957;
(*k*) Proceedings under the Guardianship of Minors Act 1971 and 1973;
(*l*) Proceedings under the Maintenance Orders Acts 1950 and 1958;
(*m*) Proceedings under Pt I of the Maintenance Orders (Reciprocal Enforcement) Act 1972 relating to a maintenance order made outside the United Kingdom;
(*n*) Proceedings under s.30 of the Human Fertilisation and Embryology Act 1990;
(*o*) Proceedings under the Social Security Act 1986, s.24;
(*p*) Proceedings under the National Assistance Act 1948 s.47;
(*q*) Proceedings under the Crime and Disorder Act 1998 for:
  (i) a Child Safety Order or for a Parenting Order made in proceedings for a Child Safety Order; or
  (ii) an Anti-Social Behaviour Order or Sex Offender Order made in relation to a child, and any associated Parenting Order; or
  (iii) a Parenting Order made on the conviction of a child but only where the parent cannot reasonably be represented by the child's solicitor.
(*r*) Applications to the court to change the name of a child

8 Prospects of Success

It is of great significance to establish whether a case has good or poor prospects **17.30** since the commission has no power to fund a case which has poor prospects of success even though it may be desirable in many other respects that funding should be granted. The Funding Code has criteria under which prospects of success can be judged. In section 2.3 of the Code prospects of success is defined as the likelihood of the client of obtaining a successful outcome in the proceedings assuming the case were determined at Trial or other final hearing.

"Guidance may give examples of what may constitute a successful outcome for different types of proceeding". The Section continues by expressing different degrees of strength of prospects:

Very good   80% or more

Good   60% to 80%

Moderate   50% to 60%

Borderline not **POOR** but because there are difficult disputes of fact law or expert evidence, it is not possible to say that prospects for success are better than 50%

Poor   Clearly less than 50% so that the claim is likely to fail

Unclear   The case cannot be put into any of the categories set out above because further investigation is needed

The concept of prospects of success involves a consideration of the likelihood of succeeding at a first instance trial rather than of achieving a settlement and it is intended to be an objective test.

As indicated above, in addition to the prospects of success test, there are also cost benefit tests which requires an objective approach towards assessing cost benefits of any particular set of proceedings. In several of the above sets of criteria it will be noticed that the private client test is the appropriate costs benefit test and where this applies the benefits to be gained from the proceedings must justify the likely costs "such that a reasonable private paying client would be prepared to litigate, having regard to the prospects of success and all other circumstances". This is the usual test for family cases unless there is a public interest element where the public interest cost benefit test would then apply. For further information on this test, please see section 5 of the Funding Code Guidance.

9   Applications for Community Service Funding

17.31   There are specific prescribed forms for each type of CLS Funding and it is important that the correct form is adopted when making the application. If an application for a particular matter is made on the incorrect form, the LSC will simply return the application. For family proceedings, the usual forms are as follows:

CLS APP3   This is used for general family help and legal representation (including authorised representation) in family proceedings.

CLS APP4   This is used in connection with help with family mediation.

CLS APP5   This application form is for legal representation in Special Children Act proceedings.

There is a fax emergency application which is CLS APP6 which under 3c-123 of the Funding Code will only be accepted if the urgency of the situation is such that a decision is required before a postal application could reasonably be made and processed. Generally a fax application will only be justified when work must be undertaken within a working day of the application.

10   Costs of Funded Clients

Under the Legal Aid Act 1988

Where a client had advice and assistance prior to January 1, 2000, the costs **17.32** claim is subject to the Legal Aid Act 1988, and regs 4, 29 to 31 and Sch.6 to the Legal Advice and Assistance Regulation 1989. Guidance on the scope of this scheme and how it operates and remuneration appears under Notes for Guidance in the Legal Aid Handbook for 1998/1999.

Provision of advice and assistance between January 1, 2000 and March 31, 2000 under Pt III of the Legal Aid Act 1988 falls under the General Civil Contract and the contract specification and guidance are both set out in the contract specification in volume 2 of the Legal Services Commission Manual.

Under the Access to Justice Act 1999

The usual case where services are provided under the General Civil Contract **17.33** between the Commission and a supplier will usually involve the definition of the remuneration rate payable for the level of service provided under the contract itself.

Where legal representation is not provided under contract the rate is determined by the type of work which has been undertaken. Family work is generally remunerated under the Legal Aid in Family Proceedings (Remuneration) Regulations 1991 as amended and all non-family work is generally remunerated under the Legal Aid in Civil Proceedings (Remuneration) Regulations 1994 as amended.

Rates of remuneration are shown in Appendix 1.

Fees of counsel are governed by the Community Legal Service (Funding) **17.34** (Counsel in Family Proceedings) Order 2001 which came into force on May 1, 2001. It applies to all counsel's fees in respect of all family proceedings in the High Court, county courts and magistrates courts. It does not apply to proceedings where the length of the main hearing exceeds 10 days nor does it apply to appeals to the Divisional Court of the High Court, the Court of Appeal or the House of Lords.

As a result of these regulations graduated fees for counsel shall be the base fee or the hearing unit fee as appropriate in respect of the function for which the fee is claimed and which is specified in the schedules to the order as applicable to the category of proceedings and the Counsel instructed. This may be supplemented by a settlement supplement or additional payment, a special issue payment or a court bundle payment. The total graduated fee as prescribed shall be increased by 33 per cent in respect of all work carried out while the proceedings are in the High Court.

The regulations are relatively complex but the basic fees are set out in Appendix 2 to this chapter.

11   Costs against the Legal Services Commission

Considerable changes to the regulations relating to costs ordered to be paid **17.35** by an LSC funded client or by the LSC itself were made as a result of the provisions of the Access to Justice Act 1999, s.11 (1). Regulations made under that Act include the Community Legal Service (Cost) Regulations 2000 and the Community Legal Service (Cost Protection) Regulations 2000. These set out a procedural code which govern orders for costs against LSC funded clients and against the LSC itself. Furthermore the normal rules governing the assessment of costs which are set out in CPR, Pts 44 to 48 do not apply to the assessment of costs under these regulations (see CPR, Pt 44.17). The procedure to follow in such cases is set out in CPD, ss.21 to 23. Any costs order to be paid by an LSC funded client must not exceed the amount which is a reasonable one for him to pay having regard to all the circumstances including the financial resources of all the parties to the proceedings and their conduct in connection with the dispute to which the proceedings relate.

In *The Secretary of State for the Home Department*, ex parte *Gunn* [2001] 3 All E.R. 481; [2001] 2 Costs L.R. 263, significant guidance on the whole question of recovery of costs against the Legal Services Commission was given by the Court of Appeal and in particular the previous practice of Courts at first instance deciding whether an order should be made against the Legal Services Commission was disapproved. The Court which makes such an order should not be the Court that tried the substantive dispute but a costs judge or a district judge. In effect the Costs Regulations 2000 govern the procedure relating to these applications and the Costs Protection Regulations provide the substantive law.

17.36   The Court of Appeal in *Gunn* cited *re O (Costs: liability of Legal Aid Board)* [1997] 1 F.L.R. 465, where the Applicant for costs was a local authority and where it was held that it was not put at any disadvantage as compared with any other litigant in seeking an order against the Board simply because it was a local authority. The Court of Appeal in the Gunn case recommended that the practice laid down in *Re O* should be followed by costs judges when applications are made to them for costs against the Commission following a Court of Appeal Decision in favour of non funded parties even if they are government departments.

It is important to ensure where costs are being claimed against the LSC itself the application should be made within 3 months of the date of the order for costs and copies of the application must be served on the LSC funded client and/or the Regional Director of the LSC as the case may be. Late applications are unlikely to be accepted against the LSC itself unless the application for the funded services was made on or after December 3, 2001 and there is good reason for the delay in making the application – see CLS (Costs Protection) (Amendment no. 2) Regulations 2001.

The application for costs when made against an LSC funded client will result in the client being required to respond within 21 days of service of the application by making a statement of resources. This may or may not be accompanied by written points disputing items in the Bill of Costs. The Statement of Resources must set out details of financial resources and the expectations of the individual concerned and of his "Partner". However the resources of a partner are not treated as the client's resources if the partner has a contrary interest in the proceedings. The Statement of Resources is explained in para.22.1 of the Costs Practice Direction but basically covers a Statement of Income with capital and financial commitments during the previous year, estimated future financial resources and expectations and a declaration that the client has not deliberately foregone or deprived himself of any resources or expectations. These details are not exhaustive.

12   The Statutory Charge

The Legal Aid Act 1988, s.16 and the Civil Legal Aid (General) Regulations **17.37**
1989, Reg.85 and Pt X1 (Regs 87–99) apply to cases where a certificate was
granted for representation under that Act. Guidance as to the Statutory
Charge may be found in the Legal Aid Handbook 1998/99, *Notes for
Guidance*, Chaps 15 & 16, pp. 206 – 225 inclusive

Where the LSC funds a service for a client as part of the CLS, the unrecov-
ered cost of funding the service gives rise to a first charge on any property
recovered or preserved by the client in any proceedings, any compromise or
settlement of any dispute in relation to which the services were funded. This
is provided for by s.10 (7) Access to Justice Act 1999.

The charge does not arise in respect of the cost to the Commission of Legal
Help, except in relation to Family, Clinical Negligence or Personal Injury disputes or proceedings; Family Mediation; Help with Mediation; or Help at
Court other than in relation to Family, Clinical Negligence or Personal Injury
matters.

The Statutory Charge means a first charge on *property preserved or recov-* **17.38**
ered to meet the cost of a case to the Legal Aid Fund to the extent that such
cost is not met by the assisted person's contribution and any between parties
costs recovered. Therefore the charge will only arise if the assisted person has
been successful wholly or in part in the proceedings or has obtained an out of
Court settlement with the benefit of Public Funding.

Property has been preserved or recovered if it was in issue in the proceedings and it has been recovered by the Claimant if it was the subject of a successful claim and it has been preserved to the Respondent if the claim failed.
The charge will still arise even if the assisted person preserves only part of
what he regards as his, leaving him worse off than at the outset (*Till v Till*
[1974] 1 All E.R. 1094). What is at issue is a question of fact. It is to be determined from the Pleadings, Evidence Judgment and/or Order — see *Hanlon v
The Law Society* [1980] 2 All E.R. 199) at p.209 and also 2 W.L.R. 756. The
recovery of **possession** of property (even though the title to the property is not
in issue) can constitute recovery of property, just as the defeat of a claim by
another party to a possessory interest in the property may constitute preservation of the property (*Curling v The Law Society* [1985] 1 All E.R. 705). The
right to retain the exclusive use and occupation of a property for the period
dealing which a sale was deferred can be an interest under s.16 (6) of the Legal
Aid Act 1988 enabling the charge to attach to the property to which the interest related (*Parkes v Legal Aid Board* [1994] 2 F.L.R. 850). Also where the
dispute or proceedings result in a payment to someone other than the client
who has been funded, such as a dependent child or a creditor but the payment
is for the benefit of the client, the charge still arises on that payment (Access
to Justice Act 1999 s.10 (7)).

Exemptions from the Statutory Charge are shown in Reg.44 of the **17.39**
Community Legal Service (Financial) Regulations 2000. They are:

(*a*) Periodical payments of maintenance;

(*b*) where the charge is in favour of the supplier, the funded client's
home;

(*c*) their personal possessions and tools of trade unless exceptional in
number or quality;

(*d*) interim payments in Inheritance Act proceedings;

(*e*) the first £2,500 or, if the Certificate was granted on or after December 3, 2001, £3,000 of any property recovered or preserved in most family proceedings;

(*f*) 50 per cent of any redundancy reward;

(*g*) any Employment Appeal Tribunal awards;

(*h*) any property subject to a Statutory Prohibition against assignment.

The LSC announced in May 2002 that it had revised its view on the operation of the statutory charge on pension sharing and pension attachment orders. When a court determines an application for a pension sharing or attachment order any property recovered or preserved as a result of its determination is exempt from the statutory charge apart from any lump sum order payable under a pension attachment order.

17.40   The Statutory Charge also applies to the rights of a legally funded client under any compromise arrived at to avoid or bring to an end the proceedings for which that person has been funded. Proceedings do not have to have been commenced for the charge to apply. If a settlement is reached either before or during the proceedings, the charge will affect all property received by the assisted person whether or not it was claimed in the potential or actual proceedings (*Van Hoorn v The Law Society* [1985] Q.B. 106. Legal advisors have a duty to the Legal Aid Fund not to manipulate the destination of money or property so as to avoid the Statutory Charge. (*Manley v The Law Society* [1981] 1 All E.R. 401).

The charge applies to the whole proceedings and not merely that part of the proceedings in which a recovery was made (*Hanlon v The Law Society* [1980] 2 All E.R. 199). It also applies not only to the costs of the whole proceedings covered by the certificate but also to those covered by any amendments and it may be therefore desirable for a separate certificate rather than an amended certificate to be issued in certain circumstances where that is possible. If, however, one certificate covers more than one action, cause or matter under the Civil Legal Aid (General) Regulations 1989, reg.46 (3), the statutory charge will only apply to those proceedings in which the recovery is made. It is also important to recognise that for the purposes of calculating the amount of the charge, the cost of funding services does not include the costs of assessment proceedings under the CPR or taxation proceedings in the House of Lords nor are the costs of drawing up a bill part of the costs of assessment proceedings and so those costs will form part of the deficiency to the Fund and therefore part of the statutory charge.

17.41   The charge belongs to the Commission except where it arises in respect of the costs of Legal Help or Help at Court, in which case it belongs to the supplier. But if having received Legal Help or Help at Court there is then another level of service, and the client goes on to recover or preserve property, the charge will be in favour of the Commission (see reg.45 Community Legal Services (Financial) Regulations 2000).

The Statutory Charge will still apply where the property is recovered or preserved following the discharge or revocation of a legally funded client's certificate. (reg.49, Community Legal Service (Financial) Regulations 2000).

Any money recovered in the dispute or proceedings including damages costs and interest must be paid to the client's solicitor unless it is either maintenance or paid into Court and invested for the client's benefit. The solicitor must report any attempt to manoeuvre around this rule (reg.18(3), Community Legal Service (Costs) Regulations 2000) and the solicitor must also report to the regional office straightaway when the client recovers or preserves property (reg.20(1)(a)). The solicitor must pass on any money recovered in the proceedings which is not exempt to the Commission. He may pass on money which has been recovered or preserved but which is exempt, to the client.

The Commission has no power to waive the charge unless it has funded legal **17.42** representation or support funding in proceedings in which it consider had a wider significant public interest and it considered it to be costs effective to fund that service or those services for a specified Claimant or claim. (reg.47, Community Legal Service (Financial) Regulation 2000).

The Commission may only defer enforcing the charge if:

(*a*) The property subject to the charge is the home of the funded client or dependence or, in family proceedings, money to be used to buy a home for the client or their dependence; and

(*b*) The Commission is satisfied that the home will provide security for the child; and

(*c*) The charge is registered (reg.52 Community Legal Service (Financial) Regulations 2000).
Interest accrues from registration of the charge of 8 per cent on the lesser of either

(i) the value of the charge; or
(ii) if the value of the property was lower at the time of recovery, the value of the property when it was recovered or preserved (Reg.53 (3), Community Legal Service (Financial (Regulations 2000 as amended).

In determining the value of the property subject to the charge for the **17.43** purpose of deciding what sum the interest should accrue upon, the Commission will take into account the £2,500 or £3,000 exemption in family cases. The client's liability to pay interest does not depend upon the funded client having signed a form agreeing to do so. This was the case under the 1989 Regulations but under the new regime this provision has been dropped.

The effect of the Statutory Charge must be explained to the client at the outset and the explanation and any advice in relation thereto should be confirmed by letter. Enclosed with such a letter should be the explanation of the basic conditions of legal funding including the Statutory Charge.

Part II

Remuneration for Legal Aid Costs

1 Costs between Parties

17.44 The Legal Aid in Family Proceedings (Remuneration) (Amendment) Regulations 1994 and The Legal Aid in Civil Proceedings (Remuneration) Regulations 1994 and The Civil Legal Aid (General) (Amendment) Regulations 1994 brought in important changes to the recovery of costs by a legally funded party under a between parties order. Instead of those costs being taxed at legal aid prescribed rates, they may be recovered at normal private rates from a paying party. The prescribed rates will only apply if the Legal Aid Fund is liable to pay the costs.

2 Costs payable by the Legal Services Commission

17.45 The question of remuneration for family proceedings and associated proceedings has gradually become more and more complex over the years and there are several categories and sub-categories of costs which cannot be set out in full detail in this Chapter simply because of their number and length. Full details of the various categories and sub-categories and the current prescribed remuneration rates may be found in Vol.2 of the LSC Manual and in s.E of Vol.1 of the Manual. For example, there are some 28 pages dealing with remuneration in s.E of Vol.1 of the LSC Manual which also contains a very helpful table listing all the various application forms for different aspects of LSC funded matters and the reference number of each form with a cross reference to the reference number by which the form was known prior to the creation of the Legal Services Commission.

Generally speaking, under the Legal Aid Act 1988 where a certificate was granted for representation under the Act the Legal Aid in Family Proceedings (Remuneration) Regulations 1991 apply to family and associated work for those periods. Where legal representation is not provided under contract under the Access to Justice Act 1999, family work is generally remunerated under the Legal Aid in Family Proceedings (Remuneration) Regulations 1991 also. There are however exceptions and reference should be made to s.E of Vol.1 of the Legal Services Commission for further details.

3 Assessment of Bills

17.46 Under the Legal Aid Act 1988 the Legal Aid Board has power to assess costs incurred under Civil Legal Aid Certificates in certain specified circumstances this power was retained in the Access to Justice Act 1999. In connection with assessments by the LSC it is very important to ensure that time limits are observed very strictly since the penalties can be very severe if they are exceeded.

The assessment limits remain as under the Legal Aid Act 1988 and any bill where proceedings have been issued and the total of the amount of the claim does not exceed £500 must be assessed by the Legal Services Commission. There is no option in this case for detailed assessment by the Courts. Any bill where proceedings have been issued and the total claim is between £500 and £1,000 may be assessed either by the Commission or by the Courts. It is for the solicitor instructed to choose which option is preferred. All other proceedings which have been issued, and where the total of the costs exceeds £1,000, must go to the relevant Court for detailed assessment, although there are provisions in special circumstances where assessment would be against the interests of the assisted person or would increase the amount payable from the Fund (see Reg.105 (3) (c)). It should also be noticed that where there is no discharge or revocation of the certificate there cannot be an assessment of costs until the conclusion of the cause or matter even if there is an order for costs an Interlocutory Application. Summary assessments are not possible in relation to publicly funded cases.

In relation to certificates issued on or after February 25, 1994 where between parties costs have been agreed and recovered the solicitor may claim his legal aid only costs from the Fund. Irrespective of the amount of thee costs, if the total of the legal aid costs claimed is up to £500 then they must be assessed, if they are between £500 and £1,000 the solicitor may decide whether the assessment should be carried out by the LSC or the Courts and if they exceed £1,000 they must be assessed by the Courts.

So far as the costs of assessment are concerned, all cost claims prepared and **17.47** submitted on or after March 18, 2000 are subject to Regs 16 of the Civil Legal Aid (General) (Amendment) Regulations 2000 and these replace Reg.113 of the 1989 Civil Legal Aid (General) Regulations. It provides that detailed assessment proceedings are deemed to be proceedings to which the certificate relates and this applies even though the certificate may have been revoked or discharged. The costs therefore must be paid from the Fund unless the Court orders otherwise and the solicitor instructed in the matter may prepare and attend on a detailed assessment without any amendment being obtained to the certificate. The costs of detailed assessment proceedings do not form part of the calculation of the statutory charge but that does not include the costs of preparing the bill by a law costs draftsman. Such fees will fall to the part of the statutory charge amount. The LSC Manual explains that in the vast majority of cases which fall within the Commission's own assessment limits (as opposed to the court's) an allowance of between 30 and 60 minutes will be appropriate for preparation of the bill. A greater time may be claimed but the bill should justify the time spent with reference to the circumstances of the individual case. Costs in family proceedings for this work are prescribed and they are only to the maximum set by the regulation. The allowance for preparation of a bill is in addition to the time allowed for checking and signing the bill in compliance with the regulations. (see *A Local Authority v A Mother and Child*, December 20, 2000, Court of Appeal).

A legally funded client having a financial interest in the assessment of his solicitor's costs has a right to attend on the detailed assessment of those costs. There are various obligations imposed upon the instructed solicitor in this respect. Having a financial interest usually relates to whether any contribution is payable or if the statutory charge will apply to the case. Revocation of a certificate does not give the funded client a financial interest because once the certificate is revoked the client is deemed never to have been a legally funded client.

The solicitor's obligations are (*a*) to supply the funded client with a copy of the Bill of Costs; (*b*) to inform the funded client of the financial interest and the right to make written representations and (*c*) to endorse on the bill whether or not the funded client has a financial interest, that the client has been supplied with a copy of the bill and has also been informed of the right to make written representations. If written representations are received from a funded client then a copy of the representations will be sent to the solicitor instructed prior to the assessment requesting comments within 21 days. Representations by a funded client may relate to the conduct of the case (for example that costs had been wasted or that work was not reasonably done) or state that there is an inaccuracy in the bill. These rights apply irrespective of whether the assessment is carried out by the LSC or by the Court. The requirements when assessment is by the Court are set out in the CPR and the associated Costs Practice Directions.

4   Other costs assessments made by the Commission

17.48   If the assessment is made in relation to controlled work (Legal Help, Help at Court and controlled representation) or authorised representation and the work is carried out under contract, the contract itself determines the assessment and appeals procedure. In the case of non-contracted work, where the costs assessment relates to advice and assistance or ABWOR provided before January 1, 2000 (or other ABWOR provided before April 1, 2000) the Legal Aid Act 1988 and its supporting regulations apply.

Approved family help is licensed work supplied under the General Civil Contract and is remunerated in accordance with articles 5 & 6 of the Community Legal Service (Funding) Order 2000. Article 6 leaves it to the contract to provide whether such costs are to be assessed by the Courts.

Specified family proceedings will be assessed by the Commission and as also will costs of support funding.

5   Detailed Assessment of Costs by the Court

17.49   Family proceedings costs are assessed by District Judges in the appropriate local court or, in the case of the Family Division in London, by Costs Officers in the Supreme Court Costs Office. There are no longer any assessments carried out by the Principal Registry of the Family Division. All these assessments are subject to the costs provisions in the CPR and their associated Costs Practice Direction.

Time Limits

17.50   CPR, r.47.17 (2) sets a 3 month time limit from the date on which the right to detailed assessment arose within which the receiving party must commence detailed assessment proceedings. CPR, r.47.8 deals with delay in the commencement of detailed assessment proceedings. A paying party may apply to the Court for an order that the receiving party commences the detailed assessment procedure. The Court may then issue an "Unless" Order requiring the proceedings to be commenced within a specified period failing which all or part of the receiving party's costs may be disallowed. If, however, the receiving party commences proceedings late but no application has been made by the paying party, the only penalty that may be imposed is the disallowance of interest on the costs for the period of delay. In publicly funded cases these rules apply as if the Commission were the paying party.

If delay is brought to the Commission's attention, the regional office will make applications to the Court under CPR, r.47.8. This enables Counsel to be paid their fees for the client's case to be balanced and monies released where the solicitor has failed to commence detailed assessment proceedings promptly. Counsel is not entitled to commence detailed assessment proceedings in their own right.

With regard to cost claims which have to be submitted to the LSC, the **17.51** Commission has been given power to sanction those who delay in submitting cost claims to it for assessment. The power is introduced by amendments to Reg.105 of the Civil Legal Aid (General) Regulations within the Civil Legal Aid (General) (Amendment) Regulations 2000. The regulation was implemented on October 31, 2000 although it actually became effective from March 18, 2000. The Commission may for good reason extend the time limit and the Regional Director may in exceptional circumstances consider whether it is reasonable both to extend the time limit and to reduce the costs but the costs must not be reduced unless the solicitor or Counsel has been allowed a reasonable opportunity to show cause in writing why the costs should not be reduced. Such a decision may be appealed to the area Costs Committee but the appeal must be commenced within 21 days of the decision by giving notice in writing to the area (Costs) Committee specifying the grounds of appeal. The Commission issued guidance on possible reductions in relation to all cost claims received on or after the October 31, 2000. Generally speaking the guidance underlines the need to apply to the regional office for an extension to any time limit before it expires although the regional office may still extend the time limit on receipt of a costs claim after the three month period provided the solicitor can show good reason. Where exceptional circumstances are held to exist which would justify extending the time in any particular case, regard will then be had as to whether to impose a penalty for late submission. The guidance shows that deductions will be imposed to a maximum of 5 per cent for bills submitted up to three months out of time. 10 per cent for bills submitted up to 6 months out of time and 15 per cent for bills submitted up to nine months out of time. If a solicitor has failed to show either good reason or exceptional circumstances, his claim for costs will be disallowed in full. Counsel's fees will be preserved, however, provided Counsel has not caused or contributed to the delay.

Entitlement to Costs

The CPR and Costs Practice Direction apply to costs in family proceedings **17.52** with effect from April 26, 1999 although one major exception to that rule is that the general principle under the CPR that costs follow the event does not apply to family proceedings. However various factors relating to an award of costs which are set out in CPR, r.44.3 (4) are applicable and these are as follows:

(i) The conduct of the parties;

(ii) Whether a party has succeeded on part of his case, even if he has not been wholly successful;

(iii) Offers to settle.

When considering conduct of the parties conduct both before and during the proceedings is taken into account as are questions such as whether it was reasonable for a party to raise or contest a particular allegation or issue, the manner in which that allegation or issue was pursued or defended and whether a successful Claimant or Applicant exaggerated his claim. It follows from this therefore that behaviour which causes delay or setting a claim at such a high level that settlement would be almost impossible or conducting the litigation in a confrontational manner is likely to fall foul of the rules and result in a penalty in costs.

CPR, r.44.3 (6) provided that the Court may make orders for a proportion of another party's costs or for a stated amount and it may also order costs from a particular date and costs which arose before proceedings had begun.

17.53 On June 5, 2000 the Family Proceedings (Amendment No. 2) Rules 1999 introduced a new set of provisions governing ancillary relief applications. It should be stressed that they do not affect any other types of family proceedings. The rules bring to ancillary relief applications case management disciplines which are Court driven. For example, one of the provisions requires an estimate of the costs incurred by each party up to the date of that hearing or appointment. This equates with the provision for estimates in general litigation which may be found in the Costs Practice Direction. The main changes as a result of these new provisions relate to offers to settle. In ancillary relief cases a payment into court cannot be made and Pt 36 of the CPR does not apply to family proceedings. These provisions are as follows: r.2.69 (1) provides for an offer to be made but it must be in writing and must be expressed "without prejudice save as to costs". The Court must unless it considers it unjust order the party whose offer is beaten to pay the costs incurred after the date beginning 28 days after the offer was made. In cases where both parties make offers and the award exceeds both offers providing the offers were made under r.2.16 (1) the Court may order interest on the whole or part of any sum recovered at a arte of up to 10 per cent above base rate for some or all of the period after which the offer was made and it may order indemnity costs beginning 28 days after the offer was made and interest on those costs at a rate not exceeding 10 per cent above base rate.

Basis of Assessment

17.54 Under the CPR there are two bases under which costs may be assessed. They are the standard and the indemnity basis. Normally costs ordered to be paid by one party to another will be on the Standard Basis as will costs payable out of the Fund. Under CPR, r.44.4 the Court will not allow costs which have been unreasonably incurred or an unreasonable amount whether they are on the standard basis or on the indemnity basis. Under CPR, r.48.3 where the amount of costs is to be assessed on the standard basis, the court will only allow costs which are proportionate to the matters in issue and if there should be any doubt as to whether costs were reasonably incurred or were reasonable and proportionate in amount that doubt must be resolved in favour of the paying party. In the case of the indemnity basis, the resolution of the doubt is in favour of the receiving party and proportionality does not apply at all. It is clear therefore that costs awarded on the indemnity basis are likely to be considerably more generous than those awarded on the standard basis.

Unlike the situation prior to the introduction of the CPR, the Court of Appeal has made it clear that the purpose of Indemnity based costs in circumstances where a Defendant is held liable for more than the offer made under Pt 36 by a Claimant was compensatory and was neither punitive nor indicative of the Court's disapproval of the Defendant's conduct (see *McPhilmey v Times Newspapers and Others* (4) [2001] 2 Costs L.R. 295.) This novel approach to the Indemnity Basis under the CPR was emphasised in *Petrotrading Inc. v Texaco Limited* [2002] 1 Costs L.R. 60 where it was held that the ability of the Court to make orders for costs on the indemnity basis should not be regarded as penal because orders for costs, even on the indemnity basis, never compensate a Claimant for having to come to court.

In this connection it is worth noting that pre-CPR case law so far as procedural matters are concerned, appears to have little or no authority under the new regime — see *Reid Minty (a firm) v Taylor* [2002] 1 Costs L.R. 180 where costs had been sought on the Indemnity Basis but the Judge refused on grounds that such costs were only relevant where there is some sort of moral probity and conduct is only amoral condemnation but the Court of Appeal in October 2001 overruled the Judge saying that the CPR was a new procedural code and that the new rules are not to be taken "as embodying the baggage of the old rules".

Proportionality

The CPR introduced the concept of proportionality on a formal basis and its **17.55** importance so far as costs, which are to be assessed on the standard basis are concerned cannot be overemphasised. In *Jefferson v National Freight Carriers Limited* [2001] 2 Costs L.R. 321, the Court of Appeal made it abundantly clear that the Courts had a duty to consider the levels of costs at an early stage in the proceedings. Lord Woolf commended a statement in a judgment by Her Honour Judge Holton on June 22, 2000 when the judge said that in particular in modern litigation with the emphasis on proportionality there is a requirement for parties to make an assessment at the outset of the likely value of the claim and of its importance and complexity and then to plan in advance the necessary work, the appropriate level of person to carry out that work and the overall time which would be necessary to complete it. This ties in closely with the provisions in s.6 of the Costs Practice Direction dealing with Estimates of Costs.

When considering proportionality CPD, para.11.1 states that the Court will have regard to CPR, r.1.1 (2) (C). This is part of the overriding objective and states that costs must be proportionate.

(*a*) to the amount of money involved;

(*b*) to the importance of the case;

(*c*) to the complexity of the issues;

(*d*) to the financial position of each party.

However, CPD, para.11.1 goes on to say that the relationship between the total of the costs incurred and the financial value of the claim may not be a reliable guide. A fixed percentage must not be applied in all cases to the value of the claim in order to ascertain whether or not the costs are proportionate. CPD, para.11.2 accepts that there will be costs which will inevitably be incurred in any proceedings which are necessary for successful conduct of the case and that solicitors are not required to conduct litigation at rates which are uneconomic! It suggests that in a modest claim the proportion of costs is likely to be higher than in a large claim and they may even equal or possibly exceed the amount in dispute

The Assessment

17.56   The procedure is exactly the same for family proceedings as it is in all other civil proceedings. A Costs Judge or District Judge or a Senior Executive Officer may carry out assessments of family bills although there are jurisdictional limits with regard to the latter. If there are costs as between solicitor and client in family proceedings only Costs Judges and District Judges are able to carry out detailed assessments of such costs.

Detailed assessment proceedings are commenced by the service of a Notice of Commencement of Detailed Assessment Proceedings accompanied by the Bill of Costs showing the claim for costs and the bill must follow substantially the formula set out in the Costs Practice Direction. The detailed requirements are set out in s.4 of the Costs Practice Direction. In addition to the bill the necessary vouchers for disbursements including fee notes of Counsel should be served with the bill. All legal aid authorities should accompany the Notice of Commencement of Detailed Assessment Proceedings. Written evidence as to any other disbursement which is claimed and which exceeds £250 must accompany the notice as must a statement giving the name and address for service of any person upon the receiving party intends to serve the Notice of Commencement. This process represents a very considerable change from the procedure for commencing taxation which was in force prior to the introduction of the CPR. The most important aspect is to note that the Court does not become involved at all in the process (unless there are particular specific applications to be made) until a request is made for a detailed assessment hearing.

17.57   Within 21 days after the date of service of the Notice of Commencement and accompanying documentation, the paying party must serve Points of Dispute on the receiving party and any other parties involved but again these points are not at this stage sent to the Court.

CPR, r.47.9 sets out the procedure for serving Points of Dispute and it also deals with the consequences if Points of Dispute are not served. The importance of serving Points of Dispute cannot be stressed too much. In the first place if a party served Points of Dispute after the period prescribed of 21 days, that party not be heard further in the detailed assessment proceedings unless the Court gives permission. Failure to serve Points of Dispute will prompt a receiving party to file a request for a Default Costs Certificate and this in effect means that the costs will be assessed as claimed. However if a paying party served Points of Dispute before the receiving party has obtained a Default Costs Certificate, the Court is prevented from issuing such a certificate.

Requests for Default Costs Certificates are made in accordance with Costs Practice Direction, s.37 and they must be made in writing in Form N254 and must be signed by the receiving party or the party's solicitor. Applications to set aside Default Costs Certificate under CPR, r.47.12 may be made in accordance with s.38 of the Costs Practice Direction and once again the application must be in writing and it must be supported by evidence. Generally speaking a Default Costs Certificate will be set aside only if the Applicant shows good reason for the Court to do so and if he files with his application a copy of the bill and a copy of the Default Costs Certificate together with a draft of the Points of Dispute he proposes to serve if the application to set aside is granted. It is also open to the Court to order the defaulting party to pay costs and to pay an amount on account before any costs are assessed. If a Default Costs Certificate is set aside then the Court will give directions for the management of the detailed assessment proceedings.

Once Points of Dispute have been served, it is open to the receiving party **17.58** to prepare Replies to those Points of Dispute. He is not obliged to prepare Replies but if he does decide to do so, they must be served within 21 days after service on him of the Points of Dispute.

Once the exchange of Points of Dispute and Points of Reply has been completed, the receiving party is at liberty then to request a detailed assessment hearing. He must file such a request within three months of the expiry of the period for commencing detailed assessment proceedings, which itself is three months from the date of entitlement to the costs. If the receiving party fails to file a request in time, the paying party may apply for an order requiring the receiving party to file the request within such time as the Court may specify. Once again, on hearing such an application the Court may direct that unless the receiving party requests a detailed assessment hearing within the time specified by the Court, all or part of the costs to which the receiving party would otherwise be entitled will be disallowed (CPR, r.47.14 (4)). Finally it should be remembered that only items specified in the Points of Dispute may be raised at the hearing unless the Court gives permission for other points to be dealt with.

When applying for a detailed assessment hearing the receiving party must **17.59** lodge the following:

(*a*) A copy of the Notice of Commencement of Detailed Assessment Proceedings

(*b*) A copy of the Bill of Costs

(*c*) The document giving the right to detailed assessment

(*d*) A copy of the Points of Dispute, annotated as necessary in order to show which items have been agreed, their value and to show which items remain in dispute and their value

(*e*) As many copies of the Points of Dispute as there are persons who have served Points of Dispute

(*f*) Copy of any Replies served

(*g*) A copy of all Orders made by the Court relating to the costs which are to be assessed

(*h*) Copies of the fee notes and other written evidence as served on the paying party in accordance with the provisions relating to Notice of Commencement of Detailed Assessment proceedings

(*i*) Where there is a dispute as to the receiving party's liability to pay costs to the solicitors who acted for the receiving party, any agreement, letter or other written information provided by the solicitor to his client explaining how the solicitor's charges are to be calculated

17.60   (*j*) A statement signed by the receiving party or his solicitor giving the name, address for service, reference and telephone number and fax number of

- The receiving party
- The paying party
- Any other person who has served Points of Dispute or who has given notice to the receiving party under para.32.10 (1) (*b*) of the Costs Practice Direction that he has a financial interest in the proceedings and giving an estimate of the length of time the detailed assessment hearing will take

(*k*) Where the application for a detailed assessment hearing is made by a party other than the receiving party, such as the documents set out above as are in possession of that party

(*l*) Where the Court is to assess the costs of an assisted person or LSC funded client,

       (*a*) The Legal Aid Certificate, LSC Certificate and all relevant Amendments, Authorities and any Certificate of Discharge or Revocation

       (*b*) A certificate of the Sch. to the Costs Precedents (see para.17.61) as shown by Precedent F (3)

       (*c*) If the assisted person has a financial interest in the detailed assessment hearing and wishes to attend the postal address of that person to which the Court will send notice of any hearing

       (*d*) If the rates payable out of the LSC Fund are prescribed rates, a Sch. to the Bill of Costs setting out all the items in the bill which are claimed against other parties calculated at the legal aid prescribed rates with or without any claim for enhancement

       (*e*) A copy of any Default Costs Certificate in respect of costs claimed in the Bill of Costs

17.61   In connection with the above the Precedent F (3) of the SCCO precedents is a Precedent showing the form of certificate applicable to LSC Funded cases which ought to be endorsed on the bill. It is in the following form:

> Certificate as to interest of assisted person/LSC funded client pursuant to Regulation 119 of the Civil Legal Aid (General) Regulations 1989.
>
> I certify that the assisted person/LSC funded client has no financial interest in the detailed assessment.
>
> or
>
> I certify that a copy of this bill has been sent to the assisted person/LSC funded client pursuant to Regulation 119 of the Civil Legal Aid (general) Regulations 1989 with an explanation of his/her interest in the detailed assessment and the steps which can be taken to safeguard that interest in the assessment. He/she has/has not requested that the Costs Officer be informed of his/her interest and has/has not requested that Notice of the Detailed Assessment Hearing be sent to him/her.

The certificate should be signed and dated.

With regard to points (*b*) the document giving the right to detailed assessment may be one or more of the documents set in Costs Practice Direction, para.40.4, but in the case of LSC funded clients it will either be a copy of the Judgment or Order giving the right to detailed assessment or it will be a Notice of Revocation or Discharge of the LSC Certificate.

The reference to the Sch. to the Legal Aid Costs in (l) (*d*) relates to the situation where between parties costs have been claimed but the between parties costs have to be recosted in effect and set out in a separate schedule showing the value of those costs calculated at legal aid prescribed rates with or without enhancement.

Variation of a Bill of Costs

If a party wishes to vary his Bill of Costs or his Points of Dispute or Replies   **17.62** an amended or supplement a document must be filed with the Court and copies of it must be served on all other relevant parties (CPD, para.40.10 (1)). Although permission is not required to vary a Bill of Costs or other documents the Court may disallow the variation or permit it only upon conditions including conditions as to the payment of any costs caused or wasted by the variation.

The Court will list a hearing date and must give at least 14 days notice of the time and place for the detailed assessment to every person named in the statement which was lodged with the Court under para.40.2 (j) of the Costs Practice Direction. Normally speaking the Court will require the papers to be filed in support of the Bill not less than 7 days before the date for the detailed assessment and not more than 14 days before that date (CPD, para.40.11).

The Detailed Assessment Hearing

In the case of a bill which is opposed, the hearing will take place before the   **17.63** appropriate Costs Officer who will hear arguments on both sides and will determine whether any disallowance or reduction in the sums claimed in the Bill of Costs are appropriate. A note of any decision will be made on the bill. In the case of unopposed bills which will usually be those bills containing legal aid only costs, *i.e.* costs payable only by the LSC, the procedure is slightly different. In this case the assisted person's solicitor may commence detailed assessment proceedings by filing a request in the relevant practice form and this request must be filed within three months after the date when the right to detailed assessment arose. A copy of the request for detailed assessment must also be served on the assisted person. where the assisted person does not wish to attend, the Court will on receipt of the request for assessment, provisionally assess the costs without the attendance of the solicitor unless it is considered that a hearing is necessary. After the Court has provisionally assessed the bill it will return it to the solicitor. The Court will fix a date for an assessment hearing if the solicitor informs the Court within 14 days after he receives the provisionally assessed bill that he wants the Court to hold such a hearing.

In the case of a legally funded client having a financial interest in the proceedings, the Court will not provisionally assess the bill but will proceed in the normal way outlined above to set a date for the detailed assessment.

Costs of Detailed Assessment Proceedings

Normally speaking in accordance with CPR, r.47.18 the receiving party's enti-   **17.64** tled to the costs of the detailed assessment proceedings unless the provisions of any act or of the rules or any relevant practice direction provide otherwise, or the Court makes some other order in relation to all or part of the costs of the proceedings. When deciding to make some other order the Court must have regard to all the circumstances including the conduct of all the parties, the amount by which the Bill of Costs has been reduced (if any) and whether it was reasonable for a party to claim the costs of a particular item or to dispute that item.

There is a procedure under CPR 47, r.19 where either party may make a written offer to settle the costs of the proceedings which gave rise to the assessment proceedings but this rule does not apply where the receiving party is an assisted person.

6 Appeals

17.65 Important changes have been made by the CPR to the practice in connection of Appeals (under the old rules the terminology referred to "Review"). Previously the same Costs Officer who had carried out the detailed assessment (Taxation) was the officer who also heard a review of that assessment. The position under the CPR is that an appeal lies from the District Judge or Costs Judge direct to a single Judge. However, before an appeal can take place, permission must be obtained either from the Costs Officer or, if permission is refused by the Costs Officer, from the higher court. The procedural position is governed by CPR, r.52 and its associated Practice Direction.

The situation is again different where an appeal is sought from an authorised Costs Officer in detailed assessment proceedings. The procedure here is governed by CPR, r.47.20 and the Costs Practice Direction at s.47. In the case of appeals from Authorised Court Officers (previously Taxing Officers) there is no requirement to obtain permission or to seek reasons for an appeal. In the first place an Appellant must file a notice which should be in Form N161 (an Appellant's Notice). This should be accompanied by a suitable record of the Judgment appealed against. Where reasons given for the decision have been officially recorded by the Court, an approved transcript of that record should accompany the notice. Where there is no official record, either the Officer's comments written on the bill or the advocate's notes of the reasons as to why the Appellant was unrepresented will suffice. In this connection it is the duty of any advocate for a Respondent to make his own note of the reasons promptly available free of charge to an Appellant where there is no official record or where the Appellant was unrepresented.

The appeal will be heard by a Costs Judge or a District Judge and will be a re-hearing, whereas an appeal under CPR, r.52 is a review and not a complete re-hearing.

7 Disciplinary Powers of Costs Officers

17.66 The CPR give Costs Officers powers to deal with misconduct or neglect in the conduct of proceedings and to impose personal liability for costs upon solicitors and Counsel. For guidance on Wasted Costs Orders see *Langley v M W Water Authority* [1991] 3 All E.R. 610; *Re a Barrister (Wasted Costs Order) (no. 1 of 1991)* [1992] 3 W.L.R. 662; *Ridehalgh v Horsefield and Watson v Watson* [1994] 2 F.L.R. 351 and *R. v M* [1996] 1 F.L.R. 750. In legal aid cases see Civil Legal Aid (General) Regulations 1989, Reg.109 and *Davy-Chiesman v Davy-Chiesman* [1984] 1 All E.R. 321. The detailed wasted costs provisions are dealt with in CPR, r.48.7 and s.53 of the Costs Practice Direction. Such orders can be made at any stage in the proceedings up to and including proceedings relating to the detailed assessment of costs. Either the Court may make a Wasted Costs Order against a legal representative on its own initiative, or a party may apply for a Wasted Costs Order by filing a Pt 23 application or by making an application orally in the course of any hearing. (see CPD, r.53.3). It is appropriate for the Court to make a Wasted Costs Order against a legal representative only if the legal representative has acted improperly, unreasonably or negligently and, by his conduct, caused a party to incur unnecessary costs and, in these circumstances, it is just to order him to compensate that party for the whole or part of those costs. Under CPD, r.53.6 as a general rule, the Court will consider whether to make a Wasted Costs Order in two stages:

(*a*) In the first stage the Court must be satisfied that it has before it evidence or other material which, if unanswered, would be likely to lead to a Wasted Costs Order being made; and

(*b*) The Wasted Costs proceedings are justified not withstanding the likely costs involved.

At the second stage the Court will consider after giving the legal representative an opportunity to give reasons as to why the Court should not make a Wasted Costs Order, or whether it is appropriate to make a Wasted Costs Order.

8   Litigants in Person

CPR, r.48.6 deals with cases where the costs of a Litigant in Person are to be paid by any other person. Such costs cannot be allowed except in the case of a disbursement at more than two thirds of the amount which would have been allowed if the litigant in person had been represented by a legal representative. The costs allowed to the litigant in person shall be such costs which would have been allowed if the work had been done or the disbursements made by a legal representative on the litigant in person's behalf, the payments reasonably made by him for legal services relating to the conduct of the proceedings and the costs of expert assistance in connection with assessing the claim for costs. (For the details of this aspect of the matter see Costs Practice Direction, para.52.1).   **17.67**

The two thirds rule applies only where the litigant in person can show that he has suffered financial loss. In the event that he is unable to show such financial loss, the amount allowed to him in respect of the time spent reasonably doing the work is £9.25 per hour (para. 52.4, Costs Practice Direction). If a litigant in person is allowed costs for attending at Court to conduct his case he not also allowed a witness allowance in respect of such attendance in addition to those costs.

A litigant in person includes a company or other corporation which is acting without a legal representative and a barrister, solicitor, solicitor's employee or other authorised litigator who is acting for himself. However, a solicitor who is represented in the proceedings by his own firm, or by himself in his firm name, is not for the purposes of CPR, r.48.6, a litigant in person.

The Court Structure

Divorce county courts are designated in the Civil Courts Order 1983 (SI 1983, No. 713) which is periodically amended. Not all divorce county courts have district registries as shown by the following list.

The Children (Allocation of Proceedings) Order 1991 (as amended), art.2 distinguishes between divorce county courts, family hearing centres and care centres. The Principal Registry has jurisdiction as all three. Lambeth County Court and Woolwich County Court may both hear applications under CA 1989, s.8 despite the fact that they are neither divorce county courts nor family hearing centres.

"Divorce town" means a place at which sittings of the High Court are authorised to be held outside the Royal Courts of Justice for the hearing of matrimonial proceedings (FPR, r.1.2(1)).

"Court of trial" means a divorce county court designated by the Lord Chancellor as a court of trial pursuant to the Matrimonial and Family Proceedings Act 1984, s.33(1) and, in relation to matrimonial proceedings pending in a divorce county court, the Principal Registry is treated as a court of trial having its place of sitting at the Royal Courts of Justice (FPR, r.1.2(1)). All divorce county courts are designated courts of trial (Civil Courts Order 1983, art.7).

Divorce County Court	*District Registry*	*Family Hearing Centre*	*Care Centre*	*Divorce Town*
Aberystwyth	*	*		
Accrington				
Aldershot and Farnham				
Altrincham				
Barnet		*		
Barnsley	*	*		
Barnstaple	*	*		
Barrow-in-Furness	*			
Basingstoke	*	*		
Bath	*	*		
Bedford	*	*		
Birkenhead				
Birmingham	*	*	*	*
Bishop Auckland				
Blackburn	*	*	*	*
Blackpool	*			
Blackwood	*	*		
Bodmin				

Divorce County Court	District Registry	Family Hearing Centre	Care Centre	Divorce Town
Bolton	*	*		
Boston	*			
Bournemouth	*	*	*	*
Bow		*		
Bradford	*	*		
Brecknock	*			
Brentford		*		
Bridgend	*			
Brighton	*	*	*	*
Bristol	*	*	*	*
Bromley				
Burnley	*			
Burton upon Trent				
Bury	*	*		
Bury St Edmunds	*			
Caernarfon	*	*	*	*
Cambridge	*	*		
Canterbury	*	*	*	*
Cardiff	*	*	*	*
Carlisle	*	*	*	*
Carmarthen	*	*		
Central London Civil Justice Centre				
Chelmsford			*	
Cheltenham	*			
Chester	*	*	*	*
Chesterfield	*	*		
Chichester	*	*		
Chorley				
Colchester	*			
Consett				
Conwy				
Coventry	*	*	*	*
Crewe	*	*		
Croydon	*	*		
Darlington	*	*		
Dartford		*		
Derby			*	
Dewsbury	*	*		
Doncaster	*	*		
Dudley	*	*		
Durham	*	*		
Eastbourne	*			
Edmonton				
Epsom				
Evesham				
Exeter	*	*		
Gateshead				
Gloucester	*	*		
Great Grimsby	*	*		

Divorce County Court	District Registry	Family Hearing Centre	Care Centre	Divorce Town
Guildford	*		*	*
Halifax		*		
Harlow	*			
Harrogate	*	*		
Hartlepool	*			
Hastings	*			
Haverfordwest	*	*		
Haywards Heath				
Hereford	*			
Hertford				
High Wycombe				
Hitchin		*		
Horsham				
Huddersfield	*	*		
Huntingdon				
Ilford		*		
Ipswich	*	*	*	*
Keighley	*	*		
Kendal	*			
Kettering				
Kidderminster				
King's Lynn	*	*		
Kingston upon Hull	*	*	*	*
Kingston upon Thames	*	*		
Lambeth				
Lancaster	*	*	*	*
Leeds	*	*	*	*
Leicester	*		*	*
Leigh				
Lewes				
Lincoln	*		*	*
Liverpool	*	*	*	*
Llanelli				
Llangefni		*		
Lowestoft	*			
Ludlow				
Luton	*	*	*	*
Macclesfield	*	*		
Maidstone	*	*		
Manchester	*	*	*	*
Mansfield	*	*		
Medway	*	*	*	*
Merthyr Tydfil	*			
Middlesbrough (see Teesside)	*			
Milton Keynes	*		*	*
Morpeth				
Neath and Port Talbot				
Nelson				
Newcastle upon Tyne	*	*	*	*

Divorce County Court	District Registry	Family Hearing Centre	Care Centre	Divorce Town
Newport (IOW)		*		
Newport (Gwent)		*	*	
Northampton	*		*	*
North Shields				
Norwich	*		*	*
Nottingham			*	
Nuneaton				
Oldham	*	*		
Oxford	*	*	*	*
Penrith				
Penzance				
Peterborough	*	*	*	*
Plymouth	*	*	*	*
Pontefract	*	*		
Pontypridd	*	*	*	*
Portsmouth	*	*	*	*
Preston	*			
Rawtenstall				
Reading	*	*	*	*
Redditch				
Reigate				
Rhyl	*	*	*	*
Romford	*	*		
Rotherham		*		
Runcorn		*		
Salford	*			
Salisbury	*	*		
Scarborough	*	*		
Scunthorpe	*			
Sheffield	*	*	*	*
Shrewsbury	*			
Skipton		*		
Slough		*		
Southampton	*	*		
Southend on Sea	*	*		
Southport	*			
South Shields				
St Albans				
St Helens	*			
Stafford	*			
Staines				
Stockport	*	*		
Stoke-on-Trent	*	*	*	*
Stratford-upon-Avon				
Sunderland	*		*	*
Swansea	*	*	*	*
Swindon	*	*	*	*
Tameside				
Taunton	*	*	*	*
Teesside	*		*	*

Divorce County Court	District Registry	Family Hearing Centre	Care Centre	Divorce Town
Telford		*	*	
Thanet	*			
Torquay	*			
Trowbridge				
Truro	*	*	*	*
Tunbridge Wells	*			
Uxbridge				
Wakefield	*	*		
Walsall	*	*		
Wandsworth		*		
Warrington	*	*	*	*
Warwick				
Watford		*	*	
Wellingborough				
Welshpool and Newtown	*	*		
West London				
Weston-super-Mare				
Weymouth and Dorchester	*	*		
Whitehaven	*			
Wigan	*			
Willesden		*		
Winchester	*			
Wolverhampton	*	*	*	*
Woolwich				
Worcester	*	*	*	*
Worksop				
Worthing	*			
Wrexham	*	*		
Yeovil	*			
York	*	*	*	*

Appendix 2

Forms

List of forms

1   General form of petition
2   Adultery particulars
3   Unreasonable behaviour particulars
4   Desertion particulars
5   Two years' separation and consent particulars
6   Five years' separation particulars
7   Petition for nullity of marriage (incapacity or wilful refusal)
8   Certificate with regard to reconciliation
9   Notice to be endorsed on document served on a person under disability
10 Affidavit by a person who is authorised to conduct proceedings on behalf of a respondent who is under disability
11 Affidavit of deemed service
12 Affidavit of personal service of petition
13 Application to dispense with service
14 Supplemental petition
15 Application to amend petition or answer
16 Application to file supplemental petition
17 Notice of absence or withdrawal of consent
18 Application to file an answer out of time
19 Application to proceed on answer alone
20 Application to proceed by way of undefended cross decrees
21 General notice of application
22 General form of summons
23 Application to appoint medical inspector(s)
24 Order for directions as to the trial of an issue
25 Form of issue
26 Form of order on issue
27 Endorsement on affidavit
28 Application for evidence by affidavit
29 Affidavit of personal service of order
30 Affidavit of service of order on solicitor
31 Application for rehearing (county court)
32 Application by notice to attend before the judge in High Court
33 Application to make decree absolute by party against whom decree pronounced
34 Application to expedite hearing of petition
35 Application to expedite decree absolute
36 Application to dismiss petition
37 Order for sale

A2.01   Form 1 General form of petition (FPR, Appendix 2)

IN THE   COUNTY COURT,
                                                  [DIVORCE REGISTRY],
                                                  No of
                                                  Matter

THE PETITION OF   SHOWS THAT—
(1) On the   day of   20   the
petitioner   was lawfully married to
                                                  (hereinafter called the respondent)

at

(2) The petitioner and the respondent last lived together as husband and
wife at [*state the last address at which they have cohabited*].

(3) The court has jurisdiction under article 2(1) of the Council Regulation
on the following ground(s) [*tick/mark applicable box*]:

[ ]   (a) The Petitioner and Respondent are both habitually resident in
          England and Wales.

[ ]   (b) The Petitioner and Respondent were last habitually resident in England and Wales and the [Petitioner/Respondent] still resides there.

[ ]   (c) The Respondent is habitually resident in England and Wales.

[ ]   (d) The Petitioner is habitually resident in England and Wales and has resided there for at least one year immediately prior to the presentation of this petition. [*Give the address(es) where the petitioner lived during that time and the length of time lived at each address.*]

[ ]   (e) The Petitioner is domiciled and habitually resident in England and Wales and has resided there for at least six months immediately prior to the presentation of the petition. [*Give the address(es) where the petitioner lived during that time and the length of time lived at each address.*]

[ ]   (f) The Petitioner and Respondent are both domiciled in England and Wales.

[*Or if none of the above apply*]

[ ]   (g) The court has jurisdiction other than under the Council Regulation on the basis that no Contracting State has jurisdiction under the Council Regulation and the [Petitioner/Respondent] is domiciled in England and Wales on the date when this petition is issued.

(4) There is [are] [no [*or state number*] child[ren] of the family now living] [namely [*state the full names (including surname) of each child and his date of birth or, if it be the case, that he is over 18 and, in the case of each minor child over the age of 16, whether he is receiving instruction at an educational establishment or undergoing training for a trade, profession or vocation*]].

(5) [*In the case of a husband's petition*] No other child now living has been born to the respondent during the marriage so far as it is known to the petitioner [*or in the case of a wife's petition*] No other child now living has been born to the petitioner during the marriage [except [*state the name of any such child and his date of birth, or if it be the case, that he is over 18*]].

(6) [*Where there is a dispute whether a child is a child of the family*] The petitioner [respondent] alleges that   is [not] a child of the family [because [*give full particulars of the facts relied on by the petitioner in support of his or her allegation that the child is or, as the case may be, is not a child of the family*]]. [*Note: Appendix 2 to FPR does not state that particulars have to be given.*]

(7) There have been no other proceedings in any court in England and Wales or elsewhere with reference to the marriage [or to any child of the family] [or between the petitioner and the respondent with reference to any property of either or both of them] [except [*state the nature of the proceedings, the date and effect of any decree or order and, in the case of proceedings with reference to the marriage, whether there has been any resumption of cohabitation since the making of the decree or order*]].

(8) There are no proceedings continuing in any country outside England and Wales which relate to the marriage or are capable of affecting its validity or subsistence [except [*give particulars of the proceedings, including the court in or tribunal or authority before which they were begun, the date when they were begun, the names of the parties, the date or expected date of any trial in the proceedings and such other facts as may be relevant to the question whether the proceedings on the petition should be stayed under Schedule 1 to the Domicile and Matrimonial Proceedings Act 1973*]].

(9) There have been no applications under the Child Support Act 1991 for a maintenance assessment in respect of any child of the family [except [*give the date of any such application and details of any assessment made.*)]]

(10) [*In the case of a petition for divorce based on 5 years' separation*] The following [*or* No] agreement or arrangement has been made or is proposed to be made between the parties for the support of the respondent [*or* the petitioner] [and the children of the family] [namely [*state details*]].

(11) [*In the case of a petition for divorce*] The said marriage has broken down irretrievably.

(12) [*See forms 2-6*] [*or, where the petition is not for divorce or judicial separation, set out the ground on which relief is sought, and* **in any case** *state with sufficient particularity the facts relied on but not the evidence by which they are to be proved*].

The petitioner therefore prays—

(1) That the said marriage may be dissolved [*or* declared void] [*or* annulled] [or that he [she] may be judicially separated from the respondent] [*or as the case may be*].

(2) [*Where appropriate*] That　　　　　　　　　　may be ordered to pay the costs of this suit.

(3) That he [she] may be granted the following ancillary relief, namely [*state particulars of any application for ancillary relief which it is intended to claim*]:

(a) maintenance pending suit;
(b) periodical payments;
(c) secured periodical payments;
(d) a lump sum;
(e) property adjustment;
(f) periodical payments, secured periodical payments and lump sum for the said child[ren];
(g) a pension sharing order.

The names and addresses of the persons who are to be served with this petition are [*give particulars, stating if any of them is a person under disability*].

　The petitioner's address for service is [*where the petitioner sues by a solicitor, state the solicitor's name or firm and address, or, where the petitioner sues in person, state his place of residence as given in paragraph 3 of the petition or, if no place of residence in England or Wales is given, the address of a place in England or Wales at or to which documents for him may be delivered or sent*].

Dated this　　　　　　day of　　　　　　20

Note: Under the FPR further information is required in certain cases.

A2.02　　**Form 2 Adultery particulars** *(MCA 1973, s 1(2)(a))*

The respondent has committed adultery [with [*state name if the person is to be named*] (hereinafter called the co-respondent) and the petitioner finds it intolerable to live with the respondent.

Particulars

On the [　　　　] day of [　　　　] 20[　　　　] at [　　　　] the respondent committed adultery [with the co-respondent] and has cohabited and committed adultery [with the co-respondent] since that date at the said address [*or* on the [　　　　] day of [　　　　] 20[　　　　] the respondent gave birth to a child of whom the petitioner is not the father].

Form 3 Unreasonable behaviour particulars (*MCA 1973, s 1(2)(b)*)　　　　**A2.03**

The respondent has behaved in such a way that the petitioner cannot reasonably be expected to live with the respondent.

Particulars

    (*a*) The respondent is a man of violent and ungovernable temper particularly when in drink.

    (*b*) The respondent is abusive to the petitioner using obscene language towards her in front of the children of the family to their distress.

    (*c*) The respondent is financially irresponsible. The petitioner only discovered that the respondent had ceased making mortgage repayments to the [　　　　] Building Society when possession proceedings were served upon her.

    (*d*) On the [　　　　] day of [　　　　] 20[　　　　] the respondent struck the petitioner in front of the children of the family in the kitchen with a saucepan, causing severe bruising.

    (*e*) On the [　　　　] day of [　　　　] 20[　　　　] the respondent informed the petitioner that he had formed an association with another woman at his place of work.

    (*f*) As a result of the respondent's aforesaid behaviour the petitioner left the respondent on the [　　　　] day of [　　　　].

[*The above particulars are, of course, illustrative only and follow the style of drafting suggested on pp [000]-[000]*]

Form 4　Desertion particulars (*MCA 1973, s 1(2)(c)*)　　　　**A2.04**

The respondent has deserted the petitioner for a continuous period of at least two years immediately preceding the presentation of this petition.

Particulars

The respondent left the matrimonial home at [　　　　] on the [　　　　] day of [　　　　] 20 [　　　　]. The petitioner had given the respondent no cause to leave and did not consent to the separation. There has been no resumption of cohabitation since that date.

A2.05　　**Form 5　Two years' separation and consent particulars** (*MCA 1973, s 1(2)(d)*)

The parties to the marriage have lived apart for a continuous period of at least two years immediately preceding the presentation of this petition and the respondent consents to a decree being granted.

Particulars

The parties to the marriage separated on the [　　　　　] day of [　　　　　] 20[　　　　　] since which date there has been no resumption of cohabitation.

A2.06　　**Form 6　Five years' separation particulars** (*MCA 1973, s 1(2)(e)*)

The parties to the marriage have lived apart for a continuous period of at least five years immediately preceding the presentation of this petition.

Particulars

The respondent left the then matrimonial home on the [　　　　　] day of [　　　　　] 20 [　　　　　] and has lived separate and apart from the respondent since that date [save for the period from the [　　　　　] day of [　　　　　] 20[　　　　　] to the [　　　　　] day of [　　　　　] 20 [　　　　　] when the parties resumed cohabitation with a view to effecting a reconciliation].

A2.07　　**Form 7　Petition for nullity of marriage (incapacity or wilful refusal)**

(*Heading as in* **Form 1**)
THE PETITION OF *R Y*　　　　　　　　　　　　　　SHOWS THAT—
(1) On the　　　　　day of　　　　　　　　　　　　　20　　，
　　　　　　　　　　　　　　　　a ceremony of marriage was in fact
　　　　　　　　　　celebrated between thepetitioner *R Y* and *X Y*
　　　　　　　　　　　　　　　　(hereinafter called the respondent)
at (*follow marriage certificate precisely*).
　　(2) to (10) *as in* Form 1. (*Paragraph* (11) *does not apply.*)
　　(12) [*If on the ground of wilful refusal*] The said marriage has not been consummated owing to the wilful refusal of the respondent to consummate it.
　　(*Set out the facts relied on.*)
　　[*If on the ground of incapacity*] [In the alternative] the said marriage has not been consummated owing to the incapacity of the respondent [petitioner] to consummate it.
　　(*Set out the facts relied on.*)
　　The petitioner therefore prays—
　　(1) That the said marriage may be annulled.
　　(*The remainder as in* Form 1)

Form 8   Certificate with regard to reconciliation   **A2.08**
(*Form M3 of FPR, Appendix 1*)

IN THE   COUNTY COURT.
                                                  [DIVORCE REGISTRY]
                                                              No of
                                                             Matter
Between   Petitioner
and   Respondent
[and   Co-Respondent].

I the solicitor acting for the petitioner in the above cause do hereby certify that
I have [*or* have not] discussed with the petitioner the possibility of a reconciliation and that I have [*or* have not] given to the petitioner the names and
addresses of the persons qualified to help effect a reconciliation.

Dated this   day of   20

Signed

Solicitor for the Petitioner.

Form 9   Notice to be endorsed on document served on a person under   **A2.09**
disability under FPR, r 9.3
(*Form M24 of FPR, Appendix 1*)

To   of
TAKE NOTICE that the contents of purport of this document are to be communicated to the respondent [*or as the case may be*], the said   , if he
is over 16 [*add, if the person to be served is by reason of mental disorder within
the meaning of the Mental Health Act 1983 incapable of managing and administering his property and affairs*: unless you are satisfied [after consultation with
the responsible medical officer within the meaning of the Mental Health Act
1983 or, if the said   is not liable to be detained or subject to guardianship under that Act, his medical attendant]* that communication will be
detrimental to his mental condition].

* *Delete these words if the document is served on the responsible medical officer
or medical attendant.*

Form 10   Affidavit by a person who is authorised to conduct proceedings on   **A2.10**
behalf of a respondent who is under disability (*FPR, r 9.3(1) and 2(2)*)

1.   , of [*address and description*] make oath and say as follows:

   (1) That I am [the person authorised under Part VII of the Mental
       Health Act 1983 to conduct these proceedings on behalf of the res-
       pondent   *or* in whose care the Respondent   is

or with whom the respondent   resides [*or as the case may be*]].

(2) That   is a person detained under the Mental Health Act 1983 [*or* suffering from mental disorder] and has been a patient in   Hospital since the   day of   20 , [and is under my care at (*address*)].

(3) That a copy of the petition for divorce [or nullity] [*or as the case may be*] of   bearing date the   day of   20 , together with a notice of [proceedings] and form of acknowledgment of service was served on me [by post] [personally] on the   day of   20 , at   . The said copy petition was endorsed with a notice in Form M24 of Appendix 1 to the Family Proceedings Rules 1991.

(4) That after consultation with   the medical attendant of the said   [*or* the responsible medical officer of the said   within the meaning of the Mental Health Act 1983] I decided that the communication of the contents of the petition and documents served therewith in this cause would [not] be detrimental to the mental condition of the said   [for the following reasons, namely   ] and that I have therefore [not] communicated the contents and purport of the said petition and other documents to him [her].

Sworn, etc.

A2.11   Form 11   Affidavit of deemed service (*FPR, r 2.9(6)*)

(*Heading*)

I *A B* of   in the County of   solicitor [*or as appropriate*] make oath and say as follows:

1 I have the conduct of these proceedings on behalf of the petitioner.

2 The petition seeks the dissolution of the petitioner's marriage to the respondent on the basis [*as the case may be*];

3 On the   day of   20 I sent by pre-paid post in an envelope addressed to the respondent at [*address*] a copy of the petition filed in this suit together with Forms M4, M5 and M6 prescribed by Appendix 1 to the Family Proceedings Rules 1991.

4 On the   day of   20 I received a letter from solicitors consulted by the respondent, a true copy of which is now produced and shown to me marked '*A B* 1', indicating that the respondent had sought their advice in relation to the petition;

5 I verily believe that the respondent has received the copy petition sent to him on the   day of   20 notwithstanding that no acknowledgment of service has been returned to the Court.

Sworn etc.

Form 12   Affidavit of personal service of petition   A2.12

(*Heading*)

I *A B* of   in the County of   [*description*] make oath and
say as follows:

1 That I am over sixteen years of age and [acting as agent for the peti-
   tioner] *or* [employed by   of   solicitor for the
   above-named petitioner].

2 That I did on the   day of   20   serve a copy of
   the petition a true copy of which is annexed hereto and marked 'A'
   together with a notice of proceeding in Form M5 with acknowledgment of service in Form M6 attached [a copy] [or copies] of the statement as to arrangements for children in Form M4] [and a medical
   report] [and   a notice of issue of a public funding
   certificate] on the respondent [*or* co-respondent]   by
   delivering the same to the said respondent [*or* co-respondent] personally at

3 [*Paragraph as to identity (see below) in the case of a respondent
   spouse*]

Sworn at   in the
County of   this
day of   20
Before me
Officer of a Court, appointed by the Judge to take Affidavits.

This affidavit is filed on behalf of the petitioner.

PRECEDENTS OF PARAGRAPH AS TO IDENTITY

Identity by photograph

That the photograph annexed hereto marked 'B' is a photograph of the person
whom I served as the said respondent and who at the time of the said service
in my presence signed the back of the said photograph.

When petitioner attended at time of service and identified respondent

That at the time of the said service the petitioner was present and pointed out
to me the said as his wife [*as the case may be*].

Where process server knows personally the person served

That I know and am [have been] personally acquainted with the said respondent [for   years] and know him to be the husband of the petitioner
[*or*, know her to be the wife of the petitioner].

Identity by admission of person served

That at the time of the said service on the said respondent, he [she] admitted
to me that he [she] was the said respondent and signed in my presence the statement annexed hereto and marked 'B' in acknowledgment of service of the
copy petition and of admission of identity.

A2.13   Form 13   Application to dispense with service

(*Heading*)
[*First paragraph as in form 3*]

that service of a copy of the petition herein on the respondent [co-respondent] be dispensed with.

[*Remainder as in form 3*]

A2.14   Form 14   Supplemental petition

(*Heading*)
Dated this   day of   20

The supplemental petition of (*name of petitioner*) shows that: On   20   the respondent: (*set out details of allegations relating to matters occurring after date of petition*)
    The petitioner therefore prays as before

(*Signed*)

Solicitor for the petitioner (*or as appropriate*).

Note: If the original petition was for judicial separation and the Petitioner now seeks a divorce, the prayer would be 'the petitioner therefore prays that the marriage be dissolved'. Any further prayers for costs, custody or other relief should also be included.

A2.15   Form 15   Application to amend petition or answer

(*Heading*)
[*First paragraph as in form 21*]

that the Petitioner [Respondent]   be at liberty to amend the petition [answer] herein [*herein state the amendment required*] [*add where applicable, and that re-service of the petition [answer] be dispensed with*].

[*Remainder as in form 21*]

A2.16   Form 16   Application to file supplemental petition

(*Heading*)
[*First paragraph as in form 21*]

that the Petitioner be at liberty to file a supplemental petition herein.

[*Remainder as in form 21*]

Form 17   Notice of absence or withdrawal of consent   **A2.17**

(*Heading*)

Take notice that I do [the respondent does] not consent to a decree of divorce being granted in this cause *or* I withdraw [the respondent withdraws] the consent to a decree of divorce being granted, which consent is referred to in the petition in this cause.

Dated this   day of   20

[Solicitors for] the respondent

To the Court and to the petitioner.

Form 18   Application to file an answer out of time   **A2.18**

(*Heading*)
[*First paragraph as in form 21*]

that the respondent be at liberty to file an answer to the petition herein [notwithstanding that directions for trial have been given] [notwithstanding that the time limit for doing so has expired].

[*Remainder as in form 21*]

Form 19   Application to proceed on answer alone   **A2.19**

(*Heading*)
[*First paragraph as in form 21*]

    1) that the proceedings arising from the prayer of the petition be stayed

    2) that the cause proceed on the prayer of the respondent's answer.

    3) that in the event that the respondent shall fail to apply for directions for trial within [28] days of the date hereof the petitioner shall have liberty to apply to rescind this order.

    4) that there be no order as to the costs of this application [nor any costs inter partes on the grant of the decree]

[*Remainder as in form 21*]

Form 20   Application to proceed by way of undefended cross decrees   **A2.20**

(*Heading*)
[*First paragraph as in form 21*]

1) that the answer be amended to delete paragraphs—

   (*delete paragraphs denying that the marriage has irretrievably broken down or seeking rejection of the prayer of the petition or dismissal of the petition*)

2) [that the reply be struck out]

3) the suit proceed undefended to cross decrees on the prayers of the petition and answer.

4) in the event that either party shall fail to apply for directions for trial within [28] days of the date hereof the other party shall have liberty to apply to rescind this order

5) that there be no order as to the costs of this application [nor any costs inter partes on the grant of the decree.]

[*Remainder as in form 21*]

A2.21 Form 21   General notice of application

(*Heading*)

TAKE NOTICE that the petitioner [*or as the case may be*] intends to apply to the [Judge] [District Judge] of this Court at
   Or, to a [Judge at the Royal Courts of Justice, Strand, London WC2.] [District Judge at the Divorce Registry, First Avenue House, 42/49 High Holborn, London, WC1V 6NP], on   the   day of
, 20   , at   o'clock for [an order that]
[on the following grounds]

Dated this   day of   , 20

(*Signed*)

Solicitor for the petitioner [*or as the case may be*].

To the District Judge
and to the [respondent]

A2.22 Form 22   General form of summons

(*Heading*)
Let all parties concerned attend the Judge   , [in Chambers] [Court]]
at
   Or, the Judge in Chambers [Court] at the Royal Courts of Justice, Strand, London WC2
   Or, the District Judge at
   or, one of the District Judges at the Divorce Registry at Somerset House, Strand, London WC2,

on   day the   day of   , 20   , at   o'clock on
the hearing of an application on the part of the Petitioner [*or as the case may
be*] [for an order]
Dated this   day of   20

This summons was taken out by
of   , solicitor for the
To

Form 23   Application to appoint medical inspector(s)   A2.23

(Heading)
[*First paragraph as in form 21*]

to determine whether medical inspector(s) should be appointed to examine the
parties to this cause and to report to the Court the result of the examination
[*or* that medical inspectors be appointed to examine the parties, etc].

[*Remainder as in form 21*]

Form 24   Order for the directions as to the trial of an issue   A2.24

(*Heading*)
Upon Hearing
and Upon Reading
It is Ordered:

1 That an issue [as to whether *X Y* is a child of *C D*; as to whether *X Y*
   has been treated as a child of the family; as to whether A *B* was habitually resident in England and Wales for a period of one year ending
   with the date of presentation of the petition, *or as the case may be*] be
   tried;

2 That A B be the plaintiff and C D be the defendant [*or as the case may
   be*] in the said issue;

3 That the issue be heard by a Judge in open court [*or* in chambers] on
   oral evidence [*or as the case may be*];

4 That the issue be settled by a District Judge of this court;

5 [That the cause be stayed pending the determination of the said
   issue;];

6 That the costs of this application be costs in the issue. Dated
   the   day of   , 20

A2.25 **Form 25** **Form of issue**

(*Heading*)

WHEREAS A *B* the plaintiff in the issue affirms, and *C D* the defendant in the issue denies, that [*X Y* is a child of *C D; X Y* has been treated as a child of the family; A *B* has been habitually resident in England and Wales for a period of one year ending with the date of presentation of the petition; *or as the case may be*]
    AND WHEREAS by order dated the   day of   , 20 ,
it was ordered that an issue be tried herein.
Therefore let the same be tried accordingly.
Settled
District Judge

Dated this   day of   , 20

A2.26 **Form 26** **Form of order on issue**

(Heading)

Upon Reading the issue herein
    Upon Hearing Counsel for the parties and Having Taken the oral evidence of *A B* and *C D*
    It is Declared that [X *Y* is a child of *C D; X Y* has been treated as a child of the family; *A B* has been habitually resident in England and Wales for a period of one year ending with the date of presentation of the petition; *or as the case may be*]
    And it is Ordered that the defendant do pay the plaintiffs costs of the issue (*or as appropriate*)

Dated this   day of   , 20

A2.27 **Form 27** **Endorsement on affidavit**

(Practice Note 23 July 1983) [1983] 3 All ER 33
Party: Petitioner
Deponent: A R Smith
No of Affidavit: Second [in ancillary relief application]
Sworn: 5.11.02
Filed: 8.11.02

A2.28 **Form 28** **Application for evidence by Affidavit**

(*Heading*)
[*First paragraph as in form 21*]

that on the hearing of this cause the evidence of the petitioner [*or*   a witness for the petitioner] be given by affidavit a draft of which is exhibited to the petitioner's affidavit in support of the application filed herewith.

[*Remainder as in form 21*]

Form 29   Affidavit of personal service of order   A2.29

I,
of
[Process Server] [Solicitor] make oath and say as follows:—
  (1) I did on the   day of   , 20   , at   , personally serve the above-named [petitioner] [respondent] with a sealed true copy of the order dated the   day of   , 20   ], a copy of which is now produced and shown to me marked 'A'.
  (2) service was effected by [*detail the circumstances under which service was effected*].
  (3) I am satisfied that the person whom I served was the [petitioner] [respondent] because (*detail the circumstances under which identification was satisfied: see form 12*]).

Form 30   Affidavit of service of order on solicitor   A2.30

I,
of
[Process Server] [Solicitor] for the [petitioner] [respondent] make oath and say as follows:
  (1) I did on the   day of   , 20   , serve   , solicitors for the above-named [respondent] in this cause with a sealed copy of the order dated the   day of   , 20   , a copy of which is now produced and shown to me marked 'A' [by leaving it at   , being the address for service in the cause, with a [   ] employed by the said solicitors] [*or* by posting it first class mail at the post office at   in a prepaid envelope addressed to the said   , at   being the address for service in the cause], [or by delivering it to the document exchange at which the said solicitors have numbered box [   ]] [or by sending it by fax in accordance with RSC, Ord 65, r 5(2B)]
  Sworn, etc.

Form 31   Application for re-hearing (county court)   A2.31

(*Heading*)
[*First paragraph as in form 21*]

for an order for the re-hearing of this [*state nature of proceedings*] tried by the [judge] [district judge] on the   day of   , 20   .
  The grounds of this application are:

[*Remainder as in form 21*]

A2.32   Form 32   Application by notice to attend before the judge in High Court

(Heading)
TAKE NOTICE that the [respondent] intends to apply to the Judge [in Chambers] [under section 10(1) of the Matrimonial Causes Act 1973] for [the recission of the decree of divorce in this cause] on the grounds that [the petitioner misled the respondent, etc] [*or as the case may be*].

   AND FURTHER TAKE NOTICE that you are requested to attend before the Judge at
on   day the   day of   20   , at   o'clock on the hearing of this application by the [respondent].

Dated this   day of   20

[Solicitor for the] [respondent].

A2.33   Form 33   Application to make decree absolute by party against whom decree pronounced

(*Heading*)
[*First paragraph as in form 21*]

that the decree nisi pronounced herein on the   day of
20   , against the [petitioner] [respondent] be made absolute the [petitioner] [respondent] not having made any such application.

[*Remainder as in form 21*]

A2.34   Form 34   Application to expedite hearing of petition

(*Heading*)
[*First paragraph as in form 21*]

that directions be given to expedite the hearing of the petition.

[*Remainder as in form 21*]

A2.35   Form 35   Application to expedite decree absolute

(*Heading*)
[*First paragraph as in form 21*]

that the court do abridge the time for making absolute the decree nisi pronounced herein on the   day of   20   , and that the petitioner do have leave to make the said decree absolute [forthwith] *or* [on the   of   20   ].

[*Remainder as in form 21*]

Form 36   Application to dismiss petition   A2.36

(*Heading*)
[*First paragraph as in form 21*]

that the petition dated the   day of   , 20   , be dismissed
[and that the petitioner pay the costs of the proceedings], on the grounds
that [   ]

[*Remainder as in form 21*]

Form 37   Order for sale   A2.37

The property known as   [registered at HM Land Registry under
title number   ] be sold forthwith by private treaty and the following
consequential provisions shall apply;

(*a*) the said property shall be sold for such price as may be agreed
between the parties or in default of such agreement as determined by
the Court;

(*b*) The [petitioner's]/[respondent's] solicitors shall have the conduct of
the sale;

(*c*) the said property shall be offered for sale by [   ]/[such estate
agents as may be agreed between the parties or in default of such
agreement as nominated by the Court];

(*d*) to proceeds of sale of the said property shall be applied as follows:

(i) the discharge the mortgage secured thereon in favour of
the   Building Society;

(ii) in payment of the [petitioner's]/[respondent's] solicitors' conveyancing costs and disbursements;

(iii) in payment of the costs of [*estate agents*];

(iv) in payment to the [petitioner]/[respondent] of the lump sum of
£   [referred to in paragraph [   ] of this order] [*or as
appropriate*];

(v) in payment of the balance to the [respondent]/[petitioner].

Form 38   Mesher order   A2.38

With effect from [the making of this order]/[the date of decree absolute] the
property known as [registered at HM Land Registry under title number   ]
shall be held by the petitioner and the respondent upon a trust of land as
beneficial tenants in common in equal shares [*or as appropriate*] and upon the
following terms and conditions:

(*a*) The [petitioner]/[respondent] shall occupy the said property to the
exclusion of the [respondent]/[petitioner] until sale;

(*b*) The said trust shall not be carried into effect without the consent of both parties or further order until either:

  (i) the children] of the family shall have attained the age of eighteen years and completed [his]/[her]/[their] full-time education [*or as appropriate*], whichever shall be the later;

  or

  (ii) the death of the [petitioner]/[respondent]; or
  (iii) the remarriage or cohabitation of the [petitioner]/[respondent] with another [man/woman] as man and wife for a period of [   ], whichever shall first occur.

(*c*) The [petitioner]/[respondent] shall with effect from the date of this order be responsible for all payments of capital interest and interest on the mortgage in respect of the said property secured in favour of the   Building Society and the [petitioner]/[respondent] shall have credit in respect of one-half of the element of repayment of capital comprised in such payments made by [him]/[her] from   20   to the date of sale;

(*d*) The [petitioner]/[respondent] shall be responsible for all maintenance and decorative repairs to the said property;

(*e*) The cost of insuring the said property and of any structural repairs shall be shared equally [*or as appropriate*] between the petitioner and the respondent provided that no works of structural repairs shall be carried out to the said property save by agreement between the parties or by further order of the court.

There be liberty to apply as to the implementation of the terms of this order.

A2.39   Form 39   Order for deferred charge

The [petitioner]/[respondent] shall within days [of the date of this order]/[after the date of decree absolute herein] transfer to the [respondent]/[petitioner] all [his]/[her] legal and beneficial interest in the property known as [registered at HM Land Registry under title number   ] and that as from the date of the said   transfer the said property do stand charged by way of legal charge in favour of the [petitioner]/[respondent] with a lump sum [of £   ]/[of one-third [*or as appropriate*] of the [gross/net] proceeds of sale] provided always that such charge shall not become enforceable until:

(*a*) the death of the [respondent]/[petitioner]; or

(*b*) the remarriage or cohabitation of the [respondent]/[petitioner];

  or

(*c*) upon [his]/[her] vacating the said property; or

(*d*) upon the date when the youngest child of the family attains the age of eighteen years or completes [his/her] full-time education.

Form 40   Consent application for maintenance pending suit   A2.40

by consent that the respondent do pay or cause to be paid to the petitioner as from the   day of   , 20 (*date of the presentation of the petition or such other later date*), maintenance pending suit at the rate of £   per [*week*] payable weekly until the date of final decree and thereafter interim periodical payments at the rate of £   per [week/month] until further order.

Form 41   Consent application for periodical payments order   A2.41

by consent that the respondent do pay or cause to be paid as from the   day of   , 20   , periodical payments to the petitioner during their joint lives until such date as she shall remarry or further order at the rate of £   [per week/annum] payable [weekly *or* monthly] [in advance] and as from the   day of   , 20   , periodical payments for the benefit of the child of the family [*AB* born   ] until he/she shall attain the age of [17] years or cease full-time education whichever shall be the later or further order at the rate of £   per week/annum payable [weekly *or* monthly] [in advance].

Form 42   Limited term periodical payments order   A2.42

IT is ORDERED that the [petitioner/respondent] do pay or cause to be paid to the [respondent/petitioner] periodical payments at the rate of £[   ] per annum payable [weekly/monthly] [in advance] from [   ] during joint lives until the   day of   20   or until the [respondent's/petitioner's] [earlier] remarriage or further order whichever shall be the earlier whereupon the [respondent's/petitioner's] claims for periodical payments and secured periodical payments shall stand dismissed and the [respondent/petitioner] shall not be entitled to make any further application in relation to the marriage under the Matrimonial Causes Act 1973, s23(1)(*a*) or (*b*) [and it is directed pursuant to the MCA 1973, s28(1A) that the [petitioner/respondent] shall not be entitled to apply for an extension of the term of the above order].

Form 43   Lump sum order   A2.43

The [petitioner/respondent] do pay or cause to be paid to the [Respondent/Petitioner] a lump sum of [£   ] payable within [three months] of the date of final decree hereon AND IT IS DIRECTED that interest shall be payable on the said lump sum by the [petitioner/respondent] at the rate applicable for the time being to a High Court judgment debt [from the date of this order until the date at which the said lump sum falls due for payment] [[and] in default of payment as aforesaid by way of a further instalment of the said   lump sum order from the date on which the said lump sum falls due for payment until the date of payment to the [Petitioner/ Respondent]].

A2.44   Form 44   Dismissal of claims

IT is ORDERED [*save as aforesaid*] that all claims of the petitioner [*and of the respondent*] for maintenance pending suit, periodical payments, secured periodical payments, lump sum, property adjustment and pension sharing orders [*or as appropriate*] shall be dismissed and neither the petitioner nor the respondent [*or as appropriate*] shall be entitled to make any further application in relation to the marriage under the Matrimonial Causes Act 1973, s23(1)(*a*) or (*b*).

A2.45   Form 45   Order under Inheritance (Provision for Family and Dependants) Act 1975, s 15

IT is ORDERED pursuant to the Inheritance (Provision for Family and Dependants) Act, s 15, the court considering it just to do so, that neither the petitioner nor the respondent shall on the death of the other be entitled to apply to the court for an order under s 2 of that Act.

Form 46—Form A: Notice of [intention to proceed with] an application for ancillary relief

Notice of an Application for Ancillary Relief

	In the
	County Court

Case No. *Always quote this*	
Applicant's Solicitor's reference	
Respondent's Solicitor's reference	

Name and Address of
Respondent(s) / Respondent(s) Solicitor

The marriage of   **and**

Take Notice that

The Applicant intends **to apply** to the Court for:

☐ an order for maintenance pending suit   ☐ a periodical payments order

☐ a secured provision order   ☐ a lump sum order

☐ a property adjustment order   ☐ an order under Section 24B, 25B
                                                                          or 25C of the Act of 1973

If an application is made for any periodical payments or secured periodical payments for children:

■   and there is a written agreement made before 5 April 1993 about maintenance for the benefit of children,
tick this box ☐
■   and there is a written agreement made on or after 5 April 1993 about maintenance for the benefit of children,
tick this box ☐
■   but there is no agreement, tick any of the boxes below to show if you are applying for payment:

☐   for a stepchild or stepchildren

☐   in addition to child support maintenance already paid under a Child Support Agency assessment

☐   to meet expenses arising from a child's disability

☐   to meet expenses incurred by a child in being educated or training for work

☐   when either the child **or** the person with care of the child **or** the absent parent of the child
is not habitually resident in the United Kingdom

☐   other (please state)

Signed: **Dated:**

[Solicitor for the Applicant]

The court office at

is open between 10 am and 4 pm (4.30 pm at the Principal Registry of the Family Division) Monday to Friday. When corresponding with
the court, please address forms or letters to the Court Manager and quote the case number. If you do not do so, your correspondence
may be returned.

Form A   Notice of an Application for Ancillary Relief   7 November 2002
Quantum Skip (version 2.02) from Class Publishing

A2.47   Form 47—Form B: Notice of application under FPR, r. 2.45 to consider financial position of Respondent

Notice of an application under Rule 2.45

In the	County Court
Case No. *Always quote this*	
Applicant's Solicitor's reference	
Respondent's Solicitor's reference	

The marriage of   and

Take Notice that

The Respondent intends to apply to the Court under section 10(2) of the Matrimonial Causes Act 1973 for the Court to consider the financial position of the Respondent after the divorce.

Signed: **Dated:**
[Solicitor for the respondent]

The court office at

is open between 10 am and 4 pm (4.30 pm at the Principal Registry of the Family Division) Monday to Friday. When corresponding with the court, please address forms or letter to the Court Manager and quote the case number. If you do not do so, your corrrespondence may be returned.

Form B   Notice of an Application under Rule 2.45   7 November 2002
Quantum Skip (version 2.02) from Class Publishing

Form 48—Form E: Financial statement

FINANCIAL STATEMENT

Applicant

In the	
	County Court
Case No *Always quote this*	

Between

Applicant	
Solicitor's ref.	

and

Respondent	
Solicitor's ref.	

Please fill in this form fully and accurately. Where any box is not applicable write "N/A". You have a duty to the court to give a full, frank and clear disclosure of all your financial and other relevant circumstances.

A failure to give full and accurate disclosure may result in any order the court makes being set aside.

If you are found to have been deliberately untruthful, criminal proceedings for perjury may be taken against you.

You must attach documents to the form where they are specifically sought and you may attach other documents where it is necessary to explain or clarify any of the information that you give.

Essential documents, which **must** accompany this Statement, are detailed at questions 2.1, 2.2, 2.3, 2.5, 2.14, 2.18 and 2.20.

If there is not enough room on the form for any particular piece of information, you may continue on an attached sheet of paper.

> This statement must be sworn before an Officer of the Court,
>
> a solicitor or a Commissioner for Oaths
>
> before it is filed with the Court
>
> or sent to the other party
>
> (see page 20).

Form E
Quantum Skip (version 2.02) from Class Publishing

1.1

7 November 2002

Form 48—Form E: Financial statement continued

Part 1 General information

1.1 Full name

	Day	Month	Year			Day	Month	Year
1.2 Date of birth					**1.3 Date of marriage**			

1.4 Occupation

1.5 Date of the separation

	Day	Month	Year

Tick here ☐ if not applicable

1.6 Date of the

Petition			Decree nisi/ Decree of Judicial Separation			Decree absolute		
Day	Month	Year	Day	Month	Year	Day	Month	Year

1.7 If you have remarried, or will remarry, state the date

Day	Month	Year

1.8 Do you live with another person? ☐ Yes ☒ No

1.9 Do you intend to live with someone within the next six months? ☐ Yes ☒ No

1.10 Details of any children of the family

Full names	Date of birth			With whom does the child live?
	Day	Month	Year	

1.11 Give details of the state of health of yourself and the children

Yourself	Children

Form 48—Form E: Financial statement continued

1.12 Give details of the present and proposed future educational arrangements for the children.

Present arrangements	Future arrangments

1.13 Give details of any Child Support Maintenance Assessments or Child Maintenance Orders made between the parties. If no assessment or agreement has been made, give an estimate of the liability of the non-residential parent under the Child Support Act 1991 in respect of the children of the family.

1.14 If this application is to vary an order, give details of the order that is to be varied and attach a copy of the order. Give the reasons for asking for the order to be varied.

1.15 Give details of any other court cases between you and your husband/wife, whether in relation to money, property, children, or anything else.

Case No.	Court

1.16 Specify your present residence and the occupants of it and on what terms you occupy it (e.g. tenant, owner-occupier).

Address	Occupants	Terms of occupation

Form 48—Form E: Financial statement continued

Part 2 Financial Details   *Capital: Realisable Assets*

* If you have obtained a valuation within the last six months attach a copy. If not, give your own estimate of the property value. A copy of your most recent mortgage statement is also required.

2.1   Give details of your interest in the matrimonial home.

Property name and address	Land Registry Title No.	Nature and extent of your interest	* Property value

Mortgagee's name and address	Type of mortgage	Balance outstanding on any mortgage	Total current value of your beneficial interest

NET value of your interest in the matrimonial home **(A)**	£0

2.2   Give details of all other properties, land, and buildings in which you have an interest.

Property name(s) and address(es)	Land Registry Title No.	Nature and extent of your interest	* Property value

Mortgagee's name(s) and address(es)	Type of mortgage	Balance outstanding on any mortgage	Total current value of your interest

TOTAL value of the above (not including the matrimonial home)	**(B1)** £0

Form 48—Form E: Financial statement continued

2.3 Give details of all bank, building society, and National Savings accounts, in credit, which you hold or have an interest in. Include all PEPs, TESSAs and ISAs. For joint accounts, give your interest and the name of the account holder. If the account is overdrawn, include in Liabilities section at 2.12.

You must attach your bank statements covering the last 12 months for each account listed

Name of bank or building society including Branch name	Type of account (e.g. current)	Account number	Name of other account holder (if applicable)	Balance at the date of this Statement	Total current value of your interest
				(B2)	
			TOTAL value of your interest in ALL accounts		£0

2.4 Give details of all stocks, gilts and other quoted securities which you hold or have an interest in. Do not include dividend income as this will be dealt with separately later on.

Name	Type	Size	Current value	Total current value of your interest
				(B3)
		TOTAL value of your interest in ALL holdings		£0

2.5 Give details of all life insurance policies which you hold or in which you have an interest, including those that do not have a surrender value, for each policy. *You must attach any surrender value quotations*

Policy details including name of company, policy type and number	If policy is charged, state in whose favour and amount of charge	Maturity date			Surrender value	Total current value of your interest
		Day	Month	Year		
						(B4)
	TOTAL value of your interest in ALL policies					£0

Form 48—Form E: Financial statement continued

2.6 Give details of all issues of National Savings certificates which you hold or have an interest in.

Name of issue	Nominal amount	Current value	Total current value of your interest
			(B5)
TOTAL value of your interest in ALL your certificates			£0

2.7 Give details of all National Savings bonds (including Premium bonds) and other bonds which you hold or have an interest in.

Type of bond	Bond holder's number	Current value	Total current value of your interest
			(B6)
TOTAL value of your interest in ALL your bonds			£0

2.8 Give details of all monies which are OWED TO YOU. Include sums owed in director's or partnership accounts.

Brief description of debt	Balance outstanding	Total current value of your interest
		(B7)
TOTAL value of your interest in ALL debts owed to you		£0

Form 48—Form E: Financial statement continued

2.9 Give details of all of cash savings held in excess of £300. You must state where it is held and the currency it is held in.

Where held	Amount	Currency	Total current value of your interest
		TOTAL value of ALL your cash	**(B8)** £0

2.10 Give details of personal belongings individually worth more than £500. Include cars (gross value), collections, pictures, jewellery, furniture, and household belongings (this list is not exhaustive).

Item	Sale value	Total estimated current value of your interest
TOTAL value of your interest in ALL personal belongings		**(B9)** £0

2.11 Give details of any other realisable assets not yet mentioned, for example, unit trusts, investment trusts, commodities, business expansion schemes and futures (this list is not exhaustive). This is where you must mention any other realisable assets.

Type	Current value	Total current value of your interest
TOTAL value of your interest in ALL other realisable assets		**(B10)** £0

Now add together all the figures in the previous total boxes (B1 to B10) to give the TOTAL current value of ALL your interest in realisable assets.

(B)	**£0**

Form 48—Form E: Financial statement continued

Part 2 Financial Details   *Capital: Liabilities*

2.12   Give details of any liabilities you have. Exclude mortgages on property dealt with above. Include money owed on credit cards and store cards, bank loans, hire purchase agreements and any overdrawn bank or building society accounts.

Liability (i.e. total amount owed, current monthly payments and term of loan/debt)	Current amount	Total current value of your share of the liability
TOTAL value of ALL your liabilities		(C1) £0

Part 2 Financial Details   *Capital: Capital Gains Tax*

2.13   If any Capital Gains Tax would be payable on the disposal now of any of your realisable assets, give your estimate of the tax.

Asset	Capital Gains Tax	Total current value of your liability
TOTAL value of ALL your Capital Gains Tax liabilities		(C2) £0

Now add together C1 + C2 to give:-
TOTAL net value of your liabilities   **(C)**   £0

Now take the liabilities total from the realisable
assets total (A + B - C), to give:-   **(D)**   £0
TOTAL net value of your personal assets

Form 48—Form E: Financial statement continued

Part 2 Financial Details *Capital: Business Assets*

2.14 Give details of all your business interests.

You must attach a copy of the last 2 years accounts and any other document on which you base your valuation.

Name and nature of your business	Your ESTIMATE of the current value of your interest	Your ESTIMATE of any possible Capital Gains Tax payable on disposal	Basis of valuation *(No formal valuation is is required at this time)*	What is the extent of your interest?	Total net current value of your interest
TOTAL current value of your interest in business assets **(E)**					£0

2.15 List any directorships you hold or held in the last 12 months.

Form 48—Form E: Financial statement continued

Part 2 Financial Details

Capital: Pensions (including SERPS but excluding basic state pensions)

2.16   Give details of your pension interests.

If you have been provided with a valuation of your pension rights by the trustees or managers of the pension scheme, you must attach it. Where the information is not available, give the estimated date when it will be available and attach the letter to pension company or administrators from whom the information was sought. If you have more than one pension plan or scheme, you must provide the information in respect of each one, continuing, if necessary, on a separate piece of paper. If you have made Additional Voluntary Contributions or any Free Standing Additional Voluntary Contributions to any plan or scheme, you must give the information separately if the benefits referable to such contributions are separately recorded or paid. Please include any SERPS.

Information about the scheme(s)

Name and address of scheme, plan or policy	
Your national insurance number	
Number of scheme, plan or policy	
Type of scheme, plan or policy *(e.g. final salary, money purchase or other)*	

CETV - Cash Equivalent Transfer Value

CETV Value	
The lump sum payable on death in service before retirement	
The lump sum payable on death in deferment before retirement	
The lump sum payable on death after retirement	

Retirement Benefits

Earliest date when benefit can be paid	
The estimated lump sum and monthly pension payable on retirement, assuming you take the maximum lump sum	
The estimated monthly pension without taking any lump sum	

Spouse's Benefit

On death in service	
On death in deferment	
On death in retirement	

Dependant's Benefit

On death in service	
On death in deferment	
On death in retirement	

TOTAL value of your pension assets **(F)**   £0

Form 48—Form E: Financial statement continued

Part 2 Financial Details   *Capital: Other Assets*

2.17 Give details of any other assets not listed above.
Include the following (this list is not exhaustive):

  *   Unrealisable assets.

  *   Share option scheme, stating the estimated net sale proceeds of the shares if the options were capable of exercise now, and whether Capital Gains Tax or Income Tax would be payable.

  *   Trust interests (including interests under a discretionary trust), stating your estimate of the value of the interest and when it is likely to become realisable. If you say it will never be realisable, or has no value, give your reasons.

  *   Specify also any asset that is likely to be received in the forseeable future, any assets held on your behalf by a third party and any assets not mentioned elswhere in this form held outside England and Wales.

Type of asset	Value	Total net value of your interest

TOTAL value of your other assets   **(G)**   £0

TOTAL value of your net assets (excluding pensions) **(H)**   £0
(D + E + G)

TOTAL value of your net assets (including pensions) **(I)**   £0
(F + H)

Form 48—Form E: Financial statement continued

Part 2 Financial Details *Income*

2.18   Earned Income: Give details of your gross and net   *You must attach your last three payslips and your*
income in the last financial year, and in the current   *P60 for the most recently completed financial year.*
financial year.

Nature of income *(e.g. salary, bonus)*	Last financial year		Current financial year *(estimated for the whole year)*	
	Gross	Net	Gross	Net

2.19   Additional Income: benefits, etc. Give details and the value of all benefits in kind, perks, or other
remuneration not disclosed elsewhere, received in the last financial year and current financial year.

Nature of income	Last financial year	Current financial year *(estimated for the whole year)*

Form 48—Form E: Financial statement continued

2.20 Self-employed or partnership income: Give details of annual net profit or loss for the last two accounting years, your share of this figure and tax payable to date of the last accounts and the estimate of income since that date. State the date on which your accounting year begins. Year 2 should be the most recent year, Year 1 the previous year. Please state the "from" and "to" dates for the years concerned.

You must attach the accounts for the last two completed accounting years.

Nature of income and date your accounting year begins	Details of the last two accounting periods					
	Net profit/loss		Your share of profit/loss		Tax payable by you	
	Year 1	Year 2	Year 1	Year 2	Year 1	Year 2

Net income SINCE date of last accounts and estimate for the whole year	
Net income	Estimate

2.21 Investment income (e.g. dividends, interest). Give details of net income received in the last financial year, and in the current financial year and state whether it was paid gross or net of income tax. You are not required to calculate any tax payable that may arise.

Nature of income and the asset from which it derived	Paid gross or net (delete that which is not applicable)	Last financial year	Current financial year

2.22 State benefits (including state pension). Give details of all state benefits received in the last 52 weeks.

Nature of income	Total income received in the last 52 weeks

Form 48—Form E: Financial statement continued

2.23 Any other income. Give details of any other income received in the last 52 weeks.

Nature of income	Total income for the last 52 weeks

Part 2 Financial Details   *Summaries*

2.24 Summary of your income

Your estimate of your current annual net income from all sources (2.18 - 2.23)	Your estimate of your net income from all sources for the next 52 weeks
	(J)

2.25 Summary of financial information

	Reference of the section on this statement	Value
Net value of your interest in the matrimonial home	A	£0
Total current value of all your interest in the other realisable assets	B	£0
Total net value of your liabilities	C	£0
Total net value of your personal assets	D	£0
Total current value of your interest in business assets	E	£0
Total current value of your pension or transfer values	F	£0
Total value of your other assets	G	£0
Total value of your net assets (excluding pension)	H	£0
Total value of your net assets (including pension)	I	£0
Your estimated net income for the next 52 weeks	J	£0

Form 48—Form E: Financial statement continued

Part 3 Requirements *Income Needs*

3.1 Give the reasonable future income needs of yourself (e.g. housing, car, etc.) and of any children living with you or provided for by you. This may be expressed as annual, monthly or weekly figures (state which), but you should not use a combination of any of these periods.

Item	Income needs of yourself	Amount
	Total income needs of yourself	£0

Item	Income needs of child(ren) living with you, or provided for by you	Amount
	Total income needs of children	£0

	Total income needs	£0

Form 48—Form E: Financial statement continued

Part 3 Requirements   *Capital Needs*

3.2 Give the reasonable future capital needs of yourself and of any children living with you, or provided for by you.

Item	Capital needs of yourself	Cost
	Total capital needs of yourself	£0

Item	Capital needs of child(ren) living with you, or provided for by you	Cost
	Total capital needs of children	£0
	Total capital needs	£0

Form 48—Form E: Financial statement continued

Part 4   Other Information

4.1   State whether there has been any significant change in your net assets during the last 12 months, including any assets held outside England and Wales (e.g. closure of any bank or building society accounts).

4.2   Give brief details of the standard of living enjoyed by you and your spouse during the marriage.

4.3   Are there any particular contributions to the family property and assets or outgoings, or to family life that have been made by you, your partner or anyone else that you think should be taken into account? If so, give a brief description of the contribution, the amount, when it was made, and by whom.

4.4   Bad behaviour or conduct by the other party will only be taken into account in very exceptional circumstances when deciding how the assets should be divided after divorce. If you feel it should be taken into account in your case, identify the nature of the behaviour or conduct.

Form 48—Form E: Financial statement continued

4.5   Give details of any other circumstances which you consider could significantly affect the extent of the financial provision to be made by or for you or for any child of the family e.g. earning capacity, disability, inheritance prospects or redundancy, remarriage and cohabitation plans, any contingent liabilities. (This list is not exhaustive).

4.6   If you have remarried (or intend to) or are living with another person (or intend to) give brief details, so far as they are known to you, of his or her income and assets.

Annual Income		Assets	
Nature of income	Annual Income (state whether gross or net, if known)	Item	Value (if known)
Total income *(Gross)* *(Net)*	£0 £0	Total assets	£0

Form 48—Form E: Financial statement continued

Part 5 Order Sought

5.1 If you are able to at this stage, specify what kind of orders you are asking the court to make, and state whether at this stage you see the case being appropriate for a "clean break". (A "clean break" means a settlement or order which provides, amongst other things, that neither you nor your spouse will have any further claim against the income or capital of the other party. A clean break does not terminate the responsibility of a parent to a child.)

5.2 ** If you are seeking a transfer or settlement of any property or other asset, you must identify the asset in question.

5.3 ** If you are seeking a variation of a pre-nuptial or post-nuptial settlement, you must identify the settlement, by whom it was made, its trustees and beneficiaries, and state why you allege it is a nuptial settlement.

** **Important Note:** Where 5.2, 5.3 (above) or 5.4 (overleaf) apply, you should seek legal advice before completing the sections.

Form 48—Form E: Financial statement continued

5.4   **   If you are seeking an avoidance of disposition order, you must identify the property to which the disposition relates and the person or body in whose favour the disposition is alleged to have been made.

Sworn confirmation of the information

I   *(the above named Applicant)*

of   make oath and confirm that the information given above is a full, frank, clear and accurate disclosure of my financial and other relevant circumstances.

Signed	Dated

Sworn by the above named Applicant at

on

before me

A

Address all communications to the Court Manager of the Court and quote the case number from page 1. If you do not quote this number, your correspondence may be returned.

The Court office at

is open from 10 a.m. to 4 p.m. (4.30 p.m. at the Principal Registry of the Family Division) on Monday to Friday only.

Form 49—Form F: Notice of allegation

Notice of Allegation in Proceedings for Ancillary Relief

In the	
	County Court
Case No. *Always quote this*	
Applicant's Solicitor's reference	
Respondent's Solicitor's reference	

The marriage of   and

Take Notice that

This statement has been filed in proceedings for ancillary relief:

Signed: **Dated:**
[Respondent/Solicitor for the respondent]

If you wish to be heard on any matter affecting you in these proceedings you may intervene by applying to the court for directions regarding:

- the filing and service of pleadings
- the conduct of further proceedings

You must apply for directions **within eight days** after you received this Notice. The period of eight days includes the day you receive it.

The court office at

is open between 10 am and 4 pm (4.30 pm at the Principal Registry of the Family Division) Monday to Friday. When corresponding with the court, please address forms or letters to the Court Manager and quote the case number. If you do not do so, your correspondence may be returned.

Form F   Notice of allegation in proceedings for ancillary relief
Quantum Skip (version 2.02) from Class Publishing

7 November 2002

A2.50   Form 50—Form G: Notice of response to first appointment

Notice of response to First Appointment	**In the**	
		County Court
	Case No. *Always quote this*	
	Applicant's Solicitor's reference	
	Respondent's Solicitor's reference	

The marriage of   and

Take Notice that

At the First Appointment which will be heard on

at   pm

the Applicant will not be in a position to proceed on that occasion with a Financial Dispute Resolution appointment.

Dated:

The court office at

is open between 10 am and 4 pm (4.30 pm at the Principal Registry of the Family Division) Monday to Friday. When corresponding with the court, please address forms or letters to the Court Manager and quote the case number. If you do not do so, your correspondence may be returned.

Form G Notice of response to First Appointment   *7 November 2002*
Quantum Skip (version 2.02) from Class Publishing

Form 51—Form H: Costs estimate

Ancillary Relief Costs Estimate of *[Applicant] *[Respondent]

In the	
	*[County Court] *[Principal Registry of the Family Division]
Case No. *Always quote this*	
Applicant's Solicitor's reference	
Respondent's Solicitor's reference	

(delete as appropriate)*

The marriage of   and

PART 1

		Prescribed Rates for publicly funded services £	Indemnity Rates £
1.	Ancillary relief solicitor's costs *(including VAT)* including costs of the current hearing, and any previous solicitor's costs		
2.	Disbursements *(include VAT, if appropriate, and any incurred by previous solicitors)*		
3.	All Counsel's fees *(including VAT)*		
	TOTAL		

PART 2

4.	Add any private client costs previously incurred *(in publicly funded cases only)*		
5.	GRAND TOTAL		

PART 3

6.	State what has been paid towards the total at 5 above		
7.	Amount of any contributions paid by the funded client towards their publicly funded services		

NB   If you are publicly funded and might be seeking an order for costs against the other party complete both rates.

Dated:

The court office at

is open between 10 am and 4 pm (4.30 pm at the Principal Registry of the Family Division) Monday to Friday. When corresponding with the court, please address forms or letters to the Court Manager and quote the case number. If you do not do so, your correspondence may be returned.

Quantum Skip (version 2.02) from Class Publishing
Form H   Costs Estimate

A2.52   Form 52—Form I: Notice of request for periodical payments order at same rate as order for maintenance pending suit

---

Notice of request for periodical payments order at same rate as order for maintenance pending suit (Form I)

Notice of Request for Periodical Payments Order at same rate as Order for Maintenance Pending Suit

In the	
	*[County Court] *[Principal Registry of the Family Division]
Case No. *Always quote this*	
Applicant's Solicitor's reference	
Respondent's Solicitor's reference	

(*delete as appropriate)

The marriage of   and

Take Notice that

On   1999 [20   ] the Applicant obtained an Order for you to pay maintenance pending suit at the rate of £

The Applicant having applied in his/her petition (answer) for a Periodical Payments Order for himself/ herself has requested the Court to make such an Order at the same rate as above.

What to do if you object to this Order being made.

If you object to the making of such a Periodical Payments Order, you must notify the District Judge and the Applicant/Respondent of your objections within 14 days of this notice being served on you. If you do not do so, the District Judge may make an Order without notifying you further.

The court office at

is open between 10 am and 4 pm (4 30pm at the Principal Registry of the Family Division) Monday to Friday. When corresponding with the court, please address forms or letters to the Court Manager and quote the case number. If you do not do so, your correspondence may be returned.

Form I Notice of Request for Periodical Payments Order at same rate as Order for Maintenance Pending Suit (12.00)   *Printed on behalf of The Court Service*

Form 53—Form M1 - Statement of information for a consent order (*FPR, r 2.61*)

A2.53

In the

County Court

No. of matter

Between

Petitioner   *Solicitor's ref*

and

Respondent   *Solicitor's ref*

Statement of information for a consent order

Duration of Marriage
Give the date of your marriage and the date of the decree absolute (if pronounced)

Ages of parties
Give the age of any minor (i.e. under the age of 18) or dependant child(ren) of the family.

Petitioner _____   Respondent _____

Child(ren) _____   _____   _____   _____

Summary of means
Give, as at the date this statement is signed overleaf:

*(1) the approximate amount or value of **captial resources**. If there is a property give its net equity and details of the proposed distribution of the equity.*

*(2) the **net income** of the petitioner and respondent and, where relevant, of minor or dependant child(ren) of the family.*

*(3) the value of any benefits under **a pension scheme** which you have or are likely to have, including the most recent valuation (if any) provided by the pension scheme.*

***Note:** if the application is only made for an order for interim periodical payments, or for variation of an order for periodical payments, you only need to give details of 'net income'.*

	(1) Capital Resources *(less any unpaid mortgage or charge)*	(2) Net income	(3) Pension
Petitioner			
Respondent			
Children			

Where the parties and the children will live
Give details of the arrangements which are intended for the accommodation of each of the parties and any minor or dependant child(ren) of the family.

M1 Statement of information for a consent order (Family Proceedings Rules) (D81)   Laserform International 9/01

Form 53—Form M1 - Statement of information for a consent order (*FPR, r 2.61*) continued

Marital plans

Please tick box and, if appropriate, give the date of the marriage if you know it.

	No intention to marry or cohabit at present	Has remarried	Intends to marry	Intends to cohabit with another person
Petitioner	☐	☐ Date of marriage:	☐ Date of marriage:	☐
Respondent	☐	☐ Date of marriage:	☐ Date of marriage:	☐

Notice to Mortgagee

These questions are to be answered by the applicant where the terms of the order provide for a transfer of property.

Has every mortgagee (if any) of the property been served with notice of the application?   Yes ☐   No ☐

Has any objection to a transfer of property been made by any mortgagee, within 14 days from the date when the notice of the application was served?   Yes ☐   No ☐

Notice to Pension Fund or Insurance Scheme

These questions are to be answered by the applicant where the terms of an order under section 23 of the Matrimonial Causes Act 1973 include provision by virtue of section 25B and section 25C of that Act.

Has every Trustee or Manager of any pension fund, insurance scheme or similar arrangement been served with notice of the application and notice under Rule 2.70 (4)(a)(b) and (c) of the Family Proceedings Rules 1991?   Yes ☐   No ☐

Has any objection to an order under section 23 of the Matrimonial Causes Act 1973 which includes provision by virtue of section 25B and section 25C of that Act been made by a Trustee or Manager within 14 days from the date when the notice of the application was served?   Yes ☐   No ☐

Other information

Give details of any other especially significant matters.

Signed

[Solicitor for] Petitioner

Date

[Solicitor for] Respondent

Date

Form 54   Originating summons under s 17 of the Married Women's   A2.54
Property Act 1882 (High Court)
(*Form M23 of FPR*)

In the High Court of Justice
Family Division
[District Registry]
In the Matter of an Application by
under s 17 of the Married Women's Property Act 1882
Between   Applicant
and   Respondent
   Let   of
attend before District Judge   in chambers at the Divorce Registry,
42/49 High Holborn, London, WC1V 6NP, [*or as the case may be*] on
day, the   day of   , 20   , at   o'clock, on the hearing of
an application by   for an order in the following terms:-
[*here set out terms of order sought*]

Dated this   day of   20

This summons was taken out by

[Solicitor for] the above-named applicant

To the respondent
TAKE NOTICE that:—

1   A copy of the affidavit to be used in support of the application is
    delivered herewith.

2   You must complete the accompanying acknowledgment of service
    and send it so as to reach the Court within eight days after you receive
    this summons.

3   If you wish to dispute the claim made by the applicant you must file
    an affidavit in answer within 14 days after the time allowed for
    sending the acknowledgment of service.

4   If you intend to instruct a solicitor to act for you you should at once
    give him all the documents served on you, so that he may take the nec-
    essary steps on your behalf.

A2.55   Form 55   Appeal from district judge in county court

Notice of appeal from district judge when case proceeding in a county court

[Heading as for main case]

TAKE NOTICE that the [Respondent/Applicant] will apply to one of the judges of this Court in Chambers at [*address*] on [*date*] for an order that the order of District Judge [*name*] whereby it was ordered that [*set out parts of order appealed against*] be set aside and for an order that [*set out order sought*].

And that the [Respondent/Applicant] be ordered to pay the costs of the appeal and below.

GROUNDS OF APPEAL

The district judge erred in that:

[Set out grounds relied on.]

Form 56   Penal notice endorsed on a decree or order (county court)   A2.56

To :
of :

You must obey the directions contained in this order.
   If you do not, you will be guilty of contempt of court and may be sent to prison.

Dated :
District Judge

Form 57   Penal notice endorsed on a decree or order (High Court)   A2.57

If you the within-named   neglect to obey this decree [*or* order] by the time stated [*or* disobey this decree [*or* order]] you may be held in contempt of court and liable to imprisonment.

A2.58   Form 58   Specimen orders under FLA 1996, Part IV)
(*Form FL404*)

Orders made on applications for non-molestation orders and occupation orders (Form FL404)

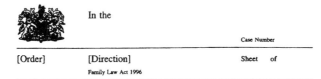

In the

Case Number

[Order]   [Direction]   Sheet   of

Family Law Act 1996

Form 58   Specimen orders under FLA 1996, Part IV) continued
(*Form FL404*)

	In the	
		Case Number
[Order]	[Direction]	Sheet of
	Family Law Act 1996	

Ordered by   [Mr] [Mrs] Justice

[His] [Her] Honour Judge

[Deputy] District Judge [of the Family Division]

Justice[s] of the Peace

[Assistant] Recorder

Clerk of the Court

on

Form 58   Specimen orders under FLA 1996, Part IV) continued
(*Form FL404*)

<u>Orders under Family Law Act 1996 Part IV</u>

(*General heading followed by Notice A or Notice B and numbered options as appropriate*)

<u>Notice A – order includes non-molestation order – penal notice mandatory</u>

Important Notice to the Respondent [name]

This order gives you instructions which you must follow. You should read it all carefully. If you do not understand anything in this order you should go to a solicitor, Legal Advice Centre or Citizens Advice Bureau. You have a right to ask the court to change or cancel the order but you must obey it unless the court does change or cancel it.

You must obey the instructions contained in this order. If you do not, you will be guilty of contempt of court, and you may be sent to prison.

<u>Notice B – order does not include non-molestation order – *penal notice discretionary</u>

Important Notice to the Respondent [name]

This order gives you instructions which you must follow. You should read it all carefully. If you do not understand anything in this order you should go to a solicitor, Legal Advice Centre or Citizens Advice Bureau. You have a right to ask the court to change or cancel the order but you must obey it unless the court does change or cancel it.

You must obey the instructions contained in this order. *[If you do not, you will be guilty of contempt of court, and you may be sent to prison.]

Form 58   Specimen orders under FLA 1996, Part IV) continued
(*Form FL404*)

<u>Occupation orders under s33 of the Family Law Act 1996</u>

1.   The court declares that the applicant [name] is entitled to occupy [*address of home or intended home*] as [*his/her*] home. **OR**

2.   The court declares that the applicant [name] has matrimonial home rights in [*address of home or intended home*]. **AND/OR**

3.   The court declares that the applicant [name]'s matrimonial home rights shall not end when the respondent [name] dies or their marriage is dissolved and shall continue until ... or further order.

It is ordered that:

4.   The respondent [name] shall allow the applicant [name] to occupy [*address of home or intended home*] **OR**

5.   The respondent [name] shall allow the applicant [name] to occupy part of [*address of home or intended home*] namely: [*specify part*]

6.   The respondent [name] shall not obstruct, harass or interfere with the applicant [name]'s peaceful occupation of [*address of home or intended home*]

7.   The respondent [name] shall not occupy [*address of home or intended home*] **OR**

8.   The respondent [name] shall not occupy [*address of home or intended home*] from [*specify date*] until [*specify date*] **OR**

9.   The respondent [name] shall not occupy [*specify part of address of home or intended home*] **AND/OR**

10.   The respondent [name] shall not occupy [*address or part of address*] between [*specify dates or times*]

11.   The respondent [name] shall leave [*address or part of address*] [forthwith] [within ___ [*hours/days*] of service on [*him/her*] of this order.] **AND/OR**

12.   Having left [*address or part of address*], the respondent [name] shall not return to, enter or attempt to enter [or go within [*specify distance*] of] it.

Form 58 Specimen orders under FLA 1996, Part IV) continued
(*Form FL404*)

Occupation orders under ss35 & 36 of the Family Law Act 1996

It is ordered that:

13. The applicant [name] has the right to occupy [*address of home or intended home*] and the respondent [name] shall allow the applicant [name] to do so. **OR**

14. The respondent [name] shall not evict or exclude the applicant [name] from [*address of home or intended home*] or any part of it namely [*specify part*]. **AND/OR**

15. The respondent [name] shall not occupy [*address of home or intended home*]. **OR**

16. The respondent [name] shall not occupy [*address of home or intended home*] from [*specify date*] until [*specify date*] **OR**

17. The respondent [name] shall not occupy [*specify part of address of home or intended home*] **OR**

18. The respondent [name] shall leave [*address or part of address*] [forthwith] [within ___ [*hours/days*] of service on [*him/her*] of this order.] **AND/OR**

19. Having left [*address or part of address*], the respondent [name] shall not return to, enter or attempt to enter [or go within [*specify distance*] of] it.

Occupation orders under ss37 & 38 of the Family Law Act 1996

It is ordered that:

20. The respondent [name] shall allow the applicant [name] to occupy [*address of home or intended home*] or part of it namely: [*specify*]. **AND/OR**

21. [One or both of the provisions in paragraphs 6 & 10 above may be inserted] **AND/OR**

22. The respondent [name] shall leave [*address or part of address*] [forthwith] [within ___ [*hours/days*] of service on [*him/her*] of this order.] **AND/OR**

23. Having left [*address or part of address*], the respondent [name] may not return to, enter or attempt to enter [or go within [*specify distance*] of] it.

Form 58   Specimen orders under FLA 1996, Part IV) continued
(*Form FL404*)

Additional provisions which may be included in occupation orders made under ss33, 35 or 36 of Family Law Act 1996

It is ordered that:

24.   The [*applicant [name]*] [*respondent [name]*] shall maintain and repair [*address of home or intended home*] **AND/OR**

25.   The [*applicant [name]*] [*respondent [name]*] shall pay the rent for [*address of home or intended home*] **OR**

26.   The [*applicant [name]*] [*respondent [name]*] shall pay the mortgage payments on [*address of home or intended home*]. **OR**

27.   The [*applicant [name]*] [*respondent [name]*] shall pay the following for [*address of home or intended home*]: [specify outgoings as bullet points].

28.   The [*party in occupation*] shall pay to the [*other party*] £   each [*week, month, etc*] for [*address of home etc*].

29.   The [*party in occupation*] shall keep and use the [*furniture*] [*contents*] [*specify if necessary*] of [*address of home or intended home*] and the [*applicant [name]*] [*respondent [name]*] shall return to the [*party in occupation*] the [*furniture*] [contents] [*specify if necessary*] [*no later than [date/time]*].

30.   The [*party in occupation*] shall take reasonable care of the [*furniture*] [*contents*] [*specify if necessary*] of [*address of home or intended home*].

31.   The [*party in occupation*] shall take all reasonable steps to keep secure [*address of home or intended home*] and the furniture or other contents [*specify if necessary*].

Form 58   Specimen orders under FLA 1996, Part IV) continued
(*Form FL404*)

Duration

Occupation orders under s33 of the Family Law Act 1996

32.   This order shall last until [*specify event or date*]. **OR**

33.   This order shall last until a further order is made.

Occupation orders under ss35 & 37 of the Family Law Act 1996

34.   This order shall last until [*state date which must not be more than 6 months from the date of this order*].

35.   The occupation order made on [*state date*] is extended until [*state date which must not be more than 6 months from the date of this extension*].

Occupation orders under ss36 & 38 Family Law Act 1996

36.   This order shall last until [*state date which must not be more than 6 months from the date of this order*].

35.   The occupation order made on [*state date*] is extended until [*state date which must not be more than 6 months from the date of this extension*] and must end on that date.

Form 58   Specimen orders under FLA 1996, Part IV) continued
(*Form FL404*)

Non-molestation orders

It is ordered that:

38.   The respondent [name] is forbidden to use or threaten violence against the applicant [name] [and must not instruct, encourage or in any way suggest that any other person should do so]. **AND/OR**

39.   The respondent [name] is forbidden to intimidate, harass or pester [*or [specify]*] the applicant [name] [and must not instruct, encourage or in any way suggest that any other person should do so]. **AND/OR**

40.   The respondent [name] is forbidden to use or threaten violence against the relevant child(ren) [name(s) and date(s) of birth] [and must not instruct, encourage or in any way suggest that any other person should do so]. **AND/OR**

41.   The respondent [name] is forbidden to intimidate, harass or pester [*or [specify]*] [the relevant child(ren) [name(s) and date(s) of birth] [and must not instruct, encourage or in any way suggest that any other person should do so].

A2.59 **Form 59 Certificate as to postponement of statutory charge**

IT IS CERTIFIED that for the purpose of the Community Legal Service (Financial) Regulations 2000 and Access to Justice Act 1999 [that the lump sum of £[   ] has been ordered to be paid to enable the [Petitioner/ Respondent] to purchase a home for [himself/herself] [or [his/her] dependants]] [that the property at [   ] has been [preserved/recovered] for the [Petitioner/Respondent] for the use as a home for [himself/herself] [or [his/her] dependants]].

A2.60 **Form 60 Pension sharing order**

BY CONSENT] IT IS ORDERED that:
[1] [Unless the [Respondent]/[Petitioner] predeceases* the [Petitioner]/ [Respondent] prior to the implementation of this order in which event only it shall not be carried into effect] there be provision by way of pension sharing in favour of the [Petitioner]/[Respondent] in respect of the [Petitioner]/ [Respondent]'s rights under [his]/[her] pension arrangement[s] with ['] in accordance with the [annex[es]] to this order.

Form 61—Form P1: Pension sharing annex

Pension Sharing Annex under Section 24B of the Matrimonial Causes Act 1973 (Rule 2.70 (14) FPR 1991)	**In the** *[County Court] *[Principal Registry of the Family Division]

Case No. *Always quote this*	
Applicant's Solicitor's reference	
Respondent's Solicitors' reference	

The marriage of

Take Notice that:

On [*date*] the court

- made a pension sharing order under Part IV of the Welfare Reform and Pensions Act 1999.

- [varied] [discharged] an order which included provision for pension sharing made under Part IV of the Welfare Reform and Pensions Act 1999 and dated [*date*].

This annex to the order provides the person responsible for the pension arrangement with the information required by virtue of The Family Proceedings Rules 1991 as amended.

1. Name of the Transferor:

2. Name of the Transferee:

3. The Transferor's National Insurance Number:

4. Details of the Pension Arrangement and Policy Reference Number:

   (or such other details to enable the pension arrangement to be identified).

5. The specified percentage value of the pension arrangement to be transferred:

   (The specified amount required in order to create a pension credit and debit should only be inserted where specifically ordered by the court).

   In accordance with The Divorce etc. (Pensions) Regulations 2000 the court has specified that the benefits shall be valued as at the following date:

Form P1 Pension Sharing Annex under Section 24B of the Matrimonial Causes Act 1973 (Rule 2.70 (14) FPR 1991) (12.00)

Reproduced by Addleshaw Booth & Co

Form 61—Form P1: Pension sharing annex continued

6. Pension Sharing Charges:

   (*Delete as appropriate)

   It is directed that:

   *The pension sharing charges be apportioned between the parties as follows:

   *The pension sharing charges be paid in full by the transferor.

The court is satisfied that the person responsible for the pension arrangement has furnished the information required by Regulation 4 of the Pensions on Divorce etc. (Provision of Information) Regulations 2000 and, that it appears from the information that there is power to make an order including provision under section 24B (pension sharing) of the Act 1973.

THIS [ORDER] [PROVISION] TAKES EFFECT FROM

To the person responsible for the pension arrangement:
(*Delete as appropriate)

1. *Take notice that you must discharge your liability within the period of 4 months beginning with the later of:

   - the day on which this order or provision takes effect; or,

   - the first day on which you are in receipt of -

     a.　this [order] [provision] for ancillary relief, including the annex;

     b.　the decree of divorce or nullity of marriage; and

     c.　the information prescribed by Regulation 5 of the Pensions on Divorce etc. (Provision of Information) Regulations 2000.

2. *The court directs that the implementation period for discharging your liability should be determined by regulations made under section 34(4) or 41(2)(a) of the Welfare Reform and Pensions Act 1999, in that:

Form 62—Form P2: Pension attachment annex   A2.62

Pension Attachment Annex under
Section 25B or 25C of the
Matrimonial Causes Act 1973
(Rule 2.70 (15) FPR 1991)

In the	
	*[County Court]
*[Principal Registry of the Family Division]	

Case No. *Always quote this*	
Applicant's Solicitor's reference	
Respondent's Solicitors' reference	

The marriage of

Take Notice that:

On [*date*] the court

- made an order including provision under section [25B] [25C]* of the Matrimonial Causes Act 1973.

- [varied] [discharged] an order which included provision under section [25B] [25C]* of the Matrimonial Causes Act 1973 and dated [*date*].

(*delete as appropriate)

This annex to the order provides the person responsible for the pension arrangement with the information required by virtue of The Family Proceedings Rules 1991 as amended.

1. Name of the party with the pension rights:

2. Name of the other party:

3. The National Insurance Number of the party with pension rights:

4. Details of the Pension Arrangement and Policy Reference Number:

    (or such other details to enable the pension arrangement to be identified).

5. *The specified percentage of any payment due to the party with pension rights that is to be paid for the benefit of the other party:

    *The person responsible for the pension arrangement is required to:

    (*delete as appropriate)

    In accordance with The Divorce etc. (Pensions) Regulations 2000 the court has specified that the benefits shall be valued as at the following date:

Form P2 Pension Attachment Annex under Section 25B or 25C of the Matrimonial Causes Act 1973 (Rule 2.70 (15) FPR 1991) (12.00)

Reproduced by Addleshaw Booth & Co

Form 62—Form P2: Pension attachment annex continued

To the person responsible for the pension arrangement:
(*Delete if this information had already been provided to the person responsible for the pension arrangement with Form A or pursuant to FPR 2.70(11))

1.   *You are required to serve any notice under the Divorce etc. (Pensions) Regulations 2000 on the other party at the following address:

2.   *You are required to make any payments due under the pension arrangement to the other party at the following address:

3.   *If the address at 2. above is that of a bank, building society or the Department of National Savings the following details will enable you to make payment into the account of the other party (e.g. Account Name, Number, Bank/Building Society/etc. Sort code):

Note: Where the order to which this annex applies was made by consent the following section should also be completed.

The court also confirms:
(*Delete as appropriate)

-   *That notice under Rule 2.70(11) of the Family Proceedings Rules 1991 has been served on the person responsible for the pension arrangement and that no objection has been received under Rule 2.70(12).

-   *That notice under Rule 2.70(11) of the Family Proceedings Rules 1991 has been served on the person responsible for the pension arrangement and that the court has considered any objection received under Rule 2.70(12)(b)

Form 63—Letter to pension provider seeking disclosure of information   **A2.63**

Dear Sirs

[*Party with pension rights*]
[*Name and reference number for pension arrangement*]

We act for [*party with pension rights*] in divorce proceedings and would be grateful if you would supply us with the following information in relation to the above pension arrangement pursuant to the Family Proceedings Rules 1991, r 2.70(2):

1 The CETV value of pension rights or benefits accrued under the above arrangement;

2 A statement summarising the way in which the valuation referred to in paragraph 1 is calculated;

3 The pension benefits, which are included in the valuation referred to in paragraph 1;

4 Whether you offer membership to a person entitled to a pension credit and, if so, the types of benefits available to pension credit members under that arrangement;

5 Whether you intend to discharge your liability for a pension credit other than by offering membership to a person entitled to a pension credit; and

6 The schedule of charges which you will levy in accordance with the Pensions on Divorce etc (Charging) Regulations 2000, reg 2(2).

Under the Pensions on Divorce etc (Provision of Information) Regulations 2000, reg 2[(5)/(6)], the information must be provided within [*see note 2*] of the date of this request.

We would be also be grateful for the following additional information, which our client is also required by the Family Proceedings Rules 1991, r 2.61B to provide to the court and [his wife/her husband]:

7 The lump sum payable on death in service before retirement;

8 The lump sum payable on death in deferment before retirement;

9 The lump sum payable on death after retirement;

10 The earliest date when benefit can be paid;

11 The estimated lump sum and monthly pension payable on retirement, assuming that the maximum lump sum is taken;

12 The estimated monthly pension without taking any lump sum;

13 The spouse's benefit on death in service;

14 The spouse's benefit on death in deferment;

15 The spouse's benefit on death in retirement;

16 The dependant's benefit on death in service;

17 The dependant's benefit on death in deferment;

18 The dependant's benefit on death in retirement.

We look forward to hearing from you. Please quote our above reference.

Yours faithfully

Notes:
(1) This specimen letter attempts to collate the information required by section 2.16 of Form E and FPR, r 2.70(2). It is submitted that section 2.16 (which predates the Family Proceedings (Amendment) Rules 2000 (SI 2000/2267)) requires revision.

(2) The time limit for supplying the information required by FPR, r 2.70(2) is three months of the request or (if needed in connection with proceedings) six weeks (or such shorter period as may be specified by the court). Where the request relates to information other than a valuation, the time limit is one month.

A2.64   Form 64—Draft joint letter of instruction to expert

Dear Sirs

Mr and Mrs [   ]
[Address of property to be valued]

We act for [   ] in connection with divorce proceedings. [   ], solicitors, of [   ] (tel: [   ], ref: [   ]) act for [   ].

We are writing jointly to request that you prepare a valuation of the property referred to above which is owned in the [sole/joint] name[s] of [/ the parties] on the basis of the open market value of the property in its current condition with vacant possession.

We should be grateful if you would ensure that your valuation report complies with Part 35 of the Civil Procedure Rules and that:

1 The report is addressed to [   ] County Court and not to either of the instructing firms.

2 The report contains details of your qualifications and of any literature or other materials upon which you have relied in making your report.

3 The report must contain a statement setting out the substance of all material instructions (written or oral) and should summarise the facts in the instructions which are material to the opinions in your report, making clear which of the facts stated are within your own knowledge. We anticipate attaching a copy of this letter of instruction should suffice, unless it is necessary for you to make further enquiries.

4 Where there is a range of opinion on the matters dealt with in your report, you summarise that range of opinion and give reason for your

own opinion. If you are not able to give your opinion without qualification, you state the qualification.

5 The report must contain a statement that you understand your duty to the court and that you have complied with your duty and will continue to comply with that duty.

6 The report must contain a statement of truth as follows:

"I confirm that, insofar as the facts stated in my report are within my own knowledge, I have made clear which they are and I believe them to be true and that the opinions I have expressed are represent my true and complete professional opinion".

We suggest that you contact [   ] direct on [   ] and [   ] direct on [   ] to arrange a convenient time for you to inspect the property. [Both parties wish to be present]. [   ] is currently living in the property.

There is a court appointment in this matter listed on [20   ]. In order to make best use of that court hearing, it would be helpful if we could have your report by [   ]. If this presents you with any difficulties, we should be grateful if you would contact [   ] of [   ] and [   ] of [   ] as soon as possible. In any event, please contact us to agree your fee in advance. Mr and Mrs [   ] will each be directly responsible to you for half of your fee.

Yours faithfully

Solicitors for [   ]   Solicitors for [   ]

Appendix 3

2001 No. 830
LEGAL AID AND ADVICE, ENGLAND AND WALES
The Legal Aid in Family Proceedings (Remuneration) (Amendment) Regulations 2001

Made	*8th March 2001*
Laid before Parliament	*9th March 2001*
Coming into force	*2nd April 2001*

The Lord Chancellor, in exercise of the powers conferred upon him by sections 34 and 43 of the Legal Aid Act 1988,[1] having had regard to the matters specified in section 34(9) of that Act and having consulted the General Council of the Bar and the Law Society, and with the consent of the Treasury, makes the following Regulations:

Citation, commencement and interpretation

1.—(1) These Regulations may be cited as the Legal Aid in Family Proceedings (Remuneration) (Amendment) Regulations 2001 and shall come into force on 2nd April 2001.

(2) In these Regulations, any reference to a regulation or Schedule by number alone is a reference to the regulation or Schedule so numbered in the Legal Aid in Family Proceedings (Remuneration) Regulations 1991.[2]

Transitional provision

2. These Regulations shall apply to work carried out on or after 2nd April 2001 and in relation to work carried out before that date the Legal Aid in Family

---

[1] 1988 c. 34. Sections 34 and 43 were amended by the Courts and Legal Services Act 1990 (c. 41), Schedule 18 paragraphs 60 and 63 and the Family Law Act 1996 (c. 27), Schedule 8 paragraph 44, Sections 34 and 43 are repealed (together with other provisions) by Part I of Schedule 15 to the Access to Justice Act 1999 (c. 22), which was brought into force on 1st April 2000 by the Access to Justice Act 1999 (Commencement No. 3, Transitional Provisions and Savings) Order 2000 (S.I. 2000/774), but subject to savings. Section 43 is an interpretation provision and is cited because of the meaning given to "regulations".

[2] S.I. 1991/2038; the relevant amending instruments are S.I. 1996/650 and 1555 and 1997/2394.

Proceedings (Remuneration) Regulations 1991 shall have effect as if these Regulations had not been made.

Amendments to the Legal Aid in Family Proceedings (Remuneration) Regulations 1991

3.—(1) In regulation 2(1), in the definition of "the relevant authority", for "taxing officer" there shall be substituted "costs officer" and for "taxation" (in both places where it occurs) there shall be substituted "detailed assessment".

(2) In regulation 2(2), the word "and" at the end of sub-paragraph (a) shall be deleted and after that sub-paragraph there shall be inserted—

"(aa) the expressions "detailed assessment", "costs judge" and "costs officer" shall have the meanings given to them in Part 43 of the Civil Procedure Rules 1998[3]; and".

4.—(1) In regulation 3(4)(bb)—

(a) after "Schedule 2, shall" there shall be inserted ", subject to paragraph (4A),";

(b) "for franchisees" shall be deleted;

(c) for the words from "(other than the Board)" to "Legal Aid Act 1988" there shall be substituted "who is authorised to carry out work in family proceedings by a contract with the Legal Services Commission"; and

(d) for "work done by franchisees" there shall be substituted "such work".

(2) In regulation 3(4)(c)(iii), the words after "circumstances of the case" shall be deleted.

(3) After regulation 3(4) there shall be inserted—

"(4A) Except in relation to prescribed family proceedings in a magistrates' court, where paragraph (4)(bb) applies and the relevant work is done by a member of a relevant panel the relevant authority shall, subject to paragraph (4B), allow whichever is the higher of—

(a) an amount 15% higher than the amount in Schedule 1A or (as the case may be) 2A(a) which he would have allowed but for this paragraph and paragraph (4)(c); and

(b) if he decides to award such an amount, a larger amount than that specified in column 2 or column 3, as the case may be, of Parts I, II, III and V of Schedule 1A or (as the case may be) 2A(a), awarded in accordance with paragraph (4)(c).

(4B) Paragraph (4A) shall not apply in relation to any item if, but for that paragraph, the relevant authority would, in accordance with regulation

---

[3] S.I. 1998/3132.

3(4)(c), have allowed a lower amount for that item than the one in Part I, II, III or V of Schedule 1A or 2A(a).".

(4) In regulation 3(8) for "R.S.C., Order 62" there shall be substituted "Parts 43 to 48 of the Civil Procedure Rules 1998".
(5) After regulation 3(8) there shall be inserted—

"(9) In this regulation—

(a) "relevant panel" means—

(i) the Solicitors' Family Law Association Accredited Specialist Panel; or
(ii) in relation to work done under a certificate which includes proceedings relating to children, the Law Society's Children Act Panel; and

(b) "proceedings relating to children" means proceedings in which the welfare of children is determined, including, without limitation, proceedings under the Children Act 1989[4] or under the inherent jurisdiction of the High Court in relation to children.".

5. In Part V of Schedules 1 and 2—

(a) for the heading "TAXATION AND REVIEW OF TAXATION" there shall be substituted "DETAILED ASSESSMENT AND APPEAL IN RELATION TO DETAILED ASSESSMENT";

(b) for "taxation", wherever it occurs, there shall be substituted "detailed assessment"; and

(c) in item 19 of Schedule 1 and item 20 of Schedule 2, for "Review by district judge or judge" there shall be substituted "Appeal to costs judge, district judge or judge".

6.—(1) For Parts I to III of Schedule 1A there shall be substituted—

"SCHEDULE 1A
CARE PROCEEDINGS

PART I
PREPARATION

Column 1	*Column 2*	*Column 3*
	High Court	*County court or magistrates' court*
ITEM		
1. Writing routine letters	£4.70 per item	£4.10 per item
2. Receiving routine letters	£2.35 per item	£2.05 per item
3. Routine telephone calls	£4.70 per item	£4.10 per item
4. All other preparation work including any work which was	£73.15 per hour	£64.90 per hour

---

[4] 1989 c. 41

Column 1	Column 2	Column 3
	High Court	County court or magistrates' court
reasonably done arising out of or incidental to the proceedings, interviews with client, witnesses, and other parties; obtaining evidence; preparation and consideration of, and dealing with, documents, negotiations and notices; dealing with letters written and received and telephone calls which are not routine	(£77.85 per hour for a fee-earner whose office is situated in the Legal Services Commission's London Region)	(£68.20 per hour for a fee-earner whose office is situated in the Legal Services Commission's London Region)
5. Travelling and waiting	£35.75 per hour	£32.45 per hour

PART II
CONFERENCES WITH COUNSEL

Column 1	Column 2	Column 3
	High Court	County court or magistrates' court
6. Attending with counsel in conference	£41.25 per hour	£36.30 per hour
7. Travelling and waiting	£35.75 per hour	£32.45 per hour

PART III
ATTENDANCES

Column 1	Column 2	Column 3
	High Court	County court or magistrates' court
8. Attending with counsel at the trial or hearing of any cause or the hearing of any summons or other application at court, or other appointment	£41.25 per hour	£36.30 per hour
9. Attending without counsel at the trial or hearing of any cause or the hearing of any summons or other application at court, or other appointment	£73.15 per hour (£77.85 per hour for a fee-earner whose office is situated in the Legal Services Commission's London Region)	£64.90 per hour (£68.20 per hour for a fee-earner whose office is situated in the Legal Services Commission's London Region)
10. Travelling and waiting	£35.75 per hour	£32.45 per hour".

(2) For Part V of Schedule 1A there shall be substituted—

"PART V
DETAILED ASSESSMENT AND APPEAL IN RELATION TO
DETAILED ASSESSMENT
(HIGH COURT AND COUNTY COURT ONLY)

Column 1	Column 2 High Court	Column 3 County court
17. Preparing the bill (where allowable) and completing the detailed assessment (excluding preparing for and attending the hearing of the detailed assessment)	£35.75–£99.85 per hour	£35.75–£56.95 per hour
18. Preparing for and attending the hearing of the detailed assessment (including travelling and waiting)	Discretionary	Discretionary
19. Appeal to costs judge, district judge or judge (including preparation)".	Discretionary	Discretionary

7.—(1) For Schedule 2A there shall be substituted—

"SCHEDULE 2A
PRESCRIBED FAMILY PROCEEDINGS

(a) High Court and county court proceedings

PART I
PREPARATION

Column 1	Column 2 High Court	Column 3 County court
1. Writing routine letters	£7.05 per item	£6.15 per item
2. Receiving routine letters	£3.50 per item	£3.10 per item
3. Routine telephone calls	£7.05 per item	£6.15 per item
4. All other preparation work including any work which was reasonably done arising out of or incidental to the proceedings, interviews with client, witnesses, and other parties; obtaining evidence; preparation and consideration of, and dealing with, documents, negotiations and notices; dealing with letters written and received and telephone calls which are not routine	Where proceedings were conducted in the divorce registry or in another court on the South Eastern Circuit at the time when the relevant work was done: £78.40 per hour All other circuits: £73.05 per hour	Where proceedings were conducted in the divorce registry or in another court on the South Eastern Circuit at the time when the relevant work was done: £68.50 per hour All other circuits: £64.80 per hour
6. Travelling and waiting time in connection with the above matters	£35.75 per hour	£32.45 per hour

PART II
CONFERENCES WITH COUNSEL

Column 1	Column 2	Column 3
	High Court	*County court*
7. Attending counsel in conference	£41.25 per hour	£36.30 per hour
8. Travelling and waiting	£35.75 per hour	£32.45 per hour

PART III
ATTENDANCES

Column 1	Column 2	Column 3
	High Court	*County court*
9. Attending with counsel at the trial or hearing of any cause or hearing of any summons or other application at court, or other appointment	£41.25 per hour	£36.30 per hour
10. Attending without counsel at the trial or hearings of any cause or the hearing of any summons or other application at court, or other appointment	Where proceedings were conducted in the divorce registry or in another court on the South Eastern Circuit at the time when the relevant work was done: £78.40 per hour	Where proceedings were conducted in the divorce registry or in another court on the South Eastern Circuit at the time when the relevant work was done: £68.50 per hour
	All other circuits: £73.05 per hour	All other circuits: £68.80 per hour
11. Travelling and waiting	£35.75 per hour	£32.45 per hour

PART V
DETAILED ASSESSMENT AND APPEAL IN RELATION TO DETAILED ASSESSMENT

Column 1	Column 2	Column 3
	High Court	*County court*
18. Preparing the bill (where allowable) and completing the detailed assessment (excluding preparing for and attending the hearing of the detailed assessment)	£35.70–£99.85 per hour	£35.70–£56.95 per hour
19. Preparing for and attending the hearing of the detailed assessment (including travelling and waiting)	Discretionary	Discretionary
20. Appeal to costs judge, district judge or judge (including preparation)	Discretionary	Discretionary

(b) Magistrates' court proceedings

Preparation	£48.95 per hour - (£52.25 per hour for a fee-earner whose office is situated in the Legal Services Commission's London Region)
Advocacy	£61.90 per hour
Attendance at court where counsel assigned	£33.30 per hour
Travelling and waiting	£27.50 per hour
Routine letters written and telephone calls	£3.80 per item - (£4.00 per item for a fee-earner whose office is situated in the Legal Services Commission's London Region)".

Signed by authority of the Lord Chancellor

David Lock
Parliamentary Secretary, Lord Chancellor's Department

Dated 8th March 2001

We consent,

Greg Pope

Jim Dowd
Two of the Lords Commissioners of Her Majesty's Treasury

Dated 8th March 2001

These Regulations, which amend the Legal Aid in Family Proceedings (Remuneration) Regulations 1991 (S.I. 1991/2038), introduce new rates of remuneration for representation in family proceedings which is still being provided by suppliers with a family contract with the Legal Services Commission, under Part IV of the Legal Aid Act 1988. Part IV of the 1988 Act was repealed by the Access to Justice Act 1999, but is saved in relation to transitional cases by the Access to Justice Act 1999 (Commencement No.3, Transitional Provisions and Savings) Order 2000 (S.I. 2000/774). The rates also apply, by virtue of the Community Legal Service (Funding) Order 2000 (S.I. 2000/627), to representation in family proceedings provided under contract as part of the Community Legal Service, under Part I of the Access to Justice Act 1999.
    These Regulations also—

(a) introduce an uplift of 15% in cases where the supplier is a member of the Solicitors' Family Law Association Panel or, in relation to proceedings relating to children, the Law Society's Children Act Panel; and

(b) make some amendments reflecting changes in terminology brought about by the Civil Procedure Rules 1998.

Appendix 4

Application for ancillary relief

2.61A—(1) A notice of intention to proceed with an application for ancillary **A4.01** relief made in the petition or answer or an application for ancillary relief must be made by notice in Form A.

(2) The notice must be filed:

(a) if the case is pending in a divorce county court, in that court; or

(b) if the case is pending in the High Court, in the registry in which it is proceeding.

(3) Where the applicant requests an order for ancillary relief that includes provision to be made by virtue of section 25B or 25C of the Act of 1973[1] the terms of the order requested must be specified in the notice in Form A.

(4) Upon the filing of Form A the court must:

(a) fix a first appointment not less than 12 weeks and not more than 16 weeks after the date of the filing of the notice and give notice of that date;

(b) serve a copy on the respondent within 4 days of the date of the filing of the notice.

(5) The date fixed under paragraph (4) for the first appointment, or for any subsequent appointment, must not be cancelled except with the court's permission and, if cancelled, the court must immediately fix a new date.

Procedure before the first appointment

2.61B—(1) Both parties must, at the same time, exchange with each other, and each file with the court, a statement in Form E, which—

(a) is signed by the party who made the statement;

(b) is sworn to be true, and

(c) contains the information and has attached to it the documents required by that Form.

(2) Form E must be exchanged and filed not less than 35 days before the date of the first appointment.

(3) Form E must have attached to it:

(a) any documents required by Form E; and

(b) any other documents necessary to explain or clarify any of the information contained in Form E.

(4) Form E must have no documents attached to it other than the documents referred to in paragraph (3).

(5) Where a party was unavoidably prevented from sending any document required by Form E, that party must at the earliest opportunity:

(a) serve copies of that document on the other party; and

(b) file a copy of that document with the court, together with a statement explaining the failure to send it with Form E.

(6) No disclosure or inspection of documents may be requested or given between the filing of the application for ancillary relief and the first appointment, except—

(a) copies sent with Form E, or in accordance with paragraph (5); or

(b) in accordance with paragraph (7).

(7) At least 14 days before the hearing of the first appointment, each party must file with the court and serve on the other party—

(a) a concise statement of the issues between the parties;

(b) a chronology;

(c) a questionnaire setting out by reference to the concise statement of issues any further information and documents requested from the other party or a statement that no information and documents are required;

(d) a notice in Form G stating whether that party will be in a position at the first appointment to proceed on that occasion to a FDR appointment.

(8) Where an order for ancillary relief is requested that includes provision to be made under section 25B or 25C of the Act of 1973, the applicant must file with the court and serve on the respondent at least 14 days before the hearing of the first appointment, confirmation that rule 2.70(4) has been complied with.

(9) At least 14 days before the hearing of the first appointment, the applicant must file with the court and serve on the respondent, confirmation of the names of all persons served in accordance with rule 2.59(3) and (4), and that there are no other persons who must be served in accordance with those paragraphs.

Expert evidence

2.61C CPR rules 35.1 to 35.14 relating to expert evidence (with appropriate modifications), except CPR rules 35.5(2) and 35.8(4)(b) apply to all ancillary relief proceedings.

The first appointment

2.61D—(1) The first appointment must be conducted with the objective of defining the issues and saving costs.

(2) At the first appointment the district judge—

    (a) must determine—

        (i) the extent to which any questions seeking information under rule 2.61B must be answered; and

        (ii) what documents requested under rule 2.61B must be produced,

      and give directions for the production of such further documents as may be necessary;

    (b) must give directions about—

        (i) the valuation of assets (including, where appropriate, the joint instruction of joint experts);

        (ii) obtaining and exchanging expert evidence, if required; and

        (iii) evidence to be adduced by each party and, where appropriate, about further chronologies or schedules to be filed by each party;

    (c) must, unless he decides that a referral is not appropriate in the circumstances, direct that the case be referred to a FDR appointment;

    (d) must, where he decides that a referral to a FDR appointment is not appropriate, direct one of the following:

        (i) that a further directions appointment be fixed;

        (ii) that an appointment be fixed for the making of an interim order;

        (iii) that the case be fixed for final hearing and, where that direction is given, the district judge must determine the judicial level at which the case should be heard; or

        (iv) that the case be adjourned for out-of-court mediation or private negotiation or, in exceptional circumstances, generally;

    (e) must consider whether, having regard to all the circumstances (including the extent to which each party has complied with this Part, and in particular the requirement to send documents with Form E), to make an order about the costs of the hearing; and

    (f) may—

        (i) make an interim order where an application for it has been made in accordance with rule 2.69F returnable at the first appointment;

        (ii) having regard to the contents of Form G filed by the parties, treat the appointment (or part of it) as a FDR appointment to which rule 2.61E applies;

        (iii) in a case where an order for ancillary relief is requested that includes provision to be made under section 25B or 25C of the Act of 1973, require any party to request a valuation under regulation 4 of the Divorce etc. (Pensions) Regulations 1996[2] from the trustees or managers of any pension scheme under which the party has, or is likely to have, any benefits.

(3) After the first appointment, a party is not entitled to production of any further documents except in accordance with directions given under paragraph (2)(a) above or with the permission of the court.

(4) At any stage:

(a) a party may apply for further directions or a FDR appointment;

(b) the court may give further directions or direct that the parties attend a FDR appointment.

(5) Both parties must personally attend the first appointment unless the court orders otherwise.

The FDR appointment

2.61E—(1) The FDR appointment must be treated as a meeting held for the purposes of discussion and negotiation and paragraphs (2) to (9) apply.

(2) The district judge or judge hearing the FDR appointment must have no further involvement with the application, other than to conduct any further FDR appointment or to make a consent order or a further directions order.

(3) Not later than 7 days before the FDR appointment, the applicant must file with the court details of all offers and proposals, and responses to them.

(4) Paragraph (3) includes any offers, proposals or responses made wholly or partly without prejudice, but paragraph (3) does not make any material admissible as evidence if, but for that paragraph, it would not be admissible.

(5) At the conclusion of the FDR appointment, any documents filed under paragraph (3), and any filed documents referring to them, must, at the request of the party who filed them, be returned to him and not retained on the court file.

(6) Parties attending the FDR appointment must use their best endeavours to reach agreement on the matters in issue between them.

(7) The FDR appointment may be adjourned from time to time.

(8) At the conclusion of the FDR appointment, the court may make an appropriate consent order, but otherwise must give directions for the future course of the proceedings, including, where appropriate, the filing of evidence and fixing a final hearing date.

(9) Both parties must personally attend the FDR appointment unless the court orders otherwise.

Costs

2.61F—(1) At every court hearing or appointment each party must produce to the court an estimate in Form H of the costs incurred by him up to the date of that hearing or appointment.

(2) The parties' obligation under paragraph (1) is without prejudice to their obligations under paragraphs 4.1 to 4.11 of the Practice Direction relating to CPR Part 44.".

[1] sections 25B and 25C were inserted in the Act of 1973 by section 166(1) of the Pensions Act 1995 (c. 26).back
[2] S.I. 1996/1676.back

Index